INDUSTRIAL RELATIONS

to

HUMAN RESOURCES

and

BEYOND

ISSUES IN WORK AND HUMAN RESOURCES

Daniel J.B. Mitchell, Series Editor

INDUSTRIAL RELATIONS

— *to* —

HUMAN RESOURCES

— *and* —

BEYOND

*The Evolving Process
of Employee Relations
Management*

Bruce E. Kaufman
Richard A. Beaumont
Roy B. Helfgott

Editors

M.E. Sharpe
Armonk, New York
London, England

Library of Congress Cataloging-in-Publication Data

Kaufman, Bruce E.
    Industrial relations to human resources and beyond: the evolving process of
employee relations management [edited] by Bruce E. Kaufman, Richard A.
Beaumont, and Roy B. Helfgott.
        p. cm. — (Issues in work and human resources)
    The essays in this volume were commissioned in honor of the seventy-fifth
anniversary of Industrial Relations Counselors, Inc. (IRC) and were intended for
delivery on September 11, 2001 at Princeton at a commemorative symposium which
was suspended.
    Includes bibliographical references and index.
    ISBN 0-7656-1205-4 (alk. paper)
    1. Personnel management—United States—History. 2. Industrial relations—United
States—History. I. Beaumont, Richard A. II. Helfgott, Roy B. III. Industrial Relations
Counselors, Inc. IV. Title. V. Series.

HF5549.2.U5 147 2003
658.3—dc21   2002030689

Contents

**Section III. Human Resource Management
in the Twenty-First Century**

List of Tables and Figures

Tables

Figures

Foreword

There is always a tendency to assume that the way things are is the way they have always been. Particularly in the United States, human resource practices are often described in timeless and placeless terms. There are particular human resource policies that "work," and there is little point in considering alternatives.

In fact, American human resource practices have evolved over long periods and have frequently been influenced by forces external to the firm. Wars, depressions, and political and social currents have been part of the development process. Once that basic fact is understood, further change can be anticipated. To understand the present and the future and to explore the likely direction of employment policies within firms, it is necessary to study the evolution of those policies.

In the current volume, readers will find a series of papers that do just that. These essays examine how we arrived at our current set of human resource practices. In doing so, they help us look to the future.

Other symposia have explored human resource policy in the light of history. This one, however, was able to draw on a particular focus, thanks to the sponsorship of Industrial Relations Counselors, Inc. (IRC). In deciding to examine its own history, IRC inherently fostered a larger examination of the development of human resource practices in the twentieth century. The fact that a particular organization—and in particular, individuals associated with that organization—played an important role in evolving management practices is itself an important lesson. The outcomes we see today were not simply the product of blind and deterministic forces. There is always the potential for people of vision to help shape the nature of the employment relationship.

Daniel J.B. Mitchell
Series editor

Preface

Bruce E. Kaufman, Richard A. Beaumont,
and Roy B. Helfgott

The essays in this volume were commissioned in honor of the seventy-fifth anniversary of Industrial Relations Counselors, Inc. (IRC), and were intended for delivery at a commemorative symposium at Princeton on September 11, 2001 (more about this in the Introduction). IRC, established by John D. Rockefeller, Jr., in 1926, was unique as the first organization dedicated to providing expert consulting and research on labor and industrial relations matters and to promoting progressive management methods to improve the hitherto contentious relationship between employers and their employees. Throughout its history, IRC has significantly influenced both private practice—in many of the country's leading employers—and public policy in the field known today as human resource management.

This book seeks to expand our knowledge of history, contemporary practice, and future challenges in employer-employee relations—a chronicle of the people, ideas, forces, and developments that gave birth to industrial relations and guided its evolution to contemporary human resource management. Whatever the label given to this field, one challenge has remained paramount—balancing the interests of employers and employees and finding methods to promote a more productive, satisfying, and rewarding workplace for all parties. Although the modern-day workplace still has not fully achieved the vision that many hold for it, no one will be able to finish this volume without being impressed and gratified by the immense progress that has occurred during the twentieth century.

Many thanks must be extended to the several authors who have contributed to this volume from academia and from Organization Resources Counselors, Inc. (the organization formed by IRC to continue its for-profit work). The help and support of the editorial staff, including Jane Bensahel, Joy Correge, and especially Bernadette Steele, made this volume possible. Our thanks. We also wish to express gratitude for the efforts of several members of the staff who had prepared to present summaries of the papers at the symposium but, due to the tragic events of the day, could not— including Patricia Frisbie and Maria Tsiadis, who also helped enormously in the planning, organization, preparation, and management of the meeting, for which we are more than grateful.

INDUSTRIAL RELATIONS

to

HUMAN RESOURCES

and

BEYOND

1

Introduction

Roy B. Helfgott

By the dawn of the twentieth century, the United States had become a major industrial nation and economic power. Technological change brought greater capital intensity of production and economies of scale and, with the expansion of markets, gave birth to giant corporations with hired managers that supplanted small-scale owner-operated businesses. The concepts of laissez-faire and individual initiative, which permeated employer thought and behavior, meant that each business owner should be free to run his enterprise as he saw fit without interference from government or workers. The employer's authority in the workplace was almost absolute, and labor was treated as just another commodity to be hired and fired as needed and purchased as cheaply as possible. There were no personnel policies, and control of the workforce was left in the hands of foremen, which was supposed to lead to efficiency but instead resulted in labor conflict and poor work performance. Unions tried to organize workers but faced fierce employer resistance.

A handful of employers, such as Filene's department store in Boston, sought to treat workers differently, but the major captains of industry clung to the laissez-faire model. By the 1920s, however, there had been a break in their ranks, as John D. Rockefeller, Jr., chastened by the "Ludlow Massacre" at a Rockefeller holding, sought to emphasize the mutual interests of employers and employees, treat workers fairly, and provide them with a voice in the workplace. This movement led to the establishment in 1926 of Industrial Relations Counselors, Inc. (IRC), which provided the intellectual underpinnings to management efforts to advance progressive human resource policies and practices within American industry.

A symposium at Princeton University to commemorate the seventy-fifth anniversary of the founding of IRC was scheduled for September 11 and 12, 2001. The opening session was under way when news of the tragic events at the World Trade Center and the Pentagon was received. Under the circumstances, the proceedings were suspended. The symposium would have been a significant event. This book presents what would have been its contents: essays by academic experts that trace developments during the twentieth century in various areas of human resource management, as well as a practitioner view, from staff members of Organization Resources Counselors, Inc. (ORC), of the current state of human resource (HR) policies and practices and the outlook for the future. Before turning to these topics, I first present a brief outline of IRC's history so that the reader will be better able to appreciate the role of IRC in these developments.

A Brief History of IRC

Although officially born in 1926, IRC's roots go back to a 1914 violent strike at the Colorado Fuel and Iron Company (CF&I), during which nearly a dozen women and children died. This event, dubbed the "Ludlow Massacre," brought John D. Rockefeller, Jr., the major stockholder, into disrepute. Rockefeller, who had left company operations to local management, sought the advice of William Lyon Mackenzie King, former minister of labour of Canada, who formulated a plan that granted workers the right to appeal grievances and established a joint industrial council of employees and management. This "employee representation plan" spread among progressive companies both inside and outside the Rockefeller network. In 1919, ten of these companies formed the Special Conference Committee, whose representatives met periodically to discuss labor policies. The group developed what has become known as "welfare capitalism," which emphasized the stake of workers in the system. These companies also led in the creation of the new field of personnel management.

In 1922, an "industrial relations staff" was established in the office of Rockefeller's attorney, Raymond B. Fosdick, to provide expert investigation and help to introduce progressive labor policies. It was incorporated in 1926 as a separate nonprofit organization, Industrial Relations Counselors, Inc., to "advance the knowledge and practice of human relationships in industry, commerce, education, and government."

In 1922, an industrial relations (IR) section also was established within the Economics Department of Princeton University with Rockefeller support. Subsequently, IRC helped to set up additional IR centers at the University of Michigan, California Institute of Technology, Stanford University, Massachusetts Institute of Technology, and Queens University in Canada. Later, IRC established the C. J. Hicks Memorial Fellowships in Industrial Relations at each of these universities. In the 1970s, an IRC professorship in industrial relations existed at the Colgate Darden School, University of Virginia.

Between 1927 and 1932, IRC maintained a branch office at the International Labour Organisation in Geneva and conducted research on social insurance programs in European countries. In the 1930s, IRC's research unit was on loan to the executive branch of the U.S. government and played a pivotal role in the development of the nation's social security system.

Rockefeller was IRC's principal support for a decade, after which it expanded its consulting activities. In the mid-1950s, however, it ceased all consulting activities, which were transferred to a separate for-profit corporation, now called Organization Resources Counselors, Inc., and the ideals and concepts of IRC have become part of ORC's mission.

With the upsurge of unionism in the 1930s, IRC aided companies in effecting smooth labor-management relations and offered guidance to the nation in terms of labor policy. IRC promoted job evaluation as a means of rationalizing company wage structures and promoting internal equity, and as World War II loomed, it helped to establish compensation structures to support effective operation of the defense effort. During the war, it explored wage stabilization efforts, and as the need for IR competence became a matter of national priority, it began to offer training courses in IR. Over the years, thousands of IR/HR specialists were graduates of these courses, with many of them becoming the HR leaders in major corporations.

Even before the civil rights crusade gained momentum, IRC was working to open economic opportunities to African-Americans, and its 1959 publication, *Employing the Negro in American Industry*, became a guide to management as it established nondiscriminatory hiring in the 1960s. In that decade, IRC research focused on two areas: (1) the interaction between new technology and progressive human resource management and (2) a balanced national labor policy. It also began a symposium series that explored the significance to HR of the latest developments in the behavioral sciences. For the past decade, it has been issuing *IR Concepts*, occasional papers on important current issues affecting human resource policy and practice.

Contents of This Book

This book commemorates IRC's founding. It is divided into three sections: Section I—The Early Stages of Welfare Capitalism and the Birth of IRC and Human Resource Management; Section II—History and Development of Human Resource Management, with chapters by academic experts in the field; and Section III—Human Resource Management in the Twenty-First Century, with essays by practitioners in the field.

Section I. The Early Stages of Welfare Capitalism and the Birth of IRC and Human Resource Management

In Chapter 2, I provide an overview of the political, economic, social, and cultural backdrop of the 1920s, the decade of IRC's birth. The 1920s witnessed a burst of innovative behavior in the United States that diverged from European and British traditions. The creation of a consumer society was one way we deviated from Europe, where class-riven societies could not envisage the "lower orders" driving automobiles or wearing clothing undistinguishable from their "betters."

The United States followed a policy of isolationism. It turned away from Europe, not only politically but also culturally, asserting an "American" culture, and it was an incredibly creative period for American literature, music, and the physical and social sciences. Radio, motion pictures, and sports became part of the new consumer society.

Attempts to improve the relationship between a company and its employees symbolized another American effort to turn away from old-world models. John D. Rockefeller, Jr., and his advisor, William Lyon Mackenzie King, tried to steer a course different from that of Europe's class struggle and American employers' laissez-faire doctrine. Rockefeller sought to establish a labor-management relationship based on mutual interest and obligations, to curb management's authoritarian power, to treat workers fairly, and to give them a voice in the determination of the conditions under which they worked. This distinctive American approach envisioned by Rockefeller, however, crumbled in the Great Depression as jobs disappeared, wages were cut, employer pension plans went bankrupt, and the misery of the times made workers psychologically ripe for unionization. In place of the philosophy of mutual interests of employers and employees came an adversarial labor-management system under government aegis.

In Chapter 3, Professor Bruce E. Kaufman explores IRC's impact on modern HR, which he traces to Rockefeller's recognition of the need for cooperation between labor and management and a shift from the traditional employer workplace autocracy to representative democracy. King's employee representation plan, which provided for joint governance, was implemented at CF&I and then at the Bayonne refinery of Standard Oil Company of New Jersey. Jersey Standard adopted one of the most forward-looking industrial relations programs in the nation, a model for the "welfare capitalism" of the 1920s. IRC was established to advance this concept of mutual gain through cooperation between management and employees. Kaufman concludes that the birth and development of IRC over the past three quarters of a century are noteworthy on many counts. Its creation signaled a movement away from disregarding labor questions to a new conceptualization in which the management of labor is considered a matter of strategic importance that requires executive attention and professional administration.

IRC played a crucial role in developing, propagating, and implementing the new progressive IR strategy and counseled companies to see employees as human beings and assets rather than commodities and a short-run expense and as stakeholders rather than "hired hands." It advocated forms of collective dealing with workers and told employers that they had a social/ethical responsibility toward labor and the community. IRC's history is a testament to the success it and progressive management have had in transforming American industrial relations to a more scientifically based, professional, humanistic model.

Section II. History and Development of Human Resource Management

In Section II, noted academics chronicle the evolution of the employer-employee relationship and focus on specific areas of IR/HR policies and practices. The section begins with Chapter 4, in which Professor Bruce E. Kaufman examines the concept of a unity of interest between management and employees. Kaufman notes that IRC's birth was an outgrowth of four decades of effort to find a solution to the "Labor Problem," the epic struggle between labor and management over control of the processes of production and distribution. Rockefeller, King, and Clarence Hicks broke with the employer laissez-faire autocratic view and promoted one that recognized areas of activity in which the interests of labor and management coincide.

This "employers' solution" sought not only to preserve capitalism and the employer's ability to run the enterprise but also to resolve labor problems through a reform program to increase both efficiency and employee satisfaction by fostering workplace cooperation based on promoting identity of interest (goal alignment) between employer and employees. The unity of interest philosophy and associated management practices—articulation of a formal labor policy, setting up an industrial relations department, gain-sharing forms of compensation, provision of employee benefits, employment security, limits on supervisory power, and a nonunion system of employee representation—were propagated by IRC. The ideas behind today's concepts of high-performance organizations remain remarkably similar to those promoted by IRC and the progressive firms of the 1920s.

Professor Sanford M. Jacoby presents a history of the human resource function in Chapter 5. At first, human resource decisions were left to first-line supervisors, but this led to high turnover rates, and so some companies introduced employment departments to handle these functions. Labor-market tightening, labor unrest, and intrusion of the federal government during World War I led additional companies to establish personnel departments and to have them take over more of the foreman's domain with central hiring, disciplinary rules, training, performance evaluation, and rationalized wage structures.

The Great Depression led to government regulation and encouragement of trade unions, and personnel management coordinated corporate labor policies. In the 1950s and 1960s, management saw itself as having responsibilities not only to stockholders but also to consumers, the public, and employees, thus boosting the status of the human resource management function (HR). The emergence of the behavioral sciences produced a split between labor and employee relations, narrowing the former's responsibilities to collective bargaining and contract administration. With the growing importance of the internal labor market, HR concentrated on management development, training, and communications. In the 1970s, HR focused on dealing with worker dissatisfaction and the application of new forms of work organization in nonunion plants, which expanded the organizational development staffs within HR. In the 1980s, HR departments became less influential as enforcement of federal regulations eased, unionism declined further, and the labor market loosened. Corporate restructuring and demands for higher returns led companies to view employees as costs and to allow line managers to assume greater control. To survive in this short-term-oriented organizational milieu, HR moved from an employee focus to a business orientation.

Chapter 6 traces the rise of employee benefits and social insurance. Professor John F. Burton, Jr., with the assistance of Professor Daniel J.B. Mitchell, sees them as an important component of the welfare capitalism that emerged in the 1920s. Their growth has been phenomenal: In 1929, employee benefits paid for by employers and employer contributions to social insurance represented only 1.3 percent of wages and salaries, but by 1999 this had increased to 18.4 percent. The three major forces driving the growth of employee benefits have been government policies, labor unions, and organizations such as IRC that sponsored the idea of a progressive relationship between management and workers.

Rapid industrialization caused a problem of work accidents, and the first form of social insurance to emerge was workers' compensation. In the 1920s, some progressive employers began to provide employee benefits. The Depression led to the Social Security Act of 1935. Social Security benefits were supplemented by union-negotiated pensions. Unable to obtain national health insurance, unions negotiated health-insurance coverage with employers. Nonunion firms followed suit, and employer-provided health insurance became the norm. Burton and Mitchell end by raising the question of why health insurance should be part of a person's employment package, as other industrial nations have health insurance funds run through government or quasi-public institutions.

Professor Daniel J.B. Mitchell analyzes twentieth-century pay practices in Chapter 7 and discerns the societal, economic, business, and union influences on industry compensation programs. At the beginning of the century, there were four types of compensation arrangements: (1) time-based wages, (2) social welfare benefits, (3) explicit incentive programs, and (4) those that share organizational risk with the employees. At the end of the century, he finds that the same four categories apply, although with somewhat different emphasis.

In the pre–New Deal period, employers were in a laissez-faire situation with regard to their pay-setting decisions. The Great Depression dramatically altered compensation policy, as unions began to play a major role in pay setting. A concern about the equity of pay structures resulted in job evaluation, with its rating of jobs on the basis of skill, responsibility, and conditions. Over time, however, it has lost favor for many reasons, including its subjectivity in practice, the constraints of finely differentiated job titles and narrowly defined jobs, and the new concept of comparable worth. In recent years, as membership has declined, union influence on compensation has diminished, and in the 1980s, unions even acquiesced to risk-sharing plans. The data show a trend toward more flexible pay arrangements and a shift in compensation toward the pay-for-performance emphasis of the 1920s.

As he reviews trends in equal employment opportunity in Chapter 8, Professor Jonathan S. Leonard notes that the idea that women and minorities might have a right not to be subject to discrimination is of relatively recent vintage. World War II was an anvil for change, with the federal government forging a new role with President Roosevelt's Executive Order 8802, which barred discrimination by race, creed, color, or national origin in federal employment and defense contracts. Extreme wartime labor shortages also pressured industry to hire those previously excluded.

The campaign against discrimination always has depended upon a balance of commitment bred of goodwill and compulsion based on strong law. In the 1940s, public opinion did not support a law to compel action, but blacks made significant progress through improvement in education and migration to industrial jobs in the North. Progressive managers, who saw themselves as following proper human resource practices, also opened doors to blacks, according to the 1959 IRC monograph, *Employing the Negro in American Industry*.

Title VII of the Civil Rights Act of 1964, which prohibited discrimination on the basis of race, color, creed, national origin, and sex, was the keystone of the campaign to bar employment discrimination. Black economic progress in the years following passage of Title VII was fostered by the indirect effect of judicial interpretations of Title VII to promote affirmative action, but the term evokes controversy, because it runs up against the deeply held American belief in individual merit. Leonard concludes that discrimination policies will be stronger where they are seen as applying generally rather than being specifically targeted at narrow groups.

In Chapter 9, Professor Daphne G. Taras examines the concept of "voice" in the North American workplace. She sees it as containing two elements: employee representation, which lasted between 1919 and 1935 and sought to give workers collective participation in setting the terms and conditions of their employment, and the newer concept of employee involvement, which recognizes that workers' creative talents can be harnessed for the good of the enterprise. Employee representation emanated from William Mackenzie King's recommendation to John D. Rockefeller, Jr., to set up an enterprise-based plan of representation. The Wagner Act of 1935, however, ended nonunion employee representation, despite IRC's efforts to distinguish it from "company unions."

After World War II, the notion of achieving higher performance and enhanced productivity through motivation and investment in people grew. In the 1970s, the concept of the high-performance workplace, including teams, job enlargement, greater worker authority, use of gain sharing, investment in training, and creation of greater trust between workers and managers, became popular. In the 1980s, Japanese approaches, e.g., quality circles and just-in-time inventory control methods, evoked interest, and new nonunion high-performance workplaces that utilized autonomous work teams and performance-based compensation were established. Since then, employee involvement (EI) has spread through industry, but its legality has been threatened by the Wagner Act prohibition against employers discussing with employees any issues that fall within the domain of collective bargaining, even absent a union.

New industrial relations issues have arisen with increased international trade and investment, and Professors Morley Gunderson and Anil Verma, writing in Chapter 10, see labor standards as the most pressing one. Labor standards are set in three ways. The first, the market mechanism, relies on demand and supply to determine pay and labor allocation, thus ensuring efficient utilization of labor and production of items that consumers want. However, markets have imperfections, and even perfectly functioning ones can produce outcomes that are efficient but not necessarily what society would consider fair. The second mechanism, employee representation, mitigates market forces by providing a bargaining mechanism and/or ensuring due process to employees. Some argue, however, that unions also reduce the managerial flexibility and organizational competitiveness needed for joint survival of employers and employees. Third are laws that regulate the employment relationship, govern collective bargaining, set wages and hours, ban discrimination, and establish social insurance. By establishing a floor below which market transactions are not allowed to occur, labor regulations and legislation provide a safety net when the market mechanism creates disadvantages for workers.

Freer flow of goods, capital, people, and ideas across borders has enhanced the role of the market mechanism, and collective bargaining is on the defensive. Unions have been unable to attain any form of transnational collective bargaining, and plummeting membership in many countries means they are less able to set national standards. Domestic regulative initiatives also are inhibited by fear of repelling investment. Thus, there is pressure to set international labor standards to inhibit competition based on low wages and poor working conditions.

In Chapter 11, Professor Paul S. Adler examines work organization—the determination of who performs what tasks and how these activities are coordinated. Studies by IRC, in 1964 and 1988, that analyzed the effects of changing technology captured the key issues: (a) modern technology tends to reduce physical effort and increase mental effort; (b) automation displaces the direct human production role, and workers become more like technicians; (c) automation increases the share of skilled workers relative to unskilled workers, of maintenance jobs relative to production jobs, of technicians and engineers relative to blue-collar workers, and of service jobs relative to manufacturing jobs; (d) the environment of most jobs becomes more pleasant and safer; and (e) new group relationships are formed based on work coordination. The pressure of market competition, however, may at times distort these positive trends. Adler concludes, however, that hidden beneath a seemingly cyclical process is an underlying trend toward what he dubs "collaborative control," based on stronger, broader, and more "modern" forms of trust and cooperation.

Section III. Human Resource Management in the Twenty-First Century

We turn next to what the future may hold, as seen by members of the staff of Organization Resources Counselors, Inc. The first of the three chapters in this section reports on an IRC-commissioned survey of senior human resource and line executives in ten major global corporations. The second focuses on three crucial areas of human resource policy: compensation policy and practice, international compensation, and equal employment and diversity programs. The third chapter identifies major challenges facing the human resource management function and offers insights on how to balance their demands with the needs of the organization's employees.

The IRC survey, discussed in Chapter 12 by Richard A. Beaumont, Carlton D. Becker, and Sydney R. Robertson, explores three themes: (1) how the HR function adds value to the enterprise, (2) how the HR function today differs from the past, and (3) what will be required of it in the future and how it should prepare to meet those challenges. The role of the human resource function has shifted from administrator of policies and programs and an employee advocate to a strategic business partner that contributes to the bottom line by building an organization capable of rapid and continuous change on a global scale and to a facilitator of employee self-service.

HR is poised to step into the gap created by the decimation of the ranks of midlevel managers and the growth of more complex organizations to become the "Great Integrator"—a translator of strategy into effective organizational forms, processes, and talent pools; a communicator that reinforces the strategic message of line management; and a moderator of the natural tensions between potentially competing constituencies. Critical new priorities will include developing global leaders, reskilling the workforce, and strengthening employees' commitment.

Compensation has been profoundly affected by economic and technological change, and in the first part of Chapter 13, William N. Brown examines the issues confronting compensation strategy and design in the twenty-first century. While compensation policy and practice in the past were largely shaped in reaction to outside forces (government, unions), the twenty-first century will see them more tailored to internal concerns (support of strategic business plans, accumulation of complex knowledge, and competitiveness). To do this will require that companies consider an array of questions about the greater use of equity, the appropriate degree of compensation risk, how to best reflect shareholder value, and other issues. He concludes that the nature of compensation will continue to move toward broader eligibility for those programs that reward employees for their work and provide an entrepreneurial connection to the company, as well as a greater respect for employees' opinions about programs that impact them.

As companies become global, so do their workforces. Unable to recruit highly skilled personnel in all countries in which they operated, multinationals have always turned to expatriates, that is, people who work outside their home country, to fill such positions. Today, executive career paths often include an expatriate assignment. In the second part of Chapter 13, Geoffrey W. Latta explores the challenges in managing this employee group. Differences in standards of living, attitudes, and culture between home and assignment locations raise roadblocks to the global mobility of personnel, as do their fears of what happens when they return—their overseas experience won't be utilized, jobs at home will be less challenging, and their employee networks will have been weakened. Companies that can demonstrate that assignments abroad will concretely help an employee's career can generally attract people to accept them.

A greater problem is remuneration—how to structure a compensation package that both provides sufficient inducement to the employee to accept a foreign assignment and is affordable for the company. For the vast majority of companies, the solution is to pay on a home build-up or balance sheet approach for straightforward out-and-back assignments. The balance sheet retains the expatriate at his or her home-country salary and grading structure, sometimes with a foreign service premium, and pays, in addition, a series of allowances to cover differences between home and the assignment location in the cost of goods, housing, transportation, children's education, etc. The underlying principle is to provide broad comparability with home life-style and costs—to make the individual "whole." Despite changes that may occur in the Eurozone, the balance sheet approach, which has several advantages over other approaches, will continue to be the method of choice for most overseas assignments.

Whether operating globally or domestically, organizations find that their workplaces are no longer homogeneous by age, sex, or ethnic group, and their labor forces will become even more diverse as the twenty-first century progresses. Roderick O. Mullett examines this subject with respect to the United States in the last part of Chapter 13. Viewing the changing scene, he notes that the anti–affirmative action forces have achieved considerable success, particularly in the courts. In terms of societal mores, intentional discrimination is generally perceived to be unethical, but empathy with the disadvantaged has eroded as people perceive reverse discrimination. Further eliminating discriminatory attitudes in the workplace is more difficult, as blatant discriminatory behavior has largely disappeared but more subtle and tenacious systemic discrimination still exists and is hard to identify. Current equal employment opportunity (EEO) compliance systems and diversity efforts also have inherent flaws and face particular obstacles. Mullett describes the elements of a successful Diversity system and provides some practical advice on how to handle increased tensions that arise out of the events of September 11. Short-term labor-market fluctuations have largely deterred corporate America from making Diversity a priority, but Mullett concludes that as an untapped tool for increasing organizational effectiveness, it should be a management priority.

Section III closes with Chapter 14, "Challenge and Balance," in which Richard A. Beaumont identifies ten significant challenges that demonstrate management's need for thoughtful, skilled, professional HR staffs: (1) continual reskilling of the workforce in response to technological and economic change; (2) a simultaneous shortage of talented personnel with critical skills and surpluses of other types of labor that threaten the traditional doctrine of equality of treatment; (3) income distribution and a growing public reaction against a system in which the ratio of pay of the highest job to the lowest is greater than it has ever been; (4) the employee quest for security, which could lead to employees with common occupational interests or characteristics banding together for what they perceive as their mutual advantage; (5) social security and retirement programs that face future difficulties as a result of changing demographics; (6) the importance of EEO and diversity programs to ensure effective workplaces as work becomes more team-based and cooperative; (7) corporate governance—determining the proper roles of boards of directors and their members; (8) organization and structure as companies move further from the classical authoritarian model to an ever more flexible and democratic one; (9) the risk that HR professionals face as they stand up for what they see as the proper course, and the need to know how to marshal arguments to balance immediate business needs with sound long-range human resource needs; and (10) the social behavior of companies wherever they operate and good corporate citizenship. He concludes that we are entering an era in which the human resource function, best able to deal with these challenges, can be fundamental to business success and should be a partner in the development of strategies responsive to the human/social realities faced by business.

In Conclusion

Lastly, in Chapter 15, "In Conclusion—Transiting from the Past to the Future," Richard A. Beaumont notes that as we close this story of the rise and development of progressive industrial relations and human resource management, we must salute John D. Rockefeller, Jr. He learned from the tragedy of Ludlow and sought to establish a labor-management relationship based on mutual trust and obligations, to treat employees fairly, and to give them a voice in the determination of the conditions under which they worked. In this endeavor, Mr. Rockefeller displayed great courage as he broke with the other captains of industry, who clung to their laissez-faire, authoritarian views. Yet, it was his vision that ultimately triumphed within American management.

The forces that have shaped the course of human resource management—and will continue to shape its evolution in the future—include changes in markets and technologies, the flux in social thinking on the roles of organizations and people, and the attitudes of employees concerning their work, their organizations, and their managers. In the last couple decades, the rate of market and technological changes has outstripped the ability of many companies to modify their resources/organizations and, in particular, management and employee attitudes/behaviors in response to such changes. Thus they experience "implicit disequilibrium." It will be HR's role not only to orchestrate continuous change in the midst of disequilibrium but also to identify for management the trends and developments that are likely to impact the organization in the future. Mindful of the concepts of John D. Rockefeller, Jr., industry must balance market demands with employee needs, and we see that in the twenty-first century, the human resource function will play a key role in achieving that balance.

The Early Stages of Welfare Capitalism and the Birth of IRC and Human Resource Management

The United States in the 1920s

Breaking with European Traditions

Roy B. Helfgott

The Roaring Twenties: Jazz, Prohibition, Laissez-Faire, and "Normalcy"

It was the Roaring Twenties, the Jazz Age. The decade began in 1920 on an ominous note with a bomb explosion on Wall Street that killed 30 people and injured 100, but things settled down after that. America had returned to "normalcy" and was keeping cool with Coolidge, yet people craved excitement. The Census of 1920 revealed that for the first time, the United States was an urban nation, and half the population was first or second generation. People were still moving west—California's population increased by two thirds during the decade, making it almost equal to that of Texas. The most populous states remained New York, Pennsylvania, Illinois, and Ohio, and the northeast quadrant continued to dominate the nation's manufacturing and, indeed, its total economy.

In politics, the Republican Party, devoted to laissez-faire, was in control throughout the decade. Disillusioned with the results of the First World War and Wilson's failure at Versailles, the nation in 1920 elected the Republican ticket of Warren Harding and Calvin Coolidge by seven million votes over the Democratic slate of James Cox and Franklin Roosevelt. The Teapot Dome Scandal rocked the new administration, but President Harding conveniently died and was succeeded by the impeccably honest Calvin Coolidge. In 1924, a third party appeared on the scene when a coalition of farmer groups, liberals from both major parties, and the Socialists supported Senator Robert La Follette (Republican, Wisconsin) on the Progressive ticket, but Coolidge garnered four and a half million votes more than La Follette and Democrat John W. Davis combined. In 1928, Republican Herbert Hoover won by a tidy six million votes over the Democrats' "happy warrior," Al Smith of New York, who even lost some southern states because he was Catholic. Not all was calm in the decade as passions were inflamed by the Sacco-Vanzetti case, in which two Italian-immigrant anarchists in Massachusetts were convicted of murder and subsequently executed.

Hypocrisy reigned as alcohol was illegal but the nation was awash in bathtub gin; the speakeasy became a national institution and the hip flask a part of a man's dress. Prohibition also bred the bootlegger, organized crime flourished, and Al Capone ruled Chicago, which culminated in the infamous "St. Valentine's Day Massacre" in 1929. The story was similar with respect to sexual expression—in practice, people engaged in it within and outside of marriage, but books, such as D. H. Lawrence's *Lady Chatterly's Lover* and Frank Harris' *My Life and Times*, were banned as pornographic.

Women had won the vote, and in 1924 two states, Wyoming and Texas, elected female governors. Women bobbed their hair, raised their hemlines, put on silk stockings, smoked cigarettes, and became flappers. Young people were dancing the Charleston and smooching in the rumble seats of their jalopies.

Times were good. World War I may have devastated Europe, but the United States emerged a greater economic power. The decade opened with a sharp postwar depression, but that was followed by a spectacular economic boom. Incomes rose, consumption jumped, investment soared, jobs were available, and electricity was brought into the rural areas of the North (but much less so in the South). Technological and organizational changes increased industrial efficiency, and productivity rose between 1919 and 1929 at an average annual rate of 2.3 percent. While Germany and other nations were ravaged by inflation, here consumer prices actually declined from 1920 to 1929 by more than 10 percent. As a result, real wages were rising. At the same time, work hours were being reduced, with Ford Motor Company taking the bold step in 1926 of cutting its workweek from six to five days.

Emergence of a Consumer Society

Thus, Americans both could afford to buy things and had time in which to enjoy them, and industry obliged by turning out a plethora of products, including new ones such as radios and refrigerators. A consumer society was taking shape, and a cult of salesmanship arose, exemplified by Bruce Barton, who established the leading advertising agency, and Edward Bernays, Freud's nephew, who became the first public relations guru. Chain stores were expanding and installment buying became common, enabling people with modest incomes to savor the plentitude bursting forth from the factories.

Mass production and mass consumption differentiated the United States from Europe, where class-riven societies could not envision the lower orders enjoying the better things of life. In Britain, snob appeal had surfaced early, as shown by the attacks on ready-made clothing that alleged it could be made for the "tasteless" middle class but not for a "gentleman." The automobile is a prime example of the difference—Britain became known for the Rolls Royce and Germany for the Mercedes, but here, Henry Ford's assembly line had converted the automobile from a plaything of the rich to a means of transportation for the average family. Indeed, Ford and General Motors opened plants in Britain and Germany in the 1920s to cater to their middle-class markets.

Even at home, the mass market was attacked for entailing a production system that, it was charged, deskilled and demeaned workers. The negative views centered on the assembly line, even though it was not typical of industrial work. But even Taylorism and Fordism, the epithets hurled at American production methods, involved a trade-off: As Peter Drucker has pointed out, by raising the productivity of manual work, they had converted the "laborer" into a semiskilled worker with a middle-class standard of living (Drucker 1970).

Whatever the criticisms, Americans were falling in love with the automobile. That industry became the nation's largest, roads and highways were being built at a frantic pace, and filling stations were popping up, as were tourist courts to accommodate vacationers driving through the country. The automobile also had social consequences: For one thing, it ended rural isolation, as farmers could now drive into town; for another, many people were taking motor trips on Sunday instead of attending church as they formerly had.

A lot of people were enjoying life as never before, and the national mood exuded confidence. Boosterism was the order of the day, and small businessmen in Rotary and Kiwanis clubs and local chambers of commerce promoted that confidence. Business was booming and people were buying into it, that is, buying shares of stock in American corporations, the prices of which were zooming upward. The great bull market was in full swing.

Those Left Out

Not everyone, however, fully participated in the prosperity. Mill towns of New England were decimated as the cotton-textile industry moved south to be closer to its raw material and to tap cheaper labor. The lumber industry in the West was in a slump. Coal mining in Pennsylvania and West Virginia fell upon hard times as the use of oil spread. Rural areas, however, were faring worst as prices for agricultural goods plummeted—even after some recovery, farm prices in 1927 were only two thirds of what they had been in 1920. Government rebuffed farmers' pleas as President Coolidge twice vetoed the McNary-Haugen bill to aid agriculture because it contained price-fixing features that ran counter to his laissez-faire views. It was not until 1929 that the

Agricultural Marketing Act, designed to ensure farm price stability, was adopted, but by then the nation was on the verge of plunging into depression.

The urban-rural split was also cultural. Freud and psychoanalysis might be the vogue in urban America, but rural folk had never heard of him, nor were they reading Hemingway and Fitzgerald. Those in the South and Midwest, in particular, read the Bible and believed its every word. Darwin's theory of evolution may have called into question the faith of people in cities, but not in rural America, where John T. Scopes was convicted—in the world-famous 1925 trial that pitted Clarence Darrow against William Jennings Bryan—for violating Tennessee's prohibition of teaching ideas that ran counter to the biblical account of man's creation. Darrow also had been the defense attorney the year before in the other spectacular trial of the decade, the "thrill" murder case involving two very bright Chicago boys, Nathan Leopold and Richard Loeb.

There was an ugly side to cultural conflict. Although big business was allied with immigrant groups to keep America's doors open, nativist sentiment against those from southern and eastern Europe, abetted by a postwar Red Scare, led to legislation ending free immigration and setting up an ethnically biased admissions policy. There was a resurgence of the Ku Klux Klan, its ranks swelling to four million by 1924, but the new Klan was different from that of the nineteenth century. First, it was now strong in the North as well as the South, and in urban areas as well as rural, with large memberships in Chicago and Detroit. Second, its animus had spread beyond African-Americans to include Roman Catholics and Jews, and there was considerable violence against Catholics. The power of the Klan was demonstrated in 1925 when forty thousand hooded Klansmen marched down Pennsylvania Avenue in the nation's capital to the cheers of the crowds. Meanwhile, Henry Ford was preaching virulent anti-Semitism in his newspaper, the *Dearborn Independent*.

Catholics and Jews might suffer from employment and residential discrimination, but Americans of African decent bore the brunt of bigotry. They were the poorest of the rural poor in the South, with many reduced to sharecropping and living in virtual economic slavery. Blacks had begun to migrate north as industrial jobs were opened to them, but now they found that progress was moving at a snail's pace, if not receding. "Jim Crow" ruled the day and such laws were reintroduced in many communities. Calvin Coolidge was the first president in the twentieth century not to be a racist, and indeed, to be sympathetic to blacks, but in line with his overall policy of not interfering with existing conditions, he took no actions to advance their interests. Loss of hope led to Marcus Garvey's brief black-nationalist "Back to Africa" movement. In the face of a less-than-friendly trade-union movement, organizations such as the National Association for the Advancement of Colored People and the National Urban League looked to industry for leadership in ending discrimination in employment. But very few employers hired blacks for jobs other than those in the unskilled categories.

Turning Inward Politically and Culturally with a Burst of Creativity

The nation, of course, existed in a wider world, but with the rejection of Woodrow Wilson's League of Nations, it withdrew as much as it could from it, that is, aside from the Western Hemisphere. We did not hesitate, for instance, to intervene in the affairs of Central American and Caribbean nations, including sending troops to occupy some, and we even dispatched a thousand marines to China in 1927 to protect American property. Events elsewhere in the world, however, only contributed to the quest for isolation, as we can see by focusing on 1926, the year that Industrial Relations Counselors, Inc. (IRC), was founded.

Benito Mussolini was consolidating power in Italy, building a new antidemocratic system, "fascism," featuring the corporate state. In the Union of Soviet Socialist Republics that had replaced the Czarist Russian Empire, Joseph Stalin was preparing his brutal collectivization and industrialization programs. The German Weimar Republic was admitted to the League of Nations, but a disgruntled war veteran, Adolf Hitler—head of a small party called the National Socialists—was haranguing crowds, preaching hatred of Jews and German revanchism. Even Great Britain was wracked by a general strike, and economist John Maynard Keynes, who had warned of the dangers of the Versailles Treaty, published another seemingly prophetic book, *The End of Laissez-Faire*. Less prophetic was the award of the Nobel Peace Prize to Artiste Briand of France and Gustave Stressemann of Germany for having negotiated the Locarno Pact, which was supposed to ensure peace between the two nations.

The United States turned away from Europe culturally also, repudiating English and European traditions and asserting an "American" culture, which involved a shift of dominance from staid Boston to polyglot New York, as Ann Douglas (1995) has shown. Long the nation's financial and business center, New York City—IRC's home—now was the center of publishing, advertising, fashion, radio, music, and art as well. Its population doubled between 1910 and 1930 as it drew both immigrants from abroad and creative people from small towns across the nation. Symbolic of its cultural preeminence was the founding in 1925 of a new magazine, *The New Yorker*, which became the reading matter of the nation's sophisticates.

Not everyone, of course, moved to New York and Chicago: Boston and Philadelphia remained cultural centers but more regional. The South, moreover, enjoyed a literary renaissance. William Faulkner of Mississippi became one of the nation's top authors, and a southern literary movement, agrarianism, arose, centered around Vanderbilt University and the journal, the *Fugitive*.

American literature blossomed, and authors, although dubbed "the lost generation" by Gertrude Stein, became famous as book buying by the growing middle class—facilitated by the new Book-of-the-Month Club and Literary Guild—became part of the consumer society. Newspaper circulation boomed as the tabloid appeared, and magazines, both old—*The Saturday Evening Post*—and new—*The Reader's Digest*—flourished. The New York literary scene was both exciting and prodigious. Franklin P. Adams and his cronies held their roundtables at the Algonquin, the Fitzgeralds drank themselves blooey, Edna St. Vincent Millay burned her candle at both ends, and Edmund Wilson recorded it all in his journals. The action was not limited to midtown or Greenwich Village, for uptown the great "Harlem Renaissance" was in full bloom, featuring writers and artists such as Countee Cullen, Charles Johnson, Claude McKay, and Langston Hughes. Everyone was partying and having a swell time, especially the city's flamboyant mayor, Jimmy Walker.

It was an incredibly creative period. In 1926, Americans were reading Fitzgerald's *The Great Gatsby*, John Dos Passos' *Manhattan Transfer*, Theodore Dreiser's *An American Tragedy*, and the poetry of Robinson Jeffers, Edna St. Vincent Millay, T. S. Eliot, and Ezra Pound. That year saw the publication of Ernest Hemingway's *The Sun Also Rises*, Stephen Vincent Benet's *The Spanish Bayonet*, William Faulkner's *Soldier's Pay*, Hart Crane's first collection of poems, *White Buildings*, and e. e. cummings' *Is 5*. The 1926 Pulitzer prizes went to Sinclair Lewis for *Arrowsmith* in fiction, but he refused it, to George Kelley for *Craig's Wife* in drama, and to Amy Lowell for *What's o'Clock* in poetry. In the nonfiction area, Will Durant's *The Story of Philosophy* was published.

The lights of Broadway were ablaze in 1926. Mae West starred in *Sex,* and George and Ira Gershwin had a new hit, *Oh, Kay!* with its feature song, "Someone to Watch over Me." Richard Rodgers and Lorenz Hart's *The Girl Friend* and Anita Loos's *Gentlemen Prefer Blondes* played to packed houses. Dramas included Sidney Howard's *Ned McCobb's Daughter*, starring Alfred Lunt, Eugene O'Neill's *The Great God Brown*, and Jim Tully/Frank Dazey's *Black Boy*, about heavyweight champion Jack Johnson and starring Paul Robeson. Not everything was serious—*Abie's Irish Rose* entered its sixth year, becoming Broadway's greatest success.

In the visual arts, Edward Hopper was still painting realistic cityscapes,

Charles Sheeler made industry his subject matter, Georgia O'Keefe and Stuart Davis were innovating new forms and styles, and Peter Arno started drawing cartoons for *The New Yorker*. Americans blazed new paths in architecture in the form of the skyscraper and also in the work of Frank Lloyd Wright, who sought to harmonize buildings with their landscapes. New York's women's apparel industry moved uptown and began to challenge other cities, even Paris, as a fashion center.

Symphony orchestras were being established across the nation, but the most significant musical innovations came in the form of jazz and the attempts to combine it with classical music, e.g., George Gershwin's "Rhapsody in Blue." The top jazz artists were black and included King Oliver and his Creole Jazz Band, Louis Armstrong and Fletcher Henderson, Bessie Smith (the "empress of the blues"), and Duke Ellington. Jazz may have been born in the South, but the Cotton Club and other Harlem nightspots became the jazz centers of the 1920s. At the same time, dance innovations by Martha Graham were gaining recognition.

Radio broadcasting, for which the first license had been issued in 1920, became a stellar feature of popular culture, but it took second place to the motion picture, which by 1926 had become the nation's fifth-largest industry. Some twenty thousand theaters, many resembling modern palaces, dotted the landscape, and every little town could boast at least one. The movie actor became a celebrity, and one of the most memorable events of 1926 was the funeral of the "Latin Lover" who had enthralled American women, Rudolph Valentino. One third of American films were still made in New York, but California's Hollywood had become the world's film capital and helped to turn Los Angeles into a big city. In this arena, the United States reigned supreme—three quarters of all films shown in the world in 1926 were American. The industry rose to new heights as the silent era gave way to the "talkie" with the 1927 release of *The Jazz Singer*, starring Al Jolson.

Another form of popular culture, sports, exploded. While many people still engaged in sports themselves, most participated as spectators, and attendance at athletic events became part of the new consumerism. In 1926, Babe Ruth hit 47 home runs in the new Yankee Stadium and led the Yankees to another pennant, but they lost the World Series, 4–3, to the St. Louis Cardinals. The highlight of the year was Gene Tunney's defeat of Jack Dempsey for the world heavyweight boxing championship. It was quite a year: Gertrude Ederle swam the English Channel; in tennis, Helen Wills again won the American women's single championship, and the United States defeated France to win the Davis Cup; in golf, Walter Hagen won the PGA, but Bobby Jones took the U.S. Open; Alabama beat Washington, 20–19, in college football's Rose Bowl; and Red Grange played for the New York Yankees in a new sport—professional football. It also was the era of the sportswriter, and fans avidly read the columns of Grantland Rice, Damon Runyon, Ring Lardner, Paul Gallico, and John Kieran.

American accomplishment extended to the social and physical sciences. Ruth Benedict and the young Margaret Mead were advancing the relatively new field of anthropology. The Regional Planning Association of America came into being, with Lewis Mumford as its secretary and leading advocate of urban design. Two physicists won Nobel Prizes—Robert A. Millikan in 1923 and Arthur H. Compton in 1927. Another physicist, Robert Goddard, successfully fired the world's first liquid-fuel rocket in 1926. His work would not bear fruit for decades, but the nation was moving quickly into the airplane age. That same year, the Army Air Corps was established and the Air Commercial Act, which provided federal aid to airlines and airports, was passed. The law ran counter to the prevailing laissez-faire view, but subsidies to private industry were essential if aviation was to progress, since the only profitable area of commercial flying was bringing in booze from Canada and Mexico. Meanwhile, Charles Lindbergh was preparing for his historic 1927 flight across the Atlantic.

Innovations in Industrial Relations

Interesting things were happening in the industrial relations arena, too. The 1920s were not fruitful for unionism, as membership, which had shot up during the war, peaked at 5 million in 1920. Employers took advantage of a two-year depression to press the open-shop drive, and a number of court decisions went against unions. By 1923, membership had plummeted to 3.6 million. The sharpest drops were in the recently organized sectors, e.g., manufacturing. The membership of the International Association of Machinists, the major union in the metalworking industries, fell from 330,800 in 1920 to 77,900 in 1924.

Even in the prosperous period of 1923–29, union membership declined a further 200,000 in the face of a 3 million increase in nonagricultural employment. Some unionized industries were migrating from old production centers; in others, technological change eliminated the need for skilled workers. A number of unions were racked by internal dissension as the Communists tried to gain control, and others were infiltrated by racketeering elements.

Part of the problem facing unions was that management was attempting to improve conditions on the job and, in so doing, prove to employees that unions were not necessary to their welfare. Some companies also provided "voice" to employees through workers councils or employee representation plans. With the new management approaches and rising real earnings, unions found it difficult to organize in large manufacturing companies, so trade unionism continued to be basically a skilled-worker movement. The only industries with sizeable degrees of penetration were railroads, the building trades, and printing.

The railroad industry, the major form of transportation, saw significant developments. The shop-craft unions and the companies engaged in union-management cooperation. The federal government entered the scene in 1926 with the Railway Labor Act (RLA) which was designed to stabilize relations by setting up a system of mediation, arbitration, and fact finding to prevent strikes that would disrupt service. The RLA also facilitated the railroad brotherhoods' dominance by forcing management to recognize and bargain with them.

Trade unionism may have atrophied in the 1920s, but innovations in business were as dramatic as those in the cultural areas. Management became recognized as a profession, and colleges began to offer courses in the new discipline. With financial aid from John D. Rockefeller, Jr., an industrial relations section was established within Princeton University's economics department.

With the firm having grown to the size of a giant multi-establishment corporation, problems of control and coordination abounded. There were many experiments in organizational design, but the most famous was that of Alfred P. Sloan, Jr., at General Motors. Influenced by the DuPont system, Sloan created the concept of decentralized administration and operation coupled with centralized control and review, which permitted the separate parts of GM to work toward common goals. To the concept of decentralization into product divisions, DuPont then added the notion of profit-center accountability—each division was given a certain amount of resource investment, and its subsequent performance was measured and controlled by judging the rate of return on that investment.

Systematic management control became the norm, and much of industry used Frederick Taylor's scientific management approach (see Chapter 3, p. 42). There were contrasting views, such as Mary Parker Follett's "integrative unity," but the greatest challenge came accidentally as a result of a study undertaken in 1924 at the Hawthorne Works of Western Electric to test the relationship between worker efficiency and environmental factors, such as plant illumination and rest periods. Further study at Hawthorne, under the direction of Elton Mayo, led to the concept of "social" as well as "economic" man, that is, that workers were interested in aspects of the job beyond the amount of money it provided. Viewing the organization as a social system gave birth to the human relations movement. Some companies, particularly as the new staff function of industrial relations expanded, began to focus attention on the work group and on meeting employees' social needs.

The attempt to improve the relationship between a company and its employees was furthered by the founding in 1926 of IRC by John D. Rockefeller, Jr., "to advance the knowledge and practice of human relationships in industry, commerce, education, and government." Its trustees included industrial and educational leaders. IRC was the first and, at the time, only organization in the United States engaged in industrial relations research and application. With a top-notch staff, IRC pioneered progressive human resource policies through a wide swatch of American industry, eventually conducting studies and making recommendations for organizations outside the Rockefeller circle of interest.

IRC also symbolized another American attempt to turn away from old-world models. Given Europe's feudal history, the working class that arose with industrialism was drawn to Marx's concept of incompatibility between the interests of capital and labor and the need to replace capitalism with socialism. We seemed headed in that direction, too, as labor strife marked the opening of the twentieth century. Industry adhered to laissez-faire views, hiring and firing workers in response to production needs and ferociously resisting unionism. A trade-union movement, the American Federation of Labor (AFL), based on the British craft model, was expanding. A Socialist Party arose, and it quickly drew followers as it entered the political arena and elected mayors in a number of cities and two members of Congress (New York, Wisconsin); its 1912 presidential candidate, Eugene Victor Debs, secured 6 percent of the vote. (The Socialists, however, had peaked by World War I.) There even was an excursion into syndicalist revolutionary unionism, with the Industrial Workers of the World proclaiming it "was building the foundation of a new society within the shell of the old."

Yet, American history differed from that of Europe. The United States was unencumbered by a feudal class tradition, it eschewed the European concept of citizenship determined by bloodline, and it preached, if it did not practice, the equality of all people. At its founding, the nation was basically one of small, independent farmers, and the concept of an independent yeomanry persisted, even with the rise of industry. This history seemed to offer a possibility of a distinctive American approach to the relations between workers and employers.

Rockefeller recognized that possibility following the events at Ludlow in 1914 and abandoned the laissez-faire approach to seek a labor-management relationship based on mutual interests and obligations. Rockefeller stated his views succinctly in the first principle of what he called his creed: "I believe that Labor and Capital are partners, not enemies, that their interests are common, not opposed, and that neither can attain the fullest measure of prosperity at the expense of the other, but only in association with the other" (Fosdick

1956, 186). His associate, Clarence J. Hicks, pointed out that although employees and employers had conflicting interests in some areas, they had joint ones in many others, but it was up to management to promote mutuality of interest by curbing the authoritarian power of supervisors and listening to employees.

Rockefeller's second principle also sets a distinctive course: "I believe that every man is entitled to an opportunity to earn a living, to fair wages, to reasonable hours of work and proper working conditions, to a decent home, to the opportunity to play, to learn, to worship and to love as well as to toil; and the responsibility rests as heavily upon industry as upon government or society, to see that these conditions and opportunities prevail" (ibid.). He also believed that workers should have a voice in determining the conditions of their employment, but without the intrusion of a third party.

IRC sought to spread Rockefeller's creed through industry. Its very first publication, in 1927, was *Vacations for Industrial Workers*, a radical idea at the time. IRC also opened an office at the International Labour Organization in Geneva to conduct research on European social insurance programs. Through its consulting activities, it promoted pension plans, employee services, safety programs, supervisory training in human relations, and employee voice through employee representation plans (ERPs). Indeed, ERPs spread among progressive companies. While trade unionism declined during the 1920s, ERPs burgeoned and by 1928 covered 1,548,000 workers, a number equal to 44.5 percent of total union membership. Clearly, ERPs competed with unions as a device for providing voice in the workplace.

The End of This Innovative American Decade

Then suddenly, the situation changed, and this fascinating decade came to an end on October 29, 1929, "Black Thursday," when the stock market came crashing down from its speculative heights. Everything was turned upside down as the "era of permanent prosperity" gave way to that of the Great Depression. Businesses that had been efficient and profitable organizations yesterday found that no one wanted their products today. Workers who had been diligent and faithful were out on the street as their employers' orders disappeared. Worst of all, the nation's morale, including that of the business community, was shattered, as no one knew what to do about the Depression. The public's faith in laissez-faire was shaken to its foundations. In the industrial relations arena, the distinctive American approach envisioned by Rockefeller crumbled as jobs disappeared, wages were cut, employers' pension plans went bankrupt, and the misery of the time made workers psychologically ripe for unionization. In place of the philosophy of mutual interests of employers and employees came an adversarial labor-management system under government aegis.

It had been a glorious decade in which the United States had forged a distinctive economy and culture. For the next decade and a half, we endured depression and war but sprang back and reached ever-new heights—economically and culturally—and finally broke the race barrier that had divided us and moved toward a nation of equality for all. As we survey the changes in industrial relations over the past three quarters of a century, we find that many of Rockefeller's objectives have been achieved. The American workplace is much improved, employees are decently remunerated, they have protection against adversity, and their grievances are heard even in nonunion situations. Paradise has not been achieved, however, so let us at this symposium explore what aspects of the IRC objectives have meaning for us today.

By an eerie coincidence, this chapter, which includes a paean to New York City, was being delivered as the twin towers of the World Trade Center were attacked on September 11, 2001.

Industrial Relations Counselors, Inc.

Its History and Significance

Bruce E. Kaufman

*In research of this kind, we are aiding the whole cause of
industrial liberalism.*
Arthur Young in a 1926 letter to John D. Rockefeller, Jr.

The twentieth century witnessed many revolutions, but surely one of the most important and far-reaching took place in the conditions of work and the management of labor. At the beginning of the century, America was still in the early phase of transition from an agrarian to an industrial economy. For the wage-earning labor force, work hours often stretched to twelve a day, pay for many manual workers was barely enough to support a family at a subsistence level, and personal injury, termination without notice, and rough and insensitive treatment were everyday perils. In the common law of the period, the employment relationship was governed by the doctrine of "master and servant," a phrase that accurately captures both the spirit and practice of labor management at most companies of the period.

These conditions did not disappear overnight, and indeed, elements continue to exist in some contemporary workplaces in this country. But viewed over the long run, a remarkable, almost night-and-day transformation has taken place in the quality of people's work lives and in the practice and philosophy of labor management. Employees today enjoy a standard of living, a package of benefits, a safer and more pleasant (or at least less onerous) work environment, and legal protection against inhumane, unscrupulous, and discriminatory treatment that would have been unimaginable to early-twentieth-century workers. The philosophy and practice of people management in the workplace have also undergone a similar transformation, captured by the modern ideas that employees are no longer "hired hands" but "human resources" and managers should function as "leaders" and not "bosses."

Any account of this revolution in the workplace must highlight a large and diverse group of actors and developments. Certainly on this list would be labor unions and collective bargaining, government-enacted labor and employment laws, court rulings that expanded employees' workplace rights and protections, and the pressure exerted by various social reformers and religious and civic groups on behalf of improved workplace conditions. Also commanding attention would be the breathtaking technological advances, greater macroeconomic stability and reduced levels of unemployment, higher levels of education, a more open and meritocratic society, and greater sensitivity and commitment to human rights and values.

But also deserving to be on this short list would be another actor—employers—and another development—the philosophy and practice of progressive labor management. It is to this duo that the chapters in this volume pay tribute, with a special emphasis on one of the leading catalysts for change and proponents of progressive management—Industrial Relations Counselors, Inc.

As explained in the Introduction, Industrial Relations Counselors, Inc. (IRC), was organized in New York City in 1926 under the sponsorship of John D. Rockefeller, Jr. The impetus for the formation of IRC was Mr. Rockefeller's deep interest in promoting a more liberal and constructive approach to the management of employer-employee relations—a cause he had become a convert to as a result of his wrenching experience ten years earlier with a bloody miners' strike now popularly known as the "Ludlow Massacre." IRC was chartered as a nonprofit management research and consulting organization and, in this capacity, was the first of its kind in the nation. Its declared mission was to "advance the knowledge and practice of human relationships in industry, commerce, education, and government." The term "industrial relations" in IRC's title was intended to be construed broadly—as per common usage at that time—to include all subjects and practices related to work and the employment of labor, including what is known today as human resource management, while the word "counselors" was that era's term for consultants or advisors.

Mr. Rockefeller established and funded IRC with the intent that the organization would provide him with useful advice and counsel on employer-employee relations in his many business interests. But in keeping with his dedication to philanthropy and promoting the social good, he also intended that IRC serve a broader mission and constituency. A significant cause of friction and enmity between management and labor, he believed, was poor communication and inaccurate information about actual workplace practices and conditions. Thus, part of IRC's mission was to carry out a wide-ranging research and publication program, disseminating to companies and the public at large through newsletters, reports, and books the results of in-depth surveys and investigations on industrial relations topics. At the time, neither universities, government, nor other private agencies performed more than a smattering of such research, and IRC's work was therefore not only pioneering but also frequently authoritative.

Rockefeller also saw that many of the nation's leading businessmen, even when sincerely committed to improving their industrial relations programs, were often woefully ignorant of labor conditions in their own companies, had little knowledge of "best practice" personnel procedures, and had nowhere to go to obtain advice and guidance. Thus, a second part of IRC's mission was to serve as an industrial relations consultant to companies, providing in-depth, confidential reports and recommendations to top management on overall labor policy and all aspects of personnel/human resource practice. Many of America's leading companies established their first personnel/industrial relations department, pension system, and supervisor training program on the recommendation of IRC.

In the early 1930s, Mr. Rockefeller began to phase out his financial support for IRC, believing that the organization had proven its value and could successfully generate enough funds to operate on a self-supporting basis. He was correct in this surmise, but inevitably the pressure of raising additional revenue led IRC to gradually shift more of its emphasis in succeeding years to the consulting and training side of the business. Eventually, in the early 1950s, to avoid potential dispute over its nonprofit tax status, the consulting activities were spun off to a for-profit sister organization—initially called "Industrial Relations Counselors Services, Inc." (IRCS) and later "Organization Resources Counselors, Inc." (ORC), while IRC continued to carry forward the research and publication program.

For another twenty years, IRC produced a steady stream of newsletters, reports, and books on a wide array of industrial relations topics, keeping the profession up-to-date on the big issues of the day—automation, equal opportunity, a guaranteed annual wage, and a host of other subjects. But IRC's research and publication activity began to gradually slacken as the organization entered the 1970s, which reflected both financial constraints and the fact that the research void so noticeable in industrial relations in the 1920s and 1930s was now being more ably filled by numerous universities, government agencies, and private organizations. By the end of the 1990s, IRC had become largely inactive, its name and legacy known to only a small circle of academics in business and labor history and client companies that continue to receive occasional IRC newsletters and reports.

Although IRC's current contribution to the cause of progressive management and improved employer-employee relations is modest, its historical contribution is large indeed. Thus, it seems particularly fitting on the occasion of IRC's seventy-fifth anniversary to take a retrospective look at its founding, activities, and accomplishments and to place these in their larger historical significance. This is the task of this chapter.

Antecedent Events and People

Industrial Relations Counselors, Inc., was one player in a much larger, unfolding drama in industrial America. Appreciation of the role played by IRC, and its contribution to the outcome, requires that we go back in history to the late nineteenth century, starting with the advent of what was popularly known as the "Labor Problem."

The Labor Problem

For a roughly forty-year period stretching from 1880 to 1920, the number one domestic issue in the United States was the "Labor Problem." The labor problem was originally conceived in unitary terms—the titanic struggle between Labor and Capital over control of production and the distribution of the fruits thereof. It was propelled into the national consciousness in the 1880s and 1890s by bloody labor strikes, such as at Homestead and Pullman, that escalated into pitched battles, mass destruction of property, considerable loss of life, and, not infrequently, intervention by state and federal troops to restore order. These strikes, and other attendant acts of violence and sabotage, continued through the first two decades of the twentieth century, which led the U.S. Commission on Industrial Relations to declare in 1916, "The question of industrial relations assigned by Congress to the commission for investigation is more fundamental and of greater importance to the welfare of the Nation than any other question except the form of government" (U.S. Congress 1916, vol. 1, 1). Scarcely before the ink was dry on these words, strikes, labor violence, and widespread fear of revolution escalated even further with the advent of World War I, culminating in 1919 with the Seattle general strike, nationwide strikes in the steel and coal industries, thousands of other walkouts, and widespread hysteria that Russian-inspired Bolshevism was threatening to subvert American democracy.

Although strikes and other forms of conflict were at first taken as the defining feature of the Labor Problem, a broader, more expansive view emerged as the nation moved into the twentieth century. Increasingly, people no longer talked about *the* Labor Problem but instead used the plural version labor problem*s*. The "problems" perspective gained currency because people came to realize that numerous other serious shortcomings and maladjustments were present in the employment relationship besides conflict and that these problems adversely impacted all parties to the employment relationship—employers, employees, consumers, and the public. Examples included rampant employee turnover and absenteeism, great waste and inefficiency in production, poverty-level wages for many manual workers, twelve-hour days and seven-day workweeks, tens of thousands of industrial fatalities, and near complete absence of rights and voice in the workplace.

The cause of labor problems and their real-life nature at the turn of the twentieth century can be appreciated with greater insight by an example. In his autobiography, Don Lescohier describes the working conditions and management methods at the Detroit Stove Works where he worked as a young man in 1900. Lescohier was so appalled by conditions he encountered there that he quit, dedicated his life to making things better, attained a Ph.D. in economics from the University of Wisconsin, and became the first full-time university professor to teach personnel management at an American university. He says of work life and human resource management at the Detroit Stove Works:

Working in factories during the 1890s, or indeed, up to the time of the First World War, was very different from working in factories today. In the first place, the method of hiring the unorganized was for foremen to come to the front gate of the plant around 7 a.m., look over the gang of men congregated outside the gate, pick out men he knew or thought he wanted, or motion to this man or that, without interviewing, to come through the plant gate. It was a good deal like a butcher picking out particular animals from a herd.

When he got as many as he wanted he led them to his department, assigned them their work, with perhaps momentary interviews to find out whether they had any experience in the kinds of work in his department. Ordinarily a man hired in this process did not know what his pay would be until he got his wages on payday. If you asked the foreman that question when you were hired you would, ordinarily, be shown the gate. Complete submission of unorganized workers to the company was the expectation of the Detroit Stove Works. Like hundreds of other common laborers I had heard the foreman say to me: "Put on your coat," which meant that you were fired. You did as he said.

In the basement of the building where I worked at that time was a grinding room. The only artificial light was old-fashioned gas lights, one above and between each pair of grinding wheels. It was in almost complete darkness—say dark twilight—since the gas flames gave so little light. You had to walk slowly and keep a hand out in front of you to avoid falling over a truck handle or other obstruction. One man, I remember, broke his leg by falling over a truck handle in that dark passage.

The employees in that place were all old men, not strong enough any more to do the harder work of most common laborers. They got $1.25 for ten hours' work in that department.

The stock room where I worked was a corner partitioned off from the metal polishing department. On the side toward the polishing room were large removable windows which allowed light to come through the stock room to the polishers—who were skilled union men. The windows also let in the south and southwest summer breezes. The polishers asked to have the windows opened each day during the summer so they could feel those breezes. The company refused. The polishers went out on strike to force the company to remove the windows. When one union struck, they all did. So a plant with 2,500 employees was tied up for three days over this simple grievance. But striking was the only grievance procedure the men had and only the union men had that.

There were a lot of accidents in the stove works—no fatal ones that I know of. But there were emery wheel burns, bad cuts often three or four inches long from the edges of sheets of steel, burns from hot iron in the foundry, loss of fingers or toes. At sixteen years of age one of my duties was first aid for the injured. No one gave me any instructions and the medical supplies consisted of a bottle of oil, some unsterilized waste, and some unsterilized cotton bandage cloth, kept in an ordinary cupboard. [1960, 32–34, modestly condensed from the original]

Solutions to Labor Problems

Lescohier's experience at work was not unique nor were the management methods and organization of work. From this description, it is self-evident why the nation had serious labor problems and why turnover, waste, low morale, conflict, and workplace fatalities were rampant. Because of the breadth and depth of labor problems, much public and private attention was devoted to finding a solution. Although a wealth of diverse viewpoints and proposals were put forward, three broad positions on the continuum of opinion are identifiable. The two endpoints were defined by a status quo conservative/reactionary position based on principles of laissez-faire, freedom of contract, and Social Darwinism on one end and on the other end by a revolutionary movement to replace capitalism with a version of socialism or syndicalism (Bendix 1956; Fine 1956). In the middle were a large number of social/economic reformers who sought to maintain basic American political and economic institutions but also to smooth the "rough edges" of class conflict and harmonize the relations between Capital and Labor through new devices such as collective bargaining, government protective labor legislation, and progressive methods of labor management. I briefly review each.

Laissez-Faire, Freedom of Contract, and Social Darwinism

On one endpoint of the continuum of thought, albeit a position with many adherents, was a distinctly conservative, sometimes reactionary, position built on a melding of the economic theory of laissez-faire, the legal theory of freedom of contract, and the social theory of Social Darwinism. People in this group tended to believe that society was ordered by natural, God-given law and that harmony would prevail but for defects of human character and willful violations of this law—a view consistent with and reinforced by the then widespread Calvinist religious belief in salvation through hard work and individual initiative. Labor problems such as unemployment, low work effort, and poverty, for example, were typically ascribed to personal short-comings of workers, such as laziness, intemperance, and lack of initiative, while problems such as strikes and labor unrest were the product of agitators and organized interest groups intent on subverting American institutions. That some people rose to become "captains of industry" while others remained day laborers all their life was likewise the operation of the Darwinian law of "survival of the fittest" and was God's providential way of promoting social progress and survival of the species.

From this point of view, efficiency and justice could best be obtained by promoting Adam Smith's system of "natural liberty" through a highly de-centralized market economy—efficiency because the combination of private property, freedom of contract, and competition provides the maximum in-centives and opportunities for people to create wealth and engage in person-ally responsible behavior and justice because competition ensures that every person is paid commensurate with their contribution to production, and any party who feels ill-treated can easily find alternative employment. Labor unions, government regulation, and softhearted business reformers were typi-cally regarded as misguided and often harmful and thus to be condemned. Representative of this conservative viewpoint in the late nineteenth century is economist Arthur Latham Perry (1878), who maintains that the solution to the worker's problems is "to look out for his own interest, to know the market-value of his own service, and to make the best terms for himself which he can; . . . [T]he remedy . . . is not in arbitrary interference of govern-ment in the bargain, but in the intelligence and self-respect of the laborers" (p. 200). He goes on to condemn collective bargaining and strikes as "false in theory and pernicious in practice . . . they embitter relations between em-ployers and employed . . . and rarely or never are permanently advantageous" (p. 204). Also illustrative is this statement by railroad magnate George Baer: "The rights and interests of the laboring man will be protected and cared for, not by labor agitators, but by the Christian men to whom God in His infinite wisdom has given the control of the property interests of the country" (quoted in Commons 1913, 63).

Socialism and Syndicalism

On the other end of the spectrum were radical solutions to the Labor Problem, such as socialism and syndicalism. Although neither doctrine enjoys more than fringe support today, in the late nineteenth and early twentieth centuries, they were far more popular, evidenced by the millions of votes Socialist candidates regularly received in political elections. Socialists and syndicalists thought the Labor Problem was an inherent feature of capitalism and that workers and employers were separated by a deep and unbridgeable conflict of interest. They further thought that the concentration of property in the hands of the capitalists, the effective control of the government by the rich and powerful, and the workers' lack of any resource except perishable labor tilted the conflict of interest so far to the disadvantage of workers that they became "wage slaves," suffering the extremes of exploitation, mistreatment, and subordination. From this perspective, reform was a short-run palliative and the only real solution was to abolish capitalism and/or the wage system.

Toward this end, socialists advocated resolving the Labor Problem by having the working class control the state and replacing private ownership of the means of production with state ownership. These steps would end the conflict of interest (because capitalists are eliminated and the state manages industry as the agent of the working class) and ensure workers the full fruits of their labor (since the working class owns all the means of production and therefore receives the total income); thus, true "industrial democracy" prevails (since workers control industry through the state). Syndicalists, on the other hand, thought the source of the Labor Problem was deeper than capitalism and arose from the inherent nature of the wage system. Whether the means of production are owned by capitalists or the state makes no difference in this view; the result will be the same since those in control of industry will of necessity face two pressures—to hold down wages and working conditions in order to provide funds for capital investment and to exert control over workers and "boss" them. Thus, the solution is to abolish the wage system by having all capital communally owned and operated in the form of worker cooperatives ("syndicates"), thus in effect making individual workers shareholders and turning the enterprise into an employee-managed enterprise (a nineteenth-century version of an employee stock ownership plan)). Illustrative of these points of view, labor radical and Socialist Party candidate for U.S. president Eugene Debs stated in 1911, "In the struggle of the working class to free itself from wage slavery, . . . the simple question is can the workers fit themselves, by education, organization, co-operation, and self-imposed discipline, to take control of the productive forces and manage industry in the interest of the people and for the benefit of society? . . . [In socialism] there would be no 'bosses' and no 'hands,' but men instead—free men, employing themselves cooperatively under regulations of their own" (1948, 340–41).

Reform Methods: Unions, Legislation, Management

Between the two extremes of unregulated profit seeking and the abolition of capitalism were situated a broad array of reform movements. These reform movements had their roots in the late nineteenth century but flowered in the first two decades of the twentieth century in what is now popularly called "the Progressive era." The Progressives were drawn largely from the growing ranks of the urban middle class, the professions, and salaried management and were often imbued with a strong streak of reformist Christianity known as the "Social Gospel." Their socioeconomic position and more liberal religious bent gave them both a significant stake in stabilizing and preserving the prevailing political/economic order and an outlook that was more educated, rationalistic, and humanistic. Their outlook is well captured by Progressive economist John R. Commons' statement that his goal was to "save capitalism by making it good" (1934, 143) and by William Lyon Mackenzie King's declaration that "an industrial system characterized by antagonism, coercion, and resistance must yield to a new order based upon mutual confidence, real justice, and constructive good-will" (1918, 10).

The Progressives and their allies charted three different broad approaches to solving the Labor Problem. These became known, respectively, as the *workers' solution*, the *employer's solution*, and the *community's solution* (Watkins and Dodd 1940; Kaufman 1993).

The *workers' solution* to the Labor Problem was trade unionism and collective bargaining. Trade unionism was largely of working-class origins, a number of unions were avowedly socialistic, and the labor movement was regarded by many conservatives and businesspeople as a propagator of labor monopoly and class warfare. But a number of Progressives saw that the labor movement could be an important instrument for defusing the Labor Problem and bringing greater economic stability and social justice to the workplace. Toward this end, they sought to make an alliance with the more moderate wing of the labor movement, including a number of "business unions" in the American Federation of Labor (AFL) and "responsible" union leaders, such as the AFL's Samuel Gompers and the Mine Workers' president, John Mitchell. Moderate business unions, the Progressives thought, could help solve the

Labor Problem in two ways: by equalizing the bargaining power between Capital and Labor and by introducing democracy into industry. Equal bargaining power, achieved through collective negotiation with the employer and the threat of striking, would help end exploitation, sweat-shop conditions, twelve-hour days, and the constant threat of discharge, while industrial democracy would be achieved by using collective bargaining to give workers a voice in the determination of workplace rules and due process in the resolution of disputes. The net effect would be to reduce the breadth and depth of open conflict between Capital and Labor by promoting "a constitutional form of organization representing the interests affected, with mutual veto, and therefore with progressive compromises as conflicts arise" (Commons 1913, 140). Unions do not eliminate class conflict in this view, but they help to bridge it through negotiated compromise.

The *workers' solution* of trade unionism blossomed in practice and in Progressive thought beginning in the last decade of the nineteenth century. The *community's solution* followed in the early part of the twentieth century. The community's solution to the Labor Problem entailed law and regulation, principally in the form of protective labor legislation (e.g., minimum wages, prohibition of child labor) and social insurance programs (e.g., accident, unemployment, and old-age insurance). As seen by Progressive reformers, the interplay of competition and profit seeking in unregulated labor markets led to a number of grievous social ills. Since trade unions represented only about 5 percent of the workforce at the turn of the century, an alternative method was needed to equalize the bargaining power of these disadvantaged groups, establish a minimum level of labor conditions throughout industry, and provide welfare benefits that individual firms either could or would not. Thus, in the first decade of the twentieth century, a movement developed in American society for greater government regulation of labor conditions and provision of social welfare benefits, spearheaded by a new organization established in 1906 called the American Association for Labor Legislation (AALL) and a coalition of liberals and progressives from industry, academe, social work, and religious groups. Illustrative of their philosophy is this statement by Thomas Adams and Helen Sumner in their book *Labor Problems* (1905, 15): "The true ideal of society is not laissez faire, but economic freedom, and freedom is the child, not the enemy, of law and regulation." Despite considerable political agitation and political lobbying, the actual progress of reformers in implementing the community's solution to labor problems was quite modest before World War I, blocked by conservative Supreme Court decisions and public opinion (the largest gain was in state-enacted workers' compensation laws, followed by a few state minimum-wage laws for women).

The third approach to reform that developed in the early twentieth century to resolve the Labor Problem was the *employers' solution* of progressive labor management (Jacoby 1985; Kaufman 2001). Up to the period of World War I, the practice of labor management in American industry was marked by authoritarianism and insensitivity, a "commodity" conception of labor, "drive" methods of work motivation, and lack of any systematic, formalized personnel procedures. Most employers, to quote one nineteenth-century observer, thought that their relation to the workers was "a purely economic one—they considered them not as men, but as a means of accumulating capital" (Gilman 1899, 10). Said a factory owner looking back on the period, "One of the great evils that grew out of the [pre–World War I] system was the tendency of those who employed labor to buy it just exactly as they would the machinery and materials required; to obtain it at the lowest possible price and get as much out of it as they could" (quoted in Smith 1960, 263). And prevailing economic conditions and social mores allowed employers to strike a very hard bargain.

In the two decades prior to World War I, millions of immigrants poured into the United States, predominantly from southern and eastern Europe, often illiterate, unskilled, and non–English-speaking, and from pre-industrial peasant societies. This flood of new labor-force entrants, coupled with significant laborsaving (and deskilling) technological change and recurrent periods of recession and depression, made unskilled and semi-skilled labor a "buyer's market" and, in most years, gave employers the upper hand in bargaining. (Skilled craft workers exercised more control over labor conditions, but their ranks were dwindling in relative terms.) The result was not only the long work hours, low pay, and primitive working conditions previously described in the quote from Lescohier but also an autocratic, arbitrary, and dehumanizing exercise of authority. The employment relation at the time was legally conceived as one of "master and servant" and "employment at will." This, along with the surplus of job seekers and the tendency of native-born Americans to regard many of the new immigrants as a lower grade of humanity, made it possible for employers to rule the shop in a largely unrestricted fashion—to "drive" workers to exert maximum effort through rough language, threats of firing, and termination of workers for any infraction of work rules, complaints about working conditions, or interest in unions. Not only did employers rule the shop with a heavy hand, often they dominated local communities, built as they were around a steel mill, coal mine, or textile mill, and used their control of company housing and local judges and sheriffs to further consolidate their control over labor (Fitch 1924). After a tour of coal-mining towns in West Virginia, Senator Robert Wagner remarked, "Had I not seen it myself, I would not have believed that in the United States there were large areas where civil government was supplanted by a system that can only be compared with ancient feudalism" (quoted in Huthmacher 1968, 64).

The first stirrings of reform in the manner in which companies managed their employees began in the last decade of the nineteenth century. As described in the next chapter of this volume, engineers and progressive employers began to experiment with different forms of compensation, such as profit sharing and differential piece-rate systems, in an effort to promote greater work effort and better align company and worker objectives. It was thus in 1895 that Frederick Taylor, later to be recognized as the father of scientific management, published his first article, entitled "A Piece Rate System, Being a Partial Solution to the Labor Problem." Over the next decade, he extended his theories, which he detailed in 1911 in the book *Principles of Scientific Management*. Taylor argued that industrial management involved scientific principles and that the discovery and implementation of these principles would dramatically increase efficiency and output, provide the basis for much higher wages (thus uniting the interests of Capital and Labor in greater productivity), and eliminate injustice and rancor by basing shop rules and operations on objective criteria. Toward this end, he advocated a wide range of "efficiency devices," such as time-and-motion study, instruction cards for performing each task, and a system of functional foremanship.

A second avenue of reform in labor management also emerged in the late 1890s and came to be known as the "industrial welfare" movement (Tone 1997; Mandell 2002). Forward-looking, socially minded employers began to provide employees with a variety of nonwage benefits, such as company-sponsored social events, libraries and reading rooms, an in-plant doctor or nurse, and subsidized coal and food. In large companies, these new programs were administered by a newly hired "welfare secretary" and often staffed by a person (typically female) from a social-work background. As described by one proponent of welfare activities (Gilman 1899, 358), they were intended as a "healing measure" and "can hardly fail to bring him [the employer] nearer as time goes by to a living sympathy with these men and women of like passions with himself" (p. 358). The motivation, in turn, was often couched in terms of moral responsibility, although they also clearly served a business objective (e.g., reducing turnover, increasing employee loyalty). Thus, in this spirit, the same author states, "The employer here recognizes a moral obligation, incumbent upon the successful producer, to give a share of his fortune to his fellow-workers . . . his large moneyed ability seems to him to impose the responsibility of that finer justice which men call generosity" (ibid., 27–28).

A third area of innovation in labor management became visible in the early 1910s—the creation of an "employment management" staff function in large companies (Jacoby 1985). Before this time, companies did not have any kind of personnel department or staff nor did they have any kind of standardized, written company guidelines or employment polices. Rather, company executives typically delegated to the plant superintendent responsibility for establishing and administering labor policy and managing the workforce; most often the superintendent delegated the day-to-day operational aspects of personnel management, such as hiring, firing, rates of pay, and resolution of grievances, to individual foremen and gang bosses. This system allowed company executives and plant superintendents to focus on other areas of the business deemed more crucial, such as finance and production, but also caused them to be largely divorced from events and conditions on the shop floor. The actual management of labor also suffered because the system was highly decentralized and largely uncoordinated; management methods were haphazard and generally based on customary procedures or personal whim, and the foremen often exercised their authority in a "hard-boiled," insensitive, and often discriminatory way that bred much resentment and feelings of injustice among the workers. This system was gradually recognized as highly inefficient and a major cause of labor conflict, which led to reform efforts. One tack was to create an "employment management" department in the plant or firm through which hiring decisions were coordinated (a broader-based personnel department was a still-later innovation, first appearing in the late 1910s). Another was to create some kind of shop committee or "conciliation council" to resolve disputes before they boiled over into strikes and violence. Although obviously of great promise for the future, as of 1915, these initiatives remained rudimentary and were adopted in some form by only several dozen progressive employers.

Thus, among the great mass of American employers, the management of labor was still practiced much as it had been one and two decades earlier—it was haphazard, heavily autocratic, and regarded as of little strategic importance. Other than the introduction of a smattering of welfare programs and the practice of an enlightened paternalism among some employers, little attempt was made in a positive direction to foster cooperation, promote justice and goodwill, and gain commitment of the employees to a common purpose. Rather, most employers were still wedded to the doctrines of laissez-faire, freedom of contract, and Social Darwinism and managed their employees in this spirit. The traditional personnel functions of attracting, retaining, and motivating workers were thus largely accomplished for manual employees through punitive and coercive methods, such as the threat of unemployment and driving methods of supervision, while threats to the employer's authority were met with quick termination and grievances with the rejoinder: "If you don't like it here, quit and go somewhere else." Not surprisingly, employees responded in kind with sky-high rates of job turnover, soldiering on the job, numerous strikes and refusals to work, and simmering interest in union organization.

Thus, despite more than three decades of public alarm over the threat posed by the Labor Problem and the beginnings of reform along three fronts, the specter of class war continued to haunt American society on the eve of World War I. As the nation entered the year 1914, little did it know that the Labor Problem would spawn a cataclysmic event in the coalfields of Colorado that would galvanize the son of America's richest industrialist to abandon conservatism and take up the reform of industrial relations through the employers' solution of progressive management. This transformative event was the Ludlow Massacre, and born out of it a decade later was Industrial Relations Counselors, Inc.

The Ludlow Massacre

In the summer of 1913, the United Mine Workers Union began extensive organizing efforts among the miners in the southern coalfields of Colorado (Gitelman 1988). Several months later, the union presented a list of eight demands to the companies, including union recognition, a 10 percent increase in wages, the eight-hour day, abolition of armed mine guards, and compliance with Colorado mining laws. The companies refused to discuss the demands, and on September 23, more than eight thousand miners went on strike. Because the companies owned the housing, the striking miners and their families were forced to leave the coal camps and live in a makeshift tent colony.

Violence quickly broke out, and the state militia was called in to restore order. Hostility between the militia and miners grew during the winter, and on April 20, 1914, a pitched battle erupted. By the end of the daylong shootout, the troops had killed ten men and one child and had burned the tent colony to the ground. The next day, two women and eleven children, who had hid in a hole under one of the tents to escape the gunfire, were discovered to have suffocated during the fire. The killings were dubbed the "Ludlow Massacre" and quickly sparked an orgy of burning, looting, and killing across the coalfields of Colorado.

Word of the disaster quickly spread across the nation, leading to widespread outrage and condemnation of the companies. The focal point of the public's ire was the Rockefellers, the largest shareholders of the Colorado Fuel and Iron Company (CF&I) and thus the ones many people held ultimately responsible for the disaster. This judgment was formed on two counts. First, CF&I was the largest employer involved in the strike, and it was presumed that the Rockefellers (Sr. and Jr.) controlled the company's labor policy and influenced the negotiating position of the companies. Second, John D. Rockefeller, Jr. (hereafter, "Rockefeller"), had earlier testified to a congressional committee on the strike and seemed to have only sketchy knowledge of the situation, reaffirmed his belief that the workers were satisfied with labor conditions at CF&I and had been coerced into striking by union agitation and misinformation, refused to intercede with CF&I executives to promote a compromise solution, and took a hard-line position against any dealings with the union.

Rockefeller was excoriated in the press, received death threats, and was denounced by demonstrators outside his office in New York City. His first response was to deny responsibility as he had delegated labor policy and conduct of the strike to CF&I executives in Denver and, hence, had little direct knowledge or control. Rockefeller also pointed out that the battle had been waged by the state militia, not personnel of CF&I, and the killings of the women and children were an accident, albeit a terrible one. While true as literal statements of fact, this position did little to defuse the criticism and, indeed, only led to further attack for his apparent lack of concern for the treatment of workers in his employ and unwillingness to become involved even after disaster had struck. To many people, Rockefeller appeared to be a remote, insensitive capitalist who was wedded to maintaining the open shop regardless of the human costs, and thus they assigned to him and his family a majority of the blame for the outcome.

Looking back on the situation, Rockefeller's legal advisor and business counselor, Raymond Fosdick, concluded that he was indeed innocent of much of this criticism but that Rockefeller had nonetheless erred, partly because he badly misperceived the true facts surrounding the strike, relying as he had on reports and assurances from CF&I executives several thousand miles away, and partly because CF&I executives and several of his close business advisors in New York were "unquestionably bred in the paternalistic spirit" and hence steered him toward too hard and uncompromising a stance (Fosdick 1956, 145). Fosdick—later to play a key role in the formation of Industrial Relations Counselors, Inc.—conceded that the miners did in fact have many legitimate grievances, even though labor conditions at CF&I were generally superior to those at other companies. He says,

> The location of the camps and the unnatural growth of the communities soon created a kind of feudal autocracy in which the various companies acted not only as employer but also as landlord, merchant, legislator, and indirectly as priest and teacher. The situation at its best was unsatisfactory, and oftentimes this concentration of power led to serious negligence and

abuse on the part of company officials. There was no adequate contact between employer and employee, no machinery for the adjustment of grievances, indeed no appreciation of the significant place of labor in cooperative enterprise. [Ibid., 144]

He goes on to say,

According to the company's officers, there was no need for a grievance procedure; the miners were contented with conditions in the Colorado Fuel and Iron Company, and if misunderstanding arose they were free to come as high as the president himself with their complaints. But few of the miners were willing to risk the ire of a pit boss who had been bypassed, to say nothing of assistant managers and superintendents, and there was the further danger of being blackballed as a union sympathizer. Thus the operators who spoke so confidently about the universal satisfaction among their employees were actually in no position to know the facts. [Ibid., 146–47]

As the condemnation and criticism rained down upon him, however, Rockefeller had little grasp of these realities, having had little interest or experience in labor matters and never having been closer to the mines than Denver where the CF&I board of directors met. However, confident in the correctness of his position, and convinced that the public would exonerate him and the Rockefeller family if they only knew the true facts, Rockefeller decided to sponsor an impartial investigation of the events in Colorado by an expert in the field of industrial relations. On the advice of Charles Eliot, president of Harvard University, Rockefeller in June 1914 invited William Lyon Mackenzie King to direct the investigation. The choice, in Fosdick's words, "could not have been more fortunate" and seemed to be the work of "some rare providence" (ibid., 153). Indeed, the selection of King changed the course of American industrial relations and led directly to the founding of IRC.

King and the Rockefeller Plan

William Lyon Mackenzie King was a Canadian of about the same age as Rockefeller. He had done graduate work at the University of Chicago and at Harvard on labor problems, participated in the social-work program at Hull House, and then moved back to Canada, where he amassed considerable experience and public recognition for his work in industrial relations, culminating in his selection as minister of labour in the federal government in 1909 (McGregor 1962). Fortunately for Rockefeller, King lost his cabinet position in 1911 when the Liberal Party lost control of Parliament, making him available for the Colorado investigation.

As Fosdick notes, "more important than King's professional training was the fact that he was a man signally qualified to influence JDR Jr." (1956, 154). By all accounts, Rockefeller took to King immediately, and the two formed a lifelong bond of friendship and trust. The charge given to King was to advise Rockefeller on, "the discovery of some organization or union, or at any rate of some mutual relationship of capital and labor which would afford to labor the protection it needs against oppression and exploitation, while at the same time promoting its efficiency as an instrument of economic production" (quoted in Gitelman 1988, 45). In August 1914, King responded with a six-Page letter outlining a plan of employee representation.

In his letter, King proposed that the miners at CF&I choose in secret-ballot elections representatives from among their ranks. These representatives would, in turn, meet with company officials on a regular basis to discuss all matters of mutual interest, including terms and conditions of employment and outstanding grievances. The aim, said King, was to foster greater cooperation, mutual understanding, and sense of justice by providing a mechanism for direct communication between the company and miners, a method for collective dealing with labor, and a forum for the airing of disputes and dissatisfactions. The virtue of the plan, said King, was that it steered a middle course between the two extremes of individual bargaining and collective bargaining with a national union. Importantly, King insisted the plan contain a guarantee that the company would follow a practice of nondiscrimination with respect to union membership and that employees could serve as representatives regardless of union affiliation (Gitelman 1988).

Rockefeller accepted King's idea, worked to convince CF&I executives to accept it, and in September 1915, personally accompanied King to the coalfields of Colorado to pitch the plan to the company's employees. After two weeks of visits to coal camps and miners' houses, Rockefeller asked the employees to vote on acceptance of King's plan. Of 2,846 ballots cast, 2,404 were in favor.

Rockefeller was aware, however, that the new representation plan could easily fail for lack of careful and adroit leadership, so he recruited Clarence Hicks to administer the plan at CF&I. Hicks was, in the words of Fosdick, "a warm and energetic man and one of the pioneers in the field of industrial relations" (1956, 164). Another attribute that Hicks shared with King and Rockefeller was a strong religious bent. Hicks had begun his career with the YMCA (Young Men's Christian Association), working with railroads to improve lodging and recreation facilities for the train crews while away from home, and was later recruited by the International Harvester Company to serve as an executive in charge of its fledgling industrial relations program. After CF&I, Hicks in 1918 went to Standard Oil (New Jersey) and developed one of the most extensive and successful industrial relations programs in any American company of the period. On his retirement in 1933, he joined the staff of IRC and in 1936 became chairman of the board of trustees.

The employee representation plan at CF&I received great national attention. Some critics, of course, remained unimpressed. For example, Samuel Gompers, president of the American Federation of Labor, asked, "What influence can such a pseudo union have to insist upon the remedying of a grievous wrong or the attainment of a real right?" (quoted in Fosdick 1956, 166). Many industrialists, on the other hand, regarded the plan as a radical, utopian step that undermined management authority and opened the door to unionism and bolshevism (Ching 1953, 29). But the majority of Americans regarded the "Rockefeller plan" as a progressive, forward-looking innovation in industrial relations, and Rockefeller's sponsorship of the plan and visit to Colorado did much to win him back public favor. As Fosdick observed of the CF&I plan, "It represented the beginnings of a new attitude of responsibility and cooperation on the part of employers" (1956, 166). In this respect, he was also correct in observing, "The younger Rockefeller had come a long way since 1913" (ibid., 165).

Labor Troubles at Jersey Standard

The strike at CF&I was not the only labor trouble dogging Rockefeller. In 1915 and again in 1916, violent strikes erupted at the Bayonne, New Jersey, refinery of the Standard Oil Company of New Jersey ("Jersey Standard"). The labor policies of the company, and the cause of the strike, vary only in the details from the case of CF&I. As described by Gibb and Knowlton (1956, 135–52, 570–95), the Rockefellers had a long-standing policy, communicated to Jersey Standard's board of directors and top executives, that pay was to be kept at or above the market level and workers were to be treated fairly. But beyond these broad guidelines the Rockefellers did not go, nor did they express any interest or concern about the implementation and administration of labor relations. Much the same attitude and policy were adopted by the company's executives, with the result that no standardized or written employment rules or guidelines existed, nearly all operational aspects of labor practice were delegated to individual foremen, and no mechanism for the resolution of grievances or bottom-to-top communication existed.

The first strike began on July 15, 1915, and quickly escalated into a pitched battle, replete with massive destruction of property, numerous deaths, and use of the National Guard to restore order. As described by Gibb and Knowlton, "[R]ioting and destruction began—the worst the East Coast had seen in many years. . . . The city of Bayonne became a battle camp and the refinery a fortress under siege" (ibid., 143). This first strike was eventually subdued and order restored. The company refused throughout to meet with the strike leaders but did at the end grant a wage increase. Then in October of 1916, another strike of similar proportions broke out, leading to more deaths and destruction. The Rockefellers, of course, were again the object of much public criticism.

The ostensible cause of the strikes was a demand for higher wages, but Gibb and Knowlton conclude the real reasons lay elsewhere. They state, "The basic cause of the uprisings was the yawning administrative chasm that separated Bayonne management and the men. Jersey Standard's honorable tradition of fair play to the contrary notwithstanding, no workman at the Bayonne refinery had any effective way by which he might air his grievances. . . . [T]he men at Bayonne knew, if the directors did not, that long before they reached the front office with their complaints they would have ceased to hold their jobs. . . . Here the only recourse was to the strike; the men submitted to the leadership of rabble-rousers, radicals and incompetents because there was no effective alternative" (ibid., 570).

Once the strike began, the company fought back with all of the resources available to it. Gibb and Knowlton say, "The directors, like other men of that day and later, were imbued with fervent belief in their right to protect their property at any cost. They were bitterly opposed to any collective action by the men that had its origins in leadership from outside the company. . . . They were convinced that the men who had provoked and prolonged the violence were not only radical reformers but enemies of the United States" (ibid., 150–51).

If the younger Rockefeller had any thoughts that the events in Colorado were somehow an isolated or unique occurrence, the back-to-back strikes at Jersey Standard surely disabused him of this notion. In fact, the historical record shows that his thinking on industrial relations was already undergoing a profound metamorphosis—a metamorphosis that the labor troubles in Bayonne only gave greater speed and urgency to.

Spokesman for a New Partnership in Industry

Under King's tutelage, Rockefeller's perspective on industrial relations underwent a marked transformation in the period from 1914 to 1916. Paying homage to King's influence, Rockefeller remarked many years later, "I needed education. No other man did so much for me. He had vast experience in industrial relations and I had none. I needed guidance" (quoted in Fosdick 1956, 161).

Several years after the CF&I strike, King set down his philosophy on industrial relations in his book *Industry and Humanity* (1918). Although it received only lukewarm reviews then and is seldom referenced today, the book is nonetheless a valuable statement of King's perspective on labor-management relations—a perspective of interest in its own right but more so since Rockefeller largely took it as his own. Illustrative of the kernel of King's philosophy is this passage:

> To reconcile Labor to innovations and to efficiency methods of one kind or another; and to win Labor's co-operation with the other parties to Industry, in an endeavor to further to the utmost a common aim, two things are necessary. Labor must be given an understanding of industrial processes as a whole, and also a direct interest in the success of undertakings as a whole. A *common knowledge and a common interest* are essential to call forth the highest effort toward a common end. Moreover, since Industry implies co-operative effort, regard must be had for men in their collective capacity. To concede to Labor some element of control, as respects both industrial conditions and industrial rewards, is necessary to afford a common knowledge and a common interest. Control is a matter of government. Therefore, . . . there must be some understanding of the methods of government in Industry whereby functions are easiest co-ordinated, and principles most effectively applied. [Pp. 195–96, emphasis in original]

It is evident from these remarks that the central goal King sought to promote was genuine *cooperation* between the parties to industry, for out of cooperation grows greater efficiency, larger profits and wages, and conditions of justice and mutual goodwill. He recognized that in the short run, the employment relationship is characterized by a conflict of interest between Labor and Capital, causing each to struggle against the other to the detriment of society and their own long-term well-being, and that typically the individual worker comes to the struggle in the weaker position. To replace conflict with cooperation, the central need is to make Labor and Capital partners in the industrial enterprise so that they share a common, rather than opposed, interest. Genuine partnership, however, requires that each share in the gains and losses of the enterprise and in the determination of policy and day-to-day operations. Looking at the workplace in political terms, King saw the need to shift from the traditional workplace-governance model of employer autocracy to one of representative democracy. Toward this end, he advocated establishing a formal system of employee representation in the firm— a device he thought essential to promoting shared purpose, a better balance of power, and greater trust and confidence.

A contentious issue facing both King and Rockefeller was their stance on trade unionism and collective bargaining. From an early age, King saw the necessity of trade unionism and defended the workers' right to collective bargaining. In *Industry and Humanity*, he states his position in these words:

> The right of association and of organization by workers is a fundamental right. Denial or interference with this right is provocative of much ill-will in Industry. With organization is necessarily associated representation. . . . Methods adopted to effect and promote organization are not infrequently open to question, on the part of both Labor and Capital; but questionable practice and the principle of organization are not one and the same thing, and should be kept separate and distinct. No handicap could be severer than the atom-like position of many an isolated worker in the struggle against forces of world-wide competition. . . . Far-reaching social gains may accrue from wisely promoted association and co-operation begotten of the necessities of isolation. [P. 137]

While King defended the right of workers to join unions and collective bargaining and roundly denounced employers' efforts to thwart employees' desire for independent representation, his enthusiasm for unionism was nonetheless qualified. He realized that workers were driven to unions by the exploitative and autocratic practices of employers and, thus, unions were necessary to protect and advance the workers' interests. But his long-term goal remained fostering cooperation and unity of interest between Capital and Labor, and for this purpose, he realized unions were often not well suited. Part of the reason relates to the "questionable practices" that unions pursue—most importantly the closed shop but also the sympathy strike and secondary boycott. But more fundamentally, King thought that unions were by their nature bargaining organizations driven to gain more from the employer through an adversarial "win-lose" contest. While this approach was often necessitated by the workers' underdog status and employers' intransigence, it nonetheless undercut the long-run goals of cooperation, shared purpose, and mutual gain. Thus, he says,

> Instead of a united control expressive of a harmony of interests among partners, it is a struggle for supremacy of control, in which the parties are arrayed as opposing forces, conspiring and combining against each other like so many warring nations. A militant Trade-unionism claims exclusive right to speak in the name of Labor and to enforce its newly acquired control by the weapon of the strike, regardless altogether of the interests and well-being of Capital, Management, and the Community. [Ibid., 243]

Recognizing that workers needed representation in order to have their voices heard, but leery of the excesses and shortcomings found in a number of unions (such as the UMW in Colorado, which he thought was run by "a lawless and irresponsible group"), King was naturally led to propose to Rockefeller a compromise solution. This solution turned out to be a management-crafted employee representation plan that provided for joint governance, a more equal balance of power, and a forum for mutual discussion and resolution of grievances, while at the same time, it avoided the militancy and worst practices of some of the unions. With the employee representation plan, King thus tried to steer American industrial relations onto a "middle course" to resolve the Labor Problem, using employee representation as a means to pass between the Scylla of employer autocracy and the Charybdis of union adversarialism and restriction. Toward this end, he was astoundingly fortunate, for he found a patron who was not only one of the most influential businessmen in the country but also a "born-again" convert to the cause.

The first public confirmation of Rockefeller's conversion to a distinctly more progressive philosophy of industrial relations was in his testimony to the presidential-created Commission on Industrial Relations on January 25, 1915. The Commission was a seven-person investigative body appointed in 1913 to determine the causes of the profound labor unrest sweeping the nation. After the disaster at Ludlow, the Commission decided to take an in-depth look at events there and, as part of its inquiry, invited Rockefeller to testify.

The impact of King on Rockefeller's thinking was immediately apparent. In his testimony nine months earlier to a congressional committee, Rockefeller had disavowed responsibility for the labor practices of companies under his control, had strenuously defended the principle of the open shop, and dismissed strikes as the work of agitators. In his opening statement to the commission, he takes an entirely different tack. Regarding labor unions, he says, "I believe it to be just as proper and advantageous for labor to associate itself into organized groups for the advancement of its legitimate interests as for capital to combine for the same object. . . . whatever their specific purpose, so long as it is to promote the well-being of the employees, having always due regard for the just interests of the employer and the public, leaving every worker free to associate himself with such groups or to work independently, as he may choose, I favor them most heartily." With regard to the strike in Colorado, he says, "Its many distressing features have given me the deepest concern. I frankly confess that I felt there was something fundamentally wrong in a condition of affairs which rendered possible the loss of human lives, engendered hatred and bitterness, and brought suffering and privation upon hundreds of human beings." And on his responsibility toward industrial relations, he states with regard to the situation at CF&I, "I determined that in so far as lay within my power I would seek means of avoiding the possibility of similar conflicts arising elsewhere, or in the same industry in the future. . . . The correspondence will show that, in addition to having taken steps as early as the beginning of June last, to secure Mr. King's services, I also sought and obtained advice with respect to machinery for the prevention and adjustment of industrial differences, to which I invited the consideration of the officers of the Colorado Fuel and Iron Company" (U.S. Congress 1916, vol. 8, 7764). He then goes on to describe the representation plan (ibid., 7766).

Although critics such as the commission's chair, Frank Walsh, were not impressed with Rockefeller's new approach to industrial relations, most of the other commissioners were, as were much of the press and public. Commissioner John R. Commons, for example, is reported as saying that "he thought Mr. R's statement the best thing he had heard anywhere in the way of a pronouncement on the question of unionism" (McGregor 1962, 133).

In subsequent years, Rockefeller broadened and elaborated his philosophy on industrial relations, moving it closer and closer to that of his mentor, King. For example, he expounded his views in an article entitled "Labor and Capital—Partners" in the January 1916 issue of the *Atlantic Monthly*. In it he says,

> Our difficulty in dealing with the industrial problem is due too often to a failure to understand the true interests of Labor and Capital. . . . Much of the reasoning on this subject proceeds upon the theory that the wealth of the world is absolutely limited, and that if one man gets more, another necessarily gets less. . . . If this theory is sound, it might be maintained that the relation between Labor and Capital is fundamentally one of antagonism, and that each should consolidate and arm its forces, dividing the products of industry between them in proportion as their selfishness is enforced by their power. But all such counsel loses sight of the fact that the riches available to man are practically without limit, . . . and to promote this process both Labor and Capital are indispensable. If these great forces cooperate, the products of industry are steadily increased; whereas, if they fight, the production of wealth is certain to be either retarded or stopped altogether, and the wellsprings of material progress choked. The problem of promoting the cooperation of Labor and Capital may well be regarded, therefore, as the most vital problem of modern civilization. [Reprinted in Rockefeller 1923, 39–40]

Also echoing King are these thoughts on labor unions:

The development of industry on a large scale brought the corporation into being, a natural outgrowth of which has been the further development of organized Labor. The right of men to associate themselves together for their mutual advancement is incontestable; and under our modern conditions, the organization of Labor is necessary just as the organization of Capital; both should make their contribution toward the creation of wealth and the promotion of human welfare. The labor union, among its other achievements, has undoubtedly forced public attention upon wrongs which employers of to-day would blush to practice. But employers as well as workers are more and more appreciating the human equation, and realizing that mutual respect and fairness produce larger and better results than suspicion and selfishness. . . . To say that there is no way out except through constant warfare between Labor and Capital is an unthinkable counsel of despair. [Ibid.]

Rockefeller thus avows the right of workers to join unions and recognizes both their necessity and contributions but nonetheless finds that they come up short as an effective, long-run solution to the Labor Problem. So, what is the solution? He first diagnoses the problem and then offers the solution. On the diagnosis, he pinpoints miscommunication, unsettled grievances, and the unjust distribution of the product between profit and wages. On these points he states in the article, "Most of the misunderstanding between men is due to a lack of knowledge of each other. When men get together and talk over their differences candidly, much of ground for disputes vanished." And on distribution he says, "Assuming that Labor and Capital are partners, and that the fruits of industry are their joint product, to be divided fairly, there remains the question: What is a fair division? The answer is not simple—the division can never be absolutely just." And on grievances, "Much unrest among employees is due to the nursing of real or fancied grievances arising out of the daily relations between the workmen and the petty boss" (ibid., 44, 45, 57).

Regarding the solution to the Labor Problem, he states,

The problem [is] how to promote the well-being of each employee; more than that, how to foster at the same time the interest of both the stockholders and the employees through bringing them to realize the fact of their real partnership [and] the discovery of some mutual relationship between Labor and Capital which would afford to Labor the protection it needs against oppression and exploitation, while at the same time promoting its efficiency as an instrument of economic production. [Ibid., 47–48]

The device he then goes on to describe is the employee representation plan at CF&I:

> The industrial machinery which has been adopted by the Colorado Fuel and Iron Company and its employees is embodied in two written documents. One of these documents is a trade agreement . . . setting forth the conditions and terms under which the men agree to work. . . . The other document is an "Industrial Constitution" setting forth the relations of the company and its men. . . . Every employee is protected against discharge without notice, . . . [and it] facilitate[s] the adjustment of disputes and the redress of grievances. . . . [T]he plan gives every employee opportunity to voice his complaints and aspirations, and it neglects no occasion to bring the men and the managers to talk over their common interests. . . . The plan is not a panacea; it is necessarily far from perfect, and yet I believe it to be a step in the right direction. [Ibid., 50–53, 56, 61]

Implementing the New Program

Rockefeller continued to write and speak on his new vision of industrial relations and became something of an evangelist for employee representation. The danger existed, of course, that his words were little more than lofty-sounding but largely empty rhetoric. The evidence, however, is that he in good faith "walked the talk." Three pieces of evidence support this view: the pressure he brought to bear on other Rockefeller-connected companies to adopt a more progressive industrial relations policy and, in particular, employee representation; his break with conservative industrialists at President Wilson's industrial conference in 1919 over the issue of employee representation; and his establishment of the consulting and research organization, Industrial Relations Counselors, Inc. The first two are examined briefly in this section, while the third occupies the remainder of the chapter.

A New Industrial Relations Program at Jersey Standard

In the aftermath of the two Bayonne strikes, Rockefeller was determined that Jersey Standard would put its labor relations on sounder and more progressive footing. Although the directors of Jersey Standard realized that something had to be done to prevent another disastrous strike, they were not prepared by either training or sympathy to fundamentally change the company's labor policy. At this point, according to Wall and Gibb (1974, 131), Rockefeller chose to actively intervene in the company's affairs—one of the few times he did so in his life.

Rockefeller suggested to Jersey executives that they bring Hicks from Colorado to conduct a two-month investigation of the company's labor practices and write up his findings and recommendations in a report. After some debate, this was done, and Hicks arrived in 1917. Hicks proposed that Jersey Standard follow CF&I and establish an employee representation plan—an industrial relations practice that in the context of the times was not only unproven and highly unusual but widely regarded in business circles as dangerously radical. But with Rockefeller's encouragement, the company board of directors assented, subject only to the condition that Hicks leave CF&I and come to New Jersey to assume responsibility for Standard Oil's industrial relations program. Hicks agreed, and indicative of the importance attached to the new industrial relations program, his position of executive assistant reported directly to the company's president, Walter Teagle (Hicks 1941).

Under Rockefeller's encouragement, Teagle's support, and Hicks' direction, Jersey Standard put in place one of the most forward-looking, advanced industrial relations programs to be found in the United States and a model for what was to become known as the "welfare capitalism" movement of the 1920s (Jacoby 1997; Kaufman 2001). The centerpieces of the program were (1) a new labor relations philosophy, described by Hicks as founded on "faith, harmony, and the golden rule" (quoted in Talbot 1982, 65), and (2) establishment of a formal plan of employee representation in the company's major domestic facilities. The representation plan established joint management-employee councils at individual refineries and plants. Once a year, however, all employee delegates met with company executives for an evening banquet at Standard Oil headquarters at 26 Broadway in New York City. Such a gathering was so unusual, given the chasm that separated management and workers at most companies of the period, that the first banquet in 1918 was featured in newspaper articles across the country (Wall and Gibb 1974, 132).

Soon thereafter, Hicks engineered adoption of a variety of other progressive measures, including a written employee handbook. an annuities plan for all employees sixty-five years of age with twenty or more years of service; substantial death, accident, and sickness benefits; an eight-hour day and one day a week off; creation of a personnel and training department; a stock ownership plan; a companywide safety program; a commitment to tie wage levels to the cost of living; a paid employee-suggestion program; a company magazine; a forum for grievances (through the representation plan); and prohibition of layoff without cause. In terms of both management practice and the daily work life of employees, however, perhaps the most profound change was the decision to take the right to hire and fire away from the foremen and centralize it in the newly created industrial relations department. Reviewing these developments, Gibb and Knowlton state, "The conclusion is scarcely debatable that in one mighty surge of effort the Jersey directors, prodded by Rockefeller, Jr., and led by Hicks, had pushed the company almost overnight to a position where it could be regarded not just as a good employer but as among the most progressive in the field of labor relations in America. No one of the many measures adopted in this year of great transitions was unprecedented, but the comprehensive scope and the total effect of all the efforts imparted to company policy an almost revolutionary character" (1956, 578–79).

As noted earlier, the animating goal of all of these new labor practices was to move from a zero-sum, adversarial employment relation to a coopera-tive, positive-sum relation—on the presumption that the higher cost of the new industrial relations program would more than pay for itself in the form of greater productivity, lower turnover, and more effective collaboration. Another indirect benefit, it should be noted, was that the new practices would also remove many of the dissatisfactions that create a demand for union rep-resentation. In the words of Gibb and Knowlton, "There was a ready, if un-spoken appreciation of the fact that the new plans and practices were suffocating by sheer weight of generosity the forces of unionism within the company" (ibid., 585).

As all parties recognized, complete cooperation and unity of interest are impossible in any industrial enterprise, but the evidence is clear-cut that the industrial relations program Hicks put in place went a considerable distance toward these goals. One testimonial, for example, is an article entitled "Thirty Years of Labor Peace," featured in the November 1946 issue of *Fortune* maga-zine. The author states of Jersey Standard, "Jersey appears to have achieved a contract with its manpower that is more profound than any to be found elsewhere in U.S. industry." He goes on to say, "The plan of industrial rela-tions introduced at Jersey in 1918 is probably the most profound illustration of one of the two fundamental ideas propagated among U.S. wage earners: that there is an inherent harmony of interest between capital and labor" (p. 167). The proof of the assertion, the author notes, is that even in the rush to organize during the years of the New Deal in the 1930s and World War II in the 1940s, Jersey employees voted in repeated National Labor Relations Board NLRB elections to keep their representation plans (transformed into inde-pendent local unions after passage of the Wagner Act) rather than affiliate with an AFL or a CIO union. As the author of the *Fortune* article remarked, "The philosophy of capital-labor harmony as conceived by Jersey may be said to have filtered right through the Wagner Act" (p. 211).

Under Rockefeller's influence, as well as the more general economic and political events taking place in the years surrounding World War I, a number of other companies adopted all or significant parts of the new industrial rela-tions paradigm. In the oil industry, for example, representation plans were soon established at eighteen companies (Gibb and Knowlton 1956, 591), while more than twenty mining companies in Colorado adopted representation (Fosdick 1956, 168). A number of companies outside the oil industry, such as International Harvester, AT&T, and U.S. Rubber, also voluntarily adopted wide-ranging industrial relations programs, including employee representation (Scheinberg 1986; Kaufman 2000). Less auspiciously, employee representation also received additional impetus by the actions of the National War Labor Board and other agencies during World War I when, in an effort to forestall strikes and labor unrest, they ordered "shop committees" (a variant of the Rockefeller representation plan) established in more than two hundred plants. The companies that voluntarily adopted the new labor policy were, of course, only a very small minority among American employers, and not all of them were as well managed or committed as Jersey Standard. And success was not always permanent or in full measure, per Fosdick's observation that "in many other companies where vigilance was much less pronounced, the [representation] plan far too often disintegrated into a mere formality" (1956, 173). Given these caveats, when evaluated against the labor situation then prevailing across most of America, the breadth as well the depth of change in both the philosophy and practice of industrial relations that occurred in the few years that followed the Ludlow Massacre must nonetheless be rated as profound.

The Washington Industrial Conferences

In 1919, the United States experienced an unprecedented wave of strikes and labor unrest, including headline events such as the Seattle general strike, Boston policemen's strike, and industrywide walkouts in coal, steel, and railroads. In addition to intense shop-floor conflict, the nation was also gripped by a near-hysteria over the perceived threat posed to American democratic institutions by Bolshevism and other radical movements. In response, President Wilson convened an industrial conference in Washington, D.C., in the fall of 1919 to consider the causes of labor unrest and make recommendations for changes in national labor policy (Gitelman 1988). The conference was composed of representatives of employers, organized labor, and the public. John D. Rockefeller, Jr., was one of the public delegates.

The conference was riven by disagreement, with the employer advocates of the open-shop principle on one side and union proponents of collective bargaining on the other. As before, Rockefeller sought to chart a middle course between these two extremes, in the process staking out a position that was for that period quite liberal and which earned him a national reputation as a progressive leader in industrial relations.

Rockefeller introduced a resolution that in the first instance, sided with the labor group and advocated adoption of language that committed the nation to support the principle of employee representation in industry. This part of his resolution read as follows: "Resolved, that this conference recognizes and approves the principle of representation in industry under which the employees shall have an effective voice in determining their terms of employment and their working and living conditions." But Rockefeller also resisted efforts of organized labor to promote a union form of collective bargaining over others. Thus, he included a second clause that sought to ensure free choice of representational form. It read, "Be it further Resolved, that just what form representation shall take in each individual plant or corporation, so long as it be a method which is effective and just, is a question to be determined by the parties concerned in the light of each particular instance" (quoted in Gitelman 1988).

After introducing his motion, Rockefeller addressed the delegates. The scene was described in the October 25, 1919, issue of *Survey* magazine:

> A dramatic moment in a conference replete with the picturesque was signaled when John D. Rockefeller, Jr., first of all arose in his seat to speak in behalf of the resolution. Judge Gary, who ordinarily occupied a chair nearby, was conspicuously absent. In a full rich voice, Mr. Rockefeller read his argument. In the course of his address he made statements and used phrases which have a memorable suggestion of that great coal strike in 1914 in which he was a prominent, if an unwilling actor. "Representation is a principle which is fundamentally just and vital to the successful conduct of industry," said Mr. Rockefeller. "This is the principle upon which the democratic government of our country is founded. Surely it is not consistent for us as Americans to demand democracy in government and to practice autocracy in industry. With the developments in industry what they are today there is sure to come a progressive evolution from autocratic single control, whether by capital, labor, or the state, to democratic cooperative control by all three. . . ." The incident closed with the labor group clapping, as he sat down, the man they had damned from one end of the country to the other five years ago. [p. 36]

After much debate, Rockefeller's resolution was modified and then displaced by another, to which he gave his support. In spirit and substance, it committed the nation to a labor policy that was a long distance from the model of autocracy and employer "divine right" that still prevailed throughout much of industry. It stated, "The right of wage earners to organize in trade and labor unions, to bargain collectively, to be represented by representatives of their own choosing in negotiations and adjustments with employers, and in respect to wages, hours of labor, and relations and conditions of employment is recognized. This must not be understood as limiting the right of any wage earner to refrain from joining an organization or to deal directly with his employer if he chooses" (Gitelman 1988, 316).

Rockefeller was the first to speak in favor of this resolution. A majority of the employers' group opposed it, however, and it and subsequent permutations were thus defeated. At the end, the conference failed to reach agreement on any statement of policy and adjourned.

President Wilson asked the public group to form a second industrial conference and again endeavor to agree upon a statement of principle regarding national labor policy. Of the fifteen members, Rockefeller emerged as the leader and most influential voice. With King in the background, Rockefeller again pushed the principle of employee representation and won consent of the group to make it the central recommendation of their report. When issued to the public in early 1920, the industrial conference recommendation elevated the experiment of employee representation—conceived only seven years earlier in the shadow of the Ludlow Massacre—to a basic principle of American industrial relations. In so doing, it also elevated Rockefeller to a widely acknowledged position as the leader of the progressive wing of employers. The fact that the conference report was not carried forward into law does not obscure the major contribution Rockefeller and King had made to reshaping industrial relations along more progressive lines.

The Path to Industrial Relations Counselors, Inc.

The events of the preceding years had taught Rockefeller two important lessons. The first was that neither he nor fellow business leaders could any longer ignore industrial relations or relegate it to a minor concern to be handled by foremen and other lower-level subordinates. The second was that executives of large companies needed expert advice on labor, both to have a firm foundation of facts upon which to make decisions and to gain counsel on the best procedures and practices in industrial relations. But while business leaders had engineers, accountants, and bankers to turn to for counsel in others areas of business activity, in the labor area there was a notable void.

At first, Rockefeller relied on King to fulfill these roles. King had originally been hired under the auspices of the Rockefeller Foundation to conduct research on the labor question and provide a report and recommendations (McGregor 1962). As the situation at CF&I unfolded, King's role quickly evolved, however, to one of personal labor advisor and investigator. It was thus King whom Rockefeller dispatched to Colorado in 1914 to learn the true state of facts about the strike and to whom he repeatedly turned to for advice and counsel on the representation plan, policy toward organized labor, and position to take in public statements and testimony on labor. Likewise, when the strikes at Jersey Standard broke out in 1915–16, as well as at another Rockefeller-connected company (the Davis Coal & Coke Company), it was King whom Rockefeller dispatched to apprise him of the situation and the best course of action. During 1917, King remained in Canada a good deal, working on his book and running for Parliament (unsuccessfully). With the entry of the United States into the war in late 1917, however, industrial relations controversies mushroomed, and for the next eighteen months, King again devoted much time to counseling Rockefeller and making field investigations. Besides Rockefeller-controlled companies, such as the Consolidated Coal Company and Standard Oil of New York, King made investigations and reports of, and provided counseling services to, a wide range of well-known American companies, including Bethlehem Steel, General Electric, International Harvester, and Youngstown Sheet & Tube (Gitelman 1988, 253–62).

Political events in Canada in the fall of 1918, as well as the completion of his book *Industry and Humanity*, began to pull King away from Rockefeller, however. The leader of the Liberal Party in Canada, Sir Wilfred Laurier, was considering retirement and told King that he would support him as his replacement. Then in early 1919, Laurier died and King found himself waiting in the wings as the new leader. After an extended trip to Europe in the summer of 1919, King returned and in August was elected party leader and, subsequently, prime minister. Although King and Rockefeller would continue to correspond and occasionally meet in person, the ability of King to serve as his industrial relations consultant was at an end.

King could never be replaced in whole, but Rockefeller was fortunate to find another man of exceptional capability who also shared King's progressive vision of industrial relations. This was Raymond Fosdick. Rockefeller and Fosdick met in 1910 while serving on a grand jury investigating the white slave traffic (Fosdick 1958, 124). When Fosdick returned from Europe at the end of World I, having served as deputy secretary for the League of Nations, he decided to return to the practice of law and joined with Chauncey Belknap (former secretary to Justice Holmes) and James Curtis (former assistant secretary of the treasury) to found the law firm of Curtis, Fosdick, and Belknap (Fosdick 1958, 214; Belknap 1976, 9–10). Fosdick's first client was Rockefeller.

Fosdick had previously worked with King on industrial relations matters for Rockefeller but had no special training in the area (labor law at the time did not exist as a field). But with King largely gone, Rockefeller now made Fosdick his "eyes and ears" on labor relations developments at his various business interests. According to Belknap, "Mr. Rockefeller one day asked

Mr. Fosdick to check into a report that a corporation in which the Rockefellers were financially interested was operating on a twelve-hour day, seven-day week. Fosdick's investigation confirmed the report; as Mr. Rockefeller's representative he succeeded in bringing about a change for the better" (1976, 10).

Belknap states that soon "similar assignments multiplied." Certainly the most complex and potentially explosive situation Fosdick was asked to investigate was the perilous state of labor relations at the Consolidated Coal Company, a Rockefeller -company and the largest producer in the upper Appalachian area. King had done an extensive field investigation in 1919 and had given Rockefeller a written report and recommendations. Among other things, King advised Rockefeller that resistance to the United Mine Workers union in several divisions of the company was not only pointless, given the degree of strength the union enjoyed with the miners, but also counterproductive, since the union served as a stabilizing force in the industry (King 1919). But he found that the company officials were intent on pursuing a policy of hard-boiled anti-unionism and in general did not appear receptive to his more liberal recommendations. Over the next two years, relations further soured, particularly with the onset of depression in 1920, vast overcapacity in the industry, and wage reductions of 30 to 40 percent. As a 1924 IRC consulting report on Consolidated Coal Company stated, "The Consolidated Coal Company is probably faced with as complex a labor problem as ever confronted an industrial company" (p. 38).

Rockefeller asked Fosdick, a member of Consolidated's board of directors, to do another field investigation. In his final report, Fosdick (1921) is blunt and honest with Rockefeller about the failures of the company, the bankrupt state of the employee representation plans earlier installed, and the reasons why the workers are demanding union recognition. Here are some illustrative excerpts:

> I do not see that any improvement in the industrial situation in the Pennsylvania division has taken place since Mackenzie King's visit. . . . The men have not a word to say as regards either their working or living conditions. There are no committees of miners waiting on the management with grievances and no attempt on the part of the management to find out what the men desire or are thinking about. Union agitators are run out of company towns by force; indeed, intimidation is the principle method of the company to prevent organization and to secure compliance with the will of the officials. . . . In August 1921 a reduction in wages was put arbitrarily into effect without consultation with the men. . . . If the men could have been consulted about the cut in advance, instead of having it jammed down their throats, no valid criticism could now be aimed at the reduction. The utter

lack of such machinery in the Pennsylvania field, however, and the absence of any desire on the part of the management to cooperate with the men in matters of this kind, make it impossible to entertain any great hopes of good understanding, or to relieve ourselves from the charge of acting unfairly toward the employees.... There is just one word that describes the situation in Pennsylvania and that is "autocracy.... It is difficult to find words strong enough to condemn a situation such as this. It is not only undemocratic and un-American, but it is contrary to every principle of free government.

It was out of Fosdick's work on the Consolidated Coal Company that the germinal seed that later grew into Industrial Relations Counselor's, Inc., was planted. In a letter written to Rockefeller on June 2, 1921, Fosdick states,

Ever since I talked with you at Seal Harbor [Maine] last summer, I have been impressed—I was almost going to say depressed—by the load of responsibility that you are carrying in connection with industrial questions, as well as the magnitude of your opportunity to influence the evolution of industrial relations throughout the world. The position which you occupy is absolutely unique; and I doubt whether the fortuitous currents of history will ever again give a single individual the power you possess. You not only practically own a number of worldwide industrial enterprises, but you are the largest single shareholder in many others, and what you do in relation to these enterprises is going to affect, for better for worse, the whole course of industrial development for generations.

As I have thought of this matter in the last eight or nine months, I have frankly wondered whether you had at your command the kind of machinery through which you could adequately meet these responsibilities. You have, of course, taken steps of tremendous significance in the direction of getting facts and applying them practically to your industries. Mr. King, Mr. Hicks, and others—but especially Mr. King—have from time to time looked into particular questions for you, and just now I am conducting, at your suggestion, a study of profit sharing and plans of stock purchase by employees. But all of this has been and is to a certain extent sporadic. You have no highly specialized machinery *constantly* at work through which you can not only get current information as to industrial conditions, but can find out, on the basis of expert information, what policies are adapted to particular situations, and how these policies can best be promoted among the executives of your industries. Without such machinery, constantly at work for you—multiplying your eyes and ears and reflecting your liberal point of view in the enterprises for whose industrial conditions you have the chief responsibility—your vast influence, I fear, will be to some extent dissipated.

Fosdick then goes on in several sections of the letter to outline in more detail the purposes, functions, and structure of this proposed organization. He lists three purposes: (1) provide expert investigation, (2) help to introduce approved policies, and (3) keep in constant touch with these policies after introduction. He next discusses the organization of the staff and proposes six divisions of work: (1) labor maintenance (wages, hours, etc.), (2) research and statistics, (3) safety and health, (4) women's work, (5) industrial risks, and (6) community conditions. Regarding the relationship of the new consulting service to Rockefeller's existing businesses, he suggests the staff "could be organized independently with offices apart from your own, under some such name as the Industrial Relations Corporation, or it could be attached directly to your office." Finally, Fosdick addresses the economic contribution of the new organization and its likely start-up cost. He says of the former, "The economic importance of this kind of research cannot be over-estimated. Indeed what I am talking about is not primarily a *welfare* proposition. It is not merely a sentimental approach to the problem of industrial relations. It is based on the hardest kind of economic facts. Generally speaking, industrial relations work is only on a sound basis when it improves the conditions of production at the same time that it benefits the wage earners" (emphasis in original). With regard to the latter, he states at the end of the letter, "The beginning should be small and modest—three or four men at the outside, perhaps not more than two or three. . . . The cost including office expenses and travel ought not to run above $30,000 or $35,000 a year."

Apparently, Rockefeller had not approved of Fosdick's proposal by the late fall of the year, for he again broaches the subject in his final report on the Consolidated Coal Company (1921). He pitches it to Rockefeller in the context of the situation at Consolidated:

> [N]o more serious problem is presented than the wage disputes which are coming up for settlement. . . . In regard to all of these wage matters I feel that we have not at hand a sufficient body of information to enable us to give intelligent options. Certainly, as a director of the Consolidated Coal Company I could not now determine with any degree of justice what the mining wage for the next two or three years ought to be, and yet, on April 1 I shall be called upon to express a pretty conclusive opinion on the subject. The competitive nature of the industry, the desirability of underselling England in shipping coal to South America, the competitive relationships between non-union and union fields, the necessity of paying wages which will conform with minimum health and decency standards—all these questions enter into the conclusion and must be carefully weighed.
>
> My chief recommendation, therefore, is that a study should be started immediately of the whole wage and industrial situation . . . by an indi-

vidual or staff competent to consider the tangled technical questions which it involves. . . . If such a study is to be made in an impersonal, detached way, it will have to be instituted by some prominent stockholder who will use its results for his own information and use his information in effecting the decision of the Board of Directors. [Pp. 23–25]

Fosdick must have received encouragement from Rockefeller, because in a letter dated December 2, 1921, he discusses with Rockefeller the person he thought best matched to head the organization. He states, "The man I have in mind to start the job is Mr. George J. Anderson, who is now the Managing Director of the New York Employing Printers Association. I have canvassed the field very broadly and I do not believe there is a better man than he." Fosdick also counsels Rockefeller that a man of Anderson's caliber will be "high-priced" and cites a salary figure in the $15,000 range (IRC 1976). (The price level in 2000 is approximately ten times higher than in the mid-1920s, making Anderson's salary in constant dollars roughly $150,000.)

Shortly thereafter, Rockefeller gave the go-ahead, and a separate industrial relations section, referred to early on by Fosdick as a "Bureau of Industrial Relations" and more generally thereafter as the industrial relations "staff" or "section," was established within the law firm of Curtis, Fosdick, and Belknap. Anderson was also hired, and within a year the staff had grown to six in number.

In his first annual report to Fosdick, Anderson briefly describes the activities of the staff during 1922. Chief among them was a document entitled "Labor Policy in the Bituminous Coal Industry," prepared after two months of intensive study and printed for public distribution, which Anderson stated to be "the first comprehensive study of its kind for the bituminous coal industry." Other activities related to the coal industry included frequent consultations with the National Coal Association (an employers' group); a field investigation of the strike conditions in Somerset County (Pennsylvania); consultation with West Virginia coal operators on ongoing negotiations; conferences with the secretaries of labor and commerce; and "repeated conferences, memoranda and correspondence concerning detailed situations of labor policies in the coal companies with which we are primarily concerned." Also under way were several major initiatives in the oil industry, including comprehensive surveys of industrial relations practices at Standard Oil of New Jersey, Standard Oil of Indiana, and the Elk Basin oil fields of Wyoming. A third industry in which Rockefeller had major interests was railroads, and here the Bureau made an investigation and report on the strike at the Western Maryland. A project at the steel works of CF&I was also initiated. Finally, Anderson notes that a small library was started and "consultations given to officers of the National Personnel Association, Industrial Department of the Federal Council of Churches, U.S. Bureau of Labor Statistics, and other interests" (Curtis, Fosdick, and Belknap 1922).

In 1923, the industrial relations section continued to grow and take on new projects. The annual report lists ten staff members and expenses of $52,000. Of the staff, the person with the most visibility besides Anderson was Glenn Bowers, who authored numerous articles on industrial relations trends and developments in management periodicals (e.g., *Industrial Management*) over the course of the 1920s. The research and consulting activities of the staff continued to be centered on the coal & oil industries, where Rockefeller had extensive interests. Staff consulted with Rockefeller-controlled companies (e.g., Consolidated Coal, Davis Coal and Coke) on wage policy and gave expert advice to the National Coal Association, the American Petroleum Institute, and the U.S. Coal Commission. Links were also made with the newly established American Management Association and the Industrial Relations Section at Princeton University (discussed in more detail later in the chapter) (ibid. 1923).

Most significant, however, was the strong research and investigation program carried out in 1923. Completed during that year were five highly detailed surveys of industrial relations practices/policies at individual companies/divisions (Standard Oil of New Jersey, the Elk Basin oil fields, Davis Coal and Coke, Midwest Refining Company, and Standard Oil of Indiana). The reports were commissioned by the individual companies and provided a confidential, in-depth examination of the state of their industrial relations and a set of recommendations for management action. The first report, on Jersey Standard, comprised three volumes with more than 250 pages of analysis, 20 tables, and 15 charts. In addition to the company surveys, the staff also completed eight smaller research memoranda, on topics such as company pensions and immigration policy, and fourteen "comments" (ibid.)

In 1924, George Anderson resigned to become vice president of industrial relations at the Consolidated Coal Company, and Arthur Young was hired to take his place. Just as Rockefeller had earlier gone to the International Harvester Company to recruit Hicks, now he returned to Harvester to recruit Young, who was then in charge of the company's industrial relations program. (Rockefeller and Cyrus McCormick were brothers-in-law, which partly explains the close links.) Young was also well connected and influential in the progressive wing of the management movement of that period, serving as a director of the newly founded American Management Association (AMA). Under Young's direction, the industrial relations "bureau" continued to grow. In 1924, the staff grew to fourteen full-time people, and the budget increased to $58,000 (ibid. 1924).

During 1924–25, another four industrial relations surveys were completed, in most cases of similar size and detail to the original Jersey Standard report. For the first time, companies independent of Mr. Rockefeller began to ask for an industrial relations audit. In terms of staff time and financial resources, the largest commitment was to a several-month-long investigation of industrial relations practices for the Hawaiian Sugar Planters Association (a consortium of pineapple growers). Participating in this survey as a contract consultant was Henry Metcalf, president of the Personnel Research Federation; and Mary Gilson, formerly a well-known industrial relations manager for Joseph & Feiss Company (a firm in the vanguard of progressive scientific management), who came on as a full-time staff member and investigator (Gilson 1940). Commenting on these reports, Young states in an internal report (IRC n.d.), "Our whole objective may be said to be to aid our clientele by counsel, based on observation and impartial analysis, in order that they may see in perspective conditions as they exist and visualize the advantages to all parties in the industrial equation which are derived from sound human relationships and a heightened morale within a company."

Several dozen other research memoranda were completed in these years, as were two larger unpublished research reports. The first was "Employee Stock Ownership," the second "Profit Sharing and Financial Incentives for Executives."

Also of note, the 1924 annual report lists all the conferences and meetings attended by the industrial relations staff. After only two years of operation, the links with other management organizations and companies were rapidly widening. Listed, for example, are the AMA, the National Industrial Conference Board, Young Men's Christian Association (YMCA), Women's Trade Union League, Association of Collegiate Schools of Business, American Iron and Steel Institute, National Safety Council, and the Special Conference Committee (SCC, to be discussed in more detail shortly).

Industrial Relations Counselors: Birth and Activities

Through 1925, the industrial relations staff was still housed within the law firm of Curtis, Fosdick, and Belknap. Looking back, Fosdick recalled,

> [O]ur staff, under Mr. Young, continued also to expand, and soon it outnumbered the law staff of my firm. My law partners began to wonder what kind of an office they were running and whether the tail wasn't wagging the dog. So in 1926 I suggested to Mr. Rockefeller that we incorporate the activity, and move the staff out of the law office into quarters of its own.

Mr. Rockefeller approved the suggestion and also agreed to contribute to the support of the program until the income from counseling, together with contributions from individuals and companies, could provide an adequate budget. (Fosdick 1951, 2)

Industrial Relations Counselors, Inc., was thus incorporated on May 1, 1926, and had its offices at 165 Broadway in New York City. (The law firm was located at 61 Broadway, while Rockefeller's offices were at 26 Broadway, as was the office of Edward Cowdrick, secretary of the Special Conference Committee.) Later, IRC moved to Rockefeller Center, where it and ORC now reside.

Several aspects of the new organization deserve note. The first is the adopted name of *Industrial Relations Counselors.* Due to changes in usage, the meanings of these terms are not as evident today as in 1926. The term *counselors*, for example, is that period's term for *consultants.* In current practice, the term *industrial relations* generally connotes unionized employment situations and, in this context, is often treated as synonymous with *labor relations.* But this was not the case in the 1920s, and not until the early 1960s (Kaufman 1993). Rather, *industrial relations* was defined quite broadly to cover all aspects of the employment relation; subsumed employer-employee relations in union and nonunion contexts and in private, public, and nonprofit sectors; and included all aspects of personnel/human resource management and labor relations. Thus, the twenty-fifth anniversary *Conference Proceedings* published by IRC (1951) contains this statement (inside front cover): "In terms of content 'industrial relations' has come to include all contacts between labor and all grades of management, which are connected with or grow out of employment. Specifically, it covers items usually classified as personnel work, such as recruiting, hiring, placement, transfer, training, discipline, promotion, layoff, and termination of employees." The mandate of IRC, as seen at the time, was thus as broad as the employment relationship and clearly gave emphasis to both the management and employee sides of that relationship.

The second aspect of note is the intended purpose to be served by IRC. On this matter, Belknap states,

Scientific research in medicine was a familiar activity as conducted, for example, in the laboratories of the Rockefeller Institute for Medical Research. ... But how could scientific research on the relations between the workers in a coal mine or an oil refinery and their employers be conducted? There was no supporting precedent, but we decided that it should be possible to show that for such research the laboratory was the coal mine or the oil refinery itself. Accordingly, the corporation was organized with a charter stating that its purpose was "to advance the knowledge and practice of human relationships in industry, commerce, education, and government." [1976, 11]

A third noteworthy point is that IRC was founded as a nonprofit corporation. Mr. Rockefeller always indicated that he desired IRC to eventually become financially self-supporting, but he had no desire to make a profit from the work of the organization. His goal was, rather, that IRC make its services as widely available as possible to clients and the public and that its reputation for neutral, fact-based research not be compromised by the profit-seeking motive. In fact, over the course of the first decade of IRC's existence, Rockefeller donated $1.3 million to fund the organization's activities and cover revenue shortfalls. In the mid-1930s, he ended direct contributions to the organization.

A fourth point of note concerns the leadership structure and executive personnel of IRC. As set up, the corporation was governed by a board of trustees. Raymond Fosdick was chairman of the board from 1926–36, after which he became president of the Rockefeller Foundation. He was succeeded as chairman by Clarence Hicks (1936–44), Bryce Stewart (1945–54), Thomas Roy Jones (1954–64), Albert Masters (1964–67), and Logan Johnston (1967–77). The position of board chair was left vacant after this date.

A three-person executive committee oversaw the administration and operation of IRC, but in practice, effective control was exercised by the director—a title later changed to president. Arthur Young was the first director, a post he held until 1934 when he resigned to take the position of vice president of industrial relations at the United States Steel Corporation. Young was succeeded, in chronological order, by T.H.A. Tiedemann (1934–51), Carroll French (1951–62), Rowland Burnstan (1962–63), Richard Beaumont (1964–73), Leo Teplow (1975–79), Sydney Briggs (1979–81), Charles Tasso (1981–93), Calvin Reynolds (1993–96), and Roy Helfgott (1996–present). Tiedemann had been Hicks' assistant at Jersey Standard; French also started at Jersey Standard (director of training and personnel) but was serving as director of the Industrial Relations Division at the National Association of Manufacturers when he was appointed president of IRC (after an earlier stint on the IRC staff). French had also obtained a Ph.D. at Johns Hopkins University in 1922 and authored a well-recognized research monograph on the early experience with employee representation (French 1923).

Beginning in 1930, IRC created a new position of "director of research." The first person to hold this job was Bryce Stewart (1930–52). He was followed by Howard Kaltenborn (1952–58), James Taylor (1958–60), Roy Helfgott (1967–68), and Richard Beaumont (1961–64, 1970–present).

The IRC board of trustees included prominent industrialists and educators, often with a tie to the Rockefeller family, the Rockefeller or SCC network of companies, or the Rockefeller-connected university network. At IRC's founding, for example, board members included Owen Young (chairman, General Electric), Cyrus McCormick (chairman, International Harvester), Arthur Woods (vice president, CF&I), and Ernest Hopkins (president, Dartmouth College). At the time of IRC's twenty-fifth anniversary in 1951, the board was composed of Tiedemann, Stewart, Walter Teagle, C. Canby Balderston (dean, Wharton School, University of Pennsylvania), Thomas Roy Jones (president, Daystrom, Inc.), Theodore Petersen (president, Standard Oil of California), Rueben Robertson (chairman, Champion Paper Co.), Winthrop Rockefeller, and R. Douglas Stuart (vice chairman, Quaker Oats Co.).

A fifth point concerns the intended activities and programs of IRC. In an undated internal IRC memorandum, Arthur Young states on this score,

> The two general types of activity of Industrial Relations Counselors, Inc. are *research* in the field of personnel management and industrial relations and consulting *services* primarily for industrial concerns. The research work includes studies and reports of a technical nature in all factors of the industrial relations program, such as unemployment insurance, employee stock ownership, vacations with pay for factory workers, financial incentives for executives, industrial pensions, etc. The consulting service includes recommendations based upon special studies of one or more factors of the industrial relations program, reports of current developments in the field of industrial relations generally and consultation on such problems as may be presented by client companies. A complete survey of important operating units and personnel of a company is regarded as a necessary preface to counseling services. This usually involves a field study by one or more members of the staff. [Emphasis in original]

A sixth point that deserves to be highlighted is that IRC was the first organization of its kind to be established in the United States and, probably, in the world. When originally set up in 1922 within the Curtis, Fosdick, and Belknap law office, there was no other organized center in the country for expert consulting and research on labor and industrial relations matters—indeed, the very concept of a field and practice of industrial relations was at that point only a few years old and still had an uncertain future and a small base of corporate practitioners and adherents. As described more fully below, only two universities in the early 1920s (Princeton and the Wharton School of the University of Pennsylvania) did organized research and information dissemination on industrial relations, and both had ties to Rockefeller and IRC. Thus, employers, unions, or government agencies that desired factual information or expert advice on industrial relations would have found at this time that academe had little to offer, particularly of a more constructive, practical nature.

Likewise, neither government nor private industry provided much in the way of expert research and consulting on the "employer's solution" of modern industrial relations management. The U.S. Bureau of Labor Statistics was the major source of government-provided data and reports on labor conditions, but its resources were limited, the focus of its work was on more aggregative, economywide developments, and it did relatively little on management practices/policies per se. In industry, groups such as the Personnel Research Federation and the National Industrial Conference Board (NICB) sponsored occasional surveys and reports on company employment practices, but their research staff and resources were quite limited. In the consulting arena, when interest in industrial relations first gained momentum between 1917 and 1919, with the crisis precipitated by wartime conditions, a number of "labor consultants" quickly appeared. Their motives, objectivity, and qualifications were frequently questionable, however. In this vein, noted labor economist John R. Commons observed of the period, "It is astonishing what easy marks for experts many employers had become in the summer of 1919. From all sides and several vocations these experts were coming in and setting themselves up. They got long-distance calls from employers to hurry up and come at once. They lifted the employer's pocket at will" (1921, viii). The establishment of Industrial Relations Counselors and its progenitor in the law office of Curtis, Fosdick, and Belknap thus was not only a "first" but helped fill what was then a notable void.

A final point concerns the place of IRC in the spectrum of management thought and practice, circa the 1920s and 1930s. By nearly all accounts, IRC was a spokesman for and representative of the liberal/progressive wing of American employers—reflecting as it did the philosophy and program of its patron, John D. Rockefeller, Jr. (Rubinow 1934; Bernstein 1960). At the time, there was no such thing as a monolithic employer class or uniform management philosophy toward labor relations. Arrayed along the continuum of opinion/practice, starting on the right (conservative) and moving to the left (liberal), were employers' associations, such as the National Metal Trades Association (NMTA), followed by the National Association of Manufacturers (NAM), the NICB, the National Civic Federation (NCF), the American Management Association, the Special Conference Committee, and the Taylor Society (Harris 1982; Jacoby 1985).

Companies affiliated with the NMTA and NAM, for example, were typically "traditionalists" with respect to the management of labor and "belligerents" with respect to unions (Harris 1982; Jacoby 1985). But emerging out of World War I—with important roots in the Rockefeller/ King response to the earlier disaster at CF&I—was an alternative labor strategy that was far more progressive and enlightened (Kaufman 2001). As described in more detail in the next chapter, the fundamental goal of this new strategy was to achieve competitive advantage by achieving labor's goodwill and cooperation, thus promoting greater productivity and firm performance. To obtain labor's goodwill and cooperation, however, firms had to shift from an employment strategy that views workers as commodities and a short-run expense to be minimized to a "human capital" conception in which labor is treated as a long-run asset embodied in human beings with psychological needs for respect, security, justice, and self-realization. Doing so, maintained King (1918, 103–4) and Hicks (1941, 77), would create a "unity of interest" between employers and workers that leads to a host of desirable outcomes and behaviors—greater work effort, reduced turnover, more efficient plant operations, and higher morale and esprit de corps—and the possibility of a "win-win" outcome of higher profits and wages. Key to achieving cooperation and a unity of interest was a variety of new human resource practices, but Hicks gave greatest emphasis to two: employee representation and employment/income security programs (ibid., 79–110). With respect to unions, this new strategy also adopted a far more liberal view—the right of employees to join unions was recognized, but if they chose not to (certainly management's desired outcome), it would not be because they were deterred by fear and coercion but rather because the companies had won their loyalty and allegiance through superior conditions and square dealing.

This alternative employment strategy, adopted by the minority of leading employers in the 1920s, gradually became known as "welfare capitalism" (Jacoby 1997). Few movements in industry have generated as much controversy and debate, both at the time and among modern-day business and labor historians. To critics on the left, welfare capitalism was largely a defensive, albeit relatively sophisticated, effort to keep out unions and government and accomplished relatively little of lasting value (Dunn 1926; Gitelman 1988); to critics on the right, it was a costly, impractical, and dangerously radical departure from sound management principles and opened the doors to unionism (Ching 1953; Jacoby 1985). Other observers, however, have reached a far more positive conclusion. Writing at the time, for example, economist Sumner Slichter called welfare capitalism "one of the most ambitious social experiments of the age" (1929, 432), while William Leiserson concluded after a review of labor developments in the 1920s, "When the accomplishments of Personnel Management [the welfare capitalism employment strategy] are recapitulated . . . the result is bound to be an impressive sum" (1929, 164).

Industrial Relations Counselors, Inc., along with other Rockefeller-connected organizations and like-minded progressive groups, was at the center of the welfare capitalism movement. Illustrative, for example, is the fact that no other company had a greater influence on IRC than Jersey Standard and, in the words of one well-known labor historian, Jersey Standard was "the most ambitious and enduring monument of the welfare capitalism of the twenties" (Bernstein 1960, 166). Although the welfare capitalism movement was badly damaged and discredited by the economic and political events of the Great Depression and New Deal of the 1930s, in retrospect, a good case can be made that the basic management philosophy and strategy propounded by IRC and management progressives of the period are in fundamental respects the foundation for the modern "high-performance" workplace model that represents current "best practice" in American industry and industrial relations (Kaufman 2001 and Chapter 4 in this volume).

In what follows, I examine in broad outline the major activities and accomplishments of IRC since its birth to the present. This narrative is split into two parts for expositional purposes: 1926–45 and 1946–present. I also assess the historical significance of these activities and the extent to which IRC maintained fidelity to the original credo of industrial relations as propounded by Rockefeller and King. I would characterize this credo, in a sentence, as a progressive humanistic approach to management that seeks to promote a mutual-gain outcome through improved, science-based industrial relations policies/practices and a "people strategy" that emphasizes development of a fuller, deeper cooperation and unity of interest between management and employees. I note that in reconstructing this record, the task is made difficult because relatively few internal memorandums and little working correspondence of the officers and staff of IRC have survived to the present day. Use is thus made of several other sources to fill in the gaps, principally the collection of consulting reports completed by IRC for clients, published books and monographs, and a modest amount of unpublished materials from the IRC library and other sources.

Consulting Services

As previously indicated, the vision of the founders of IRC was that it would pursue two primary lines of activity. From these it was to earn sufficient funds to operate on a break-even basis. The first of these lines of pursuit was provision of consulting services to employers and other organizations (defined broadly to include training services); the second was industrial relations research. I examine these in this order.

For the first several years after the industrial relations "section" was established at Curtis, Fosdick, and Belknap, the staff worked only on consulting projects for Rockefeller-connected companies. But soon word spread and requests came in from companies outside the immediate Rockefeller network. The consulting program in its initial years involved two lines of work. The first and most important was the conduct of in-depth industrial relations surveys (or "audits") at specific companies; the second was providing more informal, ongoing advice and consultation on specific industrial relations issues. Little evidence on the nature or extent of the latter activity survives, so I concentrate on the former.

Industrial Relations Surveys

During the last half of the 1920s, IRC performed approximately two large-scale industrial relations audits per year and, over the course of its first nine years, completed a total of twenty-four. Through the 1920s, the bulk of the companies were in the petroleum and coal industries, but then other industries began to be represented. From 1926 to 1930, for example, audits were performed for Marland Oil (later Continental Oil); White Star Refining; Buffalo, Niagara and Eastern Power; Standard Oil of California; American Bemberg; and Radio Corporation of America. With the coming of the New Deal in 1933 and the rather unsettled, even tumultuous, nature of industrial relations in this period, corporate interest in labor practices picked up, and IRC completed another seventy-two audits by early 1940. Major companies represented include International Shoe, American Tobacco, General Foods, U.S. Steel, Quaker Oats, American Can, and A. E. Staley. Particularly in the early years, the audits were massive undertakings (in bound form they appear similar to a Ph.D. dissertation), typically took several months to complete, utilized several staff members, and involved extensive on-site visits and interviews. An indication of the cost is provided in the 1923 annual report (when the staff was still with Curtis, Fosdick, and Belknap), which lists the expenses for completed surveys as between $5,000 and $6,500. The price tag for the industrial relations survey for the Hawaiian Sugar Planters Association, on the other hand, was much higher—quoted by Young in his proposal to the growers at $25,000 (reflecting the fact that eight staff worked on the project for a number of months, most of them in Hawaii with family brought along). The reports were strictly confidential between the client and IRC.

A better sense of the nature and contributions of the early industrial relations audits can be gained by a closer examination of the first one completed after the founding of IRC in 1926 (eight had been previously completed by staff of the law firm). Done for the Ohio Oil Company, it comprised three volumes and 290 pages and was largely the work of Charles Mills, Albert

Regula, and Murray Latimer. Individual chapters were provided on the following aspects of industrial relations:

- Organization and administration
- Employment, wages, and hours
- Training and education
- Accident and fire prevention
- Medical service, insurance, and mutual benefit association
- Housing, sanitation, service features, and employee activities
- Savings and investment plans
- Pensions
- Joint relations

These were preceded by an extensive overview of the history of the company, its principal lines of business, and recent operating and financial results (the subjects of Volume 1). Each chapter was organized into three parts: good practice, present conditions, and conclusions and recommendations. These three sections of each chapter were then summarized and condensed in tabular form as an "executive summary."

Arthur Young wrote a three-page "Forward" to the report, and it is useful to provide an extensive quotation, both for its historical interest and relevance for present times and debates. He states,

> In all industrial organizations, even with the maximum application of mechanical power and processes, the attainment of results is ultimately dependent upon human labor, in its many variations of skill and experience, from roustabouts to president.
>
> In the Ohio Oil Company as in most industrial organizations the money spent on human labor as expressed by payroll expenditure represents the largest single item of operating expenses. It gives promise therefore of yielding the greatest economic return by the application of organized methods of administration.
>
> The accumulated experience with methods of control and coordination of the labor force in industry is defined by the term labor administration. From a technical standpoint labor administration has to do with the intricate and complex problem of obtaining the most effective use of the labor force or securing the maximum return from payroll expenditures. It ranks in importance, therefore, with production, finance, and other major functions of management.
>
> There are, however, other compelling aspects in the maintenance of harmonious relationships throughout any industrial organization.

The overwhelming speed of events and changing conditions in the past ten years have emphasized the dependence of society upon modern industry, have brought business activities under the pressure of public opinion as never before, and have focused attention upon the social status of the individual. This combination of circumstances requires acceptance by management of a broadened responsibility and a general recognition of imposed trusteeship.

It is with a balanced consideration of economic return, social interest and individual well-being that Industrial Relations Counselors have approached the preparation of this report and have drawn the conclusions. . . . This report is not submitted with thought of complete finality in the solution of the many complex problems. It is intended, rather, to establish a working basis for the continued study and constant application necessary for the ultimate solution of labor problems within the company. [Portions deleted from the original]

It is evident that Young hits upon—in at least embryonic form—many themes that remain current today: the importance of labor (human resources) to organizational effectiveness and competitive advantage; the need to give labor administration (human resource management) a weight in corporate affairs equal to production and finance; the idea that maximum efficiency depends on correctly adjusting both the technical and social/psychological sides of the labor equation; the challenge posed to management by rapid economic change; recognition that corporations have a social responsibility in the treatment of labor that transcends narrow consideration of maximum profit; adoption of a "stakeholder" view of the employment relationship in which economic returns are balanced against concerns for employee well-being and the general public interest in justice and humane workplace conditions; and the recognition that there is no "one best way" or "final solution" to labor problems but, rather, a process of steady, incremental progress.

A review of the report reveals many interesting aspects about both prevailing labor management practices in the mid-1920s at a representative large company and the nature of the recommendations put forward by IRC. With respect to "organization and administration," for example, the report indicates that the company had no centralized staff function responsible for the conduct of industrial relations, no enunciated labor policy, nor any written guidelines or rules governing the terms and conditions of employment or procedures of industrial relations (IR). Under "good practice" (a 1920s version of "best-practice benchmarking" used today) and "recommendations," the IRC investigators list centralization of labor relations activities under one executive; a direct reporting relationship between the IR executive and the company president; the IR executive and personnel serving in a staff capacity under the direction of the line managers; adoption of written, consistent labor guidelines; and determination of policies and procedures through consultation with lower ranks of subordinates. On the latter point, the authors of the report state, "Labor policy has vastly more chance of intelligent, willing, and thorough execution when it is not handed down simply as a fiat of management but is adopted after a consultation with those whom it affects" (p. 2).

In the area of employment, the report notes that the company delegates hiring, termination, and pay decisions to local officials; no policy exists on promotions; race and sex discrimination are practiced (few Negroes are hired, unmarried women are preferred for the office); and employment procedures are generally "rule of thumb." Recommendations include, for example, introduction of job analysis, noting, "Good practice in employment procedure requires that every job to which human energy is applied shall be analyzed and described. To hire employees without specifications would be similar to picking drilling tools from the stock room without knowing whether they were for a cable or rotary job." The report also counsels an end to all forms of discrimination, stating, "Since sex or race distinctions and religious, fraternal or union affiliations do not necessarily affect the character of an employee's work there should be no discrimination for such reasons" (p. 13).

On wages and hours, the report highlights a number of deficiencies. The IRC investigators found, for example, that 56 percent of nonsalaried employees continued to work seven days a week, ten hours a day; many production workers were given at most two holidays (Christmas and July 4) at reduced pay; wage rates showed considerable nonsystematic variation within occupation and across location; and often men doing similar work received significantly different pay. The report notes that these conditions created widespread perceptions among employees that discrimination was practiced. Thus, the IRC report recommends abolition of the seven-day workweek, written policies on holidays and vacations, setting of wage rates using job classification and standardization, a general wage increase to bring the company's pay scale up to market levels, and use of wage surveys to maintain comparability.

A third area that draws attention regards employee benefits. According to the IRC report, the company has a rudimentary pension plan that is "distinctly unsatisfactory" on account of being unsystematic (each case is considered individually with no formal guidelines), temporary (all pensions commitments are for a year only), uncertain (no guarantee of payment upon retirement), and underfunded. IRC thus recommends that the company invest in an expert actuarial study to lay the groundwork for a major reform of its pension system. (Performing such actuarial studies became a major area of consulting practice for IRC and led to its involvement in the development of the federal Social Security program, as discussed shortly.)

The final area of human resource practice considered in the report is "joint relations." In discussing "good practices," the report starts out with this declaration: "Employers and employees alike want a spirit of cooperation in the day to day relationships on the job. It is impossible to have this spirit without some organized form of personal contact between the managing group and the men in the ranks" (p. 283). Under "present conditions," the report notes that employee relations are dealt with on an individual basis with no avenue for appeal or consultation other than the "open door" to management. It also notes, "In no instances in wage and hour adjustments have employees been consulted regarding their opinions of policy or procedure. Neither have there been conferences between groups of employees and management concerning operating problems." In its recommendations, the IRC staff states, "There is abundant proof that human relations in a company can be immeasurably strengthened by some form of joint conference. . . . It is recommended that the high executive officers of the company now adopt the policy statement that some form of employee representation is desirable" (p. 287).

It is unknown how many of the recommendations in the report were adopted by the company, but certainly it is fair to say that had they all been implemented, the result would have been a near-revolution in the firm's labor policy and practices. This example also illustrates my earlier claim about the overarching strategy IRC adopted toward improved industrial relations—the introduction of systematic, science-based IR practices (a formal labor policy, actuarial study of the pension system) in combination with a humanistic "people strategy" based on concepts of social responsibility, fair-dealing, and esprit de corps that together are meant to achieve greater cooperation between managers and employees, higher organizational performance, and a better work experience for employees. All of these elements are well represented in the report.

It is interesting to compare the industrial relations audits done in the late 1920s with those done two decades later, as they demonstrate both elements of constancy and change in the consulting practice of IRC and the major industrial relations issues of concern to business executives. In terms of the reports themselves, those of the mid-1940s and later are frequently considerably shorter in length (often about 100 pages), more frequently focus on a specific IR subject (e.g., a corporate pension plan) rather than the entire IR program, largely omit the detailed overview of the company's operating and financial results, and largely drop the numerous tables and charts and accompanying detailed statistical information. While the 1920s IR surveys closely resembled an investigative report by a government commission, the reports in the 1940s and 1950s had become closer to a business report with a more compact, tightly focused statement of the problem and attendant set of recommendations.

In terms of content, the IRC consulting reports show both elements of stability and change. For purposes of comparison, here is the list of major topics considered in the *Industrial Relations Survey* done for the Standard Oil Company of Ohio in 1949. The report is organized into seven major sections:

    I. Top Management Responsibility for Industrial Relations
    II. Industrial Relations Organization
    III. Status, Functions, and Development of the Supervisory Organization
    IV. Compensation Policies and Procedures
    V. Relationships with Organized and Unorganized Employees
    VI. Employment and Related Activities
    VII. Accident Prevention and Employee Benefits and Services

Most of these subject areas roughly correspond to subject areas in the Ohio Oil Company report but are broader in scope. The section on employment, for example, covers subjects such as employee selection, performance appraisal, and seniority, transfers, and promotions—subjects largely missing from the 1926 IR survey. The section on benefits is also much broader in scope, featuring subsections on topics such as disability benefits, the hospital and surgical expense plan, and group life insurance. Illustrative of the evolution of business and industrial relations, there are also topic areas that were important in the 1920s that no longer were by the late 1940s. Company housing is one example, hours of work is another (it gets two pages in the 1949 report). Finally, both the 1926 and 1949 audits have a section on joint relations, but the former focuses on the nonunion employee representation plan, while the latter focuses on collective bargaining with independent labor unions.

The nature of the recommendations to senior management also evolved in interesting ways over this two-decade period. In the 1920s, the challenge was to get companies to establish their first IR department; in the 1949 report, a corporate IR department is in place but the company is being pushed to establish a training department within it and to better communicate changes in corporate IR policy to plant-level managers. Similarly, in the 1920s, the challenge was to take the right to hire and fire away from the foreman; in the late 1940s, the challenge was to restore the morale and authority of supervisors in light of union encroachment and the increased hiring of college graduates into entry-level management jobs. Another example is in the compensation area, in which in the 1920s, the push was to formalize and systematize the wage structure, while in the late 1940s, the report counsels top management to push greater decision making on compensation to the plant level in order to better fit compensation to local and individual needs.

The final aspect of the IRC consulting reports that merit mention is what they reveal about the organization's attitude and approach to unions and collective bargaining. The reports are particularly interesting in this regard, given that they were prepared and presented with strict confidentiality, thus giving the IRC staff considerable confidence that they could present their viewpoint to management without fear of public disclosure.

A prominent and influential line of academic research holds that a major purpose—possibly the overriding purpose—of Rockefeller, King, and IRC was to help corporate America practice successful union avoidance (e.g., Gitelman 1988). The internal consulting reports of IRC reveal, however, a markedly different picture. The stance taken by the IRC staff in the reports I have read is, without exception, neutral on the question of union organization and repeatedly stresses that the matter is to be determined by employees. Where unions are present, the IRC staff always take the position that management's job is to create a positive relationship with the union, or at least learn to live with it for the long term; advice or intimation that the union could somehow be made to go away is never even obliquely proffered, even in the context of adopting positive employment practices (such as the adoption of an employee representation plan).

In the first year of IRC's operation, Arthur Young told the president of the Hawaiian Sugar Planters Association in a private letter (contained in the IRC survey report to the company), "You need have no fear of embarrassment from the attitude of any member of our staff in regard to Labor Union activities. Our viewpoint is necessarily not partisan." The evidence from internal reports and correspondence is that the organization consistently hewed to this line. Indeed, according to several people long associated with IRC, the organization was viewed as too liberal or "union friendly" by a significant portion of the business community.

In no report that I have examined did IRC counsel a company to adopt an employee representation plan, or any other industrial relations practice, to either directly or indirectly avoid unionization. During the 1920s and early 1930s, most companies it worked with had no union organization among the employees and little history thereof. In the consulting reports, therefore, the topic of unions was, at most, mentioned in passing. Thus, in the Ohio Oil Company report of nearly 300 pages, the history and experience with unions occupy part of one page. In the section where the IRC staffers recommend the adoption of an employee representation plan, no mention of unionism, or the avoidance thereof, is in any fashion made. Rather, the rationale advanced to management for employee representation is "a properly functioning employees' representation plan should enlist the cooperation of every employee and officer in a united effort to improve all phases of the business" (p. 289).

Another example is the report done in 1930 for the American Rolling Mill Company (ARMCO). The company had in years past bargained with the Amalgamated Association of Iron, Steel, and Tin Workers but had broken off bargaining relations and operated nonunion. The IRC report briefly discusses this history but makes no further mention of unions or collective bargaining. It does counsel the company to strengthen its system of nonunion employee "advisory committees," noting, "The advisory committees in reality are affording only a one-way channel for intercourse, namely, from the management to the employees. Under the present set-up it would be practically impossible in case of labor difficulties to convince the public that the machinery provided affords adequate protection. . . . The management-employee relations should be organized so that representatives will fearlessly and frankly air each real or fancied problem." The benefit to the company of ensuring that "employees have an equal voice and vote with the management" is never even obliquely related to avoiding unions but, rather, is couched in terms of increased cooperation and unity of interest: "Experience has shown that the added recognition and responsibility given representatives will exert a sobering influence and will increase the belief of the body of employees in the honesty of purpose of the company and the oneness of interest of the management and employees" (p. 257).

Further evidence comes from the period of the mid-1930s when the unionization drive in American industry was particularly strong. In a November 1934 report of industrial relations practices at SKF Industries, the staff noted that the company had suffered several recent strikes, had recently withdrawn recognition from a labor union, and appeared determined to maintain an open shop. It might be expected that the IRC staffers would recommend installation of an employee representation plan, if not to directly counter the union threat, then to indirectly avoid it by giving workers an alternative forum for voice and the resolution of grievances. But instead, the report counsels management that "the establishment of joint relations through employee representation would seem to be inadvisable at this time, but the door should be left open to any plan which the employees may propose." The reason given has nothing to do with unionism, however, but with the fact that the company did not have the necessary foundation upon which to build a successful program for joint dealing and cooperation due to "the present composition of the [management] organization, the absence of a background of foremen training and the general lack of understanding of personnel management . . ." (p. 20). The report thus recommends that the achievement of better employer-employee relations be obtained through other means, such as reform of the company's personnel practices and procedures, investment in an education and training program, and reorganization of the mutual benefit association.

IRC also took a strong position that employers should in all respects follow the law as regards employee free choice and right to collective bargaining. In a June 1934 report prepared for the Kaufmann Department Stores, the IRC counselors state, "The existing representation plan . . . is in reality a 'company union' of the type that has been repeatedly condemned by the National Labor Board. . . . It is *recommended* that the management take advantage of the amendment provision in the plan to effectuate revisions that will bring the plan in harmony with the official interpretations of section 7(a) of the National Industrial Recovery Act and in line with the experience gained by many progressive companies in the administration of plans during a period of years prior to the Recovery Act" (pp. 24–25). Parenthetically, the report also notes that the company had hired "under-cover men" to spy on employees and states to management, "The employment of so-called 'under-cover men' by management is an old-line, outworn practice long since abandoned by most progressive companies. . . . It is *recommended* that the employment of under-cover men be abandoned through-out the company" (p. 26, emphasis in original).

Also illustrative is this passage from a November 1935 report prepared for the American Tobacco Company. Remarkably, the IRC staff began their report to management with this statement: "It was felt initially that it was more than probable that in organization [an independent union] rested the only hope of tobacco workers for improvement of their lot." The report goes on to say that the staff investigators found that the employee relations climate was much better than expected and, thus, unionization might not be foreordained. But they then counsel management that "the decision as to organization is one that rests entirely with the employees themselves. The trend of legislation and public opinion support the right of employees to organize and to bargain collectively with their employer through representatives of their own choosing, with the emphasis on the free choice of employees in this regard. . . . It is because of this conviction that a major recommendation of this report is to the effect 'that the company continue to shape the course of its future relationship with employees with the fundamental principle of nondiscrimination'" (p. 2).

Finally, it is also the case that once a company had a union, IRC consistently counseled management to view the collective bargaining relationship as a permanent, long-run part of employee relations and to take a proactive approach in dealing with the union to foster as much cooperation and trust as possible. In a report prepared for the Dominion Coal Company in 1941, for example, IRC staff notes the vexatious state of labor relations at the company arising from numerous wildcat strikes by the local union and the militant attitude of the local leadership. Rather than counsel management in ways to get rid of or undercut the union, the report counsels management that "it seems logical to assume, therefore, [based on the number of dues deductions cards signed] that the UMWA will continue indefinitely as the employees' bargaining agency. The company's policy should be based on this assumption, and every possible effort should be made to establish and promote orderly procedures for collective bargaining with the UMWA. To this end it will be necessary for the management to develop new attitudes and practices. . . . These are admittedly enormously difficult tasks and can be achieved only by the application of sound labor policies over a period of years" (p. 32).

IRC Training Programs

A second area of consulting services (broadly defined) that IRC provided to industry was training programs in various phases of industrial relations. A continuous theme in the consulting reports to management is the need to strengthen the capabilities of the industrial relations function and staff. Doing so, IRC claimed, not only lead to improved employer-employee relations but also would gain the confidence and support of top management. To promote this goal, IRC began to offer training programs in the late 1930s, but it was only in the 1940s and later that training became a major initiative, earning IRC a reputation as one of the leading providers of industrial relations training in the nation.

The largest and most significant program was a two-week "IRC Management Course in Industrial Relations." The first such course was begun in 1943, with an enrollment of sixty people (all men) from middle to upper IR positions in industry (IRC 1943). Daylong seminars were held on all the major phases of industrial relations work, often taught by IRC staff—including in the first year Clarence Hicks (who died the subsequent year), Bryce Stewart, T.H.A. Tiedemann, and Carroll French. In 1948, the course was located in Williamsburg, Virginia, where it was subsequently offered numerous times through the 1980s. In addition to the Williamsburg course, for many years IRC offered periodic training courses on industrial relations in various cities throughout the country.

Relationship with the Special Conference Committee

In 1919 at the initiative of A.C. Bedford, president of Jersey Standard, ten large corporations agreed to form a group called the Special Conference Committee (SCC), composed of the chief executive and person in charge of industrial relations, for the purpose of having regular meetings to discuss all matters of mutual interest concerning labor (U.S. Senate Committee on Education and Labor 1939, 16781; Scheinberg 1986). The ten companies were in the vanguard of the progressive management movement in the 1920s and were the leading practitioners of welfare capitalism. Members included Standard Oil (New Jersey), Bethlehem Steel, International Harvester, U.S. Rubber, General Motors, DuPont, Goodyear, General Electric, Westinghouse, and Irving Trust Bank. Later AT&T (1925) and U.S. Steel (1934) were added as members. (Of the original ten members, General Motors was something of an outlier, as it continued to use fairly traditional labor practices.) Collectively, the SCC companies employed 1.3 million people in the mid-1930s, or roughly 5 percent of private nonagricultural employment. Clarence Hicks served as chairman of the group until his retirement from Jersey Standard in 1933, and Edward Cowdrick served as secretary (beginning in 1923). The group decided to keep their meetings confidential, so the existence of the SCC was only revealed in 1937 during the investigations of the LaFollette Civil Liberties Committee, a subcommitee of the Senate Committee on Education and Labor, chaired by Robert M. LaFollette, that began an investigation of employer antilabor practices in 1936.

Cowdrick was an influential force in shaping progressive industrial relations practices in the 1920s and 1930s but has gone largely unrecognized in historical accounts. Cowdrick was a journalist for a Denver newspaper whose balanced accounts of the Ludlow situation caught the attention of Rockefeller and King. They hired him to replace Hicks at CF&I and, several years later, brought him to New York City as an "industrial consultant," where he took on the duties of secretary to the SCC. Cowdrick authored a number of articles and a book (1924) on industrial relations subjects but, for the most part, chose to operate quietly behind the scenes advising and consulting with SCC companies and other progressive employers. As part of his duties with the SCC, he conducted studies and surveys on personnel/IR topics requested by member companies, consulted with them on an invited basis, and authored a regular "Cowdrick letter" with information and advice to client companies on new events and developments both in labor and in Washington, D.C. He thus played an important role in coordinating the IR programs of the SCC network of companies and in disseminating/developing information on "best practice" personnel procedures.

According to IRC research consultant James Tower (personal interview), who worked with him in his later years, Cowdrick's approach to industrial relations was pragmatically progressive; he only consulted with companies that he felt were "above board"; and while he did not view AFL-type unions with much favor, he nonetheless thought that unions "could be worked with."

The conventional wisdom holds that the principal function of the SCC was union avoidance (Scheinberg 1986; Gitelman 1991). According to Tower, this view is skewed because the SCC companies—once past the unsettled period around 1919–20—faced a small and diminishing union threat until 1933 and the advent of the New Deal (also see Nelson 2000). Rather, the companies' continued participation in the SCC was motivated in larger part by their common decision to pursue a course of progressive employment relations, or "industrial liberalism," as a competitive strategy. This view is supported by the following observation in the LaFollette Committee report: "Throughout the material in the files of the Special Conference Committee we find a constant emphasis on the necessity for cooperation between employers and employees in industry. The 'cooperative' method appears as the desideratum of sound industrial relations" (U.S. Senate Committee on Education and Labor 1939, 16789). Thus, the primary purpose of the SCC was to support this strategy by providing a meeting place for top-level executives to learn about, discuss, and take back to their member companies information on labor market trends, "what works and doesn't work" in personnel/IR practice, and political developments affecting labor at the state and federal levels. Several of the SCC's unpublished annual reports survive, and they are largely devoted to a summary of the subjects just described, while overt anti-unionism or discussion of union avoidance practices are almost completely absent. (Annual reports for 1933–36 are provided in the LaFollette Committee report; reports for several earlier years are available at the Hagley Library, Wilmington, Delaware.) These companies were not keen to have collective bargaining (although Gerard Swope of GE reportedly told AFL President Green in the late 1920s he would collectively bargain with a union if only it would be structured along industrial lines [Loth 1958]), but their position in the vanguard of employers—coupled with their progressive philosophy—made unionism in practice largely a moot issue.

The SCC and IRC were established as separate, independent groups and had offices at different locations in New York City. They were, nonetheless, closely linked due to their close Rockefeller ties and common philosophy and strategy on industrial relations. Internal IRC records indicate, for example, that Arthur Young was a regular attendee at SCC meetings and that he on occasion sent SCC reports related to some labor relations issue to client companies. Interestingly, the two groups seemed to have pursued parallel research/consulting programs.

As indicated above, throughout the 1920s, the SCC sponsored periodic reports and surveys for member companies on a variety of industrial relations subjects. Several have survived, such as a rather voluminous report done on methods of wage payment at member companies, a series of six case-study reports on employee representation plans at SCC companies, a report on the labor-management cooperation program at the B&O Railroad, and a report on the labor policies of Mitten Management, Inc. (operator of the Philadelphia Rapid Transit Company). (The wage payment study is in the Bethlehem Steel Company records at Hagley Library; the other reports are in the IRC library.) At the same time, IRC was also conducting similar research, such as on pensions and profit sharing (unpublished reports). The basis for this division of labor is unknown, although SCC did predate IRC by several years and for that reason had a head start. Whatever the case, this division of labor explains two apparent anomalies. One is that very few of the SCC companies asked IRC to do an IR audit of their company (Jersey Standard being an early exception), even though these companies would have been the most likely candidates, given their strong interest in IR policies/practices and links to the Rockefellers. Presumably the explanation is that the companies were already getting their consulting/research needs taken care of through Cowdrick and the SCC (and, possibly, being in the vanguard of employers they may not have felt the need for a complete IR audit). A second anomaly is that IRC never published any type of research report or other material on employee representation plans, despite the fact that these plans were in the early years at the heart of IRC's program for improved industrial relations. A partial explanation is that, as indicated above, in the late 1920s the SCC conducted its own survey work on the performance of the plans and distributed lengthy reports to members.

The LaFollette Committee was hostile to employers and, according to Tower, took a "prosecutorial" stance when it interviewed Cowdrick and, in general, sought to present the SCC in a bad light. Although the anonymous existence of the SCC, and its large and influential corporate membership, has suggested to many that it operated principally as an employer network bent on subverting unionism and controlling labor markets (Scheinberg 1986; Gitelman 1988 and 1991), the voluminous documentary evidence assembled and published by the Committee provides very little support for this contention. Despite losing its cloak of confidentiality and acquiring an unsavory reputation in some circles, the SCC continued in existence, and Cowdrick continued to lead it until just before his death in 1951. As described shortly, IRC then took over responsibility for coordination and administration of SCC meetings and affairs.

Research

The second major area of activity performed by IRC has been in industrial relations research. The evolution of the research function is described in these words in an internal memorandum:

At first only studies of industrial relations programs of single companies were carried on. Continuing counseling relationships with companies grew naturally out of the survey work. Next, research in special subjects was undertaken as an indispensable accompaniment of the survey and counseling activities. With the increasing volume of surveys, studies of company problems, and special research, an industrial relations library, headed by a trained librarian, became necessary. Finally, the news letter and industrial relations memorandums were initiated as a means of helping the staff and contributor companies keep abreast of the increasingly complex developments in legislation and company and union activities. The organization is unique in the breadth of its programs of integrated activities and its policy of basing research upon actual practice. [IRC 1940]

In its earliest years, IRC did a smattering of research work, but most of the staff and time were devoted to the consulting work. In the late 1920s, however, IRC significantly expanded its research work and, in the process, earned a reputation during the 1930s as one of the leaders—arguably *the* leader in certain areas—in applied research on industrial relations. Illustrative are these statements: "One has learned to expect any publication of Industrial Relations Counselors, Inc. to be an event in its field" (*Personnel*, February 1938), and "I feel the present staff is as able as can be found in the field of industrial relations. Its research work, particularly in the field of unemployment insurance, has surpassed in quality anything that has been done in the United States" (Isador Lubin, Commissioner, U.S. Bureau of Labor Statistics, personal letter, 1934).

Making Its Mark: Pensions and Unemployment Insurance

The area of industrial relations practice that IRC carved out as the major focus of research, and for which it earned a national reputation as the leading authority, was with respect to employee benefits and, most particularly, pensions and unemployment insurance. Two factors seemed to have pushed IRC in this direction. One was that progressive employers saw unemployment and old-age insurance programs as serving important strategic IR goals. Of most importance, writers of the period clearly saw that instability of employment and employees' fear of job loss threatened to scuttle attainment of the central goal of welfare capitalism—achievement of goodwill, cooperation, and unity of interest (Commons 1919; King 1918, 158). They further realized that the ability of most private employers to provide insurance plans, particularly with respect to unemployment, was limited and, thus, some form of government participation was necessary. Unemployment and old-age insurance also promoted other IR goals, such as reducing turnover, fostering higher morale, and providing a socially responsible way to retire "superannuated" workers who were too old to perform a regular workload. The second reason, alluded to above, is that client companies for whom IRC did consulting work often came back wanting expert advice on pensions and other insurance programs, which inevitably led the organization to build up expertise in this area. The volume of work in the pension area grew so rapidly that, according to an internal memorandum, "it is probable that Industrial Relations Counselors, Inc. now does more work of this kind than any other American organization" (IRC 1940).

The IRC research program in benefits and social insurance programs was spearheaded by two IRC staff members, Murray Latimer and Bryce Stewart. Also heavily involved, and contributing nationally recognized research, were Mary Gilson and Thomas Spates (Gilson 1940; Spates 1960).

Latimer was only twenty-five when he joined IRC, coming from Harvard as an instructor in finance (Domhoff 1996, 133). He gained practical experience in the pension area in his first assignments with IRC as a pension consultant/ designer for Jersey Standard and several other companies. After becoming a nationally recognized authority on pensions through his work with IRC, he left in 1936 and headed the Railroad Retirement Board. Economist Edwin Witte, a key player in the drafting of the Social Security Act, said of Latimer, "It was agreed by everyone consulted that the best person in the field [of old-age pensions] was Latimer" (Witte 1963, 29). Stewart, in turn, was a Canadian and already prominent when he came to IRC in 1927. He had served as director of the National Employment Service of Canada, came to the United States to design and administer the unemployment insurance plan for the Amalgamated Clothing Workers Union, and then obtained a Ph.D. in labor economics. He stayed with IRC until his retirement in 1952 (with a brief stint as deputy minister of labour in Canada during WWII), becoming its director of research in 1930. Famous labor economist John R. Commons referred to Stewart as "the leading authority in the country on unemployment insurance" (1934, 200).

Listed in Table 3.1 are the books and monographs produced by the staff of IRC during the 1930–40 period on various aspects of unemployment insurance and pensions. It is fair to say that these works collectively represented the "state of the art" in the 1930s in terms of thinking and practice on these two subjects.

This large-scale research activity required extensive funding, much of which came from grants from the Rockefeller Foundation. As these IRC books began to appear, calls started to come in from state governments and, later, the federal government for expert help in drafting unemployment insurance and social security legislation. IRC provided consulting advice to the states of New York, Minnesota, and Wisconsin, for example, and once the Wiscon-

Table 3.1

IRC Publications on Unemployment Insurance and Pensions: 1930–1940

B.M. Stewart and Associates, *Unemployment Benefits in the United States*, 1930, 727 pp.

M.B. Gilson, *Unemployment Insurance in Great Britain*, 1931, 560 pp.

T.G. Spates and G.S. Rabinovitch, *Unemployment Insurance in Switzerland*, 1931, 276 pp.

M.W. Latimer, *Trade Union Pension Systems*, 1932, 205 pp.

C.A. Kiehel, *Unemployment Insurance in Belgium*, 1932, 509 pp.

M.W. Latimer, *Industrial Pension Systems*, 1933, 2 vols.

O. Weigert, *Administration of Placement and Unemployment Insurance in Germany*, 1934, 241 pp.

Industrial Relations Counselors, Inc., *An Historical Basis for Unemployment Insurance*, 1934, 306 pp.

Industrial Relations Counselors, Inc. and others, *Administration of Public Employment Offices and Unemployment Insurance: Canada, France, Sweden, and Switzerland*, 1935, 397 pp.

B.M. Stewart and Associates, *Planning and Administration of Unemployment Compensation in the United States*, 1938, 665 pp.

M.W. Latimer and K. Tufel, *Developments in Industrial Pensions under the Social Security Act*, 1940, 88 pp.

sin unemployment insurance law was passed, Stewart drafted three reports for the state industrial commission on proposed methods of administration (Domhoff 1996). When the Roosevelt administration came into office, IRC staff were soon called to Washington to participate in a number of New Deal initiatives. In 1933, for example, Stewart was appointed to an advisory council for the U.S. Employment Service, while Latimer served on a similar council with the Department of Labor. Shortly thereafter, Stewart, Latimer, and J. Douglas Brown (director of the IR section at Princeton University) worked together to create a retirement system for railroad workers (the Railroad Retirement Act).

The apogee of their involvement in the Washington legislative process, however, was in the research and drafting work done on the Social Security Act. Stewart, Latimer, and Brown all held high-level appointments on the Committee on Economic Security, the group appointed by Roosevelt to develop legislation, and all three testified before Congress. The central role played by IRC in the development of this landmark legislation is indicated by Witte when he remarks, "Almost the entire staff of the Industrial Relations Counselors, Inc. was placed on the payroll of the Committee on Economic Security, so that the arrangement (allowing Stewart to remain in New York and use IRC staff) in effect amounted to employing the Industrial Relations Counselors, Inc. to make this study" (1963, 29).

In terms of the legislation that ultimately was voted into law, IRC won the war but lost several important battles. IRC "won the war" in that the Social Security Act was successfully signed into law, despite widespread doubt that the legislation was politically feasible and the strong opposition of more conservative business groups (e.g., the NAM). In the drafting of the legislation, however, the position taken by IRC staff came into conflict with the position of the "Wisconsin" group associated with John Commons. IRC staff favored a single national system for both the old-age and unemployment insurance programs and joint contributions from employers and employees; the Wisconsin group favored individual state-run programs and no employee contributions. Latimer and Brown prevailed in this battle with respect to the old-age insurance part of the Social Security Act, but Stewart lost in the design of the unemployment insurance program (Witte 1963; Domhoff 1996).

Unemployment compensation and old-age insurance were not the only topics that brought IRC staff to Washington during the New Deal. Arthur Young, for example, held several positions, such as on an advisory council for the U.S. Employment Service and on a committee for the Veteran's Placement Service (Domhoff 1996,144). And Clarence Hicks, who joined IRC in 1933 after his retirement from Jersey Standard, served as a staff member of the Labor Advisory Board, created by Roosevelt to help settle labor disputes arising from provisions of the National Industrial Recovery Act.

It is thus a remarkable accomplishment that an organization founded less than ten years previously, with only a director, a handful of staff, and a modest budget, was catapulted by the quality and timeliness of its research into a top policy-making position in the federal government. In this regard, Young observes in a letter written to Fosdick at the end of 1933, "The timeliness and character of the research work of Industrial Relations Counselors, Inc. has resulted in inescapable demands on the staff for service to various government agencies and officials arising out of the emergency problems confronting them. . . . Since June 1933 there has come what amounts to an overwhelming demand for personal participation by staff members and the conduct of special research studies from cabinet officers, federal departments, and bureaus and special committees" (quoted in ibid.).

Employee Representation and the National Labor Relations Act

The progressive employers connected with the SCC and IRC put together a comprehensive package of new, innovative IR practices, but the two components given most emphasis were employee representation and employee benefit plans. These two IR practices suffered widely divergent fates during the New Deal years, however. As just described, IRC supported government programs of old-age and unemployment insurance and emerged triumphant in gaining such programs, albeit in a modestly different form than originally advocated. With respect to employee representation, on the other hand, IRC and associated groups suffered a resounding and hard-to-stomach defeat.

In 1915 at CF&I, the program of industrial relations reform promoted by Rockefeller and King largely contained one arrow in the quiver—the plan of employee representation. After World War I, other new IR practices were added, such as a personnel department, expanded welfare benefits, employment security, and limits on the power of foremen to hire and fire. Although contemporary management scholars are prone to paint the IR programs of employers of that period as largely of a piecemeal, reactive nature concerned with record keeping and company picnics (Dulebohn, Ferris, and Stodd 1995; Schuler 1995), the evidence is quite the opposite for the vanguard of progressive SCC companies. These companies made a deliberate strategic choice to gain competitive advantage by moving to a cooperative/harmony-of-interest model of employee relations, and they put together a synergistic bundle of IR practices to accomplish this goal (Kaufman 2001). Although there were now more "arrows in the quiver," employee representation, according to both contemporary and modern observers, continued to be the linchpin or "crown jewel" of the welfare capitalist IR model (Leiserson 1929; Bernstein 1960; Kaufman 2001).

In the immediate period following World War I, a faddish "bubble" developed in which employee representation, or "plans of industrial democracy," was widely touted and adopted in industry (Lichtenstein and Harris 1993). After this bubble was deflated in the early 1920s—due to a combination of economic depression, shallow commitment among many employers, and representation's not-always-evident payoff, the movement consolidated and registered modest growth through the 1920s. At the end of the decade, several hundred representation plans were in operation, covering 1.2 million workers. These plans were concentrated among large manufacturing firms, utilities, railroads, and a modest number of small- to medium-sized firms with owners committed to progressive industrial relations, with the SCC companies in the vanguard.

The experience with employee representation was checkered, and not all observers reached positive conclusions. IRC staff researcher Gilson, for example, recounts in her autobiography that by the late 1920s, "I no longer had faith in company unions. I was convinced that our group must pay more than lip service to the idea of working toward real industrial democracy in industry" (1940, 269). In a similar vein, John Carmody, who served as vice president of industrial relations at the Rockefeller-owned Davis Coal & Coke Company and ran a representation plan at the company, observed, "Now, those of us who have helped organize company unions, and who have worked with them over the years, as I have done in industry, know that they are innocuous, that they are straw men" (NLRB 1985, 339). Modestly more positive, but with significant reservations, was an in-depth evaluation of the representation plan at CF&I by Benjamin Selekman and Mary Van Kleeck (1924). But a number of other knowledgeable people saw a substantially more positive picture (Kaufman 2000). After a detailed investigation, for example, Carroll French concluded, "The meetings of the joint committees have been remarkably successful. . . . [T]he burden of the evidence and testimony as to the results of the shop committee agree that it has made for a better relations between management and men" (1923, 75–76). Likewise, one of the periods most expert and disinterested observers of employee representation, William Leiserson, also reached a notably upbeat conclusion. He states,

> The unskilled and semi-skilled working people of this country, in the last six years, have obtained more of the things . . . out of employee representation plans than they have out of the organized labor movement. . . . There is even evidence that these workers sometimes deliberately prefer company unions to the regular trade unions. The reason is that they think employee representation is doing what the unions have failed to do. [1928, 127]

Although the employee representation movement broadened considerably beyond the Rockefeller/SCC network of companies, theses companies nonetheless defined its central core and continued to be its strongest proponents. Not unexpectedly, therefore, employee representation was also adopted and endorsed by Industrial Relations Counselors, Inc., and IRC played a significant role in promoting the concept and spreading it to a wider constituency in industry.

As already noted, IRC never published a report or a book on employee representation. Given that employee representation was arguably the central IR innovation espoused by IRC, this omission appears anomalous at first. I believe the reason is that up to the beginning of the Depression in late 1929, IRC did not have the staff or resources to undertake a significant research/ publication program (recalling that the first published monograph was not until 1931), and after the Depression commenced, interest in employee representation declined and the importance of employment/income stabilization commensurately rose. Also of relevance, IRC was able to promote employee representation through other channels, such as books (French 1923), speeches at conferences by Hicks, Young, and other staffers, and articles in practitioner publications. Illustrative, for example, is the session devoted to employee representation at the 1928 annual YMCA industrial relations conference at Silver Bay, New York, and the series of articles published in the journal *Personnel* (February 1928).

Evidence contained in the IRC consulting reports suggests, however, that the organization was a consistent proponent of employee representation to its corporate clients, albeit with two important caveats. The first is that the relative emphasis given to employee representation in the reports declines over the course of the 1920s. In the early years (1923–25), the IR audits—after a review of the company's business and overall labor policies—typically began with a large chapter devoted to "joint relations" and, in particular, the case for employee representation. Later in the decade, the "joint relations" chapter tended to move to the back of the reports and be much shorter in length. Then as the Depression deepened in the early 1930s, a "joint relations" chapter was on at least one occasion omitted altogether (the report did, however, continue to recommend employee representation, albeit in abbreviated treatment in a different section). Not unexpectedly, with the onset of the New Deal in 1933 and the labor turmoil that ensued, "joint relations" once again moved to the front of the reports and employee representation was discussed in greater detail.

These trends can be interpreted in various ways. One interpretation is largely negative—that employee representation was losing momentum or "stalling out," or that other IR practices (e.g., employee benefits) were found to be more effective or popular and thus were "crowding out" employee representation. Another interpretation, more neutral or even positive, points to two other developments: (1) the amount of attention given to employee representation naturally tended to decline as the practice became established and routinized and (2) the emphasis given to employee representation in the survey reports varied with the economic environment and the labor problems facing management. This suggests that the relative decline in emphasis given to representation was a rational business response to the improved tenor of joint relations in the latter 1920s and to the appearance of mass unemployment in the early 1930s. Evidence does not permit a definitive conclusion, but I judge elements of both explanations were at work. Certainly an entirely or predominantly negative conclusion is not supported. Even in the depth of the Depression, for example, a 1931 IRC report to Standard Oil

Company of Ohio states, "Employee representation has been outstandingly successful where the plan has been properly conceived and operated and where it has been adopted by a management which recognizes the principle that, in the last analysis, policies to be ultimately successful must work to the well-being of employees as well as the company" (p. 25). The report goes on to recommend adoption of a representation plan, even though in an earlier IRC report in 1928 the company was judged not ready for representation. A second piece of evidence is from six case-study reports of employee representation at SCC companies prepared by Cowdrick in 1928. The reports conclude that employee representation had performed relatively well to that point and certainly give no indication that enthusiasm or commitment to representation was flagging. In the "Conclusion" to the report on International Harvester, for example, Cowdrick states, "Enough good results, however, can be traced back directly to the works council plan to corroborate to the satisfaction of a fair-minded observer the testimony of the Harvester management that representation has played an important part in the advantages that have occurred both to the company and to the employees since its adoption" (pp. 41–42). Finally, Hicks reaffirms his support of employee representation when he calls it, "the most significant development in American industrial relations during the past twenty years" (1928, 94).

The second caveat concerning IRC's commitment to employee representation is that the organization consistently withheld recommendation of representation where it judged that the situation was not ripe for success due to ongoing labor strife, unsupportive management, or the primitive nature of personnel practices. Several examples from IRC surveys have already been provided along this line.

Given this background, in the early spring of 1933 as Franklin Roosevelt came to office as the new president of the country, no one at IRC, or indeed in the nation, could have anticipated that in a little more than three years, employee representation plans would be declared illegal and ripped up root and branch. Certainly there was some drift in opinion against employers who used representation plans (also called, more pejoratively, "company unions") as an overt union-busting device, illustrated, for example, by favorable public reaction to the Supreme Court's decision in the Texas and New Orleans Railroad case in 1930 (to disestablish a company union forced on employees in place of independent union representation). But the progressive welfare capitalist companies associated with IRC and the SCC had eschewed such heavy-handed tactics, and their representation plans had heretofore been cited as models of enlightened management.

The downfall of employee representation involves a complex interplay of economic and political events and contains several significant ironies. This story is told elsewhere in much greater detail (Kaufman 2000), so only the barest account is offered here. The catalyst was passage in early summer of 1933 of the National Industrial Recovery Act (NIRA), which was legislation hastily crafted and enacted to promote economic recovery. The aim of the NIRA was to cartelize product and labor markets in order to stabilize prices and wages, thus stopping the destructive process of deflation. An additional goal was to redistribute income from capital to labor in order to promote greater household purchasing power and aggregate demand. To accomplish this, firms were allowed through industry associations to set prices and production quotas, while the Act sought to promote unions and collective bargaining to stabilize and advance wages (and shorten hours). Toward this end, a Section 7(a) was included in the NIRA that declared as national labor policy that workers have the right to join labor organizations of their own choosing and engage in collective bargaining without coercion or interference.

The enactment of the NIRA, the inclusion of Section 7(a), and the popular belief that the president's economic recovery program depended on widespread adoption of collective bargaining led to a massive surge in union organizing. Most employers were strongly anti-union and sought to deflect the union drive. To do so, many engaged in a two-pronged strategy: using union-suppression tactics (e.g., firing union supporters) to squelch worker organizing while quickly setting up an employee representation plan—claiming that these "company unions" satisfied the NIRA's intent to promote "collective bargaining" (broadly defined). More progressive companies, such as among SCC members, were largely spared large-scale labor unrest and organizing drives in the 1933–34 period but nonetheless revised their representation plans to make them more closely conform to the collective bargaining model promoted by the NIRA (e.g., by signing written contracts with employee councils).

Senator Robert Wagner, a friend of organized labor and a drafter of the NIRA, grew increasingly hostile toward employers and "company unions" because, in his view, they were overtly thwarting employees' right to organize and the economic purpose of the NIRA, which was to promote economic recovery through wage stabilization and income redistribution via bona fide collective bargaining. He thus introduced legislation in 1934 that sought to strengthen the protection of labor's freedom of association and right to collectively bargain. In it he included a Section 8(a)(2) that declared it an illegal "unfair labor practice" for an employer to operate a "dominated" (i.e., company-created and -supported) employee representation plan or committee for purposes of dealing with employees on matters concerning terms and conditions of employment. To the surprise of most people, and the great consternation of employers, a revised version of the bill—called the National Labor Relations Act (NLRA, or Wagner Act)—passed both houses of Congress in the spring of 1935 and was signed into law by President Roosevelt. The act made it public policy to encourage and protect the practice of collective bargaining, while it outlawed the Rockefeller-type employee representation plan. Equally surprising, the Supreme Court in 1937 upheld the constitutionality of the NLRA, and over the next decade, Section 8(a)(2) of the act was repeatedly and aggressively used to root out employee representation plans (estimated to cover two and a half million workers in 1935), leaving practically none in existence by the end of World War II.

Several aspects of this story are noteworthy as they pertain to IRC. First, while IRC was enjoying the triumph that went with the passage of the Social Security Act in 1935, in the same year it experienced the defeat that went with enactment of the National Labor Relations Act and the demise of employee representation.

Second, a question arises as to IRC's involvement in political efforts to defeat or amend the NLRA. As previously documented, IRC was heavily involved in the development of the Social Security Act, but this entrée was ostensibly in a research capacity and was thus consonant with its stated principle of nonpartisanship. The development of the Wagner bill, however, was done among a close circle of people associated with the senator and sympathetic to organized labor and involved no explicit research component (Casebeer 1987). IRC thus had no opportunity to play a role in the development of the legislation.

Regarding lobbying and political efforts to defeat/amend the bill, evidence indicates IRC also remained uninvolved and tried assiduously to remain so as a matter of policy. One important factor in this regard was that from the beginning of the NIRA experiment, John D. Rockefeller, Jr., unlike many of his fellow industrialists, publicly supported Section 7(a) and its encouragement of representation in industry. In a radio address in August 1933, he told the nation, "A further and fundamentally important advantage growing out of the National [Industrial] Recovery Act is the hastening of the day when labor shall have proper and adequate representation in industry. For nearly twenty years I have been an ardent advocate of that policy." Part of his support for Section 7(a), however, was based on the fact that while it promoted representation of employees, it allowed free choice as to the particular form representation takes. Thus, in this regard, he stated, "Whether the workers shall have a voice in industry through some such representation plan or through some kind of trade unionism is a question which the workers in each plant should be free to determine. The National [Industrial] Recovery Act makes this choice possible, and is all the stronger in that it refrains from specifying the adoption of any particular form of collective bargaining" (Rockefeller 1933).

A second factor behind IRC's nonpartisan position was Rockefeller's dread of having his good name and liberal IR reputation suddenly sullied by charges that he or his associates were subverting Section 7(a)'s protection and encouragement of workers' right to join unions. This fear is clearly revealed in a letter from Fosdick to Rockefeller, written in March 1934. Fosdick states,

> One of my responsibilities in the twenty-one years in which I have been associated with you has been to point out possible dangers ahead in connection with your multifarious interests. The country is at the moment witnessing a head-on collision between the labor union and the company union. Your position has always been clear, i.e., that you stood for adequate *representation* no matter whether it was by one method or another. We have always tried to hold the scales evenly as far as the management of Industrial Relations Counselors was concerned, and we have friends on both sides of the fence.
>
> In the heat of the present controversy, . . . I am not entirely convinced that the detached attitude which we have thus far held can be maintained. Mr. Hicks with entire frankness has pointed out to me that the very nature of the work of Industrial Relations Counselors implies a sympathy toward the company union which as an organization we do not have toward the labor union. If this is true—and I fear it may be—it is possible that the charge might be made that you were financing an organization to fight union labor, and you might thereby be maneuvered into an uncomfortable public position. . . .
>
> Of course, I am not saying that you *would* be dragged in. Industrial Relations Counselors might—and indeed probably can—steer clear of this fighting issue in the future as we have in the past. I feel I have the duty, however, just to mention the possibility of unpleasantness. [Emphasis in original]

The evidence indicates that IRC and its staff did indeed remain uninvolved, and, remarkably for an organization linked to a rich industrialist and the cause of employee representation, it escaped nearly all criticism or public suspicion during the tumultuous and highly partisan labor turmoil sweeping the nation in the mid-1930s. No one representing IRC, for example, testified before Congress during the hearings on the bill in 1934–35, nor did IRC take a position on the NLRA in several unpublished memorandums to clients. IRC "Memorandum to Clients" Nos. 8, 9, 11, and 13, written in the first half of 1935, all gave fairly detailed accounts (4–9 pages in length) of the provisions of the NLRA and the prospects for passage of the legislation, but none expressed an evaluative position on the legislation or counseled clients to take political action. The only quasi-exception to this statement is in IRC's Memorandum No. 9, dated March 27, 1935, which states,

> Spokesmen for employee representation plans in a number of steel plants testified before the committee March 26, asserting that many thousands of employees were satisfied with employee representation plans as a method of collective bargaining. Frequently proponents of such plans have been ineffective in their testimony. . . . However, it is hoped that certain amendments which have already been considered by the committee will be adopted. These amendments are designed principally to ensure recognition of employee representation plans not dominated by management. [P. 8]

Not only did IRC remain outside the battle on the NLRA, but also the people most closely associated with it kept a low profile. Neither Hicks nor Cowdrick, for example, testified at the congressional hearings on the NLRA, nor were they or other Rockefeller-connected people later exposed in the LaFollette Committee hearings as among the "belligerent" opponents of the NLRA (U.S. Senate Committee on Education and Labor 1939). Hicks and Cowdrick did, however, work behind the scenes in Washington to influence New Deal labor policy, principally through the Industrial Relations Committee of the Business Advisory Council (BAC). The BAC was a forty-one-person council, created in 1933 and chaired by Gerard Swope of GE, to advise the secretary of commerce. It quickly became a center for corporate lobbying and political action in the Roosevelt administration. The BAC created an Industrial Relations Committee, chaired by Teagle of Jersey Standard, to work on labor issues, and Teagle made the people from the SCC companies members of the committee and asked Cowdrick and Hicks to coordinate the committee's activities (Domhoff 1990).

The SCC companies, and individuals such as Hicks and Cowdrick, quietly lobbied behind the scene for defeat of the NLRA and coordinated testimony against it in the congressional hearings in 1934–35. But among the business groups active in Washington politics at this time, the Rockefeller-connected people active in the BAC were clearly in the moderate/liberal camp regarding labor policy in general and the NLRA in particular. Although not eager to see the extension of AFL-style independent unionism with its associated "evils" of the closed shop and antiquated craft structure, they were nonetheless open to dialogue and compromise with the leaders of organized labor and were prepared to support legislation that provided a stronger guarantee of workers' right to organize. This position is clearly stated in several letters Hicks wrote to Wagner in 1934 (contained in the Wagner papers at

George Washington University). In these he voices support for Section 7(a) of the NIRA and the necessity of independent representation for workers employed at companies that used fear and intimidation tactics. But Hicks pleads with Wagner to recognize that the employee representation plans at companies such as Jersey Standard serve a useful purpose for both employers and employees and, accordingly, to revise the language of the bill to allow these plans to survive. Arthur Young—speaking in his new capacity as vice president of industrial relations at U.S. Steel—takes a stronger stand in opposition to the bill in his testimony to Congress, but he does so less on a general hostility to collective bargaining than on the above-mentioned "evils" (the closed shop and craft structure) and the bill's antagonistic stance toward employee representation plans (NLRB 1985).

I note, finally, that Rockefeller also chose not to publicly oppose Wagner's bill, even though it conflicted with the principles on employee representation he enunciated at the second 1919 industrial conference and threatened to eviscerate the CF&I-type employee representation plan. Rockefeller's position in 1919 was that public policy should promote greater access to all forms of employee representation, but Wagner's bill sought to favor one form of representation (union) at the expense of another (the employee representation plan). Had Rockefeller chosen to take as forceful and public a stand in 1934 in support of *all* forms of employee representation as he had in 1919, the outcome of the political battle might have been far different and more balanced.

To the people in the Rockefeller/SCC/IRC camp, the demise of employee representation created strong feelings of irony, injustice, and some bitterness. From their point of view, organized labor and its allies had won through partisan politics what they could not win by direct appeal to workers—the triumph of the independent union over the employer representation plan (Nelson 2000). They were also galled by the caricature of company unions as toothless "shams," when in their opinion the record clearly showed that employee representation among progressive firms had led to a considerable improvement in employee relations and conditions of work. And then there was the perceived injustice and one-sidedness of the NLRA—unjust because it purported to promote and protect employee free choice but, in fact, restricted free choice by eliminating the option of a Rockefeller-type representation plan in order to foster trade unionism and one-sided because it declared illegal employer domination but left untouched union domination (e.g., the closed shop).

Despite this welter of negative feelings, after enactment of the NLRA, spokesmen in the IRC camp adopted a constructive and even modestly positive line on the issue of employee representation. Hope was expressed, for example, that if the plans were stripped of overt forms of employer domination, they would pass muster with the National Labor Relations Board (French 1937). Notice was also taken of the effort among some SCC employers, such as Jersey Standard and DuPont, to convert representation plans into independent local unions (Jacoby 2000). Also noteworthy, IRC consistently counseled employers in internal memorandums to hew to the new requirements of the NLRA, even if they seemed draconian or counterproductive. And finally, the view of IRC stalwarts was that Section 8(a)(2) was manifestly unjust in principle and harmful in practice and, for these reasons, would eventually be amended. Stated Clarence Hicks, "Any legislation that aims to prevent such friendly intercourse [between employers and employees] is bound to be modified" (1941, 94). More than six decades later, however, Hicks' prophecy remains unfulfilled.

Other Research Accomplishments

Returning to the research function of IRC, in the 1930s, there were four other accomplishments deserving mention. The first was the establishment of a research and consultation relationship with the International Labour Organization (ILO). Rockefeller had strong interests in international affairs and encouraged IRC to extend its work in industrial relations to the international arena. Accordingly, in 1927, IRC opened a branch office at the ILO's headquarters in Geneva, Switzerland, and maintained a full-time staff person there (Thomas Spates). The IRC office served as an informal clearinghouse for the exchange of American and foreign developments in the labor area and assisted ILO officials in dealing with inquiries about U.S. industrial relations. The office was closed in 1932.

A second research development was the initiation of a "newsletter" and "memorandum" series. Regarding the former, beginning in January 1936, IRC distributed a periodic newsletter of 5–6 pages in length on current industrial relations events/trends to contributing companies, university industrial relations sections, and other interested parties. With respect to the latter, memorandums called "Industrial Relations Memos" (or "Memorandum to Clients" until 1939), were issued at a rate of 6–12 a year, generally ran 8–10 pages in length, and dealt with current topics of interest, such as apprentice training, wage incentive plans, prospective labor legislation, and developments in collective bargaining.

The third development of note is the role that IRC played in the founding of the nation's first university-level units (sections) devoted to research and teaching in industrial relations. In his autobiography, Clarence Hicks recounts his dismay at the way the typical "labor problems" course was taught in universities. He says of the instructors of such courses, "Their approach in this latter case [the labor problems course] has been theoretical and usually under the direction of a professor of economics who, in most cases, has had but little practical touch or experience" (1941, 140). Hicks was also dismayed by the one-sided approach they typically took to the subject, giving most of the time to the subject of trade unionism and emphasizing the positive virtues thereof, with correspondingly little time or positive perspective given to the industrial relations programs and accomplishments of employers.

To help remedy this situation, Hicks took the lead in establishing six industrial relations sections at major universities: Princeton, MIT, Stanford, Michigan, California Institute of Technology, and Queens (Canada). A seventh was planned for Wisconsin, but it never came to fruition (ibid., 150). The first IR section was established at Princeton in 1922, while the others were set up in the 1930s. To finance the operations of the IR sections, Hicks obtained substantial gifts from Rockefeller. The sections were intended to promote research in all phases of industrial relations, but per Hicks' vision, the "employer's solution" of progressive IR management was given greater emphasis (relative to other university programs). Toward this end, a library was established at each section to collect and disseminate a wide range of IR materials, including extensive company publications and records. Also, at Princeton, starting in 1931, an annual conference was held for high-level IR executives, an event which IRC personnel attended and participated in. Upon Hicks' death in 1944, fellowships in his name were established at each section.

Two other universities also had discernible ties to IRC. The first was the Wharton School of Business and Commerce at the University of Pennsylvania. An "industrial research unit" was established in 1921, and its director, Joseph Willits, had close links to the Rockefeller interests and later served as director of the Social Science Research Council, a Rockefeller-funded foundation. C. Canby Balderston, dean of the Wharton School in the 1930s, served on the IRC board of trustees, and both Balderston and Herbert Northrup authored IRC monographs (Balderston 1937; Northrup 1946). The second university was Cornell. In the early 1940s, Walter Teagle, chairman of the board at Jersey Standard, urged Cornell to establish an IR section and donated funds to work up a preliminary plan (Hicks 1943). The end product was the New York State School of Industrial and Labor Relations, established in 1945.

The fourth research development deserving mention is IRC's own library. The organization hired a full-time professional librarian—later to grow to a staff of four full-time librarians—and developed in the pre-WWII years one of the nation's most extensive collections of industrial relations books, periodicals, and other publications. These materials supported the research and consulting activities of IRC and were also available to client companies, university researchers, and public persons. The bulk of these materials were later donated to the library of Cornell University.

Readjustment and Retrenchment

In many respects, the 1930s represent the high-water mark for IRC's research program. Going into the 1930s, IRC was one of the very few organizations conducting high-quality, objective research on industrial relations topics. There was thus a large void, made even larger by the events of the New Deal, and IRC was well positioned to fill it. But by the end of the decade, the landscape had changed and IRC was forced to shift gears.

Two factors came into play. The first was that many new organizations and agencies, such as in government and universities, began to pursue extensive, large-scale research in industrial relations. The field thus became much more crowded, highlighted in these words in an internal IRC report (1940): "Having pioneered in research in social security and allied subjects, Industrial Relations Counselors, Inc. now finds that many agencies with vast research resources are now at work in that field." The second factor was that IRC's financial position was under increasing pressure, forcing cutbacks in the research program. During the 1930s, the Rockefeller Foundation gave IRC more than $90,000 to fund completion of the ten volumes earlier listed. But these funds ran out toward the end of the decade and were not renewed. As earlier indicated, Rockefeller also phased out his personal contribution to IRC in the mid-1930s, which in past years had been at an annual level of $100,000–$150,000 ($1.0–$1.5 million in current dollars). The bright spot, according to the above-cited memorandum, was that "shortly after the decline in income began, the demand for surveys mounted and the requests for surveys in 1938–39 were unusually great." Although not mentioned in this memorandum, IRC also had modest success in recruiting companies to enter into a long-term "client" relationship, where for a modest annual fee (typically in the $1,500–$2,000 range), the company would receive all IRC publications and be entitled to ongoing consulting advice. In the mid-1930s, IRC had a dozen client companies, a number which then grew to forty-nine by 1953.

IRC was forced to make major readjustments. According to the memorandum, "The organization has adapted itself to these conditions by limiting the scope of its projects, reducing the staff on special studies and transferring much personnel to survey work (the staff had grown to approximately forty in number), engaging persons with special knowledge of particular subjects for temporary assignments instead of making permanent appointments, and giving more research to contributing companies with the hope of encouraging their continued support." As just indicated, IRC thus chose to cut back its research program and concentrate the bulk of its resources on the survey work—work that was both in increasing demand and a revenue generator. It also decided to shift its research focus, in these words, "to the practical administrative aspects of industrial relations, an area in which little effective work is being done. A series of monographs on such topics has recently been initiated. The monographs average from fifty to seventy-five pages and are designed to aid industrial relations executives and in the teaching of the subject." The irony facing IRC in adopting this course of action was duly noted at the time: "The decline in income comes just at the time when the organization had just begun to capitalize on its accumulated experience" (ibid.).

On top of these difficulties, one other development also took its toll on the IRC research program. With the outbreak of World War II, numerous IRC staff members were recruited into government work or the armed forces. Not only were staff resources seriously depleted, even paper to print new books was unobtainable due to wartime rationing. On the potentially positive side, the advent of industrial unionism and wartime wage-price controls led to a substantial increase in demand for job evaluation studies, and IRC developed an expertise in this practice area in the 1940s that closely rivaled its reputation in the pension area in the 1930s. But in this case, relatively modest published research was generated (Balderston 1940; Gray 1943).

Thus, starting in the latter part of the 1930s, IRC's research program was both cut back in scope and redirected to shorter, more practitioner-oriented studies. IRC also increasingly contracted out the studies to outside authors, such as university professors in the labor area. Illustrative are monographs by C. Canby Balderston (1937, the Wharton School) on profit sharing, Herman Feldman (1939, Dartmouth) and Richard Lester (1939, Princeton) on the case for and against experience rating in unemployment insurance programs, and Sumner Slichter (1939, Harvard) on economic factors affecting wartime industrial relations policies.

This shift in research strategy, while perhaps inevitable and in certain respects meritorious, nonetheless brought with it several significant long-term problems. One was wastage of accumulated knowledge and human capital. As the 1940 IRC report states, "The combined experience and training of the staff members and their knowledge of industrial relations in American industry are without parallel. The same is true of the body of information in the files which includes survey, pension, and other reports for more than a hundred companies." But the new research strategy had no way to effectively use these resources. A second problem was the belief that ongoing, staff-conducted research was a crucial ingredient to maintaining leading-edge consulting services. The internal memorandum states in this regard, "No doubt for a time the survey work could be done on a self-supporting basis, but ultimately its quality would deteriorate. Like clinical work in medicine, this clinical work in industrial relations must be based on continuous study." Finally, the de-emphasis of research and the growing reliance on consulting-generated income threatened IRC's nonprofit status. In the late 1930s, the Internal Revenue Service raised this issue but chose not to pursue a legal challenge. This problem, however, would come back again.

Post–World War II Developments and Activities

In the first two decades of its existence, IRC had carved out a national reputation for excellence in consulting and research in industrial relations. It proved, however, an ever-larger challenge in the decades following World War II to preserve this momentum. The first casualty was the consulting program, which in the 1950s had to be spun off to a sister organization. For the next two decades, IRC continued a visible and active program of research and training, but by the 1980s, these also began to noticeably slacken. One culprit was lack of financial resources; another was a gradual loss of competitive advantage in a more crowded and fast-changing marketplace. Despite a number of fund-raising initiatives and new research and training strategies, IRC's programs and activities slowly contracted until, by the 1990s, the organization was largely inactive. With the death of Winthrop Rockefeller in 1973, IRC also lost the last direct link to the Rockefeller family. In the next section, I briefly recount these events and trends.

Consulting

The consulting function of IRC grew in relative importance during the 1940s and 1950s. In 1936, for example, 41 percent of IRC's income came from consulting; by 1946, the proportion had risen to 78 percent and remained in that vicinity for years hence. This trend, as earlier indicated, reflected in part the decline in individual financial contributions to IRC, largely from Rockefeller, and in funds obtained from research grants. But another part was attributable to a growing demand for IRC's consulting services. From 1926 to 1936, IRC completed 73 consulting reports, which then increased to 275 between 1937 and 1946 and to 354 between 1947 and 1957. The growing demand for IRC's consulting services also led to the opening of a branch office in Toronto, Canada, in the early 1950s and to consulting activity in Europe, Asia, South America, and the Middle East.

One consequence of this relative shift in income and activity was renewed attention from the Internal Revenue Service regarding IRC's nonprofit status.

After considerable debate and analysis, the board of trustees of IRC decided in 1953 to separate the research and consulting activities into different organizations. The research function remained a part of IRC, while the consulting function moved to a new for-profit organization called Industrial Relations Counselors Services, Inc. (IRCS). Initially, the entire capital stock of IRCS was held by IRC, although over the years IRCS/ORC ownership has subsequently become much more widely spread (partly through employee stock ownership). In 1969, the name of IRCS was changed to Organization Resources Counselors, Inc. (ORC). ORC to this date continues to carry out a wide-ranging consulting practice both in the United States and a variety of other countries. Through the year 2000, its chairman and CEO was Richard Beaumont, who also served as research director of IRC. The professional staff of ORC numbers approximately 130.

As described earlier, the consulting reports done by IRC in the first decade of its life were in the form of a broad-ranging "survey of industrial relations" at the client company and were massive reports in terms of length, detail, and statistical investigation. By the 1950s, it was no longer necessary to "sell" clients on the need for an IR/HR function and program, so the focus and format of IRC's consulting reports changed accordingly. Increasingly, the reports no longer canvassed the broad domain of industrial relations practice at a client company but, rather, focused on specific IR practices and issues, such as job evaluation, attitude surveys, and employee turnover. Nor were they nearly as lengthy and detailed. One of the last general "IR surveys" to be done, for example, was for the Riverside Cement Company in 1959. The entire report ran 34 pages.

Another consulting-related activity performed by IRC—and later transferred to ORC—was sponsorship of the Cowdrick Group (and related subgroups). As noted earlier, Edward Cowdrick served as secretary of the Special Conference Committee until his death in 1951. Shortly thereafter, IRC took on the responsibility of acting as the organization's "secretariat," and the SCC's name was changed to the Cowdrick Group in his honor. In 1946, a separate Cowdrick Training Group was established, and later the Overseas Cowdrick Group was created. With the proliferation of groups, the original SCC organization became known as the Cowdrick Main Group. As of 1963, the Main Group had grown to thirteen companies, but only Western Electric and Union Carbide were new additions since the 1920s. Today twenty-three companies belong to the Cowdrick Main Group. The Group typically meets in New York City and has two-day programs on current human resource/industrial relations topics of interest to member companies. IRC/ORC will perform periodic canvasses (surveys) for the Cowdrick Group companies when a request is made for more data or information on a particular topic.

A second consulting-related activity carried forward by IRC from earlier decades was management training. The "IRC Management Course in Industrial Relations," started in 1943, was offered annually and then semiannually at Williamsburg, Virginia, through the 1980s. More than six thousand managers participated in the programs. A variety of other more topic-specific seminars and training programs (e.g., supervisor training) was also provided over the years by IRC and, later, ORC.

Research

With the split-off of the consulting function to IRCS/ORC, the core activity of Industrial Relations Counselors, Inc., shifted toward research and, secondarily, education. Until the mid-1970s, IRC was able to produce a steady stream of books, monographs, and special reports. Indeed, the decade of the 1960s saw the greatest number of publications of any decade in IRC's history.

From 1926 to 1946, IRC produced a total of twenty-eight published research works. As already noted, the dominant topics of research in this period were pensions and unemployment insurance. From 1947 to 1959, the rate of publication fell off significantly, with only ten works appearing. The single greatest number of publications was again in the area of pensions and old-age insurance, but collective bargaining subjects also bulked large, and a significant study on "Employing the Negro in American Industry" was also completed. Then over the short span of 1960–70, IRC produced a spurt of twenty-three more publications on a diverse range of subjects, including various facets of collective bargaining and labor relations, incentive forms of compensation, employee benefits, productivity, and automation. Research output then dropped precipitously. Over the remainder of the 1970s, only five publications appeared, and in the 1980s and 1990s, only two more works were published. The last research publication of IRC was in 1994, entitled *Report on the IRC Survey of Employee Involvement.*

A number of developments contributed to these trends. One was financial. The relative dearth of research publications in the 1947–59 period is explained in an internal IRC report (1957): "Until very recently, virtually the only source of funds available to IRC has been the contributions of a limited group of companies, totaling only a small fraction of the amounts available in the earlier years. This reduction in funds precluded the undertaking of further large-scale research projects requiring substantial financing and long-range assignment of staff." Under the direction of IRC Research Director Richard Beaumont, an intensive campaign was begun in the early 1960s to raise a substantial pool of funds to support a much expanded research program. According to a 1970 internal report, "An intensive but short-term effort to gain research support from industry was successful in raising between $150,000 and $170,000 in annual contributions from individual companies. Most of this money was contributed on a five-year basis." IRC had been successful in getting more than thirty corporations to pledge five-year gifts to underwrite a reinvigorated research program. The product was nearly two dozen books, monographs, and published reports over the decade.

At the end of the five years, however, most of the contributing companies chose not to renew their pledges, and IRC funds for research shrank considerably. An effort was subsequently launched to raise a multimillion-dollar endowment for IRC, but restrictive rulings by the Internal Revenue Service aborted this initiative. The situation as of the early 1970s was thus summarized this way: "The sources of income currently available to IRC are inadequate to maintain its research effort. At present, the organization is drawing on its general fund for current operating expenses to cover a restricted and minimum research activity. Within a year at the most, this reserve fund will be exhausted, and a real question will then arise as to whether IRC can continue as an effective research organization" (ibid. 1970). This question was answered largely in the negative, for in the years afterwards, IRC's research output dropped sharply and effectively ceased after the mid-1990s.

A second development that hit IRC hard was a gradual loss in competitive advantage in the research marketplace. Before World War II, few universities or government agencies conducted rigorous IR research of a "prac-ademic" nature (i.e., high-quality, scientifically respectable research on relatively applied issues of labor practice and policy). IRC was thus in a unique position to fill this research void, situated as it was with unparalleled links to the business world but also possessing a highly trained and competent staff of researchers. In the post-WWII era, IRC's research strategy continued to be focused on serving this "prac-ademic" market, in effect occupying a middle ground between universities and government agencies on one side and industry trade groups on the other. As one example of this strategy in action, in 1962 IRC launched an annual program of "Symposia on Advanced Research in Industrial Relations." The idea was to bring university researchers and IR executives from industry together to "bridge the historical gap between academic research and its application in the workplace." Toward this end, several books were published in the 1960s in which academic researchers and industry executives explored the interface between IR theory and practice.

While sound in principle, this strategy ran into two problems. The first was that the major "customer" of this kind of research—corporations in industry—proved in the main unwilling to financially underwrite it over the long term. The second was that the cost and resources necessary to mount a large, ongoing IR research program rose sharply with the advent of computers, large-scale surveys, and ever-increasing statistical sophistication. IRC thus found its research program increasingly squeezed on one side by diminishing sources of revenue and on the other by mounting costs and resource demands. The result, as already noted, was that by the early 1980s, IRC's formal research program had largely come to an end.

Finally, note must be made of a third development that negatively impacted the viability of both IRC's consulting and research activities in the last three decades of the century. Into the 1960s, the term "industrial relations" continued to be interpreted in the academic and practitioner worlds as a broad-based concept that included both personnel/human resource management (HRM) and union-management (labor) relations. Thereafter, however, usage changed, and increasingly "industrial relations" narrowed in meaning to include only the subject of labor relations, while personnel/HRM became established as separate entities (Kaufman 1993). Thus, while in the early 1960s the top executive in charge of the employment function at many corporations still carried the title "Vice President, Industrial Relations," by the early 1980s, this title had all but disappeared, replaced by "Vice President, Human Resources." As "industrial relations" became associated with "union-management relations," as the unionized share of the workforce continued to shrink (to only one in ten private sector workers by 2000), and as the locus of new, leading-edge employment practices and organizational innovations shifted to HRM, an organization named "Industrial Relations Counselors" inevitably began to look to the corporate and public eye as increasingly time-worn and out of the HRM mainstream. These perceptions, whether true or not, became a growing handicap.

IRC's only ongoing publishing activity in the 1990s was a periodic newsletter to client companies, called *IR Concepts*, which discussed current events and policy issues in industrial relations. In 2000, ORC assumed sponsorship of the *Journal of Organizational Excellence* (formerly the *National Productivity Review*), but while this development considerably renewed the research emphasis in the organization, it was under the label of ORC, not IRC. IRC also funded and published a major study in 1994 of employee involvement programs in sixteen companies (IRC 1994). On occasion, IRC also provided financial support to universities for research in industrial relations. In 1973, for example, IRC funded a professorship in industrial relations at the Colgate Darden School of Graduate Business Administration at the University of Virginia. And returning to its roots in 1997, IRC helped fund a conference in Banff, Canada, on the subject of "Nonunion Employee Representation" (Kaufman and Taras 2000)—the IR innovation pioneered by John D. Rockefeller, Jr., William Lyon Mackenzie King, and Clarence Hicks in the mid-1910s that not only led to the birth of IRC but also fundamentally changed the course of management and industrial relations in this country.

As this volume goes to press, discussions are under way at IRC on initiatives to renew the organization's research program. Should these bear fruit, the seventy-fifth anniversary of IRC will be a time not only for celebration of past accomplishments but also of future contributions.

Conclusions

Industrial Relations Counselors, Inc., was officially born seventy-five years ago, but its roots extend back more than a decade earlier to one of the great tragedies in American labor history, the "Ludlow Massacre." The Colorado coal strike, and the loss of life and destruction of property flowing from it, brought wealthy industrialist John D. Rockefeller, Jr., face-to-face with the Labor Problem. Like most other employers of that era, Rockefeller's initial response to the disaster was to absolve management of any responsibility, point the finger of blame at union agitators and political radicals, and stand firm for the principles of the "open shop" and liberty of contract. The course of history changed, however, when through good fortune and sound instinct, Rockefeller invited Canadian labor expert William Lyon Mackenzie King to come to America and serve as his industrial relations advisor. King guided Rockefeller onto a new path of industrial relations that was for the era markedly reformist and progressive.

The hallmark of this new IR strategy was a more scientific, humanistic, and long-run-oriented approach to the management of labor. This strategy sought to transform Labor and Capital from adversaries caught in a "zero-sum" struggle over control of the workplace and the distribution of revenues to partners working cooperatively to generate "positive-sum" outcomes of greater efficiency and profit, higher wages and improved working conditions, and an expanded sense of justice and human well-being for all. The initial innovation developed by King and adopted by Rockefeller to promote this new partnership was a formal plan of employee representation. Later, it was supplemented by a number of additional management initiatives, including a written labor policy and set of employment standards, establishment of an industrial relations department, use of new personnel management methods such as job evaluation and foreman training, efforts to promote job security, and adoption of gain-sharing forms of compensation and a variety of employee benefits.

When King returned to Canada in 1919 to resume a career in national politics, Rockefeller searched for new counsel on industrial relations matters. He at first relied on legal and business advisor Raymond Fosdick and then, upon Fosdick's suggestion, created in 1922 a staff of IR advisors within Fosdick's law firm, Curtis, Fosdick, and Belknap. Four years later, with Rockefeller's financial support, the IR "section" in Curtis, Fosdick, and Belknap was transferred to a new nonprofit consulting and research organization, Industrial Relations Counselors, Inc.

The birth of IRC in 1926 and its growth and development over the succeeding three quarters of a century are noteworthy on a number of counts. As pointed out in this chapter, for example, Industrial Relations Counselors, Inc., has the distinction of being the first IR consulting and research organization to be established in this country. Not only is this an important event in its own right, but it also signals a fundamental transition point in the approach of American employers to the management of industrial relations. Where industrial relations was once routinely regarded as of secondary importance and something to be handled by foremen and supervisors, the founding of IRC signaled a new conceptualization in which labor management is considered a matter of strategic importance requiring executive attention and professional administration.

IRC also played a crucial role in propagating, developing, and implementing the new, more progressive IR strategy developed by Rockefeller, King, and Clarence Hicks. IRC was first used principally by Rockefeller to promote improved IR practices at companies directly under his control or influence, but within a few years IRC was being increasingly called upon by a wide range of other companies to survey their IR program and recommend changes. Many companies at IRC's recommendation established their first IR department, introduced an employee representation plan, established a pension program for retired employees, and in numerous other ways improved their personnel programs. This consulting activity continues to this day, albeit under the auspices of IRC's sister for-profit organization, Organization Resources Counselors, Inc.

Also deserving note is that in its consulting work—and overall philosophy of industrial relations—IRC was a leader in the liberal/progressive wing of employers. IRC, for example, consistently counseled companies to look at employees as human beings and assets, not as commodities and a short-run expense; encouraged management to view employees as stakeholders, not "hired hands"; counseled employers that they had a social/ethical responsibility toward labor and the community; advocated various forms of collective dealing with workers; consistently supported freedom of association and the right of workers to collective bargaining; and forswore overt and covert methods of union avoidance and opposed repressive methods, such as yellow-dog contracts and labor spies. IRC's liberal, socially progressive stance on industrial relations was also mirrored in the decision to locate a branch office in Geneva, Switzerland, in order to coordinate research and consulting with the ILO.

Not only IRC's consulting work in industry was pathbreaking and highly influential, so too was its research work on matters of national IR policy and practice. Particularly during the 1930s, IRC was widely acknowledged to be a center of excellence in IR research and home of the nation's foremost experts on industrial pensions and programs of unemployment insurance. During this period, IRC published nearly a dozen research books and monographs on these two subjects that were regarded at the time as the "state of the art," and IRC staff, such as Bryce Stewart and Murray Latimer, played key roles in the Roosevelt administration in the development of the Social Security Act and other related New Deal legislation. In later years, IRC's publication program continued to fill a valuable "prac-ademic" middle ground in IR research, providing companies and policy makers with research reports and studies that were scientifically informed but written to be of direct use in the world of practice.

Today IRC is largely inactive, its consulting and training programs taken over by ORC and its research and publication programs at a standstill for lack of funds and staff. One could interpret this as a sign of failure, but the reverse is more nearly the case.

IRC was born out the nation's desperate need in the early twentieth century to resolve the Labor Problem. The Labor Problem could have been dealt with in a variety of ways that would have been destructive of American institutions and at odds with fundamental American political and social beliefs—for example, reactionary suppression along Fascist lines or a Socialist nationalization of industry. But John D. Rockefeller, Jr., and other forward-looking employers in the 1910s charted a middle course of reform that at once defused the Labor Problem through a new strategy of progressive management and, at the same time, preserved the basic institutional/political structure of the country. Industrial Relations Counselors, Inc., was one important player in the unfolding of this strategy.

History has shown that progressive management by itself cannot be counted on to fully resolve labor problems and balance the interests of labor, capital, and the public, and thus, enduring improvements in industrial relations also require the complementary contributions of organized labor and government. But looking over the course of the twentieth century, one cannot help but be impressed with the tremendous advances made in all aspects of employment and feel that progressive management has played a large part in this outcome. Viewed in this manner, IRC's much-diminished activity is a testament to the measure of success it and the progressive management movement have had in transforming American industrial relations—now more often called human resource management—into a more scientifically based, professional, and humanistic model. The Labor Problem is not eliminated, but it is considerably tamed and shorn of its most serious excesses. IRC was a pioneer and leading force in this tremendously positive development.

Acknowledgments

The author acknowledges with appreciation the helpful comments of Richard Beaumont, Roy Helfgott, and William Domhoff on earlier drafts of this chapter. Domhoff also generously shared materials from the Robert Wagner papers.

Section II

History and Development
of Human Resource Management

4

The Quest for Cooperation and Unity of Interest in Industry

Bruce E. Kaufman

The parties to industry are in reality not enemies, but partners;
they have a common interest; no one can get
on without the others. . . . Success is dependent on the
cooperation of all.

—John D. Rockefeller, Jr. (1923)

To reconcile Labor to innovations and efficiency methods of
one kind or another; and to win Labor's co-operation with the
other parties to Industry, in an endeavor to further to the
utmost a common aim, two things are necessary. Labor must be
given an understanding of industrial processes as a whole, and
also a direct interest in the success of undertakings as a whole.
A common knowledge and a common interest are essential to
call forth the highest effort toward a common end. Moreover,
since Industry implies co-operative effort, regard must be had
for men in their collective capacity.

—William Lyon Mackenzie King (1918)

To the extent that American employers recognize the common
interests of management and men and invite their employees to
co-operate with them through representatives of their own
choice, to that extent American industry will pass from the
stage of autocracy and its counterpart, antagonism, to one of
friendly co-operation. . . . With an increasing emphasis on the
unity of interest of all levels of employees, the effectiveness of
American industry will provide a standard of work and living
which will be as satisfying as it is secure.

—Clarence Hicks (1941)

As described in Chapter 3, the birth of Industrial Relations Counselors, Inc. (IRC) in 1926 was an outgrowth of a four-decade-long struggle to find a solution to what was widely referred to as the "Labor Problem." Chapter 3 also detailed the numerous proposed "solutions" to the Labor Problem that were advanced by various parties during the 1880–1920 period, such as socialism, trade unionism, government regulation, and laissez-faire "survival of the fittest" capitalism. One such approach was what became known as the "employers' solution," and it was out of this stream of thought and practice that IRC had its origins and to which it also made significant contributions. The employer's solution sought to preserve capitalism, a market economy, and the employer's authority to run the enterprise but, at the same time, to also resolve labor problems through a wide-ranging reform program that was intended to achieve a "double win" of increased efficiency in production and greater harmony between employers and workers.

The employers' reform program was not a monolith, for various proponents came to it with differing social philosophies, theories of management and economy, and a variety of particularistic programs, activities, and practices. In this chapter, I look at one particular philosophy and set of practices associated with the employer's solution to labor problems—those espoused by the founders and leaders of IRC. As the three quotes featured at the beginning of the chapter illustrate, the philosophy propounded by the key men associated with the birth and early years of IRC for achieving the win-win of greater efficiency and harmony centers on two overarching ideas. The first is that both organizational effectiveness and individual satisfaction from work are promoted by fostering greater *cooperation* in the workplace; the second is that cooperation is promoted by a closer *unity of interest* (or "goal alignment" in modern terms) among the parties to industry. The early leaders of IRC thought greater cooperation and a closer unity of interest in industry could be accomplished by a number of devices, such as profit sharing, employee welfare benefits, and improved personnel programs. The practice that they gave the highest priority, however, was joint dealing between management and workers through *employee representation*.

This chapter explores both the theory and practice of cooperation and unity of interest as espoused by IRC's founders and leaders. The next section describes why cooperation is vital to organizational effectiveness; the conditions that impede cooperation; and how goal alignment promotes improved cooperation. The discussion then demonstrates that these basic principles of organizational practice are not a twentieth-century invention but, rather, were grasped in rudimentary form by the Greek philosophers and, later, various writers in the 1800s. The chapter then traces the evolution of thought through successive stages of development, looking briefly at the contributions of thinkers such as Mary Parker Follett, Elton Mayo, Douglas McGregor, and modern writers on the "high performance" workplace. The conclusion is that while the quest for cooperation and unity of interest in industry is still an unfolding endeavor, considerable progress in both theory and practice has been made, spurred in part by the contributions of IRC and its leading figures.

Cooperation and Unity of Interest: Insights from Theory

As shown in a later section, people have been contemplating the factors that lead to efficient and effective organizations for more than two thousand years. The need to attain cooperation among the participants and a commitment to a common purpose has figured prominently in these discussions. Advances in modern economics and organization science, however, have pushed these insights considerably beyond the stage of common sense and practical experience. Indeed, at least seven Nobel prizes have been awarded in the last thirty years to people writing on aspects of economic organization. This section describes some of the most important findings and implications of this literature with regard to cooperation and unity of interest, albeit at an elementary and nontechnical level.

The logical first question concerns why multiperson organizations and, correlatively, an employer-employee relationship exist in an economy. After all, for centuries most production that was traded in a market was performed by individual farmers, artisans, and craftsmen, such as the butcher, brewer, and shoemaker celebrated by Adam Smith. It was Smith (1776) who pinpointed one condition that fosters larger-scale multiperson organizations—division of labor. He noted that specialization of tasks in production can dramatically increase the productivity of labor and hence the "wealth of nations." His classic example was the manufacture of pins, in which ten people working together at specialized tasks (e.g., the drawing of the wire, the shaping of the head) are able to produce many hundredfold more pins than the same ten people employed as independent producers and responsible for performing all aspects of the manufacturing process.

Smith assumed without questioning the matter further that the manufacture of pins would take place in a firm directed by an entrepreneur/manager and would utilize the labor of paid employees. Writing nearly a century and a half later, however, Ronald Coase (1937), in a famous article, called this assumption into question. Coase posed the provocative question "Why are there firms?" which is to say, why isn't all production carried out in one-person firms, like the seventeenth-century artisans and craftsmen, and then traded through markets to other producers higher in the production chain until a finished product for consumers is completed and ready for sale? It is true, Coase noted, that division of labor makes it more efficient to have one person draw the wire and another shape the head of the pin, but this fact does not mandate that production take place in a multiperson organization. It could equally well be accomplished by having the ten workers form separate sole proprietorships and have the person who draws the wire sell his product to the person who shapes the head, who then sells it to the next person in the chain of production, and so on until at the end the finished pin is sold to consumers by another single-person firm (or series of single-person firms).

Coase's question has led to a burgeoning line of inquiry that still proceeds today. The consensus is that there are two principal factors that together determine whether production and exchange take place through markets or within multiperson organizations (Williamson 1985; Furubotn and Richter 1997).

The first and necessary condition is the existence of significant interdependencies in the production process, or what economists call *complementarities, nonseparabilities,* and *indivisibilities* (Alchian and Demsetz 1972). A production process contains interdependencies when the contribution/performance of one factor input is dependent on that of another (often referred to as a *team* form of production). One example from sports of such a production process is the performance of a football team; another from industry is the manufacture of automobiles in a modern assembly plant. In both cases, effective performance by all team members is required if successful production is to occur. Conversely, if even one person fails to satisfactorily do his/her job, then total output declines more than proportionately, perhaps falling even to zero (e.g., a car will not run if one worker fails to properly install an engine part).

The second condition is what is commonly referred to as "bounded rationality," meaning imperfect information and limited human cognitive abilities (Simon 1982; Williamson 1985). Bounded rationality is the opposite of complete or "full" rationality as presumed in standard microeconomic theory (e.g., perfect information, omniscient and costless decision-making ability). Bounded rationality promotes the organization of production into multiperson firms because lack of information and costly/impeded decision making significantly raise the costs of negotiating and enforcing contracts between the parties to a market exchange, thus raising the costs (generally called *transaction costs*) of using the market and giving an advantage to concentrating exchange and production within a firm (thus avoiding transaction costs). Stated another way, bounded rationality favors "make" over "buy."

Economists have shown that if the production process is completely separable (so individual contributions to production are completely identifiable and independent) and economic agents possess full rationality (including perfect information), then production and exchange will be carried out in a perfectly decentralized economy composed of M single-person firms and N consumers. This economic system corresponds to an Arrow-Debreu model of general equilibrium, in which all economic activity is coordinated by the "invisible hand" of the price system (Cheung 1983; Demsetz 1991). In this model, no employment relationship exists and there is thus no need for a human resource management function (since there are no employees, only single-proprietorship firms like the family farm). Furthermore, economists have also shown that this economy yields the most efficient allocation of resources and maximizes consumer well-being.

It is important to note that cooperation is still crucial to the success of this type of economy, although it is cooperation of an impersonal, highly decentralized nature. Each economic agent has different preferences (utility functions) and is in competition with other agents for scarce resources, thus giving rise to a conflict of interests among individuals. But as Adam Smith first deduced, the beauty of the price mechanism, when embedded in a system of "perfect liberty," is that the invisible hand of self-interest operating through competitive markets is able to coordinate production and exchange in such a way that it creates a social "harmony of interests" out of individual conflict of interests—a harmony of interests because all sides gain the maximum from trade, given their initial factor endowments. This outcome is achieved by cooperation, only it is cooperation writ large (at the level of society) in that each economic agent fully plays by the rules of the game, respects all property rights, and avoids opportunistic or illegal acts that promote individual self-interest at the expense of the interests of everyone else.

The American economy prior to the Civil War largely resembled the individualistic, highly decentralized economy described above. By the turn of the twentieth century, however, the structure of the economy had changed dramatically. Increasingly, production was centered in large plants and firms, often with hundreds and thousands of employees under the direction of an entrepreneur and/or salaried cadre of managers (Nelson 1975). In place of individual craftsmen, artisans, and farmers of yesteryear were giant firms such as Standard Oil, United States Steel, and the Pennsylvania Railroad. And with the rise of these giant firms, along with the concomitant growth of a wage-labor force, the various labor problems previously described also grew in breadth and intensity. Conflict of interest among the parties seemed to swell to threatening and even revolutionary size, impelling social reformers and forward-looking employers to search for new ways to promote cooperation and a sense of shared purpose.

What fueled the growth of large multiperson organizations, and why did labor problems suddenly become endemic and virulent? Modern economic and organization theory supplies answers to these questions. We start with the growth of firm size.

The key development leading to large firms and the growth of an employer-employee relationship is technological change, bringing with it greater capital intensity of production and economies of scale. Invention and innovation in the nineteenth century led to an amazing burst of technological advances in production. Starting with the steam engine and powered mechanical looms in the early part of the century, the technology of production pushed forward at a rapid rate with the discovery and advancement of railroads, steelmaking, oil refining, electricity generation, mechanized farm equipment, and automobiles. The hallmark of these new technologies and products was that they required large outlays of financial and physical capital. To obtain the requisite financial capital, sole proprietorships and partnerships evolved into the limited-liability joint-stock corporation in which ownership was decentralized among thousands of individual shareholders while control over business operations was vested in a cadre of salaried managers (Chandler 1962). Likewise, to exploit the new technologies, firms built large-sized factories, multistate railway networks, and large underground mines and generating plants, bringing together under one management hundreds and thousands of employees. These large agglomerations of capital and labor soon displaced smaller-scale producers because they realized lower costs of production through economies of scale. Part of these economies came from spreading large overhead costs, but another came from the synergies provided by interdependencies in production. In team forms of production, complementarities and indivisibilities allow increases in production more than proportionate to the increase in capital and/or labor inputs, leading to decreasing unit costs over a considerable range of output (Alchian and Demsetz 1972).

Technological change, together with the expansion of markets and the development of the corporate form of business, thus made the single proprietorship of Adam Smith's day uneconomic. In its place were a growing number of large corporations and industrial trusts, employing hundreds and thousands of workers in large-scale plants, mills, and mines. These new giants of industry gave rise to great economic and political debates. Economists and politicians alike were torn about the virtues of the new industrial system: awed by its tremendously higher productivity but fearful of its impetus toward monopoly and political domination. Of equal importance, the advance of large-scale capital-intensive industry also seemed to bring with it numerous labor problems and an entirely new set of management dilemmas.

Instead of coordination of production and exchange through the invisible hand of the price mechanism, industry was now faced with the complex and unfamiliar task of coordinating a far-flung, highly interdependent production process through an entirely different mechanism—the "visible hand" of management authority and control. Not surprisingly, given the size of many of these giant corporations and trusts, coupled with bounded rationality and relatively primitive methods of communication, severe inefficiencies and wastage often occurred. And to further complicate matters, management authority and control were challenged by widespread apathy and overt hostility on the part of labor—evidenced by the rising crescendo of strikes, employee turnover, and soldiering on the job.

The key insight provided by modern economic and organization theory is that the very force that made possible large-scale industry and much-advanced standards of living—new technology and associated production interdependencies and economies of scale—also created (in conjunction with bounded rationality) the conditions that led to widespread organizational inefficiencies and labor problems (Miller 1991). Arising from this paradox, and growing out of the search for solutions, were numerous new management ideas and practices, including those pioneered by IRC.

In an Adam Smith economy of decentralized production and exchange, self-interested competition is a virtue that leads via the "invisible hand" to a social optimum in terms of efficiency and resource allocation. When interdependencies in production start to bulk large, however, entrepreneurs gain a cost and profit advantage over rivals by organizing team forms of production, or what we earlier called multiperson organizations. One feature of such organizations is the employer-employee relationship—the employer being the owner of the firm and the "boss" while the employees are "hired hands" who exchange their labor for a certain rate of pay and work for the owner at his/her direction and discretion.

The owner of the enterprise faces a number of challenges in achieving efficiency and maximum profit. These challenges are often identified with the central tasks of management—identified by Fayol (1916), for example, as forecasting, planning, organizing, commanding, coordinating, and controlling. Without denying the importance of these functions, the modern theory of organizations points out that there is yet another central challenge that all owners/managers must confront, and one that Rockefeller, King, and Hicks of IRC all came to realize early in this century. This central challenge is achievement of maximum cooperation among the parties to industry and construction of a shared sense of purpose or unity of interest.

An oft-used and highly productive tool of modern economics and management is game theory. Game theory shows that all hierarchical multiperson organizations face two broad sets of "managerial dilemmas" that individually and collectively impede intraorganizational cooperation and, hence, organizational effectiveness and efficiency. The challenge of management is to overcome these dilemmas (Miller 1991).

It is evident, first of all, that when the production process involves significant interdependencies, intraorganizational cooperation assumes great significance. For example, the probability of a scheduled flight from Los Angeles to New York being safe, on time, and hassle-free is commensurately higher the greater the degree of cooperation among the managers, pilots, flight attendants, ground crew, and mechanics. Should any one of these agents shirk their responsibilities or otherwise fail to perform their jobs, the performance of the entire team suffers, as do the costs and profits of the organization and the pool of resources available for future team (employee) compensation. Attaining maximum cooperation in the enterprise is thus a crucial ingredient to business success.

But attaining and maintaining a high level of cooperation among employees and between employees and managers/owners is difficult. One source of such difficulty is popularly referred to as the "free rider" problem. As shown by the best known of all game theory models, the Prisoner's Dilemma, it is often rational and in the short-run interest of individual participants in a team production system to loaf, soldier, and otherwise not carry their full weight (Furubotn and Richter 1997). Since the production process is interdependent, it is impossible for management or fellow workers to fully identify each worker's individual contribution to production—a problem then exacerbated by bounded rationality. Each participant knows that full cooperation by everyone will maximize organizational performance and the pool of potential profits and wages, but individuals are nonetheless tempted to be a free rider and loaf—on the expectation that all others remain diligent and the size of the "pie" thus remains largely unaffected. Of course, what is self-interestedly rational in the short run for one participant is similarly rational for all other participants, leading all to loaf and condemning the organization to a serious shortfall in productivity and performance.

Another source of noncooperative behavior arises from what is popularly called the principal-agent problem in organizations (ibid. 1997). As typically described, the principal is the owner/manager of the firm who hires an agent (the employee) to perform job tasks at the principal's direction in exchange for a sum of money. In a fully cooperative arrangement, the agent would faithfully and diligently perform all job tasks in order to maximize the profits of the enterprise. But with bounded rationality and differences in preferences (utility functions), the agent faces strong incentives to pursue his/her interests at the expense of those of the owner. For example, the owner has a strong interest in maximum profit since profits redound to him/her, but the employee has little or no interest in maximum profit since he/she is paid a wage per hour regardless of firm performance (at least above the bankruptcy level). Thus, the agent will rationally decide to work only at half speed, come in late, or take a lackadaisical attitude toward product quality, knowing that bounded rationality keeps the principal from fully detecting his/her malingering and/or malfeasance. Of course, all employees face the same incentives, leading to the potential of widespread underperformance of work and diminished cooperation.

A third source of noncooperative behavior arises from intraorganizational bargaining over the distribution of rewards from production (Miller 1991). In an Adam Smith economy, individual productivity is independent and identifiable and thus accurately compensated through the forces of market competition. But in an interdependent production process with bounded rationality, individual contributions are neither clearly discernable nor capable of determination by market forces. For this reason, individual rewards among employees and the overall split of revenues between profits and wages have to be determined through a process of overt or covert bargaining. But bargaining leads to a variety of behaviors inimical to cooperation and optimal firm performance. In the presence of bounded rationality, for example, each person is tempted to conceal or distort information in an effort to increase his or her "take" from the bargaining process (e.g., by exaggerating his or her contribution to production or minimizing the contribution of workmates). Likewise, bargaining leads to the development of adversarial attitudes, jealousies, and hard feelings that also undercut cooperation and team performance. In the worst-case scenario, the pathologies of intraorganizational bargaining can so polarize an organization that its very survival is called into question.

We see, then, the paradox previously mentioned. Large-scale multiperson organizations hold out the promise of a significantly higher level of productivity relative to an Adam Smith economy of small-scale sole proprietorships, but this promise of higher productivity is itself threatened by forces that can easily undermine the intraorganizational cooperation upon which the superior performance hinges. The challenge facing owners/managers is thus how to overcome these negative forces and promote and maintain a high level of cooperation in the enterprise.

Modern theory suggests that these managerial dilemmas may be at least partially solved through a variety of means (ibid.). In the presence of bounded rationality, none will be completely effective, but considerable progress in the direction of greater cooperation and organizational performance can nonetheless be accomplished. Here is a brief sampling:

- Promote employment security, advancement from within, and a longer-term employment relationship.
- Promote greater vertical and horizontal communication in the organization.
- Align employer and employee goals and objectives through compensation practices that promote mutual sharing of financial gains and risks.
- Create an organizational culture that stresses shared values, teamwork, the importance of employees as a major stakeholder of the organization, and a commitment to fair treatment.
- Reduce power and status differentials.
- Establish a strong ethos of trust and avoid undermining it by unilateral or opportunistic actions.

One other management practice that has the potential to significantly improve cooperation is various forms of employee participation and representation. We highlight these, given their centrality to the progressive management program advanced by IRC and its principal figures (e.g., Rockefeller, King, and Hicks).

Avoidance of the managerial dilemmas just highlighted is greatly facilitated by what North and Weingast termed "setting a precedent of responsible behavior [and] appearing to be committed to a set of rules that he or she will consistently live up to and enforce" (cited in Miller 1991, 225). The ability to build trust, commitment, and effective communication through personal face-to-face interaction is quite limited in a large far-flung organization. Thus, managers must find some other way to make a credible commitment to employees that they intend to follow a long-term policy of cooperation and mutual gain. As suggested by Miller (1991) and Kaufman and Levine (2000), a particularly visible and substantive "signal" is for management to establish a formal program of (nonunion) employee representation and to delegate to the councils and committees jurisdiction and at least some decision-making power over various matters of joint interest. The commitment becomes more credible the greater the power and range of issues delegated to employees and the longer and more steadfastly the employer engages in good-faith interaction with the employee representatives.

Critics point out that pursuit of this logic would suggest that employers who are genuinely interested in securing the fruits of cooperation should embrace genuine collective bargaining with an independent labor union (since the contract is legally enforceable and thus of still greater credibility). This argument has merit and some empirical support (Freeman and Rogers 1999). A variety of counterarguments also exist, however. Unionism, for example, may on net reduce the likelihood of cooperation and unity of interest by fostering an adversarial "we versus them" attitude. Theory (Hirsch 1991) also suggests that through a "median voter" process, unions may also be led to pursue an opportunistic, short-run wage policy of "rent seeking" (trying to capture as much profit as possible without driving the firm into bankruptcy) that effectively destroys the basis for a long-run mutual-gains relationship. The bottom line from a theory perspective appears to be that some form of employee representation has the potential to strengthen the bonds of cooperation and avoid a suboptimal Prisoner's Dilemma outcome, but whether a union or nonunion type of representation is preferable has to be based on the empirical evidence.

The State of Theory and Practice a Century Ago

These organizational principles, and the ideas that underlie them, have been grasped at some level for more than two thousand years (as demonstrated in the next section). But however obvious they appear in hindsight, their discovery and implementation proceeded at a glacial pace for most of civilized history. Indeed, they remain only imperfectly accomplished today at even leading companies and are hardly implemented at many others.

Looking back a century, most companies were structured and run in ways that were in many respects the antithesis of the model just outlined. It is no wonder, in turn, that the Labor Problem loomed large on the national scene and enterprises were rife with inefficiency and enmity. The Ludlow Massacre—the event central to the conversion of John D. Rockefeller, Jr., to the cause of progressive management and the formation of Industrial Relations Counselors, Inc.—was in this respect only the tip of a very large iceberg. To better appreciate the tremendous distance traveled in terms of both organizational theory and practice, it is useful to briefly look back at the situation that prevailed in American industry one hundred years ago, and then to trace the development of more progressive thought and practice from ancient times to the present.

Workplace Theory and Practice Circa 1900

The philosophy and practice of management and industrial relations a century ago were in many respects vastly different from those of today. As described in Chapter 3, social doctrines of laissez-faire and Social Darwinism were widely shared, while in the legal sphere the dominant ideas were the sanctity of liberty of contract and the "master and servant" nature of the employment relationship. Together, these doctrines provided the intellectual and legal foundation for a largely unrestricted system of employer autocracy in the internal governance of the firm and an unregulated system of wage/employment determination in which labor is treated as a commodity to be bought as cheaply as possible and used only as long as necessary.

In theory, this system was thought to promote efficiency and justice for all. That is, efficiency is promoted because unfettered competition provides maximum incentives and pressures for employers to conserve scarce resources and wisely manage production, while employees are led to work diligently, move from areas of labor surplus to areas of labor scarcity, and acquire new skills and talents. Justice and fair treatment are also promoted because, on one hand, the competition for jobs and workers forces both sides to the employment relationship to meet "best practice" and provide the other a "square deal"; on the other hand, the ability of the employee to immediately quit the job and the firm to fire the worker gives each side an effective escape route from oppression and poor performance. Cooperation in this model is not something that management has to consciously "engineer" but, rather, automatically flows out of the invisible hand of self-interest, competition, and survival of the fittest—regulated by strict enforcement of property rights, the sanctity of contract, and the practice of Christian virtue and personal responsibility (Bendix 1956; Fine 1956).

In practice, the virtues of the traditional employment model were far less compelling and the defects far more obvious and manifold. An important defect of the traditional model is that labor markets were far more imperfect than envisioned by the proponents of laissez-faire (Kaufman 1997). One-company towns, collusive practices by employers' associations, segmented labor markets due to ethnic and gender discrimination, and a chronic oversupply of labor from mass immigration and recurrent recessions/depressions caused competition to be both impeded and tipped against the individual worker. As a result, wages were low, hours long, and safety and health conditions often woefully inadequate. The forces of competition, the "exit" option of looking for a different job, and Christian morality also frequently proved a weak defense against the arbitrary and sometimes oppressive exercise of the employer's authority in the firm. While freedom of contract and employment at will were putatively evenhanded toward the interests of employer and employee (since both parties had equal right to walk away from the employment contract), the reality was that individual workers needed the job far more than the firm needed the worker. The resulting inequality of bargaining power inside the firm created conditions of autocracy reminiscent of the divine right of kings" in fourteenth-century England—an autocracy sometimes practiced benevolently but too frequently manifest in "drive" methods of motivating workers (e.g., use of threats, rough language, and fear of termination), arbitrary and discriminatory rules and treatment, and little opportunity for voice or redress of grievances (Leiserson 1922; Jacoby 1985).

The traditional philosophy of management and practice of industrial relations led to much conflict between labor and capital and poor work performance and morale in the enterprise. In this regard, Clarence Hicks says of the autocratic method, "A barren ground for developing real co-operation, autocracy breeds resentment in those who come under its domination. This resentment may not be apparent, and at times may not be fully recognized by the worker himself, but it is inevitably reflected in lowered morale and efficiency." He goes on to say, "A growing feeling today is that there must be some better way of dealing with employees" (1941, 67).

Indeed, as the Labor Problem grew in breadth and depth of intensity in the latter part of the nineteenth century, a number of alternative diagnoses and solutions were advanced. One line of thought held that the interests of Labor and Capital are inherently antagonistic and the only solution to the Labor Problem is to abolish capitalism and/or the wage system and replace them with socialism, syndicalism, or workers' cooperatives.

A second line of thought, less radical than the first, sought to maintain capitalism and the wage system but "level the playing field" for workers by promoting widespread trade unionism and collective bargaining. In this scenario, Labor and Capital continue to have (largely) opposed interests but through collective bargaining work out a compromise (or "armed truce") that provides more equitable and efficient terms and conditions of employment and a measure of joint governance in the firm and democracy in industry. Hicks describes this basis for the employer-employee relationship as "two antagonistic parties in industry" in which "Labor and Capital [are] each selfish, hostile, and determined to secure all it can for itself" (ibid., 67). In his view, trade unionism and collective bargaining are "the natural results of the autocratic attitude of many employers. . . . If employers assume an autocratic attitude, employees are bound to organize for defense and aggression" (ibid., 69, 76). He further observes that collective bargaining has served a positive and constructive function for all parties, noting, "There is much to be said for this movement and for the results it has accomplished for working men" (ibid., 69).

While Hicks sees unionism as a necessary counterweight to employer autocracy, he does not believe it is the best solution to the Labor Problem or the method that best serves the long-run interests of labor, capital, and the community. The reason, he states, is that collective bargaining rests on reciprocal use of force and coercion by both employer and union and that "such a basis has yet to demonstrate that it is an effective foundation for co-operation. . . . [T]he repeated 'alarums and excursions' of hostile armies play havoc with the finer arts of peace" (ibid., 76, 77). Restated, the problem with collective bargaining, in his view, is that it undercuts cooperation and firm performance because its methods are inherently adversarial and restrictive—an approach that perhaps gains more for the employees in the short run but at the expense of diminished productivity and wage growth in the long run.

A Third Way: a Cooperative Unity of Interest

Hicks, in tandem with Rockefeller and King, thus came to advocate a third approach—what Hicks called the "unity of interest of all employees." He says of this approach, "Management, on its part, is no longer the unquestioned dictator, but can be increasingly regarded as the agent that brings employee, owner, and consumer together in a mutually beneficial relationship. Such a relationship requires co-operation on all sides to be successful, but most of all it requires the co-operation of the two active partners, management and men, and in promoting this co-operation management has the obligation of initiative" (ibid., 77). According to Hicks, cooperation and unity of interest are not a utopian dream, as evidenced by his statement that in a large section of industry, "real unity of interest exists and friendly relations prevail" (ibid., 69). On the other hand, Hicks also appears to recognize that a unity of interest is an ideal to be worked toward but never fully and completely accomplished (similar to the theory of perfect competition in economics), and that the baseline condition in the employment relationship is one of conflict of interest. In this vein, he quotes a conference report endorsed by Rockefeller: "It is idle wholly to deny the existence of conflicting interests between employers and employees. But there are wide areas of activity in which their interests coincide. It is the part of statesmanship to organize an identity of interests where it exists in order to reduce the area of conflict" (ibid., 78).

In this spirit of pragmatic reformism, Rockefeller, King, and Hicks took the initiative in reconstructing the traditional employment relationship from one of autocracy and two antagonistic parties to the third approach of cooperation and unity of interest. As detailed in Chapter 3, their reform effort began at the Colorado Fuel and Iron Co. (CF&I) (the scene of the Ludlow Massacre); was soon introduced in a deeper, more integrated manner at the Standard Oil Co. (New Jersey); and quickly metamorphosed into a major component of and inspiration to the 1920s progressive management movement now popularly called "Welfare Capitalism" (Jacoby 1997; Kaufman 2001). And IRC was a central conduit through which the new unity of interest philosophy and associated management practices were propagated to other companies both inside and outside the Rockefeller network.

These new industrial relations practices included the articulation of a formal labor policy, establishment of an industrial relations department to oversee and administer human resource practices, use of gainsharing and profit-sharing forms of compensation, provision of extensive employee benefits, promise of employment security, promotion from within, an effective program of employee communication, management training programs in human relations, and limits on supervisor power to discipline and discharge. At the apex of these innovations was a nonunion system of employee representation, modeled on the original plan of representation introduced by Rockefeller, King, and Hicks at CF&I. It was first and foremost through the representation plan that cooperation and unity of interest were to be accomplished, allowing as it did a forum for mutual discussion, joint dealing, communication, employee voice and participation, and problem solving in a nonadversarial climate. Then the mutual interests were further strengthened by the practices previously mentioned—giving employees a financial stake in the performance of the firm, having the firm take care of employee welfare needs (insurance, medical and dental care, safety, etc.), promoting employee loyalty through employment security and promotion from within, and using communication devices (e.g., a plant magazine) to foster greater employee understanding of the company's business strategy, financial results, and operational problems.

All of these measures entailed additional expenditures, curbed management power and authority, and had an uncertain payoff. But they were nonetheless seen by Rockefeller, King, and Hicks as a good long-run investment for the company—and a source of higher living standards, security, and job satisfaction for employees—because they created a high-performance organization that tapped the powers of cooperation and common purpose to gain competitive advantage through higher productivity, better quality, and superior innovation.

Innovative and far-reaching as this new management philosophy and set of industrial relations practices were, they were not entirely new inventions of Rockefeller and associates, nor were they the final word on these matters in subsequent years. The next section places the contributions of Rockefeller, King, Hicks, and IRC in a larger context, tracing both the origins of the cooperative unity of interest idea and its evolution to the present day.

The Evolution of Thought on Cooperation and Unity of Interest

As earlier indicated, the importance of cooperation and unity of interest for successful organizational performance is not a new or revolutionary idea. From the dawn of human civilization, rulers of city-states and generals of armies have described their benefits. In his treatise *Oeconomicus* (from which the English word "economics" is derived), for example, the Greek philosopher Xenophon describes how coordination and cooperation of soldiers and sailors are crucial to military success (e.g., the quickest ship has sailors that "sit on the benches in order, moving their bodies forward and backward in order, and embarking and disembarking in order"), a lesson which he then applies to the successful management of an estate (Pomeroy 1994, 115). Similarly, Plato pays tribute to unity of interest when he asks Glaucon, "What can we describe as the greatest good for the constitution of a city?" and then answers, "Community in pain and pleasure acts as a bond of union, does it not, when all citizens as far as possible experience the joy and pain virtually at the same advantages and losses? . . . a city, in fact, which most nearly resembles a single human being" (Laistner 1974, 98, 99).

Moving forward in time, in the early nineteenth century, it is possible to find clear statements about the importance of cooperation and shared purpose in industrial enterprise. For example, early-nineteenth-century industrialist and social reformer Robert Owen stresses the importance to industrial success of obtaining human cooperation in these words: "You will find from the commencement of my management I viewed the population [labor force], with the mechanism of every other part of the establishment, as a system composed of many parts, and which it was my duty and interest so to combine, as that every hand, as well as every spring, lever, and wheel, should effectually cooperate to produce the greatest pecuniary gain" (Wren 1997, 287–88).

At nearly the same time, English engineer Charles Babbage (1833) wrote of the harm done by conflict of interest between employer and employee in these words: "A most erroneous and unfortunate opinion prevails amongst the workmen in many manufacturing countries, that their own interest and that of their employers are at variance. The consequences are, that valuable machinery is sometimes neglected, and even privately injured . . ." (p. 250). Presaging Frederick Taylor by nearly seven decades, Babbage then proposes that this gulf can be overcome by some form of gainsharing or incentive pay, saying, "It would be of great importance, if, in every large establishment the mode of payment could be so arranged, that every person employed should derive advantage from the success of the whole . . ." (p. 251), later stating the benefit to be that "every person engaged in it would have a direct interest in its prosperity . . . and an immediate interest in preventing any waste" (p. 257). Babbage also anticipates Clarence Hicks' contention that a unity of interest largely obviates the workers' need for trade unions when he states, "Another advantage . . . would be the total removal of all real or imaginary causes for combinations. The workmen and the capitalist would so shade into each other—would so evidently have a common interest, . . . that instead of combining to oppress one another, the only combination which could exist would be a powerful union between both parties to overcome their common difficulties." Finally, Babbage also anticipates the idea that a cooperative approach to employment relations, while perhaps reducing the employer's share of profit in the short run, leads to larger profits in the long run because of superior growth and productivity (now popularly called a "mutual gain" outcome). Thus, he states, "It is quite true that the workmen would have a larger share [of profit] than at present: but, at the same time, it is presumed that the effect of the whole system would be that . . . the smaller proportion allowed to capital . . . would yet be greater in actual amount" (p. 258).

Moving forward a half-century, we come to the birth of management as a recognized field of study and practice. Various writers (e.g., Duncan 1989, 3) on the subject place the birth of the field in the year 1886, marked by the publication of industrialist Henry Towne's paper, "The Engineer as an Economist," in the proceedings of the American Society of Mechanical Engineers. Towne's paper is considered the beginning of the management field, given his counsel that the function of engineer and businessperson be united in one person (thus combining technical expertise with the practical knowledge of business methods) and his claim that "the matter of shop management is of equal importance with that of engineering . . . and the management of works has become a matter of such great and far-reaching importance as perhaps to justify its classification also as one of the modern arts" (p. 429). Presented here in roughly chronological order from the 1880s to the present are significant writers/thinkers on the subject of management and, in particular, the importance of cooperation and unity of interest in industry and methods to achieve them.

Nicholas Gilman

The first person to mention is Nicholas Gilman, a writer and consultant on business whose name today is little known. Gilman wrote two books that directly addressed industrial cooperation and unity of interest. The first, published in 1889, provides the first in-depth analysis of profit sharing and its potential to resolve the Labor Problem. Gilman locates the source of the Labor Problem in the wage system. He states, "However finely men may talk about the identity of interests of capital and labor, it remains a natural and an inevitable fact, that, under the wages system, there is a constant clashing of interests between the employer and employed" (p. 52). He goes on to elaborate, "The 'antagonism,' which is real and natural, is the opposition of the buyer and seller of labor, of the employer and the employee: the one seeks to obtain labor at a low price, the other seeks to dispose of his labor at a high price. The divergence of interests is palpable" (p. 413).

Unlike other critics of industry, Gilman does not believe it is necessary to abolish the wage system by a system of worker cooperatives or some form of socialism. Instead, he concludes that the fundamental problem is "the decay of feeling of partnership prevalent in earlier and simpler days, when business establishments were small, when the master often worked with the man, and product sharing was common" (p. 413) and that "a sharing of profits, since a sharing of products is now out of the question, is, on general grounds, the most likely solution of the problem" (p. 414). The virtues of profit sharing, according to Gilman, are that it provides greater motivation to employees to work for the good of the enterprise; preserves the system of private enterprise, competition, and management control; makes labor compensation vary automatically with the prosperity of the firm and leads to risk sharing among the parties; and promotes closer feelings of partnership and shared purpose. Finally, like Babbage before him, he emphasizes that profit sharing leads to a long-run win-win outcome in that not only does the employee gain higher pay but also "the tendency of Profit Sharing is to enlarge the disposable profits to such a degree that the employer is better off financially than before" (p. 416).

Gilman's second book of note is *A Dividend to Labor*, published ten years later (1899). His focus is now considerably wider, including not only "direct" payments ("dividends") to labor in the form of profit sharing and gain sharing but also "indirect" payments through voluntary employer "welfare" expenditures. Examples of the latter include insurance against accidents, ill health, and old age; in-plant medical services; employer-provided schools and libraries; and workmen's clubhouses and social events. These industrial welfare programs were at this time in their infancy, and Gilman's comprehensive coverage is the first of its kind. Gilman cites the "personal alienation of the employer from his fellow-men whom he engages to work for him" as the principal cause of the "trouble and conflict in the labor world" (p. 15). This alienation can be partly overcome by a sharing of financial rewards, but Gilman concludes that pure profit sharing is "a counsel of perfection" and needs to be supplemented by other "indirect" forms of employer expenditure. He states that to obtain labor peace and hearty cooperation, the employer has to become "moralized"—has to shift from viewing employees as a commodity and the employment relationship from a strictly dollars-and-cents perspective to one that regards workers as fellow human beings for whom principles of justice and fair dealing are important. Toward this end, Gilman counsels employers to invest in "welfare institutions" because they both win labor's "good-will" and raise the efficiency of the employer's "living machinery." He thus concludes, "Where the banner of welfare-institutions is firmly erected, . . . the deep consciousness of a common life, the full recognition of a common aim, and the just division of a common product, the industrial members work together as one body—head and heart and hand agreeing in one conspiracy of benefit" (p. 361).

Frederick Taylor

Frederick Taylor is one of the most famous men in the annals of management thought and is widely known as the "father of scientific management." Through midlife he was an engineer and, later, a business consultant and writer.

Like Gilman, Taylor saw the method of wage payment as a fundamental cause of the Labor Problem. He started out with a different approach to solving it, however, and his thinking then evolved over the next two decades until he had developed what he claimed to be an entirely new system of management.

His first published article was in 1895, entitled "A Piece Rate System, Being a Partial Solution of the Labor Problem." He begins, "The ordinary piece-work system involves a permanent antagonism between employers and men, and a certainty of punishment for each workman who reaches a high rate of efficiency." He goes on to say, "The system introduced by the writer, however, is directly the opposite, both in theory and results. It makes each workman's interests the same as that of his employer" (p. 856). His new system rested on three parts: (1) determination of piecework prices through time and motion study of each elementary part of the production process; (2) a differential piece-rate system that pays a high price per unit when the work is finished in the shortest possible time and a low rate if it takes longer; and (3) paying employees on day work according to the skill and energy devoted to the job and not according to the position filled.

In the next decade and a half, Taylor refined and expanded his new theory of management and then explained it in detail in the book *The Principles of Scientific Management* (1911). In the first sentence of Chapter 1, Taylor states, "The principal object of management should be to secure the maximum prosperity for the employer, coupled with the maximum prosperity for the employee" (p. 9). But he notes that the traditional system of management often results in much the opposite—that conditions of "war" often prevail between management and workers and the workers deliberately soldier (underwork) on the job ("in many instances do not more than one-third to one-half of a proper day's work"). The result is a lose-lose outcome, since the firm suffers from low productivity and has less surplus to pay workers as wages. The fundamental cause of the problem, he claims, is the traditional system of "rules of thumb" management.

The remedy to industrial inefficiency and "war," says Taylor, lies in systematic management and the realization that management is a true science. Toward this end, he sought to develop new methods of management based

on scientific principles, such as time and motion study, functional foremanship, the standardization of tools, differential piece-rate pay systems, and
instruction cards for workers. But he then warns readers, "The mechanism of
management must not be mistaken for its essence, or underlying philosophy" (p. 128). And what is this philosophy? He earlier states it thus: "Scientific management . . . has for its very foundation the firm conviction that the
true interests of the two [employers and employees] are one and the same"
(p. 10). To achieve the desired unity of interest between management and
workers, Taylor claims management must follow "four great underlying principles: the development of a true science, the scientific selection of the workman, his scientific education and development, and intimate friendly
cooperation between the management and the men" (p. 130). Successful implementation of the philosophy and methods is sufficiently complex that Taylor
maintains it requires a "complete mental revolution" on the part of management
and employees. But if accomplished, the result is a great increase in productivity, a substantial increase in pay for employees, and "justice for all parties through
impartial scientific investigation of all the elements of the problem" (p. 139).

Mary Parker Follett

In the development of management thought, one of the deepest and most
penetrating of the early thinkers was Mary Parker Follett. Indeed, one author
has called her "the prophet of management" (Drucker 1995).

In her paper "Business as an Integrative Unity" (reprinted in Metcalf and
Urwick 1940), Follett states, "It seems to me that the first test of business
administration, of industrial organization, should be whether you have a business with all its parts so co-ordinated, so moving together in their closely
knit and adjusting activities, so linking, interlocking, interrelating, that they
make a working unit—that is, not a congeries of separate pieces, but what I
have called a functional whole or integrative unity" (p. 71). How can management construct an integrative unity? She says, "Capital and labor must
fight or unite. . . . We want to do away with the fight attitude, to get rid of
sides" (p. 73). The key to this transformation, Follett claims, is "when you
have made your employees feel that they are in some sense partners in the
business, they do not improve the quality of their work, save waste in time
and material, because of the Golden Rule, but because their interests are the
same as yours" (p. 82).

Like Taylor, Follett suggests a number of concrete steps to follow in
order to create a unity of interest. But her perspective is much different,
given that Taylor approached the issue as an engineer and Follett as a political scientist and former social worker. While Taylor emphasized "laws

of science" and individual initiative, Follett emphasizes participative management and achievement of group consensus. Conflict, in her view, comes from two sides approaching an issue as a zero-sum game to be resolved through the exercise of power—what one side wins, the other loses. This, she says, is the fundamental defect of trade unions and collective bargaining. The better approach, Follett claims, is to try to get the parties to reframe the dispute as an exercise in problem solving and then cooperate together in a search for a positive-sum (win-win) solution. Toward this end, she advocates extensive two-way communication in the business organization, ongoing conferences between managers and workers through employee representation committees and other devices, and eliminating as much as possible artificial distinctions between management and labor. With regard to the latter, she counsels that authority and power in the organization be based on knowledge and the "law of the situation" rather than invested in certain persons because of their rank or position.

Chester Barnard

One of the most famous and widely read management books of all time is *The Functions of the Executive* (1938) by Chester Barnard. Barnard brought to the book keen insights developed from both his years as president of the New Jersey Bell Telephone Company and wide-ranging reading in the social and behavioral sciences.

Barnard defines organizations as "associations of cooperative efforts" (p. 4) and "a system of consciously coordinated activities or forces of two or more persons" (p. 73). He claimed that all organizations have three universal elements: (1) willingness to cooperate, (2) common purpose, and (3) communication. Regarding the first, Barnard recognizes that in a free society, an organization can only attract and retain participants if people see that membership advances their individual interests. Thus, every organization has to offer inducements to participation, some of a largely objective nature (e.g., the level of wages, quality of working conditions) and others of a more subjective nature (e.g., the social atmosphere, community reputation of the company). The second factor, common purpose, is the objective around which cooperative effort is organized. While individual goals often differ from the organization's goal, the function of the executive is to harness the former to the latter through both proper inducements and "persuasion" (changing subjective attitudes of members so that they identify more closely with the organization and its survival and growth). Finally, the third factor, communication, is the mechanism that ties together and integrates individual motives with organizational goals. In this respect, the executive uses communication both to coordinate cooperative effort and to provide the motivation and rationale for such effort (pp. 83–91).

Barnard has thus combined and synthesized elements of Taylor and Follett and also added his own unique perspective. Like both of these earlier writers, Barnard portrays cooperation as the essential ingredient in organizational life and effective cooperation as the key to organizational survival and growth. Like Taylor, Barnard emphasizes the important role that incentives play in motivating individuals to pursue a common purpose; like Follett, he also emphasizes the importance of using executive persuasion and communication to create an integrative unity through creative reduction of overt conflict and inculcation of feelings of organizational loyalty and commitment. More so than these other writers, Barnard also emphasizes the interaction that takes place between changes in the environment external to the organization and the cooperative equilibrium internal to the firm (e.g., the disruptive effect business cycles have on established systems of cooperative effort) and the crucial role of effective executive leadership in defining the organization's purpose and harnessing diverse people and resources to attainment of this common end.

Elton Mayo

Spanning chronologically the work of Barnard was that of Elton Mayo and colleagues of the Harvard-centered human relations school (e.g., T.N. Whitehead, Fritz Roethlisberger). Although Mayo began writing on industrial problems in the early 1920s, it was only with his interpretation of the famous Hawthorne experiments in two books (1933 and 1945) that his fame and influence spread widely.

The Hawthorne experiments took place at the Hawthorne, Illinois, plant of the Western Electric Co., starting in 1927. According to Mayo (1933, 99), Western Electric was by all accounts a model employer, and morale at the plant was high. Yet the research team from Harvard found widespread evidence of deliberate restriction of output on the part of employees, as well as other negative behaviors such as frequent absenteeism and nonattention to work tasks. Mayo and colleagues set out to discover the source of these problems.

He states in this regard, "Every social group . . . must face and clearly state two perpetual and recurrent problems of administration. It must secure for its individual and group membership: (1) the satisfaction of material and economic needs, and (2) the maintenance of spontaneous co-operation throughout the organization." He goes on to say, "Our administrative methods are all pointed at the materially effective; none, at the maintenance of cooperation. . . . Problems of absenteeism, labour turnover, 'wildcat' strikes, show that we do not know how to ensure spontaneity of co-operation; that is, teamwork" (1945, 9). Breaking with Taylor, however, Mayo categorically rejects that financial incentives can provide the stimulus for effective collaboration. Instead, Mayo and colleagues find that cooperation depends first and foremost on a sense of social identity among group members and feelings that they are integrated into and have a stable place within the group. These feelings, in turn, are to a significant extent nonlogical in nature.

Mayo's diagnosis of labor problems is thus fourfold: (1) industrialism has unleashed major forces of change that disrupt social groupings both external to and within work units; (2) the disruption of social groups creates a psychological condition of "anomie" (rootlessness and alienation); (3) anomie undercuts spontaneous collaboration and leads to a variety of work and social pathologies (turnover, etc.); and (4) management efforts to impose a technological, rational order to production further fragment social cohesion and exacerbate anomie. Thus, he states, "Human collaboration at work . . . has always depended for its perpetuation upon the evolution of a nonlogical social code which regulates the relations between persons and their attitudes to one another. Insistence upon a merely economic logic of production— especially if the logic is frequently changed—interferes with the development of such a code and consequently gives rise in the group to a sense of human defeat" (1933, 120).

The lesson for management theory, according to Mayo, is that the factory is not only a technological/economic system but also a social system and that effective cooperation can only be gained when an equilibrium or *modus vivendi* is worked out between the logic of efficiency and the nonlogic of worker sentiments. With respect to management practice, Mayo's research pointed to the importance of interpersonal relations, sociopsychological skills training for leaders, recognition of informal work groups and their norms, interviewing and counseling so that workers have an opportunity to vent and release emotions, and the importance of social over economic determinants of work effort.

McGregor, Argyris, and Likert

Moving a quarter century forward, we come to significant figures in management thought circa the early 1960s. Three examined here in modest detail are Douglas McGregor, Chris Argyris, and Rensis Likert. They represent the turning point from the human relations school to the new field of organizational behavior (OB).

In *The Human Side of Enterprise* (1960), McGregor writes, "There is no question that important progress has been made in the past two or three decades. . . . A tremendous number of policies, programs, and practices which were virtually unknown thirty years ago have become commonplace. . . . It [management] has significantly reduced economic hardships, eliminated the more extreme forms of industrial warfare, provided a generally safe and pleasant working environment, *but it has done all of these things without changing its fundamental theory of management*" (p. 45, emphasis in original).

McGregor labels the traditional theory of management "Theory X" and contrasts it with a new "Theory Y." He lists some of the assumptions of Theory X: (1) humans have an inherent dislike of work, (2) people must be controlled or coerced to work toward organizational goals, and (3) the average person lacks ambition and prefers to be told what to do. Given these assumptions, Theory X leads to a style of management that emphasizes top-down control, carrot-and-stick reward systems, and tight supervision—features that McGregor claims lead to low morale and work effort, unnecessarily high turnover, low rates of organizational learning, and wastage of many talents and ideas of the workers. The new Theory Y approach to management makes much the opposite assumptions: (1) people have a natural inclination to work, (2) people will exercise self-control when committed to a goal, (3) rewards that satisfy self-actualization and ego needs are often stronger motivators than monetary rewards, and (4) most people have untapped creative potential.

These assumptions lead to a different style of management. McGregor states in this regard, "The central principle which derives from Theory Y is that of integration: the creation of conditions such that members of the organization can achieve their own goals best by directing their efforts toward the success of the enterprise" (p. 49). Integration, McGregor claims, cannot be ordered by an authority figure but arises from subordinates' commitment to and internalization of organizational goals as their own. He goes on to describe the implications for a wide array of personnel practices, such as performance appraisal (less a control device, more of a learning device), salary determination (de-emphasize wage differentials as a motivational tool), and employee participation (promote more of it).

Another significant book of this period was *Integrating the Individual and the Organization* by Chris Argyris (1964). As the title suggests, the main thesis Argyris advances is that organizations perform better when their structures and control systems are closely aligned to the needs, aspirations, and capabilities of the people employed in them. Labor problems and low organizational performance, he claims, stem from the fact that traditional work organization and management practices—e.g., narrow specialization of labor (allowing use of only a limited range of ability), a hierarchical chain of command (making employees dependent and passive), and top-down decision making (placing all responsibility for thinking with higher levels of management)—trap people at an immature stage of sociopsychological development and lead to personal frustration, dissatisfaction, and withdrawal. The purpose of integration is thus to achieve a closer harmony between the structures/practices of organizations and the psychosocial needs of employees, allowing workers to move to a more mature stage in their personality and promoting, thereby, more functional and effective behaviors (e.g., higher job satisfaction, lower turnover, greater work effort).

A third influential book of this period was *New Patterns of Management* by Rensis Likert (1961). Based on more than a decade of research at dozens of companies, Likert sounds this now-familiar theme: "The high-producing managers have developed their organizations into highly coordinated, highly motivated, cooperative social systems. Under their leadership, the different motivational forces in each member of the organization have coalesced into a strong force aimed at accomplishing the mutually established objectives of the organization" (p. 100). Like a number of the other writers just reviewed, Likert emphasizes that a unity of interest is best built on psychosocial grounds. Thus, summarizing the research evidence, he states, "This provides the basis for stating the general principle which the high-producing managers seem to be using and which will be referred to as the *principle of supportive relationships*. This principle . . . can be briefly stated: The leadership and other processes of the organization must be such as to ensure a maximum probability that . . . each member . . . view the experience as supportive and one which builds and maintains his sense of personal worth and importance" (p. 102, emphasis in original). Among the concrete implications for management, Likert claims one of the most important is that "the form of organization which will make the greatest use of human capacity consists of highly effective work groups linked together in an overlapping pattern" (p. 162).

Contemporary Writers and the HPWS

Many of the ideas of these earlier writers have been incorporated into modern management thought and further developed into new theories and concepts. Illustrative of this process, and the important role that cooperation and unity of interest continue to play in modern management, is the burgeoning literature on the "high-performance work system" (HPWS).

The HPWS, also known as a "high-commitment" work model, is not the work of any one person but, rather, reflects the contributions of many people in both the United States and other countries (Appelbaum and Batt 1994). An early contribution came from the work of Eric Trist and colleagues in the United Kingdom on "socio-technical" work systems. In the United States,

Louis Davis and Richard Walton were early pioneers, the former emphasizing the redesign of jobs and the latter the shift from control to commitment as a principle for coordinating and motivating work. Popular books, such as *In Search of Excellence* (Peters and Waterman 1982), also contributed to development of the HPWS paradigm by emphasizing the important role that a people-centered strategy can play in generating superior organizational performance. The titles of more recent books, such as *Competitive Advantage Through People* (Pfeffer 1994), *Ultimate Advantage* (Lawler 1992), and *The Mutual Gains Enterprise* (Kochan and Osterman 1994), all speak to this theme.

Nadler and Gerstein (1992, 118) define the HPWS as, "an organizational architecture that brings together work, people, technology, and information in a manner that optimizes the congruence or 'fit' among them in order to produce high performance in terms of the effective response to customer requirements and other environmental demands and opportunities." Relative to earlier models, the HPWS more explicitly rests on notions of complementarity and interdependency in organizations, thus leading to an emphasis on exploiting synergy through congruence and fit. The model also gives greater weight to an external focus on meeting the needs of customers and suppliers and aligning strategy with the economic and social environment.

The important role of organizational complementarities in the HPWS paradigm, and the consequent emphasis on promoting cooperation and unity of interest, is well illustrated by these comments of Trist (1981). He first describes the traditional organization:

> Traditional organizations are also characterized by maximum work breakdown, which leads to circumscribed job descriptions and single skills—the narrower the better. Workers in such roles are often unable to manage the uncertainty, or variance, that characterizes their immediate environment. Layer upon layer of supervision comes into existence supported by a wide variety of specialist staffs and formal procedures. A tall pyramidic organization results, which is autocratically managed throughout, even if paternalism is benign. [P. 43]

Then he says of the new HPWS-type organization:

> The new paradigm, by contrast, gives first place to coping with the manifold interdependencies that arise in complex organizations. It values collaboration between groups and collegiality within groups. . . . The new paradigm imposes the additional task of aligning [the organization's] . . . purposes with the purposes of the wider society and also with the purposes of [its] members. . . . This leads to a flat organization characterized by as

much lateral as vertical communication. A participative management style emerges with the various levels mutually articulated rather than arranged in a simple hierarchy. [P. 43]

Numerous other writers strike the same themes. For example, Beer and Spector (1984) list sixteen assumptions or concepts that provide the foundation for a high-performance approach to organizational design and human resource practice. Other authors (Nadler and Gerstein 1992; Pfeffer 1994) assemble different lists, but they have much in common. Included among them are the following (not all are listed for sake of brevity):

1. The organization is a system.
2. People have higher commitment when they get to participate in decision making and problem solution.
3. Organizational effectiveness is maximized by achieving a state of fit among components of the system.
4. Organizations have cultures that facilitate or impede collaboration and adaptation.
5. People have a need for achievement and desire to grow.
6. In the long run there is a coincidence of interests between employees, management, and shareholders.
7. Effective cooperation is facilitated by the development of trust, tolerance, and respect.
8. Organizations have diverse "stakeholders" that need voice and recognition of their distinct interests.
9. Employees are motivated by more than financial incentives.
10. Problem solving is preferable to conflict.
11. Power equalization inside the organization promotes trust and collaboration.
12. Open communication is also crucial to trust and commitment.

Scanning this list, unity of interest and cooperation are explicitly mentioned in items 6 and 7, while the others in various ways contribute toward their accomplishment. Other writers (e.g., Appelbaum and Batt 1994; Delaney and Godard 2001) also make a "unitarist" perspective on the employment relationship a central feature of the HPWS, suggesting that a common intellectual thread exists between the early-twentieth-century writings of Rockefeller, King, and Hicks and modern management thinking on high-performance work practices.

Of course, caveats and qualifications are also required. As Appelbaum et al. (2000, 25–26) note, for example, in the 1920s, the focus was more on achieving high performance by motivating greater physical work effort, while in the 1990s it shifted toward eliciting greater creativity and information sharing. Also, Appelbaum and Batt (1994) observe that there are at least two different versions or permutations of the HPWS—one they call a "lean production" model and the other a "team production" model. The latter makes greater use of a "human capital" strategy to attain high performance and thus gives greater emphasis to cooperation and unity of interest, while the former emphasizes gaining production efficiency through technological and engineering solutions (akin to 1920s-era scientific management) and thus gives relatively less weight to these issues. Another difference is that terms such as "cooperation" and "unity of interest" used in the 1920s are often relabeled and sometimes given modestly different interpretations today. Cooperation, for example, is now often referred to as "collaboration" or "teamwork," while unity of interest becomes "integration" and "goal alignment." And, finally, some features of the HPWS emphasized today, such as self-managed work teams, were not well developed in this earlier era. Teams or "work gangs" certainly existed, but most were directly controlled by supervisors and foremen, and self-managing groups of skilled craft workers were being replaced in factories by semiskilled workers employed in individually organized assembly and machine jobs.

Another common link between the past and present concerns the strategic use of human resource management practices to achieve high performance and cooperation/unity of interest. A common theme in modern discussions of the HPWS, for example, is the importance of adopting individual HR practices, such as in selection, compensation, and training, that mutually reinforce each other and exploit complementarities and synergies (McMahan, Bell, and Virick 1998). Balderston (1935) provides evidence that this idea was already being practiced, albeit in more rudimentary form, in the late 1920s by leading Welfare Capitalist employers. In his case study investigation of the employment practices of twenty-five leading companies, he found they had put together a bundle of thirteen HR practices, and he described these practices as an "integrated" approach and "composite program" aimed at "getting men to work together effectively" (p. 290). Also illustrative of these links between present and past is the adoption of individual HR practices, such as employment security and gain sharing, that are a mainstay in modern HPWS plants. These same practices were first systematically introduced into industry in the 1920s by progressive employers affiliated with the Special Conference Committee and the Welfare Capitalist movement (Kaufman 2001).

Note, finally, that of all HR practices the one that is perhaps the linchpin of the modern HPWS is employee involvement. Cappelli and Neumark have recently said, for example, "It seems fair, therefore, to assert that the central research hypothesis being tested in prior research on high-performance work practices is whether employee involvement is associated with improved organizational performance" (2001, 742). But the potential payoff to greater employee involvement is not at all a new idea—it was one of the major rationales put forward by Rockefeller, King, and Hicks in the late 1910s for adoption of employee representation plans in industry. It appears, therefore, that the employment model pioneered by IRC in the 1920s—built around the principles of cooperation and unity of interest—not only was pathbreaking then but also remains central to progressive, leading-edge management thought as we enter the early twenty-first century.

Conclusion

The Ludlow Massacre forced John D. Rockefeller, Jr., to confront the Labor Problem in a close and personal way. It was evident that "business as usual" threatened the very social fabric of the nation and could spell personal disaster for the family name and fortune, so he searched for a solution to the bitter relations and bloody conflict bedeviling not only his companies but many others. The dominant strategy counseled and adopted by fellow industrialists of the time was bare-knuckled resistance to trade-unionist and political "agitators" and continued adherence to the time-honored doctrines of laissez-faire, freedom of contract, and "master and servant." On the other side, of course, were loud voices crying for measures that went to the other extreme, such as nationalization of industry, abolition of the wage system, and control of industry by workers' cooperatives.

Luckily for Rockefeller and the nation, he chose a middle path—one clearly reformist and even tinged with radicalism to fellow industrialists but, at the same time, one that met the problem in a substantive way while still preserving basic American political and economic institutions (and, cynics would say, the family fortune). Upon the able advice of men such as William Lyon Mackenzie King, Rockefeller became a convert to the then-fledgling, scarcely developed cause of progressive management in industry (or the "employer's solution" to labor problems). Under King's guidance, and later as implemented by men such as Clarence Hicks at the Standard Oil Co. (New Jersey), Rockefeller introduced a host of new practices and programs in an effort to improve relations between management and the workers. Most prominent was a system of employee representation, but also included were other advanced features such as establishment of an industrial relations department, an employee handbook with written policies and procedures, above-market wages, use of job evaluation methods to determine pay differentials, employment security, promotion from within, a variety of insurance and medical benefits, a savings and stock purchase plan, and training of supervisors in human relations practices. All of these industrial relations innovations within a decade became standard features in the Welfare Capitalism model of employment relations pioneered by America's leading edge of progressive employers.

More important than any one technique or program, however, was the guiding philosophy and purpose of Rockefeller's new industrial relations strategy—a philosophy underlying the Welfare Capitalism movement, taken up by Industrial Relations Counselors, Inc., and made the backbone of its work. Stated in a sentence, this new philosophy was to resolve the Labor Problem by management initiatives that transformed the employment relation from a win-lose proposition featuring intense adversarialism, conflict of interest, and considerable waste and inefficiency to a high-performance outcome based on extensive worker-management cooperation, unity of interest, and mutual gain. The programs and practices enumerated above were the concrete methods used to attain this end.

As earlier pointed out, Rockefeller and advisers were not the first ones to grasp the importance and positive impact on organizational performance of effective cooperation and sense of shared purpose. The idea in embryonic form goes back to the pre-Christian Greek philosophers and was clearly anticipated and discussed by various writers before the birth of the modern field of management in the late nineteenth century. Since then, it has become one of the foundation stones of modern management thought, albeit in different guises and achieved through a panoply of different methods. The ideas of cooperation and unity of interest can be traced through the writings of famous management thinkers such as Frederick Taylor, Mary Parker Follett, Elton Mayo, and Douglas McGregor, culminating in today's management literature on the high-performance workplace.

The quest to transform the employment relationship from a zero-sum to a positive-sum outcome can, in general principle, only be lauded. In this spirit, the contributions of progressive management thinkers, and the work of IRC in particular, toward this goal are notable and praiseworthy. Of course, as with all human endeavors, actual practice seldom fully lives up to theory, and accomplishment generally falls short of expectation. Great ideas can also be used for less than admirable ends by shortsighted persons and under the crush of events.

Certainly the quest for cooperation and unity of interest in industry exemplifies both these positive and negative sides. On the positive, one can hardly doubt that great strides have been made over the last century in improving the management of industrial relations and, more particularly, fostering greater cooperation and shared purpose in organizations. The Labor Problem, considered by many people to be the nation's most serious social malady a century ago, has largely faded from sight. Further, there can be little argument that cooperation and unity of interest are worthy goals and, if done correctly and in the right spirit, do indeed contribute to more efficient workplaces and more satisfying work experiences.

But there are also drawbacks and shortcomings. Critics note, sometimes with considerable merit, that a large gap can exist between the rhetoric of cooperation and unity of interest and the reality of everyday life in the workplace. In many companies there remain basic enduring conflicts of interest between employers and workers, and cooperation is born more out of economic necessity and the heavy hand of management domination than out of a genuine sense of shared commitment and teamwork. At a conceptual level, many "pluralist" industrial relations scholars also believe the "unitarist" employment model is inherently flawed and prone to a short half-life of success. From their perspective, cooperation and shared purpose can only arise when both employees and the employer interact with each other from a position of equality and security. Otherwise, management is given the opportunity and power to take self-interested, shortsighted actions (e.g., layoffs, work intensification) that benefit it at the expense of employees—actions that quickly undercut the culture of cooperation, trust, and mutual gain that are essential to an effective HPWS organization (Voos 2001). A successful HPWS model, as they see it, thus depends on some form of independent union representation and collective bargaining, or perhaps a European-type works-council organization. But in the view of the critics, one purpose of an HPWS strategy—often unstated but nonetheless real—is to undercut worker interest in unions and thus avoid collective bargaining (Gitelman 1988).

The position taken on this debate by John R. Commons—early-twentieth-century labor economist and person widely considered to be the father of the field of industrial relations—is also the one subscribed to in broad outline by Rockefeller, King, and Hicks. Commons (1919) welcomed management effort to foster cooperation and construct a unity of interest and accepted with equanimity workers' decision not to seek union representation if they are satisfied with prevailing employment conditions. The key requirement, however, is that management gain cooperation and unity of interest through a positive win-win approach of persuasion rather than a negative win-lose approach centered on coercion. Where the latter is practiced, high performance is gained at the expense of employee interests and human values, and trade unionism should be a readily available option. While Rockefeller, King, and Hicks had deep reservations about particular union practices and behaviors, they nonetheless took a progressive position on this matter that was much closer to the position enunciated by Commons than the far more belligerent anti-union position of most of their management colleagues.

Out of the disaster of the Ludlow Massacre in 1914, therefore, grew a new approach to industrial relations that markedly transformed the employment relationship in modern industry. This new approach is based on attaining high performance in industry by substituting mutual gain, cooperation, and unity of interest for the traditional model that rested on conflict of interest, adversarialism, and a win-lose approach. Although these ideas were not entirely new at the time, nor fully developed or institutionalized in succeeding years, certainly their spread and adoption in American industry were materially promoted by the work of Industrial Relations Counselors, Inc. Modern management and the practice of progressive employment relations thus owe much to IRC and its pioneering founders.

Acknowledgments

The author acknowledges with appreciation the contributions of George Strauss to an earlier version of this chapter.

5

A Century of Human Resource Management

Sanford M. Jacoby

It is an irony that most histories of personnel management are ahistorical, presenting the field as a succession of techniques and philosophies divorced from the historical context that produced them. Scientific management, human relations, employee participation—they march on, one after the other, with the narrative providing little or no perspective on the societal and economic forces that produced these movements. Standard histories of personnel management also have little to say about the personnel manager's role inside the corporation, e.g., relationships with other managers or influence (or lack thereof) on business decisions and strategies (Ling 1965; Milton 1970; Nestor 1986).

This discussion takes a different approach. It embeds personnel managers—and the firms employing them—in the cultural trends of American society. It argues that the role and status of personnel management *inside* the firm have always depended critically on forces *outside* the corporation, such as labor markets, government regulation, unions, and social norms of what constitutes "fair" employment. When there are labor shortages, new laws to comply with, or threats from unions—that is, when the external environment creates uncertainty—personnel managers have found themselves in relatively powerful positions, with a role in strategic decisions and with substantial budgets. But when the external environment is relatively stable and predictable, personnel management has usually been low man on the corporate totem pole. Thus, the power and influence of personnel management are dependent on external triggers rather than forces within personnel management itself.

Why have personnel managers historically been such a weak group within management? First, they deal with qualitative or "soft" problems (the Japanese would say "wet") in a world dominated by those who think in quantitative terms. Second, as the succession of philosophies indicates, personnel managers, unlike engineers or accountants, have never developed an intellectually consistent paradigm for asserting their professional legitimacy. Thus, when personnel professionalization does emerge—and we will examine this phenomenon—it has typically been a defensive strategy devoid of theoretical content. Finally, personnel managers are in an ambiguous social role— between employees and line managers—causing them to be distrusted by both sides. Their ambiguous role is reinforced by the prevailing norm of U.S.-style capitalism that shareholders are the organization's principals, managers their agents, and employees a factor of production with no stakeholder claims. But as we will see, the primacy of shareholders has itself sometimes been challenged, and when that has occurred, it has been associated with an accretion of power for personnel managers.

The Roots of Personnel Management

In the late nineteenth century, when the United States was becoming an industrial society, companies—even large ones—rarely took a systematic approach to managing their employees. Most were content to leave daily production and employment decisions in the hands of their first-line supervisors—their foremen—and sometimes even contracted out to these foremen all managerial responsibilities for a given operation or department. But as technologies and organizations became more complex, this decentralized approach created problems (Nelson 1975). The flow of production was hindered by a lack of coordination between various departments, and data on costs were not kept or were gathered irregularly. The result was that firms found it difficult to increase throughput speed, which, as historian Alfred D. Chandler (1977) has argued, was the key to corporate growth and to mass production and distribution.

Between 1880 and 1920, the systematic management movement (of which Frederick Taylor's scientific management was one strand) began to introduce new methods of coordination and control to industry, systems that told foremen and skilled workers how to schedule production and the order in which to perform operations. The new systems also included cost accounting and the creation of staff departments to handle technical and administrative duties (Litterer 1963). By and large, however, the new systems left untouched the foreman's control over the hiring, firing, training, and payment of workers.

There were, however, two incursions into the foreman's empire. First, industrial engineers introduced various incentive wage schemes that, it was hoped, would boost productivity and thereby raise wages sufficiently to head off any incipient labor unrest (Taylor 1895; Thompson 1914). Second, some companies took the industrial engineers' approach to production—orderly procedures, accurate records, and the departmentalization of routinized functions—and applied it to their hiring practices. They created so-called employment departments that interviewed prospective employees, kept track of "problem" workers, and assigned new hires to departments where they were needed. One of the earliest of these departments was established at Goodyear in 1900 (Eilbirt 1959; Jacoby 1985).[1]

The late nineteenth and early twentieth centuries were an era of recurring political and labor unrest in both the United States and Europe. In the United States, socialist and anarchist ideas were popular, not only among immigrants but also with native workers and farmers. Craft unions periodically engaged in bitter disputes with employers; unorganized workers sometimes went on strike or simply quit their jobs in search of better ones. Labor turnover rates were extremely high by modern standards, a situation that was exacerbated by the foreman's hire-and-fire approach. Middle-class reformers searched for ways to ameliorate these problems, inspired by religious and secular ideas of "uplift" and by the legislative experiments being tried out in Europe (Wiebe 1967; Rodgers 1998).

The religious impulse to minister to industrial workers found expression in a variety of turn-of-the-century movements, including the Social Gospel of reform Protestantism, Catholic mutual aid societies, and Quaker communitarianism. One of the earliest organizations to get involved in outreach and uplift activities was the Young Men's Christian Association (YMCA), which in the 1870s set up special rooms in railroad stations for prayer meetings and Bible classes for railway workers. In 1888, railroad magnate Cornelius Vanderbilt erected a large building to house the programs the YMCA had organized for his employees. By this time, the YMCA's approach had begun to blend religiosity with recreational activities. Vanderbilt's YMCA building contained game rooms, libraries, lunchrooms, bowling alleys, a gymnasium, and a chapel. The idea spread rapidly, and by 1901, some ninety railroad buildings had been constructed on different lines, each administered by a "secretary" appointed by the YMCA's national Railroad Department. These secretaries were, in a sense, corporate welfare managers, indirectly employed by the company but paid by the YMCA (Jacoby 1985 56–60). Heading the Railroad Department for many years was a Wisconsin-born lawyer named Clarence J. Hicks, who believed that the employer-supported YMCA recreational activity was "not a philanthropy, but simply a good business for the railroad company." It was "based upon unity of interest between employer and employees" (Hicks 1941, 21).

Some companies preferred to organize their own uplift activities—what came to be known as "welfare work"—rather than have the YMCA do it for them. Welfare work ran the gamut from pecuniary incentives, such as profit-sharing, pension, and stock bonus plans, to programs more directly aimed at the worker's character, such as thrift clubs, citizenship instruction, company recreational activities, company housing, and company medical facilities. Occasionally, elected employee representatives were placed in charge of these activities, as with the Filene Cooperative Association, founded in 1905. More commonly, employers hired specialized welfare secretaries who had backgrounds in social work, settlement work, journalism, and the ministry. Reflecting their backgrounds and their desire to have greater influence in the companies that employed them, welfare workers at an early stage sought to professionalize their activities through such organizations as the American Institute for Social Service and the National Civic Federation.

Welfare workers rarely became involved in daily employment decisions about the hiring, firing, and payment of employees. Their focus was on the employees' extra-work activities, including their home activities. At Ford Motor and other companies, welfare workers practiced "home visiting," which brought the welfare workers into the employee's home to check up on illnesses, offer advice on hygiene and housekeeping, and extend a bit of familial warmth from an otherwise impersonal corporation. As in social work, this sympathetic and nurturing role was often filled by women.[2]

The family theme extended to the employer as enlightened paterfamilias. Many employers supported welfare work out of a paternalistic sense of duty and a religious belief that great wealth carried great responsibilities. John D. Rockefeller, Jr., a devout Baptist, was chastened by the horror of the Ludlow Massacre and the public's condemnation of his seeming aloofness. He became an ardent advocate of welfare work, which he saw as a form of stewardship, the "duty of everyone entrusted with industrial leadership to do all in his power to improve the conditions under which men work and live" (Jacoby 1985, 51). For Rockefeller, this duty included the provision of employee representation to employees at his Colorado Fuel and Iron Company and at Standard Oil of New Jersey. To oversee these efforts, Rockefeller hired Clarence J. Hicks, who later would become an executive of the Rockefeller-funded Industrial Relations Counselors, Inc. (Gitelman 1988).

Social reformers concerned about unemployment and dead-end jobs also contributed to the emergence of personnel management. Believing that the foreman's crude motivational and hiring methods contributed to high rates of turnover and unemployment, they advocated the transfer of the foreman's powers to new personnel departments that would assign workers to jobs that were appropriate for them. They also advocated more sophisticated selection methods, including psychological tests, to identify employee skills and aptitudes (Baritz 1960; Kevles 1968; Jacoby 1985, 65–93).

Thus, the strands that would compose the personnel management movement came together on the eve of America's entry into the First World War.

Efficiency, administrative specialization, uplift, and vocational guidance all fed into a growing recognition that America's large and midsize companies needed to pay more attention to how they managed their employees. There was a belief that professionalization of personnel management—hiring specialized, educated employees—would humanize industry and bring a more enlightened approach. Yet prior to the war, only a minority of firms translated these ideas into action. The vast majority of employers retained traditional methods of workforce management. Labor was cheap and readily available, and foremen complained about having to take orders from soft-handed college graduates. As a result, most large companies lacked personnel departments, and while welfare work was more prevalent, employees resented its intrusive paternalism (Nelson and Campbell 1972).

Wartime Watershed

As labor markets tightened after 1915, employers were confronted with a host of problems that, while not entirely new, were of such magnitude as to cause them to reconsider their traditional approach to employment management. Unemployment rates fell to the lowest levels since the 1880s, turnover rates skyrocketed, and productivity sank. Meanwhile, labor unrest was widespread and strikes became commonplace. In fact, the ratio of strikers to all workers between 1916 and 1921 was at the same level as during the more famous strike years of 1934 and 1937. On top of this, the federal government for the first time took an active role in regulating the national labor market. It established administrative machinery for settling labor disputes and enforced new standards regarding overtime pay, the eight-hour day, safety and sanitation, and minimum wages (Jacoby 1985, 136, 142). Each of these factors—labor shortages, labor unrest, and government regulation—in itself was sufficient during later years to compel employers to establish new personnel departments or to boost the status and resources of those departments already in existence. What made the war period unusual was the combination of these factors and their intensity.

The years from 1916 to 1920 witnessed a veritable personnel boom as companies rushed to create personnel departments that would help them recruit and retain workers, maintain labor peace, and comply with government regulations. Between 1915 and 1920, the proportion of firms with more than 250 employees that had personnel departments increased from roughly 5 percent to about 25 percent. The rapid growth created a new occupation almost overnight. Five hundred persons attended the first national conference of personnel managers held in 1917, and close to three thousand were present when another conference was held in 1920. These new managers came from diverse backgrounds. Some were former social workers or educators, but most had previously been employed in industry—as welfare workers, safety experts, salespersons, and attorneys. Inevitably, turf disputes broke out between the new personnel managers and line managers, especially foremen, and with industrial engineers and production officials who were reluctant to change traditional methods and were quick to blame personnel managers for driving up costs and being too "soft" in dealings with employees. Personnel managers responded by forming professional organizations to bolster their status, including the National Association of Employment Managers, which after several name changes became the American Management Association in 1923 (ibid., 137, 161).

Despite the griping, the new personnel managers made substantial inroads into the foreman's empire. The biggest changes were the adoption of central hiring offices, rules for disciplining and dismissing workers (which usually involved a role for the personnel manager), record keeping for employment and wages, and more systematic approaches to training, performance evaluation, and promotion. Some companies introduced formal job analysis to aid in employee selection and to rationalize the hodgepodge of wage rates that existed in many companies. A few hundred firms established their own employee representation plans; others were compelled to do so by the War Labor Board and other agencies. As a result of these changes, companies found themselves better able to retain employees, control costs, and raise employee morale. Workers came to feel more attached to the companies that employed them; their jobs began to look more like careers. These changes reduced the potential for labor unrest by replicating within the firm many of the unions' own protective structures and by removing the most egregious workplace problems (ibid., 141, 149).

The Special Conference Committee (SCC) and Welfare Capitalism of the 1920s

During these tumultuous years, some large employers felt the need to more decisively shape the course of events and set an appropriate direction for the personnel movement to follow. One result was the formation of the National Industrial Conference Board in 1916, an effort led by Magnus W. Alexander of General Electric (who also was one of the first to demonstrate the existence and costliness of labor turnover). Another was the creation in 1919 of the Special Conference Committee (SCC), made up of executives—CEOs and personnel managers—from ten of America's leading industrial corporations. The SCC had close ties to the Rockefeller interests. Clarence J. Hicks was the SCC's chairman from 1919 to 1933, during which time he also headed the personnel department at Standard

Oil of New Jersey. The SCC was headquartered in the offices of Raymond Fosdick, who was a Rockefeller attorney in New York (Gitelman 1984; Jacoby 1985, 184).[3]

In addition to New Jersey Standard Oil, the SCC companies included Bethlehem Steel, DuPont, General Electric, General Motors, Goodyear, International Harvester, Irving National Bank, Standard Oil of Indiana, and Westinghouse. U.S. Rubber joined in 1923, AT&T in 1925, and U.S. Steel in 1934. The SCC adopted a set of principles based on the belief of John D. Rockefeller, Jr., that "the only solidarity natural in industry is the solidarity which unites all those in the same business establishment" (Jacoby 1985, 181–83). Each of the SCC companies had employee representation plans that sought to offer a corporatist alternative to craft or industrial unions. The firms also were leaders in the introduction of pecuniary welfare benefits—pension plans, paid vacations, health insurance, profit sharing—that were seen as a less paternalistic alternative to welfare work. Finally, the SCC companies all had personnel departments, which made sure that employees received steady jobs, similar pay for similar work, and reasonably fair treatment from their supervisors. Several of the SCC companies, like others in the vanguard of welfare capitalism, also made efforts to stabilize employment so as to reduce frictional and seasonal unemployment. One of the SCC companies, General Electric, even adopted its own private employment guarantee (unemployment insurance) plan. This plan was consistent with a core principle of SCC-style welfare capitalism—that business, through good personnel management, could solve problems such as unemployment and old-age insecurity without government intervention as in Europe (Nelson 1969, 21; Jacoby 1997).[4]

The SCC emphasized that the job of the personnel manager was to supply tools for line managers to use. It wanted the personnel movement to get away from the idea—popular among liberals in the movement—that the personnel manager was an independent professional, a third force in the firm who could overrule line managers in favor of employees. The SCC was in favor of returning power to foremen but training them to use it. In part, this reflected a desire to curtail what were seen as excesses of the wartime period; in part, it reflected the search for a way of managing what were becoming increasingly decentralized companies (Chandler 1956). This combination of employee representation, welfare benefits, career jobs, foreman training, and a pure staff-type of personnel administration would become the exemplar for large progressive companies in the 1920s and 1930s. The SCC disseminated its ideas through the YMCA, which in the 1920s held regular conferences for personnel officials; through the American Management Association, whose board it controlled; and through Industrial Relations Counselors, Inc. (IRC), founded in 1926 by John D. Rockefeller, Jr., to provide research and consulting services to the SCC and other companies, especially in areas such as old-age pensions and employment stabilization.[5]

Yet most employers of the 1920s failed to follow the example set by the SCC and IRC. After the war, the same forces that had driven the formation of personnel departments went into reverse: Labor markets softened, labor unrest subsided, and government unwound its wartime regulations. Some companies that had adopted personnel departments and other reforms as a temporary expedient now cut their budgets and let their programs lapse. Others, which had never implemented personnel reforms, now felt little pressure to do so in the changed atmosphere of the 1920s. By 1929, about 40 percent of industrial firms employing more than a thousand workers had personnel departments. Many of these departments were rather powerless as compared to their wartime counterparts. While personnel managers tried to defend their budgets using hard data such as figures on labor turnover and its attendant costs, their pleas now fell on deaf ears.

On the other hand, the use of pecuniary welfare benefits became more popular in the 1920s, with around a quarter of large firms offering paid vacations in 1929. More costly and complex parts of the SCC's "welfare capitalism" remained relatively rare, however. In the mid-1920s, only 245 firms had active pension plans, and only 399 had company unions. Thus on the eve of the Great Depression, American industry comprised three kinds of firms: a vanguard made up of the SCC companies and some other even more progressive companies such as Kodak, Procter & Gamble, and Dennison Manufacturing; a group of laggards that had personnel departments but failed to empower them or to adopt welfare programs or company unions; and a group of traditionalists—the vast majority—whose personnel policies in 1929 were much the same as they had been thirty years earlier. These traditionalists came from highly competitive industries that were under intense economic pressure in the 1920s. Their response to this pressure was an intensification of the foreman's drive system and an aggressive pursuit of the open shop, decisions that would come back to haunt them in the 1930s (Jacoby 1997, 23–31).

The Turbulent Years

After the stock market crash in 1929, some large companies tried to keep their workforces intact using the employment stabilization techniques that had been promoted during the 1920s. Personnel management organizations such as the Personnel Research Federation, the American Management Association, and IRC worked with municipal, state, and national officials to encourage employers to produce for inventory, undertake repairs, or engage in worksharing so as to avoid layoffs (Domhoff 1996, 138). But the remedies were feeble in face of the Depression's severity, and by the fall of 1931, layoffs reached catastrophic levels. Included in the layoffs were some personnel managers (around 5 percent of the personnel departments in existence in 1929 were eliminated by 1933); other personnel departments shrank as employers cut back on or discontinued welfare benefits and formal systems for employment administration. Employer groups such as the SCC worried that "radical legislation" such as government-funded unemployment insurance might soon be enacted, and they were right to worry: Despite the promises of welfare capitalism, only a third of large firms offered unemployment relief to their employees, and only a handful had formal insurance plans (Jacoby 1985, 207–23). Early in 1933, liberal economist William Leiserson gloomily wrote that the "depression has undone fifteen years or so of good personnel work," and he warned that "labor is going to look to legislation and not to personnel management for a solution of the unemployment problem" (Leiserson 1933, 114).

Passage of the National Industrial Recovery Act (NIRA) set in motion a chain of events that brought government regulation back to the labor market and rejuvenated the labor movement. Although unemployment remained high, two of the three conditions for personnel formalization were in place, and the result was another boom for personnel management. As during World War I, there was a dramatic expansion between 1933 and 1936 in the proportion of firms with personnel departments. To bolster employee morale and forestall unionization, personnel departments moved aggressively to shrink the foreman's discretion by making labor allocation (hiring, promotion, layoffs, dismissals) subject to definite rules and procedures, such as rudimentary seniority provisions, merit ratings, job evaluation, wage classification, and progressive discipline (Jacoby 1985, 226–39). In response to recommendations from IRC and similar groups, companies dusted off their foreman training programs as a first line of defense against unions. There was a moderate increase in welfare benefits such as pension plans and employment guarantees, though cash-strapped companies found it difficult to offer much at this time. Several hundred large firms also established company unions in the wake of the NIRA, a controversial move that was condemned by the burgeoning labor movement (Jacoby 2000).

Yet none of these moves was sufficient to halt the tide of union organizing or a flurry of new labor-market regulations. Close to five million workers joined unions between 1936 and 1939, notably in mass-production industries that previously had been nonunion strongholds. The Wagner Act facilitated unionization while making it more difficult for employers to initiate or maintain company unions. The Social Security Act brought government into competition with private welfare capitalism, although employer groups such as IRC, insurance companies, and well-placed managers, such as Marion Folsom of Kodak, were able to carve out a place for private provision (Jacoby 1993). By keeping public old-age benefits to a minimum, private benefits could still play a supplementary role; by providing for experience rating, there still was an incentive for private companies to stabilize employment; and by keeping government out of the health arena, private companies (including insurers) had room to maneuver. Nevertheless, the events of the mid- to late 1930s called into question large parts of the welfare capitalist agenda charted by SCC companies and IRC (Berkowitz and McQuaid 1992; Derickson 1994; Domhoff 1996, 138–54; Klein 2000).

The one part of the agenda that remained vital was to specialize and centrally coordinate corporate labor policies. Now there was a new importance accorded to personnel managers—experts capable in designing employment policies that complied with government regulations, in negotiating with unions, or in preempting union organizing. Personnel managers, said one commentator in 1937, were "rising to a place of new importance in the management function" (quoted in Jacoby 1985, 242). Under pressure from unions and from workers concerned about security, corporate personnel departments further formalized companywide procedures for hiring, promotion, and layoff. Often these procedures gave much heavier weight to seniority than ever before. Unions—or the threat of them—led personnel departments to undertake the codification of personnel procedures via handbooks and corporate conduct codes. Unions also triggered the adoption of definite procedures for discipline and dismissal, and personnel departments came to play a larger role in the disciplinary process (Jacoby 1985, 233, 243–50).

World War II saw government take an active role in coordinating the labor market, as in the previous war. Part of the government's objective was to prevent strikes from disrupting vital war industries. During the war, unions were more powerful than ever and added more than five million members to their rolls. Thus, all three growth factors were in play, and the result was a massive expansion of the personnel function. Small and medium-sized firms that had never adopted personnel departments now instituted them, while in larger companies, the status and size of personnel departments reached an all-time high. What was left of the foreman's empire was brought under the control of centralized personnel departments, and foremen were herded into training programs subsidized by government. (Some foremen angrily protested by forming their own unions.) To get control of pay structures for collective bargaining and to comply with federal wage controls, personnel departments embarked on a massive effort to rationalize pay structures via job evaluation plans. Because the War Labor Board allowed employers to circumvent wage controls with reasonable expenditures on fringe benefits, there was a massive expansion in health, hospitalization, and pension benefits during the war (ibid., 260–74).

The Golden Years: The 1950s and 1960s

The end of the Second World War led to some cutbacks in the size of personnel department budgets, but the cuts were relatively small as compared with twenty-five years earlier. Why? First and foremost, unions were now deeply entrenched in major sectors such as manufacturing, transportation, and regulated utilities. This required management attention. Second, government—through its activities to supervise union-management relations, restrain wage inflation, and regulate the provision of welfare benefits, such as pensions and health insurance—was now a permanent fixture in the labor market. Third, companies had come to accept the value of having specialized staff handle what was now a technically complex function. They also recognized that societal norms had changed such that employees had to be treated as members of the enterprise—given security and fair treatment—if a company were to be seen as legitimate and responsible. An enabling factor for this sense of responsibility was that corporate ownership was now firmly separated from management control, a phenomenon first explored by Berle and Means (1932) in the 1930s. Managers in the postwar era saw themselves as having responsibilities not only to owners (stockholders) but also to consumers, the general public, and to employees (Sutton et al. 1956). The typical mind-set of senior management had become

> an introverted corporate view . . . focused on growth, diversification and opportunity for the "corporate family.". . . It was a period when the social and legal climate encouraged management to adopt a pluralistic view of their responsibility to the various corporate constituencies. As career employees themselves, it was natural for management to identify with all constituents who were long-term investors in the enterprise and to view shareholders in the same light. [Donaldson 1994, 19]

Recognition of these facts led corporations to take seriously their responsibilities as "good" employers, which boosted the personnel function's status in the organization. Companies also responded by aligning or combining their personnel departments and their public relations departments because both were aimed at what were now perceived as "stakeholders" of the corporation (Tedlow 1979).

Another important change in the postwar era was the growing importance of psychology to personnel management. Prior to the war, psychological techniques such as selection tests and attitude surveys were used by only a handful of companies, chiefly as a guide in executive selection and for study of employee morale. Pioneering companies such as AT&T and Western Electric conducted large-scale studies of employee attitudes, as in the well-known Hawthorne experiments at Western Electric run by Harvard anthropologist Elton Mayo. Mayo's ideas—dubbed "human relations" by his followers— were a break from the reliance on economic incentives and administrative processes that had characterized the field of personnel management prior to the 1930s (Jacoby 1988). The Mayoites argued that managers should give more attention to the worker's psyche and to his personal relationships at work, especially the relationship between employee and supervisor, and worry less about pay and perquisites (Roethlisberger and Dickson 1939). During the war, the government's Training Within Industry (TWI) program used Mayo's ideas to teach nearly half a million foremen how to motivate their employees. Other behavioral scientists were employed in the Army's personnel classification and selection sections—which helped to develop vocational and IQ tests—and in the Morale Services Division and the Office of War Information, which conducted attitude surveys of soldiers and civilians (Jacoby 1997, 221–28). After the war, many of these behavioral scientists went to work in the private sector, either as management consultants or as personnel management staff. By 1948, more than 30 percent of large corporations had a psychologist on the payroll (Bennett 1948). There now was much heavier use of selection tests, attitude surveys, leadership training, and other programs based in the behavioral sciences. The academic field of personnel management increasingly became the province of applied psychologists (Kaufman 2000).

The impact of the behavioral sciences on personnel management continued to be felt well into the 1960s. Some researchers studied employee motivation and applied their insights to compensation design and work restructuring. Out of this came ideas such as "vertical job loading," which showed how routine jobs could be made more interesting while at the same time eliminating supervisory positions (Herzberg 1968). The most sophisticated elements of the behavioral sciences were directed toward managerial and professional employees and included techniques such as sensitivity training (for bolstering psychological acuity among managers) and the managerial grid (to help managers balance "people" and "production" problems). Personnel managers spearheaded corporate involvement with the behavioral sciences and used the latter's academic origins to legitimate greater spending on management training and organization development (McGregor 1960; Blake and Mouton 1964; Pearse 1964; Rush 1969).

Another development in the postwar decades was the growing gap between labor relations and employee relations. Labor relations became the province of specialists concerned with collective bargaining and contract administration, while employee relations encompassed all other aspects of the employee-company relationship. Labor relations departments were found only in unionized firms, a group whose size stopped growing in the early 1950s. As union organizing slowed and as industrial relations became more orderly and predictable, the labor relations aspect of personnel management became less important. Few labor relations managers had time to delve into the behavioral sciences and sometimes were skeptical of them, as were unions. In contrast, employee relations departments became the place where the new behavioral approach took hold—in unionized, partially unionized, and non-union companies. An example of this was General Motors, the first of the big three automobile manufacturers to develop a coherent industrial relations strategy after the war. The GM approach was Janus-like: The unions faced a tough adversary in bargaining while employees saw a kinder, gentler GM through the employee relations department. Among other things, the department was in charge of conducting attitude surveys at GM plants around the country. It also administered a contest in the late 1940s in which workers wrote essays on "My Job and Why I Like It." GM invited Paul Lazarsfeld, an eminent survey researcher from Columbia University, to analyze the data using latent structure analysis. It also hired Opinion Research Corporation to find out what GM employees thought of the contest (Evans and Laseau 1950).

Even in heavily unionized companies, labor relations no longer was the primary element in personnel management. A study of large companies found that labor relations was the dominant personnel activity in only 7 percent of surveyed companies; 55 percent did not even consider it important (Conference Board 1966, 21). Instead, personnel units reported that they were focusing much more on management development, employee benefits, training, and communications. It is interesting that companies attributed the shift in activities not only to the stabilization of labor relations but also to the fact that they had "overwhelmingly decided that going outside the company to fill vacant managerial positions is unsatisfactory. Instead they staff from within wherever possible . . . [and this requires] monetary and other incentives for good men to come into and remain with the company, developing men for the future needs of the company, and setting up more efficient systems of interunit promotion and transfer" (ibid., 28–29).

This shift of focus is hardly surprising. After all, the 1950s and 1960s were the heyday of the Organization Man—a period when companies were vastly expanding their middle management ranks (Whyte 1956). Tying the careers of those managers more tightly to the company was done partly to attract and retain scarce talent (the cohort born during the Great Depression, who were graduating from college in the 1950s, was relatively small), partly to meet the deeply felt security concerns of these "children of the depression" (Elder 1974).

The expansion of middle management occurred as U.S. companies moved decisively toward adoption of diversified, multidivisional corporate structures (the "M-form") in which a headquarters unit oversaw the activities of semiautonomous divisions (Chandler 1962; Fligstein 1985). It was also a time when companies built up their overseas operations and became increasingly multinational. With these changes came the creation of new headquarters personnel units alongside divisional and plant units; more than half the headquarters units in existence in the mid-1960s had been created after the end of the war (Conference Board 1966, 13). The headquarters units concerned themselves with companywide policy and managing executive careers, giving personnel—at least at the top—its focus on managerial employees. Thus, despite corporate decentralization, headquarters personnel staff grew during the 1960s—most corporate personnel departments were adding activities, and their staffs were growing more rapidly than their companies as a whole—and the vast majority of headquarters units felt that their status inside the organization had risen (ibid., 15, 31–37, 64–72).

It is less clear what these changes meant for divisional and unit (establishment) personnel managers, whose activities now were directed more toward rank-and-file workers and day-to-day operating issues. On one hand, these units initially grew larger as a result of decentralization; on the other hand, the divisional units came more firmly under the control of divisional and unit line managers, were focused on lower-status employees, and applied— rather than developed—administrative systems.

Some studies in the 1960s detected status anxiety among personnel managers, perhaps as a result of decentralization. The most dissatisfied personnel managers were those reporting to divisional (line) managers, more than a third of whom felt that their departments were too small and more than half of whom felt that the personnel function needed moderate to extensive change (McFarland 1962, 22–23). Not surprisingly, some personnel managers—like their forebears in the 1910s and 1920s—again turned to professionalism as a tactic to bolster their organizational influence. They joined organizations such as the American Society for Personnel Administration, sought professional certification, and sought advice and ideas from experts outside the firm (Ritzer and Trice 1969).

Yet even at the highest levels of the organization, where personnel executives reported that their influence had increased, there were indicators that all was not well. The spread of the M-form structure after the war brought with it the elevation of the corporate finance function. To modern financial managers, the firm is seen as a collection of assets. Financial tools are used to judge the performance of divisions and units, and units are bought and sold to improve overall share returns. During the 1960s, the number of mergers and acquisitions rose sharply as more firms adopted the finance model, with some of them taking it all the way to its logical conclusion—the conglomerate model of unrelated diversification. Increasingly, CEOs and presidents came not from the operating side or from sales but from finance (Fligstein 1990). For financial managers, quantitative indicators were paramount, but unfortunately, they often were not available in the personnel area (and when they were, as in management of fringe benefits such as pension plans, financial managers contested with personnel managers for control). Not surprisingly, personnel executives in the early 1960s reported more conflict with finance departments than with any other functional unit. From personnel's perspective, the problem was that "in top management about the only thing that counts is finance" (McFarland 1962, 63). From the perspective of other senior managers—including finance—the problem was that the personnel function was perceived as little more than "the administration of routine, maintenance, housekeeping tasks." It was criticized as being "not a risk taker" and "not business oriented" (Ritzer and Trice 1969, 65). The last criticism was not so wide of the mark. As companies became more finance oriented and numbers driven, personnel managers—even at the senior level—found themselves intellectually unprepared for the brave new world that corporations were entering.

Respite in the 1970s

Just when things were starting to look dicey for personnel managers, four things happened that gave them a reprieve: (1) the stock market started to drop in 1969, taking the wind out of the sails of CFOs and their obsession with mergers, acquisitions, and conglomerations; (2) there was a growing concern over worker dissatisfaction—the so-called Lordstown Syndrome or blue-collar blues; (3) companies faced increased opportunities and incentives to open nonunion facilities; and (4) government regulation of the workplace proliferated along various dimensions.

Lordstown, Ohio, was the site of a celebrated 1971 strike by young workers in a General Motors assembly plant who, although well paid, were unhappy with the intrinsic aspects of their jobs. The strike led to a new concern with the quality of working life (QWL) and to a slew of work enrichment experiments, in both unionized and nonunion settings, and in the private and public sectors. The experiments included reorganization of tasks and technology, formation of self-directed work teams, and joint problem-solving groups. At the same time, companies were trying to bring some related changes to management, seeking to improve communications among managers and between managers and their subordinates (Berg, Freedman, and Freeman 1978; Strauss et al. 1974).

For personnel managers, these efforts led to an expansion of organization development (OD) staffs, making OD among the fastest growing of new personnel activities in the 1970s. The effect was most pronounced at corporate headquarters, where personnel departments acquired new professional staff that included psychologists, sociologists, and an occasional anthropologist. As a result of these new hires, the personnel function developed expertise in the area of planned organizational change and communications. Links to university-based researchers, which were first established in the human relations era, were expanded. In parallel with corporate developments, the academic study of organization behavior (OB)—the successor to human relations—enjoyed new funding and prestige in the 1970s. Yet even as headquarters staff expanded, so did the duties of line managers, who were considered a crucial element in leading work reform activities and making them successful. Indeed, the most innovative companies were those where line managers had the most control over personnel decisions. Increasingly left out of the picture were divisional and plant personnel departments (Janger 1977, 48–49).

Although joint union-management QWL efforts were celebrated in the 1970s, many of the more advanced work reform experiments took place in new nonunion plants, such as the General Foods pet-food factory in Topeka, Kansas. Part of the explanation was that it was easier to introduce work reform in a greenfield setting, where neither workers nor first-line supervisors had established traditional attitudes and ways of doing things. Another part of the explanation was that while some unions such as the Autoworkers (UAW) were champions of QWL, many other unions—and some vocal factions within the UAW itself—were deeply suspicious of work reform, seeing it as a management effort to undermine the union (Parker and Slaughter 1988). But another factor was simply that companies in the 1970s had stepped up the pace of their union-avoidance activities such that the supply of new nonunion plants increased steadily over the decade. Union avoidance became more prevalent in the 1970s because it was easier to do—unions were weaker than before; the cost of operating union facilities rose sharply in the inflationary 1970s, thus creating an incentive to open nonunion plants; and the new behavioral approach to work organization made nonunion plants harder for unions to crack (Freeman and Medoff 1984; Jacoby 1997). Empowered workers tended to be more loyal to management and less interested in the traditional union approach, which was built around a different conception of work organization (Kochan, Katz, and McKersie 1986).

For personnel managers, the new nonunion emphasis had several consequences. It widened the divide between labor relations and employee relations: Labor relations became a less centralized and less prestigious activity while employee relations—now starting to be called human resources (HR)—gained responsibility for more dynamic endeavors (e.g., management development and strategic planning) and greater responsibility for union avoidance activities (Foulkes 1980, 70–96). Local line managers—a key element in both union avoidance and work reform—became increasingly involved in these activities, again at the expense of unit personnel departments. Now that the key players were the line managers and corporate (headquarters) HR units, friction increased between them, with line managers feeling that as in earlier eras, "headquarters" was too involved in making sure that "locals" did nothing that might entice a union into the company's facilities (Freedman 1985, 29–33).

Keep in mind that during the 1960s and 1970s, the "union question" was becoming less important because the labor force included increasing numbers of college-educated technical and professional employees, groups that traditionally had shown little interest in unions, and conversely. Managing these employees required personnel policies that promoted communication and small-group decision making, precisely the outcomes that could be achieved by the work organization and OB principles being applied to blue-collar workers (Heckscher 1988). Thus, rising education levels had the same effect as blue-collar blues: It bolstered the importance of the behavioral sciences to personnel management, thereby creating a congruence in the ways in which top-office and shop-floor employees were managed. In some companies with both highly educated and less educated employees, this congruence led to single-status personnel policies and to a greater emphasis on unifying corporate cultures.

Although unions were of lesser importance to corporate personnel managers, compliance with a myriad of new government regulations became a time-consuming task. Starting with the Manpower Development and Training Act of 1962, the federal government kept up a steady pace of regulatory innovation the likes of which had not been seen since the 1930s: the Equal Pay Act (1963), Civil Rights Act (1964), Economic Opportunity Act (1964), Occupational Safety and Health Act (1970), Equal Employment Opportunity Act (1972), Comprehensive Employment and Training Act (1973), and various executive orders, including one that established the Office of Federal Contract Compliance Programs (Dobbin 1998). Predictably, compliance with these programs had a centralizing effect as headquarters personnel departments took responsibility for record keeping and the design of corporate systems for ensuring that units complied with the law. A survey of major corporations in the mid-1970s found that compliance with EEO and occupational safety laws had become the most important change in personnel activity over the decade, with much of the activity concentrated at corporate headquarters. Said the report, "Centralization is the term executives and managers most often use to describe the developing trends in the organization of the personnel function. By greater centralization they mean the substantial new constraints they feel when hiring, firing, disciplining, directing, training, promoting and compensating subordinates" (Janger 1977, 1, 4, 63). Because of the risk of lawsuits and other negative publicity, CEOs and company presidents became involved in these activities, which resulted in closer contact between senior management and the corporate HR function. According to the report, the net effect of these regulatory changes was "an end to the 20–year trend of increasing delegation of authority over personnel matters to local [line] managers" (ibid., 1). This was, however, but a temporary respite.

Crisis and Deconstruction: The 1980s and Early 1990s

Starting in the early 1980s, the pendulum once again swung in the opposite direction, with HR departments becoming smaller and less influential in corporate affairs. All of the factors bolstering HR's role inside the corporation now turned negative. First, deregulation of transportation, communication, and other industries was initiated under President Jimmy Carter and accelerated during the Reagan years. While the employment relationship remained enmeshed in statutory complexity, federal oversight grew less rigorous (Vogel 1996). For employers, the sense of urgency faded, and this weakened HR's claim to resources that it had commanded in the 1970s. Second, unions became ever weaker in the 1980s. There was concession bargaining and continued shrinkage of private-sector unionism. Third, labor markets were loose. To extinguish inflation, the Federal Reserve Bank kept interest rates high for most of the 1980s and early 1990s, which raised unemployment. Monetary stringency combined with increased international competition and deregulation to produce a wave of permanent job losses in the 1980s, concentrated among blue-collar workers (Bluestone and Harrison 1982; Kletzer 1998).

The 1980s and early 1990s also saw a shift in corporate governance, as evidenced by the rise in hostile takeovers and the development of a more active market for corporate control. Shareholders—many of them large institutions—grew more assertive of their status as the corporation's sole residual claimants. As power shifted in the 1980s, corporations found themselves having to take on greater risk and crank out higher returns to satisfy investors and to avoid takeovers (Coffee 1988; Useem 1996). Some senior managers gave up on public ownership and took their firms private in so-called leveraged buyouts (LBOs). The quest to restructure corporations and to squeeze out higher returns shifted from blue-collar workers to middle managers, who increasingly found themselves the chief targets of industrial restructuring. The late 1980s and early 1990s saw permanent losses concentrated among managerial and professional employees. Companies that had once prided themselves on offering long-term jobs and good benefits—Kodak, DEC, IBM—now sacked thousands and shred implicit career-job contracts with their middle managers (Jacoby 1999).

For HR departments, these changes were, to put it mildly, a shock to the system, affecting each of the three main roles HR departments traditionally had played: (1) provider of services to career employees, including benefits, training, and development; (2) supplier of programs to, and monitor of, line managers; and (3) advocate of employee interests to senior executives and line managers, a role that often put HR in the middle between employees and their supervisors.

Now, all three roles were called into question. The difficult economic environment of the 1980s and early 1990s caused companies to backpedal from earlier promises of career employment and to adopt a more market-oriented set of employment practices (Cappelli 1999). Under this new approach, the huge staffs that HR had devoted to training, development, and other services were put to the knife. Having more market-oriented employment practices meant that HR departments had less to offer line managers. To cut costs of remaining programs, HR activities were outsourced whenever possible, a trend that fit with the resurgence in the 1980s of a financial approach to management, whereby corporations shed activities in which they did not have a core competence (Lever 1999). This created a boom business for compensation consultants and specialized firms providing services in payroll and benefits administration. The net result was a substantial shrinkage in the size of HR staffs and in the ratio of HR managers to employees (Csoka 1995, 11).[6]

The 1980s and 1990s also saw a new wave of organizational decentralization, continuing a process that had started in the 1960s. Decentralization was partly a cost-cutting move, intended to shrink the size of what were now perceived as bloated headquarters. It was also part of an effort to differentiate business-unit policies so as to fit units more closely to the needs of rapidly changing and increasingly diverse markets (Kramer 1998). Operating managers now became more involved in hiring, evaluating, and paying their employees. Facilitating decentralization was the greater availability of computing power throughout the organization, which allowed companies to put many of their HR systems online—from recruitment through retirement—and thus cut costs in the HR area (Yeung and Brockbank 1999). Another development that shifted power away from HR departments to operating managers was the rise of the quality and high-performance movements, a broad-based effort to improve product and service quality through employee involvement in management decisions. Unlike the QWL movement, this effort was initiated by line managers—not by HR staff—with the result that HR sometimes was viewed as irrelevant to quality efforts in the workplace. Instead of HR providing programs to line managers, the latter were taking initiative on their own (Caimano, Canavan, and Hill 1999).

Corporate restructuring and stronger alignment with Wall Street created major dilemmas for HR managers. The financial approach to management meant that decisions increasingly were based on short term considerations of costs and benefits and that these costs and benefits had to be quantifiable (Lafferty 1996). The age-old problem in HR, of course, was that while the costs were quantifiable and short term, the benefits were not. (For example, developing senior managers inside large multinational companies can take from ten to fifteen years.) It became increasingly difficult to justify such things as layoff-avoidance policies or career development programs. With employees viewed as costs and line managers taking greater control, HR managers faced a choice. They could buck the corporate trend, insist on the virtues of employee-centered HR policies, emphasize the long term, and persist in being employee advocates. Or they could shift to a more hard-headed approach, one in which they were seen as business partners with line management and strategic partners to finance and accounting. For those HR managers who wanted to keep their jobs, the decision was a no-brainer. As one HR manager said, "Our role has dramatically changed from pacifying disgruntled employees to consulting with internal customers. We have moved from being focused solely on employees to a business orientation. Being here primarily to support the business is a fundamental mindset change" (Csoka 1995, 31).

As old roles fell out of favor, it was unclear what, exactly, would be HR's responsibilities under its new role as business and strategic partner. Calling HR the business partner of line management sounded impressive, but it had the unfortunate effect of leaving line managers free to do a mediocre job of managing employees. Research showed that line managers did not have the skill sets that would make them effective supervisors. They were strong at putting technical expertise to practical use and in getting things done for customers. But they were weak at being team builders, at communicating with subordinates, and in selecting and motivating employees (Lombardo and Eichinger 1997). These were areas in which HR professionals had much to contribute, of course. But the attitude of many line managers was "Don't call us; we'll call you," and the phone never rang. Lacking external legitimators such as government and tight labor markets, HR found itself losing leverage with line managers, who viewed HR as less important than other functions inside the organization. Said one report in 1995, "HR finds itself facing a crisis of confidence and credibility with line managers and business people" (Csoka 1995, 9).

Taking a "hard" approach did have the effect of aligning HR with the dominant mind-set inside companies. As one senior HR manager said, "We want to show we are not the soft-hearted (or soft-headed) personnel directors of yore, whose only mission seemed to be making sure forms were filled out properly, taking care of the Christmas party, and sending baby gifts" (ibid., 22). But in becoming "harder" and more numbers oriented, HR unwittingly set itself up for further cuts, since the easiest figures to generate were those related to resource consumption (Pfeffer 1997). Moreover, the emphasis on "hard" implicitly gave credence to the credo of line management that there was nothing more to managing employees in a decentralized market-oriented organization than a good pay-for-performance plan. But this was precisely what Frederick W. Taylor, an industrial engineer, had argued back in the early 1900s! It was as if sixty years of research on the psychological and social complexities of managing employees had never occurred. Part of the blame lies with HR managers themselves. Many lacked an understanding of that research base, which left them unable to persuasively articulate the intellectual rationale for HR, and also left them vulnerable to outsourcing to consultants. HR managers also often lacked an understanding of basic accounting and finance (Legge 1995).

Finally, while HR managers increasingly styled themselves as "strategic partners," the reality was that the function remained shut out of important decisions at the corporate level. When it came to reviewing business units or drawing up proposals for mergers and acquisitions, corporate HR managers were uninvolved until *after* the key decisions had been made (Marginson et al. 1993; Purcell and Ahlstrand 1994). That is, they carried out but did not design strategy. HR tended to be most uninvolved in decentralized, finance-oriented, predator-acquirer companies, the sort that became more prevalent in the 1980s. Thus, despite the brave new rhetoric, HR remained a relatively low-status function.

HR Since the Mid-1990s: A New Era?

Is the pendulum again swinging in HR's favor? There is evidence to suggest that it might be, with the impetus coming again from a tight labor market.

From 1997 to 2000, unemployment dropped sharply, bringing the lowest unemployment rates since the late 1960s. Managerial and skilled workers are in great demand. One headhunting agency reported that managers at companies announcing layoff plans often find themselves with several job offers in hand before the layoffs occur. As companies scramble for help, they are bolstering the size of their HR staffs devoted to recruiting. Meanwhile, they are luring new recruits with offers of traditional career opportunities. Employers are dusting off and reintroducing old-style development and training programs intended to reassure managers and professionals of their prospects. All of this means increased work and responsibility for HR professionals. Citibank, for example, despite layoffs in the mid-1990s, expects its workforce to grow in coming years. So it recently established a formal career development program for 10,000 managers. The company's vice president for HR said, "We want to make people feel that they have a long-term career with us" (*Business Week* 1998, 67).

Although the cooling of the economy that started late in 2000 will relieve some labor scarcity in cyclically sensitive industries and regions—such as the Midwest—demography is working against quick relief for employers. During the late 1980s and early 1990s, it was feasible to lay off large numbers of expensive older workers because replacement workers from the baby boom generation were plentiful. The cohort behind the boomers—Generation X—is relatively small, however. Current estimates are that the number of thirty-five- to forty-four-year-olds will decline by 15 percent between 2000 and 2015. There is little in sight to relieve the demographic pressure on employers. The long-term rise in female labor-force participation is leveling off, while white-collar productivity gains are small (Chambers et al. 1998).

At the same time, employers are becoming ever more dependent on skilled professional, managerial, and technical employees. In the technology and service industries that increasingly dominate the economy, intellectual capital is a company's chief competitive advantage. Hence "it is no longer in product markets but in intangible assets where advantage is built and defended" (Teece 1998, 77). With this has come greater attention to HR policies that facilitate morale, creativity, and retention. As the head of HR at a software company puts it, "At 5 a.m. ninety-five percent of our assets walk out the door. We have to have an environment that makes them want to walk back in the door the next morning" (Groves 1998, D-5). In short, employer concerns with scarcity and retention are likely to persist into the next century, bolstering the role of the HR function inside organizations.[7]

New theories of business strategy reflect the growing importance of human capital and other intangible assets. They emphasize that competitive advantage lies in the possession of inimitable or nonsubstitutable resources that other companies do not possess. These include human capital, intellectual property, organizational structure (including a distinctive corporate culture or approach to innovation), and long-term relations between employees and customers. While these resources are best thought of as a complement to, rather than a substitute for, other strategies such as cost minimization or product differentiation, they do shift the emphasis in business thinking toward internal factors that make a company distinctive. They also shift strategy away from purely financial considerations to those guided more by issues of core competency and synergy. Companies are realizing that they cannot achieve synergy while treating business units as differentiated, decentralized profit centers (Barney 1991; Purcell 1995; Foss 1997).

Where these new strategies have been adopted, they have created important responsibilities for HR managers. Companies that adhere to the new approach tend to be those that are willing to make long-term investments in their employees, whether through on-the-job learning or the formation of teams and other high-performance work practices. They tend to be companies in which HR is able to hold line managers accountable for HR-related outcomes and where HR is willing and able to defend employees against poor decisions made by line managers. They also tend to be companies that take seriously the creation of strong corporate cultures that foster employee morale, creativity, and commitment. This requires extensive communication and information sharing with employees as well as extensive employee services. Thus, in companies pursuing a resource-based approach, HR managers play key roles related to recruitment and retention, organization culture and values, and fitting of human capital to business strategies (Becker and Huselid 1999; Pfeffer 1998; Reichheld 1996).

Continued labor shortages, the emphasis on intellectual capital, and new resource-based models of competition all spell good news for HR's status in the corporation. But these are fragile reeds. If companies were, in fact, becoming more focused in their business strategies, we might expect to see a rise in industrial concentration levels as firms shed unrelated units by selling to larger-share competitors (and the latter made related acquisitions). In fact, concentration ratios fell from 1980 to 1995, suggesting that the financial model remained the dominant approach to strategy in most companies, although since 1995, there has been a modest increase in concentration ratios (White 2001). And the evidence that HR is becoming more involved in strategic activities—that it is a business partner—is largely anecdotal. The few systematic studies suggest that what links there are run from business strategy to HR policy—in other words, that HR is reactive and does not shape corporate strategy. The links are rather conventional stuff, such as succession planning and tying business goals to performance criteria and rewards (Gratton et al. 1999).

Other data similarly give the impression that HR continues to occupy a secondary niche in the corporate hierarchy. First, few CEOs in the United States have a background in HR. Second, there is a higher proportion of women and minorities in HR than in other managerial specialties, which is usually a sign of an occupation's low status.[8] Third, HR managers are paid less than most other managerial specialties: For ten primary management occupations, average annual earnings for HR managers ranked eighth lowest, just slightly above purchasing and transportation but well behind information systems, marketing, finance, and operations.[9] Finally, in contrast to countries such as Japan, where HR managers usually have a seat on the company's board, only six companies out of the Fortune 1000 accord the same privilege to their own HR manager.[10]

Conclusions

Over the past century, personnel management has established itself as a necessary staff function in the managerial hierarchy. But its status and power remain precarious due to the dominance of a least-cost mass-production mindset in the first half of this century and a short-term shareholder-driven mindset more recently. Hence, HR managers have repeatedly relied on the external environment to justify their existence. When the environment is threatening—that is, when labor shortages, government, or unions are driving up the cost of labor—HR is able to garner extra resources and a more influential voice in the affairs of the corporation. In this way, HR aligns itself with the financial-quantitative ethos, using cost to legitimize itself and its resources. But HR has had a difficult time securing and institutionalizing its power during less turbulent periods.

HR's problems are partly of its own making. It does not have strong and consistent theories that would justify its expertise inside the corporation. While there have been periodic attempts at professionalization, these have backfired because the price of HR specialization has been a lack of broad business experience. While personnel managers could bolster their position by being advocates of employee voice inside the corporation, personnel managers have shied away from this role in recent years. At various times in the past, external groups have helped to bolster the function's status inside the corporation—groups such as Industrial Relations Counselors, the Silver Bay conferences started by Clarence J. Hicks, and the Committee for Economic Development. Today, however, there are few such organizations, leaving HR managers dependent on the vagaries of external events.

The future is not entirely bleak. As noted, there are new approaches to business strategy that emphasize employees as a competitive resource. There is the ever-growing importance of intellectual capital. And one senses an emerging consensus in (HR) management that something must be done to bolster the function's status inside the corporation, at the top and, especially, at divisional and plant levels. Out of that sense of crisis might possibly emerge a new model for managing an organization's human resources. It is incumbent on those of us on the "outside" to lend our expertise and support in helping to develop that new model.

Notes

1. On the use of cooperative employment bureaus by smaller companies, especially for "union busting" purposes, see Harris (2000).
2. The literature on welfare capitalism is extensive. For an overview, see Gilson (1940), Scheinberg (1966), Brandes (1976), Berkowitz and McQuaid (1978), and Jacoby (1997).
3. For more on the SCC, see Scheinberg (1966) and Ozanne (1967).
4. For example, in 1928, Arthur H. Young gave a lecture in Philadelphia on regularizing employment (Harris 2000, 316).
5. IRC was founded in 1921 as a subgroup of Raymond Fosdick's personal law firm (Gitelman 1988; Domhoff 1996).
6. The number of HR managers shrank from 130,000 to 90,000 between 1988 and 1993, especially at divisional and unit levels. See Daniel J.B. Mitchell, "Incentives and Structure: Development of Pay Practices in the Twentieth Century," in this volume.
7. As recently as 1978, the book value of property, plant, and equipment of publicly traded corporations accounted for 83 percent of the market value of financial claims on the firm. By the end of 1997, it accounted for less than one third of the market value of those claims (Blair and Stout 1999, 744).
8. "Current Population Survey," U.S. Bureau of Labor Statistics (available on the Internet at ftp://ftp.bls.gov/pub/special.requests/lf/aat11.txt) shows that in 1999, women represented 49 percent of all managers but 60 percent of all personnel and labor relations managers; for blacks, the figures are 8 percent of managers but 11 percent of personnel managers.
9. Wage data are from "Occupational Employment Statistics," U.S. Bureau of Labor Statistics, available on the Internet at http://stats.bls.gov/news.release/ocwage.t01.htm.
10. Data on corporate boards kindly provided by Caroline Nahas of Korn/Ferry.

Employee Benefits and Social Insurance

The Welfare Side of Employee Relations

John F. Burton, Jr., and Daniel J.B. Mitchell

Introduction

The primary purpose of this chapter is to examine the role of employers in the development and evolution of employee benefits and social insurance during the twentieth century.[1] Employee benefits voluntarily provided by employers are one component of welfare capitalism, a human resource (HR) strategy that emerged among progressive employers early in the century as a way "to win workers' cooperation, loyalty, and hard work through positive HR practices, such as above-market pay, job security, employee benefits, promotion from within, and employee participation plans," and to avoid unions and fend off government intervention in labor markets (Kaufman 2001). Because employer-provided benefits are often competitive with or complementary to social insurance (benefits for workers provided by insurance arrangements operated or mandated by government), we also examine the history of social insurance.

Table 6.1, which provides data from the National Income and Product Accounts (NIPA) on employer-paid employee benefits and employer contributions for social insurance,[2] illustrates the enormous growth of these expenditures in the twentieth century. In 1929, employee benefits and social insurance represented 1.3 percent of wages and salaries; by 2000, these employer expenditures had increased to 18.2 percent of payroll.[3]

We identify five historical periods: the Progressive Era (1900–1920), the Period of Normalcy (the 1920s), the New Deal and World War II Era (1930–45), the Post–World War II Era through 1990, and the Modern Era of the 1990s. (A comprehensive study would also consider various subperiods, and we recognize that other authors might select different names or dates for their primary periods.) We examine the nature and growth of employee benefit and social insurance programs and the associated political, legal, and economic factors. We also focus on specific programs (such as retirement benefits and health insurance) with particularly important developments

Table 6.1

Employee Compensation and Components, 1929–2000

Year	Wages and salaries $ Billions	Other labor income (employee benefits) $ Billions	Other labor income (employee benefits) As % of wages and salaries	Employer contribution for social insurance $ Billions	Employer contribution for social insurance As % of wages and salaries	Compensation $ Billions	Compensation As % of wages and salaries
1929	50.5	0.7	1.3	0.0	0.0	51.1	101.3
1930	46.2	0.6	1.4	0.0	0.0	46.9	101.4
1935	36.7	0.6	1.7	0.0	0.0	37.4	101.8
1940	49.9	0.9	1.9	1.4	2.8	52.2	104.6
1945	117.5	2.3	2.0	3.5	3.0	123.3	104.9
1950	147.2	4.8	3.2	3.4	2.3	155.4	105.5
1955	212.1	8.5	4.0	5.2	2.5	225.8	106.5
1960	272.8	14.4	5.3	9.3	3.4	296.4	108.7
1965	363.7	22.7	6.2	13.1	3.6	399.5	109.8
1970	551.5	41.9	7.6	23.8	4.3	617.2	111.9
1975	814.7	87.6	10.8	46.7	5.7	949.0	116.5
1980	1,377.4	185.4	13.5	88.9	6.5	1,651.7	119.9
1985	1,995.2	282.3	14.1	147.7	7.4	2,425.2	121.6
1990	2,754.6	390.0	14.2	206.5	7.5	3,351.0	121.7
1995	3,441.1	497.0	14.4	264.5	7.7	4,202.5	122.1
2000	4,837.2	534.2	11.0	343.8	7.1	5,715.2	118.2

Source: U.S. Department of Commerce, Bureau of Economic Analysis, Tables 6.3A, 6.3B, and 6.3C (wages and salaries); 6.11A, 6.11B, and 6.11C (other labor income); 3.6 (employer contribution for social insurance); and 6.2A, 6.2B, and 6.2C (compensation).

during each period. For the entire scope of our study—the twentieth century—we are especially interested in the reasons why employers generally supported the increasing importance of employee benefits.

The Progressive Era

During the Progressive Era, 1900–1920, some employers instituted a broad range of employee benefits in what was known as "welfare work," and most states adopted the first social insurance program, workers' compensation (Tone 1997, 2). The underlying impetus for these new workplace practices can be traced to the developments in the United States in the last few decades of the nineteenth century, when the nation rapidly industrialized and much of the population moved from farms to urban areas (Jacoby 1997, 3). Industrialization and urbanization were accompanied by business cycles in which unemployment and wages fluctuated widely. In the 1890s, for example, the unemployment rate averaged 4.1 percent in 1890–92 and 13.1 percent in the rest of the decade (Bureau of the Census 1975, Series D-86). These unstable labor markets adversely affected workers, in part because they could not rely on homegrown food to tide them over during downturns (Jacoby 1997, 3–4).

Large firms emerged along with moguls of industry, who amassed considerable wealth and influence. Many labor markets were more like monopsonies—where employers had superior bargaining power—than like competitive markets, where employer needs and worker desires interacted to determine working conditions. As a result, workers were subject to long hours, onerous working conditions, and—for many children and women—employment in marginal jobs.

There were very few options available for dealing with these unfavorable by-products of industrialization. Some workers who prized their independence relied on individual savings and skills to cope with the adverse conditions (ibid., 4), and the most influential employer association of the time, the National Association of Manufacturers (NAM), was content to make employees individually responsible for their own situation (Tone 1997, 35–36).

A second option was collective action by workers, an effort to offset the superior bargaining power of employers by demanding higher wages and benefits that would ameliorate the economic insecurity associated with industrialization. Unions of various types emerged, ranging from the inclusive Knights of Labor to the craft-based unions affiliated with the American Federation of Labor (AFL). Almost all employers resisted independent unions, although the NAM was particularly concerned with the union "menace." There were a number of incidents of labor violence during this period, such as the Homestead, Pennsylvania, strike in 1892, which resulted in the deaths of nine strikers and seven Pinkerton detectives hired to guard the Carnegie Steel Corporation (ibid., 16, 28).[4]

A third option was government intervention. Federal and state governments responded to the labor strife primarily by assisting employers in their efforts to break strikes. Despite this, however, governments did seek to identify and remedy some of the adverse effects of industrialization through legislation (ibid., 23, 25–28). Thus, between 1877 and 1894, all northern industrial states but Illinois passed laws mandating sanitation and safety features in factories. By the beginning of the twentieth century, twenty-eight states had child labor laws that regulated matters such as the maximum number of working hours during a day, and sixteen states limited work hours for women. The federal government also acted to a limited extent. The U.S. Department of Labor was organized in 1888 and became a source of information for reform efforts, such as the favorable study of the German system of compulsory insurance published in 1893. The NAM and other more conservative elements of the employer community worked to defeat or weaken legislation that regulated employer practices or established social insurance programs, although (as discussed below) some employers supported the enactment of workers' compensation laws.

Finally, there was a small but influential group of progressive employers that began to voluntarily improve working conditions or indemnify workers for adverse outcomes (Jacoby 1997, 4). This strategy is generally known as welfare capitalism, although the term used in the Progressive Era was "welfare work."

Welfare Work

John R. Commons (1903) coined the term "welfare work," which he defined as "all those services which an employer may render to his work people over and above the payment of wages." The meaning of "welfare" at the time encompassed those services provided by employers on a voluntary basis as opposed to benefits mandated by government, and it is not to be confused with the modern meaning of "welfare"—namely, "grudging aid to the poor" (Tone 1997, 37, 38).[5]

The scope of benefits provided by some employers under welfare work was broad. Mandell (2002, 3–4) identifies four categories: (1) programs that promoted health and safety at the workplace, such as ventilation systems, guards on machinery, clean toilets, well-appointed restrooms, and factory gardens; (2) activities that focused on health and safety in the workers' homes, including counseling for personal matters and cooking classes; (3) a wide variety of educational, recreational, and social activities that ranged from English classes to noontime dancing; and (4) financial benefit plans, such as pensions, sickness benefits, and life and health insurance.

Beginning in 1904, the National Civic Federation (NCF), which was described as the "leading organization of politically conscious corporate leaders" throughout the Progressive Era and supported voluntary labor reform by employers, assisted individual companies in providing welfare work through its Welfare Department. By 1911, it had more than five hundred employers as Welfare Department members (Tone 1997, 38–39, 45–47).

The implementation of welfare work was not confined, however, to these employers. Jacoby (1997, 13) reports the NCF counted 2,500 firms pursuing a gamut of welfare activities. These firms typically were large (more than a thousand employees); were in industries in which workers exercised some control over production processes or in which workers influenced profitability through their demeanor; were located in larger cities, where there was more competition for workers; were in the North, where the threat of labor legislation was greater; and employed a relatively large share of women. Welfare work was also more prevalent in the expansive phase of the business cycle, when labor markets were tight, and it peaked during World War I, when workers were scarce (Tone 1997, 52–63).

The employers who provided such benefits were castigated by other employers and the NAM. Tone argues, however, that all three parties were often in the same political camp in their opposition to government intervention in the workplace. For instance, NCF employers opposed universal sickness insurance, in part, they argued, because U.S. workers were fiercely independent and did not want the government involved in attempts to improve working conditions. Gertrude Beck, secretary of the NCF Welfare Department, argued that government programs would undermine workers' morale because they would be viewed as "charity," which would erode individual initiative and destroy workers' self-respect; in contrast, welfare work, which allowed workers to earn benefits such as pensions through their hard work and loyalty, would validate manhood by supplying the financial basis for independence (ibid., 35–39, 41–42, 45).

The notion that government was not the appropriate source of most forms of protection for workers also resonated with much of the labor movement. Indeed, Samuel Gompers, president of the AFL, was vice president of the NCF until his death in 1924, and at least one third of the NCF Executive Committee were union members (ibid., 46). This alliance with employers was consistent with the unions' strategy of "voluntarism," which eschewed government support and endorsed collective action by workers as the preferred means to achieve labor's goals.

Employers who did adopt welfare work expressed a variety of motives for their policy. Some claimed to be solely motivated by kindness (ibid., 63), and undoubtedly, moral obligations—often reinforced by religious beliefs— did play a role (Jacoby 1997, 14). Mandell (2002) analogizes welfare work in a company to the Victorian family: the employer as the authoritative father, the employees as the subordinate children, and the welfare manager as the mother responsible for creating a harmonious household—a role facilitated by the fact that many welfare managers were women.[6]

Most employers admitted, however, "altruism within the workplace was a profit making venture" (Tone 1997, 64). Employers felt that workers would be cheaper and more productive if they spent their careers with a single firm rather than moving among firms in an open market; they also believed welfare work would inhibit the growth of unions and government regulation of the labor market (Jacoby 1997, 4, 14).

Why did employers pay additional compensation in the form of employee benefits and services rather than just pay workers higher wages? First, welfare work may have allowed employers to pay lower wages. Employers were less risk averse than employees, and they were better able to purchase insurance on more favorable terms because of economies of scale and the reluctance of insurers to sell insurance policies to individual employees (because of the adverse selection phenomenon). Both of these factors could lead workers to accept lower wages in exchange for employer-provided benefits,[7] although employers who provided benefits claimed that they were paying the same, if not better, wages than competing firms without the benefits. Second, since benefits such as pensions and vacations were only given to long-term employees, they promoted worker loyalty to the firm (Tone 1997, 79, 87), and longer tenures made it easier for employers to increase the work pace and hasten the introduction of new technologies (Jacoby 1997, 15). Third, paternalistic employers felt they knew better than workers how to spend additional funds: Higher wages might allow workers to patronize brothels and dance halls, a detriment to worker productivity, whereas employer-provided meals, supervised recreation, and health facilities would increase productivity (Tone 1997, 79–80)—arguably a motivation more properly termed condescension and manipulation (Jacoby 1997, 15).

Retirement Benefits

Employee Benefits

Retirement benefits were the most expensive component of employee benefits. The Grand Trunk Railway of Canada organized the first pension system in North America in 1874, and the American Express Company established the first private pension plan in the United States in 1875. After the turn of the century, pension plans spread rapidly through the railroad industry, were predominately noncontributory (i.e., employers paid all of the costs),[8] and by 1920, covered 76 percent of all railroad employees. The public utilities, banking, and insurance industries also established noncontributory pension plans between 1900 and 1920, and Carnegie Steel Company set up the first enduring pension plan in manufacturing in 1901 (Latimer 1932a, 20, 27).

Latimer reports that in all U.S. and Canadian industries, employers established 12 pension plans between 1874 and 1900 and another 275 plans between 1901 and 1920; 271 were still operating in 1929 and covered 2.3 million employees, almost all (97.6 percent) in noncontributory plans (ibid., 42, 45). A few unions had also developed pension plans in this period—the Granite Cutters' plan created in 1905 was the first to actually pay benefits from a specific fund designated for pensions—and by 1920, union pension plans protected 264,700 workers, or 5.2 percent of total union membership (Latimer. 1932b, 21, 128).

Social Insurance

Between the mid-1870s and 1920, many elderly Union veterans of the Civil War received federally funded old-age pensions—"nearly two-thirds of the native white persons over sixty-five years of age," excluding the South (Rubinow 1913, 407). Rubinow predicted that these pensions would serve as an "entering wedge for a national system of old-age pensions" because the rapid decline in the number of surviving veterans would free up funds for a national scheme (p. 409). However, some scholars and reformers argue that the Civil War pensions became instead an obstacle to a broad system of pensions in the Progressive Era, repelled as many reform-minded Americans were by the "political corruption" associated with the pensions (Skocpol 1992, 532–33).[9]

Another obstacle to a federal program of national old-age pensions was its constitutionality with respect to private-sector employees. The U.S. Supreme Court's conservative interpretation of the commerce clause of the Constitution prevented enactment of any federal social insurance programs and protective labor legislation for private-sector (nongovernment) workers. (Civil War veterans had been government employees and thus escaped this constraint.) Thus, it was left to the states to legislate protection for most workers. A 1909 proposal to establish an "Old-Age Home Guard of the United States," which would permit men and women over sixty-five to enlist in order to receive pensions as "pay," was an ingenious but ultimately unsuccessful effort to finesse this constitutional issue (Rubinow 1913, 410–11).

During the 1910s, the constitutional limit on federal action prompted forty states to legislate "mothers' pensions"—financial support for widowed mothers—which, however, did not become a basis for a broad-based program applicable to workers, in part because of another legal constraint. State and federal constitutions were generally interpreted to limit efforts to regulate working conditions in the belief that such laws would infringe on the rights of workers and employees to freely negotiate contracts. Gender-based reforms, a hallmark of the Progressive Era, were a very significant exception: The courts upheld interference with "free contracts" rights to protect female workers (all being actual or potential mothers, in the courts' eyes) (Skocpol 1992, 530–31).

Workers' Compensation

Until the early twentieth century, the only remedy available for a worker injured at work was a common-law negligence suit against the employer. If the employee won the suit, the recovery could be substantial, as the damages could include compensation for lost wages and such nonpecuniary consequences as pain and suffering. However, even if the worker could prove the employer was negligent, a negligent employer had several defenses that were insurmountable legal hurdles for many workers.[10] Initial reforms took the form of employer liability acts, which eliminated some of these employer defenses. Nonetheless, employees still had to prove negligence, which remained a significant obstacle to recovery.[11] The conventional wisdom in the early twentieth century was that the average award in negligence suits was low.[12] However, the occasional large award prevented employers from being entirely satisfied with this legal remedy.[13]

Workers' compensation statutes, which provide cash benefits and medical care to injured workers, were designed to overcome the perceived deficiencies of the common law and employer liability acts. The workers' compensation principle includes liability of the employer *without fault:* The employee need not prove negligence by the employer, only that the injury is "work related" (although there are legal obstacles to meeting the work-related test, in many cases); however, the benefits paid to the workers under the program are the employer's only liability for work-related injuries and diseases. Thus, workers' compensation statutes eliminated the employee's right to sue the employer for negligence (although there are limited exceptions to this exclusive remedy doctrine).

Williams and Barth (1973) review the political and legal factors that affected the adoption of workers' compensation:

> In 1898, the Social Reform Club of New York drafted a bill proposing automatic compensation for some types of industrial accidents. This bill was opposed by various labor organizations that did not accept the concept of compensation at this time. They were fearful that State development of guildlike provisions for pensions and other welfare benefits would reduce the workers' loyalty to the unions. They supported legislation modifying the employers' common law defenses which they believed would produce court awards much higher than automatic compensation. Agitation along these lines resulted in the Reform Club's compensation bill "dying on the drawing board" and ultimately led to the passage of employer liability statutes.
>
> In contrast to this opposition by labor leaders, many private corporations, particularly the railroads, had come to favor such plans.... The National Association of Manufacturers in 1910 openly endorsed the idea of workmen's compensation legislation. They realized that employer relief funds were too costly for small manufacturers and could not provide an adequate solution to the problem of industrial injuries....

By 1910, labor had shifted its position because of the failure of liability statutes to provide a remedy, and began to work actively for compensation legislation. The National Civic Federation, which claimed to represent business, labor, and the public, managed to unify the various labor organizations and gain the attention of the State legislatures. With labor and industry lobbying for effective compensation legislation, the movement toward reform was in full swing ... [and beginning with Wisconsin in 1911,] 24 jurisdictions had enacted such legislation by 1925. [Pp. 16–18]

This account must be viewed with caution, however, as historians disagree about the role of the NCF in enacting workers' compensation legislation. Weinstein (1968) argues that the NCF support of workers' compensation laws indicated the organization's willingness to support reform legislation. Tone disagrees, claiming instead that the NCF recognized the inevitability of some form of legislation to deal with industrial accidents and thus involved itself in the reform movement to gain public approval while it weakened the legislation. The model legislation drafted by the NCF did not propose universal coverage of employees, did not make the law mandatory for employers, and did not remove all employer defenses to liability, all of which were features of the laws actually enacted by the states during this period (1997, 48–49).

Why was workers' compensation for industrial accidents—a serious problem, to be sure[14]—the first and only U.S. social insurance program adopted between 1900 and 1920, while other deleterious by-products of industrialization such as unemployment were largely ignored? First of all, workers' compensation was unique among like issues in that a legal remedy—tort suits—already existed, and, according to Berkowitz and Berkowitz (1985, 160), "workers were beginning to enjoy considerable legal success at the beginning of the compensation era," which would have become a major concern to employers. Once employers recognized the need for a concerted response to the workplace-injury problem—and presumably assumed that the solution would be costly to most employers—they saw an advantage to a government program that would mandate participation (hence cost sharing) by most private-sector employers. Otherwise, a voluntary solution would enable a recalcitrant employer to opt out and thus gain a competitive advantage over more responsible employers.[15, 16, 17]

Obstacles to Social Insurance During This Era

There were several reasons why the reform movement that emerged in 1900–1920 had only limited success in enacting effective social insurance legislation to remedy the woes of workers affected by industrialization. Workers in general were never effectively organized into a political party, as was the case in some other countries, in part because of the emphasis on individualism in the United States. The union movement was largely confined to skilled workers, and the leaders of the AFL generally opposed government solutions, reflecting both their experience with the generally hostile government interventions in strikes and their belief that provision of benefits by government would undermine their organizing ability.

There were, to be sure, proponents of social insurance legislation. The reformers included experts who belonged to organizations such as the American Association for Labor Legislation, founded in 1906 to promote social insurance and protective labor legislation (Moss 1996, 1–2). The reformers drew not only on their critical analyses of industrialism and urbanization but also on foreign models of social insurance, including pensions in Germany and workers' compensation in Britain (Tone 1997, 30). These reformers were aided by journalists, dubbed the Muckrakers.[18]

Offsetting the efforts of reformers and journalists to enact social insurance laws were employers, who (except for their mixed support for workers' compensation statutes) opposed government intervention in the labor market. Many employers, including those who were proponents of welfare work, used employee benefits as a way to reduce the threat of government regulations and social insurance programs.[19] Tone (1997, 31–33) indicates this strategy was successful: By the end of the Progressive Era in 1920, welfare capitalism had triumphed over government reform.

Government officials and bureaucrats also arguably had an impact on the reform movement. Skocpol (1992, 41) is a leading proponent of what she terms the "structured polity" approach to explaining the origins and transformations of systems of social protection. Domhoff (1996, 231) explains this approach as "meaning that social movements, coalitions of pressure groups, and political parties must be given their due" in explaining the policies pursued by government. Skocpol argued that public sentiment and organizations based on gender that intended to honor and protect soldiers (men) and mothers were the effective political forces in the United States from the nineteenth into the early twentieth century. She further argued that the dearth of social insurance programs directed at workers in general can be explained by various factors, including early democratization for white males, which discouraged U.S. industrial workers from operating as a class-conscious political force (Skocpol 1992, 50). However, Skocpol's analysis has been challenged by other scholars, probably most aggressively by Domhoff, who argues that the dearth of social legislation in the United States during the Progressive Era, relative to other countries, "is that the working class is weaker and the capitalist class stronger in the United States than elsewhere" (1996, 238). He cites as evidence U.S. employers' success in defeating the movements for health insurance, unemployment insurance, and old-age pensions and in enacting workers' compensation programs that served their interests. The clash between the explanations for the development of government programs proposed by Skocpol and her associates and the class dominance theory asserted by Domhoff resurfaces later in this chapter in analyses of the 1930s.[20]

The Period of Normalcy

Welfare Capitalism

The political environment was more conservative in the 1920s than in the Progressive Era, and the threats of unionization and government intervention were less compelling (Jacoby 1997, 20–21). As a result, many employers who had viewed welfare work as a roadblock to unions or government intervention were reluctant to continue to expend resources on employee benefits. Indeed, when a labor surplus emerged after World War I, many employers dismantled their welfare work programs (Tone 1997, 62). Mandell (2002, 9–10) explains this, in part, as the unwillingness of employers to grant welfare managers (the mothers in her analogy of welfare work to the Victorian family) the authority they demanded to implement the obligations that corporate leaders (fathers) had to their employees (children). One consequence of this resistance was that welfare managers, largely women, were replaced by personnel managers, almost exclusively men, who were thought to have expertise in the "manly art of handling men."

An elite group of companies moved from the paternalism associated with welfare work in the Progressive Era to a comprehensive version of welfare capitalism in the 1920s, which included financial benefits, career jobs, company unions, and supervisor training. Although the companies that utilized this strategy employed at most only a fifth of the industrial workforce, "welfare capitalism came to be seen as America's future" (Jacoby 1997, 20, 32).

Jacoby indicates there were a "slew of welfare programs that provided monetary benefits: pensions, stock ownership plans, paid vacations, mortgage assistance, and health insurance"; although they had several objectives, the most important was "to create a body of stable, loyal, and productive employees" (ibid., 24). Thus, employers departed from the paternalistic pattern of the Progressive Era's welfare work by limiting benefits to those employees with a minimum level of tenure and providing benefits specifically desired by the workers.

The degree to which firms practiced welfare capitalism varied considerably, from large employers who endorsed the strategy, including employee benefits and company unions, to traditional companies which adopted few or none of the practices. Firms more likely to implement welfare capitalism had relatively low labor costs, were profitable, had steady product demand, were unorganized, and had centralized personnel departments (ibid., 26–29).

One employer organization that promoted welfare capitalism in the 1920s was the Special Conference Committee (SCC), which included executives from ten of America's leading companies. The "SCC had close ties to the Rockefeller interests; until 1933 it was chaired by Clarence J. Hicks, former head of the personnel department at Standard Oil of New Jersey" (ibid., 21).[21]

The 1920s also saw the emergence of Industrial Relations Counselors, Inc. (IRC), whose origins can be traced to the 1914 Ludlow Massacre at the Colorado Fuel and Iron Company (CF&I)—a Rockefeller family holding— where twenty-four striking miners and members of their families were killed by militiamen (see Kaufman's detailed discussion of IRC's history in Chapter 3 of this volume[22]). As a result of the ensuing negative publicity, John D. Rockefeller, Jr., under the tutelage of William Lyon Mackenzie King, the future Canadian prime minister, pursued a more enlightened labor relations policy in the family properties. He later created and funded a permanent staff in 1922 to carry this work forward through research and consultation. In 1926, this staff moved from the Rockefellers' law firm of Curtis, Fosdick, and Belknap to become Industrial Relations Counselors, Inc. (Hicks 1941, 119), which was underwritten by the Rockefeller family until the 1930s.[23] IRC conducted industrial relations studies, provided technical support to employers, and published information, such as *Vacations for Industrial Workers* (Mills 1927).The combined influence of the SCC and IRC helped spread the practice of welfare capitalism during the 1920s. Kaufman, in Chapter 4 of this volume, describes the distinctive philosophy promoted by IRC and the SCC (known as the "Rockefeller approach") as the promotion of greater cooperation and unity of interest between capital and labor to achieve both greater efficiency in the firm and an elevated moral and ethical basis for the employment relationship.

Health Benefits

Employee Benefits

Until the 1920s, employer-provided private health insurance in the modern sense was virtually unknown aside from certain employer-sponsored mutual benefit associations that paid some medical expenses and/or had arrangements with associated physicians. Some firms provided or allowed workers to purchase "group health and accident" policies, but these plans typically provided limited cash payments for lost work time rather than direct medical-care reimbursement or provision (National Industrial Conference Board [NICB] 1923, 117–19; 1929b, 16; 1931, 64).[24]

Medical services provided on the job might range from first aid for a work-related injury to more comprehensive treatment, including, in a few cases, company dentists and "oculists." Company-owned hospitals were available to some railroad workers, notably those of the Southern Pacific in San Francisco. Many firms had company doctors—at least in part as a response to workers' compensation requirements—who, in some cases, also screened potential new hires "in order to place employees in their proper work." These companies saw this as a strategy to reduce total compensation costs through selective expenditures on employee benefits (NICB 1921, 5).

Social Insurance

Several proposals for state-run health insurance plans were defeated in the years during and after World War I. The origins of the plans can be traced to 1915, when a group of reformers decided that the success in persuading states to enact workers' compensation statutes should be followed by efforts to enact health insurance. The American Association for Labor Legislation took the lead in a multiyear research, publicity, and legislation-drafting project. The draft laws were enacted nowhere, however. During the war, the concept of health insurance was suspect because some of the countries with such laws were the "enemy," and the political environment in the postwar period, with its "passionate striving for 'normalcy,' " was equally inhospitable. The opposition to health insurance consisted of a formidable "united front": Employers—led by several employer organizations, including the National Civic Federation—objected to paying their 40-percent share of the program, taxpayers objected to their 20-percent share, workers objected to their share of the tax, and many workers and unions also objected to the compulsory nature of the program. Insurance carriers, who feared government competition, and the medical profession, led by the American Medical Association, which perceived a threat to doctors' professional standing and income, also strongly opposed the health insurance legislation (Rubinow 1934, 207–208, 210–215).

Retirement Benefits

IRC played an important role in promoting and evaluating employee benefits, particularly retirement benefits, as evidenced by Latimer's (1932a) comprehensive survey of pension plans. Aside from the 287 pension plans in existence by the end of the Progressive Era, Latimer identified an additional 131 plans established between 1921 and 1929, 126 of which were still operating in 1929 and covered almost 508,000 workers, 84.1 percent in noncontributory plans.[25] All the employer pension plans surveyed by Latimer that were still in operation in 1929 covered 3.7 million workers, a maximum of 14.4 percent of the workers encompassed by his study (which excluded the public sector and the professional occupations). In addition, union pension plans covered 798,700 workers by 1930, 20.5 percent of total union membership (up from 5.2 percent coverage in 1920) (Latimer 1932a, 42, 46, 54–55; 1932b, 128).

Latimer cites three employer objectives that underpinned the adoption of pensions during both the Progressive Era and the 1920s. First was the advisability of removing from service elderly persons no longer able to perform their tasks efficiently, particularly when (as on the railroads) public safety was a consideration. Second was the desire to develop a stable and competent workforce: Pensions were thought to prevent strikes and promote long, loyal, and uninterrupted service. Third, a humane method of dealing with older (and incapacitated) workers enhanced a company's reputation and its ability to attract capable workers. Latimer concludes that rarely, if ever, had pensions been established as the result of demands from employees. Nonetheless, the assumption was that pensions, once offered by employers, would be very attractive to workers (Latimer 1932a, 18–19).[26]

Latimer goes on to provide an interesting assessment of the evidence concerning the effect of pensions on employer and employee behavior. He argues that (1) pension plans have no important effect on employment stability and an equally inconsequential effect on labor mobility, (2) pension plans have little effect on reducing strikes, (3) the evidence is "hardly compatible with the theory that pensions reduced the ability of unions to organize workers," and (4) those employers with pension plans did not consequently have reduced wages. He argues, however, that the pension plans he examined had serious deficiencies, such as insecurity (due to factors such as inadequate financing) and inflexibility (due to factors such as excessive service requirements for eligibility). He then offers a comprehensive outline of an ideal pension plan with twenty-nine main features (ibid., 753, 757, 760, 784, 902–38, 945–52). The Latimer study for IRC thus provides a commendable model for analysis of employee benefits: Theories about the effect of pensions on the behaviors of employers and employees are critically examined in light of available evidence, flaws of existing plans are identified, and guidance is provided for improved pension programs.

Although pensions were the most common form of employee benefit in the 1920s, Latimer's survey indicates nonetheless that most workers did not have pension coverage and vesting was not necessarily a feature for those who did. Since high turnover rates typically characterized the workforce of that era, many workers who were employed by successive firms with pension plans did not actually collect retirement benefits even if they lived to retirement age.

The result of such limited pension protection was that many elderly men either worked until they dropped or ended up as public charges. In the pre–New Deal period, the short-term solution for elderly without means of support was typically county- or charity-operated poorhouses and old-age assistance plans. Many in the 1920s believed the underlying problem to be inadequate thrift by workers when they were young and the "contempt for the careful husbanding of ... resources" and "free spending of money" by workers (not unlike today's lament about the lack of personal saving) (NICB 1929a, 1).

To counteract these unfortunate worker habits and instill more prudent worker behavior, employers often provided and facilitated savings arrangements. These began simply as a location for workers to deposit their savings if a financial institution was not available to handle such small sums and then evolved into either more formal arrangements with banks or credit unions or company-sponsored "investment trusts" (mutual funds), sometimes with disproportionate investment in the firm's own stock. Payroll deductions were used to promote regular saving. As with modern 401(k) plans, employers sometimes subsidized employee contributions, which in some instances were based on profit sharing. Apart from paternal stimulation of thrift, employers saw such plans as promoting "harmonious" labor relations, raising worker morale, and reducing labor turnover (ibid., 27–28, 32–33, 75).

In the absence of tax incentives for employers to "pay" for benefits, firms often limited themselves to providing mutual benefit associations through which employees could take care of their own needs; in return, employers expected to garner employee gratitude without the risk of employees becoming dependent on the firm for illness, disability, or old-age support. Some firms, however, would guarantee the payment of benefits if the associations ran into financial difficulties (National Industrial Conference Board [NICB] 1923, 94–95).

Explanation of the Developments

Employee Benefits

The total cost of employer-provided benefits was $650 million in 1929, 1.3 percent of payroll (Table 6.1). Although the NIPA data begin in 1929, these relatively low costs probably were typical of the 1920s. For example, Epstein (1936, 160–61) conducted a survey of 514 large corporations in 1926 and found that, on average, employers annually spent $17.04 per worker on all their welfare work, including old-age benefits, health insurance, restaurant subsidies, baseball clubs, and the like. The largest expenditure was for pensions at an annual per capita cost of $10.75. Since large employers were more likely to provide welfare work, the average expenditures for all employers were even less.

One reason for the paucity of employer-provided benefits in the 1920s is that the threat of unions, which had induced some firms to offer benefits during the prior two decades, declined in the aftermath of World War I. But even if unions had been more powerful in the 1920s, their goal would not necessarily have been to push for employer-paid benefits, which were often seen as paternalistic and in competition with what unions could provide themselves.

Another reason is that since few employees paid income taxes, there was no incentive for employers to provide nontaxable benefits to workers. There were, to be sure, a minority of employers who provided a comprehensive set of benefits to their employees during the 1920s, in part because of a conviction that welfare benefits were a good investment. Nonetheless, most employers apparently were not persuaded that such benefits improved profitability through reduced turnover or increased productivity, nor were they driven by the typical Progressive Era paternalistic belief that such benefits promoted thrift, temperance, and moral behavior among workers.

Social Insurance

The effort to establish a social insurance program for health care was a notable failure during the 1920s. However, the federal government established three welfare programs during this period, two related to World War I—vocational education to provide trained workers for the war effort and vocational rehabilitation to provide assistance to disabled veterans—and the third—an infant and maternal health program—partly as a political response to women, who had finally earned the right to vote (Berkowitz and McQuaid 1992, 73–76). These welfare programs helped lay the groundwork for the massive expansion in government programs in the era of the New Deal and World War II.

The New Deal and World War II Era

The U.S. economy plunged into a severe depression in the 1930s, with the unemployment rate soaring from 3.2 percent in 1929 to 24.9 percent in 1933 (Bureau of the Census 1975, Series D 86). The unemployment rate remained above 14 percent until 1941, when it dropped below 10 percent for the first time in more than a decade. The Depression caused a fundamental shift in the political environment, and the business community lost prestige and influence, in part because of its reactions to the crisis, illustrated by the following passage:

> "You are always going to have, once in so many years, difficulties in business, times that are prosperous and times that are not prosperous," said Albert H. Wiggin of the Chase. "There is no commission or any brain in the world that can prevent it." Senator La Follette, startled, asked Wiggin whether he thought the capacity for human suffering to be unlimited. "I think so," the banker replied.
>
> If depression was inherent in the system, then so was recovery.... Little could be worse than trying to meet an economic crisis by passing laws. "Lifting the individual's economic responsibility by legislation," said the President of the N.A.M., "is to promote the very habits of thriftlessness in his life which produce his dependency upon such a process." [Schlesinger 1957, 178]

The Depression also significantly affected unions. As the prestige of the business community waned, the appeal of unions waxed, which helped them attract members and political support. They shifted from an organizing strategy largely confined to skilled workers to one that included unskilled workers in mass-production industries. Furthermore, the futility of trying to achieve economic gains for workers in a dysfunctional labor market led most union leaders to abandon the policy of voluntarism, in which government action was considered a threat to the benefits that unions could provide their members, and to embrace government intervention in the labor market.

One consequence was the enactment of legislation favored by unions, including the National Labor Relations Act (NLRA) in 1935, which protected the rights of workers to organize, bargain collectively, and engage in strikes. The change in the statutory framework was accompanied by Supreme Court decisions that affirmed the right of Congress to use the Constitution's commerce clause to regulate industries that affected interstate commerce. Its 1937 decision in *National Labor Relations Board* v. *Jones and Laughlin Steel Company* upheld the constitutionality of the NLRA and was one of the decisions that helped validate enactment of protective labor legislation, such as the Fair Labor Standards Act, and social insurance programs during the 1930s.

Greater government intervention and union influence were both reinforced during World War II. The unemployment rate was below 2.0 percent from 1943 to 1945 (Bureau of the Census 1975, Series D 86), and the economy

Table 6.2

Selected Components of Employer Contribution for Social Insurance, 1929–2000

Year	Wages and salaries $ billions	OASDHI $ billions	OASDHI As % of wages and salaries	Unemployment insurance (UI) $ billions	Unemployment insurance (UI) As % of wages and salaries	Employer contribution for social insurance $ billions	Employer contribution for social insurance As % of wages and salaries
1929	50.5	0.0	0.0	0.0	0.0	0.0	0.0
1930	46.2	0.0	0.0	0.0	0.0	0.0	0.0
1935	36.7	0.0	0.0	0.0	0.0	0.0	0.0
1940	49.9	0.3	0.6	1.0	2.0	1.4	2.8
1945	117.5	0.6	0.5	1.4	1.2	3.5	3.0
1950	147.2	1.3	0.9	1.5	1.0	3.4	2.3
1955	212.1	2.8	1.3	1.6	0.8	5.2	2.5
1960	272.8	5.6	2.1	2.9	1.1	9.3	3.4
1965	363.7	8.3	2.3	3.8	1.0	13.1	3.6
1970	551.5	18.5	3.4	3.7	0.7	23.8	4.3
1975	814.7	36.1	4.4	7.4	0.9	46.7	5.7
1980	1,377.4	67.2	4.9	15.7	1.1	88.9	6.5
1985	1,995.2	114.3	5.7	25.5	1.3	147.7	7.4
1990	2,754.6	170.8	6.2	21.3	0.8	206.5	7.5
1995	3,441.1	217.5	6.3	29.3	0.9	264.5	7.7
2000	4,837.2	300.1	6.2	28.5	0.6	343.8	7.1

Source: U.S. Department of Commerce, Bureau of Economic Analysis, Tables 6.3A, 6.3B, and 6.3C (wages and salaries); 3.6 (OASDHI, unemployment insurance, and employer contribution for social insurance).

was regulated to suppress excess demand through mechanisms such as wartime wage controls, which limited increases in take-home pay but allowed employers to provide additional compensation as deferred income, including pensions.

As a result, employer contributions for employee benefits increased modestly between 1930 and 1945, from 1.4 percent to 2.0 percent of payroll. However, the most striking development during these fifteen years was the increase in employers' contributions for social insurance programs, including the unemployment insurance program, from nil to 3.0 percent of payroll (Tables 6.1 and 6.2).

Employee Benefits

As the economy slid into the Depression, a few companies tried valiantly to maintain their employee benefits programs or to provide assistance to workers, including extending emergency loans or waiving rent on company housing (Bernstein 1960, 290). But most employers were overwhelmed by the adverse economic conditions, and most company-provided benefits were cancelled: Niceties such as paid vacation were often suspended or discontinued (NICB 1935, 9); group life-insurance terminations exceeded new sales during 1929–33 (NICB 1934, 28); employees covered by noncontributory pensions were required to contribute (IRC 1936); and stock purchase plans tended to be discontinued as share values declined.

The Conference Board reported that "in some cases, it was difficult to explain the situation to certain uneducated elements of the working force who could not comprehend why they were not paid in full (by the stock plans) and, consequently, employee morale suffered." Even where companies had seemingly conservative savings arrangements with local banks, bank failures sometimes led to plan terminations and employee losses (NICB 1936a, 13–14, 23). IRC suggested that the rise of unions in the 1930s was partly attributable to embittered workers who felt management had enticed them into money-losing investments (IRC 1945b, 7).

While most companies reduced or eliminated employee benefits and other components of welfare capitalism, three leading companies—Kodak, Sears Roebuck, and Thompson Products—were an exception. "These modern manors preserved an American tradition of vehement employer opposition to organized labor" (Jacoby 1997, 7) and managed to avoid both unionization and the ravages of the Depression. They shifted the emphasis from control to consent, educating their managers about human relations and weakening the foreman's coercive "drive" system. In place of discretionary benefits, they provided generous welfare plans designed to supplement social insurance. Between the 1930s and 1960s, these firms succeeded in modernizing welfare capitalism into what Jacoby terms "a kinder, gentler sort of paternalism" (ibid., 5).

Jacoby identifies other vanguard companies (including Standard Oil of New Jersey) that did not feel the Depression's full fury and could more easily avoid layoffs, deter unionization, and maintain welfare programs (ibid., 33). In addition, IRC's efforts to promote such benefits were an important counterbalance to the tendency to cut benefits because of the economic duress. Clarence Hicks, who retired from Standard Oil of New Jersey in 1933 and subsequently became the chairman of the board of trustees of IRC, provides a rationale for these benefits when he argues (1941) that security of the employee is a matter of mutual concern for workers and management because insecure workers have a costly effect on efficiency; moreover, the type of worker that values security most dearly is the most effective employee because of his foresight, reliability, and initiative. Hicks also endorses employee involvement in the development, operation, and financing of these programs and the necessity of formal rules on which workers could rely (ibid. 98–102).

This argument for employee benefits was subject to a major qualification, however, articulated by Bryce Stewart (1930), a director of research for IRC, in this comment on employer unemployment insurance plans:

> It should be emphasized that no industry can safely undertake any industrial relations scheme on a voluntary basis except in so far as the scheme pays its own way. In the degree that efficiency is promoted and unit costs are reduced by greater stability and *esprit de corps* in the employed force, such plans may be counted on to broaden in scope. In so far as the costs are uneconomic, the operation of competition will ultimately bring about deliberalization and perhaps withdrawal of the plan. [p. 221]

Retirement Benefits

Employee Benefits

Between 1929 and 1932, the number of workers covered by employer-based pension plans and the adequacy of pension benefits declined significantly. Almost 10 percent of the pension systems operating in 1929 were discontinued, closed to new employees, or suspended by 1932, the most rapid rate of decline in the entire history of the pension movement. Those plans that did continue to operate during this period were more likely to require employee contributions and, for about 30 percent of the workers, to provide reduced benefits or have more difficult eligibility requirements (Latimer 1932a, 846, 861–66). Unions also experienced severe financial difficulties with their pension plans but were hobbled by the fear that to improve their financial condition through increased contribution rates would result in large losses of members (Latimer 1932b, 124–25)

Although many employers dropped or scaled back their pensions during the Depression, a number—primarily small firms relatively unaffected by the slump in the economy—did establish new plans—a great majority of which required employee contributions (Latimer 1932a, 886). The overall trend in pension plan contraction reversed dramatically between 1932 and 1938 with the creation of 281 new private pension plans, an unprecedented period of extraordinary rapid growth. More than 75 percent of the 515 old and new plans active in 1938 were contributory, but since many larger employers still maintained noncontributory plans, only about 29 percent of all covered workers were required to pay into their pension plans (Latimer and

Tufel 1940, 7). Many of these 515 plans provided pensions that were integrated with the old-age benefits provided by the new federal Social Security system enacted as part of the New Deal (discussed below). Latimer and Tufel caution, however, that there was little prospect that the government would provide "adequate retirement provisions for the great majority of industrial workers", and therefore there would be a continuing need for private retirement systems to supplement the Social Security benefits (ibid., 44). However, critics of private pension plans argued that these plans were unable to provide much protection. Epstein (1936, 148) asserted that they covered hardly more than 10 percent of all U.S. wage earners, and that because of service requirements and other limitations, no more than 5 to 10 percent of covered workers would eventually qualify for private benefits.

Social Insurance

The reduction in pension coverage as the Depression worsened in the early 1930s, coupled with declining employment opportunities, had a devastating effect on the economic status of older workers, which ultimately gave rise to populist social movements of the elderly, such as the Townsend Crusade and its proposed $200 monthly pensions. The New Deal political response was the creation of the Social Security system.

President Franklin D. Roosevelt appointed the Committee on Economic Security (CES) in 1934 to draft the Social Security Act. The committee consisted of (1) five Cabinet members, with Secretary of Labor Frances Perkins as chair and Edwin Witte from Wisconsin as executive director; (2) an Advisory Council of distinguished individuals outside the federal government, which included Walter C. Teagle, president of Standard Oil Company and later a member of IRC's board of trustees; and (3) a Technical Board of representatives from various federal departments and agencies, among them Murray Latimer, a former IRC employee and author of its 1932 volume on pension plans, who served as chairman of the Technical Board's Old Age Security Committee. As a key member of the Technical Board, Latimer argued against exempting employers with existing pension plans from the Social Security system and testified before Congress in favor of the legislation. One of the committee's key advisers was Professor J. Douglas Brown of Princeton University's Industrial Relations Section (Witte 1962, 24, 27, 30, 158–59).

The Old Age (OA) component of Social Security covered virtually all workers in the private sector engaged in commerce and industry. Although initially funded with appropriations from general revenues, beginning in 1937 employers and employees were subjected to a payroll tax to fund the program: The contribution rate between 1937 and 1949 for both employers and employees was 1.0 percent of the first $3,000 of pay. Benefits for retired workers aged sixty-five or older began in 1935; benefits for spouses and children were added in 1939, along with benefits for survivors of insured workers. The original law did not automatically increase old-age and survivor (OAS) benefits in response to changes in the Consumer Price Index (CPI). Features of Social Security's old-age benefits (trust funds, employer and employee contributions, benefits based on earnings history, etc.) were modeled after the private sector's pre–New Deal defined-benefit pension plans (Mitchell 2001).

Unemployment Insurance Benefits

The national unemployment insurance (UI) program was a component of the Social Security Act of 1935. However, it warrants separate treatment, in part because of the important contributions to the design of the program made by IRC.

The UI program is a federal-state system. The original UI program only covered employers with eight or more employees and excluded numerous types of employment, including farm workers, service for nonprofit organizations, and governmental employment (most of these exemptions have since been removed). A federal tax is assessed against all covered employers, which is largely forgone if a state has a UI program that meets several federal standards, including the use of experience rating for determining employer assessments. This federal-state system was adopted in part because of the fear that a strictly federal system would not survive a constitutional challenge. Although Supreme Court decisions by the late 1930s would have affirmed the constitutionality of a federal UI program, the federal-state system, once in place, has persisted.

IRC was a major contributor to the development of the unemployment insurance program. Between 1927 and 1932, IRC maintained a branch office at the International Labour Organization in Geneva from which it conducted research on unemployment insurance in several European countries. One result was a series of volumes describing social insurance in various countries (Great Britain by Gilson 1931; Switzerland by Spates and Rabinovitch 1931; Belgium by Kiehel 1932). In the United States, IRC surveyed the use of unemployment benefits by companies as a means to regularize employment (Stewart 1930). As the Depression deepened and the need for unemployment insurance became more pressing, Bryce Stewart, director of research for IRC, coauthored a blueprint for reform (Hansen et al. 1934).

After President Roosevelt appointed the CES, Stewart was selected under an unusual arrangement to head the staff responsible for the study of unemployment insurance. He was never placed on the payroll of the

CES, but almost the entire research staff of IRC was. Stewart and the IRC staff remained in New York throughout their assignment for the CES, and Merrill Murray, the director of the Minnesota Employment Service and one of Stewart's coauthors of the 1934 blueprint, was hired as Stewart's principal assistant and placed in the CES office in Washington (Witte 1962, 29).

Witte's account makes numerous references to Stewart's contribution to the activities of the CES. Nonetheless, he lost on two crucial design issues. Stewart supported a federal UI program—rather than a federal-state system—and as a second choice, a federal-state system with subsidies from the federal budget rather than a self-supporting system solely financed by employer contributions (ibid., 125). Had Stewart's views prevailed, the history of the UI program might have been quite different. For example, the pressures on states to compete for employers by scaling back benefits (to reduce employers' costs) might have been muted.

Explanation of the Developments

The 1930s provided the crucible in which the primary social insurance programs for the United States were created. There is a dispute among scholars about the determinants of the contents of the unemployment insurance and old-age programs (similar to the arguments concerning the influences on social insurance during the Progressive Era). Skocpol and her associates, in their state autonomy theory, argue that elected and appointed officials represent the state (i.e., government), which has its own interests and goals and which plays a major role in shaping legislation. Orloff (1993), who presents a modified version of this viewpoint for her analysis of the 1930s, attributes the legislative enactments to "the activities of party officials, elected leaders, state bureaucrats, social scientists, charity workers, and social reformers." She denigrates the influence of business in her assessment of the enactment of the Social Security Act of 1935: "The act passed overwhelmingly, showing the weakness of U.S. business as an interest group at this juncture of American history" (ibid. 76, 297).

Domhoff (1996) supports a "class dominance" view that emphasizes the influence of business interests on American policy making; he argues that a "Rockefeller Network," which funded *inter alia* the Social Science Research Council, the Industrial Relations Section at Princeton University, and IRC, dominated decisions about the design of the Social Security Act. Berkowitz (1996) agrees that Douglas Brown and Murray Latimer, both prominent figures in the "Rockefeller Network," were intimately involved in the creation of the old-age sections of the act and that many of their preferences prevailed in its design, including a national program. However, Brown, Latimer, and Walter Teagle lost the battle on other aspects of the old-age program such as the program's funding mechanism. As for unemployment insurance, Berkowitz indicates that IRC did help write various versions of the law. However, as Witte (1962) noted, Bryce Stewart's views did not prevail on several key issues, such as the solely federal versus federal-state cooperative design dispute. Berkowitz concludes: "In the contest [concerning the design of the Social Security system], IRC won some and lost some, just as Edwin Witte did. The Rockefellers were in the arena but did not always prevail" (1996, 4).

The Post–World War II Era Through 1990

Overview of Developments

Employee benefits surged after World War II, from 2.0 percent of payroll in 1945 to 13.5 percent in 1980, and then grew more slowly until reaching 14.2 percent of payroll in 1990 (Table 6.1). The primary sources of this increase were pension and profit-sharing plans, which increased from 1.5 percent of payroll to 7.5 percent between 1948 and 1980 before declining to 5.5 percent in 1990, and group health insurance, which steadily increased from 0.3 percent to 6.8 percent of payroll between 1948 and 1990 (Table 6.3).

This period also saw substantial increases in employer contributions for social insurance, which grew from 3.0 percent of payroll in 1945 to 7.5 percent in 1990. The largest source of this growth was due to the Social Security Old Age, Survivors Disability, and Health Insurance (OASDHI) program, for which employer expenditures increased from 0.5 percent to 6.2 percent of payroll in the forty-five year period (Table 6.2). Unemployment insurance contributions as a percent of payroll actually declined through much of this period, which reflected the generally buoyant economy. The combined employer expenditures on employee benefits and social insurance programs more than quadrupled between 1945 and 1990, from 4.9 percent of payroll to 21.7 percent. As discussed below, there were significant variations among firms in the size of expenditures.

Retirement Benefits

Employee Benefits

There was an explosive growth between 1950 and 1975 in the number of workers covered by private pension plans, from 9.8 million to 30.3 million workers. Several factors facilitated this proliferation of pension plans. The

Table 6.3

Selected Components of Other Labor Income (Employee Benefits), 1948–2000

Year	Wages and salaries $ Billions	Pension and profit sharing $ Billions	Pension and profit sharing As % of wages and salaries	Group health insurance $ Billions	Group health insurance As % of wages and salaries	Other labor income (employee benefits) $ Billions	Other labor income (employee benefits) As % of wages and salaries
1948	135.5	2.0	1.5	0.4	0.3	3.5	2.6
1950	147.2	2.9	1.9	0.7	0.5	4.8	3.2
1955	212.1	5.0	2.3	1.7	0.8	8.5	4.0
1960	272.8	8.2	3.0	3.4	1.2	14.4	5.3
1965	363.7	12.8	3.5	5.9	1.6	22.7	6.2
1970	551.5	23.4	4.2	12.1	2.2	41.9	7.6
1975	814.7	52.0	6.4	25.5	3.1	87.6	10.8
1980	1,377.4	102.8	7.5	61.0	4.4	185.4	13.5
1985	1,995.2	143.9	7.2	110.0	5.5	282.3	14.1
1990	2,754.6	151.8	5.5	188.6	6.8	390.0	14.2
1995	3,441.1	186.0	5.4	256.6	7.5	497.0	14.4
2000	4,837.2	183.3	3.8	300.1	6.2	534.2	11.0

Source: U.S. Department of Commerce, Bureau of Economic Analysis, Tables 6.3A, 6.3B, and 6.3C (wages and salaries); 6.11A, 6.11B, and 6.11C (pension and profit sharing, group health insurance, and other labor income).

federal tax code was amended during World War II to clarify the favorable tax treatment of pension and welfare funds. After the war, several major unions pressed for pensions, facilitated by the National Labor Relations Board's decision in a dispute between the United Steelworkers and the Inland Steel Company that pensions were a bargainable issue. The Steelworkers and the United Auto Workers made pensions a priority demand in negotiations, which culminated in strikes won by the unions. Pensions soon spread among other unionized and unorganized industries (Stein 1979, 6–8).

Significant spokespersons in the employer community also supported the adoption of pension plans. Pension plan design was now characterized in equity terms. Rather than just terminating elderly workers when they became "superannuated," IRC (1950) advised employers that

> [pension] benefits ... should be large enough to make elderly employees, if not positively willing to retire, at least willing to acquiesce in the termination of their service without any sense of grievance and with some realization that the company has made as generous provision for retirement as could be reasonably expected. [P. 1]

The growth of pension plans in the first twenty-five years after the war was accompanied by some abuses. In response, Congress enacted the Employee Retirement Income Security Act (ERISA) in 1974, which established standards in all areas of funding and administration that significantly changed the structure of the pension system (Stein 1979, 11). For example, ERISA established minimum requirements for vesting, required employers to cover employees on a basis that did not discriminate among workers, and created the Pension Benefit Guaranty Fund (PBGC) to guarantee benefits of defined benefit plans if they are terminated.

One immediate aftermath of ERISA was a drop in new plans and an increase in terminations of plans. Stein postulates that growth in coverage could be expected to decline, as most unionized and many large firms already had pension plans of some kind (ibid., 18, 21). His predictions were actually optimistic, as the percentage of the private-sector workforce covered by employer-sponsored pension plans declined from around 50 percent in the 1970s to around 45 percent in 1988 before rebounding to about 50 percent in 2000 (Munnell, Sunden, and Lidstone 2002). Munnell, Sunden, and Lidstone attribute the stability in the overall coverage figures between 1979 and 2000 to offsetting changes for men (down from about 55 to 51 percent of all male workers) and women (up from about 36 to about 44 percent of all female workers). The extent of coverage dropped for all males except those workers in the highest earning quintile (top 20 percent) due to declines in union membership and male employment at large firms and the rapid growth of 401(k) plans, which made employee participation in pension plans voluntary. Female coverage increased because of higher earnings, an increase in full-time work, and—to a lesser extent—because of increased unionization and female employment at large firms.

Munnell, Sunden, and Lidstone further report that the existence of pension plans varied sharply by size of firm: 68 percent of large firms (more than 1,000 employees) provided pensions in 2000 as compared with only 23 percent of small firms (fewer than 25 employees). Firms with less than 100 employees accounted for about one third of full-time employees, a factor in the low overall rate (50 percent) of workforce coverage.

Munnell, Sunden, and Lidstone also document a second major shift in private pension plans in recent decades—from defined benefit plans (which generally provide retirement benefits based on final salary times a percentage that increases with each year of service) to defined contribution plans (where the employer and often the employee contribute a specified dollar amount or percentage of earnings each year into an account, the balance of which is available for the employee upon retirement). The number of active participants in defined contribution plans increased from less than 30 percent of all pension plan participants in 1975 to almost 70 percent in 1997. The most rapidly growing type of defined contribution plan is the 401(k) plan, in which participation in the plan is voluntary and the employee as well as the employer can make pretax contributions to the plan. As Munnell, Sunden, and Lidstone indicate, these characteristics of 401(k) plans "shift a substantial portion of the burden for providing for retirement to the employee" (ibid., 6–7). Despite this drawback for workers, participants in 401(k) plans as a percentage of participants in all defined contribution plans increased from about 25 percent in 1984 to about 70 percent in 1997.

Munnell, Sunden, and Lidstone further note that the framers of ERISA did not mandate employer-sponsored retirement plans and instead provided the Individual Retirement Account (IRA) for workers whose employers did not provide a plan. However, as of 1996, only about 4 percent of eligible persons contributed to an IRA. As a result, the authors conclude:

> The pension story remains the same whether or not IRAs are included in the analysis. Private pension plans provide substantial benefits to middle- and upper-income workers, but a significant portion of the workforce— particularly those with low earnings—end up without any source of retirement income other than Social Security. [Ibid., 9]

Social Insurance

Social Security benefits were considerably enhanced in the decades following World War II (Social Security Administration 2000). Coverage was extended in several steps: farm and domestic workers in 1950; most professional self-employed workers in 1954; many federal employees in 1983; and most state and local government employees in 1986 and 1990. Automatic adjustments in Social Security benefits based on increases in the CPI began in 1972, with the formula modified in 1977 and 1983. Significant new benefits were added: disability insurance (DI) in 1956 for disabled workers who were fifty to sixty-four years old and for disabled children; DI benefits for younger workers in 1960; health insurance (HI) benefits, commonly referred to as Medicare, in 1966 for persons aged sixty-five or over; and the extension of HI benefits to disabled persons in 1972. These extensions of the Social Security program led to an increase in the contribution rate for both employees and employers: from 1.0 percent of the first $3,000 of earnings in 1937–49 to 7.65 percent of the first $51,300 of earnings in 1990.

The Social Security program experienced several financial problems in the postwar period. The 1972 formula for protecting benefits against inflation was defective and, coupled with high levels of unemployment that reduced contributions, led to amendments in 1977 that increased taxes and lowered benefits, in part by changing the cost-of-living-adjustment formula (Stein 1979, 8–9). Then in the early 1980s, the OAS trust fund was depleted, in part because of the static growth of wages (IRC 1996). A commission headed by Alan Greenspan recommended changes, enacted in 1983, that *inter alia* increased the tax rate, subjected some of the benefits to taxation, and increased the retirement age in stages.

These 1983 changes were supposed to solve the Social Security funding problem for seventy-five years, but they were based on economic and demographic assumptions that were too optimistic. One consequence has been a spate of proposals to significantly reform the OAS components of the program. Boskin (1986) proposed separating Social Security into two parts, one that would base OA benefits on worker contributions and one that would guarantee a minimum adequate level of retirement income for all citizens. His proposal was followed by others from conservative groups, such as the CATO Institute, to privatize at least a portion of the OA benefits by requiring participants to establish IRAs. Privatization has not yet been adopted, however, in part because many analysts agree that "effecting a smooth transition from social security to a privatized individual annuity program would be very difficult and expensive" (IRC 1996, 6).[27]

Health Benefits

Employee Benefits

Initially, unions had little enthusiasm for the sickness plans sometimes found in the nonunion workplaces that they organized in the prewar period (Bureau of Labor Statistics [BLS] 1942, 200). These sickness plans—essentially offerings of paid sick leave and disability (not modern health insurance)—persisted through the war (IRC 1945a). However, since doctor opposition in the 1930s and 1940s defeated proposals for government-run health insurance at the national and state levels, privately negotiated health insurance became commonplace in union agreements in the postwar period.

Unions tended, where such plans were available, to tilt toward "capitation" systems such as Kaiser Permanente in California or HIP in New York. The flat costs per employee were easier to budget and negotiate (Mitchell 2001). Such arrangements later became the models for modern HMOs and managed care. Fee-for-service plans, including major medical supplements—although often negotiated by unions—were seen by organized labor as obstacles to a better system of universal coverage and capitation (IRC 1957, 28).

As unions obtained health benefits for members, many nonunion employers also began to offer health insurance. The employer-provided plans became more comprehensive in the 1950s. Major medical insurance supplements that wrapped around more basic plans—or were part of them—covered 3.6 million workers and their dependents in 1956, up from less than 300,000 in 1952 (ibid., 3).

Hicks (1941, 103–6) had been a strong early advocate for group health insurance plans. He notes that younger workers had greater concern for the cost of illness than for insecurity in old age. He observed that the cost of treating illness had mounted steadily with the advance of medical science, and the legitimate concern of employers is not just with work-related illnesses, "but in the total health picture of the employee and his family." Hicks also points out the lower costs that resulted from employer-based group health insurance.

The rapid growth of employer-provided health care benefits between the end of World War II and the 1970s was followed by a period of decline. Between 1979 and 1992, the percentage of civilian, full-time, year-round workers who received health insurance through their employers dropped from 82 percent to 73 percent, according to data cited by Gottschalk (1998), who provides this explanation:

> From the Second World War until about the 1970s, employer-based health plans covered an increasing proportion of Americans. From then onward, however, coverage began to shrink as the initiative in industrial relations shifted radically from union to nonunion firms and from labor to management in ways that would have important consequences for the private-sector safety net, including health benefits. Many nonunion firms initially provided comparable wage and benefit packages to attract the best workers and to keep unions at bay. Yet as firms became increasingly adept at slowing and then stopping the expansion of collective bargaining and union membership, the initiative in the private sector shifted. In an important reversal, innovations in labor-management relations began to originate in nonunion firms and then spread to union ones. Nonunion firms were the first to experiment widely with cutbacks in benefits and with new ways of organizing the work place and the work force, notably a greater reliance on part-time and "contingent" workers. [Pp. 13–14]

Social Insurance

The United States stands in contrast to other developed countries because of the relatively limited government role in the provision of health insurance for active workers. Almost all of the attention given this issue of American exceptionalism has been focused on the federal government. Generally, the failure of the Truman Administration to enact a federal health plan in 1949 has been taken as the turning point after which the United States decisively moved to a system of (incomplete) job-based private coverage (Poen 1979). The difficulty with that view is that by 1949, job-based health care had already become embedded in the personnel practices of many firms, especially those with union contracts. As such, the actual turning point most likely came earlier.

Our candidates for the critical point and place are California at the end of World War II. Earl Warren, the governor and a progressive Republican, formulated his own proposal for a single-payer, fee-for-service comprehensive state health plan. The Warren plan, based on a 3 percent payroll-tax split between employers and workers, was presented to the California legislature in early 1945.

It is interesting to speculate on what would have happened if Warren had succeeded in implementing his plan. Senator Robert Wagner and others in the U.S. Congress who supported government-provided health insurance might have shifted their objectives toward a federal-state partnership, perhaps using unemployment insurance as the model. A plan based at the state level might have had more appeal to conservatives in Congress than a federal program. The Truman plan of 1949 might have followed a model of supporting existing state initiatives rather than the purely federal program the president actually proposed.

Alas, Warren was unable to pass his proposal. Part of his problem was a split within organized labor. The California AFL backed the Warren plan, but the CIO insisted on a plan based on capitation rather than fee-for-service. Meanwhile, the California Medical Association, based on advice from its campaign consultant that it could not defeat the Warren proposal without an alternative model, substantially expanded its Blue Shield plan.[28]

There is a tendency to assume that the American system of incomplete employer-provided health insurance was inevitable. However, history suggests that had Warren been more careful in drafting and promoting his health proposal and had the AFL and CIO not been split, California and then the United States might have adopted a Canadian-style system of health insurance.

More recent prominent national efforts to enact health insurance include the plans proposed by President Nixon (Gottschalk 1998). The original Nixon plan proposed in 1971 required employers to pay 65 percent of the cost of the insurance premiums for employees who worked twenty-five hours or more per week. The plan would have maintained private insurance carriers, and so gained their support. It also received qualified support from the NAM and the U.S. Chamber of Commerce, although they argued that employers should bear a smaller share of the costs. The National Federation of Independent Business (NFIB) opposed the proposal, arguing that small employers could not afford the program. In addition, the labor movement and leading Democrats opposed the plan. Senator Ted Kennedy and Representative Martha Griffiths supported a national health insurance plan financed from a new payroll tax and general revenue; this would have made the federal government the single payer, eliminate commercial health care insurers, and provide all Americans with a package of benefits. After several years of stalemate, a new Nixon proposal was introduced in early 1974; the labor movement, still in favor of a single-payer model, opposed the new proposal, which now garnered the opposition of the NAM. Gottschalk asserts that the unwillingness of unions to endorse any compromise that fell short of full-blown national health insurance caused a rupture with some Democrats, including Senator Kennedy.

By the late 1970s, organized labor for the first time embraced the idea of health insurance based on mandates for employers, a strategy that might have led to the enactment of the Nixon plan if it had been adopted by unions earlier in the decade. Ironically, by the time labor was converted to the employer-mandate approach, the tide of employer interest was shifting away from providing benefits at the workplace. According to Gottschalk:

> With the retrenchment of the public-sector safety net and the decline of the unionized work force, employers began to feel less pressure to provide good benefits as a way to prevent the expansion of government programs or to compete with unionized firms for the top workers. In summarizing the tenor of a major conference in 1978 ... sponsored by the Conference Board, ... David A. Weeks concluded ... that the basic assumptions about employee benefits may no longer be true. He predicted that benefit packages would probably not continue to improve, and that employees would be required to contribute more for items like health insurance and pensions in the near future. Most significantly, he predicted that companies that were considered leaders in providing liberal benefits would no longer be given credit for their "progressiveness and farsightedness."[29] [Ibid., 13]

Workers' Compensation

Workers' compensation, the oldest of the social insurance programs, was criticized in the decades after World War II because benefits lagged behind wage increases and the proportion of the workforce covered was less than for the Social Security and unemployment insurance programs.[30] One consequence of the criticism is that the Occupational Safety and Health Act of 1970 (OSHAct) contained a section added at the insistence of New York

Senator Jacob Javits that established the National Commission on State Workmen's Compensation Law. Most of the members were Republicans screened by the Nixon White House, and many represented employers, private carriers, and state agencies—in part to ensure that the Commission did not recommend the same fate for state workers' compensation programs that had befallen state safety programs under the OSHAct—namely, federalization.

The Report of the National Commission on State Workmen's Compensation Laws (National Commission on State Workmen's Compensation Laws, 1972) was surprisingly critical of state workers' compensation programs, describing them as generally inadequate and inequitable. The Commission made eighty-four recommendations for virtually all aspects of state programs and designated nineteen of the recommendations dealing with coverage and benefit levels as essential. The Commission rejected federalization, that is, a federal takeover of state programs. However, the Commission members unanimously recommended that Congress should enact federal minimum standards for the state programs if states did not comply with the nineteen essential recommendations by 1975. The Commission offered the rationale for federal standards: Without a floor being placed under state coverage and benefits, states would be impeded from enacting adequate laws that would increase employers' costs because legislatures would be threatened by "the specter of the vanishing employer" fleeing to a lower-cost jurisdiction.

This attempt to introduce a federal presence into the workers' compensation programs was unsuccessful for several reasons. Many states improved their laws (although none complied with all nineteen essential recommendations). Senator Javits and Senator Williams from New Jersey introduced federal standards legislation that preceded the 1975 deadline and contained so many extraneous requirements that even the former chairman of the National Commission testified against the bill. Carriers and employers began to have second thoughts and eventually largely opposed the bill. The labor movement was ambivalent because most unions preferred federalization to federal standards. Furthermore, many participants in state workers' compensation programs, including attorneys, agency administrators, and lobbyists, resisted the loss of state control over the program. Eventually, the political climate turned more conservative and the moment for realigning the control of workers' compensation passed.

Explanation of the Developments

The postwar decades were generally prosperous. There were recessions, but the unemployment rate never exceeded 10 percent in any year between 1945 and 1990, and there were extended periods of prosperity, most notably the

1960s, when the longest peacetime expansion until then took place. Super-imposed on these business cycles were several secular economic trends that affected the development of employee benefits and social insurance programs, including the increasing competition in product markets and the growing reliance on contingent workers.

The political environment varied over these decades. To greatly simplify, the conservatives were dominant in the 1940s and 1950s (as witnessed by the enactment of the Taft-Hartley Act in 1947 and the Landrum-Griffin Act in 1959, both of which favored management over labor); liberals had considerable influence in the 1960s and early 1970s (as evidenced by the Great Society legislation under President Johnson and the OSHAct and ERISA laws under Republican Administrations); and then more conservative views prevailed for the rest of the 1970s and 1980s.[31] The most significant development concerning participants in the political process involved unions, which grew after the war to encompass about one third of the labor force by the mid-1950s, and then generally declined for the balance of the period.

Employee Benefits

The tax code was an important reason for the growth of employee benefits in the first few decades after the war. Both the union and nonunion sectors were stimulated to create health, pension, and other employee benefits. Larger firms became more aware of "tax efficiency" in their benefit offerings, probably because they had personnel managers who could understand the concept. Thus, for example, large firm pension plans tended to be noncontributory, unlike many of those in small firm plans, where employees paid their share of the pension expense in after-tax dollars (IRC 1949, 13–16).

Further changes in the tax laws may have contributed to the decline in the prevalence of employer-provided pensions later in the postwar era. The marginal tax rates for individuals were cut during the Reagan Administration in the 1980s, which reduced the incentives for employees to pressure employers to pick up a larger share of retirement plan costs. Reagan and Turner (2000, 476–77) estimate that these declining tax rates explain almost 20 percent of the decrease in private pension-plan coverage of young males between 1979 and 1988.

In the years immediately after the war, the strong union movement that emerged made pensions and other employee benefits major bargaining goals, aided by favorable court rulings that required employers to bargain about such matters. A result, in part, of the dramatic growth in union plans was that the U.S. BLS as well as private organizations such as the Bureau of National Affairs, issued numerous reports for several decades after the war that summarized the terms of union health insurance and pension plans. The 1947 Taft-Hartley Act essentially made union contracts public documents; thus, union plans were easier to report than nonunion plans, which were not public information. Such a high profile made union practices appear as norms of good practice to be emulated and helped to spread employee benefits to more and more workplaces.[32]

Although corporations that remained nonunion in the immediate postwar period were generally overlooked by industrial relations scholars or, worse, viewed as aberrant (Jacoby 1997), by the 1970s, nonunion employers had became the innovators in human resource management techniques and began a trend of shifting employee benefits expense to workers (Gottschalk 1998). This trend grew as employers sought to offset their obligations and costs under federal legislation, such as the OSHAct and ERISA, and unions, declining in strength, could offer only limited opposition.

Social Insurance

In the early postwar decades, when unions were at their peak strength and some segments of the employer community supported reform, social insurance programs expanded. After about 1970, the political environment changed, and efforts to establish new programs or enact federal standards were defeated (in some instances, facilitated by union strategic errors), and by the end of the period, important components of Social Security were threatened with privatization.

More specifically, the Social Security program was greatly expanded in the first few decades after the war, including increases in the generosity of OAS benefits and the addition of disability benefits. From the 1970s on, however, a series of funding problems forced an increase in taxes and a scaling back of the protection. By the 1980s, the program faced more fundamental challenges, such as the proposals to privatize the OA component. These proposals reflected factors such as the aging of the workforce and the changing political environment.

Several efforts to provide health care coverage for working Americans were unsuccessful. The California proposal of Governor Warren almost succeeded in the 1940s and could have established a movement toward state-level health care plans.[33] One chance for national health care reform during the Nixon Administration was scuttled in part because unions insisted on a comprehensive plan run by the government rather than using employer mandates as a primary source of the protection. During this period, many employers were willing to support the employment-based financing mechanism, and so union intransigence was a major reason why the plan failed.

Workers' compensation also had a possibility for national involvement in the 1970s, when the deficiencies of the program convinced representatives of most participants in the system—including employers—that federal standards were necessary for the survival of the program. In this instance, overly aggressive legislative proposals in Congress, lack of full support from labor (since many unions wanted complete federalization of the program), and the change in the political climate by the late 1970s doomed the effort.

The Modern Era of the 1990s

Overview of Developments

The six-decade trend of increasing rates of employer expenditures on employee benefits and social insurance programs, which began in 1929, reversed during the 1990s. Employee benefits dropped significantly, from 14.2 percent of payroll in 1990 to 11.0 percent in 2000, largely due to lower employer contributions for pensions and health insurance (Table 6.3). Employers' social insurance contributions also declined, albeit less dramatically, from 7.5 percent of payroll in 1990 to 7.1 percent in 2000 (Table 6.1). Employer's Social Security contributions remained at 6.2 percent of payroll, but there was a decline in unemployment insurance program taxes (Table 6.2) and a sharp drop in the employers' costs of workers' compensation from 2.18 percent of covered payroll in 1990 to 1.25 percent in 2000 (Mont et al. 2002, Table 13).

Expenditure rates for employee benefits were not uniform among either employers or segments of the workforce, however. Although 48 percent of all private-sector workers participated in retirement plans in 1999, for instance, participation rates noticeably varied by employee category, as illustrated by the following BLS data (2001b, Table 1):

- 79 percent of unionized vs. 44 percent of nonunionized workers
- 69 percent of professional/technical employees vs. 45 percent of clerical/sales employees and 42 percent of blue-collar/service employees
- 56 percent of full-time vs. 21 percent of part-time workers
- 81 percent of employees in large firms (with 2,500 or more employees) vs. 30 percent in small firms (with less than 50 employees)

Although 53 percent of all private-sector workers had health care benefits in 1999—somewhat higher coverage than retirement benefits—there were similar disparities in coverage by employee category and employer size:

- 73 percent of unionized vs. 51 percent of nonunionized workers
- 68 percent of professional/technical employees vs. 51 percent of clerical/sales and 48 percent of blue-collar/service workers

Table 6.4

Percentage of Total Compensation Represented by Selected Benefits, March 2001

| | Percent of total compensation* | | | | | |
| | Type of establishment | | | Number of employees | | |
Type of benefit	All private	Union	Nonunion	1–99	100–499	500+
Defined benefit retirement plans	1.0	3.9	0.6	0.7	1.0	1.6
Defined contribution retirement plans	1.9	1.6	2.0	1.7	1.9	2.3
Health insurance	5.6	8.1	5.2	4.9	6.0	6.4
Legally required benefits	8.3	8.4	8.3	8.9	8.2	7.4

Source: U.S. Bureau of Labor Statistics 2001a.
*For private-sector employers.

- 64 percent of full-time vs. 14 percent of part-time employees
- 71 percent of employees in large firms vs. 41 percent in small firms

The most prevalent employee benefits in 1999 were paid vacations and paid holidays (79 percent and 75 percent, respectively, of all private-sector workers) (ibid., Table 3). Conversely, there were limited offerings of more esoteric benefits, such as employer assistance for child care (6 percent of workers eligible), adoption assistance (6 percent), subsidized commuting (4 percent), and fitness centers (9 percent) (ibid., Tables 3–5). There were some firms in the 1990s that attracted workers with even more exotic benefits, such as corporate concierge services and lactation rooms for nursing mothers, but these benefits were uncommon and were usually found only in large firms or particular industries; for example, although 17 percent of all workers had wellness programs, these were available to 30 percent of employees in the finance, insurance, and real estate sectors (but to only 4 percent in the retail trade) and to 54 percent of employees in large firms (but to only 4 percent in small firms).

The BLS data in Table 6.4 point to the (intercorrelated) impact of size of establishment and unionization on employer expenditures for employee benefits and social insurance. The patterns for employee benefits and social insurance differ. Defined-benefit pensions and health benefits both represent a larger fraction of the compensation dollar in larger establishments and in union establishments. Defined-contribution pension expenditures are correlated positively with size, but negatively with unionization. Conversely, legally required benefits (the social insurance programs)—required for almost all employers regardless of size—are essentially the same percentage of compensation in both unionized and nonunion firms, and there is a tendency for these benefits to decline as a percentage of compensation as firm size increases.

Retirement Benefits

The share of private-sector workers who participated in pension plans increased from about 45 percent in 1990 to more than 50 percent in 2000 (Munnell, Sunden, and Lidstone 2002, Figure 1). Despite the increase in coverage, employers were able to reduce their expenditures on retirement benefits from 5.5 percent to 3.8 percent of payroll because the rise in the stock market caused many defined-benefit pension plans to be funded in excess of actuarial needs. There were no major changes in the OA component of the Social Security program during the 1990s, although the discussions of privatization continued and intensified.

Health Benefits

Employer contributions for health insurance declined after 1995, in part a temporary victory in the battle to contain costs through the implementation of managed care. In addition, some employers in the 1990s eliminated their health insurance plans, and many of the plans that did continue shifted some of the cost to employees through increased deductibles, copayments, and employee contributions toward premiums.

Congress rejected the major social insurance initiative in health care, namely the Clinton Administration's proposal of 1993–94. The plan contained a complex set of provisions and would have relied on employers to finance most of the program. While the notion of employer-based financing now garnered the support of the labor movement, employers generally opposed the legislation and private insurance carriers led a successful attack on the proposal.

Other Social Insurance Programs

The long expansion in the economy during the 1990s reduced benefit payments and employer contributions for the unemployment insurance program. The workers' compensation program also experienced lower costs as a result of an unanticipated decline in workplace injuries and a concerted effort by employers and carriers to constrict eligibility and reduce benefits (Spieler and Burton 1998). The reason for employer and insurer reform efforts was the significant increases in employers' costs and benefits in the late 1980s and early 1990s, as well as underwriting losses for the carriers. The success of the employers and carriers reflects, in part, their increasing power relative to unions in many states.

Explanation of the Developments

This discussion is abbreviated because some of the developments of the 1990s are examined in the concluding section and placed in a longer-term context. The longest period of economic expansion in U.S. history began in 1991 and lasted for the rest of the decade. The unemployment rate peaked at 7.5 percent in 1992 and then declined every year through 1999, when the rate was 4.2 percent, which resulted in a decade average of 5.8 percent. The annual increase in the CPI dropped from 5.4 percent in 1990 to 1.6 percent in 1998 before increasing to 2.2 percent in 1999, which resulted in a 3.0 percent average annual increase for the decade. Medical care costs also increased at a modest rate in the 1990s, averaging only a 5.3 percent annual increment for the decade. Perhaps the most spectacular performance of the 1990s was the stock market: The Standard and Poor's (S&P) composite index almost quadrupled during the decade, from 334.59 in 1990 to 1,327.33 in 1999. However, stock prices increased much more rapidly than corporate earnings, as witnessed by the decline in the S&P earnings/price ratio from 6.47 percent in 1990 to 3.17 percent in 1999 (Clinton 2001, Tables B-42, B-62, B-64, B-95).

The 1990s can be characterized as a decade when there were wide variations among employers in the variety of benefits provided to workers, but the overall employer expenditures of employee benefits and social insurance programs declined. There were several reasons for the overall pattern of decline and the shifts in expenditures among some categories of benefits. The booming economy and stock market reduced the funding requirements for existing programs, notably retirement benefits and unemployment insurance. In some areas, such as health care, employers shifted some of the costs to employees. For retirement benefits, there was a reduction in the relative importance of employee benefits (employer expenditures for pensions and profit sharing dropped from 5.5 to 3.8 percent of payroll between 1990 and 2000) compared with the importance of social insurance (employer contributions to OASDHI remained at 6.2 percent of payroll over this period). There also apparently were shifts among social insurance programs in expenditures for some sources of income loss. For example, while workers' compensation benefits and costs plummeted in the decade, the expenditures of the Social Security DI program increased, leading to speculation that some of the costs of work-related disabilities were shifted from the state programs to the federal program (Mont et al. 2002).

Conclusion: Employee Benefits and Social Insurance in the Twentieth Century and Beyond

This section summarizes the factors that contributed most significantly to the development and growth of employee benefits and social insurance during the twentieth century and speculates about the future of employer expenditures for them. As shown in Table 6.1, compensation (which includes employer expenditures on employee benefits and social insurance) grew much more rapidly than wages and salaries after 1929. Legally required social insurance programs, such as Social Security benefits, account for some of this trend, along with the increased spread of employee benefits, most notably pensions and health insurance in the post–World War II era. There was a reversal of this trend in the 1990s, apparently in part because employees assumed a larger share of the economic risks associated with employment. The intriguing question is whether the experience of the last decade was a temporary or permanent reversal of the long-term trend toward greater employer expenditures.

The Economic Environment

The value of human capital has increased throughout the twentieth century as workers have become better educated and better trained and, as a result, have been able to create greater value for their employers and the economy as a whole. The carnage in the workplace that resulted from workplace injuries and diseases in the early part of the century reflected many employers' practices of treating workers as expendable commodities. As workers have become increasingly skilled, employers have had greater incentives to retain current workers and their skills. Thus, fringe benefits that tie workers to a particular employer have become an increasingly rational use of resources and are likely to continue to be in the future.

Economic fluctuations have certainly influenced the developments of the twentieth century. The leading example is the Depression of the 1930s, which produced a national problem of unemployment that, in turn, created a climate for reform. The previous solutions to the unemployment problem— reliance on the private sector to produce jobs and on the limited resources of public programs and private charities to care for chronically unemployed workers—came to be considered inadequate by management, labor, and the public.

Certain economic conditions of the past decade that enabled employers to reduce their expenditures on employee benefits and social insurance appear to be transitory. For example, a repeat of the stock market's performance seems unlikely given that it derived in large part from an unsustainable rise in stock prices that outstripped the growth in corporate earnings. Moreover, while the overall rate of inflation remains low through 2002, the modest increases in health care costs of the 1990s appear to have been replaced by double-digit jumps in health care insurance premiums.

Perhaps a more permanent legacy of the 1990s is that economic incentives for corporate management underwent a transition as their financial rewards became more closely tied to performance of company stock, based on the theory it would increase the alignment of financial interests between management and shareholders. However, the unintended consequence in some firms was the irresistible urge for management to inflate short-term profits by dubious or even illegal accounting techniques in order to artificially inflate stock prices. The time horizon for corporate planning appears to have shortened as a result, and we doubt that reforms resulting from the Enron and other scandals of 2002 will appreciably correct the management myopia.

Another significant economic development of the 1990s that appears likely to persist is the increasingly competitive environment that many firms face due to deregulation of domestic industries, the increasing integration of domestic and foreign markets via globalization, and the rapid pace of technological change. The increasing competition has abetted the tendency of management to think about short-term solutions as well as encourage management to shift risk to others—notably workers. One manifestation of this shifting of risks to employees is the emergence of the corporate strategy to retain permanent employees in "core" competencies of the firm while relying on contingent workers or employees of other firms for "noncore" firm functions, such as maintenance or HRM.

The Legal Environment

In the early part of the twentieth century, the Supreme Court's interpretation of the Constitution's commerce clause severely limited the ability of Congress to regulate employers or to establish social insurance programs. Thus, workers' compensation of necessity was established for private-sector workers by state laws. In addition, both the Supreme Court and state courts limited government efforts to regulate employment relations under the guise of protecting the rights of workers and employers to sign contracts. The exceptions were confined to subsets of the workforce for whom special treatment could be rationalized, such as women and children.

The courts in the 1930s largely overturned the legal doctrines that had restricted government intervention in the labor market. The reinterpretation of the commerce clause by the Supreme Court also permitted the federal government to potentially regulate all aspects of employment relations. Indeed, the legal factor likely to represent a continuing significant influence is the constitutional principle of preemption, under which states can only regulate employment relations, including employee benefits, with the "permission" of Congress. An obvious example is the regulation of pensions, whereby ERISA precludes states from regulating employers who provide such benefits (although insurers are still subject to state regulations).

The favorable tax treatment for employer expenditures on such programs as retirement plans and health insurance stimulated the growth of employee benefits and employers' contributions to them in the post–World War II period, although undoubtedly some employee benefits would exist absent such treatment. Woodbury and Huang (1991) estimate is that if tax preferences were eliminated, employer contributions to pensions would be halved and employer contributions to health insurance would be cut by more than one fifth.

The Political Environment

Economic crises affected the political environment during the twentieth century, most notably the Depression of the 1930s, which resulted in the ascendancy of President Roosevelt and the Democratic Party. The resulting New Deal included the most fundamental changes in government intervention in employment relations in U.S. history. Other changes in the political environment have been less dramatic, although the relationship between the economic environment and the political environment still can be identified. For example, the election in 1992 of President Clinton and Democratic majorities in both houses of Congress can be attributed in large part to the recession of the early 1990s.

The 1990s nonetheless exemplify why the economic environment is not a deterministic influence on the political environment. Congress reverted to Republican control in 1994, in part because of the increasing prominence of a conservative movement led by Newt Gingrich. Many of the debates of the 1990s, such as those about deregulation and privatization, still resonate and affect decisions concerning employee benefits and social insurance.

The political process can no longer be characterized as a struggle between traditional camps or interests. For example, President Clinton was identified with the "New Democrats," who endorsed positions on issues such as welfare reform that traditionally were associated with Republican (i.e., conservative) views. As another example, health care reform was shaped by the competing interests of insurers and trial lawyers more so than by those of labor and business. Perhaps the recent experience suggests that the key participants in the political process are now interest-group representatives, consultants, and think-tank wonks (not always mutually exclusive categories).

The experiences since 1990 provide little assistance in sorting out the conflict between the theorists who argue that class explains social policy (the Domhoff view) and those who argue there is an independent role for the state (including elected and appointed government officials) in affecting policy (the Skocpol view). The first theory gains credence from the synchronous strategy of the Bush II administration to eliminate the estate tax while cutting the growth of Medicaid benefits. The second theory seems compelling in explaining the demise of the Clinton health care reforms of the 1990s: The incompetence of the team responsible for the design of the plan provides a telling example of the influence of government bureaucrats on the fate of social insurance initiatives.

Retirement Benefits

The aging workforce ensures that the issue of economic security for retirees will become more pressing in coming decades. The high rates of returns on investments, which allowed employers to reduce pension plan contributions in the 1990s, are very unlikely to reoccur in coming decades. Indeed, in the short run, the stock market decline between 2000 and 2002 will probably require significant increases in employer contributions to fund defined benefit plans, which is likely to further encourage defined contribution plans.

The OAS components of Social Security are projected to begin to run a deficit within the next twenty years, given the current levels of benefits and payroll taxes. A de facto constraint on reform is an apparent unwillingness by Congress to increase the tax rate. One possible "solution" is to further reduce the CPI formula for benefit adjustments. A more fundamental type of reform involves partial privatization of the OAS program, perhaps by allowing individuals to invest some portion of their contributions. Although there is a precedent for private-sector involvement in social insurance, such as the workers' compensation program, the proposal for privatization of OAS benefits is highly charged and seems unlikely in the near future. In any case, privatization is unlikely to reduce the amount of employer contributions to Social Security.

Health Benefits

The problems of higher costs and inadequate coverage of workers are testing the capability of the workplace-based system of health care. It is not clear whether a fundamental solution is feasible. In the meantime, the likely outcome will be even higher costs for employers, coupled with greater cost shifting to employees and diminished coverage. Those employers who continue to provide health care are likely to face additional but limited regulations, similar to those provided by the Family and Medical Leave Act (FMLA).[34] One likely result will be an increasing disparity among employers in the extent of health care benefits provided to their workers.

Health insurance is sometimes regarded as a "merit good"—something we think people ought to have regardless of their preferences. Of course, that does not explain why we think people should have it *as part of their employment compensation packages* as opposed to other sources of provision. Outside the United States, for example, there are various health insurance programs run through governments or quasipublic institutions. Nonetheless, the failure of comprehensive health care reform in the 1990s has probably doomed any comprehensive solution for the next decade. Moreover, even incremental reform will be hard to achieve, as evidenced by the 2002 struggle to add prescription benefits to the Medicare program.

Unemployment Insurance

The unemployment insurance program will experience short-term problems as a result of the 2001 recession, such as exhaustion of benefits for many long-term unemployed and the depletion of state reserves. Perhaps the most challenging issue for the UI program is the extent to which funds collected from employer and employee contributions should be diverted to uses other than ameliorating the short-term effects of involuntary job loss due to economic conditions. For example, the UI funds have been used in New Jersey to provide medical care for uninsured patients, and now there is a proposal to fund cash benefits for workers who are temporarily unemployed because of health conditions covered by the FMLA.

Workers' Compensation

The early 2000s present a challenging situation for the private insurance industry, which is experiencing serious underwriting losses. However, unlike the experience of a decade earlier, the source is not escalating losses that result from higher benefit payments. Indeed benefits and costs as a percent of payroll have declined substantially since the mid-1990s. Rather, premiums are declining in part due to the increased competition among carriers, a result of deregulation of the insurance markets in most states (Thomason, Schmidle, and Burton 2001, 287–90). Since employers are not experiencing rapidly increasing costs for workers' compensation, it will be difficult for carriers to build political coalitions to further reduce benefits and tighten eligibility standards.[35]

There appears to be no prospect in the next decade of the federal government displacing the state dominance in the workers' compensation arena. One possible source of federal intervention is the experience during the 1990s in which more disabled workers qualified for DI benefits under Social Security, while fewer workers received workers' compensation benefits. Defenders of the integrity of the DI program may view this as evidence of cost shifting between programs and may argue that states should be required to reinstate traditional standards of eligibility. Realistically, this probably is not a serious enough threat to the DI program to warrant federal intervention into the workers' compensation system.[36]

The Role of Employers

Progressive employers who were motivated by genuine concerns for workers played a critical role in the emergence of the workers' compensation program, the Social Security system, and various forms of employee benefits. However, profitability was certainly a motive as well, since firms that engaged in welfare capitalism believed that, over time, workers who were treated well and who received generous benefits would be more loyal and productive and, thus, long-run profit would be enhanced by progressive employment policies. The analogy from chess is the gambit, whereby an immediate loss of a pawn—which may exhilarate the novice who captures the prize for the moment—allows the master to control the end game.

The strategy currently motivating much of American management, however, appears to represent the collapse of the end game into the next move. Executive compensation tied to stock prices, elimination of workers who do not perform the core competencies of the firm, shifting of risk of retirement benefits to workers—all are manifestations of the emphasis on the short-term rewards, perhaps best described as corporate planning based on instant gratification.

There are, to be sure, some long-existing employers, many identified with welfare capitalism, continue to resist the addiction to short-term returns. There are certainly younger firms that have adopted aspects of welfare capitalism and have thrived.[37] Moreover, there are various employer organizations that have promoted progressive employment policies during the last century. Perhaps the leading contributor among the employer community during the formative years of welfare capitalism and the Social Security system was Industrial Relations Counselors. Indeed, IRC has been an important promoter of "welfare capitalism" throughout most of its seventy-five-year history, including the post–World War II era, when IRC's philosophy and research helped promote the spread of pensions and health insurance. Although IRC has ceased to be a dominant force in recent decades, other employer organizations such as the Business Roundtable have assumed a leading role in promoting an employer philosophy that is more focused on capturing the king rather than on gloating over the capture of the pawn or, spare the thought, on glorifying the role of the rook.

Acknowledgments

We appreciate the assistance provided by Eugene McElroy, David Bensman, Douglas Kruse, and participants in the Proseminar offered by the Rutgers University School of Management and Labor Relations.

Notes

1. Chapter 7 in this volume, by Mitchell, focuses on profit-sharing and employee ownership plans, bonuses, and other forms of incentive payment systems.

2. Unfortunately, the NIPA data make a confusing distinction between (1) workers' compensation insurance policies purchased from private carriers and workers' compensation benefits provided by self-insuring employers (which are treated as "other labor income") and (2) workers' compensation insurance policies purchased from state funds or benefits paid directly by government funds (which are treated as "employer contributions for social insurance"). We consider both these categories of employer expenditures to be forms of social insurance. The published NIPA data are not sufficiently disaggregated until 1948 to allow the construction of a "proper" series on employer contributions on all sources of workers' compensation expenditures.

3. There are two limitations to the NIPA data. The earliest year with data is 1929, and although employee benefits were a small proportion of payroll that year, there were important examples of employee benefits and social insurance in preceding decades. In addition, the NIPA data do not include employee contributions for benefits and social insurance. Before World War II, most employees did not pay income taxes, and so there were no particular incentives for employees to try to have employers pay for benefits. Such incentives did exist after the war, however: Employees' earnings were subject to tax, so they would have to purchase benefits with after-tax dollars, whereas employers' expenditures for benefits were tax-deductible. In recent decades, various tax provisions have allowed employees to purchase benefits with pretax dollars. Thus, the portion of total benefits purchased by employers and employees included in the NIPA data is likely to vary over time.

4. There were also important examples of unemployed protestors outside the union movement, such as Coxey's Army, which marched from the Midwest to the White House lawn, where federal troops disbanded the disgruntled petitioners (Dulles 1955, 180).

5. For other accounts of welfare work (or more generally, welfare capitalism), see Bernstein (1960) and Brandes (1970).

6. The Victorian family model of welfare work succeeded in many companies during the Progressive Era, although (as discussed later) it was unsuccessful after World War I.

7. A similar argument can be made for employer financing of social insurance benefits. Workers' compensation provides a good example: Moore and Viscusi (1990) estimate that workers placed such a high value on workers' compensation benefits that they accepted reductions in wages that exceeded the costs of the program to employers.

8. Latimer (1932a, 30) reported " probably more than 95 percent of all [railroad] pension payments are now being made with no cost to the employees."

9. Berkowitz and McQuaid (1992, 5–6) discuss the evolution of the pensions for Union soldiers, noting that Congress "passed an inordinate number of special acts granting pensions to people whose requests had been denied by the Pension Bureau." Moreover, the original limitation of pensions to veterans disabled by wartime injuries was dropped in 1906 to allow any Union veteran over sixty-two years of age to automatically qualify for benefits.

10. An example of the defenses available to employers was the fellow servant rule, which absolved the employer from any liability if the worker was injured through the negligence of a fellow employee.

11. As a result, the employers' liability approach was abandoned in all jurisdictions except the railroads, where it still exists.

12. The view that the pre–workers' compensation approaches were inadequate is found in the legal treatise that is currently dominant. Larson and Larson (2001, §2.05), after reviewing the results of New York and Illinois commissions that examined industrial accidents under the pre–workers' compensation approaches, concluded that, for death cases, "the precompensation loss-adjustment system for industrial accidents was a complete failure and, in the most serious cases, left the worker's family destitute."

13. The "conventional" view that workers were unsuccessful in their suits before the introduction of workers' compensation has been questioned in recent decades. Berkowitz and McQuaid (1992) indicate that by the end of the nineteenth century, employers faced legal difficulties because people regarded suits that involved industrial accidents as a way of striking back against powerful and arrogant employers. They cite Posner (1972), who studied a sample of appellate court cases between 1875 and 1905 and found that juries decided for employers in less than 10 percent of cases. Posner also found that the number of negligence suits increased from 92 to 736 per year over this thirty-year period. Because of this adverse legal experience, the expenditures of employers on industrial liability insurance increased from $200,000 in 1887 to more than $35 million in 1912 (Berkowitz and McQuaid 1992, 44–45).

14. The most hazardous time was probably about 1907, when more than seven thousand workers were killed in just two industries: railroads and mining (Somers and Somers 1954, 9).

15. Ely (1903, 405–6) discussed the "problem of the twentieth man" as a justification for government intervention in the labor market: Nineteen employers might want to improve working conditions but would be prevented by the recalcitrant twentieth employer who refuses to go along and thus gains a competitive advantage in the product market. Kaufman (1997, 36–39) further examines this rationale for government regulation.

16. Many of the early workers' compensation statutes were elective because of concerns about the constitutionality of mandatory programs. However, employers who did not elect coverage lost their common-law defenses to negligence suits and so had a strong incentive to choose coverage.

17. The necessity for reform at the state level limited the ability to deal with competition from backward firms. Employers could use their influence in business-friendly states to reduce costs by depressing benefits and then could persuade legislators in states more sympathetic to workers to hold benefits down by threatening to relocate jobs to low-benefit, low-cost states. As a result, the decentralized nature of workers' compensation probably reduced the overall adequacy of the program. Some sixty years after workers' compensation programs emerged, the National Commission on State Workmen's Compensation Laws in its report (1972, 125) attributed the general inadequacy of state laws to the likelihood "that many States have been dissuaded from reform of their workmen's compensation statute because of the specter of the vanishing employer, even if that apparition is a product of fancy not fact."

18. Weinberg and Weinberg (1961) provide a collection of articles and essays from the Progressive Era.

19. In addition, large insurance companies, such as Metropolitan Life, were able to develop methods to sell policies to individual workers and viewed government programs as a threat to their business.

20. The search for an explanation of why more social insurance programs were not enacted in the Progressive Era has spawned a variety of theories. Moss (1996, 7, note 14) discusses five schools of thought, including Skocpol's assertion that hostility against patronage politics made all proposals for public spending suspect (which Moss discounts as a factor for the failure to enact social insurance programs other than old-age pensions). Another of the five schools is the Berkowitz and McQuaid (1992, 2–3) theory that the U.S. government lacked the administrative capacity to undertake elaborate social welfare programs until well into the twentieth century, in contrast to private-sector employers, who achieved this capacity much earlier—indeed, well before 1890 for the railroads.

21. Hicks (1941, 137) refers to the organization as the "Special Conference Group" and indicates that the number of companies in the group later grew to twelve.

22. Also see Beaumont (2001, 21–26) and Domhoff (1996, 128–30).

23. John D. Rockefeller, Jr., also provided a gift to Princeton University in 1922 that established the Industrial Relations Section (Hicks 1941, 147).

24. Rates charged by insurers reportedly would be increased "when the percentage of insurance on negroes, Mexicans, or employees of the yellow race, together with women" covered by such policies exceeded a specified level (NICB 1934, 14).

25. There were also three pension plans established between 1874 and 1929 for which the date of origin is unknown (Latimer 1932a, 42).

26. Latimer's analysis of why employers adopted pension plans is consistent with what Domhoff (1996, 134) terms the "predepression thinking of the Rockefeller network on pensions."

27. Other contributions of IRC to the development of the Social Security program and its relationships to retirement benefits include the study by Stein (1979).

28. When Warren's proposal was defeated (by a single vote) in the state assembly, he immediately returned to the legislature with a more limited hospital-only plan— but that also failed. Then in 1947, recognizing that private job-based health insurance had expanded significantly absent a state plan, Warren introduced a proposal for a

state-run catastrophic health plan with a pay-or-play feature. Employers could provide the mandated coverage on their own or they would have to pay into a state fund that would provide it. This proposal was also defeated.

29. The prediction about the lack of credit for progressive employers was borne out in the debates over the proposed Clinton Health Security Act in 1993, when executives from PepsiCo and General Mills criticized the comprehensive health benefits provided by the Big Three automakers as socially and economically irresponsible (Gottschalk 1998). The opposition from significant portions of the employer community contributed to the demise of the Clinton plan, as discussed in the next section.

30. This discussion is based on the experience of coauthor Burton, who served as chairman of the National Commission on State Workmen's Compensation Laws in 1971–72. Thomason, Schmidle, and Burton (2001, Chap. 2) provide an extended discussion of developments in workers' compensation since 1960.

31. President Carter, although a Democrat, was constrained from promoting progressive legislation by serious inflation problems during his term.

32. IRC provided intellectual guidance and justification for the rapid growth of employer expenditures on retirement benefits and group health care insurance during this era. In addition, IRC played an important role in advocating flexible benefit programs in the postwar period.

33. One by-product of the enactment of ERISA in 1974 is that efforts similar to the California plans proposed by Governor Warren in the 1940s would now be impossible because states have been precluded by ERISA from regulating employer pension and welfare funds (including health care plans).

34. The Family and Medical Leave Act of 1993 *inter alia* requires employers to maintain coverage on any group health plan provided by the employer for an employee who is on a leave protected by the act. The FMLA is discussed by Willborn, Schwab, and Burton (2002, 669–80).

35. Another reason why further limitations on eligibility are less likely is that the Oregon Supreme Court held unconstitutional the simultaneous elimination of workers' compensation benefits through higher compensability standards together with the prohibition of tort suits for those workers no longer qualifying for workers' compensation benefits. *Smothers* v. *Gresham Transfer, Inc.*, 23 P. 333 (Oregon 2001) is excerpted and discussed in Willborn, Schwab, and Burton (2002, 978–85). Employers, carriers, and politicians in other states may be reluctant to squeeze more employees out of the workers' compensation system because their courts may also find the exclusive remedy provisions that protect employers from tort suits are no longer valid.

36. Ironically, state efforts to consider integration of work-related and non-work-related sources of the need for medical care (and/or cash benefits) into a unified disability program—generally referred to as "24–hour coverage"—have been stymied in part by federal law. Specifically, the Supreme Court held in *District of Columbia* v. *Washington Board of Trade*, 506 U.S. 125 (1992), that ERISA, which exempts most aspects of state workers' compensation laws from federal preemption, nonetheless preempted a District of Columbia law that required employers to maintain health insurance benefits for workers who received workers' compensation benefits, and this decision has been interpreted as prohibiting any state efforts to regulate health care for disabled workers beyond the traditional care provided by workers' compensation.

37. Continental Airlines is noteworthy because in the last decade it has simultaneously increased profits, achieved high ratings from travelers, and been rated by employees as a great place to work.

7

Incentives and Structure

Development of Pay Practices in the Twentieth Century

Daniel J.B. Mitchell

You ask me how we regulate wages; I can only reply that there is no idea in the modern social economy which at all corresponds with what was meant by wages in your day.

—Edward Bellamy writing in 1887 in the novel *Looking Backwards* about a utopia in the year 2000

We have a stable unemployment rate of around 4 percent, we have good economic growth and low inflation, this is nirvana.

—Merrill Lynch economist commenting on the actual year 2000

Any industry, to be permanently successful, must insure to labor adequately remunerative employment under proper working and living conditions, to capital a fair return upon the money invested, and to the community a useful service. . . . The soundest industrial policy is that which has constantly in mind the welfare of the employees as well as the making of profits, and which, when human considerations demand it, subordinates profits to welfare.

—John D. Rockefeller, Jr.

The point is, ladies and gentlemen, greed is good. Greed works, greed is right. Greed clarifies, cuts through, and captures the essence of the evolutionary spirit. Greed in all its forms, greed for life, money, love, knowledge, has marked the upward surge in mankind—and greed, mark my words—will save not only Teldar Paper but the other malfunctioning corporation called the U.S.A.

—Gordon Gekko, fictional financier in the 1987 film *Wall Street*

In Bellamy's famous book published in 1887, *Looking Backwards*, the main character is put into a hypnotic trance and awakes in the year 2000, amazed at the utopian social order then prevailing. In 1887, factory workers were often paid on piece rates. Scientific management was in its early days. Frederick W. Taylor and others were critical of the ways in which piece rates were being used but not of the principle that pay should reward worker performance. The idea that incomes of workers come from wages was little questioned in mainstream thought. Tensions between Labor and Capital periodically erupted into violent confrontation. The idea of a mutual interest on both sides of the employment relationship was not part of anyone's serious agenda.

Society in 2000, as envisioned by Bellamy, did not rely on wages to induce productive work. Instead it relied on social responsibility to induce work until age 45, after which workers would retire, having done their civic duty. Pay for performance was unknown in Bellamy's 2000. Everyone received an equal government credit allocation to be used for consumption. There was no analogy, therefore, to wage structure or differentials. With an equitable distribution of income, there was no tension in the workplace over division of economic rewards.

While Bellamy's book inspired a utopian social movement in his time, by the early twentieth century, others sought less radical reforms that might engender industrial harmony. Notions of a fair return to both parties, Labor and Capital, determined in a socially useful context, appealed to some major employers. The idea that as social partners Labor and Capital could interact in a manner that would determine the fair return—as well as settle other workplace issues—began to develop in the era surrounding World War I. It stood in contrast with other solutions to the Labor Problem that relied on more technical fixes: incentive schemes and efficiency enhancers such as time-and-motion analysis.

In the 1920s, groups such as Industrial Relations Counselors, Inc. (IRC), and the National Industrial Conference Board (NICB, or Conference Board) became active in promoting cooperative approaches to management beyond the simple Taylorism then in its heyday in the United States. As Clarence J. Hicks, a former IRC chairman, declared, "The field of industrial relations is . . . too young and too changing to have reached the stage of complacent satisfaction" (Hicks 1941, 122). The balance in actual human resource practice shifted over the twentieth century between alternative views of the ideal employment relationship.

A century after Bellamy wrote, and about seven decades after John D. Rockefeller, Jr., became concerned with what he called "the personal relation in industry," human resource (HR) practice seemed to be tilting again toward technical fixes. In the 1980s, the "new" approach to HR practice came under such headings as "pay for performance." In many respects, HR practice moved away from the emphasis on a more general mutuality of ongoing interests. Employees should be prepared to manage their own careers in their own interest, according to the new doctrine; human resource professionals should focus on tying policies such as pay determination to business strategy.

And it wasn't just fictional film financiers who believed that everyone should simply act in self-interest. As Jack Welch, the former CEO of General Electric, put it, "At the end of the week, we cut your paycheck. You don't owe me anything, and I don't owe you anything. We start fresh on Monday."[1] Clearly, a relationship in which neither party owes the other anything and motivation comes from short-term incentives and fear of job loss is not much of a relationship at all. It is a transaction.

The actual year 2000 turned out to be more similar to 1887 than it was to Bellamy's utopia. Pay continued as a mechanism to induce and encourage productive work. And notions of partnership between employers and employees slipped from fashion. Of course, pay practices evolved over the prior century, along with other aspects of the employment relationship. But the idea that neither side of the employment relationship owed anything to the other suggests a pulling back from the IRC vision.

A Modest (Macro) Utopia

While Bellamy hoped for a utopian future, IRC sought to apply practical knowledge and research aimed at incremental improvement. Yet in one respect, the decade leading up to the year 2000 did produce a utopia, albeit far more modest than Bellamy imagined, and one that soon began to fade. An applied macroeconomist, put into a hypnotic trance in the 1970s, might have dreamed of waking up in 2000 in a world of low unemployment—a "high-pressure labor market" was the term of art back then (Okun 1973)— but with low wage and price inflation. As fanciful as such a dream might have seemed in the 1970s, it did come to pass in the late 1990s.

Specifically, after a brief recession in the early part of that decade, the U.S. economy steadily expanded, bringing unemployment down to around 4 percent at the peak. Although employers complained of labor shortages and the need to compete for scarce help, wage inflation—and inflation generally—remained quiescent. So-called stagflation of the 1970s seemed to have vanished, along with the government wage-price controls and guidelines that went with it. The myriad decisions of employers (or, in some cases, employers and unions) on pay no longer seemed to have an inflationary tilt.

Compensation Complexity

These observations remind us that although we think of compensation mainly as a micro (firm-level) matter, it in fact has implications for national economic performance. Compensation systems create incentives, but it was increasingly recognized in the late twentieth century that these incentives go beyond inducing people to work harder. They also affect employment levels, labor force participation, job mobility, and even the amplitude of the business cycle. Compensation by 2000, in short, had come to encompass a variety of issues, some micro and some macro, that would be puzzling to any nineteenth-century observer.

Even with regard to pay for performance, a familiar nineteenth-century concept in its piece-rate format, the approach taken at the end of the twentieth century would seem exotic to a Bellamy or even a Taylor. Consider the advice offered in a guidebook on stock option plans, the rage of pay-for-performance devotees in the late 1990s given the soaring stock market of that period:

> Under the present accounting standards, where surrendered shares are not "mature," the stock swap will be considered the functional equivalent of the cash settlement of a stock appreciation right, resulting in variable plan accounting treatment (the compensation expense will be estimated at the time of grant and adjusted in each subsequent accounting period to reflect changes in the fair market value of the company's stock) and ultimately the recognition of an expense equal to the difference between the option exercise price and the fair market value of the company's stock on the date of exercise. [Rodrick 1999, 63]

The complexity of that advice—and the involvement of accountants, lawyers, and tax experts in modern compensation practices—was unknown in the late nineteenth century. And note that the advice does not address the issue of whether offering stock options will in fact achieve employer objectives regarding work motivation.

In short, if he had been able to view actual compensation systems in the actual year 2000, Bellamy might ultimately have despaired of making sense of them, much as his novel's hero had difficulty comprehending the fictional practices in the fanciful 2000 of *Looking Backwards*. Even the more practical Clarence Hicks would be puzzled, particularly by the notion that pay practices were a substitute for employee relations. We now ask much of compensation. It is supposed to motivate, attract, and retain employees, as well as deal with national social concerns. Absent other supporting institutions, that is much to ask.

Defining Compensation

Before going forward, it is necessary to define "compensation" for purposes of this chapter. If we think of compensation in its broadest sense as anything that aids in recruitment, retention, and motivation, there is little that is not potentially compensation. Nice décor, an amiable corporate culture, and perks such as workout rooms all have a potential influence on recruitment, retention, and motivation. Virtually any human resource practice could technically be included as compensation. And the modern economics literature does tend to be very encompassing.

Promotion policies, for example, are seen in that literature to be motivational "tournaments," i.e., incentives. Similarly, the threat of discharge for substandard performance is seen as a sort of performance-bound substitute that the employee can lose if adequate productivity is not maintained. For purposes of this chapter, however, arbitrary limits must be imposed on the definition of compensation. I will confine the term to instances of payouts of cash or financial assets directly to the worker or to a provider of service to the worker, whether that payment is current or deferred; look at the effect compensation has on employee behavior, whether the effect is intended or not; and define "behavior" more broadly than just effort on the job.

Four Compensation Types

Compensation arrangements can be divided into four types: (1) time-based wage, paid on a current basis, (2) social welfare benefits that are sometimes deferred, (3) explicit incentive plans, and (4) pay programs that share risk with employees.

Time-Based Wages

Since employers want effort and output from their workers, not merely time, a time-based wage raises a variety of human resource issues that economists subsume under principal/agent problems. These problems all come down to a simple question: How do you get the help to do what you want, once they are employed? With time-based wages, HR practices involving monitoring, supervision, and supplementary reward are likely to be utilized to ensure that more than mere physical presence of the worker is the end product of employment.

A basic time-based wage might be flexible or rigid in practice in either a real or nominal sense. If flexible, it might vary with individual or organizational performance but typically not through a mechanical formula. The wage—or its rate of change—might also vary with the general business cycle. Whatever variation occurred would involve subjective judgments and decisions of management officials or union and management officials through collective bargaining. Still, once it is set, the basic wage is simple for both workers and managers to understand.

The time-based wage is the default option in contemporary compensation. However, the level at which such a wage might be set relative to the outside labor market is an important HR decision with potential behavioral consequences for both employees and employers. And, of course, there typically is not one wage in an enterprise but rather a structure of wages, depending on occupation and other factors. The setting of wage differentials, and developing a program for their determination, is an important internal decision.

Social Welfare Benefits

A second, more complex form of compensation involves a social welfare function. Benefits such as pensions and health insurance fall into this category. These benefits often reflect external public policies such as tax incentives. Like time-based wages, social welfare benefits often have a certain rigidity. Your merit bonus might vary with performance, but your employer either offers you health insurance or does not. The "quantity" of health insurance received does not vary with your productivity. Absent offsetting regulation, the presence of such benefits could influence employer choice in hiring and retention. For example, younger, healthier, single workers are often cheaper in terms of their impact on health insurance than other workers. As a result, there frequently is offsetting government regulation to counteract such influences on employer behavior.

Worker behavior also can be altered by benefit offerings. If you or your dependents have health problems, you are unlikely to quit a job that provides good medical insurance, and you will be attracted to an offer of such a job. Senior workers are unlikely to quit under defined-benefit pensions as their entitlement mounts. But younger workers might be attracted to an offer from a firm with portable defined-contribution or cash-balance elements.

Individual and Small-Group Incentives

The third group of compensation arrangements—individual and small-group incentives—would be most familiar to a nineteenth-century observer. There are still individual incentive plans such as simple piece-rate systems and the more complicated differential piece-rate schemes once associated with scientific management and now newly rationalized for groups in game-theoretic terms as escapes from free riders (Peterson 1992a and 1992b).[2] Similar plans may apply to small groups where it is difficult to isolate individual contribution. Also included in this category are the kinds of commission plans used for sales personnel. Research on the "new economics of personnel" revived academic interest in use of piece rates and commissions and other incentives (Asch and Warner 1997).

Although piece rates and commission plans rely on formulas, it is also possible to provide individual rewards—such as merit bonuses—based on subjective supervisory judgments and performance appraisals. Indeed, the modern economics literature suggests that failure to allow supervisors some discretion on rewards has potential costs (Prendergast and Topel 1996). Subjective systems are likely to be used in occupations where employee outputs are not readily countable, e.g., most professional employees. A standard economic argument is that automatic plans, such as piece rates, obviate the need for supervision by being self-regulatory. But plans that are based on rewards through subjective judgment of supervisors do not obviate the need for supervision. Moreover, Taylor would not have argued that piece rates end the need for supervision; that notion is an abstraction of economists. He would have said that managerial expertise was needed but of a different kind than is used in a subjective reward system.

The IRC approach to human resource management, emphasizing the importance of good employee relations, also does not accord with a strategy relying only on a short-term incentive plan. Key figures in the founding of IRC, such as William Lyon McKenzie King, emphasized that the rewards to the parties must be adequate and were reluctant to believe that there was one right way—as Taylorists thought—to determine pay. As King puts it, "the practice [that] in the long run is apt to do most by way of promoting efficiency, through harmonizing the interests of Labor, Capital, Management, and Community, is pretty certain to be in the nature of a combination of features broader than any . . . single method" (1947, 145).

One complaint about individual piece rates and other individual rewards is that they lead to competition rather than cooperation within the workforce. Much depends on the details of the particular system. For example, a system in which the total reward kitty is rationed or in which workers are ranked against one another is more likely to foster competition than an "absolute" reward plan. A more common complaint raised about piece rates is that they lead to an emphasis on quantity over quality or to the waste of materials in an effort to build volume. The equivalent complaint concerning commissions is that sales personnel may engage in fraudulent behavior vis-à-vis consumers to generate more volume, ultimately creating potential legal liabilities for their employers. All of these complaints come down to asserting that if certain measured attributes are rewarded, employees will respond only to those measurements. They will neglect areas that are harder to calculate, a classic problem of agency relationships.

Workers may find ways of sabotaging the reward standard itself. Establishing low norms that can be readily met is one version of such manipulation. In competitive situations, output restrictions may be inevitable as piece rates are cut when earnings become "too" high relative to the outside labor market (Carmichael and MacLeod 2000). But complaints about reward criteria are not confined to systems where the reward is set by a formula. Even in subjective merit evaluations/rewards, the same issue may arise. Thus, university academics complain:

> (I)f administrators treat student evaluations of teaching as important, then teachers can be expected to react to them in ways that may be inappropriate. To instructors, generating positive student answers to questions about overall effectiveness and communication skills may smack of entertainment and dumbing down. To raise scores on the end-of-term entertainment quotient, teachers can be expected to modify student activities and grading; they can manipulate timing and procedures for student evaluations; they can drive the unhappy out of the class, with no trace showing on end-of-semester student evaluations of teaching. [Becker 2000, 114]

These types of grumbles are widespread about evaluation/reward systems; academics should not feel specially oppressed. Cynics would say that complaints arise because half of those evaluated find themselves disappointingly below the median. But no system is perfect; all create misincentives along with desirable incentives.

The ability of workers to distort incentive systems is sometimes set against management behavior that workers may regard as manipulative. Specifically, as noted above, output norms may be increased (piece rates are cut) if worker productivity rises. A consequence can be increased labor-management friction.

Finally, simple piece rates and commissions have the virtue of being readily understood. But economic analysis suggests that the resulting incentives are not likely to approximate what a costless monitoring equilibrium would bring about. Since employers cannot give the full value of the item or sale produced to employees, incentives will be inadequate relative to the ideal. Kinks can overcome this problem if they are placed correctly in the pay-to-output schedule. But perfection is unlikely to be achieved in practice (Mitchell, Lewin, and Lawler 1990, 48–51).

Risk-Sharing Plans

The fourth type of pay plan involves assumption of organizational risk by the employee. At the level of the firm, there are profit-sharing plans (those based on formulas and those based on managerial discretion), employee stock ownership plans (ESOPs), and—increasingly in the 1990s—stock option plans. The value that employees gain from these plans ultimately will depend on the economic performance of the firm, including—for the last two—the stock market's valuation of that performance. At the level of organization below the firm, e.g., a plant or division, there are various gain-sharing plans. The most commonly cited of these are Scanlon, Rucker, and Improshare plans. But many firms that use gain sharing have their own internally devised variants.

Viewed simply as large-group incentive systems, these plans all raise the issue of what economists call the 1/N problem. As N, the number of workers, grows large, the reward to any individual worker for effort becomes very small; free riding may occur. Such plans, therefore, are often viewed as requiring additional HR programs to build team spirit and peer monitoring. If successful, such programs may also overcome the overcompetitive tendencies associated with individual piece rates and may create a more cooperative atmosphere. Assuming the 1/N problem is overcome, setting production norms through time and motion becomes unnecessary. Problems of quantity over quality and excess wastage are also, in theory, eliminated by systems such as profit sharing.

The IRC approach, emphasizing employer-employee mutual interests, is compatible with programs such as profit sharing and share ownership so long as such plans are not operated without regard to the employee relations climate. HR practices that foster a sense of mutual interest may help overcome the 1/N problem of free riders. In such cases, pay practices and other HR practices reinforce one another.

There is an element in these pay plans that goes beyond incentives. If the firm does well or poorly due to reasons beyond employee control (say, a change in exchange rates), workers will receive more or less in total pay. Some risk normally borne by the firm's owners is passed to the workers as if they were investors. To the extent that workers are paid through large-group plans in lieu of regular compensation, the worker, indeed, are investors in the firm, just as are the conventional owners. They give up something currently for the prospect of eventual reward.

Note also that large-group plans, especially profit sharing, have an element of pay flexibility built in. Economists have long puzzled over the lack of auction-style flexibility of wages (Bewley 1999). Whatever the explanation, under profit sharing, the ups and downs of the firm's economic performance are reflected in pay. Thus, with such plans in force, it is as if in a standard time-based wage system, the wage level were tied to the firm's product and labor demand. In turn, pay flexibility—if widespread—has potential macroeconomic repercussions. If the macro-utopia described earlier proves ephemeral, and stagflation returns, this flexibility could provide a rationale for public policies that encourage certain kinds of large-group pay plans. That is, the plans could induce desirable employer behaviors from a social viewpoint even if employee effort remains unaffected. But evidence that associates profit sharing with employment expansion or stabilization is limited (Jones, Kato, and Pliskin 1997, 163–66).

There is evidence that pay today is less flexible, less auction-like, than it was in, say, the 1920s (Mitchell 1985). Many explanations have been offered, often emphasizing that wage cuts produce declines in employee moral and tensions between labor and management.[3] The notion that employers should concern themselves with such effects of pay decisions is in keeping with the IRC approach that stressed mutual, ongoing employee relations. Thus, the fact that wage stickiness persists, even in an era in which the ongoing employment relationship has been seen as a thing of the past, suggests that sensitivity to that relationship is not dead, even if the ties have weakened.

Compensation System Overlaps

Although we have divided compensation into four conceptual groups, there is considerable overlap between them. Even with a rigid basic wage or a simple piece rate, workers are subject to risk of layoff if firm performance is poor; risk sharing is present without a formal sharing plan. The degree of that risk for the individual worker will depend on the procedures that determine layoffs. If, as in union situations, those employees with the lowest seniority are laid off first, then senior workers are at less risk than junior workers. However, a complete failure of the firm could lead to termination of the entire workforce.

Unvested stock options—often seen as productivity enhancers—were found by employers to have the kind of antimobility (and litigation-generating effects) often associated with certain social welfare benefits (Alexander 2000; Hayes 2000). And note that virtually any benefit plan can be rationalized as providing what economists term "gift exchange." If the benefits are seen as "gravy," i.e., something provided above and beyond "normal" pay, employees might be grateful for their provision. Viewed positively, gratitude could spark increased productivity. Or in a negative sense—similar to the ersatz bond described earlier—fear of loss could induce appropriate behavior.

In summary, the types of pay described above potentially have varying degrees of incentive effects and of risk-sharing effects. Both employer and employee behaviors may be altered by the pay system. And no system, however carefully crafted, will resolve all principal/agent problems.

Public Policy Toward Compensation

There are two levels of concern about compensation arrangements, micro and societal. At the micro-level, we worry about firm efficiency. At the macro-level, we are concerned with good economic performance.

Employer-Level Rationale for Policy

Generally, we also assume that firms have built-in market incentives to be efficient. Thus, there is no obvious case for providing direct or indirect subsidies to firms to adopt particular compensation practices for pure efficiency reasons. Public policy should in general be limited to providing accurate information, as official agencies such as the U.S. Bureau of Labor Statistics (BLS) do about a variety of labor-market developments. There are also private sources of information—and firms often do rely on compensation consultants for data and analysis. But private providers—if they are in the business of selling particular plans—may not be perceived as neutral (Mitchell 1995). Noncommercial private organizations such as IRC and the Conference Board developed as information sources because they were seen as reliable. Although there is not a strong microrationale for subsidizing particular compensation systems, there are tax subsidies provided in some cases; employee stock ownership plans have received favored tax treatment since the 1970s for reasons discussed below.

Macrorationales for Policy

The macro side of compensation involves national—rather than firm-level—efficiency. Firms do not ordinarily take account of their impact on the macroeconomy; generally, no firm is large enough to have widespread macro-effects in any case. But taken collectively, particular pay practices could have such impacts. Cost inflation is an obvious example. Fear about inflation explains why the Federal Reserve closely monitors such compensation measures as the Employment Cost Index. The Fed assumes that a rise in wage costs could push up prices.

By the 1950s, there were concerns in the United States and other countries that creeping inflation had become embedded in wage and price setting (Scott 1975). Keynesian economists saw price inflation as a function of wage inflation. Unions were then prominent in wage setting and were perceived to be a major actor in the inflation process. As a well-known Keynesian put it, "What happens to prices depends on what is done about money wages by the powerful organizations, influenced by government, that determine money wage rates" (National Industrial Conference Board [NICB] 1950, 35).

Foreign countries, particularly those with "corporatist" economic systems, used "incomes policies" (wage/price guidelines) to try to reconcile low levels of unemployment with low levels of inflation. The U.S. economy was never corporatist to the degree found in Europe. But the share of compensation covered by collective agreements in the private sector probably exceeded 40 percent during the 1950s (Jacoby and Mitchell 1988).

In part because of the foreign examples, the 1960s and 1970s saw efforts by successive administrations in the United States to adopt an American version of incomes policy. The Kennedy and Johnson administrations instituted and maintained wage-price guideposts (Sheahan 1967). Nixon applied mandatory wage-price controls (Weber 1973; Weber and Mitchell 1978). The Ford administration tried exhortation. And the Carter administration tried wage-price guidelines that stood somewhere between the Kennedy and Johnson and Nixon approaches.

During the 1980s, an alternative approach was proposed. As noted earlier, profit sharing and similar plans can be viewed as providing pay flexibility. One argument was that with more flexibility and sensitivity to demand built into compensation, deflationary episodes—such as the Federal Reserve undertook in the early 1980s—would be less painful (Mitchell 1982). Another more sophisticated argument, based on microeconomic analysis, was that profit-sharing plans would lead to higher employment levels without the inflationary updraft seen in conventional wage systems. In a model put forward by Martin Weitzman, the benefit of profit sharing was its effect on employer (not employee) behavior in price setting and hiring (Weitzman 1984). These analyses led to new arguments for policy intervention in pay setting, in this case tax subsidies for profit sharing. Bills were submitted to Congress to provide tax incentives for profit sharing, but none were passed and the idea faded in the noninflationary 1990s.

Societal Rationales for Policy

A variety of justifications might be offered for the favorable tax treatment of health and welfare plans. Basically, they are regarded as "merit goods," things we just think people ought to have. Congress, in its wisdom, has decided people should have them through their employers. Stock ownership plans and, more recently, stock option plans seem to generate political support on the grounds that they will make workers into mini-capitalists. Such arguments go back to the nineteenth century when the idea was to reduce industrial and social unrest (Mitchell, Lewin, and Lawler 1990, 27–47). There was a residual element of this approach when the tax-favored treatment was first offered to ESOPs in the early 1970s.

Louis O. Kelso had been touting ESOPs as a social reform for many years on "share-the-wealth" grounds. He was able to convince Louisiana Senator Russell Long that a tax subsidy to ESOPs was warranted (Kelso and Adler 1958). Long was the son of Huey Long, the flamboyant senator and governor whose share-the-wealth political movement was prominent in the 1930s. The result was a pairing of employers seeking tax advantages and/or pay for performance with visionaries who continue to this day to issue tracts reminiscent of those published by nineteenth-century populists (e.g., Ashford and Shakespeare 1999). Despite the fervor with which ESOPs are sometimes advocated, the evidence that they raise productivity is more limited than "True Believers" care to admit (Kruse and Blasi 1997). Nonetheless, the tax expenditures directed at ESOPs totaled $1.1 billion in fiscal year 1999 (Office of Management and Budget 2000, 111).

Stock options receive favorable tax treatment because, if offered at market prices, they are not taxed until exercised and are then taxed as capital gains.[4] Yet the options have immediate value for employees (and represent costs to firms) when issued, as modern finance teaches. The fact that the value is contingent on a rise in the stock price does not mean that the option can be considered as worth zero at the time of offer. An asset that may be worth something or nothing in the future—but can never have negative value—cannot have an expected value of zero.[5] Congress seemed anxious to promote the spread of stock options to nonmanagerial workers by exempting the value of the grants to hourly workers from overtime premium requirements in 2000. But it is not only official bodies that have adopted policies intended to encourage stock option grants to employees.

The Financial Accounting Standards Board (FASB) is a nonprofit entity whose advice is generally accepted by the Securities and Exchange Commission. When FASB proposed that unexercised employee stock options be shown as liabilities on balance sheets, protests arose, although the recommendation was conceptually sound. Opponents of balance sheet treatment argued that it would discourage use of options. They wanted to obscure the information on option costs, presumably so outside stock owners would not notice, although the argument was never put that way. FASB eventually retreated from the heat. Although it is unclear that shareholders are unaware of stock option liabilities, the FASB decision was intended to encourage stock options (or not discourage them).

Policy Players

Because particular compensation arrangements are affected by public policy, a host of major players has become involved, apart from the usual coterie of "disinterested" academics and think-tank policy wonks. Business has an interest in the tax treatment of its various pay plans and the regulations that spell out eligibility for such treatment. Generally, business has opposed mandated benefit plans but does not object to (or may well favor) tax subsidies. Specialized groups have grown up around particular pay plans. For example, the ESOP Association represents the interests of firms that provide stock ownership plans.

The Process of Compensation Determination

Writing in the early 1940s, Clarence J. Hicks, chairman of the board of Industrial Relations Counselors, argued that the Wagner Act of 1935 had gone too far in promoting unions and that by the 1960s, the situation would reverse (1941, 153–73). Hicks' main concern was the process of employee representation rather than compensation per se; he was an advocate of the type of company-sponsored employee representation systems that had evolved in the 1920s. Nonetheless, the 1960s did see the beginning of a sustained decline in private-sector union representation rates. Unionization rates are now roughly comparable to what existed in the 1920s.

The union sector's influence on nonunion compensation systems—through either spillover or threat effects—has been diminished relative to the 1950s. Weakening of unions by the 1980s led to a greater union acceptance of, or acquiescence to, risk-sharing plans. For example, by the late 1990s, about one fourth of ESOP participants were covered by union-negotiated plans (Kruse and Blasi 2000, 79). More generally, compensation has shifted somewhat toward the pay-for-performance emphasis seen in the 1920s.

Because macro-shocks are still a danger—despite the euphoria of "new economy" enthusiasts of the late 1990s—I favor pay arrangements that allow some risk sharing by workers in return for more employment stability. The rest of this chapter will focus on current compensation practices, trace their origin, and then conclude with a needs assessment. It will continue to emphasize the behavioral effects of compensation but not just in the narrow sense of more effort by workers; both employers and employees have had their behaviors altered by compensation practices and public policies on compensation.

Current Trends

Although much anecdotal evidence on compensation is available, continuous, well-defined survey information is often lacking. This information deficit is especially the case with regard to pay systems such as profit sharing and piece rates. Stock options are also an example. Thus, the National Center for Employee Ownership (NCEO) reported in 2000 that between seven million and ten million workers probably received stock options, up from one million eight years earlier (NCEO 2000). Another private survey suggested that somewhere between a fifth and a fourth of nonexempt employees had stock options in 2000 (Parus and Handel 2000, 22). An official government survey of options did not exist until the late 1990s. When one did appear, it suggested a more modest use than did the private estimates.

A pilot study by BLS reported that 1.7 percent of private-sector employees had stock options in 1999. Among those employees working for companies with publicly traded stock, 5.3 percent had options. Not surprisingly, coverage by options was positively correlated with worker income and size of firm. Executives were more likely to have stock options than other employees (BLS 2000b). The impact on wage data from the omission of stock options may well have become significant in the 1990s. Researchers at the Federal Reserve, for example, believe that the omission of such data in standard measures of compensation probably caused the trend in annual wage inflation to be understated by about 0.3 percentage points by the end of the decade (Lebow et al. 1999).

The contemporary importance of social welfare benefits means that a significant part of compensation is not easy for employees to value accurately. And the cost implications of benefit changes can be difficult for employers to evaluate too. Surely these complications make recruitment and retention issues more difficult for both sides of the employment relationship.

Chamber of Commerce Data

The U.S. Chamber of Commerce has long done surveys of employee benefits. However, the scope of the survey has changed over time and access to the raw data by outsiders is limited. Although recent survey evidence from the Chamber includes some very small firms, the sample still seems biased toward larger enterprises. The basic description of the 1999 survey (of 1998 data) indicates that 619 "firms" participated. No information is given on the

Table 7.1

Chamber of Commerce Data on the Incidence and Cost of Compensation Components, 1998

Type of plan	Percentage of respondents with plan	Rough estimate of percentage of compensation for those with plan*
401(k)	81	2
Profit sharing	33	4
Stock bonus	4 }	
ESOP	11 }	
		2–3

Source: Chamber of Commerce 1999.
*Rough estimate based on dividing dollar cost for all employees and employers by percent of employers with plan and then dividing that total by an estimate of total compensation. This methodology will tend to produce overestimates for some of the compensation arrangements shown. See text for details.

number of firms invited to participate that declined. There is an indication that some of the employers surveyed were nonprofits; reference is made in the survey instrument to the Section 403(b) and 458 savings plans that cover such organizations. But such coverage details are not published.

Table 7.1 summarizes highlights of the Chamber survey. More than 80 percent of respondents had 401(k) tax-favored savings plans. Some of these accounts may contain employer stock. A third of the sample provided profit-sharing plans. This figure excludes those profit-sharing plans that were not part of deferred retirement arrangements. Thus, cash profit-sharing plans were not included. About 4 percent had stock bonus plans; it is unclear whether stock option plans were included in this category and, if so, how employers would have valued option grants for purposes of the survey. More than a tenth had an ESOP plan, although the proportion of outstanding shares owned by such plans is not indicated. No direct evidence is provided on cash incentives such as piece rates and commissions.

Chamber data on employer expenditures per employee for each compensation type include respondents that do not provide the plan in question. Those respondents will report that they spent zero on plans they do not have. Thus, the average expenditure figures will underestimate the cost to employers who do offer them. A rough estimate on the cost of particular compensation arrangements for those employers actually providing the program is also shown in Table 7.1. It was calculated by dividing the average expenditure on a plan by the proportion of employers providing that plan. The result was then divided by an estimate of total compensation. This methodology is likely to produce overestimates.[6]

Bureau of Labor Statistics Data

The U.S. Bureau of Labor Statistics' Employee Benefit Survey, summarized in Table 7.2, is based on a more elaborately constructed sample than the Chamber survey. There remain some ambiguities in the precise definitions used. But it is possible to determine a number of important characteristics of compensation practice. However, there seems little difference in the incidence of deferred profit sharing by size of business in the BLS survey.[7] Nonproduction bonuses are quite commonly used, especially for full-timers. These payments may include disparate items ranging from cash rewards for good attendance (a kind of individual incentive) to lump-sum bonuses of the type often found in union contracts (which are not individual incentives). Note that nonproduction bonuses seem somewhat more common in smaller firms—presumably with informal personnel practices—than large. It may be that smaller firms are more likely to prefer discretionary arrangements than larger ones. If so, the smaller firms can be seen as providing a kind of "walking-around money." Other BLS survey data (not shown here) suggest that nonproduction bonuses are more common in nonunion than union firms (BLS 2000a). These data also suggest interpreting the bonuses as a discretionary management reward policy since union contracts tend to include limits on management discretion.

Deferred profit sharing and ESOPs are less common in the BLS survey than in the Chamber survey. Some of the discrepancy may be due to definition. In principle, BLS includes as profit sharing only plans with a precise formula determining the share. Many firms, however, have profit sharing plans that leave the annual distribution to the discretion of the employer. Since these plans may not in fact provide distributions that fluctuate with profits, there is reason not to count them as strict "profit-sharing." Similarly, there are share ownership arrangements that are not technically ESOPs.[8]

Bureau of National Affairs Data

Unfortunately, the BLS has given up tracking union contract features, leaving the field to the private Bureau of National Affairs, Inc. (BNA). BNA data shown in Table 7.3 indicate that about a fourth of contracts in the mid-1990s had piece rates, while 4 percent had language that constrained installation of such plans. Profit sharing appeared in 8 percent of the contracts and stock purchase plans in 4 percent. It is unclear whether ESOPs are included in that category, but they probably are not. Nonproduction bonuses, other than the lump sums shown separately, were found in 11 percent of the contracts. Items such as Christmas bonuses are the major element in that category as opposed to merit rewards.

Table 7.2

Bureau of Labor Statistics Data on Incidence of Compensation Components, Selected Years

	Medium-to-large establishments*		Small independent businesses†
	Full-time employees (%)	Part-time employees (%)	Full-time employees (%)
Selected defined contribution retirement plans:			
Savings	39	13	19
Profit sharing	13	7	12
ESOP	4	n.a.	‡
Money purchase	8	n.a.	4
Tax-deferred savings:			
With employer match	46	15	20
No employer match	9	4	4
Nonproduction bonuses	42	17	48

Source: Bureau of Labor Statistics 1999a and 1999b.
*100 or more workers
†Fewer than 100 workers
‡Less than 0.5%

Table 7.3

Bureau of National Affairs Data on Union Contract Provisions, Mid-1990s: Proportion of Contracts with Selected Features

Type of feature	(%)
Profit sharing	8
Stock purchase	4
Lump sums	22
Other nonproduction bonuses	11
Piece rates	24
Limitations or bans on piece rates	4

Source: Bureau of National Affairs, Inc., 1995.

Because union contracts are negotiated to cover relatively long time horizons, union wages are often viewed as less market-responsive than nonunion. That perception does not imply that nominal union wages are never cut, however. In industries such as steel, there were dramatic wage cuts in the 1980s. But a more typical response in periods of concession bargaining was a nominal wage freeze. The distribution of wage adjustments tended to bunch at zero in periods when concessions became common. And hidden wage cuts, such as the two-tier wage plans that decrease entry pay only for new hires, also were implemented. So union pay setting may have some flexibility of the type associated with profit sharing. Hard times can produce actual and de facto pay cuts.

Summary of Current Practices

American compensation in the late 1990s had a number of pay-for-performance features. But wages were not predominantly determined by formula-driven contingent arrangements such as piece rates or profit sharing. The degree to which subjective merit judgments increasingly drove nonunion pay is hard to determine. Not all nominal merit plans involve a strong link between merit and pay. Generally, popular management literature in the 1980s and 1990s pushed the idea that pay for performance was a good thing and reported success stories of firms with such programs (Wilson 1999). (Failures were less likely to be reported.)

While it was not the case that everyone was getting stock options by the late 1990s, there was undoubtedly an increase in such arrangements, particularly in the high-tech world. Formal ESOPs seem less common than might have been gathered from journalistic accounts. Most ESOPs did not involve controlling interests in firms, although some prominent examples of majority ownership (as at United Airlines) received much attention. Discussion of the macroeconomic effects of pay systems—a hot topic in the 1980s after a period of stagflation—largely died off in the noninflationary tight labor markets of the 1990s.

Of course, the pay practices at the end of the twentieth century did not spring from nowhere. They represented a process of evolution. That evolution went beyond simple micro-incentives and optimal contracting in the economists' sense. It was also influenced by currents of fashionable thinking and academic research as well as by public policy of preceding decades. There may also have been a shift among employees toward a greater focus on monetary goals relative to softer objectives. As Figure 7.1 suggests, at least among the college educated, the 1960s hippie idealism declined in the years that followed while materialism advanced. Student goals shifted away from a "soft" developing of a meaningful philosophy of life to being well off. Pay systems may have reflected this attitudinal change. To the extent that pay systems mirror changes in employee tastes toward reward, there is rationality in their development. But what seems to have occurred in pay incentives is a mix of the rational and of the path-dependent haphazard.

Rather than try to trace each form of compensation continuously throughout the twentieth century, I look instead at two historical snapshots. Because

Figure 7.1 Goals of American College Freshmen

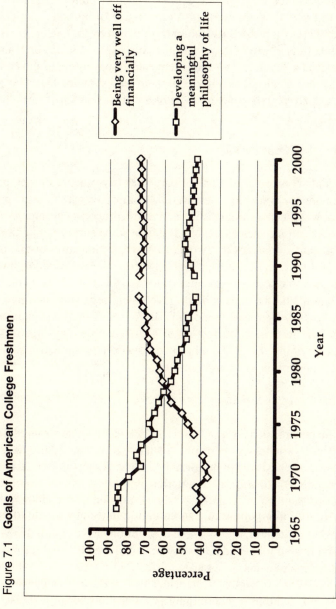

the Depression, New Deal, and World War II years are a recognized turning point for many aspects of the human resource/personnel function, the first snapshot depicts the immediate pre–New Deal years. The second then focuses on the 1950s and 1960s, a period in which the impacts of the New Deal and World War II were digested. A key source of pressure that developed between these two periods was unionization. But by the 1990s, unionization had slipped back toward levels similar to those of the 1920s. Hence, we might expect a "back to the future" tendency in pay systems and compensation practices. And, as will be seen, there was some of that. But because institutions are path-dependent, the 1990s cannot be seen as just a replay of the 1920s.

The Pre–New Deal Period

Precise data concerning the use of particular pay practices in the pre–New Deal era are not available. Then, as now, companies with unusual pay practices that were seen as progressive received disproportionate attention. However, organizations such as the NICB did do some survey work, albeit often biased toward companies that would answer questionnaires or that had high public profiles.[9] Even if biased and imperfect, this information provides a look at a world of compensation prior to tax incentives, heavy and growing unionization, and the expansion of government regulation and intervention during the New Deal and World War II. Viewed from a contemporary perspective, the most striking feature of pre–New Deal pay practices is that almost everything that is thought to be a modern pay practice was present then, although often in embryonic form.

Pre–New Deal Pay Structure

Scientific management as developed by Taylor and others required a detailed analysis of how jobs were performed. Time-and-motion studies were used to analyze the one best way of performing a particular job and for setting norms in piece rates. But apart from description of physical motion, there needed to be an understanding of what the job duties entailed. Even before World War I, provision of job descriptions had begun to develop, particularly for civil service and white-collar jobs. These descriptions were codified in ways that identified related jobs. Such information could then be used for promotions and other functions not necessarily related to pay policy.

But once the concept of systematized job descriptions developed, their potential application to determining pay structure began to be seen. Jobs could be rated numerically, based on the attributes required to perform the function. Grades and steps of the type seen in civil service could be applied in private organizations. Higher-rated jobs would be expected to pay more than lower-rated jobs. Numerical scores could be translated into monetary values. Point systems to do just that began to be applied as early as the 1920s (Benge, Burk, and Hay 1941, 13–15; Lanham 1955). However, the techniques were experimental and limited in that period. An IRC publication (1932) reviewed the literature on job analysis, primarily to catalog it. Although some of the books and articles covered linked job analysis to wage and salary administration, most of the references dealt with functions such as training, health and safety, and selection.

Pre–New Deal Social Welfare Benefits

The kinds of social welfare benefits that are today associated with employment were not prominent elements of the typical pre–New Deal employment relationship. However, there was employer interest in encouraging employee thrift; concerns about the "contempt for the careful husbanding of ... resources" and "free spending of money" by workers could be heard (NICB 1929a, 1). To counteract these unfortunate worker habits, employers often provided and facilitated savings arrangements that can be seen as predecessors of contemporary 401(k) plans. More prudent worker behavior was the goal. Yet employee thrift plans arose in part out of worker savings. Workers did try to save. Early plans were established to give workers a vehicle to deposit their savings in locations where financial institutions were not available to handle small sums.

These informal systems evolved into formal arrangements with banks or credit unions or with company-sponsored "investment trusts" (mutual funds), sometimes with disproportionate investment in the firm's own stock. Payroll deductions were used to promote regular saving. As with modern tax-favored 401(k) plans, employers might subsidize employee contributions. In some instances, employer contributions were based on profit sharing. Thus, share ownership and profit sharing were linked to savings plans in the 1920s, as they sometimes are today. But in a world in which employees did not pay income taxes, the savings arrangements of the 1920s were not tied to favorable tax treatment. Apart from thrift, employers saw such plans as promoting "harmonious" labor relations, raising worker morale, and reducing labor turnover (ibid., 27–28, 32–33, 75).

Pre–New Deal Incentives

Thanks to the popularity of Taylorism in the pre–New Deal period, use of piece rates and related incentives was widespread. Taylor's particular favored plan—the differential piece rate—was by no means the only system used, however. In fact, there was a proliferation of alternative plans with differing schedules relating pay to output. Publications for management during this era refer to incentives ranging from simple piece rates for individuals to small-group plans—for esprit de corps—with varying kinks and slopes in the pay/output schedule. Among the plans mentioned were the Rowan, Halsey, Wennerlund, Emerson, Bedeaux (or Bedaux), Haynes-Manit, Parkhurst, Gantt, Merrick, and Standard Time systems (Balderston 1930, 28, 58–76; NICB 1930c, 52–115). All claimed to be "scientific," although no one undertook rigorous statistical research to investigate which was best.

Unions sometimes resisted the use of such incentives, preferring a time-based rather than output-based system. They were particularly suspicious of complex plans devised by management under which proper compensation was hard to determine (Balderston 1930, 27). Where unions had succeeded in achieving a move to time-based wages, however, employers complained that productivity was reduced (NICB 1921, 13–14). Nonetheless, unions may well have had some success in repressing the use of piece rates and incentives. The Conference Board reported that while less than half of "wage earn-ers" in upstate New York were on time rates, about four fifths of the workers in New York City—a center of unionism—were time workers (NICB 1928a, 46). However, unions were weak in most parts of the country, limiting their influence on use of piece rates or any other pay practice.

In fact, as Table 7.4 illustrates, the use for factory workers of time rates only, i.e., not in combination with other incentive plans, was rare in larger businesses. Smaller firms were roughly as likely as others to use piece rates only. But bigger businesses more commonly used "sophisticated" plans that combined piece rates with other forms of incentives. Managers in such big-ger firms believed that by using "tact" and "gaining the workers' confidence," they could overcome employee resistance to a switch to incentives (NICB 1930c, 50–51). In a parallel with modern times, the Conference Board warned that global competition was mounting and America needed incentive sys-tems to keep up (ibid., 123).

Although explicit incentives were common, the implicit incentive of pay-ing above the going wage—what contemporary labor economists call "effi-ciency wages"—was certainly known. It has been argued that Henry Ford's famous $5 per day was an efficiency wage, promoting loyalty and creating motivation to meet production standards (Raff and Summers 1987). Ford's desire for union avoidance may also have played a role in his high-pay strat-egy. But more generally, the efficiency wage strategy could be seen as an alternative to Taylorism, with its technical approach to resolving the Labor Problem. The principle of a good wage as a part of a strategy of sound em-

Table 7.4

Use of Alternative Pay Systems, 1928

Size of establishment (workers)	Percentage of employees under different pay systems			
	Time rates only (%)	Piece rates only (%)	Piece rates and other incentives (%)	Other incentives only (%)
1–150	44.7	44.3	4.8	6.2
151–350	22.4	56.5	11.0	10.2
351–750	17.0	53.6	18.7	10.8
751–1,500	4.1	57.5	23.8	14.5
1,501 and higher	1.6	45.5	40.8	12.1

Source: National Industrial Conference Board 1930c, p. 7.

ployee relations was more in keeping with the approach of IRC that emphasized mutuality of interests of both sides of the employment relationship. Of course, employers did not have to choose one or the other approach. Ford's strategy was a mix of scientific management and mutuality, albeit without any form of the employee representation idea often associated with IRC.

Pre–New Deal Risk Sharing: Stock Ownership

The major risk-sharing systems for employees of the pre–New Deal era were stock ownership plans (although not stock options) and profit-sharing plans, both of which—as noted—were sometimes tied to thrift plans.

If strict Taylorism had been a stimulus to incentives on the individual or small-group basis, it could only have been a retarding force with regard to more widespread risk-sharing programs such as profit sharing. Taylor had condemned broad plans of risk sharing because of the free rider problem (Taylor 1911, 48). However, once Taylor and others placed the focus on using pay to raise productivity, a natural interest developed in all forms of pay plans that might have that effect.

There is a long history of attempts at worker cooperatives in the United States that could be looked at as a form of worker control akin to 100 percent stock ownership. Such cooperatives did not offer equity to outsiders. In contrast, stock ownership plans of the pre–New Deal period primarily involved companies with outside ownership and only a relatively small employee share. One survey of 20 companies with such plans in 1926 found the percentage of employee ownership of all outstanding stock to vary from 0.2 percent to 11.6 percent.[10] About $1 billion of employee-owned shares was found in another survey of more than 300 such plans in 1927. This amount was a small fraction of 1 percent of total equity outstanding (NICB 1928b, 35, 39).[11] Stock plans were mainly found in larger firms that had publicly traded shares to offer (NICB 1929c, 17–18).

Generally, what was offered was a plan whereby employees could buy shares at a favorable price or through simplified means such as payroll deduction. At General Electric, the employee thrift plan allowed purchase of company stock. In other cases, such as at Proctor & Gamble, shares were part of a profit-sharing plan, i.e., the profit-sharing bonuses came as stock. Finally, shares might be given to employees as part of bonus programs.

Share plans were not always available to ordinary employees, however; they might be applicable only to selected white-collar groups and managers. Unions generally opposed stock ownership and—not surprisingly—some employers saw such ownership as a way to avoid unionization. Employers sometimes cited generalized loyalty as a benefit to the firm. But DuPont reported that "to the average employee, ownership in the business carries but small appeal" (NICB 1928b, 131). Good public-relations value was a factor in offering some stock plans. And some employers cited share/savings plans as a source of capital. However, if the plan was actually a better source of capital than the outside market, that may have been an indication that the risk/reward being offered to employees was suboptimal from the worker viewpoint. Why should a firm be able to obtain worker-owned capital at better rates or with greater ease than capital from the external financial market?

After the 1929 stock market crash, the Conference Board decided to revisit the state of employee stock plans. Had employees become disenchanted by the plans after seeing their holdings drop precipitously in value? The difficulty with this investigation was that the Conference Board asked management, not employees, about how workers were reacting. Not surprisingly, management representatives tended to downplay the consequences of the crash. In 1930, the Conference Board thus reported: "Employee stock purchase plans have emerged from this critical period, not only unimpaired in any important respect, but actually strengthened by the trial, and now enjoying in fuller measure the confidence of both management and employees" (NICB 1930a, 34). This ludicrous conclusion carries a lesson for modern managers. If you want to know what workers are thinking about pay practices, ask *them*.

Pre–New Deal Risk Sharing: Profit Sharing

Profit sharing, as noted above, was sometimes combined with stock ownership where the two plans coexisted. But small firms, which were unlikely to have share plans, were roughly as likely as larger ones to have some version of profit sharing (NICB 1929c, 16–17). Then as now, some plans that were called "profit sharing" were not in fact linked to profits by a formula. They were discretionary bonus plans of one type or another. Profit-sharing plans, like employee stock plans, were sometimes limited to only a subgroup within the total workforce (such as managers). On the other hand, there were profit-sharing plans that covered most or all employees.

A survey by the BLS in 1917 revealed all three types of plans in operation: formula-based profit sharing, discretionary profit sharing, and profit sharing with only limited workforce coverage. The earliest plan reported in the BLS survey originated in 1886 (Emmet 1917, 8–10). One plan surveyed by BLS had in the past paid such large profit-sharing bonuses that participating employees' pay was doubled—or more than doubled—in several years. For most plans, however, the bonuses were decidedly more modest, in the range of 1 percent to 10 percent. This range seemed to be the norm in a later Conference Board study as well (NICB 1929c, 44).

Profit sharing was better established than employee stock plans at the time of the BLS survey. Perhaps for that reason, employers seemed to have a clearer grasp of the pros and cons they saw in offering profit-sharing plans. They viewed profit sharing—because it is a large-group plan—as inferior as a work incentive to individual-based systems such as piece rates. The problem of free riders was clearly recognized: "It is usually not possible to trace any direct relationship between the efforts of individual workmen and the profits that accrue" (NICB 1920, 73).

But employers also noted that piece rates could not always be applied, since there were cases when it was hard to determine output of individual workers. They reported that piece rates might have perverse effects, e.g., haste making for waste, a problem they saw profit sharing as correcting. Some of the language used by employers suggests they regarded profit sharing as promoting group cooperation. Where profit-sharing bonuses were significant, but paid only infrequently, employers saw the plans as reducing turnover, since workers had to wait until bonus time to quit if they wanted to collect. Finally, improvement in labor relations was also cited (Emmet 1917, 169–71). Unions, it might be noted, were unhappy with profit sharing, much as they were with stock plans. They liked neither the variable income entailed nor the co-opting of workers as mini-capitalists.

One element in risk sharing that was not cited by employers in the pre–New Deal period was the use of profit sharing as a form of flexible pay that could limit the need for layoffs. Interest in employment stabilization rose with the onset of the Great Depression. But this "enlightened practice," as the Conference Board called it, was linked to techniques such as forecasting the business cycle (to avoid hiring excess workers), moving redundant workers around within divisions of the firm, retraining, and similar devices (NICB 1930b, 12–35). Then, as now, reduction in weekly hours rather than workers was a common practice when demand fell; firms might initially drop to a five-day workweek in order "to conserve their working force [so] that it might function promptly when normal operation is resumed" (NICB 1929b, 57).

Employers did not explicitly discuss the possibility that pay flexibility could substitute for employment or hours flexibility. As noted earlier, there is evidence of greater downward wage flexibility than seen in current practice (Mitchell 1985). But progressive employers viewed wage cuts as bad things and resisted them in the early years of the Great Depression (Kaufman 2000, 50). There is an interesting disconnect here between economists, who in those pre-Keynesian times put much faith in wage flexibility as the solution to unemployment, and employers, who apparently did not.

Pre–New Deal Summary

American employers in the pre–New Deal period, unaffected by tax incentives and—in most cases—not imminently threatened by unionization, were in an almost laissez-faire situation with regard to the pay decisions they made. Absent external pressures, employee benefits were offered, but to a much lesser degree than exists today. In contrast, the use of explicit incentives was more widespread, particularly cash incentives such as piece rates and their Taylorist variants. Employers did not necessarily choose overtly between Taylorism—with its technical approach to solving labor problems—and the more "personal" approach, represented by IRC, that emphasized a mutual interest. They might mix and match, as at Ford with its Taylorist controls on worker effort combined with high wages and welfare benefits.

Stock ownership was offered by some larger firms, at least while the stock market was rising. Profit sharing was better established but not especially widespread. Although employers paid cash incentives for specific behavioral results, their impressions of gains for the firm from programs such as pensions or profit sharing were often more vague. Such programs were seen as morale boosters and, perhaps, turnover reducers. During this era, the use of profit sharing—a form of pay flexibility—was not discussed or even perceived by employers as an employment stabilization device. Job evaluation was used on a limited basis to determine internal pay differentials, but the practice was in its infancy.

The Post–World War II Era

The Great Depression dramatically altered labor relations and compensation policy. The public blamed business for the Depression, government intervention in the economy increased substantially, and union membership rapidly expanded. Strike activity greatly increased, and unions began to play an important role in pay setting. In 1935, for example, the BLS characterized the results of strikes involving more than half of all strikers as producing "substantial gains to workers" (BLS 1937, 70). Both government and union influence were reinforced during the subsequent World War II era of regulation of the economy for military reasons and wartime wage controls. Government efforts to avoid strike disruptions of production during the war aided union growth. In the personnel field, elements of past practice were threatened by developments during the Depression years. Employer-provided social benefits and variable elements in compensation were among the endangered species. But after the war, the former tended to be hardier than the latter.

Impact of the Economic Trauma

As the economy slid into the Depression, various company-provided benefits were cancelled. Stock purchase plans tended to be discontinued as share values declined. The Conference Board reported that "in some cases, it was difficult to explain the situation to certain uneducated elements of the working force who could not comprehend why they were not paid in full (by the stock plans) and, consequently, employee morale suffered" (NICB 1936b, 13–14). In a subsequent report, IRC suggested that the rise of unions was partly attributable to "embittered" workers who felt management had enticed them into money-losing investments (1945b, 7). Even where companies had seemingly conservative savings arrangements with local banks, bank failures sometimes led to plan terminations and employee losses (NICB 1936b, 23).

Just as stock plans suffered when stock values declined, profit-sharing plans were also often discontinued in an era of financial duress. And profit sharing was unlikely to be found in the then-growing union sector since unions—as noted earlier—disliked the income variation inherent in such arrangements. At most, unions might occasionally accept contract reopeners based on unforeseen movements in product prices or profits (BLS 1942, 46, 51). Where profit sharing continued, the idea that expected bonuses should substitute for regular wages was not accepted as good personnel practice (Balderston 1937, 60). Rather, the going rate of wages should be paid with profit sharing as an extra benefit. The Weitzman notion of the 1980s that profit sharing would generate jobs by lowering the regular wage was thus precluded.

Although large-group plans such as stock ownership and profit sharing were adversely affected by the Depression, there was nothing immediately in the economic decline that should have depressed the use of individual and small-group incentives such as piece rates. These plans were far more common than stock ownership or profit sharing. And they were much more likely to be continued (NICB 1934, 15, and 1936c, 12). Union policy on piece rates varied in this period: Some contracts restricted piece rates or demanded union participation in their operation; others were more permissive (BLS 1942, 53–61). On the other hand, bonus plans based on good behaviors such as faithful attendance were often discontinued during the Depression. Presumably with a high unemployment rate, whatever wage was paid was a sufficient "efficiency wage" to keep employees on their toes (NICB 1936c, 12). That is, the negative threat of job loss was a sufficient incentive, and an additional positive reward for general good behavior was not needed. Still, some specific behaviors, such as making cost-saving suggestions, were rewarded, generally with small bonuses (NICB 1936a).

The drop in use of certain bonuses may have been a reflection of the subjective basis for such payments. With unions now either part of the wage-setting process or threatening to become involved, employers looked for objective criteria for pay. Job evaluation to set occupational pay differentials became popular on the grounds that it would "remove all suspicion from the employee's mind that favoritism exists." In addition, management could make a better case in union negotiations because job evaluation represented "the substitution of factual data in place of personal opinion" in bargaining (NICB 1940, 4, 9).

War, Human Relations, and Fairness in Pay Setting

World War II, with its patriotic appeals for higher productivity and with union cooperation and no-strike pledges during the war effort, provided support for incentives such as piece rates. In industries where they were common, incentive pay systems persisted during the war. Unions—if they organized piece-rate industries such as cotton textiles—might insist on a voice in the system. For example, they might demand a minimum hourly wage floor or consultation before jobs were retimed after a change in production technology (BLS 1946, 10, 12). But two factors began to work against piece-rate use after the war: the spread of the human relations approach in industry and the push for economic security by unions.

The human relations approach suggested that workers could be motivated by means other than base materialism. Indeed, the very idea of simple incentives was degrading. Modern psychology could be used to design management systems that would stimulate productivity and cooperation. Initially, it was argued that wage incentives were salvageable if management used appropriate methods of worker consultation in their design. As Carroll E. French of IRC put it, "If anybody is ignored in a matter that he deems of vital interest to him, there is a resentment built up. . . . That is the crime that has been committed against American workmen by employers in instituting wage incentive plans" (quoted in Urhbrock 1935, 29).

Authorities at the War Production Board promoted incentive plans as a way of obtaining maximum production from scarce labor. A BLS study during the war noted that on the basis of industry, union status, and occupation, incentive workers earned more per hour than time workers, a finding that remains true (BLS 1943). Such a result suggests that incentive workers were more productive than time workers, possibly because of the effort-based incentives or sorting in hiring.[12] The War Production Board undoubtedly believed the former interpretation. Like French, however, it wanted such plans to be implemented only with employee or union consent (War Production Board 1945, 19).

A compendium of studies on incentives issued by IRC in 1944 emphasized the need for fairness and for dealing with union concerns in implementing such plans. For some unions, the idea of setting production standards with management raised concerns about conflict of interest in representing workers (IRC 1944; Kennedy 1945, 145). But as the human relations approach became trendy after the war, academia began to see piece-rate incentives as retrograde, although such pay systems persisted in industries such as apparel.

Equity in Wage Structure

The focus on equity and fairness spotlighted the issue of wage structure. How could wage differentials across jobs and occupations be justified, particularly in the face of the new union challenge to managerial discretion? Internal labor markets run by what has been termed "regulated bureaucracies" or "bureaucratic control" became the norm for pay setting and human resource management (Baron, Jennings, and Dobbin 1988; Milkovich and Stevens 1999). Job evaluation plans could be used within such internal markets to deal with the problem of equitable wage structures.

As noted earlier, the foundation for job evaluation had been laid earlier and existed in limited form before the New Deal. On the eve of World War II, IRC published a guide to implementation of job evaluation (Balderston 1940). The idea of grouping job attributes into various categories was well known by then. And the experiments conducted by Edward N. Hay at a Philadelphia bank would shortly evolve into the consulting firm that still bears his name and promotes the Hay system of job evaluation. Thus, the paraphernalia of contemporary systems of job evaluation—even the calculation of "compa-ratios"—were already in place (Benge, Burk, and Hay 1941, 191–94). The War Labor Board fostered job evaluation, in part as an administrative convenience. If firms could show that they had a formal plan in effect, it was not necessary for the Board to review every wage decision made within the plan. By the end of the war, plans were in operation at GE, Westinghouse, U.S. Steel, and major aircraft companies. All these plans rated jobs on skill, effort, responsibility, and job conditions, although in different fashions (Johnson, Boise, and Pratt 1946, 38).

In short, elaborate job evaluation plans and performance appraisals, often linked to time-based wages, became much more common after World War II (Kerr and Fisher 1950; Baron, Dobbin, and Jennings 1986, 361). But even in the early 1950s, many firms did not use them.[13] One survey of 1,265 firms found that more than half either had no job evaluation plan or had discontinued an earlier plan. Thirty percent either had a formal plan or were in the process of installing one. The rest either were considering a plan or had an informal one. One hang-up was union attitudes. Some unions regarded job evaluation as "hocus-pocus" and preferred to negotiate on wages, job by job. And since job evaluation typically produces a wage rate range rather than a single wage, some firms feared that unions would try to push everyone to the top rate of the range (Lanham 1955, Gilmour 1956, 188; 10, 29–30).

In fact, the union role in the postwar period was complex. Unions, like management, ultimately had to justify to workers whatever wage differentials emerged. And since unions tend to push wages above what nonunion labor markets would otherwise offer, citing the market as a rationale was not feasible. Thus, unions in steel, apparel, and other industries looked at job evaluation plans as a potential route to offering a rationale. While some unions took a hands-off approach and focused on the wage outcomes of the plans, others emphasized a need to formulate the plans *jointly* with management.

From a management perspective, a proliferation of finely differentiated job titles could lead to grievances. Slight changes in a worker's job duties would lead to union demands for reclassification. From the union perspective, finely differentiated job titles could undermine seniority in cases of either job cuts (and related "bumping" rights) or job opportunities (Gomberg 1947; Patton and Smith 1949, 76, 254–55). And in any event, job descriptions had to actually match job content where unions were involved. Arbitrators in the postwar period took the position that they would go by content (which could change over time) in deciding grievances over job classification (Baumback 1954, 6–16). Furthermore, although job evaluation plans were certainly systematic, they ultimately involved subjective ratings that could be challenged. Contemporary research indicates that job evaluation consultants can differ widely on suggested wage differentials (Arnault et al. 2001).

In some cases, the methodology of job evaluation could be excessively formalized and rigid. Was it really a "basic rule" in writing job descriptions that "each sentence should begin with a functional verb [and] the present tense should be employed throughout," as a wartime government guidebook demanded (quoted in American Society of Civil Engineers 1952, 9)? What might have seemed obvious as methodology in the 1940s became politically incorrect later. Thus, a textbook's advice to maintain separate pay scales for male and female employees and separate plans for office (often female) and production (often male) workers sparked demands for "comparable worth" and "pay equity" in the 1970s and 1980s (Balderston et al. 1949, 391). Similarly, relatively narrow job categories associated with traditional job evaluation produced demands for "broad banding" in the 1980s and 1990s. What seemed fair and efficient in one era could seem rigid and discriminatory in another.[14]

The Quest for Security

Depression trauma produced a general quest for "security." Depression fears—as reflected in union demands for security and stability—were reinforced by a demographic change in the workforce. The 1920s saw a cutoff of mass immigration to the United States, reducing the fluidity of the labor market. Immigrants already in the United States set down roots. They were not replaced by new immigrants who lacked strong family or geographic ties (Jacoby 1983).

After World War II, the quest for security at the macro level led to calls for a national "Full Employment Act" by unions, liberals, and Keynesian economists. At the micro level, unions pushed for a "guaranteed annual wage," or GAW. They wanted blue-collar workers to be treated like white-collar workers, i.e., the famous "man in the gray flannel suit" with his fixed salary and insulation from layoff. An argument was sometimes made that the micro-installation of wage and employment guarantees would itself have stabilizing macro-effects by ensuring worker purchasing power (IRC 1948b). However, while Keynesian economists pushed for fiscal policies that would bring about full employment, they did not believe it could be accomplished at the micro level. Still, they raised no objections to union-negotiated stabilization plans (BLS 1947b, 42). As it turned out, neither of these quests—macro via government fiscal policy nor micro via private bargaining—was completely satisfied. The proposed "Full Employment Act" was transfigured by a conservative Congress into just the "Employment Act of 1946." The demand by unions for a GAW was also compromised.

Some employers did concede annual hour guarantees to core workers even before America's entrance into World War II (BLS 1942, 68–70). During the war, there was a significant jump in contracts containing such provisions, although relatively few additional workers were covered (BLS 1947a, 7). Consequently, as the postwar agitation for a GAW intensified, much of the discussion in management circles was in terms of plans providing for employment and hours stabilization (IRC 1953). But as it turned out in practice, the GAW demand was often transformed into supplemental unemployment benefits, or SUB, plans. Under SUB plans, larger unionized employers operated private unemployment insurance programs for laid-off workers that supplemented state unemployment insurance payments. Layoffs could still occur—and did—but workers' annual incomes were smoothed. Pressure for a secure and nonvariable income worked against implementation or continuation of variable income programs such as piece rates or profit sharing. An exception was the use of a profit-sharing fund as a de facto SUB fund in a few cases (Frutkin 1955, 133–34).

Postwar Social Benefits

As is well known, employer-provided social benefits—especially pensions and health insurance—greatly expanded after World War II, particularly in the union sector. These benefits represented another form of security. Intended or not, such programs tended to tie workers to firms and discourage turnover. The emphasis was on fairness and equity rather than individual performance. Thus, IRC (1948a) reported that in the early postwar period, many employers were in fact supplementing their pensions with ad hoc payments due to inflation (or other factors). That is, they were making payments beyond their pension plans' requirements for reasons of equity.

An emphasis on equity runs against the use of variable pay for performance. Is it fair, for example, for an older worker who can't quite keep up with younger workers to be penalized through lower pay due to a piece-rate formula? With unions emphasizing cross-company comparisons and pattern bargaining, would it be fair for workers in one firm to earn more than identical workers in another because of differential profitability and profit sharing? Pay variation, whether across individuals, groups, or even time, can easily be seen as unfair in a world that places emphasis on security and equity.

Postwar Incentives

In the immediate postwar period, incentive wage plans such as piece rates were continued in union contracts—but with the constraints found in the wartime period. Union representatives were to be involved in programs such as

Table 7.5

**Bureau of National Affairs Data on Union Contract Provisions, Early
1960s: Proportion of Contracts with Selected Features**

Type of feature	(%)
References to piece rate or wage incentives	"about half"
Bonuses, including profit sharing	24
Escalator or cost of living adjustment	4

Source: Bureau of National Affairs, Inc., 1961.

timing of jobs despite their misgivings about being too involved in administering work standards. Minimum earnings guarantees were provided (BLS
1948a). As Table 7.5 shows, about half of contracts surveyed by the Bureau
of National Affairs in the early 1960s made reference to piece rates or wage
incentives, although some references constituted limitations. Such contracts
were found mainly in manufacturing, where output could be counted. Note
that a mention of piece rates in a contract does not mean that all workers
covered by the agreement were under piece rates. In some cases, the reference could apply only to a small subgroup.

A tension existed between the growing use of job evaluation—noted
above—and incentive systems. Individual incentive systems would create
varying differentials across workers and occupations. Advocates of job evaluation argued that appropriately constructed incentive plans could overcome
the problem. Or perhaps group bonuses instead of individual ones could preserve pay structure (Ells 1945, 46–54). But given the potential complexity of
reconciling variable pay with notions of a proper wage structure, it may have
been easier for some firms to drop incentive formulas. Time wages with periodic merit appraisals could be easier to administer. And well-documented merit
appraisals could be useful in defending adverse personnel decisions when contested before tribunals such as the National Labor Relations Board or those
handling unemployment compensation appeals (Benge 1953, 41–42).

Unfortunately, use of piece rates and similar incentives was not well tracked
in the postwar period. The BLS reported that the proportion of urban
"plantworkers" under such plans dropped from 20 percent in the early 1960s to
14 percent by the end of that decade. And the decline of such systems in manufacturing appeared to continue into the late 1970s (Cox 1971; Carlson 1982).

Postwar Risk Sharing

Just as wartime (and prewar) piece rates continued into the immediate postwar period in union agreements, so too did plans linking pay to product price

in industries such as metal mining. However, on the pricing side, contractual "escalator" provisions linking pay to the general Consumer Price Index (CPI) were becoming far more common (BLS 1948c, 41–46). While the product-price type of plan can be viewed as a gain-sharing/risk-sharing arrangement, the more common CPI-type of plan was in fact a way of shifting the risk of general inflation away from workers and to the employer. Security, rather than assumption of risk, was the more dominant theme in the union sector. Even where protection of the real wage through escalators was not required, restrictions on nominal wage reductions—as in cases when workers were recalled from layoff—were incorporated into union contracts (BLS 1948b, 6–7).

As noted, unions did not like the variability of profit sharing. And management tended to agree that workers did not want variable pay. As a 1945 report from IRC stated:

> Profit sharing does not commend itself to the wage earners. Its present position after more than a century of trial and error is insignificant. The first want of a worker is for a steady income. . . . He will accept any hand-out from profits as "gravy," but he will not be content to depend upon such a fluctuating factor as profits for any substantial part of his regular income. Profit sharing may appeal to the gambling instinct . . . but there is no considerable body of evidence that it has any more effect than a lottery ticket in inciting [workers] to greater effort. [1945a, 39]

Apart from being dubious about the utility of profit sharing as an incentive, management feared that if unions agreed to profit sharing, they would take an undue interest in sharing managerial prerogatives. Profit sharing thus came to be seen as a nonunion pay device (Jacoby 1997, 251–52). However, there were certainly union workers under some plans. The Profit Sharing Research Foundation found that 30 percent of profit-sharing plans surveyed in the early 1950s were in firms with 40 percent or more union employees. On the other hand, more than half were in firms with less than 10 percent unionization (Knowlton 1954, 10). Some written case studies pointed out that union cooperation with profit sharing promoted a good relationship, a benefit to both labor and management. It was suggested that profit sharing should be part of a package of participative practices—a theme that became commonplace by the 1990s (Tarneja 1964, 34–36, 65–77). But as Table 7.5 shows, only 4 percent of surveyed union contracts had a profit-sharing feature in the early 1960s. Union pay was more likely to be tied to the Consumer Price Index (CPI).

Stock ownership plans had fallen into disrepute in the 1930s; IRC noted in 1945 that given the woeful Depression experience, "it is doubtful whether stock ownership in the long run accrues to the employees' benefit." The same report suggested that executive stock options were largely a tax avoidance device and could not be justified unless an executive was called upon to rescue a failing business. In profitable firms, such compensation was "difficult of justification" (1945b, 18, 20). Despite these postwar views, both stock options and employee stock plans continued. And by the early 1960s, IRC took a more positive, but still cautious, approach to executive stock options. They could be helpful if used with "care and astuteness" (1963, 44).

A Conference Board study of company savings plans in the early 1960s found that most allowed employees to buy company stock. Where company stock was offered, employees often directed a large share of their savings to such stock. Evidently, Depression memories had faded by then (Fox and Meyer 1962, 48–52). Still, risk sharing was not the norm. A Conference Board study in the early 1950s of 422 companies found that only 10 percent had profit sharing and only 6 percent had a savings plan (some of which might have held company stock). But two thirds had a pension plan and more than 80 percent had health insurance (NICB 1954, 9). Programs geared to security rather than risk were what employees seemed to want and what employers wanted to offer.

As in any era, there were exceptions. The famous Lincoln Electric Company, with its strong emphasis on piece rates and profit sharing, was the subject of a sequence of Harvard Business School case studies after World War II. Its CEO initiated the firm's pay system in part because of his hostility to New Deal ideology. During the war, when Lincoln supplied the military, he feuded with the government over the bonuses paid to employees (dawson 1999, 39–41, 61–66, 79–93; Lincoln 1946, 83–88). Thus, the Lincoln pay system was intended to be the antithesis of those practices that had developed at other firms as the result of the Depression/World War II influence. Not surprisingly, Lincoln Electric received renewed prominence during the 1980s and 1990s when pay for performance was again in vogue and postwar pay practices were being questioned.

From There to Here and Onward

Compared with the 1920s, security-motivated social welfare benefits are more pervasive in the modern U.S. pay system than are pay-for-performance systems (such as piece rates, profit sharing, ESOPs, or stock options). Economists have become increasingly aware that all forms of compensation have behavioral consequences, whether or not they are labeled explicitly as "incentives." The behavioral consequences of social welfare benefits for employee hiring and retention undoubtedly outweigh the labor-market impact of explicit incentive plans simply because the former are so prevalent, in part due to tax subsidies.

Some pay incentives, notably ESOPs and stock options, benefit from favorable tax treatment. But apart from the macroconsiderations that may apply in the case of profit sharing, there is no strong rationale for this type of intervention in microlevel decision making about pay policy. I believe that making the pay system more flexible through programs such as profit sharing would be desirable from the perspective of employment stabilization. However, I also believe that the interplay of the tax code and pay policy has made the compensation system excessively complex and often opaque to both employees and employers—not a desirable outcome.

While there are always innovations in pay and HR practices, the longer history of such practices suggests an oscillation between two poles of thought. On the one hand, there are those who view the employment relationship as susceptible to a technical fix. Taylorism, pay for performance, and re-engineering fall into that category. At the other end of the spectrum are those who focus more on the "human" side of the employment relationship, as IRC did at its founding. Throughout the twentieth century, the point of median practice was influenced by great external events such as war and depression as well as internal experimentation by HR managers.

The twenty-first century began with both economic uncertainty and a war on terrorism, factors that could influence HR practices in ways that are hard to predict. But what is certain is that the American workforce is aging as the baby boomers reach their final years of employment. An aging workforce is likely to value security and stability, even within an uncertain external context. Approaches to pay and security that emphasize mutual obligation within the employment relationship will have increased appeal to such employees.

Pay policy is clearly a major decision area for human resource managers. And it is also a topic of increasing research interest to academics. An opportunity for mutual collaboration thus exists. Both academics and managers would benefit from improved and continuous data on pay practices. Both are interested in determining the impacts of alternative pay systems. In the early 1920s, Clarence J. Hicks proposed the establishment of Princeton's Industrial Relations section with the goal of gathering and disseminating current information, providing research opportunities, offering "unbiased instruction," and holding regular conferences of practitioners and scholars (Hicks 1941, 146–47). Many ideas about pay practice have changed since the 1920s. But that idea remains a good one.

Notes

1. Quoted in the online edition of the *Cincinnati Enquirer*, February 27, 2001, http://enquirer.com/editions/2001/02/27/fin_morning_memo.html.

2. The differential piece rate paid a premium once a standard, determined by time-and-motion study, was exceeded.

3. Note that morale explanations that have been traditionally used to explain reluctance to cut wages do not directly work in reverse. That is, it is difficult to argue that employee morale would be hurt by wage increases. Sluggishness on the up side, as seen during the labor shortages of the late 1990s, has not been well explained.

4. However, stock options can have calamitous tax implications for those who exercise their options but do not sell the resulting stock in a subsequent down market. Some dot-com employees who exercised in early 2000 but who didn't cash out before their stock's price tumbled faced huge tax liabilities with few assets to meet them.

5. As noted, there can be negative tax consequences if an up market is followed by a substantial stock price decline. However, a strategy of simply cashing out enough stock on exercise to pay the liability can avoid such risks.

6. To the extent that larger firms tend to provide benefits, the proportion of employers carrying the plan will be an underestimate of the proportion of employees covered in the sample. Thus, there will be an overstatement of the dollar amount provided in following the methodology described in the text. In addition, there was no direct estimate available of total compensation for employers with particular plans. Hence, the estimates of expenditure on particular plans are divided by an estimate of the total compensation for the entire sample. Plan providers, however, may well be higher payers of total compensation. Again, the methodology will produce an overestimate.

7. The table compares larger "establishments" with smaller "firms." However, while an establishment can be smaller than the firm that owns it, the firm cannot be smaller than any establishment within it.

8. The Chamber survey asks about "Employee Stock Ownership" but omits the word "Plan" from the end. Thus, arrangements other than strict ESOPs may be included.

9. The NICB relied on an Advisory Committee on Industrial Relations in the 1920s in collecting information. The committee was headed by Arthur H. Young of IRC and included Clarence J. Hicks, later chair of IRC (NICB 1929c, v–vi).

10. The actual percentages of total stock owned by employees at the time of the survey were below the figures cited in the text, since the calculation was based on actual employee ownership and "prospective" employee ownership.

11. There was about $500 billion in outstanding equity at the time (U.S. Bureau of the Census 1975, vol. II, 254).

12. If hard-working employees take jobs with piece rates—because they know they will earn premiums—while other workers take time-based jobs, it will be observed that incentive workers earn more per hour than time workers even if the incentives do not encourage more effort than would otherwise be forthcoming.

13. One factor discouraging use of job evaluation may have been the off-putting technical computations described in how-to books. One book, for example, provided an elaborate example of fitting a least-squares curve between points and wages. In the precomputer postwar period, the exercise was complex (Otis and Leukart 1948, 355–64).

14. It should be noted that advocates of comparable worth often saw use of job evaluation, but covering all occupations, as a remedy. Indeed, the failure to evaluate the jobs of "girls" was criticized in one of the first books on job evaluation (Lott 1926, 13).

8

Advancing Equal Employment Opportunity, Diversity, and Employee Rights

Good Will, Good Management, and Legal Compulsion

Jonathan S. Leonard

Introduction

One of the most controversial issues in labor policy since the 1970s has been the extent to which black economic progress toward equality with whites was due to government intervention in the workplace, to advances in education, or to the persistent forces of competitive markets (see Bloch 1994; Donohue and Heckman 1991; Freeman 1973; Heckman and Paynor 1989; and Smith and Welch 1984). In the context of this volume, the question is whether progressive (nondiscriminating) employers became prevalent enough to enable blacks to secure employment without suffering the effects of the discriminating employers that remained. A more difficult question is whether this would have occurred even in the absence of government intervention.

Certainly the historical record can be mined for some examples of progressive employers and some circumstances in which blacks progressed without benefit of legal compulsion. But after a period of intense contention over the empirical evidence, a consensus has now emerged that while educational advances and broader economic forces certainly played a role, black economic progress would not have been as rapid as it was if it had had to rely solely on the voluntary acts of progressive employers, without benefit of the threat of legal compulsion.

This chapter is concerned with the relative roles played by employers' voluntary actions and by federal law in securing black economic progress in the workplace. It first sketches the record of black economic progress—a record presented in greater detail in other reviews. It then turns to the question of how blacks made progress in an era without laws barring employment discrimination, concentrating on what drove a few early-twentieth-century employers to open their doors to blacks. I consider the role played by employee representation plans and by craft and industrial unions. I consider progressive management EEO practices in light of the history of anti-discrimination policy before and after the watershed passage of the Civil Rights Act (CRA) of 1964. The second section of the chapter deals with the impact of both the Civil Rights Act and associated affirmative action regulation. The third section then turns to the issue of voluntarism by exploring the potential role of alternative mechanisms for resolving demographic employment disputes. In particular, I examine demographic affinity groups (DAGs), placing them in the historical context of nonunion employee representation. This chapter considers some reasons for and consequences of this missing institution for demographic bargaining, in contrast to the established institutions for collective bargaining.

The Historical Record

The Record of Black Economic Progress

Black economic advance has been a product of the interplay of education, ability, migration, regulation, and economic change. Statistics on blacks' economic position in the labor market prior to 1940 are sparse. Higgs (1989) reports that black income per capita relative to that of whites increased from 24 percent in 1868, with the impediments of slavery, to about 35 percent in 1900. He also finds that this ratio stagnated between 1900 and 1940 (p. 12). Robert Margo (1990) shows that the improvement in blacks' occupational position between 1880 and 1950 resulted primarily from their migration to the North and their advance there.

Black stagnation and segregation in the South before World War II resulted from the exclusion of blacks from skilled occupations and new growing industries (Dewey 1952; Myrdal 1944; Wright 1986). This exclusion was rigidly maintained despite increases in the quantity and quality of black schooling in the South. Although helped somewhat by the tightened labor markets of World War I, blacks failed to improve economically relative to whites during the 1920s (Smith 1984) and lost ground in the 1930s with the Great Depression and shifts out of labor-intensive agriculture in the South (Myrdal 1944).

Using U.S. Census data on the ratio of black to white median earnings for full-time, full-year male workers, Glenn Cain reports that this ratio rose from 45 percent in 1939 to 62 percent by the early 1960s. WWII created a huge demand for labor that opened doors for blacks. Between 1967 and 1974, the ratio increased to 68 percent, and by the late 1970s it had reached 73 percent (Cain 1986, 708).

The oil shocks of the 1970s and the strong-dollar policy of the Reagan administration led to a secular transformation of parts of America's old industrial heartland into a rustbelt. But these were also the sectors into which blacks had moved. The industrial sectors whose burgeoning demand for labor had created opportunities for blacks now displaced them in a wave of mass layoffs and shutdowns. By the 1980s, black-male economic progress relative to that of white males suffered retrenchment because black males were heavily represented in the industries and occupations in decline (Bound and Freeman 1992).

While blacks were not heavily represented in high technology sectors by the end of the last decade of the twentieth century, they benefited from the long economic expansion that reduced unemployment to a rate not seen in three decades and began to raise the real wages of those at the bottom of the wage distribution. Among males working full-time full-year, the ratio of black to white median earnings had increased to 78 percent by the year 2000 (author's calculation with data from Current Population Survey).

Government Policy Between 1900 and 1945

The idea that employees might have a right to not be subject to discrimination is of relatively recent vintage. Changes in racial attitudes over the last century have been dramatic. One of the most remarkable accomplishments of twentieth-century America was its change from a country in which the Ku Klux Klan could march down the streets of Washington, D.C., at the beginning of the century to one in which the march through the city at the end of the century was led by Louis Farrakhan—a black not prominently featured during National Brotherhood Week.

As the U.S. economy industrialized, as the government freed the slaves and gave women the right to vote, and as U.S. society fitfully welcomed waves of diverse immigrants, it was not against the law to discriminate. The institution of slavery, which ended with the Civil War, and the Civil Rights movement of the mid-twentieth century provide the backdrop to passage of the paramount legislation barring discrimination in employment, the Civil Rights Act of 1964.

Discrimination was seen chiefly as a problem of race relations. During the first part of the twentieth century, blacks moved from the rural agricultural South to the urban industrial North. In the South, the labor force was still generally segregated. In the North, most blacks were still limited to jobs at the lowest rung of the occupational ladder.

The employment advances of minorities and women before WWII came largely in the absence of, or despite, government policy. Some state governments passed laws barring discrimination in a narrow range of sectors. An early example is Massachusetts' 1920 law barring racial discrimination in the civil service and in publicly aided public utilities (Kesselman 1946, 34).

With the desperation born of the Great Depression, the federal government dramatically increased state intervention throughout the economy. In the Unemployment Relief Act of 1933, Congress outlawed employment discrimination by race, color, or creed. Other New Deal legislation contained similar bans. Racial discrimination was banned in federal employment covered by the Works Projects Administration, the Civilian Conservation Corps, and the National Youth Administration. But all lacked a mechanism for enforcement and so had little demonstrated effect.

Between 1933 and 1941, the states of Illinois, Indiana, New Jersey, New York, Ohio, Pennsylvania, Kansas, California, and Minnesota passed laws prohibiting racial discrimination on work relief and public works projects. State laws lacked effective enforcement, complaint-processing mechanisms, criteria to determine discrimination, and sanctions (ibid., 34–35.). Again the crisis was stark, the focus narrow, and the effects limited.

The Unregulated Era

Examples of firms voluntarily employing blacks and treating them without discrimination can be found in the early part of the twentieth century and before, but these were the exceptions to the rule of pervasive discrimination. Even employers willing to hire blacks would often describe themselves as bowing to community standards that prevented them from doing so. Herman Feldman quotes a vivid example from one investigator in a large city circa 1930: "I visited the well-known factory in the city, and was told that they had quit employing Negroes. . . . They started this policy because 'the darkies were raising so much hell in town and were flocking in from the South, and the white people naturally wanted to put a stop to this' " (1931, 289). Even in the most discriminatory circumstances, there were some socially acceptable places for blacks to find employment—generally in low-skilled, low-status positions. Blacks moved from slaves to sharecroppers in southern agriculture, and into positions as maids and servants. Progression into industry was slower. Feldman writes, "Yet in the country as a whole the number of cases of concerns known to be interested in a satisfactory adjustment of the Negro in industry, even to the extent of having a policy of fair treatment on merit, is decidedly small" (ibid., 291). As the country and the South industrialized, blacks were usually barred from skilled positions but found entry into unskilled positions requiring heavy labor under harsh conditions. Employers that first moved to break the color line could, in many cases, offset community opprobrium with the economic advantage gained from having first pick of the pool of black labor, including the blacks who had managed to obtain skills despite the barriers in place.

In his excellent survey of racial employment patterns and organized labor in the first half of the twentieth century, Herbert Northrup finds blacks holding 30 percent or more of the jobs in longshoring (1944, 138). Northrup also documents firms hiring blacks in other industries, including steel and shipbuilding. The southern coal industry presents a more remarkable exception because, as Northrup notes, "segregation either by occupation or by place of work, unlike most factory industries in the South, is conspicuous by its absence in the coal mines. In mines where the two races are employed, they invariably work side by side and at the same occupations" (ibid., 159). Of course, it is no accident that blacks found accommodation in such heavy and dangerous labor. In contrast, Northrup notes, "In some industries, notably textile manufacturing, the printing trades, and clerical and white-collar pursuits, Negroes are largely excluded from employment by the decisions of management" (ibid., 6).

Even when graced with employers claiming not to practice discrimination, prospective employees cannot easily discern the employer's credibility or commitment. In his history of labor relations at International Harvester, Robert Ozanne (1967) describes the company's early formal adoption in 1919 of a written policy barring discrimination on the basis of race, sex, or membership in any labor organization as a liberal-sounding cloak to cover an anti-union open-shop policy (1967, 184). Consider this history in light of more recent naïve proposals that employers be free to discriminate (or what is the same thing, free to offer different levels of protection against discrimination). Employees would then freely choose among employers that offered the desired level of protection against discrimination. This envisions a Tiebout market in the workplace public good of fairness in employment decisions. (The level of fairness or discrimination in employment decisions can be thought of as a workplace public good. In a Tiebout model, levels of public goods are chosen through choice of community. Applied to the workplace, this model implies that with enough information, choice, and mobility across employers, employees can choose how much of a workplace public good they want by selecting among different employers.) As the Harvester case makes clear, potential employees face a severe information problem in judging the accuracy and credibility of the employer's proclaimed policy. At Harvester, ". . . no sooner was the plan adopted than its co-author, Arthur H. Young, was pressuring the manufacturing executives to cut down on the proportion of Negro employees" (ibid.).

As was common throughout northern industry, the labor shortages caused by WWI and by bars to immigration opened doors for black employment. Under the leadership of Fowler McCormick, Harvester's nondiscrimination policy ceased to be merely a cloak after 1941—this was motivated by a belief that people should be treated as individuals rather than as members of groups, according to Ozanne. McCormick carried these policies into Harvester's new southern plants in the face of concerted opposition from union locals. Unusually, McCormick opened a wide variety of jobs to blacks and trained them for skilled positions (ibid., 188–90).

Among large manufacturing concerns, Ford Motor Company and Firestone Tire are described as among the leaders in employing blacks, and in both cases, this is largely ascribed to idiosyncratic preferences by their leaders, Henry Ford and Harvey Firestone, Sr. At a time when roughly 2 percent of employees in the rubber products industry were black, Firestone's Memphis plant reached 30 percent. Firestone's interest in black employment may have been sharpened by its interest in ensuring continued supplies of raw materials from its associated Liberian rubber plantations, but other companies with similar dependencies employed far fewer blacks (Northrup 1970, 402, 405).

In Northrup's view, "Prior to World War II, Negroes came closer to job equality at the Ford River Rouge works than they did at any large enterprise know to the author or recorded in the literature" (ibid., 57). Northrup ascribes this in part to Henry Ford's independent streak and to his response to black leaders concerned with job loss during the 1921 depression (ibid., 55, 735). Even Ford's benevolence was sharply demarcated. A noted anti-Semite, even within the sphere of race relations, he was restrained by the attitudes of white employees. Ford largely limited the policy to the River Rouge plant, which accounted for 99 percent of Ford's black employees. But River Rouge stood out by employing blacks in all departments, in skilled jobs, and as foremen (Northrup 1944, 187, 189).

In terms of black employment share, the Briggs Motor Company had an even better record: In 1940, 21 percent of its employees were black, compared with 11 percent at Ford. Briggs also led in the employment of black females (Northrup 1970, 55, 62). Prior to World War II, blacks were also heavily represented at the automotive industry suppliers Midland Steel (30.5 percent black) and Bohn Aluminum and Brass (23.9 percent black), both being foundries with the most dangerous and disagreeable jobs (Northrup 1944, 188). In the South, the automobile companies, Ford included, followed community standards and avoided hiring blacks outside of a few service and menial labor jobs. On the whole, black employment expanded in growing industries.

Ford's experience at River Rouge may also have served as an example for firms in other industries, such as the Sun Shipbuilding and Drydock Company. In 1942, 10 percent of Sun's employees were black, in three integrated shipyards. Under wartime pressure to expand, Sun increased its black employment share to 43 percent in 1943. Curiously enough, most of this expansion of black employment took place in a newly opened all-black shipyard, perhaps illustrating the tenuous nature of progress in race relations. The Sun plan has also been criticized on the grounds that it was an attempt to copy the Ford River Rouge experiment of employing large numbers of blacks in order to ensure the cooperation of blacks in politics and in industrial relations. "Such allegations have been most emphatically denied by the Sun management, and no proof can be found to verify them" (ibid., 221).

What prevented these examples of private initiatives to employ blacks from serving as models for more widespread adoption? After all, in many respects, these examples were successful both in partially integrating the workplace and in making money. However, these companies still faced the weight of social opprobrium. Wright (1986) documents the failure of a number of "experiments" in which firms hired blacks but backed off in the face of strong community pressure. Warren Whatley (1990) and Thomas Maloney and Whatley (1995) find somewhat more positive effects from experimentation in their studies of the Detroit automobile industry in the 1910s and 1920s and of Cincinnati industry in 1918. Firms did change their policies toward blacks after gaining some direct experience. Maloney (1995) also found that blacks could advance more in northern meatpacking, with its greater ease of experimentation in more flexible internal hiring procedures, than in the steel industry.

Private efforts to end employment discrimination clearly extended beyond the idiosyncratic efforts of a few white employers. Blacks also attempted to organize to exert economic leverage on their own behalf rather than relying on government intervention. Both economic separatism (racial autarchy) and black boycotts of businesses that refused to hire blacks were attempted before WWII. The Vanguard League, the Future Outlook League, and the New Negro Alliance pursued such strategies with limited effect (Kesselman 1946, 33). Their leverage was constrained by limited capital and the modest income share of blacks. On the union side, A. Philip Randolph led the black Sleeping Car Porters Union, developing it into one of the first nationwide black organizations. Randolph was later to take a leading role in pushing both the AFL and then the AFL-CIO to fight discrimination.

Unions, Employee Representation Plans, and Racial Antagonism

A common path for black entry into industry was as strikebreakers (Marshall 1965). Employers seeking to divide and conquer, to drive a wedge into employee solidarity, or to break a strike played the race card. Throwing the kerosene of racial discord onto the spark of labor conflict fed the flames of long-lasting racial antagonism. The residue of this history is perhaps the most salient reason why unions even after 1964 faced difficulty reconciling the demands of black and white members. National unions attempting to voluntarily end discrimination within the union often faced distrust from blacks and resistance from many local union leaders.

The many unions that barred blacks from membership, particularly in the craft unions, set the stage for the use of black strikebreakers. Feldman (1931) reported twenty-two national unions that excluded blacks in their constitutions and numerous others that did so in practice, if not in writing (Feldman 1931, 27). The situation had changed little by 1944, when Northrup (1944) revisited the issue and found fourteen unions with provisions barring blacks, eight that tacitly barred them, and nine that only allowed them into segregated auxiliaries (Northrup 1944, 3–5). This racial discrimination was concentrated in unions of skilled craft workers, mostly AFL and railroad unions, that gained leverage with employers by restricting entry into the trades.

The CIO unions were driven to take a different position, both by ideology and by economic forces. With less ability to control the supply of labor into less skilled occupations, they faced direct competition from the unorganized, including unorganized blacks. As a result, most came to understand the necessity of organizing blacks who would otherwise have little option but to undercut their wage demands. At the same time, the industrial unions exercised much less control over whom the employer could hire.

This is not to say that all industrial unions practiced less discrimination than all craft unions, or even that all national unions agreed with the practices of their locals. The union of bricklayers and masons is an interesting exception—an AFL union with substantial black membership that fined members who discriminated against blacks. Most blacks in the construction trades were in unskilled laborer and hod-carrier positions. Some of these served as bricklayers' helpers. From this position, the nature of job interactions allowed blacks to learn the more skilled trade. At the same time, in more industrial settings, attempts to open skilled trades to blacks sometimes resulted in strikes by white employees (e.g., white workers walked out of the Bethlehem–Sparrows Point shipyard when blacks were admitted to riveting school) (ibid., 224).

Unions that barred blacks helped to create the condition in which employers used blacks as strikebreakers. Some employers using a divide-and-conquer strategy preyed on racial divisions. In an early and penetrating discussion of the uses of diversity, Feldman noted:

It may also be admitted that in the background, in varying degree, is the shrewd understanding that in time of strike, heterogeneity of race or nationality gives employers the upper hand. They have less reason to fear the cohesion that might result among workmen if they spoke a common language not understood by the employer or felt a racial bond in which he had no part. . . . In some instances, also, the possibility of using interracial jealousy among the workers themselves as a means of breaking up a long-protracted disturbance is also given an occasional thought. [1931, 272]

During the 1939 Chrysler strike, R.J. Thomas, president of the UAW-CIO, stated that the company was encouraging blacks to return to work in the hope of creating a race riot. Others interpreted this as a union threat to indeed riot if blacks did cross the picket line (Northrup 1944, 191). This makes current discussions of the benefits of diversity seem saccharine in contrast.

In this context, blacks often preferred employee representation plans and company unions to the AFL unions that had excluded them (Leiserson 1929, 156–58). During the 1922 strike by railroad shopmen, the Pullman Company moved black porters into skilled positions and later made this a permanent policy. The racist railroad craft unions subsequently made little progress in the Pullman shops, where workers supported a company-endorsed union (Northrup 1944, 81). Northrup further reports that in a 1943 shipyard election, black employees tended to vote for the company-dominated Sun Ship Employees Association rather than the competing CIO union, the IUMSWA, "because they felt a debt of gratitude to the Pew family [the company owners] for their employment opportunities. A vote for the IUMSWA was to them a vote against their benefactor" (ibid., 222).

Both employee representation plans and unions restricted an employer's discretion and subjectivity by implementing in part a rule-based system and a set of workplace employee rights. When fairly implemented, either system could offer blacks greater opportunity and protection. Not surprisingly, blacks preferred whichever system offered them greater opportunity. Given the history and the larger economic forces, this often, but not always, meant industrial unions followed by employee representation plans, since the AFL and railroad unions bore the most discriminatory legacy. The tobacco industry presents a contrasting case in which a company-dominated segregationist union lost to an integrated CIO union at Reynolds Tobacco (ibid., 116). At least one commentator claims that nonunion employee representation itself creates more liberal attitudes: "Some years ago the company put into effect a scheme of employee representation: [T]his has had the curious and unexpected effect of broadening the preoccupations of the more intelligent and skilled workers in the general direction of greater social responsibility. . . . The distinctively American population is showing signs of substituting for mere resentment a sense of the need to support the difficult work of social rehabilitation of the Mexican which has already begun" (Mayo 1929, 179).

Federal Regulation

Advancement of Equal Employment by Executive Order

World War II was an anvil of change upon which a new role for government in relations between the races was forged. Even as labor demand expanded with the nation's entry into the war, surveys indicated that 51 percent of new defense production jobs would be closed to blacks, while the black portion of the WPA rolls continued to rise between 1939 and 1942 (Kesselman 1946, 36). To protest employment discrimination at the beginning of World War II, President A. Philip Randolph of the Sleeping Car Porters Union threatened to disrupt the defense effort by staging a mass demonstration of blacks in Washington, D.C., on July 1, 1941. Less than one week before the planned rally, President Franklin Roosevelt issued Executive Order 8802—the progenitor of affirmative action—and the demonstration was called off. At the time, this Executive Order was hailed as a second Emancipation Proclamation. But accommodation was reached only under dire threat and even then was limited in nature. Executive Order 8802 barred discrimination by race, creed, color, or national origin in federal employment and defense contracts and established the Fair Employment Practice Committee (FEPC) to investigate charges of discrimination.

The tenor of the times can be judged from a few incidents. In the face of extreme labor shortages as wartime production boomed, manufacturing industries came under great pressure to open their doors to previously excluded groups. In fact, the demands of defense production were explicitly used to justify Roosevelt's Executive Order. But the largest excluded demographic group, women, was not even mentioned in the order or in the preceding New Deal legislation. When women were allowed to take over jobs previously reserved for men, it was in some unexceptional cases with the explicit condition that they withdraw to the status quo ante once the war was won. In 1943, the Packard engine plant in Detroit upgraded three black workers. This was enough to set off a wildcat strike followed by a race riot in which thirty-four people were killed and more than six hundred injured.

The FEPC immediately ran into a wall of political opposition that met every federal attempt to limit discrimination. It was starved for staff and budget. It lacked congressional authority and support. The first FEPC collapsed in 1943 in a conflict between Roosevelt's power as the chief executive and Congress's authority to legislate and budget. Roosevelt reinstituted a second FEPC by Executive Order 9346, which continued to hold hearings, investigate complaints, and seek to resolve them with the cooperation of employers. But when it failed to enlist that cooperation, the FEPC had little recourse to gain enforcement. Many employers and unions simply ignored its directives to cease discriminating. The second FEPC closed in 1946 in the absence of congressional support.

The campaign against discrimination has always depended on a calibrated balance between commitment bred of goodwill and compulsion based on strong law. In the 1940s, public opinion had yet to support a law sufficient to compel those who would discriminate. Marc Etheridge, the first chairman of the FEPC, clearly showed his own sharply circumscribed view of the limited role for compulsion in a democracy:

> Although he defended the granting of civil rights and equal opportunity to Negroes, he also affirmed his personal support of Segregation in the South. Stressing that "the committee has taken no position on the question of segregation of industrial workers," he emphasized that "Executive Order 8802 is a war order, and not a social document," and that had it [the Committee] done so, he would have considered it "against the general peace and welfare . . . in the Nazi dictatorial pattern rather than in the slower, more painful, but sounder pattern of the democratic process." [Quoted in Ruchames 1953, 28]

Although blacks made substantial economic progress during the 1940s, the direct role of federal antidiscrimination policy was limited. Reviewing the impact of the presidential FEPCs, Paul Norgren and Samuel Hill (1964) state, "One can only conclude that the twenty years of intermittent activity by presidential committees has had little effect on traditional patterns of Negro employment" (1964, 169), and "it is evident that the non-discrimination clause in government contracts was virtually unenforced by the contracting agencies in the years preceding 1961" (ibid., 171).

While antidiscrimination legislation faced a southern blockade in the Senate at the federal level, laws barring employment discrimination were enacted at the state and local levels. Starting with New York and New Jersey in 1945, eighteen states had enacted laws by 1960 that prohibited employment discrimination on the basis of race, religion, or national origin. All were outside the South. In addition, at least thirty municipalities had also enacted such laws. Many of the state FEPCs had cease-and-desist authority but rarely used it, relying instead on education, conciliation, and the threat of public embarrassment. By 1963, all but two of the state FEPCs that had previously relied solely on voluntary conciliation saw the need to add cease-and-desist authority.

While the experience of these state FEPCs has been little studied, some— including New York, in particular—seem to have had surprising success. The New York FEPC (formally the Human Relations Commission) received nearly nine thousand complaints over two decades and found probable cause for discrimination in nearly a fifth of the complaints. Almost all of these were resolved by investigation and conciliation under threat of public hearings and formal sanctions. Ultimately, only seven cease-and-desist orders were issued (Berger 1978). The experiences of these state FEPCs with their emphasis on conciliation were later to influence the creation of the federal Equal Employment Opportunity Commission (EEOC). Despite the limited enforcement tools of state FECPs, two recent empirical studies of their impact suggest they enjoyed some success in improving the economic position of blacks (Collins 2001; Neumark and Stock 2001). Clearly the process we have followed in the United States has been slow, and at times painful, but we have developed a democratic consensus against discrimination.

The Era of Voluntarism

Absent federal legislation barring employment discrimination prior to 1964, the voluntarism that characterized the first half of the twentieth century persisted into the 1950s and early 1960s. Blacks made significant progress through improvements in education and through migration to the industrial jobs in the North. Doors were opened by progressive managers who saw themselves not as social engineers but as professional managers. The Industrial Relations Counselors, Inc. (IRC), monograph, *Employing the Negro in American Industry* (Norgren et al. 1959), gives useful insights into what were then considered progressive management practices. As then Vice President Richard Nixon wrote in his preface, "A fundamental principle underlying [the nondiscriminatory employment methods adopted by 44 establishments] is that they must be motivated by genuine convictions as well as by business considerations" (ibid., vii).

What motivated managers to hire blacks in the late 1950s? Most of those surveyed in the IRC study cited the postwar labor shortage and self-interested good human resource management practices. In second place were state Fair Employment Practice laws, ignored in most later discussions of policy, and their federal and local counterparts. Almost as common a motivating factor was a principled belief that equal opportunity to all was simply the right or fair thing to do (these employers tended to be the earlier integrators). Other employers attributed their actions to pressure from organizations such as the Urban League or the NAACP, fear of adverse publicity, and a desire (in the consumer goods or services industries) to market to Negroes.

The overall tone of the 1959 IRC monograph is that the employment of blacks should be seen not as a forced result of racially targeted policies but rather as a normal by-product of the adoption of good management practices that benefit the business as a whole. As a professional analysis of the employment practices of forty-four large employers that first employed blacks during World War II, it stands apart from more recent work in this area, primarily in its much more intimate access to internal management decision making in a wider range of firms. The level of access and openness achieved by authors Norgren, Webster, Borgeson, and Patten in the IRC study has rarely been matched in subsequent research.

It is also striking that little in the intervening forty-four years would alter the prescriptions found in the 1959 study. Actually, prescription is too strong a word. The word "should" does not appear in this unabashedly pragmatic book. The authors focus instead on evidence of what works in practice, rigorously devoid of theories of organizational behavior. When compared with any recent guide to management on this issue, the fundamental advice given by IRC in 1959 remains current. A modern guide would express a less distant tone toward blacks and perhaps seem less patronizing. The modern version would make greater use of the word "diversity" without shedding any more light on the matters at issue, and it would usefully broaden the discussion to include women, the disabled, the aged, and a wider array of possible bases for discrimination. And the modern guide would certainly pay more attention to the demands of both globalization and the requirements of the law.

But the substance of IRC's 1959 prescription for effective management practice has regularly been reinvented by academic researchers, consultants, and practitioners in the intervening years. Declare top management backing. Plan. Communicate with current employees. Reach out to the community. Increase minority job applications by direct outreach to organizations, schools, and community leaders. Carefully perform initial screening, without lowering standards, or face the consequences later in job performance, job relationships, and opportunities for promotion. While specially targeted policies might be necessary at first, these should quickly be replaced by normal business practice. Avoid hiring those with little education, with a chip on their shoulder, or with a crusading attitude. Expect performance no better and no worse than that of other employees. Focus on harmonious race relations to maintain good workplace discipline and as part of an effort to ensure just and equitable treatment to all employees.

Employing the black then, becomes for the most part another aspect of good business practice. Pursued for the good of the business, with the same standards and generally the same practices that inform the rest of good human resource practice. As for the fear of suffering from poor productivity, the IRC study quotes a general manager with what the authors consider an attitude representative of those they interviewed: "Negroes are just as good as whites—they had better be or we'll get rid of them" (1959, 114). This freedom to select dominates any shortfall in average education or experience. During the 1960s, as black education and experience levels increased, the employers' discretion to select employees fell into the increasingly forceful embrace of antidiscrimination law.

Affirmative Action in the Shadow of Title VII of the Civil Rights Act of 1964

The Civil Rights Act of 1964 (CRA) marks a watershed in federal discrimination policy. Title VII of this act has been the keystone of the campaign to bar employment discrimination. The CRA established the EEOC, primarily as an agent of conciliation modeled after the earlier federal and state FEPCs. Of greater importance, the CRA established a private right to bring litigation charging discrimination, thus giving complainants the option to resolve their complaints in the courts rather than in an administrative agency.

Affirmative action in the United States has been implicitly encouraged by judicial interpretation of Title VII of the CRA and explicitly required, but not defined, by Executive Order 11246 applied to federal contractors. From its inception, the CRA has embodied a tension between words that bar employment discrimination and congressional intent to promote voluntary efforts to redress discrimination. The courts have sometimes struggled to make room for what they saw as the intent of Congress within the language of the CRA. In later cases, the U.S. Supreme Court read Section 703(J)'s bald statement that "nothing in the act shall require numerical balancing" as allowing numerical balancing as a remedy. In other cases, the Court held that the act should not be read to bar voluntary acts to end discrimination. These cases left considerable if ambiguous room for affirmative action. The threat of costly disparate-impact litigation under Title VII following the *Griggs* v. *Duke Power* case created considerable incentive to undertake affirmative action. *Griggs* was a revolutionary case. In its aftermath, every personnel decision and policy could be subject to litigation under Title VII, no matter how neutral it might appear on its face.

A rough estimate of the extent of "voluntary" (or at least nonjudicially directed) affirmative action taken in response to Title VII can be deduced from existing work on the overall impact of Title VII. Because firms directly subjected to litigation under Title VII represent such a small share of employment, the bulk of the black economic advance credited to Title VII must be due to its indirect effect in promoting "voluntary" affirmative action. For example, Freeman (1973) shows the overall impact of Title VII in the time series of black-white earnings differentials. From this, the direct impact of Title VII litigation at companies sued for racial discrimination could be subtracted. Although these impacts are substantial at the companies incurring litigation, the subsequent outward shift in the demand curve for blacks at these companies can have only a small impact on market wages, given the companies' small share of the market. Most charges of discrimination never result in litigation, and much litigation never reaches a judicial decision, leaving ambiguous interpretation and little trail. It is likely that the bulk of the changes attributed to Title VII are in a broad sense the result of affirmative action taken in response to the indirect threat, rather than the direct act, of litigation. Since the impact of Title VII is at least an order of magnitude greater than that of the contract compliance program (discussed later in this section), and only a small share of this could have occurred at companies directly litigated against, the biggest impact of affirmative action, broadly defined, very likely took place in the shadow of Title VII. To date, no one has filled in the blanks in the calculation just outlined.

The legal requirement to mitigate damages creates a paradox in which progressive management reduces the incentive for discriminating employers to change by reducing their potential legal liability. Under the CRA, as well as more generally, a plaintiff is required to mitigate damages. For example, a job applicant who is denied employment as a result of illegal discrimination is required to make efforts to find alternative employment. This concept of mitigation creates a paradox of benevolence. The greater the employment share of benevolent employers that practice progressive management and fair employment, the less the legal threat to the remaining discriminating employers. An applicant who loses a job in a world filled with discriminators will suffer great damages despite every effort to mitigate. However, in a world with few discriminators, mitigation is easy because a comparable job can readily be found at a progressive employer, so damages are reduced to negligible levels. This is another application of Becker's model of segregation. The more successful the law is in reducing discrimination, the less of a threat it presents to the remaining discriminators.

One difficulty in evaluating the impact of a national law such as the CRA is that a contemporaneous group unaffected by the law is usually lacking for comparison. In the case of Title VII, Chay (1998) overcomes this problem by examining the impact of the Equal Employment Act of 1972, which extended the reach of Title VII to smaller establishments. Chay finds that once smaller establishments came under Title VII's coverage, the relative employment and pay of blacks improved at these small establishments. Again, very little of this can be the direct result of litigation against small establishments.

The dividing line between voluntary and legally coerced action on the part of employers can be tenuous. James Heckman and Brook Paynor conclude their study of the South Carolina textile industry by stating that it "seems quite plausible that in 1965 entrepreneurs seized on the new federal legislation and decrees to do what they wanted to do anyway" (1989, 174).

Affirmative Action Through Contract Compliance

Federal contractors and first-tier subcontractors are required by Executive Order 11246 to pursue affirmative action. This policy is the direct descendent of President Franklin Roosevelt's wartime executive order barring employment discrimination among federal contractors. Because the Executive Order does not apply to all companies, it sets up a contrast that under some assumptions allows us to discern the impact of affirmative action under the contract compliance program by comparing the change in demographics at contractors with that at noncontractors.

The interpretation of such comparisons would be complicated if each employer's demographics or anticipated change in demographics affected its selection or self-selection into contractor status. However, there is no evidence of this. To the contrary, initial demographics are generally not used as a prerequisite to becoming a contractor. And, as will be explained further below, because of peculiarities in the enforcement targeting procedures used during much of the program's existence, firms with unusually low proportions of minorities or females were not likely to come under greater regulatory pressure. So, given the regulations as implemented, there was little reason for firms with low representation of minorities or females to avoid becoming a contractor. Since firms were not held rigidly to whatever promises they may have made to increase the employment of minorities or females, there was also no reason for firms that did not anticipate an increase in female or minority share to avoid contractor status. Given that enforcement creates a generalized pressure rather than a tight link between a firm's demographics and the targeting of enforcement, reverse causation is less of a concern. We can be more confident that the differences in changing demographics between contractor and noncontractor establishments/firms are not an artifact of selection or self-selection into or out of contractor status. The research on the contract compliance program allows somewhat stronger conclusions about a weaker program because it relies not just on time-series variation but also on a comparison of establishments with and without the affirmative action obligation.

Two contradictory criticisms of affirmative action have found prominent voice. The first criticism is that affirmative action goals without measurable results invite sham efforts; because these programs do not work very well, the argument goes, they should be disposed of. The second criticism is that an affirmative action "goal" is really a polite word for a quota; in other words, affirmative action works too well and therefore should be disposed of. Empirical research into affirmative action programs contradicts both criticisms. Affirmative action goals have played a statistically significant role in improving opportunities for minorities. At the same time, those goals have not resulted in "quotas" (Leonard 1985b).

Federal Contract Compliance Program regulations require that every contractor maintain an affirmative action plan consisting in part of a utilization analysis indicating areas of minority and female employment in which the employer is deficient, along with goals and timetables for good-faith efforts to correct deficiencies. To put this program in perspective, it is important to understand that through most of its history, only between four hundred and one thousand investigative officers have been responsible for enforcing compliance at any one point in time. The ultimate sanction available to the government is debarment, in which a firm is barred from holding federal contracts. In the history of the program, there have been fewer than sixty debarments. The other sanction typically used is a back-pay award. This sanction, too, is used infrequently (Leonard 1985a).

There have been several studies of the impact of the contractor compliance program (Ashenfelter and Heckman 1976; Goldstein and Smith 1976; Heckman and Wolpin 1976; Leonard 1984c; Rodgers and Spriggs 1996; Smith and Welch 1984). These studies have consistently found that employment of black males increases faster at establishments that are federal contractors than at those that are not, with the possible exception of the period during which the Reagan administration undercut enforcement. While significant, this effect has always been found to be modest in magnitude. In general, the impact on females and on nonblack minorities has been less marked than on blacks. The contract compliance program is best thought of as icing on the Title VII cake.

Between 1974 and 1980, black-male and female employment shares increased significantly faster in contractor establishments than in noncontractor establishments. These positive results are especially noteworthy in view of the relatively small size of the agency and its limited enforcement tools. First consider differences between contractors and noncontractors in the change in female and minority employment share without controlling for other possibly confounding variables. A summary measure, white-males mean employment share, declined by 5.0 percentage points among contractors compared with 3.5 percentage points among noncontractors. In other words, the contractors subject to affirmative action reduced white males' employment share by an additional 1.5 percentage points over six years. For other groups, the comparable difference in the per- centage-point change in employment share between contractors and noncontractors is 0.6 for white females, 0.3 for black females, 0.0 for other minority females, 0.3 for black males, and 0.1 for other minority males (Leonard 1984c).

Controlling for establishment size, growth, region, industry, occupational group, and corporate structure, the annual growth rate of black-male employ- ment was 0.62 percent higher in the contractor sector, and the annual growth rate of white males was 0.2 percent lower. Contractor status shifted the de- mand for black males relative to white males by 0.82 percent per year. This is less than 1 percent annually, not a dramatic change, although it can cumulate over time. Studies of earlier and later periods by Orley Ashenfelter and James Heckman (1976), James Heckman and Kenneth Wolpin (1976), and William Rodgers and William Spriggs (1976) find effects on black males of the same order of magnitude. Not surprisingly, growing establishments are better able to accommodate the regulatory pressures. Minority and female employment share increased significantly faster in growing establishments.

In addition to increasing the sheer numbers of minorities employed, the program also has had some success in helping move them up the career lad- der. Affirmative action appears to increase the demand for poorly educated minority males as well as for the highly educated. Black males' share of employment increased faster in contractor establishments in every occupa- tional group except laborers and white-collar trainees. Black females in con- tractor establishments increased their employment share in all occupations except technical, craft, and white-collar trainee. The positive impact of the contract compliance program is even more marked when the position of black females is compared with that of white females (Leonard 1984b). While some part of this appears to reflect title inflation by employers that upgraded detailed occupational categories that had a relatively high representation of minorities or females (Smith and Welch 1984), the occupational advance is accompanied by wage increases incompatible with pure title inflation (Leonard 1986). The evidence does not support the contention that this is just a program for blacks with skills. To the contrary, it helps blacks across the board. Thus, affirmative action does not appear to have contributed to the economic bifurcation of the black community.

The employment goals that firms agree to under affirmative action are not vacuous; neither are they adhered to as strictly as quotas. Affirmative action "goals" are often considered to be a euphemism for quota, which appears to overstate what the regulatory authorities actually require: good-faith efforts to meet goals that are in the first instance chosen by the employer and may subsequently be negotiated with the Office of Federal Contract Compliance Programs (OFCCP). Under the contract compliance program, firms agree to set goals and timetables. Firms that agree to increase minority employment by 10 percent will, on average, increase minority employment by about 1 percent. Employers are not sanctioned for failing to meet their goals. A good-faith effort toward compliance in practice means that firms make it about one-tenth of the way toward the stated goal. This falls well short of the rigidity expected of quotas (Leonard 1985b).

Both the contract compliance program and Title VII have been criticized for inducing firms simply to hire a "safe number" of minorities and women, irrespective of qualifications. According to this argument, whatever "quota" is imposed should be the same for firms in the same industry and region. Application of such quotas would mean that firms in the same industry hiring out of the same labor market should, over time, start to look more and more like each other in terms of the percent of women and minorities. This does not generally happen, either under Title VII or as a result of affirmative action programs (Leonard 1990).

There is some evidence that the general pressures of affirmative action have succeeded in prompting employers to search more widely but, at the same time, have been flexible enough not to impinge on the economic performance of these firms. Henry Holzer and David Neumark (1999) find that although affirmative action employers tend to hire women and minorities with lower educational qualifications, these hires do not exhibit reduced job performance.

To summarize, contractor goals do have a measurable and significant correlation with improvements in the employment of minorities and females at the reviewed establishments. At the same time, these goals are not being fulfilled with the rigidity one would expect of quotas.

Efficiency and Fairness

Classic economic models of discrimination recognize that discrimination is not only unfair, it is also inefficient. The available evidence suggests that affirmative action has helped to promote black employment and, to a lesser degree, that of females and of nonblack minorities. But by themselves, these employment gains do not tell us whether affirmative action has reduced discrimination or gone beyond that point to induce reverse discrimination. Two fundamental questions still outstanding are whether affirmative action has reduced discrimination and whether it has helped integrate society.

One method of answering the first question is to ask whether workers of various demographic groups subject to labor-market discrimination are more likely under affirmative action to be employed and paid in proportion to their productivity without regard to their race or sex. Productivity is difficult to measure, but the model for this approach is a recent paper by Hellerstein, Neumark, and Troske (1999).

Whether the employment gains associated with affirmative action and Title VII have reduced discrimination or gone beyond that to induce reverse discrimination can be addressed by asking whether industries that came under the most pressure from Title VII or affirmative action, or industries that increased their employment of minorities and women, have subsequently suffered declines in productivity. The earliest paper to use this approach of comparing relative productivity to relative wages relied on highly aggregated data and found that minority and female employment gains under affirmative action had not reduced productivity (Leonard 1984a). Direct testing of the impact of affirmative action on productivity finds no significant evidence of productivity decline, which implies a lack of substantial reverse discrimination. However, these results by industry at the state level are too imprecise to answer this question with great confidence.

Judith Hellerstein, David Neumark, and Kenneth Troske (1999) refine this approach of comparing wage differentials to estimated productivity differentials and develop much more persuasive results with a detailed study of establishments. They find that pay premiums for older workers are roughly matched by productivity increases but that the female pay penalty in the United States is generally not a reflection of lower productivity. The latter result suggests that far from imposing pervasive reverse discrimination against men, affirmative action for women has not yet succeeded in eliminating labor-market discrimination. This direction of research holds great promise to move us beyond the formulaic debates over whether the wage differences that remain between groups, after controlling for observable differences in qualifications and preferences, are due to omitted human capital or discrimination.

The political question of whether affirmative action has served to unify or divide is of continuing concern. Sniderman and Piazza (1993) conducted survey-based experiments in the United States and report that just using the term "affirmative action" is enough to provoke more discriminatory responses.

Discrimination is defined as a group problem. Members of a group are treated adversely because of their membership in the group. The relevant evidence is how members of different groups are treated. And one method of undoing the effects of discrimination calls for providing a positive counterweight based on group membership. But such a set of group preferences runs straight into conflict with a deeply rooted American belief in individual merit. Paul Sniderman and Thomas Piazza (1993) convincingly argue for the power of such beliefs and show how they undercut support for affirmative action policies that are seen as offering special treatment based on group membership. Americans do not like discrimination because it violates this norm of rewarding individual merit. But Sniderman and Piazza argue that Americans do not like the solution of affirmative action for the same reason.

Political support for antidiscrimination policies will then be stronger where these are seen as applying generally rather than being specially targeted toward narrow groups. Most Americans strongly reject strict quotas, which give the least room for individual merit. But almost all Americans are opposed to discrimination and support the fair and impartial treatment of individuals irrespective of group membership. There is wide support for business policies that embrace the meritocratic norm.

The policies promoted in IRC's 1959 monograph, *Employing the Negro in American Industry*, have been so widely embraced because they fit so well with Sniderman and Piazza's description of the dominant American norm. The IRC authors argue for general good business practice that treats all individuals fairly and without favor or bias. They dwell not on how we differ but on what we have in common. They do not ask for special treatment. They do not call for targeted policies. They do not call for managers to try to get workers to like each other just for the sake of it. Rather, they point to the more mundane but far less charged motivation of meeting the demands of managing a successful business.

The Policy Spectrum and Limits of Voluntarism

Voluntarism is sometimes offered as an alternative method to government regulation for resolving discrimination. What prospects are there for such alternative approaches to resolve discrimination disputes outside the courts and the system established by the CRA? Is there, for example, any compelling prospect that voluntary negotiations between the employer and employees, either in groups or as individuals, could fruitfully resolve demographic disputes? In the United States, the threat of litigation plays a dominant role in advancing equal employment opportunity. Richard Freeman's research (1973) has now been generally accepted as establishing that black economic progress in the labor market accelerated significantly after passage of the CRA of 1964. But legal compulsion lies along a spectrum of potential mechanisms to advance equal employment opportunity. These possibilities range from rigid quotas (is there any other kind?) at one extreme to laissez-faire at the other extreme. In between are centralized goals combined with decentralized process—embodied in play-or-pay systems—and centralized rules for process combined with decentralized goals and bargaining—as in collective bargaining.

While the law is powerful, it is also cumbersome and unwieldy. Congress is distant from the details of the workplace. Amending the CRA expends tremendous political capital and opens a Pandora's box of old wounds. The courts, of course, are attuned to the specifics of each case. But enforcement through the courts consumes time, money, and sometimes people, polarizing the parties to litigation.

Given the costs and delays of resolution in the courts, many employers have turned to various forms of alternative dispute resolution. These may help to both surface and resolve problems before they end up in court. The U.S. Postal Service is one example of a mediation service for employment disputes that has successfully reduced both the number and the intensity of disputes. Other employers have gone beyond mediation voluntarily agreed to and have required as a condition of employment the binding arbitration of all employment disputes. Of course, if the parties to a dispute individually thought it worth pouring great resources into litigation, the same Prisoner's Dilemma will lead them to pour great resources into arbitration, absent a binding commitment not just to submit disputes to arbitration but also to limit the resources committed. Indeed, over time, some involved in arbitration have come to bemoan a creeping formality and the partial re-creation of the costs and delays of a court.

The Supreme Court's 2000 decision in *Circuit City Stores* is a striking act of judicial abdication opening the door wide to laissez-faire. Any employer that dislikes the law as enacted by Congress or interpreted by the courts is now invited to choose its own judge, in the form of an arbitrator, to implement its own law, in the form of an agreement to arbitrate employment disputes—without review by the courts. The employee suffers from imperfect information and imperfect mobility, which can be expected to give the employer the advantage in this system of private justice.

One might still be able to imagine some gains from decentralization in such a system. Imagine driving down Main Street past "Help Wanted" signs, each posted with a footnote. The footnote on one sign says, "Firm A states that it pays observationally equivalent women 5 percent less than men, and in 1000 separate arbitrations the arbitrator has never found it at fault." A second sign's footnote says, "Firm B pays 2 percent less, and in 200 arbitrations it has been faulted for sex discrimination 30 percent of the time." Men and women choosing jobs in such unusually informed circumstances would know more about the employment relation they were entering into and the nature of dispute resolution at each workplace. Those seeking greater protection from an employer's potential arbitrary behavior could self-select into the more protected workplace. In a competitive market, they might even pay for such additional protection by accepting lower wages. In practice, this type of self-selection could also help explain why we seldom see such information revealed—it might attract those most likely to complain or sue. But because the same disputes are not submitted to each firm's arbitration process, the arbitration results are impossible to compare without detailed knowledge of the facts, the standards, and the process.

Play or Pay

Play or Pay represents a less extreme form of decentralization. One of the most interesting mechanisms for pursuing affirmative action can be found in the German policy to promote employment of the disabled. It is a play-or-pay policy. The German government has drawn a bright line clearly stating minimum employment share for the disabled, and employers thus face an explicit quota for disabled employment. However, together with this clear standard is a buy-out provision: Firms that do not meet their quota, for whatever reason, pay into a special government fund. This mechanism is remarkably different from those used in the United States. First, the quota is explicit and stated in terms of numerical standards rather than abstract rights. This reduces the uncertainty, risks, delays, and costs of enforcement through the courts. There is also little opportunity to argue over the existence of a hidden quota. At the same time, the buy-out provision defuses complaints about the costly burdens imposed by rigid quotas because employers experiencing the greatest difficulty or reluctance meeting the quota can buy their way out. The nearest example of a U.S. policy using a similar mechanism is the creation of tradable pollution rights under U.S. environmental law. Both mechanisms are desirable on efficiency grounds. Firms that face the greatest difficulty reaching the legal standard can buy the right to pollute (or to hire fewer disabled) from firms that can more easily meet the standard. The aggregate level of pollution (or disabled employment) can be adjusted by changing the overall standard, leaving to a decentralized market mechanism the question of which firms will pollute (or employ the disabled) and which will pay a fine. One additional benefit—the penalty paid by firms below quota goes into a fund used to support the training and rehabilitation of the disabled.

Whatever its desirability on efficiency grounds, this mechanism appears to be politically impractical in the context of race and sex discrimination in the United States. Explicitly setting quotas and putting a price on the right to employ fewer minorities or women raise the salience of the political conflicts. The current policy places only an implicit price on discrimination, but it is apparently politically advantageous to frame the discussion in terms of absolute human rights rather than to explicitly highlight the relative price society is willing to put on these rights through enforcement budgets and employment standards.

Nonunion Employee Representation for the Resolution of Demographic Disputes

Discriminating employers impose a cost on benevolent employers. Their actions can provoke passage of laws and judicial decisions that regulate the behavior of all employers, limiting the discretion of even the benevolent ones. The blunt instrument of the law is often ill matched to the subtleties and idiosyncrasies of employment relations. But the scope for voluntary action by those closest to the workplace is limited by the law.

Consider a benevolent employer that wishes to ensure that it is not discriminating. The employer might engage a counselor to meet with employees and managers to surface and confront discriminatory attitudes. An HR manager might analyze the company's statistics on personnel decisions for evidence of adverse impact. The employer might then attempt to take affirmative action to reduce apparent discrimination. But none of these steps can eliminate all legal threats to the employer of discrimination charges. Indeed, the paradox that employers have long complained of is that any of these steps might themselves be used against the employer in litigation. A nonunion employer today—which is to say most employers—that wants to reach a formal understanding with its employees to reduce apparent discrimination has no one to bargain with and no way to preserve any resulting agreement from legal challenge.

We tend to channel EEO disputes into the courts, which resolve them at great cost in terms of time, money, and polarization. Some companies have established demographic affinity groups among their employees, but these have sharply limited potential to develop into an alternative mechanism to resolve EEO disputes. They do not normally have access to internal HR information on the employment, pay, or promotions of employees. They have no legal or internal political basis for trading off the interests of different groups of workers. The problem of divergent interests between demographic groups within a workplace is not miraculously solved by organizing and dividing employees into demographically distinct groups. This may even accentuate the conflicts. Even if an agreement could be reached across such groups, nothing prevents dissatisfied members of these groups from performing an end run and taking their disputes to the courts.

Nonunion Employee Representation Groups

Since the 1970s, many large U.S. employers have organized groups of their employees into affinity or interest groups. Xerox, Corning, AT&T, Pacific Bell, DEC, Apple Computers, and other firms have on their own initiative set up employee groups for blacks, Asians, women, Hispanics, etc. By 1996, 43 percent of the Fortune 500 and the Service 500 reported having demographic affinity groups (DAGs) (Friedman 1996). These operated under a variety of names, including identity caucuses, diversity networks, and affinity groups. In some management guides, such affinity groups are held up as models for successful employee communication that engender commitment to the company; defuse racial, ethnic, or gender tensions; and help forestall and resolve conflicts. In that sense, these demographic organizations differ in intent and in import from the same employer's bowling clubs. Indeed, they echo both the intent and the tension of the Colorado Industrial Plan of John D. Rockefeller, Jr., from nearly a century ago.

In 1913, a strike by nine thousand miners against Rockefeller's Colorado Fuel and Iron Company led to violent battles in which miners and their wives and children lost their lives. This event, known as the Ludlow Massacre, raised public concern with relations between management and labor. In *The Personal Relation in Industry*, Rockefeller describes his success in defusing industrial relations conflicts by "providing for close personal contact between the duly elected representatives of the men and the officers of the company" (1923, 38). The election plan followed that proposed by William Lyon MacKenzie King in 1914 and later described in his 1918 book, *Industry and Humanity*. The Colorado Plan was administered by Clarence J. Hicks, later chairman of the board of Industrial Relations Counselors, Inc.

The Colorado Plan embodied many aspects that would be familiar to many managers today: de-emphasizing hierarchy and authoritarian control, narrowing the social distance between managers and workers, reducing arbitrary management acts, opening communication between employees and managers, providing a grievance mechanism to resolve disputes. As Rockefeller explains, "The Colorado Plan to which I have referred has been so drawn as to guard against the exercise of arrogance or oppression, by providing various channels through which the employee with a grievance can at once secure a sympathetic and friendly hearing, carrying his difficulty to the president's ear, if necessary" (1923, 40). The idea, taken at face value, is simple, powerful, and timeless. Small inevitable grievances left unresolved collect and fester, providing a fertile breeding ground for larger conflicts, as Rockefeller notes: "If [the petty grievance] is dealt with sympathetically and justly, immediately it is made known, peace, harmony and good will are readily maintained. On the other hand, if indifference is shown and lack of sympathy, the grievance is nursed and from it grows the industrial disorders which later become so acute and difficult to heal" (ibid., 41).

It is, of course, all too easy to look back on such statements with a jaundiced eye as self-serving. While Rockefeller argues passionately against viewing Labor and Capital as having competing interests, those more attuned to the role of independent unions might note that this road to labor-management harmony limits the independent exercise of power or discretion by unions, frames labor conflicts as arising from individual misunderstandings rather than underlying conflicts between management and labor as a group, leaves the government out of the picture, and preserves ultimate discretion in the hands of management. Indeed, to some degree, these concerns are reflected in IRC's own efforts to maintain distinctions between employee representation plans and company unions used to forestall unionization.

When Rockefeller writes that "men cannot sit around a table together for a few hours or several days perhaps and talk about matters of common interest, with points of view however diverse, with whatever of misunderstanding and distrust, without coming to see that after all there is much of good in the worst of us and not so much of bad in most of us as the rest of us have sometimes assumed" (ibid., 31), it can be seen both as an eternal verity for pursuit of the common good and as a more sophisticated reframing of collective conflict into a series of atomistic misunderstandings. Even the most innocent of platitudes, including in this case Rockefeller's embrace of the Golden Rule as the guiding principle for labor relations, depends on its context. The unavoidable tension here is that in labor-management relations, two things are always true: (1) labor and management always have a joint interest in growth, and (2) labor and management always have competing interests in the division of economic rents. The art of industrial relations lies in the balance.

Company unions were long thought a historical relic. Most labor lawyers could spend their careers without encountering a Section 8(a)(2) claim under the National Labor Relations Act (NLRA). Such claims charge that a company has violated the NLRA by interfering with the formation or administration of a labor organization and that the organization is dominated or supported by the company. This changed with the resurgence of employee involvement, team concept, and total quality management programs in the 1980s. In many ways, these mirrored elements of the earlier Colorado Plan and raised many of the same issues (see Kaufman and Taras 1999). In particular, some unions have seen them as a Trojan horse for management—an organization to represent workers' interests, parallel to the union but dominated by the employer and designed, in the view of some union leaders, to subvert them. For example, George Kourpias, then president of the International Association of Machinists and Aerospace Workers (IAM), vigorously and explicitly opposed team concept programs in his September 14, 1990, memo "GL-6 IAM Team Concept Policy" to IAM Grand Lodge representatives. At the same time, in many of the same unions, locals found it in their interest to participate with management in such programs. If the union does find a reason to participate, it becomes a moot issue whether the program violates Section 8(a)(2) since, as a practical matter, there is no one left in a position to object.

In this context, the demographic affinity groups of recent decades have not fallen far from the tree of Rockefeller's Colorado Plan. They stress open communication. They provide an alternative mechanism for employee voice. They are employee organizations initiated and promoted by management with a view to airing and resolving potential conflicts early and to building the trust and commitment of employees. And they preserve management prerogatives. What prospects do such institutions have for resolving EEO issues outside the courts? In contrast to the established institutions of collective bargaining, there is no support in the law for a parallel institution for demographic bargaining. Instead, EEO disputes are channeled into the legal system.

There is little empirical evidence on the impact of DAGs. A valuable recent exception by Roy B. Helfgott (2000) surveys the impact of DAGs at four workplaces and concludes that they are broadly ineffective in providing employee voice. While they may aid communication between employers and various groups, or among some subsets of employees, Helfgott finds that they are not viewed as speaking for minorities, do not solve the problems of individual employees, and do not change company policy or outcomes. Helfgott also finds that DAGs are a white-collar phenomenon, and even there only a minority of their constituents bother to join, and fewer are active. Even within the same firms, Helfgott finds an idiosyncratic record. He finds that within the same firm, members of different occupations and demographic groups differ in their expectations for DAGs, in their levels of participation, and in their views of the effectiveness of DAGs. It remains an open question, just as it did in the previous century's discussions of assimilation versus separatism, whether DAGs have promoted integration in the workplace. At least one firm saw DAGs as ineffective in promoting minorities' goals. Seeing them as ingrown and divisive, the company replaced them with a single inclusive employee group in each location composed of all employees and devoted to workplace diversity and professional growth. While diluting the salience of group-specific identity and demands, such groups may be better positioned to pursue fairness for all than fairness for any particular group. In practice, however, the flow of information seems to be one way, dominated by information from the employer to the employee concerning career advancement (Helfgott 2000, 351–58).

A number of paradoxes surround DAGs. First, they may make more salient the demographic differences across employees. An employer's decision to implement DAGs differs from that of employees to form their own, not least because it sends a message about what the employer thinks is an important and relevant dimension of its employees. Second, the companies most likely to lead in establishing DAGs probably start with some of the most progressive records. After all, if you do not hire minorities or women, you will have little use for DAGs. Third, it is possible that the most aggrieved employees, or those who identify themselves most strongly with the group, will be more likely to join and be active in DAGs, affecting their view and the degree to which they represent the group as a whole. Fourth, DAGs can be seen as Trojan horses by both sides. By establishing a set of employee organizations, management may fear sowing the seeds of organized employee power. By the same token, employees may view DAGs as merely an extension of the company's personnel office—an administrative tool to better understand, placate, influence, and perhaps gain the commitment of employees.

If the issue is employee voice and communication, the genesis of DAGs may be of secondary concern to their role in enhancing the flow of information among employees and between employers and employees. They can play a variety of roles in collecting and transmitting information. For example, because discrimination is a group phenomenon, data is needed on the treatment and outcomes of the focal group compared with similar members of other groups in order to discern patterns of discrimination—data that individuals on their own are rarely well placed to collect except from their most direct contemporaries. Different demographic groups may also have different needs, preferences, and styles of communication. In both cases, these characteristics introduce a public goods aspect to provision of information by or for the DAG. Finally, DAGs can serve simply in the limited role of a social club.

Demographic Bargaining

Employers that have established demographic affinity groups among their employees may indeed help to forestall some demographic disputes. But there is little prospect of developing DAGs into an institution for bargaining with various demographic groups of employees to resolve EEO disputes. The weaknesses of this path can be seen in its sharp contrast with collective bargaining law.

The public perception of unions is heavily influenced by the strikes that infrequently bring them into public view. But most of the time of union leaders is spent on the internal politics of administering the union, and this is almost entirely absent from public view. While the public focuses on bargaining between management and labor, the union serves the equally important function of bargaining across competing interest groups within the unionized workforce. Once certified, a union becomes the exclusive bargaining agent of the employees. The rights of numerical minorities within a union gain some protection: A union must be voted in, and it can be voted out; many unions have actively competitive internal democracies; and a union has a duty to fairly represent all employees in the bargaining unit. However, in their concern to strengthen the institution of collective bargaining as a dispute resolution mechanism, the courts and the National Labor Rleations Board (NLRB) rarely second-guess a union's internal political decisions.

In the EEO context, all employees as well as the employer can benefit from a fairer, more objective, and transparent process. Unfortunately, the more contentious of EEO issues present themselves as zero-sum games. If the job hierarchy is fixed, more promotions for one group necessarily imply fewer for another group—a recipe for conflict often met with great helpings of euphemism and ambiguity.

But unions make these kinds of tradeoffs across groups within the union every day without much notice. They are buried in contract administration or hidden in plain sight in the language of the contract. For example, it is a curiosity little remarked upon that cost of living adjustment (COLA) clauses are typically written to raise wages for all covered members by X *cents* per hour if the price index increases by Z *percent*. This is not because the contract negotiators did not know how to specify percentage rather than absolute wage increases. Why then? Look to the effect of wage compression. Over time, such clauses reduce wage inequality within the unit by generating greater percentage increases among the more poorly paid than among the better paid within the unit. In many such units, the poorly paid are more numerous. So unions can and have sacrificed the interests of one constituent group for those of others. This process has also offered unions the rare entertainment of waiting for the employer to eventually come to the table demanding higher pay for skilled employees.

Bounding the Group and Channeling Individual Leverage

The manner and degree to which the interests of individual workers are submerged into the greater good of the greater number differ sharply between collective bargaining and EEO law. Both form collectives, which stand in contrast to the dominant motif of individualism. But the process is less clearly defined and the resulting collective more transient and more porous under the CRA than under the NLRA. The NLRA lays the legal basis for an organization and an alternative dispute resolution mechanism that lives outside the courts. The CRA allows for the pursuit of a collective interest by a collective that exists in the courts—and only for the purpose of litigation.

Under Title VII of the Civil Rights Act of 1964 and related antidiscrimination statutes, members of a group that has been discriminated against can collectively share in the damages despite having no formal collective organization apart from being named in a class action. An employer may then face substantial collective liability. The identity or boundaries of such groups are not predetermined. This in itself precludes much bargaining. Typically, a plaintiff's attorney will search for evidence that alleged discrimination extends beyond a single individual. Finding such evidence, the plaintiff's attorney seeks class certification from the trial judge, a matter that is itself subject to litigation. A class action raises the stakes in litigation by multiplying potential damages, increasing the complexity and cost of litigation, and threatening more extensive changes to HR policy.

Rule 23 of the Federal Rules of Civil Procedure requires that for a class to be certified, the following four criteria must be satisfied: (1) the class is so numerous that joinder of all members is impracticable, (2) there are questions of law or fact common to the class, (3) the claims of the representative parties are typical of the class, and (4) the representative parties will fairly and adequately protect the interests of the class. In addition, part (b) of Rule 23 requires that the prosecution of separate actions by individuals would risk inconsistent adjudications, which would establish incompatible standards, and that either (1) the employer has acted on grounds generally applicable to the class or (2) the court finds that (a) the questions of law or fact common to the members of the class predominate over any questions affecting only individual members and that (b) a class action is superior to other available methods. Under these rules, individuals are allowed to opt out of the class. In some states, plaintiffs may prefer to bring suit in the state courts if these present lesser barriers to class certification or do not allow individuals to opt out.

There is a significant contrast here with the policy judgments that implicitly guide the certification of bargaining units and limit individual discretion under the NLRA. The weight of NLRB and court decisions has favored "wall-to-wall" bargaining units. This is driven not by explicit legislative mandate but presumably by a policy judgment that peaceful and productive industrial relations are more difficult to maintain in a single workplace that is splintered and whipsawed among multiple distinct unions, each of which could threaten to halt production and each of which might balk at a reasonable deal for fear of being surpassed by the others. The board and the courts have made it difficult for individuals or groups to opt out of a bargaining unit or out of collective bargaining once a union is certified. In challenges to broad bargaining units, smaller groups of skilled workers with greater leverage have typically been required by the board or the courts to submerge their own interests to the greater good of the greater number.

Hybrid forms between the extremes of collective and individual bargaining are also possible. Once bargaining begins, a union could bargain for minimum wages to be applied to the collective, leaving individual members free to individually bargain for pay in excess of this collectively bargained floor. Indeed, in a very few industries, including entertainment and the perhaps distinct subsector of professional sports, such contracts are common. It is no accident that such hybrid contracts are found where differences in leverage across individuals are great enough to threaten the integrity of the union otherwise. But such hybrids are clearly the exception.

In an underappreciated role, the union is left great discretion in the internal politics needed to balance competing interests within the union. This is perhaps the most invisible function served by unions. No parallel agency exists to balance competing interests across demographic groups within a workplace, or even to represent the interests of any one demographic group. In other words, no agency exists to forge a consensus within a demographic group in the workplace or to represent one group in discussions with other groups or with management.

In an adverse impact case, the probability of being found in violation of the law depends on a comparison across groups. For example, are women paid less than men? In such a case, if the women as a group are paid less than otherwise similar men, the employer can be liable for payments to all the women. Similarly, in class actions under Title VII, the treatment of women as a group would be compared to that of men.

The ability of individuals to opt out of a class action creates interesting incentives for employers. First, if by opting out individuals are removed from the liability phase of litigation, employers may have opportunities to increase their chances of prevailing and reduce their potential liability by encouraging opt-outs. The closest parallel in a union setting would be the employer that promotes a potential union leader into the supervisory ranks and so out of the union. Second, even if those who opt out are included in a statistical comparison, the employer may still reduce potential liability by offering a lower but certain payment to risk-averse individuals.

An employer's discretion to do good may also be limited. Consider a hypothetical case of an incumbent employee who becomes disabled. Even without legal compulsion, a benevolent employer might choose to accommodate this employee in a less demanding job—perhaps to send a message to all employees that they are implicitly insured and thus build morale, perhaps to reduce insurance premiums or to salvage some employee-specific investments, or perhaps even from some sense that it is the right thing to do. With the possible exception of the last reason, an employer has less incentive to offer the same accommodation to a new applicant as to an incumbent with the same disability. With passage of the Americans with Disabilities Act, an employer's discretion in such matters is limited. Employers are required to offer reasonable accommodations to the disabled. Employers can argue that an accommodation is too costly and thus unreasonable. But the benevolent employer that offers such an accommodation to the incumbent employee has undercut the argument that it is too costly to offer the same accommodation to a new applicant. The law may not require fairness and it may not require efficiency, but it does require consistency.

Laws designed to limit the exercise of discriminatory judgments may also limit the exercise of nondiscriminatory discretion. Consider the incentives to an employer faced with a potential case of wage discrimination but lacking clear evidence of individual productivity. Suppose that in this firm men tend to be paid more than women, but the men also tend to be in technical positions that usually require specialized training that most of the women lack. Now Fergus, who dropped out of high school, just happens to defy the odds: Despite his lack of formal training, he is such an unusual self-taught self-starter that he can easily outperform his more formally educated peers. A company free to exercise discretion promotes him into the skilled job on the spot.

In the shadow of the law, however, the same company might act differently. To accommodate Fergus' lack of a formal education undercuts its argument that women are paid less than men because they lack the requisite education. And by promoting Fergus, the company also undercuts the argument that it is too costly to use selection devices other than formal education to find those with the requisite skills. In the shadow of the law, white males who outperform their credentials increase the firm's potential legal liability. Again, the pressure will be for consistency. The firm can change the selection mechanism for all—and give Fiona the same opportunities as Fergus—or it can change the selection mechanism for none—and use neither Fergus' nor Fiona's talents, thus wasting both. Because it is the employer's discrimination that is at issue, Fergus' problem is that he cannot opt out.

Bargaining Between the Employer and the Employees

It is when we consider having one collective agency represent the interests of employees in demographic disputes and resolve internal EEO disputes that the potential for a demographic bargaining unit seems most untenable. Simply put, an institution run by majority rule is ill suited, absent other constraints, to protect the interests of demographic groups that are in a numerical minority. The slow progress of minorities and women within many craft unions and the mass of litigation charging many such unions with discrimination are testament to the limits of an internally self-regulating collective to fairly resolve internal EEO disputes.

There are, however, some exceptions to this rule, driven by either the demands of the membership or the threat of litigation. The steel industry consent decree is an example of the latter. During a long and bitter course of litigation, the Steelworkers Union, the representatives of black employees, and the major employers of the steel industry could all see a threat to their joint interest in safe working conditions and a growing business if the court imposed a solution that did not sensitively take account of the idiosyncrasies of steel production. In the shadow of that threat, the parties to that dispute crafted their own solution and redrew seniority ladders (Ichniowski 1983).

Unions have also taken a more active role in pursuing the employment rights of women and minorities when driven by a strong ideology and pulled by a large share of women or racial minorities in the workplace. As general counsel of the United Electrical Workers (UE), and later of the American Federation of State, County, and Municipal Employees (AFSCME), Win Newman led successful efforts to achieve comparable-worth pay adjustments for occupations dominated by women. At a time when comparable worth met with a chilly reception in the courts, the UE and later AFSCME were free to bargain for such adjustments within the context of their collective bargaining agreements. Although the wages of men were never explicitly reduced, it is likely that men paid for part of this wage adjustment through reduced wage growth, in the same way that more skilled workers paid for part of the greater raises enjoyed by the lesser skilled through COLA clauses. This type of EEO initiative could work in this union setting because the affected workforces had a high proportion of women and the UE had a strong ideology of equity. The AFSCME took advantage of the transparency of the public sector and the threat of public embarrassment before an electorate whose majority is female.

Conclusion

Discrimination occurs when otherwise equal individuals are treated differently on account of membership in different groups. In this sense, discrimination is inherently a group phenomenon. Evidence of employment discrimination can be sought by asking whether members of different groups are treated differently for reasons not associated with productivity differences. If discrimination builds to a headwind against a group, efforts to redress that headwind can systematically take group membership into account.

This is precisely what affirmative action is meant to do. However sensible a group-oriented solution to a group-based problem might seem to some, this collective approach conflicts with long-standing and fundamental American beliefs in a meritocracy based on the fair treatment of individuals. Beyond that, a more fundamentally conservative approach asks why state intervention and regulation are necessary.

Blacks made economic progress in the labor market without benefit of a federal law barring discrimination. Black economic progress has been fitful, but blacks made greater progress with the law. We have seen scattered evidence of voluntary decisions by employers to employ blacks without discrimination, often prompted by shortages in the labor market. But we have also seen that these early efforts usually stalled in the face of strong community pressure. The use of blacks as strikebreakers inflamed labor struggles with racial discord and left a residue of racial antagonism within some unions that lasted for another generation.

The Civil Rights Act of 1964 has been the driving force behind reduced discrimination in the workplace. It has had substantial, lasting, and pervasive effects. The concept of adverse impact developed in the Supreme Court's decision in *Griggs* v. *Duke Power* established the collective rights of members of protected groups. It also expanded the reach of the CRA into any and all employer practices or policies, however neutral they might appear on face, that might have a differential impact on the conditions of employment for minorities or women.

The bulk of the progress made under the CRA occurred at firms that were not sued. This progress occurred because of the compelling threat of private litigation under the CRA. The evidence is that firms that were never sued under the CRA changed their behavior after the CRA went into effect. The CRA can be considered an effective law that creates compelling incentives for compliance. Affirmative action is the frosting on this cake.

In the early debates over the creation of the Equal Employment Opportunity Commission, the NLRB was considered as a model. Mediation by an agency of the executive branch, rather than litigation decided by the judicial branch, was to be encouraged. While some residue of the mediation model remains in the EEOC, ultimately individuals were given the right to sue. This threat of private litigation is the fundamental lever through which the CRA has effected progress.

Alternative dispute resolution mechanisms seem sharply constrained in the case of equal employment opportunity. There is neither legal nor institutional basis for the voluntary resolution of conflicts in the workplace between the interests of different demographic groups. In the unionized sector, some legal and institutional structure exists, but minorities are reluctant to trust their fate entirely to the majority. Recognizing the same history, the courts allow members of protected groups to resort to the courts if they believe their unions have failed them. In the nonunion sector, employers that have sponsored demographic affinity groups have little to show for them.

The law barring discrimination can coerce compliance from those who would discriminate, but it is more effective when it helps to induce the cooperation of employers and enjoys the support of the public. George Meany of the AFL-CIO testified in support of the CRA of 1964 that he was happy to support a law that would give him additional leverage to help get his unions to do what he knew was right. EEO law has resulted in a number of attention-grabbing hundred-million-dollar judgments against some employers, but the bulk of the impact of the law has been felt among employers not directly involved in litigation. The law has helped some of these to do what they knew was right.

Acknowledgments

The author thanks Bruce Kaufman and Roy Helfgott for helpful comments.

9

Voice in the North American Workplace

From Employee Representation to Employee Involvement

Daphne G. Taras

The twentieth century was a fertile period of experimentation with employee voice, and many different philosophies were used to develop harmonious workplace relations in American enterprises. Employee voice was an evolving concept, moving from the initial industrial relations concern with collective representation rights to more recent human resource management formulations stressing employee involvement (EI) and participation. Industrial Relations Counselors, Inc. (IRC), was important in promoting and disseminating both employee voice concepts.

Two conceptually distinct (although heavily overlapping) elements underpinned the voice concept as it evolved in the twentieth century. The first, *employee representation*, was based on the notion that workers have a right to help determine the terms and conditions of their labor and are entitled to a fair and just workplace. Thus, the workplace was a pluralistic setting in which new ways were needed to balance the interests of owners with those of employees. This notion produced formal and sometimes complex systems of employee representation and grievance processing designed to channel and communicate the collective interests of workers on a myriad of topics. Unions as well as some companies (and the two were in competition in many cases in the first half of the twentieth century) were developing institutional forums to permit workers to be heard by their employers. In particular, employee representation vehicles in both union and nonunion settings involved the channeling of worker sentiments through their delegates or leaders, who then sought resolution from management. This approach is an "indirect" form of participation. In union settings, issues were often resolved through bargaining or formal dispute-resolution processes, but in nonunion settings, indirect participation more often occurred via discussion and consultation.

Unions and progressive employers agreed that workers had a legitimate moral, and even economic, right to speak out and participate in setting the terms and conditions of their labor. Not until 1935, with the passage of the Wagner Act, did American public policy give a legal right to unions and prescribe them as the chosen vehicle for employee representation and voice. At the same time, employer activities involving representation were severely curtailed, and unions were given, by law, the exclusive rights to this previously contested terrain. Management retreated from the formal representational field, sometimes reluctantly. Today a minority of American employers continue to run formal employee representation plans, even at the risk of incurring unfair-labor-practice charges. For other employers, the law has become an impediment to employer initiatives involving worker representation. But today, most American employers that are concerned with employee voice have sought another vision and are implementing various elements of the high-involvement workplace. They see little need to advance institutionalized forms of indirect employee representation except when the law requires bargaining with unions or mandates health and safety committees or for the solicitation of employee input on an as-needed basis. Employee representation, once at the forefront of managerial thought, has retreated into the shadowy sidelines, and another vision of voice has become prominent.

The second element, *employee involvement and participation*, recognized that the creative talents of employees could benefit the enterprise. Human resource management techniques such as recruitment, selection, and compensation systems attempted to ensure a better fit between workers and the enterprise to achieve unity of purpose (Mahoney and Watson 1993). Employees would suggest improvements and reap the rewards of their participation. Rather than treating employees as a collective, as in the first conception of voice, this second formulation emphasized production or work unit–based teams and individual systems of input through open-door policies, suggestion systems, open forums, focus groups, and topic-specific committees. Techniques, such as re-engineering and total quality management, were implemented to further integrate employee input and competitive advantage. In most firms, employee voice would be heard through "direct" forms of participation that allowed individuals to speak to managers without intermediaries. Direct employee voice, then, could motivate and increase the loyalty of workers to produce better results for the firm. Naturally, some firms also wanted to use (indirect) representation systems to increase the efficacy of participation plans but in order to do so risked violating the Wagner Act.

In this chapter I demonstrate that considerable change has occurred during the past century regarding (1) employer motivations for encouraging employee voice and (2) the institutional vehicles for the expression of voice. Because there is confusion in the literature over the appropriate labels for capturing both the motivations and vehicles, I constructed Table 9.1 to illustrate the historic progression I describe herein. Admittedly, Table 9.1 exaggerates the differences between the two concepts of voice, and in the world of work, the nomenclature, goals, practices, and techniques allow considerable overlap between one category and the other. Until the Wagner Act, there was little impediment to companies integrating both formal representation and participation, and there are cases where formal representation systems sought to solve productivity problems (e.g., Basset 1919). Even after the Wagner Act, there were (and still are) companies that tried very diligently to hear employee concerns, operate grievance mechanisms, and resolve issues related to wages and working conditions with considerable employee input. Clearly, both employee representation and participation also are efficiency responses to the complexity and size of twentieth-century firms (a point made by Verma [2000, 308] and Kaufman and Levine [2000, 159]). Both systems of voice improve communication and coordination of activities. Although representation and participation are not mutually exclusive, my point is that the historical record demonstrates that until roughly World War II, progressive management favored a model of voice that emphasized collective dealing with employees, while in the post–World War II period, the cluster of workplace voice practices developed a narrower managerialist agenda centered on productivity and firm performance. Managerial preferences and the development of new techniques of human resource management, in tandem with the constraining effects of national labor law, changed how employee voice was operationalized during a century of workplace-based practices.

The first section of this chapter documents the development of various blueprints for employee representation, emphasizing the most popular, the Rockefeller Plan. The discussion will be confined primarily to plans whose centerpieces were employee representation (as distinct from the welfare capital plans that emphasized employment benefits, insurance, health, education, and immigrant assimilation). Lessons can be learned from the implementation phase as companies voluntarily adopted representation plans designed to constructively channel employee voice and limit industrial conflict.

The second section discusses the pressures to dismantle employee representation plans and the emergence of voice in its current formulation as employee involvement and participation plans. The Wagner Act banned all "company unions,"[1] eliminating almost all nonunion systems of representing worker concerns regarding terms and conditions of employment (Kaufman and Taras 2000). American companies, including those with Rockefeller Plans, reluctantly disbanded their formal nonunion systems (Jacoby 2000). Although a remnant of the original Rockefeller Plan continues to operate in Canada at Imperial Oil, and there are modern collective representation plans in the United States airline industry subject to the Railway Labor Act, little remains of the

Table 9.1

Two Concepts of Voice

	Employee representation	Employee involvement and participation
Other terms commonly used	• Industrial democracy • Joint council • Joint committee • Shop committee	• High-involvement workplace • Employee empowerment
Goals	To foster cooperation, improved communication, and industrial harmony among competing stakeholders so that the enterprise can function without disruption	To improve ability to compete globally and increase wealth among shareholders (often including employees)
Principal issues	• Resolving employment-based issues, e.g., wages, working conditions • Focus is on industrial relations • Once workplace is more harmonious, attention may be turned to productivity	• Firm performance, employee and firm productivity • Focus is on human resource management • Removal of employment-based irritants that would lower levels of performance
Institutional vehicles for voice	• Joint councils • Joint committees • Rockefeller Plan • Industrial Plan • Employee-management advisory committees • Congressional plans • Leitch Plan, etc.	• Surveys • Open-door policies • Focus groups • Suggestion systems • Quality circles • Self-managed work teams • Employee input • Ad hoc task forces, etc.
How voice is expressed by employees	Agency model: Workers represent other workers, i.e., indirect representation through delegates	Direct: Workers represent themselves, or human resources managers represent workers
When most commonly practiced	After 1918 and before Wagner Act ban took effect in the late 1930s (although some contemporary companies continue to run these systems)	Well after World War II, although some earlier examples are evident in the literature

grand experiment with formal nonunion representation plans in American companies operating under the Wagner Act. Instead, workers' voice is expressed in nonunion companies through other mechanisms such as health and safety committees, focus groups, surveys, and work teams. Recent surveys show that the vast majority of large American firms incorporate teams into some aspects of their daily operations with considerable success (Cotton 1993; Lawler 1999).

The legitimacy of employee voice was endorsed and embedded in leading managerial practice throughout the twentieth century. The voice vehicle changed from institutionalized forums, with sometimes elaborate structures, that involved worker delegates who advocated better employment conditions, to more flexible institutional arrangements that advanced the production imperatives of the enterprise and captured the creativity of individual employees.

Part I: Employee Representation

In the early 1900s, the survival of American capitalism was viewed as more precarious than it is considered to be today. At that time, a battle raged between unions and industrialists, and solving the problems that led to periodic outbreaks of arson and manslaughter was of paramount importance. Many felt that the capitalist system and even democracy itself were at stake. Worker uprisings could be viewed as a nascent threat to order, as revolutions had profoundly changed history by overthrowing regimes in France and America, and Tzarist Russia was about to be toppled. Concerns over these instabilities affected American industrial relations. In 1910, the president of the National Metal Trades [Employer] Association warned, "Today each side is armed to the teeth, and from time to time we smell the smoke from skirmishes upon the outskirts; but the carnage of a great conflict may still be avoided. It is for us to work toward a peaceful outcome" (quoted in Harris 2000, v). The preamble to the relatively conservative American Federation of Labor constitution did not calm employer fears: "Whereas a struggle is going on in all the nations of the civilized world between the oppressors and the oppressed of all countries, a struggle between the capitalist and the laborer which grows in intensity from year to year and will work disastrous results to the toiling millions if they are not combined for mutual protection and benefit . . ." (quoted in Seager 1923, 5). Radical union leaders were becoming more commonplace (Abella 1973). The 1919 Winnipeg General Strike sent a wave of panic across the continent as unions showed they could work in concert (Bercuson 1990).

Against this backdrop, there emerged noteworthy attempts by progressive and innovative employers to demonstrate that workers could be well treated within the capitalist system. An early example is the Filene Cooperative Association, which began in the late 1880s in the Boston retail store. Eventually, this welfare and benefit program grew to more ambitious pro-

portions as the Association was given responsibility for grievance settlements and allowed to seek wage adjustments (La Dame 1930). The National
Cash Register Company was another exemplar of the era. There was a small
group of companies interested in incorporating employee representation and
voice into larger corporate welfare work, including Joseph & Feiss, Leeds and
Northrup, the Plimpton Press, and Dennison Manufacturing (Jacoby 1997, 15).
Some of these plans were implemented even without a union organizing threat
as part of the owners' commitment to running enterprises that incorporated the
views of employees. Often formal employee representation plans were preceded by the introduction of generous welfare plans (Nelson 1982; Jacoby 1997).

A unique "congressional" style of employee representation modeled after
the American government was developed by H.F.J. Porter and was then
adapted and made famous as the Leitch Plan (Leitch 1919, 340; Nelson
1982). The Packard Piano Company's plan enshrined the five principles of
industrial democracy advocated by John Leitch—justice, cooperation,
economy, energy, and service—and resulted in efficiency and increased earnings (Leitch 1919; Commons 1921, 84). Later, World War I's impassioned
discourse on world democracy brought home to many employers the need
for workplace democracy—it was difficult to treat soldiers as heroic figures
without acknowledging their rights in the workplace upon their return from
battle. This gave a boost to the Leitch Plan.

Most plans were designed to ensure cooperation and provide rudimentary
workplace justice out of a paternalistic but nonetheless genuine consideration of employee welfare (Lauck 1926). Resolving issues around wages
and working conditions absorbed most of the attention.[2] Sometimes the resulting workplace harmony also allowed productivity and morale improvements, as employee suggestions made in the spirit of collaboration and during
routinely scheduled interactions were well received by employers. Some of
these plans helped advance personnel techniques, grievance systems, training and selection improvements, suggestion and implementation plans, health
and safety committees, etc. After a comprehensive study of thirty establishments' plans in 1919, the leading industrial relations scholar concluded, "From
10 percent to 25 percent of American employers may be said to be so far
ahead of the game that trade unions cannot reach them. Conditions are better, wages are better, security is better than unions can actually deliver to
their members" (Commons 1921, 263). But the flaws in even the most well-
conceived plans became evident as many of them passed into obscurity: the
lack of management conviction over multiple generations (e.g., the Filene
Plan did not survive management succession) and the lack of sustained managerial attention to proper running of the plans (e.g., the National Industrial
Conference Board's 1922 report noted considerable degeneration of the plans

as enthusiasm waned). Often ushered in with great fanfare, some plans simply faded. But as some plans departed the scene, there always were new entrants, as enlightened owners and managers gained prominence and the benefits of employee voice in creating harmonious workplace relations became apparent.

A much larger subset of American companies neither tolerated unions nor believed in the legitimacy of collective forms of employee voice. Most industrialists responded to union threats and industrial disorder simply by refusing to recognize or deal with unions. The rallying cry for this stance was the "open shop" (Harris 2000). Typical until 1914 were the Rockefeller companies.[3] Unionization was anathema to John D. Rockefeller, Sr., who, despite his legendary philanthropy, held dear the individualistic philosophy that "the only thing which is of lasting benefit to a man is that which he does for himself" (Rockefeller 1909, 152). Rather than capitulating to union closed-shop demands intended to restrict hiring and limit managerial prerogatives, the strongest companies drove out unions, by armed conflict if required. One Rockefeller affiliate, the Colorado Fuel and Iron Company (CF&I), under an anti-union chief executive officer, hired private militia and took an extremely hard line against striking miners in Colorado. This strategy culminated in the 1914 massacre at Ludlow, Colorado (described in detail by Bruce E. Kaufman in Chapter 3 of this volume), the bloodshed of which germinated plans for a new form of industrial relations within the Rockefeller orbit.

Rockefeller and his son were absentee owners, and information about discontent among miners was considerably distorted as it made its way up the chain of command. The son had little interest in or knowledge of labor conditions even in his family's companies, shared his father's philosophies that upheld social conservatism, and even used the phrase "survival of the fittest" in a 1902 public speech (quoted in Ghent 1903, 291).[4] Thus, throughout 1913, the Rockefellers and their New York officers refused to intervene in the strike (McGregor 1962, 120). Criticism of the Rockefellers continued unabated, and finally Rockefeller initiated a publicity campaign headed by Ivy L. Lee (the founder of the modern public relations movement). The very size and fabled wealth of the Rockefellers made ruthless union suppression an unsustainable long-term strategy. The Rockefeller family, which valued its carefully cultivated reputation for philanthropy and humanitarian endeavors, was mocked and reviled because of events at Ludlow. The good works of the multimillion-dollar Rockefeller Foundation were being compromised by suspicions about the family's integrity (Fosdick 1952, 26). The sustained effort of the chair of the United States Commission on Industrial Relations to expose and vilify the Rockefellers for their role in the Colorado labor travails took its toll. Protesters encircled the Rockefellers' New York offices.

Commission investigations provided fodder for the presses. Another way would have to be found to save the reputation of the family. Although they arrived at the solution very reluctantly, giving employees voice at work seemed to the Rockefellers the only answer.

The existence of a small group of progressive employers at the vanguard of human resource practice (e.g., providing comprehensive welfare benefits and a program of employee voice) regardless of external circumstances is an enduring feature of the industrial landscape. The process of persuading a second group, a reluctant and skeptical set of owners and managers, that employee voice would be beneficial forms a more interesting story. Consider now the conversion of the more resistant companies.

Persuading the Skeptical

The most famous and most widely disseminated plan for employee representation was developed by William Lyon Mackenzie King on behalf of the beleaguered Rockefeller family.[5] To truly appreciate the vision that drove the movement toward this most popular of the company-based employee representation plans, it is imperative to understand the thinking of its principal architect.

Part of the allure of Mackenzie King's Industrial Plan had to do with his background and credentials. John D. Rockefeller, Jr., would not have likely embraced the Industrial Plan without his bedrock of faith in Mackenzie King's judgment and morality (Fosdick 1952; Scheinberg 1978, 198). Mackenzie King was forty years old, with an outstanding record in Canadian industrial relations, when he entered the Rockefeller orbit (McGregor 1962; Gitelman 1988; and documented in Mackenzie King's extraordinary Diaries). His educational credentials were beyond reproach: He received graduate training in labor economics at both Chicago and Harvard. Until his temporary fall from Canadian politics in 1911, Mackenzie King had authored every piece of Canadian industrial relations legislation as deputy minister and then minister of labor. His emphasis on mediation and conciliation were hallmarks of Canadian public policy (Craven 1980). During his years as a mediator, Mackenzie King sat with and gave de facto legitimacy to unions. He witnessed a full spectrum of behaviors among unions and had little trouble distinguishing those worthy of recognition from those he considered reckless and undeserving.

Ultimately, Mackenzie King's vision of employee voice was an amalgam of Christianity and public policy. He believed that men such as himself could develop a genuine and heartfelt understanding of the workers' plight and that workers' dire conditions should be ameliorated through direct intervention and public policy. It is critically important to appreciate that Mackenzie King embraced industrial relations as a moral imperative rather than an economic necessity.[6] He did not encourage collective bargaining as essential to economic planning or to the stabilization of wage patterns but rather as a political expedient in certain circumstances and morally correct. Delivering the working classes from unjust toil as part of a Christian mission was his idée fixe, and even though he had received significant exposure to other industrial relations approaches, he did not incorporate them into his grand mission. He chose representation as a means of empowering employees to seek the relief that met their local circumstances. In some cases, employees would use representation to advocate employment security and benefits; in other situations, they would emphasize plant safety and hygiene. Some plans would focus on productivity; others on wage gains. Sometimes the introduction of corporate employee-welfare plans occurred simultaneously, as at Standard Oil (New Jersey) and Imperial Oil (Gibb and Knowlton 1956; Ewing 1951). Representation was the vehicle for achieving a panoply of objectives.

The idea of an enterprise-specific plan of collective representation among nonunion workers clearly was not Mackenzie King's invention. During his stay in Boston, surely Mackenzie King knew of the Filene's plan. But the Industrial Plan was a unique invention, perhaps based on his early-1900s conciliation efforts in Canadian coal-mining towns. Whereas many other plans were conceived to address employee welfare concerns, the Industrial Plan originated in the interplay between employee collectives usually involved in nascent union organizing and resisting employers. What clearly distinguishes the Industrial Plan from many previous experiments with enterprise-based mechanisms was the integral role of representation and voice at the Plan's very inception. Unlike the Leitch Plan, which was modeled on government, the Industrial Plan emulated the ideal features of a nonadversarial system of industrial relations between workers and their employers.

John D. Rockefeller, Jr., wrote to Mackenzie King on August 1, 1914, asking for King's conception of "some organization in the mining camps which will assure to the employees the opportunity for collective bargaining, for easy and constant conferences with reference to any matters of difference or any grievances which may come up, and any other advantages which may be derived from membership in a union." Give my workers some of the benefits of a union, he wrote, and give me the ability to not have to deal with this particular union. Mackenzie King drafted a plan in a letter (reproduced almost in full in Taras 2000a, 234–35) detailing the attributes of the future solution to Rockefeller's search for a new type of industrial relations. If the influential Rockefellers could be persuaded to embrace a scheme of worker representation, they could blaze a trail for all of America.

Mackenzie King proposed an enterprise-based representation plan that involved the election of worker delegates to serve the interests of their wage-earner constituency, along with an equal number of manager delegates who would communicate company interests. The joint councils would emphasize "fair play," especially in determining the conditions of work and employee remuneration and in the establishment of a grievance procedure to make adjustments and settle differences. The plan could even be adapted beyond the scope of single enterprises into industry-wide councils. The original plan that was adapted for Colorado is described in detail by Rockefeller (1916), and the modern version is analyzed by Taras (2000a and 2000b).

A critical feature of the plan was the no-reprisal guarantee protecting employees who belonged to unions. However, the plan did not recognize unions as bargaining agents. Rather, any employee, whether a union member or not, could be elected to the joint council, and worker delegates of the joint council would represent all employees in their work unit. The Plan evaded the then-unthinkable prospect of union recognition by creating an alternative conception of industrial democracy. Mackenzie King had a particular antipathy to the insistence of unions that management must recognize them as a precondition to negotiation. He believed that recognition would be forthcoming when it was deserved. He was proud that he had found a solution that would be even more inclusive than unionization, and this feature was praised by the presidentially appointed Federal Commission on the Labor Difficulties in the Coal Fields of Colorado:

> Every employee has the absolute right openly to belong to a labor union or not, as he pleases; but in view of the fact that many men in the company's employ do not belong to labor unions, it offers the rights of representation, which are embodied in the company's plan to unorganized labor in its employ as well as to organized labor. In other words, as between the company and its employees, all have the right of representation, and not only those who are organized. [U.S. Congress, 64th Cong., 1st sess., Document No. 859, quoted in Mackenzie King 1918, 284]

Negotiation and recognition should be decoupled, a highly palatable stance to the majority of corporate America.

Rockefeller and his small coterie of advisors were immediately enthusiastic, but Mackenzie King knew Rockefeller's understanding of industrial relations was limited, and the first task was to tutor his new employer. Mackenzie King completely disagreed with this refusal of an absentee owner to take responsibility for ameliorating the conditions that led to warfare in the mines. The open shop was not the issue; it was the right of workers to expect better treatment. Convincing Rockefeller to embrace his Christian responsibility was the first aim of Mackenzie King's proselytizing efforts. Rockefeller's subsequent appearance at the Walsh Commission on Industrial Relations was something of a personal triumph for King. Mackenzie King heaped praise on his protégé, writing to him (February 9, 1915), "No man I have ever known has shown such splendid courage, such unswerving integrity, and such true Christian character, as you have through this fight. . . . [Y]ou will have to lead, have to be the example . . . and it is in the field of industry primarily that this leadership must be conspicuous."

The Philosophical Vision

What vision drove this most popular employee representation plan? First, industrialists must *embrace social and labor reform.* Mackenzie King urged the Rockefellers to appreciate that "investors, even such corporate investors as the Rockefeller Foundation, must share responsibility for labor conditions in the industries in which they had investments. . . . Acceptance of that doctrine meant actions in the direction of reform" (quoted in McGregor 1962, 113). This was a dramatic departure from the Social Darwinist philosophies articulated by the senior Rockefeller and heartily endorsed by his son. The younger Rockefeller's enthusiastic response to this first principle signaled a sea change in the industrial relations vision of the Rockefeller empire.

Second, with the genuine participation of leading industrialists like the Rockefellers, *voluntarism rather than statutory compulsion* was the solution. Although he was personally instrumental in drafting labor legislation, Mackenzie King's disappointing recent experiences as a Canadian politician had proved that governments come and go, whereas industrialists like Rockefeller could be a permanent force for reform. Industry could act in advance of—or even in place of—legislation.

Third, *enlightenment had to occur at the top*, and the implementation order bringing about representation had to be seen as endorsed by the highest levels—not just by the professional managers and agents but also by the owners themselves. This was a huge strength of the vision, and ultimately its greatest weakness. Very few capitalists had the time, inclination, or spirit for this type of reform. To compensate for this problem, the Rockefellers later fully supported the development of a consulting and research agency, Industrial Relations Counselors, Inc., and ensured that its board of trustees was comprised of men from industry's highest echelons. The plan would not be run by middle managers. Instead, it was imperative to find the most skilled and trusted experts, men who had the ear and support of Capital. Clarence Hicks—entrusted with implementation at CF&I and Standard Oil (New Jersey) and a host of other initiatives—and Cyrus Ching—who helped bring representation to the rubber industry—were among the experts appointed to the board. Corporate presidents frequently appeared at the inaugural meetings of these representational plans.

Fourth, and contingent on acceptance of the preceding three principles, reform of labor relations meant that *union recognition could be sidestepped* and the owners could continue to endorse the open shop. The victory of labor-management harmony over discord obviated the need for union recognition. Of paramount importance was establishing contact between workers and owners so that recalcitrant employers would come to acknowledge the value and sincerity of workers. Workers were no longer to be viewed as conspirators but as cooperators.

Fifth, the vision was rooted in *labor-management relations and the legitimacy of worker interests.* The first task was to achieve better labor-management communications and to calm the tensions in many workplaces. The enterprise would have to be saved from forces that threatened to exacerbate class warfare, and attention could be turned to the day-to-day tasks of successfully operating a business.[7] It was a declaration of neither welfare work, scientific management, nor employee involvement to enhance productivity and rationalize production but, rather, of the imperative that the voice of workers be heard. With proper facilitation, mediation, conciliation, and better communication generally, both workers and owners would then see their harmony of interests. The view that industrial relations were characterized by "irreconcilable conflict" (a vision that drove much of mainstream industrial relations) was rejected. Instead, conflict was caused by misunderstandings. Bargaining would not be necessary if communication achieved unity of purpose. Most rhetoric surrounding employee representation involved labor-management harmony, the creation of goodwill among the pillars of industry (workers and owners, with occasional reference to shareholders, the public, and government), and calming the forces propelling workers toward unionism. Mackenzie King clearly envisioned the Industrial Plan as a form of collective action, because a collectivity of workers regularly meeting with managers would bring a sustainable institutional structure into being. Its purpose? Industrial society could be a just society, a microcosm of a better society for all, and a reflection of Christian teachings about tolerance, respect, and the value of each person's contribution to the shared wealth of humanity. In the opening words of his treatise, *Industry and Humanity* (1918), Mackenzie King sets the stage for this argument:

> The existing attitude of Capital and Labor toward each other is too largely
> one of mistrust born of Fear. That was the position of the nations of Europe

before the War. If Industry is to serve Humanity, this attitude must be changed to one of trust inspired by Faith. An industrial system characterized by antagonism, coercion, and resistance must yield to a new order based upon mutual confidence, real justice, and constructive good-will. . . . Christianity differs from Heathenism in that its attitude is founded upon Faith, not upon Fear. [P. xv]

If productivity improvements result—a matter he does not address for another 200 or so pages—so much the better for demonstrating the value of employee representation and persuading corporations of its enduring worth. But productivity is not the exclusive domain of management: To Mackenzie King, all parties in society benefit from productivity, be they Labor, Capital, Management, or the Community (ibid., 254). Hence, the sooner conditions are stabilized, the sooner all parties will prosper.

Parenthetically, a sixth and secret component was that the end result could be unionization. This was neither overtly nor systematically communicated by Mackenzie King[8] nor embraced by those who later practiced the Industrial Plan. Mackenzie King privately believed that the very reasonableness of the relations that would develop between worker representatives and their employers could *foster the eventual introduction of bona fide unions* into the discussions, perhaps even leading to union recognition once employers' fears were allayed (Diary entry, February 7, 1919). He knew that introducing the full vision would be a slow process.

Implementing the Vision

Mackenzie King and other famous authorities active in the representational field, such as Clarence Hicks, John Leitch, and Cyrus Ching, knew that the implementation of any nonunion plan required careful preparation and nurturing. Ching stressed the pivotal role of "two-way communication" in employee representation plans (Ching 1973, 4, 6, 73). But how to facilitate the development of communication among adversaries? Trust had to be restored, as well as faith that the company's forum would facilitate the exchange of ideas. To lay the groundwork among miners, Mackenzie King went to Colorado with news of a $100,000 Rockefeller gift to alleviate desperate conditions among the miners, and he personally visited every community in which CF&I had mines, spoke freely with workers and their families, and toured homes, schools, mines, churches, and stores. He made friends of CF&I managers, a considerable accomplishment given the skepticism about his plan and managers' fears that their power base would be eroded by worker representation. When Rockefeller personally toured the mines and visited miners' houses, danced with wives, and gave speeches, he was met with enthusiasm. He, his new plan for representation, and his plan manager, Clarence Hicks, were all well received. This success would be leveraged throughout the Rockefeller companies. For the next decade and in various companies, the presence of staunch plan advocates who gave inspirational talks, attended employee-management meetings, and ensured a continued high regard for the plan enhanced the chances of success (Gibb and Knowlton 1956).

The Rockefeller Plan was only a qualified success in Colorado (Selekman and Van Cleek 1924; Gitelman 1988).[9] CF&I employees elected their own representatives by secret ballot, held meetings every four months, and convened joint committees to deal with industrial cooperation and conciliation issues, including dispute resolution, safety, sanitation, health, housing, recreation, and education. The two most significant features of the Colorado Memorandum were a wage guarantee and a nondiscrimination clause. The company committed itself to continue its wage rates for a two-year period, with a promise to match any wage increases in competitive areas. This is a very significant guarantee, as it is an early illustration of my argument that the success of nonunion representation depends on meeting and even exceeding wages negotiated by unions (Taras 2000b). The economic incentive for workers to turn to unions was eliminated by signing the Memorandum. Without this tension in the employment relationship, the parties could devote themselves to improved communications, justice, and restoration of trust. CF&I and other companies following the Rockefeller Plan were warned to scrupulously avoid discharging union supporters (Rockefeller 1916, 75, citing the Colorado Industrial Plan, Section III (3); Brody 1960, 227). Employee representatives also were expressly protected from company reprisal for their actions on behalf of constituents (Colorado Plan, Section III (18)). Representatives were given the right of appeal through a multistep grievance process (the same accorded other company employees), with a further right to be heard at the Industrial Commission of the State of Colorado, vested with final and binding authority on the disposition of grievances. Mackenzie King insisted on these provisions against the explicit desires of managers who feared that the joint councils could become springboards for union organizing.

Many industries were suffering from the same pressures as CF&I, albeit with less violence and bloodshed, and watched with fascination the calming of tensions in Colorado. In only three years, between 1917 and 1920, the Industrial Plan was implemented by the behemoths of industry—Standard Oil (New Jersey), Bethlehem Steel, Westinghouse, Harvester, AT&T, U.S. Rubber, and the Pennsylvania Railroad, together with all their holdings. At

Goodyear Rubber and Tire, the industrial democracy plan was proposed as the solution to the "ill will of the laboring force" (Litchfield 1946, 37). Rockefeller and his senior corporate officers promoted the new Industrial Plan throughout the Rockefeller holdings. About a year after the collapse of a bitter strike in the Bayonne refinery, the president of Standard Oil (New Jersey) directed his three New Jersey refineries, at Bayonne, Bayway, and Eagle, to implement the Industrial Plan. At AT&T, President Thayer ordered employee representation plans as "friendly organizations" to "take the place of unions" (paraphrase from quotes in Schacht 1975, 19). The goal of employee representation from the employers' perspective, according to Wisconsin Steel Company, was "a definite and durable basis of mutual understanding and confidence," and Inland Steel declared that the plans would provide "effective communication and means of contact . . . and to insure justice, maintain tranquility, and promote the general welfare" (both quoted in Brody 1960, 227). Note that the imperative to launch these plans involved industrial harmony and interactions for the purpose of setting the wages and conditions of workers. The Tayloristic productivity emphasis, very popular at the time, was largely absent from the initial commands to begin representation plans. More than a million workers experienced the Industrial Plan by the start of the 1920s, and it continued to grow in popularity.

The details of the various representation plans could be altered according to local circumstances, and the degree to which workers were involved in the early preparations of the plans also varied considerably. Some plans were drawn up by management, while others originated with "constitutional conventions" of workers and managers, who jointly drafted the details. Professional industrial relations managers such as Clarence Hicks (originally charged with managing the CF&I plan) scrutinized the plans at other Rockefeller-owned companies to ensure that they retained the "no-discrimination" features of the Colorado Plan and were drafted to suit local circumstances.

Documented early experience with the Plan throughout the Rockefeller holdings showed some (although not universal) patterns. The nonunion systems were brought into many companies during or shortly after considerable union organizing and labor unrest. Workers were positively disposed toward the representation systems, and senior managers were fiercely in favor of them (particularly when the alternative was unionization). The greatest and most concerted resistance came from foremen and supervisors who were forced to accede more authority than they desired[10] and who feared exposure of their despotic and capricious management methods. Under the plans, workers were guaranteed fairer treatment, greater wage security, freedom from discrimination, and some rudimentary industrial justice. In some cases, as in Standard Oil of Louisiana's Baton Rouge refinery, the Plan allowed for black workers from the common labor department to be heard for the first time, as blacks could elect their own representatives (Hicks 1941, 58).

The Industrial Plan's dissemination was rapid but uneven. Some industrialists were overtly hostile to representation. When Cyrus Ching and Arthur Young, both leading industrial relations specialists who had successfully implemented representation plans, spoke of their experiences to a group of senior executives in New York in 1923 or 1924, the chairman of the group put an abrupt halt to discussions, saying, "I think we've heard enough of this Bolshevik talk. Let's go on to the next order of business" (Ching 1973, 6–7). But other major American corporations, even those outside the Rockefeller empire, scrutinized the Colorado experience and sought Mackenzie King's expertise. Early examples of American industry's receptivity to the Rockefeller Plan can be sampled from the list of dozens of Mackenzie King's clients (described in detail by McGregor 1962). The introduction of employee representation was often accompanied by major reforms that greatly improved the working lives of employees (e.g., conditions were vastly improved among impoverished sugar beet workers at Great Western Sugar Company). Of course, employer receptivity to the message that employee voice should be heard was greatly enhanced by the presence of a substantial union organizing threat.[11] Mackenzie King often mediated solutions that allowed union involvement at a time when employers were not legally obliged to recognize or bargain with unions. At both Colorado and Wyoming Railway and Standard Oil of Indiana, the solution was to persuade reluctant managers to recognize unions but continue to promote the joint council (ibid., 187).

More than two hundred companies adopted the Industrial Plan in the United States. Recall that although the Rockefeller Plan was the most popular of the nonunion systems, other alternatives also spread, but to a lesser extent. For example, the Leitch Industrial Democracy Plan was implemented in a southern textile firm in 1919, in the shadow of a union organizing drive. The Plan appears to have had a positive influence on working conditions and productivity (Smith 1960, 277). It faltered, however, in 1930, when wages were rolled back against employees' wishes. Although the company president stated that "our system of employee representation contains every element of collective bargaining that has any real merit" (quoted in Smith 1960, 300), his workers felt otherwise. Workers unionized with the United Textile Workers of America and were militant enough at that point to initiate and endure a lengthy strike.

Cyrus Ching helped found a factory council at the Morgan and Wright Tire Company in Detroit for more than seven thousand employees. Once the plan became entrenched, a subcommittee was established to emphasize tire sales, with tremendous success. Ching recalls, "Someone wanted to offer a bonus to any employee who would bring in a sales contact, but I said 'No, you'll spoil it. They're doing this because they want to do something to realize that they're part of the company and they're doing something for it. And if you go giving them a bonus, then you'll spoil it.' And we never did. But it was astonishing, astounding, the leads we got on that" (Ching 1973, 67). Ching points to many other examples, particularly in U.S. Rubber, in which, after employee relations stabilized and open information sharing was achieved, there were great strides in production techniques and sales methods. At the same time, there was open discussion of wages, job protection, and seniority provisions. There also was an ironclad guarantee of third-party arbitration for any disputes that could not be resolved by the Council system, although Ching cannot recall a single case going to arbitration. Ching remained a fierce proponent of the value of third-party arbitration in nonunion plans (ibid., 71).

On the whole, the various representation plans were a qualified success throughout their early decades. They definitely required a high degree of paternalism to operate. In many cases, low attendance and apathy among workers was a serious problem. Often the devil was in the details, and plans failed because senior managers simply lacked the commitment or vision to practice the new philosophy daily. If companies failed to match the gains made by unions in comparable settings, workers quickly abandoned their interest in company-sponsored representation and shifted their allegiance to unions. While senior managers and owners were persuaded by Rockefeller's cohort that the new Industrial Plan might be indispensable to weathering the storm of industrial unrest, the lower levels of corporate America were unconvinced and sometimes obstructive. Foremen and supervisors, who believed the Industrial Plan would destroy their authority, were especially problematic. In one location, meetings were ridiculed by foremen and some executives as "Kiss Me Clubs" (Gibb and Knowlton 1956, 586).

Employee voice would be heard only if it would advance the mutual interests of workers and employers. The initial implementation of the Industrial Plan seems to have been most successful where workers had little expectation or interest in union organizing, and attention would quickly turn to improvements in safety, enhancing quality of life, and productivity. Where the Plan was viewed by workers as an overt union-avoidance or substitution scheme, the experience was more fractious. The issues tended to focus on wages and basic working conditions, with sporadic outbursts of acrimony. Industrial relations continued to be turbulent in some locations, particularly where the Industrial Plan was imposed on workers who had already expressed considerable support for unionization (Marshall 1961). According to Brody (1960, 227), many union leaders initially welcomed employee representation plans, believing that they would create institutional vehicles from which organizing could be launched and union recognition could be won. These nonunion plans would spearhead worker attempts at bargaining over the terms and conditions of employment. However, companies were more aggressively anti-union than anticipated in this scenario. Bethlehem Steel discharged union activists involved in the industrial council and attempted to hold a new election for delegates. And companies adeptly pacified workers without actually bargaining with them. Robert Ozanne's comprehensive examination of the impact of the Industrial Plan on McCormick and International Harvester (a company with a plan that changed considerably over time) concludes, "The company union of 1919–37 was clearly not an effort to extend democracy to employees but a move to establish a company-controlled substitute for outside unionism. . . . The very size and importance of the personnel department itself have mirrored the growth of the union or the threat of a union. . . . Harvester's payroll records indicate that unionism has coincided with the higher periods of real wage growth, which implies that in the absence of unions productivity gains were not automatically handed over to workers" (Ozanne 1967, 247).

As Paul H. Douglas pointed out in his 1921 attempt to assess the value of nonunion representation plans, "One must be on one's guard to distinguish between the merits of plans already in operation and the inherent worth of the system" (p. 94). In his view, all plans suffered from shortcomings (a sentiment shared by Hammer 2000). Douglas concluded that any system that relies entirely on the enlightenment and benevolence of employers is inherently flawed.[12] On the other hand, there was genuine potential in the Industrial Plan's permanent institutional structure for communication and exchange of ideas. At International Harvester, for example, the Plan was harnessed to improve the firm's business operations (Ozanne 1967). The Plan clearly was crafted to be less adversarial than a unionized relationship and also more sensitive to employees' legitimate concerns than individual employment relationships in a nonunion setting (Taras and Kaufman 1999).

One reason it is so difficult to assess the employee representation movement is the enormous breadth of activities in the field. Some plans were successful; others were not. Some were introduced in a flurry of activity designed to forestall unionization, most notably in the early 1930s with the introduction of the short-lived National Industrial Recovery Act. Other plans were genuinely meant to be major advances in the management of work and a testament to the capacity of Labor and Capital to flourish in their codependency. The tension between industrialists' wishes to bring harmony to the worksite through the Industrial Plan and their heartfelt desire to avoid its dissolution through unions led to huge variability in the degree to which companies adopted the new vision. Some companies were early adopters but then lost interest (e.g., DuPont allowed its employee councils to fade out in the 1930s; International Harvester limited its use of councils); other companies' interest waxed and waned depending on which executives had stewardship of the Industrial Plan (e.g., General Electric); and a third group became permanent devotees of employee representation (e.g., Imperial Oil in Canada and Polaroid in the United States, the latter having waged a recent losing battle against American labor-law restrictions).

A second problem for researchers is the differing aims driving the employee representation movement. For example, even within the same plan there were differences of opinion: Contrary to Mackenzie King's advice, John D. Rockefeller, Jr., and Clarence Hicks welcomed the Industrial Plan as a substitute for unionization rather than a transitional step in the evolution toward collective bargaining. While Mackenzie King saw the Industrial Plan as a halfway point in the inexorable movement toward collective bargaining, by contrast both Rockefeller and Hicks intended it as an alternative to collective bargaining.[13] Some representational plans originated in the welfare capitalist movement, while others were meant to address industrial relations concerns. But by the mid-1930s, these disjunctures and much of the debate of the time became moot—the 1935 Wagner Act simultaneously banned nonunion representation systems in the United States and mandated that employers recognize and deal with unions.

What did employee representation achieve with regard to the legitimacy of employee voice? The Industrial Plan was of immeasurable assistance in both psychologically and organizationally creating the conditions that allowed major American employers to accept the advent of compulsory collective bargaining. After many years of reflection, Cyrus Ching espoused this tribute to the plans:

> I am not advocating the factory council plan as a substitute for the labor unions of the AFL and CIO. There can be no substitute, in advancing the best interests of both workers and employers, for a democratically and intelligently run union, operating apart from the cloak of management.
>
> But the factory council idea did fill a big need in the 1920s before many employers were ready to accept unions or the theory of collective bargaining. . . . They provided a stepping-stone to the collective bargaining stage of labor relations. And they were responsible, in no small way, for the comparative labor peace of the otherwise "Roaring Twenties."
>
> [By the time the company-based plans were outlawed by the Wagner Act,] [t]he idea had outlived its usefulness, but they were of great benefit to the country at the time before the infant, collective bargaining, was able to walk. [1953, 30–31]

Some representation plans were in settings where there was no possibility of unionization other than for a small group of craft workers who could join the AFL craft unions. Many plans predated the industrial union movement, which did not sweep through industry until the 1930s and 1940s. Then, in some cases, the Industrial Plan structures actually facilitated the introduction of CIO-based industrial organizing by erasing craft-based distinctions within the workforce, as in the Bell system (Schacht 1975), the public sector, and petroleum firms (Taras and Copping 1998). By the time unions were given the legal right to be recognized (in the United States in 1935 and in Canada almost a decade later), corporations were accustomed to some collective dealing, reducing the shock of having to accommodate unions.

In a number of companies, representation plans effectively demonstrated that workers and managers had harmonious interests. From calm labor relations arose opportunities to introduce changes that would improve productivity, tackle job redesigns and processes to ensure worker health and safety, and bring about fairer systems of workplace justice. Some plans set the stage for the more production-targeted employee involvement and participation plans of the second half of the century. Clearly, the early pursuit of employee voice was a corporate labor strategy built on the idea of cooperation and a unity of interest between workers and their companies.

Institutionalizing the Vision

The final ingredient that led to the growth of employee representation was the development of a vehicle to assist in the dissemination of knowledge and experience and to impart enthusiastic endorsement of representation. The departure of Mackenzie King back to Canada (where he quickly became prime minister) left a troubling vacuum within the Rockefeller group. Expertise was desperately needed to prop up the growing appetite of other companies for information about the Plan. Clarence Hicks was ideally positioned to continue to work with the Plan, and he implemented it at Standard Oil (New Jersey) and other companies. The continuing support and interest of John D. Rockefeller, Jr., provided the advocacy necessary to persuade other industrialists and company presidents to experiment with employee representation. Socializing industrialists and members of various boards of directors was a vitally important step, a necessary precondition, to bolster the longevity of the Industrial Plan formulation of the workplace. Without reminders of the importance of the vision of employee representation, old habits sometimes died hard. It was far too easy for managers to lapse back into union-suppression tactics and lose interest in nascent representation plans. It was imperative that stewardship of the Plan be entrusted to the most enthusiastic and respected senior managers under the explicit endorsement of company owners.

The formation in 1919 of the Special Conference Committee (SCC) of executives from ten leading corporations (Standard Oil of New Jersey, Bethlehem Steel, DuPont, General Electric, General Motors, Goodyear, International Harvester, Irving National Bank, Standard Oil of Indiana, and Westinghouse, and later joined by U.S. Rubber, AT&T, and then U.S. Steel) was an important step in fostering the spread of employee representation (Ozanne 1967; Scheinberg 1986; Jacoby 1997). The SCC was chaired by Clarence Hicks, who drew on his firsthand experience in the representation field (Hicks 1941). The SCC became a useful forum for top executives to discuss their employee relations philosophies and activities. Indeed, the SCC activities still continue as The Cowdrick Group.

Companies both within the Rockefeller orbit and more broadly throughout American enterprises began to contact Hicks and Mackenzie King for advice, but Hicks was busy with Standard Oil, and Mackenzie King had long since returned to Canada. In 1922, Rockefeller asked his attorneys, Curtis, Fosdick, and Belknap, to provide such a service by forming an industrial relations department chaired by Raymond Fosdick. Fosdick was asked to investigate employment conditions as early as 1919, at "a time when labor law as we know it today, had not even been conceived. . . . [F]or many American corporations of that day industrial relations hardly went beyond distributing a turkey at Christmas" (Belknap 1976, 10). When the law firm's various reports to corporations included cautionary recommendations, "Rockefeller's backing made them cautions with a clout" (ibid.). By 1926, the department was separately incorporated under the name Industrial Relations Counselors, Inc., as a nonprofit organization for research and for maintaining a consulting service.

By the late 1930s, IRC was chaired by Clarence Hicks and had the participation of the next generation of the Rockefeller family, John D. Rockefeller III, who was a trustee. Although Rockefeller family contributions helped finance IRC, it also supplemented its budget by charging for its consulting activities to American companies. Clients requested periodic surveys of their company's industrial relations conditions (the most notable confidential reports were perhaps a series of outstanding institutionalist field studies in the late 1920s conducted by Edward Sheffield Cowdrick under the auspices of the SCC).[14] The reports' conclusions and recommendations would be used to improve employee relations. Later, Latimer's (1932) work on industrial pensions for IRC was considered as authoritative, and early studies of profit sharing (Balderston 1937, Stewart and Couper 1945, IRC 1962), job analysis and evaluation (Balderston 1940), employee stock ownership, and employment stabilization policies (IRC 1954) were influential. The IRC's emerging governing principles were articulated in its fiftieth anniversary meeting in 1976 (Teplow 1976, 5–6):

1. Long-term and sound employee relations should be established through appropriate management structures, policies, and practices.
2. Management's responsible use of authority includes recognition of the interests of employees.
3. Decision making must be based on determinable facts through investigation.
4. Confidentiality in the gathering of information must be preserved.
5. IRC reports would arise from requests from top management, and be delivered in person to top management where they would be most influential.
6. The IRC staff and trustees must consist of people of the highest competence and integrity.

Once major corporations had accepted the idea from the first era of employee representation that workers had a legitimate interest in their employing organizations and a right to be treated as more than commodities engaged in production, it was then only a small step to begin to investigate just how the employment relationship should be improved. Profit sharing, pension plans, and other vehicles for demonstrating the employers' genuine concern with workers' welfare followed. While many large companies had created such plans in the late 1910s as part of the Welfare Capitalism movement's abiding interest in charitable endeavors and corporate benevolence, the real movement toward wide scale adoption occurred only after corporations accepted moral and financial responsibilities for their workers' welfare.

Characteristic of IRC's activities was a commitment to institutional research through surveys of industry practice. First, the stature of IRC helped ensure relatively high response rates to questionnaires and the provision of highly detailed and comprehensive information from hundreds of participating companies. For example, the 1940 Latimer and Tufel study of pensions examined 466 plans, and the 1945 Stewart and Couper profit-sharing study analyzed 325 plans. Second, IRC was not only committed to examining U.S. industry practice but also looked abroad for ideas and evidence. Between 1927 and 1932, IRC maintained an office at the International Labour Office in Geneva. Third, IRC studies contained recommendations for improving industry practices. The linkage between careful research and practitioner interest and relevance was evident. Balderson motivated his study thusly: ". . . to discover what uses profit sharing may have at the present time, to what situations it is best adopted, and, from past experience with it, what mistakes should be avoided" (1937, 5). While often there was a considerable lag between academically based research and industry practice, the IRC-based studies were uniquely positioned to occur at an earlier stage. For example, in anticipation of affirmative action policies, IRC sponsored the Norgren et al. 1959 study of employment issues involving "Negro" workers.

IRC continued to advocate employee representation even in the years after the Wagner Act of 1935 curtailed such activities. Hicks continued to insist there was a separate role for nonunion employee representation plans apart from unions (Hicks 1941). When in 1945 it appeared likely that labor law reform was on the horizon, IRC issued a monograph discussing its recommendations for reform. It was a pragmatic document promoting a reasoned approach.[15] IRC argued that the Wagner Act was too restrictive in preventing discourse between managers and workers, both in a partially unionized setting and in a union-free setting:

> Not only are the majority of American wage earners not union members, but also in many plants unions are not sufficiently representative of all the employees or any group appropriate for collective bargaining to be entitled to serve as the bargaining representatives of all or any group of the employees. In such plants employers should be free under the law to collaborate and exchange ideas with individual employees or groups of employees and to establish procedures for these purposes and for the presentation and adjustment of grievances.
>
> If there is no labor organization in an establishment or if substantial numbers of employees are not represented in collective bargaining, the management should be free to suggest to the unorganized employees that they should join one or more such labor organizations as they may choose or that they should establish one or more organizations as they may decide in order to bargain collectively. The management should also be free to suggest that any such organization should be properly representative of all employee groups concerned. The management should be free to complete an agreement with any organization so formed. Some large employers in particular have found it necessary to secure expressions of employee opinion when policy on matters of mutual interest is being determined. The only effective method is conference with representatives freely chosen by the employees, who will see to it that the subject in question is discussed by the employee group and report the majority opinion. In such circumstances, government should not discourage organization, as it now does, by a too rigid interpretation of some provisions of the Wagner Act, which prevents some employers from conferring with their unorganized employees even when there is no indication that the employees wish to be repre-

sented by any organization. The Wagner Act would continue to safeguard such organizations from company domination. [IRC 1945, 24]

But IRC added a proviso that although the institutional forms for employee representation should be broadened under the law, the employer could only exercise the resulting freedoms "provided the employer does not restrict the employees' legal right of self-organization" (ibid., 28). Thus, even a decade after the passage of the Wagner Act, IRC continued to frame its support for representation plans in the context of industrial relations concerns with employment matters and industrial justice and to envision them as either a complement to unions (in the first paragraph quoted above) or a substitute for unions (in the second paragraph above). But the principle of collective dealing by employees and their right to choose their form of representation was by this time entirely taken for granted in IRC circles. Subsequent amendments to the Wagner Act did not address IRC's concerns, and restrictions on nonunion representation plans continue into the twenty-first century. By the second half of the last century, IRC had been joined in its role as disseminator of ideas by a burgeoning human resource management field with its attendant associations.

Part II: The Rise and Spread of Employee Involvement and Participation

Two major transformations severely curtailed the spread of employee representation. The first was the law. When Section 7(a) of the National Industrial Recovery Act of the early 1930s granted employees "the right to organize and bargain collectively through representatives of their own choosing" free of employer interference, huge numbers of American employers encouraged their workers to form collectives modeled after the Rockefeller Plan rather than join national unions (Bureau of Labor Statistics [BLS] 1937). By the end of 1935, there were roughly as many American workers covered by nonunion plans, the most popular of which was the Rockefeller Plan, as there were members of unions (Kaufman 2000, 24). Many of these plans were hastily conceived and poorly executed devices crafted only for union avoidance, and unions were quite justified in viewing them as a threat and urging legislators to outlaw these defective "company unions."

The National Labor Relations Act (NLRA) (Wagner Act) in 1935 was crafted to destroy the representational type of nonunion plan that was used by many companies as a substitute for unionization (Brandes 1979; Cohen 1990; Kaufman 1996). Section 8(a)(2) made it an unfair labor practice for management to dominate, participate in, or interfere with a labor organization, and

Section 2(5) defined labor organization as "any organization of any kind" that deals with matters affecting the employment relationship, such as wages and working conditions. No distinction in the law was made between successful and unsuccessful plans or between long-standing plans and hastily erected shams, and all American companies under the purview of the NLRA that operated the Rockefeller Plan were ordered to disband their nonunion systems. Despite the Wagner Act ban, there is "convincing evidence that company unions still exist," and a number of companies continue their commitment to nonunion representation even in defiance of a legislative ban (LeRoy 2000, 304; Kaufman, Lewin, and Fossum 2000). In Canada, by contrast, Mackenzie King was prime minister when a comprehensive labor bill was finally passed during World War II, and there was no restriction written into the law banning nonunion employee representation (Taras 1997).

The second transformation was managerial philosophy, which moved to embrace high-involvement systems rather than representation. Consider again the two forms of employee voice. In the representational form, exemplified by the Rockefeller Plan, employees meet with managers to discuss employee interests, air grievances, and resolve employment issues. The second form, employee involvement and participation, derives from the notion of achieving higher performance and enhanced productivity through investment in people. This form goes well beyond Taylorism and the scientific management movement of the early to mid-1900s, which tried to achieve more productive use of workers through better engineering of production and more efficient managerial techniques. The employee involvement vision actually includes workers' perspective as a central feature of the firm's transformation. While Taylorism could suggest that workers become more efficient, the employee involvement movement could help motivate workers to do so.

The writings of such luminaries in the fields of organizational behavior and industrial psychology as Elton Mayo, Kurt Lewin, Douglas MacGregor, and Frederick Hertzberg greatly influenced managerial philosophy on the treatment of workers and the practices that would achieve the best results for both the business and its employees. For example, Mayo's famous Hawthorne Experiments demonstrated the importance of human relationships at work and concluded that the interaction among workers was an important contributor to the rate at which work was completed (see, for example, Roethlisberger and Dickson 1939, chapter 20). Lewin's work revealed the importance of groups and the social setting of work. MacGregor argued that how employees were treated mattered: Greater managerial concern about employee welfare would intrinsically motivate employees. Under such circumstances, employees exercise self-direction and pursue goal attainment, limiting the need for close supervision and systems of punishment. Hertzberg argued that work could be designed so that employees could be motivated to produce out of commitment rather than pecuniary self-interest, and that if properly designed, work could be a celebration of the dignity and intrinsic worth of human beings.

While the earlier vision of voice emphasized representation and the resolution of issues related to wages and working conditions, the more recent initiatives explore the relationship between the design of work and the work unit's goal to produce tangible results. Global competition in the post–World War II era heightened the desire to improve production methods, standards, and targets. If employees could be self-directing, layers of middle management could be thinned and the need for close supervision by foreman dissipated. Productivity could improve, and unnecessary payroll costs could be reduced.

Richard Walton wrote in 1974 of eight key components of the high-performance workplace: teams, job enlargement, flexibility, greater worker authority, sharing of production and financial information, use of gain sharing, investment in training, and creation of higher trust between workers and managers (cited in Kaufman 1999, 77). According to McCabe and Lewin, "Conceptually, principles of autonomy, decentralization, and self-management guide such [participation] initiatives, together with a strong belief that they enhance employee attitudes toward work and result in improved job performance" (1992, 120). The consensus seems to be that a coherent system involves attention to recruitment and selection of capable employees; ongoing training to enable them to perform at a high level; rewarding them based on their performance; sharing information and communicating company strategies; and providing opportunities for employees to involve themselves in improving the work process (summarized in Becker and Huselid 1998).

What seems missing from some of this discussion is the need for companies, particularly those with large and complex operations, to use employee representation as a means of eliciting workers' perspectives on the employer's various activities. Direct workers' participation in workplace initiatives is not always possible—some workers with major contributions may be sidelined from discussions with managers. In some circumstances, it would seem logical, and quite beneficial, to incorporate the principles of (indirect) representation into the new high-involvement systems, but legal restrictions have contributed to the inability of American companies to successfully (and legally) amalgamate the two forms of voice.

By the 1980s, the employee involvement philosophy soared in popularity, as did the fascination with Japanese approaches involving quality circles and just-in-time inventory control methods. These and other practices in nonunion companies were studied with great interest, but representation rarely was mentioned. In Fred Foulkes' comprehensive and influential analysis of managerial practices published in 1980, attention to representation was negligible. The evidence is that many or all of the particular components of the high-performance workplace have been widely disseminated, although few companies have adopted the entire package in an integrated high-involvement system (Lawler 1999). (Indeed, a 2000 study by Blasi and Kruse concludes that popular enthusiasm for the new management style greatly exaggerates its actual penetration: Apparently only 1 percent of American establishments are running high-performance workplaces.) Specific participation programs vary widely in design, scope, and issues covered. Generally speaking, team-based approaches have dominated new practices (LeRoy 1997 and 1999), and performance-based compensation systems have flourished (Kraut and Korman 1999)—although there is virtually no evidence in the literature that corporations are using group-based performance evaluation.[16] Teams are regularly used, but performance evaluations are still conducted for individuals.

In 1989, 43 percent of nonunion production workers in manufacturing had some form of employee involvement program (Delaney, Lewin, and Ichniowski 1989). By 1994, 75 percent of aerospace employees used employee involvement, with 96 percent penetration of employers with more than five thousand employees (these studies cited in Kaufman 1999). The extent to which industry practices have been "transformed" by employee involvement varies considerably. A 1992 study found that only 7 percent of the 313 companies surveyed had high-level employee involvement, while most companies had only taken a few steps in that direction. In 1994, while more than half of companies with fifty or more employees had some form of employee involvement, only 37 percent had adopted two or more of the practices associated with high-performance workplaces (Osterman 1994). Lawler's survey of company practices in the United States (1999) showed that the vast majority of *Fortune* 100 firms use employee involvement techniques, and his survey shows significant increases in adoption even since 1987. The popularity of employee involvement apparently continues. After reviewing the substantial literature on both representation and employee involvement plans, Kaufman (1999) concluded that the number of companies that use an employee involvement plan involving representation is sizable. He estimates that in the United States, anywhere from 13.2 to 30.9 million employees are covered by these plans.

While almost half of companies had town-hall meetings, only 37 percent held regular meetings involving "a committee of employees that discusses problems with management" (Freeman and Rogers 1999). The grievance procedures employed by companies to ensure, at a minimum, some form of rudimentary justice laid out in advance of disputes vary widely. A study of seventy-eight American nonunion businesses found that about 80 percent of company handbooks specify an "open-door" policy for handling disputes, and exceedingly few companies actually allow recourse to a neutral arbitrator outside the company's employ (McCabe 1988). But this may have been changing in recent years: One of the burgeoning growth areas within the activities of members of the National Academy of Arbitrators is hearing arbitrations involving nonunion worksites.

Although the primary philosophy of employee involvement is directed toward enhanced productivity and improved work processes, it is difficult to draw a line between EI and representation matters. The Freeman and Rogers study found that in practice, 28 percent of nonunion employee involvement committees discuss wages and benefits. LeRoy's surveys of work teams found that between half and two thirds of work teams had bilateral interactions with management on matters involving the employment relationship (e.g., wages, scheduling of work, benefits, and so on). In addition, safety committees are often mandated by law for large employers, and it is quite likely that as well as safety matters, worker representatives informally discuss other issues. In my discussions with various delegates involved in safety committees, I found that nonunion employers often used safety-committee dealings to sound out employee sentiments on a variety of matters far outside the committee's purview. The title or principal mandate of a committee does not necessarily indicate its scope. But there is a decided preference among modern managers to have direct forums in which employees share their own thoughts with managers rather than the old formal systems of representation in which elected delegates speak on behalf of constituent workers.

In the arena of collective representation, however, there is little to preclude the use of both unions and high-participation workplaces. For example, Appelbaum and her colleagues (2000) demonstrated that employee involvement occurs in union settings with positive outcomes for firm performance. Thus, nonunion firms such as Polaroid, DuPont, and Efcor are perplexed that the law has limited their incorporation of formal representation systems into the high-involvement workplace, particularly when the gains of providing a more holistic system of voice seem compelling.

The confusion is evident in the empirical literature that attempts to assess the success of participation plans on outcomes such as productivity or job satisfaction. Cotton demonstrates that the field is bedeviled by an entanglement of forms and functions of participation and voice (1993, 20–31). He and his colleagues developed and tested the effects of six conceptually distinct forms of employee participation (Cotton et al. 1988; see also Batt and Appelbaum 1995 in a study asking who benefits from employee involvement). They clearly differentiated representation from other forms of participation (consultative, short-term, informal, in work decisions, and employee

ownership) and demonstrated that while some of the other forms of participation had positive effects on the outcome variables, representative participation "produced no effects for productivity or satisfaction" (Cotton 1993,
21). This is unsurprising given the argument herein that voice encompasses
many different imperatives.

In some cases, employers much preferred the productivity emphasis and
flexibility in the employee involvement approach over the more rigid "union-
like" representational plans. Imperial Oil unilaterally disbanded its Joint Industrial Council in one major refinery and replaced it with a work–team–based
approach (MacIsaac 1993, 41–42). Similarly, an American firm that was a
leading practitioner of independent local unionism until the 1960s changed
its focus from representation to employee involvement methods (Jacoby and
Verma 1992).

The employee involvement movement developed techniques for eliminating irritants in the employment relationship. Major firms introduced "justice on the job" without any form of collective representation, e.g., CIGNA's
"Speak Easy" Program, IBM's "Open Door," NBC's "Counselor System,"
the "Guaranteed Fair Treatment Procedure" at Federal Express, and Employee Committees at Polaroid (Ewing 1989). Supervisors and foremen have
been retrained in employee involvement schemes to act as "facilitators" and
"continuous improvement coaches." Personnel and human resources departments develop policies and procedures and ensure that they are applied fairly
and consistently.

Lipset and Meltz (2000) found that while half of American and Canadian
nonunion employees surveyed said their company had an employee involvement plan, only 20 percent had formal systems of nonunion representation.
IRC commissioned a study of employee involvement in American industry
(1994). Approximately 130 companies were invited to participate, and 16
large companies whose workforces included a blend of union and nonunion
workers allowed questionnaires to be sent to their employees. In all, 2,609
questionnaires were returned (a 58 percent response rate). Most collective
activity among employees involved functional work groups or departmental
teams engaged in efficiency, safety, quality, training, and cost reduction. About
15 percent reported joint employee-management committees, although dis-
proportionately more "exempt" (nonunionizable) employees participated in
joint committees than hourly workers (36 percent versus 13 percent). It is
difficult to interpret the implications of this study's findings, for the ques-
tionnaire asked workers to select and describe the one form of employee
involvement in which they were most intensely involved rather than capturing the panoply of EI devices and representation systems. The focus of this
study, even under the auspices of the very organization intended by the

Rockefellers to further the study and dissemination of representation systems, was squarely in the new school of employee involvement rather than the old tradition of employee representation (perhaps because of representation's dubious legal status).

The vehicles for dissemination of "best practices" in the participation field are now the large associations of human resource professionals and dispute resolution bodies. The growing professionalization of human resource management throughout the twentieth century has meant that firm owners and chief executives are not compelled to band together (as they did when IRC was formed) and can depend more on the skills and knowledge of human resource managers.

The issue of representation has re-emerged in recent years. But because the scope of the Wagner Act restrictions in Sections 8(a)(2) and 2(5) is so broad, they have inadvertently affected the lawful practice of some employee involvement plans. The *Electromation* case, decided by the National Labor Relations Board in 1992, sent a chill through American companies. The company Electromation was forced to disband a number of "action committees" set up to foster worker-manager communication. These committees were held to be de facto labor organizations under Section 2(5). Then working teams were disbanded in the E.I. DuPont case of 1993. Since then, more than three dozen cases have touched on this issue of where to draw the line between lawful practice of employee involvement techniques such as quality circles and joint committees (Kaufman 1999; LeRoy 1999; Estreicher 2000). Sometimes the defendant company wins, and sometimes it loses. Today the advice given to managers about avoiding unfair-labor-practice charges is that when interacting with worker groups, they must avoid all appearances of domination, limit the discussion topics to corporate matters such as profitability and continuous improvement, never discuss issues within the domain of unions (even if there is no union present in the company), and carefully consult with lawyers (Hanson, Porterfield, and Ames 1995).

In practice, it is quite difficult to create systems that fully comply with the law. Consider, for example, a team-based practice that involves production employees who make suggestions for quality improvements. Some of their recommendations might involve shift changes, gain sharing, or voluntary retirement-plan adjustments. If managers officially met with them and openly discussed their recommendations, managers would be committing an unfair labor practice by "dealing with" a labor organization on forbidden subjects.

The Wagner Act, intended to prevent sham union-substitution schemes from impeding the spread of collective bargaining, has inadvertently cast a long shadow over employee involvement. A group of firms, notably Polaroid, banded together to launch a powerful lobbying effort to amend the National

Labor Relations Act to allow workers to deal with managers in the context of employee-involvement programs. The Teamwork for Employees and Management (TEAM) Act was passed by both houses of Congress but vetoed by President Clinton in 1996 (Hein 1996; Pivec and Robbins 1996). Given the composition of Congress since the election of George W. Bush, it is unlikely that the TEAM Act proposal will be passed in the near future. American companies intending to stay within the law will have to be exquisitely sensitive to labor law in the design and implementation of any employee-involvement plans.

But although companies complain that the NLRA should be changed to allow greater freedom in determining the forms and functions of nonunion representation, there is no great outpouring of demand for the complex Rockefeller Plan of industrial representation or the Leitch Plan of workplace governance. The widespread hunger for the formal nonunion employee-representation plans was a two-year historic anachronism precipitated by the introduction in 1933 of the National Industrial Recovery Act, which compelled some form of collective action, and this great spike in interest ceased with the 1935 NLRA. When we compare Canada (which permits these plans under the law) and the United States (which outlawed them in 1935), there are very few differences (Lipset and Meltz 2000). For some rare companies, a formal representation system is integral to their philosophy of people management, but most companies would not entertain such plans. They are too complex, too difficult to administer, and too similar to collective bargaining through unions. In an empirical study of leading Canadian firms with employee involvement practices, Verma (2000) found that none of the eight firms analyzed had a formal, ongoing, and independent forum for systematic input. Most used ad hoc committees, focus groups, surveys, and task forces, but "these committees and teams were constituted at management initiative. Their membership was almost always assigned by management with minimal input by employees" (ibid., 312). Hence, even in a country that allows formal employee representation, there is little appetite for the formal representation systems.

It is ironic, though, that the representational and employee involvement streams of managerial thought have been forced into an alliance in order to lobby for the removal of restrictions in American law. Companies in the United States that tried to operationalize employee involvement—even through ad hoc and informal meetings with employees—in an attempt to mutually deal with employment issues such as wages, bonuses, pensions, shift scheduling, and so on, run afoul of the law. While I have demonstrated their different underpinnings and emphases in this chapter, there is one thing to which both groups agree: It is in their mutual interests to advocate a change in the law. Examining the history, law, and contemporary issues of this controversial subject was the motivation for the 1997 Conference on Nonunion Employee Representation in Banff, Canada, cochaired by Taras and Kaufman, which resulted in a book (Kaufman and Taras 2000). IRC provided a portion of the funding for the conference, and Roy Helfgott's involvement in the conference and subsequent publication of a summary of the conference in an IRC newsletter continued the tradition of IRC involvement in matters affecting employee voice.

Conclusions

I have traced the evolution of the managerial thought on employee voice from the initial nonunion representation systems of the early twentieth century—those that stressed communication and harmony of interests and gave workers some collective participation in influencing the terms and conditions of their employment—to the more modern employee involvement systems designed to enhance productivity and contribute to the success of the enterprise. Although both labor law and changes in managerial philosophy have made the original employee representation plans seem somewhat anachronistic today, the original contribution of companies at the vanguard of progressive management through reform of their own employment and personnel practices helped to shape industrial relations and human resources philosophies throughout much of the twentieth century. By voluntarily accepting responsibility for labor reform, these companies legitimized the idea of collective voice among employees and developed institutional mechanisms for communication between workers and managers. By convincing leading industrialists to provide a vehicle for employees to have a voice, these efforts broke with the tradition of rugged capitalism that treated workers as factors of production. In an era in which capitalists' divine right to rule their empires was a tenet of many in the industrial elite, the notion that workers' views could be relevant was a profound step forward.

Whereas Mackenzie King's vision was that the captains of industry had a moral obligation to create formal systems of employee representation, today there is little evidence of this sentiment in top business echelons. There is little evidence of the reformist spirit of "muscular Christianity" that so motivated the early employee representation movement. With private-sector union density below 10 percent, and with almost no union penetration of high technology industries, Bill Gates does not lose sleep worrying about labor unions and the fundamental rights of his employees to organize collectively. By contrast, John D. Rockefeller, Jr., did worry. It was the preoccupation of a different age, when labor unrest shook the foundations of key industries and the laws had not yet been written that limited managerial prerogatives in designing systems of voice for employees.

Today, when North American industrial leaders turn their attention to people matters, they are inclined to think about performance-based compensation, individual systems of input, and employee involvement. There remain some contemporary examples of companies deeply committed to employee representation, but most companies that adhere to the legitimacy of employee voice have turned to employee involvement and participation plans. Perhaps the decline of the union threat effect with the drop in American union density over the last three decades has made many employers more complacent about formal representation. Employee representation receives little consideration except when discussion turns to matters involving unions. Instead, progressive companies' emphasis has shifted to more flexible, decentralized, and direct forms of participation, with considerable redesign of production flows and task specifications. Companies are embracing the performance impacts of a variety of new workplace practices while retaining the now taken-for-granted notion that harmonious relations between workers and their employers is the vital base for motivating higher productivity.

And what of employee voice generally? Both the representation and participation plans rest on a shared notion that better communication and less adversarial interactions between workers and managers are essential. Perhaps the separation of representation and participation is both artificial and unnecessary and, as Verma put it, must "yield to a more integrative treatment. For employers and employees, the dividing line is frequently blurred" (2000, 319). Even Mackenzie King did not want the Industrial Plan to allow for unfettered employee voice via representation. He intended a type of voice acquired after socialization, when employees were educated to articulate their views without upsetting industrial order. This voice could be expressed once the capricious tyranny of the foreman could be curtailed through training, the creation of reasonable policies, and the direct interaction of worker delegates with senior management. Order would assert itself over chaos. Worker voice would be welcomed, particularly from workers who were immune from the blandishments of labor leaders, averse to conflict, willing to advance the interests of their enterprise, and filled with faith in their employers. Today employers hope for exactly the same outcomes, but the vehicle for achieving success is employee involvement.

Acknowledgments

Thanks to my friends Anil Verma and Morley Gunderson at the University of Toronto, James Bennett of George Mason University, and Laurie Milton, Allen Ponak, and Kelly Williams from the University of Calgary. Funding was provided by the Human Resources and Organizational Dynamics Research Grant at the Faculty of Management, University of Calgary.

Notes

1. The nomenclature of nonunion representation is confusing. Initially, supporters of nonunion plans called them works councils or shop committees and, later, joint councils, industrial councils, and employee-management associations. The term "company union" is meant to denigrate these plans by tainting them with management domination and control. Furthermore, "company union" is not the same as "enterprise union" (which, in turn, can be confused with either Japanese industrial-relations institutions or independent local unions). I prefer to avoid the term "company union" because it is not possible for such an entity to be considered a union under modern North American labor law, and as will become clear later in this chapter, the intent of too many of these nonunion plans was to allow for representation without collective bargaining. They were not unions at the time of their creation or in retrospect.

2. For example, the National Industrial Conference Board examined the Bethlehem Steel Company from 1918 to 1920 and found that of issues raised, 31 percent involved wages, 28 percent involved working conditions, 12 percent involved production methods, and 10 percent involved safety. Gibb and Knowlton (1956) found a similar pattern at Standard Oil, and there are numerous examples in the Canadian case studies of the preoccupation of nonunion plans with wages and working conditions (published in the Canadian government's journal *Labour Gazette* from 1920 to the mid-1930s).

3. The "open shop" was an absolute and unwavering philosophical commitment of the Rockefellers. Although some of the Rockefeller companies would negotiate collective agreements with unions many years before the passage of the Wagner Act, it was only when truly pressed to the wall that the Rockefeller companies would recognize unions. Even in the 1940s, Clarence Hicks, the professional entrusted with implementation of the nonunion system of representation at Standard Oil, and the chairman of Industrial Relations Counselors, wrote of his continued antipathy to the closed shop (1941, 70–77).

4. When labor relations worsened even further in Colorado, John D. Rockefeller, Jr., testified before a congressional investigating committee (April 6, 1914):

Rockefeller, Jr.: . . . [A]s part owners of the property, our interest in the laboring men in this country is so immense, so deep, so profound that we stand ready to lose every cent we put in that company rather than see the men we have employed thrown out of work and have imposed upon them conditions which are not of their seeking and which neither they nor we can see are in our interest. . . . [O]ur interest in labor is so profound and we believe so sincerely that interest demands that the camps shall be open camps . . .

Chairman: And you will do that if it costs all your property and kills all your employees?

Rockefeller, Jr.: It is a great principle.

Chairman: And you would do that rather than recognize the right of men to collective bargaining? Is that what I understand?

Rockefeller, Jr.: No sir. Rather than allow outside people to come in and interfere with employees who are thoroughly satisfied with their labor conditions—it was upon a similar principle that the War of the Revolution was carried out. It is a great national issue of the most vital kind. . . .

Rockefeller's notion was that demand for unions did not originate from within the workforce: Rather, union leaders from outside caused workers to act against their own interests and against their employers. This quote is worthy of study because it demonstrates the position of Rockefeller before circumstances forced him to become more knowledgeable about industrial relations matters.

5. The plan is variously known as the Rockefeller Plan, the Mackenzie King Plan, the Industrial Plan, the Colorado Plan, and the Joint Industrial Council Plan. These terms will be used interchangeably.

6. The impetus is similar to that underpinning the welfare capitalism movement, but Mackenzie King was more interested in representation for workers than he was in the provision of employer-promulgated welfare schemes.

7. For example, Mackenzie King wrote, "[L]et the parties to Industry recognize a mutuality, not a conflict of interest, in all that pertains to maximum production and equitable distribution of wealth, and what is the result? Immediately, fresh energies are released, a new freedom is given to the effort in Industry. Productivity is increased, as are also the respective rewards of all the parties" (1918, 172). But even in this quote dealing explicitly with productivity is an entanglement with distributive issues involving the reallocation of rewards. It is difficult to ascertain the role of productivity: Is it a goal or a welcome consequence of a well-functioning representation system ensuring a mutuality of interests?

8. There is evidence in Mackenzie King's *Diaries* that he told Rockefeller, Jr., in their first meeting together that "my sympathies had always been strongly with labour" and that "I believed in trade unions, though I thought that sometimes they were mistaken in their policies, and particularly in some of the fights that were made for recognition rather than for standards respecting conditions." Rockefeller replied that "he believed in unions himself, though he was opposed to the attitude taken by some of the leaders" (1914/1915 Special Addendum to Diaries devoted to the King-Rockefeller alliance, G-2539, p. 42) Had Rockefeller not allowed for the possibility of unions, Mackenzie King would not likely have accepted the consultancy.

9. In truth, the company owners were initially more enthusiastic about the Industrial Plan than were the workers. CF&I miners actually paid little attention to representation matters, and the company even found it difficult to get the men to vote for their representatives (Selekman and Van Kleeck 1924, 82–84). As McGregor dryly commented, "To a degree self-government had to be imposed on them" (1962, 188). McGregor felt that a full partnership between Labor and Capital was never really achieved at any of the sites, although the Plan introduced an important intermediate step in worker self-government and industrial democracy. The Industrial Plan did bring to an end the violence and misery of labor disputes, but it did not presage nirvana in Colorado. Although some strikes broke out, the ability to endure industrial discord without escalation and retaliation was a genuine departure from the past, and much of it was due to the Industrial Plan. But despite the calming of tensions, CF&I asked workers to sign "Loyalty Cards" and, even in the 1920s, employed industrial spies to monitor worker activities. The Plan came to an inauspicious end between 1933 and 1940, with some parts of the company unionizing and other parts preferring no representation at all (Gitelman 1988; Nelson 2000, 65).

10. This is a consistent finding within both the employee-representation and the employee-involvement research. Cotton (1993, 55–56) reviews some of the contemporary literature on this problem.

11. However, sometimes managers who embraced nonunion representation in the shadow of union organizing were unwilling to implement Mackenzie King's no-discrimination practice. Youngstown Sheet and Tube Company was very hostile to unions and refused to allow worker delegates to hold positions in unions, defying Mackenzie King's strong advice that they not use joint councils to combat unions. Other companies continued to use industrial spies to monitor union organizing and pinpoint activists (Gitelman 1988, 191, 324).

12. He found "grave defects" in the implementation of nonunion plans: (1) employers exerted influence over the election of worker representatives; (2) many plans discussed only trivial matters, leaving all residual matters as managerial rights; (3) management had greater weight in the design of some of the plans; (4) workers' roles were mostly advisory and their influence existed only on the sufferance of management; (5) some plans erected barriers to extensive employee participation (e.g., a workman must be employed for more than six months before being eligible for election, or barring noncitizens); (6) worker representatives conducted their affairs and modified their positions fearing company reprisal; (7) workers lacked resources to hire skilled experts to help them formulate positions and increase their capacity to bargain; and (8) they did not become active in lobbying governments for protective legislation and reform that would help workers.

13. I am fortunate as a researcher to have been allowed entree into the contemporary workings of the Rockefeller Plan through my relationship with Imperial Oil in Canada (e.g., Taras and Copping 1998; Taras 2000a). I have two conclusions about the system I observed in practice, as well as the archival materials I have been privileged to receive about other companies' usage of the Rockefeller Plan throughout the United States. First, the systems are only as good as the people involved with them. There were outstanding examples of successes of the Rockefeller Plan, just as there were dismal failures. The Plan should not be treated as an undifferentiated monolith, just as it would be naive to presume that all unions are alike. Second, managerial interest in the Rockefeller Plan was, and continues to be, inextricably linked to unionization. All documents that discuss the Plan also assess union-proneness and industrial relations tensions. Where there is a strong union-organizing threat, the Plan is most likely to be implemented with care and attentiveness to employee concerns. Both company managers and workers are vigilant in monitoring prevailing conditions in unionized sites, and wage rates for nonunion workers represented in the Rockefeller Plan either match or exceed their union cohort. Because my research program has focused primarily on the Rockefeller Plan, I may be overemphasizing features of this particular plan, and I hope that future research that is beyond the scope of this chapter's ambitions will systematically test these working hypotheses.

14. The Cowdrick reports are confidential documents of Industrial Relations Counselors. I am grateful to Bruce Kaufman for sharing six Cowdrick reports with me for this research.

15. For example, on the matter of the closed shop, IRC took the position that "any proposal completely to outlaw the closed or union shop would arouse such opposition as to prevent dispassionate consideration of more important proposals. . . . [V]oluntary agreement on union security provisions should be permitted, but union

security in all its forms should be excluded from the range of subjects upon which employers are required to bargain under penalty of being charged with an unfair labor practice" (IRC 1945, 22).

16. This conclusion was reached after I conducted an extensive search of the management literature around performance appraisal systems using ProQuest (ABI Inform). While there were hundreds of examples of individual-based appraisal systems, only a handful of articles even referred to group-based appraisals. In 1999 I asked my MBA students to locate true group-based appraisals within any firms in Calgary, and my class of sixty students was unable to provide a single example.

10

Industrial Relations in the Global Economy

Morley Gunderson and Anil Verma

The most pressing challenges—and opportunities—facing industrial relations today stem from globalization and other related forces. The discipline
of industrial relations has always emphasized that the industrial relations
system is influenced by the legal, social, and economic environment. This
environment is now global.

The international aspect, by itself, is not new. It is merely unfolding in
ways that are unfamiliar and more complex than before. The core issues are
not new—they are more old wine in new bottles. In fact, the following issues
that Industrial Relations Counselors, Inc. (IRC), dealt with in its early years
are often key policy issues today: unemployment insurance; social security;
dispute settlement; public and private pensions and retirement; worksharing;
wage-fixing legislation; income security; disability benefits; payroll taxes;
child labor; training; stock ownership, profit sharing, productivity bargaining, and wage incentive plans; the role of international organizations such as
the International Labour Organization (ILO); accommodating return to work
(at that time for war veterans); the relationship of industrial relations to
company management; unionization of professionals; hours of work and
overtime regulation; costing fringe benefits; and executive compensation
and stock options. This list reads like a research agenda for the Industrial
Relations Research Association today.

Earlier IRC studies illustrate fundamental principles inherent in current
industrial relations research. These principles often distinguish industrial relations research from the more theoretical and abstract emphasis of related
disciplines such as economics.[1] Those principles, which remain hallmarks of
good industrial relations research, involve an emphasis on the following:

- Issues of policy and practical importance
- The institutional, historical, legal, and social context in which the is-
  sues occur
- Multidisciplinary perspectives

- Objective research (given the often controversial subject matter)
- Sound data and statistical, empirical analysis
- The role of all stakeholders—labor, management, and government
- Lessons to be learned from historical experience and the experience of other countries

IRC was built on a set of basic governing concepts largely attributable to its "founders": William Lyon Mackenzie King (a former Canadian minister of labor[2] who was retained by John D. Rockefeller, Jr., to find a "better way" to do labor relations after the Ludlow Massacre); Clarence Hicks (who administered the employee representation plan set up by King); and Bryce Stewart (a former director of the Employment Service in Canada and the first IRC director of research).[3] Those basic governing principles, as interpreted by Leo Teplow (1976, 56), the president of IRC from 1974 to 1978, stressed the importance of top management support for the effective implementation of policy initiatives[4] as well as the importance of integrating employee relations into an organization's management strategy. These are generally regarded today as key elements of the effective implementation of industrial relations and human resource management practices.

Early IRC studies were set in the context of global turmoil—a world ravaged by recessions, depressions, and wars and, at the same time, dealing with the challenges and opportunities of industrialization. IRC itself was born out of conflict—the Ludlow Massacre—and stressed objective research as an important guide in its search for a "better way." IRC looked not only "inward" but also "outward" to the situation in other countries, especially Europe and Canada.[5] There was a realization then—as now—that global problems require global solutions and that considerable information can be gathered by examining the experiences of other countries. IRC's research also focused on international labor issues, including international labor standards and the corresponding role of the ILO.[6] The role of labor standards in international competition was a key issue at that time, and it remains such today. Other key issues—many of which are related to globalization (as discussed later in this chapter)—included providing jobs for a growing population, improving human resources through education and training, building safety nets to protect workers from economic disruptions, and ensuring that the gains from globalization were broadly distributed.

Particularly noteworthy for today's scholars and practitioners of industrial relations is IRC's early interest in issues of labor standards, worker voice, and fair wages. IRC has been an employers' organization right from the start, but it would be safe to say that the majority of employers at the time were not quick to espouse IRC principles of worker voice and empowerment. In formulating a vision of how to bring about change, Mackenzie King and other IRC founders did not see organized labor taking the lead in developing cooperative relations. The guiding assumption for King and his colleagues was that employers have the resources to undertake this transformation; all they needed was the will to achieve it. IRC was founded to achieve precisely this goal. Thus started a formal employer organization dedicated to improving labor standards and worker voice on the job. Employer role and, more importantly, employer leadership in labor matters continue to be debated to this day in the wake of globalization.

The purpose of this chapter is to analyze industrial relations in the global economy, focusing particularly on government-legislated labor standards, the aspect of labor legislation drawing the most attention under globalization. Labor standards legislation is first put in the context of the three main mechanisms for regulating the employment relationship: (1) the unregulated market; (2) employee representation, often through collective bargaining; and (3) laws and regulations, including labor standards legislation. The rationale and role of labor standards are then outlined and followed by a discussion of the ILO, codes of fair competition, labor standards, and international labor federations from around the time of the establishment of IRC in 1926 to the present. This is followed by a brief description of the global economic environment and its influence on the current debate on labor standards as well as its implications for industrial relations and the regulation of the employment relationship. The chapter concludes with a discussion of the appropriate response of the various stakeholders to the pressures of globalization.

The Stake of Progressive Employers in Labor Standards

In traditional employment relationships, employers and employees are generally opposed to each other's position on most matters. Early institutionalists such as John Commons and Beatrice and Sidney Webb, among others, theoretically formalized the opposing interests of employers and employees as being rooted in the roles of each party. Why then should employers be interested in labor policies that cost them resources and lower profits? The argument for employer involvement in labor welfare is that such costs are investments in future profits of the firm. The employer may not be maximizing profits for the short term by promoting good labor standards but, rather, does expect to benefit in the longer run from better relations, stability in the relationship, lower costs, quality, and productivity. This argument was rooted deeply in the philosophy of IRC. It is also an argument that can be made for proactive employer involvement in the development of international labor standards in the context of globalization and international trade.

Mackenzie King, whose leadership laid the intellectual foundation for much of IRC's work, saw corporate as well as societal prosperity dependent on empowering and co-opting workers into the larger system (King 1918). Both before and after the Russian Bolshevik Revolution of 1917, there was widespread fear within corporate and political ranks that North American workers in large numbers might espouse the romantic vision of a classless society promised by the Communist Manifesto (Bercuson 1973). The only way to neutralize this lure, in King's view, was to offer workers more voice in workplace matters and to enlist them as partners in the corporate enterprise and, by extension, in its wealth.

This larger vision for saving capitalism was extended by King in stages, first to a vision for harmonious societal relations, and then to better employment relations. The guiding philosophy for policies of worker representation first outlined in detail in the "Colorado Plan" is a direct derivative of this vision (King 1918). King passionately believed that the employment relationship need not be adversarial, a win-lose struggle for a share of a limited "pie." Good policies driven by sound theoretical and moral principles could transform the employment relationship into a positive-sum game by fostering a unity of interest between employers and employees. But this transformation could not come about without a major effort from the employers. Although King cannot be called anti-union, his vision did not leave much room for a role for organized labor in the development of a cooperative approach. The employment relationship, in his conceptualization, was very much a bilateral affair between the employer and the employee that employers needed to manage with a lofty but achievable goal in mind.

Thus, employers—who are potential opponents of any employee initiative to improve wages or working conditions—can be recast into proactive agents for the development and implementation of a strategic plan for better relations that, in return, can pay rich future dividends in terms of more productive, satisfied, and involved employees. Employers, in this view, are uniquely positioned. They have more contact with employees than does anyone else. They have better knowledge of where the business is headed and its needs along the way. Employers are also the ones charged with the duty of meeting shareholders' needs. Thus, sitting in the middle, employers are well positioned to integrate the interests of employees, management, and shareholders. All that is missing is a vision, a guiding philosophy, and an achievable action plan.

For the IRC founders, there was another rationale for promoting better labor policy among employers: reducing employer competition on the basis of lower labor standards, a possibility that is mentioned repeatedly in the international context. For King and his associates, competing in the marketplace by offering poor wages or poor working conditions was harmful to all employers. It created a pressure on employers to decrease labor standards in order to compete. King set forth the "Law of Competing Standards" (based on his observation of Gresham's Law of precious metals whereby cheaper coins drove out the dearer ones in Elizabethan England) based on his first-hand knowledge of labor markets (ibid., 53–67). He observed that left to free market forces, labor standards would gradually decline to the lowest possible denominator. He documented many anecdotal examples to back up this claim. This "race to the bottom" can be stemmed, in his and IRC's view, by employer intervention. He argued further that employers should undertake to stem this slide because doing so would secure the firm's and indeed capitalism's own future.

There are a number of parallels between the early IRC quest for employer action to secure labor standards and the current international initiatives for employer involvement in the wake of globalization (e.g., corporate codes of conduct). To begin with, many of the current social, economic, and political conditions in some developing countries are comparable to those in North America during the first two decades of the twentieth century. Many labor market institutions familiar to us today did not exist then. Internationally, there is an analogous dearth of labor market institutions that could help to establish and enforce labor standards. Many governments in developing countries are unable or unwilling to develop better standards because of lack of resources; high unemployment coupled with a perception that higher standards would have a negative impact on employment; and, in many cases, a lack of awareness or a lack of political consensus. Similarly, the organized labor movement in many countries lacks the resources to make a big impact. That leaves employers that are armed with resources, vision, and strategy in a commanding position to be proactive on labor standards.

Proponents of corporate codes of conduct have used these familiar arguments to push employers into action on establishing labor standards in their international operations. Most of the push to date is with multinational enterprises that manufacture products in low-wage countries and sell their products in high-income countries (Verma 2001). Although this sector covers only a very small fraction of workers worldwide, this development is significant because it is employer-centered in much the same way that IRC was when it got its start. Corporate codes such as the Ethical Trading Initiative (ETI), the Clean Clothes Campaign, and the Fair Labour Association (FLA) have been aimed at the growing transborder economic activity (Sabel, O'Rourke, and Fung 2000). Their member firms are drawn largely from consumer-goods industries such as clothing, shoes, toys, sports equipment, and rug weaving.

Many contemporary economists hold that lower labor standards in developing countries do not constitute an "unfair" advantage (Bhagwati and Hudec 1996; Lee 1996, 1997). Krugman (1994, 1997) has shown that labor standards are related to a nation's productivity, not its competitive advantage. Even if low labor standards cannot create a competitive advantage, they may still be subject to the pressures of "race to the bottom." At the political level, governments of large countries such as China and India, have taken the position that regulating labor standards is the sovereign responsibility of each nation.

Yet, the need to improve labor standards in many parts of the world is undeniable. The ILO, an organization with which IRC has worked closely in the past, has documented the unacceptably high incidence of child labor, forced labor, discrimination, and harassment in employment around the world (ILO 1999). Corporate codes of conduct, despite all their imperfections, offer a significant opportunity to improve working conditions for many workers around the world, just as IRC's work did eighty years ago. Corporate codes are still evolving, but they could be made more effective if some of the vision of King and lessons from IRC's field experience could be applied to these codes of conduct. Although it is hard to estimate the extent to which IRC lessons may be directly transferable to contemporary corporate behavior, it is clear that many parallels exist between the past and present situations.

Mechanisms for Regulating the Employment Relationship

The employment relationship tends to be regulated by three main mechanisms: (1) competitive forces of the unregulated market; (2) employee representation, often through collective bargaining; and (3) laws and regulations, including labor standards legislation. Specific disciplines or groups advocate individual mechanisms. For example, economists tend to emphasize the competitive forces of unregulated markets; industrial relations analysts tend to emphasize employee representation and collective bargaining; lawyers, politicians, and the general public tend to emphasize the mechanism of laws and regulation. These groups, unfortunately, tend to "talk past" each other because they fail to recognize the interrelated nature of the different mechanisms, the fact that the mechanisms can be complementary as well as alternative, and that actions through one mechanism can often by "undone" by actions through other mechanisms.

Market mechanisms rely on the forces of demand—what customers through their purchases from firms are willing and able to pay to have something produced—and supply—what labor is willing to accept as payment to produce the goods and services—to determine the pay and allocation of labor in labor markets. These simple but powerful forces ensure that labor is allocated to its most efficient use and that workers have an incentive to produce the items that consumers want to have produced. In well-functioning markets, such forces can also lead to other desirable outcomes, for example:

- Wage premiums to compensate workers for risk or other undesirable job characteristics
- An incentive for employers to reduce risk and other undesirable job characteristics to save on such premiums
- An incentive for employees to enhance their productivity through hard work and human-capital formation (e.g., education, training, mobility, job search) and to move from declining sectors and regions to expanding ones in response to wage differentials
- Promotion of meritocracy instead of discrimination, since it is costly for employers not to hire and promote the best employee or to pay members of favored groups a wage premium over what they pay members of an equally productive minority group

Continuous marginal market adjustments (e.g., small wage changes or mobility of younger persons) can also avoid the more costly inframarginal adjustments (plant closings, mass layoffs) that tend to occur when market forces are ignored and the adjustments eventually have to occur.

But market forces also have a darker side. Markets obviously have imperfections—lack of information, monopsonistic and monopolistic power, discrimination, unemployment, and underemployment. Furthermore, the behavior of individuals within markets can be influenced by factors that affect them before they enter the labor market, such as restricted educational opportunities and poverty. Even if there were no imperfections, perfectly functioning markets can lead to efficient but not necessarily fair or equitable outcomes. This is evidenced by the considerable wage polarization that is occurring and by the fact that some groups (e.g., unskilled and uneducated youths) do not seem to be sharing in the gains that are occurring, in large part because they often cannot qualify for jobs at existing wages.

Employee representation is another mechanism for regulating the employment relationship. Typically, this occurs through the form of collective bargaining with unions, but other forms of nonunion employee representation are possible (e.g., joint industrial councils, peer-review dispute-resolution panels, joint labor-management committees, European-style works councils, and nonunion professional associations).[7] Unlike the market mechanism, which responds to the need to attract and retain workers who are at the margin of decision about whether to enter or exit a firm, the collective-bargaining mechanism responds to the preferences of the median union voter, who is likely to be older, less mobile, and male—although the latter is changing as women become more prominent in unions, especially in the public sector. In essence, unions become the institutional embodiment of voice. In addition to garnering wage gains for their membership, unions can play other important roles: determine and articulate the preferences of their membership; determine the internal trade-offs that must be made by the workforce; guarantee a degree of "due process" at the workplace and protect their members against arbitrary and possibly capricious treatment on the part of some employers; inform workers of their legislated rights and provide protection against reprisals by management if those rights are exercised; and provide a degree of employment security from the vicissitudes of markets. Critics of unions argue that these occur at the expense of the managerial flexibility and organizational competitiveness deemed necessary for the joint survival of employers and their employees and that the adversarial relationship fostered by unions is antithetical to the organizational commitment and the focus on quality so crucial under global competition. They further charge that the protection of unions goes only to "insiders," with "outsiders" being even more subject to the vicissitudes of markets. Supporters of nonunion forms of representation argue that they provide an alternative way to address the concerns and needs of employees, a middle ground between the laissez-faire unregulated market and the inflexibility of traditional adversarial unionism.

Laws and regulations are a third mechanism for regulating the employment relationship. The main types of laws in the employment arena are the following:

- Collective-bargaining laws that govern the establishment and conduct of collective bargaining
- Labor standards laws that set (usually minimal) terms of employment, such as minimum wages, hours of work and overtime, termination and advance notice requirements, leave and vacation requirements, and wage claims
- Human rights and antidiscrimination legislation
- Occupational health and safety legislation
- Workers' compensation
- Social insurance

It is within this broader context of the alternative mechanisms for regulating the employment relationship that labor standards laws—a key focus of this analysis—must be viewed. Such laws cannot be viewed in isolation of the forces of markets and collective bargaining.

For better or worse, globalization—with its freer flow of goods, capital, people, and ideas[8]—has enhanced the importance of markets and competition as mechanisms for regulating the employment relationship.[9] Conventional forms of collective bargaining are on the defensive[10] and declining in most countries, with unionization rates plummeting in such countries as the United States, England, and Japan (Lipsig-Mummé 2001, 534). The main weapon of unions—the strike—has also diminished in importance (Aligisakis 1997), in large part because of the high joint cost to both parties now that consumers can readily shift to alternative products or services in the global marketplace—and once they shift, they may never come back.

Legislative and regulatory initiatives also appear to be on the defensive as countries, or jurisdictions within countries, are often reluctant to introduce or sustain costly legislative initiatives for fear that they will repel business investment and the jobs associated with that investment.[11] Some believe this will lead to a "regulatory meltdown" as countries are forced to compete away their regulations and social programs, leading to a "race to the bottom" in terms of labor laws and regulations. Others see this as just good old-fashioned competition, except that now countries simply have to be "open for business" to attract investment and the associated jobs. They believe that (1) the discipline of the market—normally thought of as applying only to employers and employees—is simply being brought to bear on government decision making; (2) regulations that serve an efficiency rationale will survive, indeed thrive, in such a competitive environment because they enhance productivity and competitiveness; and (3) regulations that merely protect the "rents" of particular interest groups will dissipate. What happens to labor standards legislation in this environment will therefore depend upon the purposes they serve and the impacts they have on the functioning of markets. It is to that dimension we now turn.

Rationale and Role of Labor Standards

Labor standards are generally regarded as providing a floor or minimum below which labor market transactions are not allowed to occur, even if voluntarily entered into by employees. Such standards are generally designed to protect the more disadvantaged workers who have little individual bargaining power under the market mechanism or who are not protected by unions through the collective-bargaining mechanism. That is, labor standards are designed to fill a void left by the lack of protection from the other mechanisms.[12]

Economic theory predicts that the market mechanism will respond by firms trying to shift the costs of higher labor standards "forward" to consumers or "backward" to the employees who benefit from the higher standards. It is increasingly difficult now, however, to pass the cost increase forward as higher prices to consumers in globally competitive markets than it was when local markets were protected by tariffs or local monopolies. Firms may be able to shift part of the cost back to the employees who are affected by the higher standards, especially since low-wage labor is a relatively immobile factor of production and cannot escape the cost-shifting. Higher minimum wages, for example, may lead to more onerous working conditions or to reductions in training opportunities if such opportunities were previously provided to workers in lieu of a higher wage. Employers may also be able to shift part of the cost of higher standards in less obvious ways, for example, by adjusting their straight-time wage portion downward to offset the impact of an overtime wage premium (Trejo 1991); shifting the cost of payroll taxes back to workers in the form of lower wages as an exchange for the benefits that are financed by the payroll taxes (Dahlby 1993); or reducing the wages of workers for whom the employer must incur costs to meet "reasonable accommodation" requirements (Gunderson and Hyatt 1996).

To the extent that firms cannot shift the cost of higher labor standards either forward to customers or backward to workers, they may substitute capital or other inputs for higher priced labor. Firms may also reduce their output as consumers purchase less of the more costly output, and some firms may even go out of business or move their business to jurisdictions that do not have such costly labor standards. The substitutions can be subtle, as, for example, when firms increase their use of nonstandard employment (fixed-term contracts, temporary-help agencies, subcontracting to the self-employed) in response to increased regulations in labor markets (Portes 1990; Lee 1997). If termination costs for potential new hires are anticipated, firms may hire fewer new workers (Lazear 1990) and, in turn, demand longer working hours from their existing workforce.

These substitution possibilities suggest that the real rationale for labor standards may be to protect the jobs of those who already have those standards and whose job security is threatened by those who do not have them. For example, minimum wages and hours-of-work restrictions were first applied to "protect" women when they first started to enter the labor market, although the real rationale may have been to protect male jobs from such lower cost labor. Developing countries accuse the developed countries of thinly disguised protectionism when trade agreements impose higher labor standards on the developing countries as a means to protect the high-wage jobs in the developed countries. Labor standards legislation may protect unionized jobs from the competition of lower cost nonunion workers. Alternatively, such legislation may be an alternative to unionization; if the state can provide such protection, there may be little demand for unions to provide it. These examples simply illustrate the proposition that the group that is being "protected" by labor standards laws may not be the disadvantaged groups to which the laws ostensibly apply.

The previous discussion assumes that the labor standards legislation imposes net costs on employers. It is possible, however, that some of the labor regulations yield benefits to employers that offset some or all of the costs.[13] For example, requirements for advance notice in the event of a mass layoff or plant closing could enable employees to engage in job search over that period, which could benefit prospective employers as well as the employees (Kuhn 1992). Workers' compensation as a "no-fault" insurance scheme, whereby injured employees are given compensation in return for giving up the right to sue their employer, may yield considerable savings to employers who would otherwise face the legal costs of the tort liability system. Protection against age discrimination may enable employees to engage with organizations in longer-term contractual arrangements that involve deferred compensation, which in turn may have positive implications for employers (Neumark and Stock 1999). Parental leave programs can improve child health and development outcomes in the early years of child development, which can save on costly programs later (Ruhm 1998, 2000). Providing an employment safety net may reduce employee resistance to technological change, trade liberalization, and other efficiency-enhancing changes.[14] It is also likely that cost advantages that arise from low labor standards may only be temporary if wages and regulations increase in response to capital moving in and increasing the demand for labor (Verma 1997, 274).

It may also be the case that "good" employers want a "level playing field" with reasonable labor standards, that is, be willing to enter into an agreement whereby they adhere to such standards and pay their share provided that their competitors also adhere to such standards and pay *their* share. In that view, legislated standards are a way of precommitting all employers to such standards. This may be a way of avoiding the "Prisoner's Dilemma," whereby cooperation yields the best outcome but each player has an incentive to defect and not cooperate (Gunderson 1999).

In essence, labor standards can serve a variety of purposes and have a variety of impacts, with those purposes and impacts being different under globalization. With increased international competition, it is less likely that the costs of labor standards in the developed countries can be shifted forward to customers and more likely that they will be shifted back to employees— unfortunately, employees whose real wages already may be eroded by the import competition from low-wage countries.[15] To the extent that such cost-shifting cannot occur and legislated standards do not yield offsetting benefits, employers will reduce their demand for the workers that are subject to the higher standards—and whose employability may already be jeopardized by increased competition from low-wage countries. In such circumstances, there will be increased pressure to have *international* standards improved so as to inhibit *international* competition on the basis of low standards. This is incredibly difficult, however, because countries are reluctant to yield any sovereignty to international organizations and because the appropriate standard for one country may not be appropriate for another—what is a floor for one country may be a ceiling for another. In such circumstances, the more developed countries will try to have higher standards imposed on the less developed countries, perhaps by making the standards part of trade agreements. This will engender the accusation of protectionism from the developing countries—especially since the developed countries exhibit this intense interest in the well-being of workers in the less developed countries at just the time that low-wage labor in the less developed countries is becoming a threat to the developed countries. Dealing with these issues is a major challenge to industrial relations under globalization. In that vein, it is instructive to understand how these issues have evolved since the start of IRC in 1926.

The ILO, Codes of Fair Competition, and Labor Standards

Around the time of the establishment of IRC in 1926, the United States was in the midst of an economic boom that followed the turmoil of World War I (1914–18). The earlier era of globalization, which had begun around the mid-1850s and was associated with the fall in transportation costs and rise of international markets, was coming to an end, with deglobalization setting in until the 1950s.[16] Protectionism was on the rise, as was isolationism, especially on the part of the United States.

The International Labour Organization was established as part of the Treaty of Versailles in 1919. This was part of broader but generally ill-fated attempts to establish international institutions such as the League of Nations. The ILO, however, had precursors that advocated international institutions to protect workers from the pressures of international competition.[17] Reflecting the foundations set by these earlier endeavors, the ILO took the stance that if labor markets were becoming global, then labor protection should be global. Also, lasting peace would be attained only if there was social justice.

Specifically, there were three main motivations behind the establishment of the ILO.[18] The first was humanitarian—to ameliorate the injustice, hardship, and privation faced by large numbers of working people and their families. The second was political—to facilitate world peace by reducing the social unrest and possible revolution that could emanate from social injustice and poor working conditions. The third was economic—to "level the playing field" with respect to humane working conditions by reducing the disadvantage that a country would face if it adopted social reform that was not adopted by its competitors.[19]

One half of the members of the Governing Body of the ILO were government representatives, a quarter were workers' representatives, and a quarter were employers' representatives. The United States did not join the ILO until 1934, under the presidency of Franklin D. Roosevelt (withdrawing again for a brief period from 1977 to 1980).

From its inception, the ILO has not had power to impose sanctions for failure to adopt its policies—a reflection of the reluctance of individual states to give up sovereignty. Rather, it relies on noncoercive measures: moral suasion, the "court of public opinion," cooperation, technical assistance, and publications and reports on policies and practices in different countries. The hope is that enlightened countries, along with enlightened employers, will voluntarily follow the recommended practices.

Largely in response to the growth of multinationals in the second wave of globalization that followed World War II, the ILO adopted in 1977 a Declaration of Principles Concerning Multinational Enterprises and Social Policy (after a resolution adopted in 1971).[20] The Declaration is a detailed set of paragraphs that emphasizes such principles as freedom of association, nondiscrimination in employment, employment security, information sharing, consultation, adherence to local laws, preferences for local employees, training of local employees, provision of wages and standards that are at least as good as those provided locally, and refraining from threats to transfer operations so as to influence bargaining.

Many of these principles are also emphasized in the voluntary Guidelines on Multinational Enterprises adopted in 1976 by the Organization for Economic Cooperation and Development (OECD) and revitalized in June 2000.[21] These codes of fair competition for multinationals cover nine policy areas, with employment and industrial relations issues having the most comprehensive set of guidelines. The guidelines generally recommend following the host-country laws; however, where there is no clear legislation, the guidelines recommend a set of "best practices."

The ILO has always emphasized a voluntary, cooperative approach. In its 1994 annual report, it specifically rejected the use of trade sanctions against countries that did not adopt its labor standards to equalize social costs (i.e., it rejected the notion of requiring social or labor protection clauses as part of trade agreements). It emphasized that labor standards must reflect the differing ability of countries to afford those standards and that trade liberalization would help to improve development, living standards, and job creation—"a rising tide raises all boats."

The ILO further reinforced its position with its 1998, Declaration on Fundamental Principles and Rights at Work, obliging all members to follow and promote four core rights: (1) freedom of association and the right to bargain collectively, (2) the elimination of forced or compulsory labor, (3) the abolition of child labor, and (4) the elimination of employment discrimination.

Assessing the effectiveness of these voluntary codes of fair competition is beyond the scope of this analysis. Bellace and Latta (1983, 74) conclude, "It has become increasingly evident that generally worded voluntary guidelines cannot persuade a MNC [multinational corporation] to adopt a behavior which it believes to be unjustified or to its economic disadvantage." However, the issue still remains as to whether they do have positive impacts in spite of their voluntary nature.

International Labor Federations

When multinationals became prominent after World War I, unions responded through a variety of international labor federations.[22] National unions from specific industries or trades (e.g., printing, metalworking) had already made an attempt at this in Europe around the turn of the century by establishing a number of International Trade Secretariats (ITS), largely to exchange information. In some cases (e.g., in the auto industry), the secretariats had established "corporation councils," which were composed of national unions from the various countries in which a specific multinational operated, with the long-term objective of engaging in collective bargaining. As John P. Windmuller (1987, 27) points out, however, "in no instance has any council yet succeeded in obtaining employer recognition as an international bargaining agent."

These secretariats were followed by the International Federation of Trade Unions (IFTU), which consisted of mainly national trade-union federations, including the American Federation of Labor. Its purpose was somewhat broader: to comment on economic and social policy issues, to conduct and publish research, and to provide strike assistance for affiliates. The IFTU was replaced in 1945 by the World Federation of Trade Unions (WFTU), which tried to be an all-encompassing body and unsuccessfully attempted to absorb the International Trade Secretariats. In reaction to the Communist dominance of the WFTU, unions from the Western democracies left and in 1949 formed the International Confederation of Free Trade Unions (ICFTU), primarily to deal with the coordination of information, to lobby, and to represent union interests in social and economic affairs.

The history of the international labor federations and transnational collective bargaining (or the lack thereof) highlights the difficulties of a coordinated trade-union response to multinationals and global competition. It is difficult enough to coordinate bargaining across industries and trades within a country. As Helfgott (1983, 83) points out, on a transnational basis the barriers are probably insurmountable and include differences in customs, laws, cultures, and bargaining structures; ideological and other differences across unions that guard their autonomy; and legal limitations on transnational bargaining and striking.

The Global Economic Environment of the Current Debate

As indicated, the issue of labor standards and the global economy is *the* key issue today in the area of industrial relations and the global economy. Like all industrial relations issues, it must be understood in the context of changes in the economic environment—a fact that is always emphasized by industrial relations researchers and that has always been emphasized by IRC in its international research endeavors. Key aspects of the global economic environment that have important implications for labor standards include trade liberalization and increased flows of capital—physical, financial, and human.

Trade liberalization, as manifest in reductions in tariff and nontariff barriers to trade, has been a feature of international agreements, such as the General Agreement on Tariffs and Trade (GATT), as well as regional trade agreements, such as the 1989 Free Trade Agreement (FTA) between the United States and Canada and the subsequent 1993 North American Free Trade Agreement (NAFTA), which also includes Mexico. Similar arrangements are occurring through Mercusor (Argentina, Brazil, Paraguay, and Uruguay), the Andean Pact (Bolivia, Colombia, Ecuador, Peru, and Venezuela), and CARICOM (Caribbean Basin countries), as well as possible extensions to a Western Hemisphere agreement as advocated by former President George Bush in his 1990 Enterprise for the Americas Initiative. The European Union represents a stronger form of integration: a customs union with free internal trade, a common external tariff, open internal mobility of labor, and a common currency. The FTA and NAFTA entail only free trade and reduced restrictions on capital flows, although there have been some recent discussions about creating a common currency through "dollarization."

Globalization also involves increased capital flows in various forms. Financial capital can flow quickly and directly to countries with the best investment opportunities, leading to the specter of capital flight and its associated instability but also providing potential stability by immediately arbitraging investment opportunities. Foreign direct investment in the form of foreign ownership of physical capital is increasingly prominent as multinationals diversify their operations around the world and more frequently outsource their operations to offshore production facilities. Plant investment and location decisions are increasingly made on a global basis. Human capital is becoming more mobile, especially professional and technical workers (including information-technology workers) as well as executives—leading to issues associated with the "brain drain."

Implications for Industrial Relations

Accompanying all the changes in the flow of goods, capital, and labor have been a variety of other interrelated changes that pressure labor markets and industrial relations. Dramatic technological change, especially that associated with the computer revolution and the information economy, has created related demands for knowledge work. Developed economies have generally undergone industrial restructuring, most notably from manufacturing to services—"high-end" professional, technical, and financial services as well as "low-end" personal services provided to those at the high end. Mergers and acquisitions are commonly used to facilitate economies of scale and scope for the global economy. At the other end of the spectrum, small firms have become the engine of growth and job creation, often as "upstream" suppliers to the larger organizations that increasingly subcontract and outsource. Deregulation and privatization have also been significant features of that restructuring, especially in the public sector.

These global and other related pressures have led to other important changes in the industrial relations system. Labor flexibility and adaptability have become key to enabling employers to quickly respond to changing circumstances. Wage polarization has worsened in developed countries due to technological change—which is skill-biased—and imports from low-wage developing countries—which have restricted the low-wage labor market in developed countries. Broader-based job classifications are more widely used, with employees often engaged in multitasking and teams, as well as job rotation and multiskilled training, to perform a wider range of tasks. Employee involvement in such processes as quality circles has increased as employers recognize the importance of competing on the basis of quality and tapping the discretionary effort of employees. Flexible work-time arrangements are more widespread as are various forms of nonstandard or contingent employment, including limited-term contracts, part-time work, temporary-help agencies, self-employment, home work, and telecommuting. Compensation is more often geared to performance, and pattern bargaining is often breaking down. Unions have declined in many countries, as have the number of strikes, likely reflecting the fact that organizations can shift their operations to other countries, or if they cannot, customers may permanently shift their purchases if production is interrupted by a strike.

Implications for Global Responses

Ironically, the global imperatives are placing the collective-bargaining and labor standards legislative mechanisms on the defensive at just the time when they may be needed most—to deal with the adjustment consequences of globalization, especially at the international level. There have been a number of responses to these challenges—although each of the responses poses challenges of its own. The responses include actions of the ILO and other international organizations; social labeling, often under the pressure of NGOs (nongovernmental organizations); voluntary codes of corporate conduct; social clauses as part of trade agreements; and international cooperation among unions.

As indicated previously, global problems require global solutions, and the ILO is obviously an international organization structured to deal with global solutions to labor issues. In that vein, the recent challenges could breathe new life into the ILO. The ILO does exercise considerable influence through moral suasion and encouragement of cooperation by means of its technical assistance and its publications and reports. It has also promulgated core labor rights in the areas of freedom of association, forced or compulsory labor, child labor, and employment discrimination. The issue here is whether moral suasion and reliance on voluntary actions without formal sanctions are sufficient.

Social labeling has been advocated and would require that certain products be labeled as to the working conditions under which they were produced—for example, "this product was not produced with child labor" (Freeman 1994, International Labour Office 1997). An international organization like the ILO could provide "quality" endorsement, such as "this product was produced under working conditions meeting ILO quality standards." This would be akin to quality standards (e.g., ISO 900) that are sought after in product markets or to such existing labeling practices as health and safety warnings, food labels that display the nutritional contents or such warnings as "best consumed before such and such a date," or the "made with union labor" labels in clothing. The social label would provide a product endorsement but leave it up to consumers to decide if they will ultimately purchase the product based on its "social content" and not merely its price.

Voluntary corporate codes of conduct have been adopted, especially among large multinationals that are sensitive to public opinion.[23] Usually, these codes have been adopted to thwart pressure from consumer advocacy groups that threaten boycotts or adverse publicity campaigns (Erickson and Mitchell

1996)—thus, it could be argued that the codes are not entirely voluntary. The corporate codes can be particularly important for those multinationals that invariably are the high-paying firms in the local economy where they operate their own plants but whose subcontracting to locally owned and managed operations can spawn "sweatshop" conditions.

The inclusion of social clauses or labor standards in trade agreements—that is, requiring countries to adhere to a set of labor standards as a precondition for entering into a trade agreement—is a more contentious international initiative.[24] In theory, such initiatives can have stronger sanctions because violating those principles could be grounds for abrogating the trade agreement. Furthermore, the fact that it is part of an international trade agreement can bring stronger international public opinion to bear on the issue and provide formal mechanisms for dealing with disputes in this area. Parties in one of the countries that participate in the trade agreement may also have an incentive to bring forth a complaint to the extent that they can benefit by having the higher labor standards imposed on their trading partners. This also highlights the concerns that such practices are simply thinly disguised protectionism designed to reduce competition on the basis of labor costs (Bhagwati 1994).

The North American Agreement on Labor Cooperation of NAFTA is an example of a social clause that is part of a trade agreement. It obliges each party to enforce its own existing labor standards (Compa and Diamond 1996; Diamond 1996). The Social Charter of the European Union establishes a set of mutually recognized labor standards as well as a Social Fund to assist the poorer countries in upgrading their standards (Due, Madsen, and Stroby-Jensen 1991; Rhodes 1992; Kenner 1995). Trade agreements in Latin America and the Carribbean are including side agreements on labor policy (Aparicio-Valdez 1995), and pressure exists in the World Trade Organization to include such clauses in its rules (De Wet 1995, Maskus 1997).

Stronger forms of international unionism have also been advocated as a way of dealing with the pressures of globalization. There is a well-known adage in trade-union circles that it is necessary to organize up to the level of the product market in which the labor is involved otherwise, any higher costs imposed by unions will simply lead to a shift of consumers to the lower-priced products of the nonunionized part of the industry. If the product market is now global, then it may be necessary to organize at the global level. As discussed previously, however, this is very difficult in practice given the different laws and regulations in the various countries as well as the unwillingness of national unions to give up any autonomy to international bodies—in fact, the trend is in the other direction. In Canada, for example, the proportion of union members belonging to unions headquartered in the United

States had fallen from 65 percent in 1969 to 30 percent by 1998 (Murray 2001, 97). International cooperation and coordination efforts among unions do occur to a greater degree than in the past, but this does not translate into international unionism.

Concluding Observations on Implications for Stakeholders

Clearly, it is not likely that international responses to the labor issues associated with globalization will come to any great extent from either the legislative mechanism or the collective-bargaining mechanism at the international level. Furthermore, these mechanisms are on the defensive domestically at the national level, given trade liberalization and the greater international mobility of physical and financial capital. This leaves the market mechanism as having greater influence in governing the employment relationship in this "new world of work." To the extent that this diagnosis is correct, it raises the question of what the implications are for the different stakeholders in the employment relationship (Gunderson and Verma 1992).

For *individual workers*, the main implication is the importance of acquiring the human-capital skills (e.g., education, training, job search techniques, and mobility) valued in the market and gearing those skills toward dealing with the market needs for flexibility and adaptability. This can mean, for example, the acquisition of generic, generally usable skills that will prepare the worker for ever-changing job requirements—preparation for "learning how to learn" and relearn in a world of lifelong learning and knowledge work.

For *unions*, the imperatives of globalization highlight the need to concentrate on aspects of their role that do not imply large cost increases for employers, (e.g., refrain from the threat of a strike to garner wage gains) (Gunderson and Verma 1999). As already discussed, it is not feasible to pass those cost increases on to consumers who are no longer forced to buy in a tariff-protected market from firms with local monopoly power, large fixed worksites, and no option to relocate to other jurisdictions or outsource offshore. The world of work is now different. Unions are more likely to survive if they concentrate on their less costly "voice" function, articulating the preferences and trade-offs of the rank and file and trying to ensure a degree of due process at the workplace in a nonadversarial fashion. In such circumstances, managerial resistance will likely be minimal and unions will not be "pricing themselves out of the market."

For *governments*, the imperatives of globalization imply that their policy initiatives in the labor area should be geared toward active adjustment assistance that facilitates the allocation of labor in the direction of market forces rather than toward passive income maintenance that encourages labor to remain in declining sectors or regions. This means, for example, focusing on the provision of labor market information (including forecasts of shortages); providing uniformity in such areas as trades certification and occupational certification and licensing; requiring information on such factors as occupational hazards; facilitating pension portability; and providing "one-stop, single-wicket" outlets for labor market information and programs.

Governments also have a legitimate role to play in assisting disadvantaged workers and in providing a social safety net, especially given the decline of the traditional safety net of the extended family. This role of governments, however, can be jeopardized by global imperatives. As discussed previously, given the mobility of all forms of capital—financial, physical, and human—governments will find it increasingly difficult to sustain a tax base and at the same time to impose costly regulations that assist the disadvantaged. The only immobile factor of production that cannot escape the tax is low- and middle-wage labor, but these groups are already hit hard by skill-biased technological change and import competition from low-wage countries. In such circumstances, assisting the disadvantaged will be increasingly difficult, compounded by the fact that any local jurisdiction that does so might serve as a "magnet" to attract more of the disadvantaged.

This is a legitimate concern, especially because greater adherence to the market mechanism is likely to create more disadvantaged persons who are bypassed by the system and because the mechanisms of legislation and of collective bargaining are less able to blunt the negative consequences of markets for the disadvantaged. This does suggest, however, that governments should *focus* their more limited role in the particular direction of assisting the disadvantaged rather than dissipating it in areas that can already be handled by the market mechanism. There is also the possibility that well-functioning tight labor markets can do more to help the disadvantaged since employers may be seeking them out to fill labor shortages. Being sought after by employers is probably preferable to receiving assistance from public funds.

For *employers*, the imperatives of globalization have a number of implications for their relationship with employees. While the increased importance of market forces may tip the balance of power in their favor, it is a power that can be used responsibly or opportunistically. Using it opportunistically is likely to increase the demand for unionization and government regulation (in spite of their costs) in order to redress the imbalance of power— this being the main rationale for unions and government regulation in the first place. Nature abhors a vacuum, and if employers leave a vacuum in the area of responsibility to employees, it will be filled by other mechanisms. The more responsible actions involve increased attention to the needs of employees (especially with respect to education and skill development) and recognition that labor is a resource to be optimized rather than simply a cost to be minimized. If product and capital prices are largely fixed in world markets, then the strategic use of human resources becomes one of the few sources of competitive advantage left for employers. This is especially true for higher-wage developed countries, which cannot compete with less developed countries on the basis of a low-wage strategy, particularly now that those low-wage countries are changing from low-productivity to high-productivity countries. Strategically maximizing the discretionary effort of employees becomes key to sustaining a high-wage, high-productivity economy. It is important for employers to also recognize that commitment is a double-edged sword: If they expect commitment and loyalty from employees, then they must also provide a degree of commitment and loyalty to their employees. Employee involvement in the decision making of firms can be an important ingredient, as can benefits programs (some in the form of a safety net) and "family-friendly" workplace practices, given the dominance of the two-earner family. Flexible work-time arrangements can help families balance the demands of the workplace and of the family. Ensuring that human resource issues are an integral part of the business strategy of firms, and not simply an afterthought, can also facilitate a responsible approach to employee relations.

Clearly, the response of the different stakeholders to the employment issues that emerge under globalization will shape the industrial relations system of the new millennium. The new system that emerges will also provide strong evidence of the pros and cons of markets as a mechanism of social ordering. The employment relationship will be fundamental to that evaluation—and it will be a fundamentally different relationship.

Notes

1. The importance of practical experience over abstract knowledge was emphasized by Clarence Hicks when he wrote, "Reading will become increasingly important as the literature of the field expands, and textbooks on sociology, psychology and economics are helpful *if not taken too seriously*; but in any profession dealing with human beings there can never be a substitute for personal contacts and experience" (1941, 63, emphasis added).

2. William Lyon Mackenzie King—not to be confused with his grandfather, William Lyon Mackenzie, the rebel who tried to win self-government for Canada in 1837—organized the first Department of Labour in the federal government under Wilfred Laurier in 1900. He became the first deputy minister of labour and gained fame for his conciliation efforts in solving labor disputes. In 1909 he became the first minister of labour. He lost his seat in Parliament, however, in 1911 when the Liberal government was defeated. In 1914 he accepted the post with the Rockefeller Foundation. Subse-

quently, he became prime minister of Canada from 1921 to 1948, except for the brief period from 1931 to 1935.

3. The use of Canadians in these key roles at that time attests to the outward and international orientation of IRC—an orientation that appears to be sustained today as evidenced by the fact that three of the contributors to this volume are Canadian—and most of the others are "honorary Canadians" in the sense that they have worked with Canadians on industrial relations issues!

4. This was also emphasized by Clarence Hicks when he stated, "But where the chief executive became concerned about the people he employed, he was able to pioneer in making the individual count" (ibid., 19).

5. In listing the key ingredients for a member of the industrial relations profession, Clarence Hicks emphasized "a sustained effort to keep aware of new developments in other companies and other industries and in labor legislation at home and abroad" (ibid., 135).

6. Between 1927 and 1932, IRC maintained a branch office at the ILO (even though the United States was not a member at that time) that conducted research, especially on national employment exchanges and unemployment in European countries, and served as a source of information for the ILO on U.S. employee relations (Teplow 1976, 6).

7. For a discussion of these forms of nonunion employee representation, see Kaufman and Taras (1999, 2) as well as the various papers in the symposium they organized, which were published in Kaufman and Taras (2000).

8. For an expanded discussion of these and other factors that have enhanced global integration, see, for example, Gomez and Gunderson (2002) and the literature cited therein.

9. This is emphasized in the various international studies in Wever and Turner (1995).

10. The pressure on unions in developed countries is particularly great since the private sectors that are subject to the greatest degree of import competition from low-wage countries tend to be the tradable goods sectors that are heavily unionized (Gunderson and Verma 1994).

11. For discussions, see Gunderson (1998 and 1999), as well as Gunderson and Riddell (1995) and the references cited therein.

12. For discussions of the role of labor standards in the international context, see Ehrenberg (1994), Fields (1995), Gadbaw and Medwig (1996), Gunderson (1998 and 1999), Herzenberg and Perez-Lopez (1990), ILO (1997), Langille (1996), and Maskus (1997), OECD (1996).

13. As the first director of research at IRC, Bryce Stewart, stated, "Labor standards enter into competition only when they increase unit cost of production. . . . Is it not conceivable that a nation may be progressive in at least a considerable range of labor standards and still be at no competitive disadvantage?" (1927, 179).

14. See Charnovitz (1987 and 1992), Rodrik (1997), Schoepfle and Swinnerton (1994), and Sengenberger and Campbell (1994).

15. According to the Heckscher-Ohlin Theorem of economics, countries will export goods that embody factors of production for which they are abundantly endowed and import goods for which they have scarce factor endowments. Developed economies have an abundance of technology, capital, and human capital and, hence, have a comparative advantage in capital-intensive high-technology production. Less developed countries have an abundance of low-wage labor and natural resources and,

hence, have a comparative advantage in exporting natural resources and labor-intensive exports. Over time, however, they often adapt the new technology and move up the value-added chain.

16. The evolution of globalization is discussed in "Globalization: Context and Practicalities" (2001) and references cited therein.

17. For discussions of these early endeavors and the early years of the ILO, see, for example, Alcock (1971), Hansson (1983), Johnston (1970), and Leary (1996).

18. These motivations and a brief history of the ILO are provided on its Web site at http://www.ilo.org/public/english/about/history/htm.

19. As stated on the ILO's Web site (http://www.ilo.org), "Because of its inevitable effect on the cost of production, an industry or country adopting social reform would find itself at a disadvantage vis-à-vis competitors." And as originally stated in the Preamble to the Constitution of the ILO, "The failure of any nation to adopt humane conditions of labour is an obstacle in the way of other nations which desire to improve the conditions in their own countries."

20. For discussion of the ILO and Organization for Economic Cooperation and Development codes of fair competition, see Bellace and Latta (1983), Blainpain (2000), Gunter (1992), Helfgott (1983), and Rowan and Campbell (1983).

21. The revitalization essentially involved a set of implementation procedures by which governments establish national contact points to resolve cases and make public their recommendations to the companies. While the guidelines are nonbinding, they can be used to expose companies and the national contact points if they are not followed. (See the Web page http://oecd.org/daf/cmis/cime/mneguide.htm.)

22. These are discussed in Helfgott (1983), Northrup and Rowan (1979), and Windmuller (1992).

23. Corporate codes are discussed, for example, in various articles in Blainpain (2000) and in Compa and Darricarrère (1996).

24. The history of including social clauses in trade agreements is discussed, for example, in Kochan and Nordlund (1989), Servais (1989), Swinnerton and Schoepfle (1994), Valticos (1969), and van Liemt (1989).

11

Toward Collaborative Interdependence

A Century of Change in the Organization of Work

Paul S. Adler

The Puzzle

Work organization denotes how tasks are grouped into jobs and how activities are coordinated across these various jobs. It is an important factor that shapes (and is shaped by) both workers' values and behavior and managers' policies in human resource management and industrial relations. The reciprocal effects of these three (clusters of) variables—work organization, worker attitudes, and management policies—shape key dimensions of organizational performance such as turnover, satisfaction, and efficiency.

Given the importance of work organization, it is regrettable that there is so little agreement about its underlying determinants or its evolution. We have many studies of the evolution over time of management *doctrines* of work organization—from scientific management to human relations, job enrichment, sociotechnical systems (STS), total quality management (TQM), and business process re-engineering (BPR). But we lack systematic studies of the corresponding *practices*, so we do not know how extensively these doctrines were implemented. We have numerous *fragments*—accounts of the evolution over short time periods of specific facets of work organization in specific firms, occupations, and industries. But we lack a common theoretical *frame*, so we do not know how to weave out of these fragments a compelling characterization of the broader trends.

In the absence of reliable data, we are forced to rely on anecdotal evidence. Consider this worker's recollection of his father, who was a trimmer for Cadillac from its very early years:

> I remember seeing him one time in the factory and he wore a leather apron which was filled with all types of needles, round and semicurved and long and short and thick and thin, and he had a thread in this pocket. And I

remember he used to say that he would take a bolt of cloth and some springs, some mohair and tacks and a hammer and his needles and go into a car and trim it from one end to another. . . . He had a half dozen pairs of shears and he used to have yellow chalk that had string around it and it used to hang from a cord around his neck and he would stick it in his pocket. My father would draw the patterns out for the cushions and the various other pieces of upholstery that was necessary for the trimming of the automobile. Then came the automatic cutters or machine cutters and the scissors got rusty around the house. . . . Then came sewing machines and my father no longer sewed. Then came men who just tied springs together, and my father was no longer in spring tying. Gradually he lost all the components of his trade. [Quoted in Peterson 1987, 38]

Faced with eloquent stories such as these, scholars have divided into three broad camps. A first camp reads such accounts as evidence of a broad trend toward the deskilling of jobs, the degradation of labor, and the alienation of workers. They point to the progressive elimination of artisans in the occupational structure and to the narrowing of skills and discretion for a broad range of jobs. A variant of this thesis acknowledges the emergence of some small, highly skilled groups and posits an overall polarizaton of the skill distribution.

A second camp points to some facts left out of this autoworker's account and reaches very different conclusions. First, the starting point of this story leaves out the much larger number of entirely unskilled laborers who typically worked alongside these craftsmen or on farms. It also leaves out the many workers who chafed under the exploitation of craftsmen operating as inside contractors. And it leaves out the many children working in huge textile mills—the eight-year-old girls working under abominable conditions for fifteen hours a day and earning $2.40 for a six-day week (Van Norst and Van Norst 1903, chap. IX). And second, the Cadillac worker's story leaves out much of the subsequent evolution of work organization. Alongside the demise of craft, the auto industry, like many others, saw a huge increase in machine operators, technicians, and clerks. These workers were less skilled and less autonomous than the trimmer had been, but they were far more skilled than most of the laborers they replaced in the occupational structure, and they were increasingly at ease with the functional interdependence that replaced the trimmer's autonomy. Some scholars therefore argue that the central tendency of work organization of the twentieth century was a path of progress toward higher skills and broader interdependence.

Yet a third camp, faced with both the lack of systematic data and the great variety of situations and trajectories, sees no consistent trends at all. Indeed, looking across workplaces and industries at any given time, we observe a huge range of variation. Given the lack of data and the powerful arguments marshaled by the other two camps, these scholars argue that there is no meaningful long-term aggregate trend.

I believe that notwithstanding the gaps in our knowledge, we can advance some reasonably well-grounded broad generalizations about these trends. To do so, however, we need a story line about the long-run evolution of work organization that can acknowledge the merit of all three camps' arguments. This chapter advances such an interpretation, focusing on the United States. In the first part, I present the main pieces of the puzzle. In the second part, I discuss how we might make sense of these pieces. A conclusion summarizes the key trends and argues that the story of work organization in the twentieth century is one of a zigzag path toward more collaborative interdependence. My argument is more speculative in some places and more empirically grounded in others. My goal is to lay out a theoretical account that can frame productive debate and serve as a fruitful source of hypotheses for future research.

Pieces of the Puzzle

The purpose of this first part is to present the main pieces of the puzzle—the key facts on which broad agreement seems possible across otherwise divergent points of view. The sections in this part address, in turn, the state of work organization at the end of the nineteenth century, subsequent changes in the broad structure of the economy, the key vectors of change in work organization, the sequence of innovations in work organization, and the diversity of forms of work organization at the end of the twentieth century.

The Starting Point: Work Organization in the Late Nineteenth Century

First, two contradictory and equally mythical images of work organization during the nineteenth century should be set aside: that it was centered around independent artisans and that it was a structure of direct, simple control by owners. In reality, during the bulk of the nineteenth century, work organization took four very different forms:[1]

1. A large but shrinking *self-employed* category composed mainly of farmers, but also including considerably smaller contingents of artisans and shopkeepers
2. A traditional sector of *external subcontracting* in the "sweated trades," which produced mainly consumer goods such as clothing, boots, shoes, and toys

3. A small but growing sector of *direct* employment and control in new larger-scale plants, often found in chemical production, as well as (quasi)monopolistic service operations such as the post office
4. A heterogeneous sector of *indirect* employment and control via internal contractors of various kinds, in (a) industries derived from domestic production, such as textiles; (b) industries founded on a craft basis, in traditional assembly operations (e.g., shipbuilding, coachbuilding), metalworking, and nontraditional assembly, and others such as glass; and (c) gang-work industries, such as in mining and the docks[2]

The overall trend during the nineteenth century was clearly to the expansion of the types 3 and 4 factory sectors. However, even in the 1880s, the typical factory was little changed from a century earlier. It remained "a congeries of craftsmen's shops rather than an integrated plant" (Nelson 1975, 3). Plants were still very small, and their owners were preoccupied with financial problems, ignorant of supervision and personnel relations as distinct administrative functions. In most industries, foremen and skilled workers controlled the pace of work, the flow of materials, and the choice of methods. Inside contractors still often controlled the hiring, firing, pay, and work of subordinate helpers and laborers. Production technology was still mainly in the form of hand tools. Authority relations were relatively personalized and often coercive. Production know-how was largely tacit. Most firms had little by way of formalized procedures. Only very few had adopted the extensive standardization that was the pride of the American system of manufacture. Beyond the shop floor, accounting and sales were the only well-established functions; but given the small average firm size, these functions were typically assured by just one or two trusted employees. In comparison with contemporary organizations, inefficiencies abounded.

As the nineteenth century drew to a close, the process of industrialization and centralization accelerated. Over the last decades, average firm size doubled in many industries.[3] Direct employment (type 3) grew in its total share. Work organization emerged as a central problem for management and as the object of wide-scale debate and struggle.

The Twentieth Century: The Evolution of the Broader Context

Before proceeding to the heart of the matter, it may be useful to remind ourselves of the main lines of evolution of the structure of the U.S. economy and labor force during the twentieth century. I summarize this evolution under eight broad headings.[4]

First, the century saw a huge change in the structure of the U.S. labor force. While the male labor-force participation rate fluctuated between 75 percent and 80 percent over the century, the female in wage labor participation grew from around 19 percent in 1900 to 30 percent in 1950 and 60 percent in 2000. The huge influx of immigrants around the turn of the century gradually subsided. Of males over twenty-one years of age, 24 percent were foreign-born in 1900, but this declined to only 11 percent in 1950 and 7 percent in 1970 and then rose modestly to some 9 percent by 2000. The industry distribution of the labor force shifted considerably, with a continuous decline in the share of agriculture, an increase and then a decrease in the share of manufacturing, and an increase in the share of services.

The occupational distribution evolved in parallel—see Table 11.1. The shares of farmers and of laborers in both farming and manufacturing declined dramatically. Paralleling the evolution of manufacturing, the shares of craftsmen and operatives first grew and then fell. There was strong, sustained growth in the share of clerical and professional-technical categories and more modest growth in the share of service, sales, and managerial occupations.

Second, the average education level of the labor force increased, and here too the change was dramatic. The fraction of seventeen-year-olds who had completed high school grew from 6 percent in 1900 to 57 percent in 1950 and continued to grow to more than 80 percent by the end of the century. Despite this huge increase in supply, investment in high school and college education continued to yield a sizable positive return (Goldin and Katz 1999), which suggests that at least some of this increase in education levels reflected increasing skill requirements rather than pure screening and credentialism (Abramowitz and David 1996). As Goldin and Katz write, the most plausible explanation for this pattern is that "technological change and capital deepening have both served to increase the demand for higher-skilled labor over the long run" (1999, 25–26).

Third, continuing the trends characteristic of the prior century, the proportion of self-employed progressively declined. Over the course of the 1800s, this proportion had progressively fallen from more than 80 percent to less than 40 percent, and this share would continue to shrink, reaching less than 7 percent by the end of the twentieth century.

Fourth, the size of firms and establishments grew. In part, this was due to the contraction of the traditional farm sector. However, even within the non-farm sector, there was a considerable increase in the average size of firms and of establishments—although this trend seems to have leveled off in the last couple of decades (Pryor forthcoming).

Fifth, alongside growth in firm size, the century seems also to have wit-

Table 11.1

Evolution of the Occupational Structure of the U.S. Labor Force

Category	Percent of U.S. labor force, by year										
	1900	1910	1920	1930	1940	1950	1960	1970	1980	1990	2000
Clerical	3	5	8	9	10	12	14	18	17	18	14
Professional, technical	4	5	5	7	7	9	11	14	15	17	19
Service (excl. private household)	4	5	5	6	7	8	8	11			
Private-household workers	5	5	3	4	5	3	3	2			
Service (incl. private household)	9	10	8	10	12	11	11	13	13	13	14
Salesworkers	5	5	5	6	7	7	7	7	11	12	12
Operative and kindred	13	15	16	16	18	20	19	18			
Laborers (excl. farm and mine)	12	12	12	11	9	7	5	5			
Operatives and laborers (excl. farm and mine)	25	27	28	27	27	27	24	23	18	15	14
Managers, administrators, proprietors	6	7	7	7	7	9	8	8	10	13	15
Craftsmen, foremen	11	12	13	13	12	14	14	14	12	11	11
Farmers	20	17	15	12	10	7	4	2			
Farm laborers and foremen	18	14	12	9	7	4	2	1			
Farmers and farm laborers	38	31	27	21	17	11	6	3	3	3	3

Source: U.S. Bureau of the Census.

Note: Data for 1980 and later combine operatives and laborers, do not distinguish private-household workers, and do not distinguish farm laborers from farmers and farm managers.

nessed growth in the density of market transactions between firms. The interindustry division of labor deepened with the proliferation of new classes of consumer and producer goods and services. The connections linking these industries became denser.

Sixth, unions grew, then shrank. Only 3 percent of the labor force belonged to unions in 1900. In the subsequent years, that rate rose slowly, then increased dramatically after passage of the Wagner Act in 1935 to reach 25 percent of the total workforce in 1956. The rate then began to decline, slowly at first but then accelerating after 1980 to 14 percent at century's end. The threat of unionization nevertheless continued to influence management in relatively unionized industries and regions, and unions continued to shape law and regulations.

Seventh, government became a progressively larger factor in the economy, both directly and indirectly. Direct employment in federal and state government grew almost continuously—from 3.8 percent of the labor force in 1900 to 10.1 percent in 1950 and to 15.1 percent in 1999, leveling off toward the end of the century. Total government expenditures grew from 8 percent of U.S. gross domestic product in 1913 to17.5 percent in 2000 (Maddison 1995, 65). The state's indirect influence also grew as both work organization and employee and industrial relations were progressively legalized by a growing panoply of laws and regulations that constrained management practices in these domains.

Finally, over the course of the twentieth century, work organization in the United States was disrupted by two periods of macroeconomic dislocation (the 1930s, the 1970s and 1980s) and by two world wars. The economic downswings brought widespread unemployment and destruction of capital. The wars—fought elsewhere—had almost counterbalancing effects in strengthening the hand of workers in their conflicts with management.

Four Vectors of Change

Within these broader contextual trends, four vectors of change characterized the evolution of work organization over the course of the twentieth century: greater specialization, development of managerial techniques of coordination and control, automation, and the rationalization of management authority. Most observers would agree with these descriptors, but their significance continues to be debated.

Specialization

First, as average firm size grew, workers found their tasks and roles progressively specialized.[5] This specialization provoked considerable debate. On the one side, protests were common against the division of craft labor. The shoemakers were affected early, as reflected in the eloquent testimony to an 1879 congressional committee by Charles Litchman, a grand secretary of the Knights of Labor and a leader in the Knights of St. Crispin, which sought to organize shoemakers in the 1860s and early 1870s:

> By the subdivision of labor a man now is no longer a tradesman. He is part of a tradesman. In my own trade of shoemaking, twenty years ago the work was done almost entirely by hand, and the man had to learn how to make a shoe. Now, with the use of machines of almost superhuman ingenuity, a man is no longer a shoemaker, but only the sixty-fourth part of a shoemaker, because there are sixty-four subdivisions in making shoes; a man may work forty years at our trade, and at the end of forty years he will know no more about making the whole shoe than when he commenced the business.[6]

The primary significance of this specialization lay in the associated loss of economic independence. The demise of domestic and handicraft forms of production and their replacement by specialized functions in large-scale factory production meant, above all, greatly reduced opportunities for economic independence. In the latter part of the nineteenth century, the contrast between these trends and the dominant ethos of economic independence provoked growing protests. These protests continued into the early years of the twentieth century. The term "slavery" was often used to condemn wage labor as a long-term status (Rogers 1974). By the mid-twentieth century, however, economic independence was a remote prospect: Independent farmers and domestic production had all but disappeared. While craftsmen remained a sizable component of the labor force, they became increasingly dependent on facilities provided by large employers.[7] In the latter part of the twentieth century, concerns about loss of economic independence were more commonly voiced by professionals such as lawyers and doctors who protested the growth of larger professional firms and of the corporate employment of professionals.

On the other side of this debate, observers such as John Dewey and Jane Addams saw a more positive social potential in this more extensive division of labor. The old "rugged individualism" of the farmer and artisan-craftsman was being replaced by a "new individualism" that was less parochial and more organically tied to a broader community (Dewey 1930). Addams wrote:

> A man who makes, year after year, but one small wheel in a modern watch factory, may, if his education has properly prepared him, have a fuller life

than did the old watchmaker who made the watch from beginning to end. It takes thirty-nine people to make a coat in a modern tailoring establishment, yet those same thirty-nine people might produce a coat in a spirit of "team work" which would make the entire process as much more exhilarating than the work of the old solitary tailor, as playing in a baseball nine gives more pleasure to a boy than that afforded by a solitary game of handball. [1902, quoted in Rogers 1974, 82]

Contrary to the view expressed by Litchman, Dewey and the other pragmatists suggested that automation too contributed to this "fuller life": As engineers, technicians, blue-collar workers, clerks, or managers, a growing proportion of the labor force found themselves designing, maintaining, and using technology, thus creating an intimate link between the worker and society's growing body of scientific and technological knowledge.

Coordination and Control

Specialization provoked (and was provoked by) management efforts to improve the coordination and control of work. Alfred D. Chandler (1962, 1977) shows how management progressively tamed the challenges of operating more efficiently with higher fixed costs, faster throughput, and greater scale and scope. Hobsbawn's (1964, chap. 17) analysis of nineteenth-century Britain suggests that management efforts to improve the coordination and control of work were also causally intertwined with the evolution of owners' values from custom to profit and with the replacement of noneconomic labor-control mechanisms by economic ones. The impact of these combined forces was, in a first phase, that "managers learned the value of intensive rather than extensive labour utilization" and, in a second phase, that they "discovered genuinely efficient ways of utilizing their workers' labour time ('scientific management')" (ibid., 406–407). (In Marx's terminology, the "real subordination of labor to capital," with the associated focus on "relative surplus value," progressively replaced "formal subordination" and "absolute surplus value" as the key axis of development.)

As a result, after considerable struggle in the late nineteenth and early twentieth centuries, much of the day-to-day control of the work process shifted to management. Inside contracting (type 4 workers) largely disappeared. The ranks of foremen swelled, and as Frederick Taylor had recommended, the work of these foremen was progressively specialized into a panoply of roles filled by a growing group of engineers, technicians, and clerical employees.[8] The ratio of nonproduction to production employees in manufacturing rose from 10 percent in 1899 to 22 percent in 1947 and to 33 percent in 1980 (Bureau of the Census 1992; Melman 1951, vol. 1, table 1). Notwithstanding press accounts of "delayering," it is not clear that the trend changed much in the last two decades of the century (Gordon 1996).

Automation

Automation was the third major vector of change. The average stock of equipment per worker increased by a factor of about seven over the century.[9] The degree of automation of transformation, transfer, and control functions varied considerably across industries. Scranton (1997) is surely correct that images of the assembly line and of the oil refinery's flow process should not blind us to the continuing importance of custom and small-batch production. But even custom manufacturing and similar service-sector activities enjoyed a considerable infusion of automation over the course of the century (Blackburn, Coombs, and Green 1985).

Debate raged throughout the century over the impact of automation on work. This is hardly surprising, since automation in these debates often stood as a proxy for—or indeed as the main driver among—the entire constellation of forces shaping work. These debates thus mirrored the more general disagreements over the evolution of work organization. From the shoemakers of the late nineteenth century to computer programmers in the late twentieth, some observers argued that automation has primarily a deskilling effect—at least under capitalist conditions—while others saw a predominantly upgrading effect, and yet others saw no generalizable pattern.

Two studies by Industrial Relations Counselors, Inc. (IRC), the first in 1964 and the second in 1988, analyzed automation's impact on work organization in a range of settings.[10] With hindsight, the IRC studies appear to have characterized accurately the broad pattern of effects. The 1964 study, in addressing both employment security and work organization, concluded that these effects were primarily benign (Beaumont and Helfgott 1964, 218–37):

- "Generally, but far from universally, modern technology tends to reduce physical effort and increase mental effort. It also demands greater versatility on the part of those who do the work. . . . Each member of the workforce now has to relate his performance to the entire operation, rather than to a specific task, and this necessitates change in the employee's perception of work".
- Automation displaces the direct human production role—workers become more like technicians—with titles such as instrument mechanic replacing electrician or pipefitter; workers need greater versatility, especially where production and maintenance tasks are combined.

- Automation tends to increase the employment share of certain types of workers: skilled relative to unskilled, maintenance relative to production, technical and engineering relative to blue-collar, and service relative to manufacturing.
- Sometimes automation brings a polarization of jobs' skill requirements, leading to greater employment shares at the top and the bottom of the scale.
- The environment of most jobs becomes more pleasant and safer.
- Industrial relations challenges are substantial, in particular because "it may not longer be feasible to abide by seniority as the mechanical determinant in job placement." Unions and management will need to find a way to recognize the importance of trainability.
- "Old work groups are now broken up"—but "new group relationships are evident. . . . Not only does each crew member have to understand his own responsibilities and tasks, he also has to coordinate his efforts with those of his coworkers, particularly in diagnosing and correcting machine breakdowns"
- Negative factors were often salient during transition periods but tended to disappear with time; nevertheless, an increase in shift work seems unavoidable, and in highly automated facilities, boredom at work constitutes a major challenge.

Some twenty years later, the findings were remarkably similar in general tone (Helfgott 1988, 67ff.):

- "Computer technology is having a profound effect on the nature of jobs and the ways in which work is organized. The scope of jobs is expanding. Workers are being trained to be more versatile and are being accorded greater responsibility and control over their work."
- "The work environment also is undergoing change, becoming safer and cleaner."
- "Operators will not gain control [over production processes] if management is reluctant to allow them such control. Some managements, however, have been more willing to share power with their employees, pointing to a movement toward a more versatile, higher skilled work force."
- "Not all types of jobs benefit from new technology in terms of skill." Numerical control of machine tools, for example, turns machinists into machine tenders. But the subsequent generation of technology—CNC— usually brings some programming back to the shop floor.
- "Since programming a robot is not difficult, many companies find that

it makes sense to train production workers as programmers." If programming of NC machine tools is often performed by white-collar technicians, "the explanation lies in the labor relations area—a management
desire to keep programming out of the bargaining unit in unionized situations. This desire is based on the fear that if the job is in the bargaining
unit, it will be subject to stringent rules on demarcation and seniority
bumping procedures, which could threaten flexibility of operations and
result in extraordinary training costs and inefficient operations as untrained
workers bump into positions involving programming."

- Broader job classifications allow production workers to do some maintenance and setup.
- A common problem was social isolation in the factory because human-
manned workstations become physically farther apart. Therefore, more
enlightened managers allowed music and created employee involvement teams.

The Changing Nature of Authority

Over the course of the century, the nature of managerial authority changed
profoundly. The arbitrary authority of the "foreman's empire" and the "drive
system" was progressively replaced by more bureaucratic forms of discipline (Nelson 1975, chap. 3). This change was due partly to the rising power
of unions and partly to management's quest for more control over the details
of unit operations. The general cultural evolution of society towards greater
respect for the individual must surely have contributed too.

Using Weberian categories, we could say that at the beginning of the century, management's power was largely coercive. As such, it was often contested or fatalistically accepted. Sometimes it was accepted on traditional or
even charismatic bases. Over the subsequent century, coercive and traditional
forms of authority were largely displaced by reliance on rationality. This
rationality took two different forms—formal and substantive. Formal rationality, by far the predominant one, was expressed in the use of bureaucratic
procedures and market exchange to exercise more effective control, ensure
efficiency of operations, and improve profitability. Substantive rationality
was expressed in the efforts of a growing minority of firms to create a community of purpose within the organization—a focus on consent based on
common commitment to a superordinate value.[11] Debate continues about
whether this mutation in the nature of authority constituted a civilizing process or a means by which workers' subjectivity could be yoked to the imperatives of profit.

The evolution of authority was expressed in the changing nature of the effort-wage bargain. Erratic preindustrial norms of work intensity progressively dissipated, and new norms of time discipline were progressively internalized (E.P. Thompson 1967). The term "driving" was often a contraction for "slave driving," but workers progressively grew accustomed to "wage slavery" and to the remoteness of any prospect of economic independence. As a result, the idea of management determining methods and speed of work became less foreign and less objectionable.

Protest sometimes flared against the specific forms of work imposed by management (notably in the 1930s and 1970s). But as unions gave workers the means by which to demand compensation for work intensification, protest was generally replaced by negotiation. In the last decades of the century, Japanese-inspired production management techniques such as TQM sought to eliminate yet more of the remaining "pores" in the working day (and to replace unproductive with productive effort). This ratcheted up once again norms of work intensity (Adler 1993; Kenney and Florida 1988). By the end of the century, however, unions were too weak to assure that workers shared in the associated productivity increases (Osterman 1999, 111).

A Sedimented Sequence of Innovations in Work Organization

The state of work organization at the end of the twentieth century not only reflected the evolution of the broader context and the four general vectors of change described in the previous two sections; it also reflected the sedimentation of a series of organizational innovations. As pointed out at the beginning of this chapter, it is difficult to assess how pervasive these innovations became in practice. But in tracing the evolution of these innovations, we are arguably tracing at least the leading edge of the changes in work organization.

Several researchers have identified this sequence of innovations by analyzing the content of articles in management journals (Abrahamson 1997; Barley and Kunda 1992; Guillén 1994). Their findings suggest that we can group these innovations in two broad categories, each associated with a different type of "rhetoric": one group emphasized formal rationality and aimed to ensure coordination and control, and the other emphasized substantive rationality and aimed to ensure employee commitment. Their analyses suggest that these two types alternated in their relative importance over the century. Changes in rhetoric correspond (roughly) to the state of the Kondratieff long wave.[12] New rhetorics tend to emerge at the troughs and peaks of cycles. Commitment was valued when business was headed into difficult times, but control was valued when business prospects were turning more favorable.[13]

The beginning of the 1872–94 Kondratieff downswing saw the emergence of the first in this sequence of innovations—*welfare work*. Welfare work, or "betterment," did not touch work organization directly but aimed instead to shape values, build basic skills, and improve physical health, and thus to promote loyalty. It used company schools, employee magazines, company churches, and company cafeterias. While some of the specific practices of early welfare work subsequently disappeared, many others persisted and were developed further by the human relations wave (discussed below).

The beginning of the 1894–1921 upswing saw the emergence of *scientific management*—a family of innovations designed to systematize management from the shop floor to the executive suite. On the shop floor, scientific management introduced techniques of production planning, work analysis, time standards, piece rates, etc. These were deployed not only in manufacturing but also in clerical occupations. The legacy of these innovations persisted. In their classic study of an automobile assembly plant in the 1950s, Walker and Guest (1952) quote workers describing work organization in terms we could have heard in 1930—or in 2000:

> Foreman: The line here, the moving line, controls the man and his speed. Then no matter how slow a man is, he has to keep moving. We're all human, we like to go as slow as we can unless we are pushed, and this line controls him perfectly.
> Worker: The line speed is too great. More men wouldn't help much. They'd just expect more work out of an individual. There's an awful lot of tension. The work isn't hard, it's the never-ending pace. The guys yell "hurrah!" when the line breaks down. It's not the monotony, it's the rush, rush, rush. On the line you're geared to the line. You don't dare stop. If you get behind you have a hard time catching up. [Pp. 40, 51–52]

Comparable accounts could be offered of work in call centers a half-century later. Incoming calls are automatically routed to employees within a couple of seconds of concluding the preceding call. The employees respond to the calls by reading from prepared scripts. Their bonuses depend on individual productivity. The quality of service is monitored secretly by supervisors who listen in to the conversations (Frenkel et al. 1999).

In the management superstructure, this wave of formal rationality innovations led to the definition of functional departments and differentiated roles for staff and line functions. Over subsequent decades, the legacy was extended in elaborate systems for formal planning, budgeting, and control.

From early on, some scientific management proponents were eager to combine it with welfare work. Joseph & Feiss Company in Cleveland, Ohio, was a notable example. Under the leadership of the company's vice president, Richard A. Feiss, the implementation of scientific management was very rigorous. The piece-rate system, for example, was very detailed. The sizable Planning Department ensured smooth high-velocity operations. But Feiss's commitment to welfare was equally rigorous—especially after a strike in 1909 against the wage system and work rules. In 1913, Feiss hired Mary Gilson to head a new Employment and Service department (he rejected the welfare label because it suggested philanthropy). Gilson helped organize a wide array of welfare measures both at work—testing, promotion ladders, elimination of foremen's favoritism—and outside work—dances, picnics, choral societies, clubs, an orchestra, and athletic programs, as well as home visits and other activities designed to promote the "mental, moral and spiritual advancement" of workers. Gilson later went on to join IRC (Nelson 1975, 78; Goldberg 1992).[14]

The beginning of the 1921–44 downswing witnessed the emergence of the *human relations* school of thought. It sought to broaden the role of the personnel function and to infuse concern for employee commitment into the fabric of daily work. The associated innovations included ability testing for selecting employees, individual performance records, employee satisfaction surveys, coaching in supervisory skills, and the nonunion employee representation plans promoted by IRC.

These ideas grew in relevance over time. Their legacy was particularly strong in the management of less-routine operations such as craft, R&D, and professional work. Notwithstanding much early and some later mutual hostility, proponents of human relations and of scientific management often joined forces in the design of formalized personnel management systems, including compensation and performance incentives and suggestion systems. The Gilbreths represented an early version of this synthesis, with their focus on active worker involvement in scientifically grounded quality-improvement efforts. Later syntheses were associated with Allan Mogenson, the Training Within Industries program during World War II, and W. Edwards Deming.

At the beginning of the 1944–71 upswing, a wave of *systems rationalization* innovations appeared that built on the scientific management legacy: operations research, management science, strategic business units as a common corporate structure, and the further refinement of business planning and control systems. As this phase built momentum, it encompassed efforts to rationalize relatively nonroutine activities, with the introduction of formalized R&D budgeting and project management approaches and the use of matrix structures.

Sometimes proponents of systems rationalization rode roughshod over the welfare work and human relations legacy. In particular, one reading of contingency theory seemed to justify a Theory X disciplinarian approach to the management of routine operations. There were also, however, many initiatives that sought synergy. Many discussions of matrix management, for example, were attentive to its human dimensions—dealing with ambiguity, ensuring appropriate upward influence, and so forth. And in the nonroutine parts of corporate operations, contingency theory authorized a more employee-centered approach.

The beginning of the downswing that started around 1971 witnessed a resurgence of interest in commitment in the form of *employee involvement* (EI), as expressed in the themes of quality, culture, and empowerment. Building on the work of Maslow, Argyris, and McGregor, this wave was often framed in opposition to the scientific management legacy. Sociotechnical systems theory (STS), a common reference point, popularized the idea that the human costs of excessively standardized and fragmented work would eventually lead to losses in productivity and quality—and that this would occur not only in nonroutine tasks but even in routine work. Proponents advocated the adoption of forms of organization that would give workgroups and individuals far greater autonomy in determining work methods and far less specialization in their job assignments:

> The work force of the new plant [and office] is organized into teams responsible for segments of the workflow. They are delegated many self-supervisory responsibilities. They make internal work assignments, make production trade-off decisions, diagnose and solve production problems, and select personnel replacements to their team. Support functions such as quality control and maintenance are integrated into team responsibilities. Team members are paid for acquisition of additional skills, not for doing a particular job. Common parking lots and cafeterias and other symbols de-emphasize status. Employees do not punch the time clock. Supervisors are expected to be facilitative, exercising progressively less direction and control as team capacities develop. Employees exercise voice over a wide range of conditions that affect them. Finally, and critically important, the organization is characterized by very high expectations about task performance and about people treatment. [Lawler 1979, 2]

Sometimes these new tactics for eliciting commitment were combined with ideas from the formal rationality traditions of scientific management and systems rationalization. Two such families of synthesis can be noted.

First, in routine operations, scientific management ideas could be combined with EI ideas. Even if the result was not the kind of autonomous teams advocated by STS or found in refinery control rooms, such syntheses could nevertheless support high levels of worker commitment. For example, TQM in mass-production industries often took the form of empowered teams (strong on commitment) themselves using standard quality improvement tools (strong on formal rationality). NUMMI provides an example. NUMMI is a GM-Toyota joint venture producing Corollas, Geos, and Toyota light trucks in Fremont, California. It has operated under day-to-day Toyota management since opening in 1984. Here is how one worker analyzed the effects of the rigorous implementation of the Toyota production system at NUMMI:

> The work teams at NUMMI aren't like the autonomous teams you read about in other plants. Here, we're not autonomous because we're all tied together really tightly. But it's not like we're just getting squeezed to work harder, because it's us, the workers, that are making the whole thing work— we're the ones that make the standardized work and the kaizen sugges-tions. We run the plant—and if it's not running right, we stop it. At GM-Fremont, we only ran our own little jobs. We'd work really fast to build up a stock cushion so we could take a break for a few minutes to smoke a cigarette or chat with a buddy. That kind of "hurry up and wait" game made work really tiring. [Adler 1993, 145–46]

A second family of syntheses built on the systems rationalization efforts to bring some discipline to nonroutine operations. EI in this context meant that staff could be actively mobilized to develop collectively their own for-mal methodologies and procedures. The general idea of process mapping— a tool used by both scientific management and STS—was brought into nonroutine operations in such forms as IDEF, CMM, ISO 9000, and clinical guidelines in medicine.

I would conjecture that since the mid-1990s, the Kondratieff wave might have resumed an upswing, and I would note that in this period we saw a resur-gence of control-oriented innovations under the banner, of *business process re-engineering, outsourcing,* and *networks.* The focus here was on radically rationalizing the scope and processes of work: Downsize so as to focus on core competencies, and outsource the rest. A first phase of this cycle seemed delib-erately scornful of the human dimension. Layoffs and downsizing cuts were trumpeted as signs of re-invigorated management recommitment to share-holder value. But within a couple of years, business process re-engineering (BPR) champions were embracing STS ideas on how to configure jobs in the re-engineered organization (Champy 1995; Hammer 1996). The literature on outsourcing reflects this continuity of commitment themes within innovations that are predominantly or initially control-oriented, with its attention to building trust and commitment with suppliers. The literature on knowledge management combines a systems-rationalizing focus on IT infrastructure and a commit-ment focus on "communities of practice."

By Century's End

All these innovations—from the coercive to the consensual, from the ad hoc to the bureaucratic—were deposited like layers of sediment in the evolution of forms of work organization. We do not have data that allow us to compare directly the early years of the twentieth century with the later ones, but sur-veys by Osterman (1994, 1999) and Lawler and his colleagues (1998) give us some economy-wide data on the recent past.[15]

At the close of the century, most blue- and white-collar employees had at least a moderate degree of discretion over their work activity. Few had either very much or very little control, as reflected in closeness of supervision, discretion over pace, or discretion over methods—see Table 11.2.[16]

By century's end, work organization commonly involved some form of off-line problem-solving groups for at least half the core employees in some 57 percent of establishments. Job rotation, too, was similarly common in more than 55 percent of establishments. Self-managed work teams were com-mon in 38 percent and TQM practices in 57 percent. Some 39 percent of establishments used three or more of these practices for more than half their core personnel. These data probably exaggerate the prevalence of these prac-tices because respondents relabeled conventional practices to make them appear in conformity with current management fads. However, it is difficult to imagine that comparable practices were anywhere nearly as widespread fifty or one hundred years ago.

This mix of forms of work organization was reflected in the range of HR/IR policies. These policies can be grouped into three broad categories: flows (recruiting, promoting), rewards, and voice.

- *Flows:* Whereas Henry Ford boasted that assembly-line workers could be recruited from among the least educated, auto assembly plants at the end of the century demanded that even applicants for assembly-line jobs have a high school education and strong interpersonal and teamwork skills, as well as a capacity to learn new skills.[17] Given such changes, it was logical that internal labor markets proliferated in large and me-dium-sized firms, replacing reliance on the external labor market with internal development and promotion.[18] Moreover, the focus of this train-ing seems to have evolved: By the end of the twentieth century, training focused not only on job skills but also on team building, quality statis-tics, and group decision-making and problem-solving skills (see Cappelli

Table 11.2

Degree of Control over Work by "Core" Employees

	Percent of establishments responding		
	All core occupations	Blue-collar core workers	Professional/technical core workers
Closeness of supervision:			
Complete	5.87	5.88	4.81
Large	24.26	14.96	20.56
Moderate	53.02	61.95	43.08
Small	16.60	16.91	30.65
None	0.25	0.29	0.90
Discretion over pace:			
Complete	6.63	7.11	12.80
Large	24.31	16.80	37.55
Moderate	36.75	47.42	28.95
Small	19.98	15.75	9.19
None	12.32	12.91	11.52
Discretion over work method:			
Complete	4.81	3.13	8.97
Large	39.86	39.88	45.77
Moderate	37.04	39.70	32.59
Small	14.21	11.24	12.67
None	4.07	6.05	0.00

Source: Osterman National Survey of Establishments 1994 (cited in Cappelli et al. 1997, 100).

Note: Core occupations are the largest group of nonsupervisory, nonmanagerial workers in the surveyed establishment directly involved in making the product or providing the service. Blue-collar workers were 42.5% of core occupations, sales were 19%, service were 18.3%, and professional/technical were 14.3% (Osterman 1994, 175).

et al. 1997, chap. 4; see also Educational Quality of the Workforce survey on the Internet at http://www.irhe.upenn.edu/centers/ctrs-prog3.html).

- *Rewards:* Reflecting the importance of skill formation for firms' competitiveness, skill-based pay systems for at least some employees were found in more than 60 percent of large companies. And reflecting the growth of teamwork, rewards for performance of the workgroup, the plant, and the firm were growing more common. Osterman's (1994) survey shows that some 45 percent of establishments offered employees some form of profit sharing.
- *Employee Voice:* Here the picture was more mixed. Lawler's survey shows that by century's end, most firms gave more than 80 percent of their employees information on corporate and unit-level operating results, and most firms gave more than 60 percent of their employees

information on business plans. It is difficult to imagine that the corresponding figures for a century earlier were that high. However, provision of such information is a very weak indicator of employee voice. Union and nonunion forms of representation are a more robust indicator, but these were in decline for most of the latter part of the twentieth century. Legal protection of employee rights did increase over this same half-century, but the courts are a relatively inaccessible forum for most employees. At the end of the twentieth century, the voice gap—the unfulfilled demand of workers for participation and representation— seemed pervasive (Freeman and Rogers 1999; but see Kaufman 2001 for a more moderate assessment).

Making Sense of the Pieces

Making sense of the evolution of work organization has proven difficult. In this second part of the chapter, I advance an interpretation that has the advantage of acknowledging the merits of both optimistic and pessimistic accounts. The following sections address, in turn, prior interpretations of this evolution, the key dimensions of work organization, the technically induced tendencies in the evolution of work organization, the socially induced tendencies, and finally, the combination of these tendencies in workers' experience of work.

Four Generations of Research

Prior to the Second World War, research on the history of work organization was scattered between two poles. At one pole, there was a growing body of applied managerial literature. At the other pole, commentators and critics attempted to characterize the trends they observed in terms inherited from the broad-scale theories of Marx, Weber, and Durkheim. In the United States, the first major scholarly work that focused on work organization was perhaps the research by Roethlisberger and Dickson (1939), in collaboration with Elton Mayo. (Another notable landmark was Gulick and Urwick 1937.) However, even in this work, only scant attention was paid to the history and determinants of work organization per se.

Since the Second World War, scholarly research on trends in work organization has gone through four major generations. Let us briefly review them; we will see how this evolution has both clarified and obscured our object of analysis.

The first generation, in the 1950s and 1960s, was dominated by authors such as Blauner (1964), Woodward (1965), Touraine (1954), and Mallet

Table 11.3

Woodward's Typology of Production Systems

	Unit production	Mass production	Continuous process
Number of management levels	3	4	6
Supervisor span of control	23	48	15
Ratio of direct to indirect labor	9:1	4:1	1:1
Ratio of managers to total personnel	Low	Medium	High
Production worker average skill level	High	Low	High
Formalization of procedures	Low	High	Low
Centralization	Low	High	Low
Amount of verbal communication	High	Low	High
Amount of written communication	Low	High	Low
Overall structure	Organic	Mechanistic	Organic

Source: Woodward 1965.

(1963), who, despite their differences, all saw a curvilinear trend in work organization. In a first phase, the shift from unit and small-batch production to mass production led to narrower, less-skilled jobs. In a second phase, the shift to more automated continuous-flow production led to broader jobs and upgraded skills. Woodward's analysis was particularly cogent: Table 11.3 summarizes her key conclusions. Like others of this generation of research, she argued that automation, by encouraging a shift toward continuous-flow production, would restore craft forms of work and an associated "organic" form of organization.

The advance of automation over the century did indeed shift some mass-production activities to continuous-flow forms. Moreover, under the impact of computer-integrated manufacturing, even highly differentiated production sometimes came to resemble continuous flow (Adler 1988). In other respects, however, this prognosis missed the mark. First, the focus on manufacturing ignored the rapid growth of the service sector, where mass-production forms of clerical work proliferated. Second, on closer examination, work in continuous-flow processes looked less like traditional craft than had been predicted, and the associated organizational forms looked less organic. The kinds of skills involved were those of the technician rather than the craftsman (Barley and Orr 1997). While some operational decision making was indeed decentralized, decision premises were often rigorously defined by a growing panoply of formal procedures.

The second generation of research emerged in the 1970s and reflected a changed social context. Less-skilled workers had played a prominent part in the resurgence of social conflict in the late 1960s, and their demands often targeted alienating and oppressive work organization rather than compensation. Moreover, scholars were impatient with the internal limits of the older research whose optimism seemed based almost exclusively on the potential effects of automation in a narrow band of continuous-process industries. This second generation argued that automation's potentially favorable effects on work organization were rarely realized. Often inspired by Marx's analysis of the labor process, authors such as Braverman (1974) in the United States, Freyssenet (1974) in France, Nichols and Beynon (1977) in the United Kingdom, and Kern and Schumann (1972) in Germany all argued a common thesis: Capitalist societies tend to deskill work and narrow job responsibilities in their constant search for lower production costs and for greater control over a potentially recalcitrant labor force.

This second generation attacked what they saw as the technological determinism of the first generation. The implementation of the same technology, they argued, would have very different effects in different types of societies. In capitalist societies, interests of workers and capitalists diverge over the intensity of work and over control in the labor process. Given the structurally subordinate place of workers in such a society, the overall effect of technological advances could therefore only be a long-run decline in average skill and discretion. (For some authors, this trend was combined with the creation of a smaller number of highly skilled positions in a polarization scenario.) The assembly line was the key image of the future of work for these researchers.

The polemical intent of this deskilling proposition was fairly evident. In the absence of systematic statistics, case studies were used to great effect to show (a) a frequent gap between workers' capabilities and job requirements (skill underutilization); (b) instances where management's drive for profitability and control did seem to lead to deskilling; and (c) other instances in which managerial ideologies and political concerns led to deskilling at the expense of efficiency.[19]

There was, however, a glaring discrepancy between the second generation's predictions and the reality as evidenced in the long-run trends in occupational distributions and in the broader sets of case studies such as IRC's. A third generation of research thus emerged, marked by a move away from the analysis of broader trends and big generalizations. Some authors attempted to renew research of a first-generation kind, with arguments about the emergence of flexible specialization or postindustrialism; but now, in tune with a growth of skepticism among currently influential thinkers concerning anything resembling historical laws of development, the focus was often on the political contingencies governing evolutionary trajectories. The focus shifted to the local dynamics of change, and for this contextualist generation, which attained dominance in the late 1970s and early 1980s, there was no valid generalization possible concerning long-run trends in work organization.

This skepticism generated valuable research into the social construction of skill labels—the idea that the distinction between skilled and unskilled is often more political and ideological than economic and technical. The research also explored the host of local factors that shape work organization such as the balance of political power, union organization, and local labor and product market conditions. The group around the French journal *Sociologie du Travail* can, in this respect, be compared to the research of Richard Edwards (1979) in the United States and Duncan Gallie (1978) in Great Britain (see also the collection edited by Knights and Willmott 1986) in their common focus on the impact of relative bargaining power and specific market conditions on automation, staffing, and labeling. This generation saw work organization as if through a kaleidoscope—constantly shifting configurations, forming no overall tendency.

Most recently, a fourth generation has shifted attention away from work organization as an object of study. The shift can be traced in the decline of two fields of research, industrial sociology and industrial relations. Work organization was a central term in the field of industrial sociology. With the turn to subjectivity and language in sociology, studies of work increasingly focused on issues of identity and Foucault-inspired research on managerial discourse. More fundamentally, the field of industrial sociology has declined in centrality within sociology; in tandem with this decline, we have seen the rise of organizational research in business schools.

Work organization was also a central issue in the field of industrial relations, but it, too, has been in decline. As Kaufman (1993) showed, industrial relations lost its legitimacy when interdisciplinary studies fell out of favor in universities. The main centers of continued research (at Sloan, Wharton, Cornell, Berkeley, etc.) seem to function increasingly at the margins of the established and ascendant disciplines. Industrial relations maintains a niche in economics (expanding modestly with the rise of personnel and organizational economics), but it too has largely migrated into business schools.

Translated into a business school setting, the "work" part of work organization has disappeared to the benefit of a focus on the issues of more direct salience to managers—the "organization" part (Barley 1996). Industrial relations has mutated into human resource management. What remains has bifurcated:

- On the macro side, work organization is addressed by studies of organization design as part of the field known as organization theory. Increasingly, however, the focus of organization theory research has shifted from the plant or establishment—the level of analysis favored by Woodward's generation—to the top-level structure of the corporation, to broader industry-level processes of institutional structuring, and to ecological processes driving the fortunes of whole populations of organizations.

• On the micro side, work organization is addressed by studies of job design as part of the field known as organizational behavior. These studies focus on the individual or the work team. They aim at a social-psychological understanding of work experience, and in particular those subjective features of work that lead to high versus low levels of commitment, alienation, satisfaction, and so forth. Over the decades, this research has given impetus and theoretical shape to the human relations and EI movements. However, this research has tended to leave aside, as too macro and sociological, efforts to characterize broad trends in work organization.

The cumulative result of this evolution in scholarly approaches is a remarkable degree of both disinterest and confusion relative to the question of the long-term trends in work organization. The disinterest can perhaps be explained by the progressive weakening of unions. As long as unions gave voice to protests over changing forms of work organization, scholarly work on the issue had a strong raison d'être. Today, as compared to fifty or even one hundred years ago, such interest is much weaker—as witnessed by the decline in the frequency of congressional hearings and of studies funded by public agencies. The confusion, by contrast, must be explained in more properly theoretical terms—the subject of the following sections.

A Theoretical Framework

The confusion over trends in work organization is, I believe, due in large part to reliance on competing but equally truncated views of the nature of the forces that shape work organization:

• Some observers see work organization as an essentially *technical* system: On this view, work organization is shaped primarily by technology, instrumental rationality, and efficiency considerations, even if it has, in turn, important social and psychological consequences.
• Other observers interpret work organization as a *social* system: As part of the structure of ownership and control within the firm, work organization is both the site and the object of often-conflicting interests between workers and managers.[20]

Reading the research described in the earlier section, it is difficult to avoid the conclusion that there is merit to both these views, and from this observation, I draw a simple conclusion: Work organization is located at the intersection of these two clusters of forces. The evolution of work organization reflects *both* technical exigencies and opportunities for improved efficiency *and* the social imperatives associated with the prevailing patterns of ownership and control (property rights and the associated decision-making rights). Taking this as my starting point, the following sections argue that technical and social forces impart distinct and often contradictory tendencies to the evolution of work organization. The trends we actually observe reflect the relative strength and interacting effects of these tendencies.

In order to describe these trends with any precision, we first need to define more specifically what we mean by "work organization." As I will use the term, work organization has two main components, the skills required of workers in their jobs and the relations that coordinate activity in these jobs.[21]

- *Skills*: Work organization is, first, a matter of how tasks are organized into jobs. From the workers' point of view, this aggregation defines the skills they need in their relationship to the objects of their work and to the tools they use. Skills vary in many concrete ways: We can distinguish manual from cognitive skills, technical from social skills, task skills from learning skills, etc. Abstracting from these concrete differences, skill can be reduced to, and measured by, required education and training time.[22]
- *Work Relations*: Work organization is, second, the fabric of relations that link different jobs and workers. This too is a multifaceted notion. Broadly we can distinguish three key dimensions of work relations: relations that workers have with others in their immediate work unit, the horizontal coordination of this unit with other work units, and the vertical authority relations by which these units' activities are coordinated and controlled. Abstracting from these concrete differences, work relations are often reduced to, and measured by, autonomy. I will argue below, however, that autonomy is merely the converse of interdependence and that the latter concept gives us a better vantage point from which to assess changes in work relations.

The Impact of Technical Forces

Let us take first the technical forces acting on work organization and identify some of the tendencies that can be attributed to them. (We will return in the next section to the impact of the social forces.) By mobilizing science and technology in the service of greater instrumental rationality and improved efficiency, modern industry progressively transformed both the skills and the relations components of work organization. Even though the rate of change varied greatly across firms and industries, I think we can advance some fairly robust generalizations concerning the overall direction of these transformations during the twentieth century.

In a nutshell, these technical forces pushed in the direction of a progressive upgrading of skill requirements and a progressive loss of autonomy through a broadening and tightening of the web of interdependencies in work relations. This generalization does not apply to all cases. Some forms of technical change created low-skill and isolated machine-tending or ancillary jobs, but these appear to have been exceptions to the broader pattern.

The Impact of Technical Forces on Skill Requirements

The main effect of technical forces on skill requirements was a gradual shift upwards in the level of education and training required in most jobs. First, technological change over the last century led to a shift of jobs out of manual occupations and into occupations that, on average, had higher skill requirements, most notably technical, professional, and managerial occupations. Second, skill requirements increased for most individual occupations, both manual and nonmanual. The breadth of jobs typically narrowed (i.e., specialization increased), but the associated deskilling effect was in most cases outweighed by greater depth of knowledge. Such seems to be the most plausible interpretation of the general increase in educational and training requirements found in most occupations. Notwithstanding the recent disturbing trend toward a polarization of incomes and wealth, the skill requirements of jobs themselves have not been polarizing but have been gradually increasing across the board. There are some exceptions to this generalization, and there remain lots of very-low-skill jobs in the United States, but these are proportionately fewer today than fifty or one hundred years ago.[23]

Viewed more concretely, skills requirements evolved from manual to cognitive and social, reinforcing the need for higher levels of education. Automation contributed to the "abstraction" of work (Adler 1986; Zuboff 1988). The task of "direct" labor—in manufacturing, but also in activities such as drafting—shifted from direct contact with the raw material to indirect contact via complex technical systems. The associated skills changed from manual and tactile to the intellectual mastery of symbolic representations and of mental models of the production process. With this shift, experience-based training became relatively less important and formal education relatively more so. The growth of indirect tasks within manufacturing and service industries (staff roles in engineering, accounting, etc.) and of high-end "symbolic analyst" services (law, consulting, etc.) reflected this abstraction of work and contributed to the corresponding rise in education requirements.

Social skills also grew in importance. First, as we will discuss further below, teamwork became more common in both manufacturing and service sectors. Second, the growth of service industries meant that a growing number of employees found themselves in direct contact with customers. Education— if not the content, then the associated personal and interpersonal disciplines— helped large masses of workers acquire the interaction skills needed in such settings.

The Impact of Technical Change on Work Relations

The main effect of technical change on work relations was to further encourage a longer-term shift away from autonomy and toward greater interdependence. As indicated above, I believe that a focus on autonomy, while informative, has the limitation of being backward-looking. It allows us to discern what was lost, but it does not give us a conceptual vantage point from which to identify the evolving forms of interdependence that replaced the lost autonomy.[24]

As noted earlier, if we go back 150 or 200 years, a large proportion of workers were independent producers, either on small farms or in small artisanal shops. By 1900, most people were no longer economically independent; nevertheless, in their day-to-day work, they often made their own decisions about what to do, when, and how. Over the subsequent decades, the scientific management revolution and its systems rationalization extensions swept through most of U.S. industry. As a result, workers no longer controlled their own work, and control was increasingly lodged in a network of specialists and managers and embodied in technology and procedures (thus the rising administrative/production ratios noted earlier).

In this process, the autonomy of workers to choose their own tools and procedures was progressively eroded. For most of our species' existence, tools were sufficiently rudimentary that they could be created by the individual worker or workgroup for their own use. Over the past century or so, by contrast, tools have increasingly taken the form of complex systems, and an extensive social division of labor has made tool development the object of distinct industries. Moreover, under a more extensive division of labor within the individual firm, formalized procedures—also developed by specialist experts, often located outside the focal firm[25]—typically tell the worker how to use these tools.

Interdependence thus overtook autonomy in all three dimensions: the individual work unit, the horizontal relations between work units, and the vertical relations within and across work units. Let us review these in turn.

Within the individual work unit, the evolution of interdependence appears to have been more complex. In a first phase, the individual replaced the group as the basic unit of work organization. Scientific management sought to eliminate work gangs so as to give management more control over the individual's work. The effort appears to have been successful. Time-and-motion analysis and other forms of job analysis proliferated in both manufacturing- and service-sector work during most of the first half of the century (Baron, Dobbin, and Jennings 1986). In a second phase, the human relations movement taught managers to be attentive to the individual employee and to their social relations at and outside work. On these foundations, the later phase of sociotechnical systems theory helped popularize teams (Pasmore, Francis, and Haldeman 1982). These teams were rather different in their responsibilities than traditional teams or pre–scientific-management gangs. They were more likely to choose their own leaders, participate in setting work goals, do their own quality control, meet to solve problems, do routine maintenance, assign daily tasks, and schedule time away from work (Appelbaum and Berg 2000, 126).

While social forces clearly play a role in this evolution (I return to them below) and management fads too (traditional arrangements are sometimes simply relabeled), technical forces appear also to have contributed to this shift from the individual to the work team. In places such as banks, insurance companies, manufacturing plants, and chemical refineries, automation eliminated many stand-alone manual tasks, which left workers with the new role of overseeing large-scale automated systems, and in many cases, this system-controller role could more effectively be played as a team. Moreover, in many industries, an increasingly demanding competitive environment forced an acceleration in the rate of change in task content, and it often became technically more efficient to give groups of workers primary responsibility for working out how they would adjust to these changes rather than forcing them to wait for a staff specialist to reorganize their tasks for them. This enrichment of workers' tasks is the kernel of truth to the proposition advanced by Woodward and echoed by Helfgott (1988, chap. 10) that automation leads to a shift from mechanistic to organic structures within firms.

The second dimension of work relations is the horizontal relationship between specialized units. The trend over the last century was toward ever-greater interdependence in these relationships, as each unit became increasingly specialized and therefore dependent on a larger number of other units. Here, too, technical factors were important drivers. As knowledge accumulated, its progress naturally created new specializations, and the effective use of this new knowledge required new coordination efforts. Reflecting the broader contextual changes over the twentieth century discussed above, this process was played out in four successively broader spheres: within firms, between firms, between industry and the public sector, and between countries. Let us briefly review them in turn.

- *Within Firms:* There were a growing number of specialized skills needed to cope with an increasingly complex world. New job titles proliferated, and new functional departments were created. Sometimes the best way to ensure teamwork between these specialized skills was to group them in one work unit. Often, it was more sensible to organize them into specialized units and establish appropriate coordination mechanisms between the units. In either case, interdependence was both broadened and tightened.[26]

  More generally, firms introduced a panoply of organizational mechanisms aimed at ensuring closer coordination. As discussed in standard organization theory texts (e.g., Daft 1989; Mintzberg 1979), these mechanisms included hierarchy, standards, plans and schedules, and mutual adjustment.[27] In their more elaborate form—which emerged in the systems rationalization phase—they included overlay, matrix reporting hierarchies, in which individuals and units report simultaneously to more than one manager. This enables coordination in more than a single dimension, such as function, product, and geography. Firms also introduced sophisticated planning and control tools for a host of different types of temporary organization forms: project teams, task forces, etc. The history of work organization in the twentieth century was in considerable measure a history of increasingly sophisticated coordination and control mechanisms.[28]

- *Between Firms:* Firms became increasingly dependent on suppliers for specialized inputs of machinery, components, and services. The recent trend toward outsourcing is only partly fad; it is also the continuation of a long-term trend toward the increasing specialization of industries. Indeed, most of the growth of the service sector over the century was due to firms outsourcing tasks to more knowledgeable and efficient specialist service firms. A broad range of mechanisms developed—from product standards to partnership-style relationships—to ensure cost-effective coordination with such specialized supplier firms. Workers increasingly found themselves interacting directly with suppliers and customers.

- *Between Industry and the Public Sector:* Firms were increasingly dependent on noncorporate suppliers for access to scientific and technological information. One manifestation was the growing interconnection of high technology industry and university researchers. Another was the growing frequency with which workers enrolled in community college courses to learn the latest production techniques and technologies.

- *Between Regions:* Over the longer period, the United States in particular, and the world economy in general, also saw growing interdependence across regional and national boundaries.[29] Interregional trade and investment links grew more numerous. Not surprisingly, trade issues and adjudicating bodies naturally appeared ever more frequently on the front pages of our newspapers. And workers were increasingly likely to find themselves talking to a visitor from an overseas sister plant, supplier, or customer.[30]

The third dimension of work relations is the vertical structure of authority. Clearly, this structure is strongly influenced by the second set of forces—the social structure—which we will examine in the following section. But this authority structure also has a properly technical aspect. The function of management in the capitalist firm is not only (exploitative) command but also (productive) coordination. Under the impact of technical forces, this dimension of work relations also witnessed progressive differentiation and growing integration.

Three forces that encourage vertical differentiation are worth highlighting:

- As the knowledge embedded in specialized economic units accumulated, hierarchies of expertise formed. Thus, even where the role of exploitative command was minimal, complex vertical relations emerged. In consulting, accounting, and law firms, for example, junior associates report to, and rely on guidance from, senior associates, who in turn have a similar relationship to junior partners, who in turn have a similar relationship to senior partners. Similar hierarchies characterize other knowledge-intensive operations, such as scientific research and engineering.
- Not only technical expertise but also, properly, managerial expertise grew in importance as the complexity of business management techniques grew. Professional training for managers grew in importance. To be sure, this training was partly for credentialing and screening, but it was also for the technical skills needed of both individual contributors and managers in finance, accounting, marketing, operations, and the other business functions.
- Moreover, to the extent that the firm incorporated a growing number of specialized units within itself, it needed more middle managers to coordinate between the units.

Against these forces, some observers argue that the accelerating rate of change and the growing complexity and uncertainty of the business environment have recently encouraged the decentralization of decision making within firms and a concomitant delayering of the organization chart. Compelling evidence of any widespread trend to delayering is, however, lacking. Moreover, just as with autonomy in horizontal coordination, the hypothesis of delayering in vertical structure is probably ill-conceived. Operating units may well require greater decision-making power to deal with their increasingly complex and uncertain tasks, but this increase in decision making seems to have taken place within a broader organizational context within which higher levels of the organization set many of the key parameters (in March and Simon's [1958]) terms, decision premises). In a non-zero-sum view of power (as articulated by Tannenbaum and Kahn 1957, for example), we would say that both lower and higher levels saw their effective power increase.

The more plausible generalization is, therefore, that the growing differentiation of the vertical authority structure required, in turn, increasingly intensive forms of vertical coordination and integration, both within and across the corporation's business units:

- Within work teams, employee involvement was increasingly valued as a means by which to ensure operations flexibility and quality and performance improvement. This involvement in turn required extensive supervisory support—smaller, not larger, spans of control (Gittell, forthcoming).
- Within individual businesses, Appelbaum and Berg (2000, 130) find that even in so-called self-directed team settings, more than 85 percent of workers communicate daily or weekly with managers in their unit and 43 percent with managers outside their unit. Moreover, such communication is more, rather than less, frequent in self-directed team settings compared to traditional work settings. It is no less frequent in highly automated steel than less automated apparel.
- Across units within the larger corporation, planning and control systems grew in sophistication. The administrative burden they represented led larger firms to decentralize wherever possible, most notably in the form of the multidivisional corporation. In general, however, these divisions shared important interdependencies, and their relations could therefore not be simply reduced to market-style interfaces. On the contrary, the planning and control systems of multidivisional firms grew increasingly sophisticated in their recognition of these horizontal linkages, in the forms of matrix management, core competencies, and horizontal strategies.

- In general, lower levels of the organization appear to have been drawn into more active roles in the planning cycle—in contrast with the earlier mix of more autocratic forms of planning and lack of planning.[31] This trend seems to have characterized both relations between work teams and their supervisors within individual organizational units and relations between the higher levels of the management hierarchy. Corporations learned to exploit the autonomous strategic learning of business units (Burgelman 1983). Even in the top-down form of strategy process, lower levels of management appear to have played an increasingly active role.

In sum, the vertical dimension of work organization saw three simultaneous changes: (a) increased centralization of power—insofar as fewer decisions were taken in complete autonomy by lower levels of the authority hierarchy; (b) increased participation—insofar as lower levels came to have more influence on decisions; and (c) reduced centralization of operational decision making—insofar as formalized decision rules allowed higher levels to delegate operational decisions to lower levels without loss of control.

The Impact of Social Forces

So far, I have argued that technical forces shaping the evolution of work organization pushed in the direction of skill upgrading and broader interdependence in work relations. But what about the other set of forces shaping work organization—the social forces? These social forces can, of course, be analyzed under many different lenses. For the purposes of the present chapter, however, I will concentrate on the generally capitalist character of the structure of ownership and control in the U.S. economy. If our task is to understand the main lines of evolution over a whole century of change in work organization, this structure is arguably the most pertinent. It is "deeper"—in the sense of deep versus surface structure in structural linguistics, and of Bhaskar's (1978) realist theory of science—than other dimensions of social structure and is therefore likely to be relatively more important in shaping broad trends. The basic social structure of our modern capitalist society can be summarized under two broad headings: competition between firms and a wage-based employment relationship within firms.[32] What do we know about the nature and impact of the trends engendered by these structures?

First, as a result of these two basic features, capitalist firms are far more aggressive than enterprises in precapitalist societies in the rational efficiency-oriented development and use of science and technology. All the tendencies attributed to technical forces in the discussion above were reinforced by (a) the pressure created by competition, (b) the opportunities created by the centralization of power within the firm, and (c) the progressive displacement of custom by instrumental rationality in the service of maximum return on investment.

Second, under the pressure of market competition between firms and the structure of managerial authority within firms, each of the trends in work organization we have noted so far—trends that were largely benign—was partially undermined and significantly distorted. The reason is not hard to see. The wage relationship reflects a society divided into employees and owners. Managers owe ultimate allegiance to the firm's owners. Under the pressure of competition, and independently of their personal attitudes and values, managers are therefore sometimes forced to impose owners' interests against workers.' The vagaries of product, factor, and financial markets sometimes encourage or force firms to lay off employees, and the brutal, unforgiving nature of competition forces firms to cut costs wherever possible. In this process, stakeholders other than owners—most notably, subordinate employees—are often short-changed.

Views differ on the extent of divergence of workers' and owners' interests. The labor process theorists' neo-Marxist assumption is that workers' interests are essentially and universally divergent from managers.' By contrast, the unitarist (Guest 1989) and pragmatic reformist views (Kaufman, chap. 4 of this volume) hold that "there can be some degree of mutuality of interest between workers and employers, as both benefit from work restructuring. Management can gain increased efficiency by allowing workers more satisfying jobs and greater autonomy" (Helfgott 1992, 18). Of the two views, the latter seems empirically far more plausible. However, there remains an important kernel of truth in the neo-Marxist view: It is surely a hallmark of the capitalist form of social organization that this mutuality of interests is realized only intermittently rather than being a regularity that is systematically reproduced.[33]

Take skill upgrading: Even though their long-run competitive success requires skill upgrading, firms are often loath to invest in the required training because workers could take the resulting "human capital" out the door to a better-paying job down the street.[34] Moreover, skilled workers typically have more power than unskilled workers, and therefore managers' control over the shop or office floor is easier to ensure when jobs require less skill and employees are more easily replaced. Managers were thus often tempted to dummy down equipment and job responsibilities and to deskill work. More advanced tools afford the opportunity to leverage others' expertise in the performance of one's work; but since these tools are deployed as the property of the firm's owners, their design, selection, and implementation often served owners' interests at the expense of workers. Since the employment contract is "incomplete"—leaving managers the task of ensuring that the capacity to work is effectively translated into work effort—tools are often used to coerce more effort from recalcitrant workers rather than to enable committed workers to better master their tasks—even though the latter approach is often more technically productive. Some of the cases documented by the labor process researchers are convincing in this regard.

Similarly with work relations: Interdependence does not always take a collaborative form. The asymmetry of power between employees and owners and the competitive relations between firms mean that interdependence often takes the form of asymmetrical and oppressive dependence. We can see this tension in all three dimensions of work relations; again, let us review them in turn.

First, managers under short-term cost-reduction pressure often manipulate teamwork to create peer pressure. Peer pressure can temporarily improve productivity, even though it can be debilitating in the longer term. Under pressure for short-term results, managers often find the temptation of such manipulation irresistible. When workers accept team responsibility for work outcomes, they have to negotiate among themselves a new balance of individual autonomy and team authority. The search for that delicate balance can easily be derailed, and the authority of the team has frequently turned into a nasty war of worker against worker (see, for example, Barker 1999).

Second, under the pressure of competition, horizontal specialization can degenerate into adversarial rivalry. Supplier firms' interests do not always align with customers,' and when push comes to shove, potentially fruitful partnerships often fragment under the pressure of competitive rivalry. Horizontal relationships within the firm are also vulnerable to the pressures of competition—in particular, competition among managers for promotion opportunities. In some circumstances, horizontal interdependence appears to workers as mutually beneficial teamwork; but in other circumstances, it is turned into a weapon against workers—who, like managers, must compete against each other in the external and internal labor markets. Outsourcing and globalization are often used as a threat in order to "divide and conquer" (Bronfenbrenner 2000).

Third and most obviously, the function of the vertical hierarchy in a capitalist firm is double: a productive function of coordinating activities and providing specialized expertise and an exploitative function of squeezing more effort from employees. A form of society such as ours—in which workers' and other stakeholders' interests are structurally subordinate to those of owners'—constantly reproduces conditions conducive to a slide from collaborative hierarchy toward the exploitative, autocratic, command-and-control form of hierarchy.

The net effect of these various social forces is that work organization and HR/IR policies attempt to bridge objectives that are sometimes incompatible. To take a simple example, the firm may need a high level of worker commitment to quality and innovation but may find itself in a situation where a sizable proportion of the labor force must be laid off and where senior management acts autocratically in proceeding with these layoffs. This potential incompatibility is at once trivial and fundamental. It is trivial, because most decision making involves trade-offs. But it is fundamental too because the nature of the trade-offs in question here makes any compromise inherently unstable (Hyman 1987). The firm is simultaneously a purposive community and a structure of domination and exploitation. Managers' values may incline them to privilege one facet or the other, but the reality of capitalist competition imposes a double bind from which no management, no matter how enlightened, can escape.

Work and Workers at the Intersection of Technical and Social Forces

In a nutshell, then, work organization has been buffeted between the longer-term technical-productive advantages of upgrading and collaboration and the shorter-term socioeconomic advantages of deskilling and autocratic domination. What do we know about the resulting trends? These trends, I submit, reflect a basic asymmetry: The technical forces progress in a cumulative manner, but the social forces reproduce a relatively stable basic social structure.[35] The result appears to have been that (a) the technically driven tendencies toward upgrading skills and broadening interdependence prevailed in the aggregate and over the longer term of the twentieth century, but (b) the social forces left their mark on this evolution, simultaneously accelerating and retarding it, making its progress sometimes too slow and other times too rapid, and leaving numerous small and several huge pockets of backwardness.[36]

Moreover, even the progressive aspects of this evolution were not without their downsides for workers. Upgrading skills and broadening interdependence tend to undermine established communities of solidarity, constantly putting workers and unions on the defensive, and they do this in several ways. Upgrading often replaces old union craft workers with young non-union technicians. Teamwork often replaces clearly delineated supervisory accountability with diffuse team accountability. New patterns of horizontal specialization undermine old bargaining units. New collaborative hierarchies ask unions to become partners, even though the need for tough-minded adversarial bargaining has hardly diminished.

These multifarious changes in work organization did not only affect the external conditions under which workers work; they also affected workers' values and their social identity. As E.P. Thompson argued relative to an earlier phase of (British) industrial history, the new conditions of industry required "new disciplines, new incentives, and a new human nature upon which these incentives could bite effectively" (1967, 57). What effects have the twentieth century's changes in work organization wrought on workers' "human nature"? In the absence of compelling evidence, I offer four conjectures.

First, upgrading and interdependence progressively raised workers' level of intellectual sophistication and broadened their worldview. Education levels rose and communication and travel costs fell. People experienced an increasingly global web of interdependence in their work:

- As noted in the first IRC report: "It is evident from study observations that work group horizons are now broader in many instances, because any one segment of work is no longer limited to a group of men doing similar jobs. The 'group' today is an assembly of men working relatedly on a complex of jobs in a department or on a shift, and new and different types of individual interaction occur" (Beaumont and Helfgott 1964, 232–33).
- Moreover, this "group" was not restricted to the peers within the firm: In their work practice, workers experienced a growing interdependence across firms. In the words of one worker I interviewed at NUMMI:

> In 23 years working for GM, I never met with a supplier. I never even knew their names except for the names on the boxes. Now, we're working with suppliers to improve our products. Workers sit down with our engineers and managers and the supplier's people and we analyze defects and develop improvement proposals. We even do that with the equipment vendors. Stuff like that gives us a better perspective on how our jobs relate to the whole process.

And more: The "group of men" referred to by Beaumont and Helfgott often evolved into a group in which men and women collaborated. At century's end, gender segregation was still pervasive at the level of individual narrowly defined occupations (Bielby and Baron 1986), but the growth of women's labor-force participation rates over the century nevertheless drew increasing proportions of men and women into mixed-gender interdependent work relations.

These various changes sometimes undermined old sources of worker identity and solidarity, but they also created broader solidarities and thus greater potential for enlightened action on a broader scale.

Second, changes in work organization reshaped workers' subjective identity. Lewchuk (1993) describes the changes wrought in the early days of the auto industry to one of the most sophisticated of these identities, that of the nineteenth-century artisan. Norms of masculinity among these artisans emphasized the value of independence in the work process. As Montgomery put it, the "manly" worker "refused to cower before the foreman's glare—in fact, often would not work at all when a boss was watching" (1979, 13–14). Once Ford had put in place an extensive division of labor and the assembly line, management worked assiduously to inculcate new norms. These norms emphasized values such as hard work under monotonous conditions, contributions to the creation of useful products, a fraternal community of Ford employees, and provision materially and spiritually for one's family. These values were actively propagated by Ford's infamous Sociology Department. Lewchuck marshals evidence, albeit fragmentary and anecdotal, that the combination of work experience and management indoctrination did indeed lead to the progressive, if partial and refracted, internalization of these values by workers and to corresponding change in workingmen's identity. I would add that the new norms were perhaps all the more significant—and simultaneously more difficult to propagate—because they emphasized values of interdependence and other-directedness rather than autonomy and self-regard—and thus were marked as feminine rather than masculine.[37] Under the impact of these various forces—plus, surely, the effect of the feminist movement itself—traditional values evolved and new identities emerged. One NUMMI worker described his personal evolution in these terms:

> I wish you could talk to the guys' wives about the changes they've seen [in workers' behavior between the GM-Fremont days and NUMMI]. I was a typical macho horse's ass when I worked at GM-Fremont. My typical line coming home was: "Work sucks, so get my dinner and get out of my way until I cool off." Now I'm much more of a partner around the house. I help wash the dishes and take the clothes hamper out to the washer because I'm so used to working cooperatively with my team at the plant. I bring a spirit of cooperation home with me rather than dump my work frustrations all over my family. [Adler 1993, 148–49]

Third, upgrading and interdependence made workers increasingly intolerant of autocratic management in firms. As Roy Helfgott put it: "I do not want to posit a strict doctrine of technological determinism, for other factors are at play in advancing new approaches to work organization. . . . [But the] new technology, which requires greater cooperation among all members of the workforce, helps undermine authoritarianism" (1988, 78). Protests against autocratic management are hardly new; they were numerous even among the immigrant workforce of the early twentieth century. Indeed, IRC owes its existence in large measure to such protests by the largely immigrant workers of the minefields of Colorado.[38] Such struggles were not, however, the norm: Outside the artisan category, fatalistic acquiescence was probably more typical. Consider this story from Ford in about 1915, as recalled by a Ford office worker, for what it tells us about this acquiescence:

> Despite a safety device, a foreign worker cut off his finger at his machine. Plant superintendent P. E. Martin and his assistant Sorenson wanted the worker to show them how it happened so the device could be corrected. The workman showed them and cut off another finger. "He understood," Brown related, "they actually wanted him to demonstrate how he cut the tip of his finger off." [Meyer 1981, 172]

Such heart-rending premodern subservience is unthinkable in today's auto plants (see, for example, Hamper 1992). Workers became less tolerant of autocratic management, and notwithstanding the recent decades' decline in union power, the twentieth century witnessed a corresponding democratization of workplace relations.

And finally, workers grew increasingly intolerant of the economic insecurity that is characteristic of the worker's status in a capitalist economy. As one of the founders of IRC, Clarence Hicks, wrote:

> Present-day managements have come to the realization that the security of the employee is a matter of mutual and not solely individual concern. The repercussions of insecurity in human psychology are manifold. In a day when the co-ordination of human effort in industry has reached an extremely elaborate state, the fear of lost income and dependency has a costly effect on the efficiency of operations. Further, the type of employee most effective in the modern corporation is just that which values security most dearly. Human personality is not divided into watertight compartments. Foresight, reliability, and initiative in protecting one's family and dependents are the same foresight, reliability, and initiative that make one a valuable employee. [1941, 98]

The most recent decade saw a decline in employment stability—albeit a modest one and for men only (Schultze 2000)—and arguably younger workers today are relatively less concerned with job security and more concerned with career opportunity. Foresight, reliability, and initiative are thus perhaps now being played out on a broader stage. But there is no evidence that workers have become more accepting of their economic vulnerability.[39]

Conclusion

The puzzle with which this chapter began was how to incorporate into a single narrative several contradictory but partially valid views of the long-term evolution of work organization. The first part of the chapter laid out some of the pieces of the puzzle; the second part proposed a solution. I argued that, on the one hand, the technical exigencies pushing toward higher skills and broader interdependence made employee commitment an increasingly important condition for effective operations; on the other hand, the capitalist social structure worked sometimes to reinforce, but sometimes to undermine, that very commitment. I also argued that there was a basic asymmetry between the technical and the social forces, and that this asymmetry explains the dominance of the technical forces in the longer-term trends.

This suggests that the sequence of work organization innovations (discussed in the first part) does not merely represent a pendulum swinging between formal and substantive rationality, between control and commitment. My narrative suggests that hidden beneath this cyclical process, there is an underlying trend toward what we might call collaborative interdependence. Evidence for this underlying trend can be found if we look more carefully at the sequence of innovations:

- Note, first, that in the sequence of normative approaches—from welfare work to human relations to employee involvement—there is a clear shift from the earlier reliance on paternalism to relatively impersonal, bureaucratic norms of procedural justice, to an emphasis on empowerment and mutual commitment. The quality of commitment sought in each successive wave of substantive-rationality innovation seems to have implied a shift from traditional blind trust to a more modern reflective form of trust (Adler 2001). In its evolution, work organization sought progressively deeper forms of subjective implication of the individual worker.
- Second, the sequence of normative innovations is also notable in engaging progressively more directly with work and work organization: Welfare work did not seek to modify the core of work organization; human relations addressed mainly supervision; EI brought concern for commitment into the heart of work organization.
- Finally, the sequence of control innovations—from scientific management to systems rationalism to re-engineering—seems to have become increasingly hospitable to commitment-oriented variants. Within two or three years of publishing a text that popularized a rather brutally

Figure 11.1   **A Trend Toward Collaborative Interdependence**

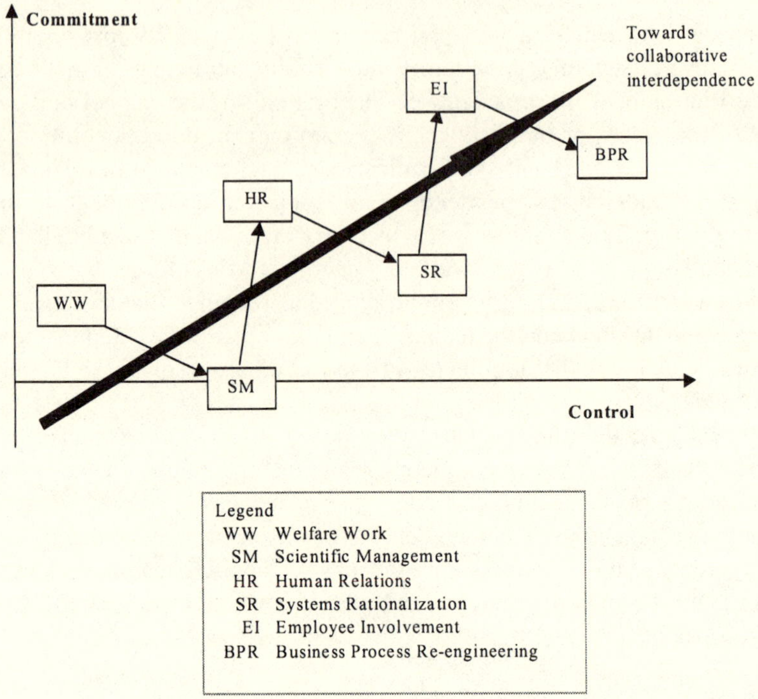

Legend
WW   Welfare Work
SM   Scientific Management
HR   Human Relations
SR   Systems Rationalization
EI   Employee Involvement
BPR   Business Process Re-engineering

coercive method of business process re-engineering (Hammer and Champy 1993), both James Champy and Michael Hammer published new volumes (Champy 1995; Hammer 1996) stressing the importance of the human factor and the need for job redesigns that afford employees greater autonomy. The undeniably autocratic character of much early re-engineering rhetoric and its rapid "softening" compares favorably with more unilateral and enduring forms of domination expressed in post–World War II systems rationalism. It compares even more favorably with the even more unilateral and rigid rhetoric in turn-of-the-century scientific management, which had softened its relations with organized labor only after nearly two decades of confrontation (Nyland 1998).

Synthesizing these observations, we might chart the evolution of innovations not as a pendulum swing but rather as shown in Figure 11.1.

Clearly there is a gap, often a huge one, between the rhetoric of work organization as expressed in management literature and the reality of work organization as experienced by workers. And just as clearly, there is a gap between the emergence of an organizational innovation and its diffusion through industry. However, this long-term evolution of rhetoric and the associated innovations both reflected and reinforced a real trend to greater reliance on consent and trust. It reflected the evolving expectations of an increasingly educated workforce and the evolving needs of increasingly interdependent forms of organization. And it reinforced that trend because the emphasis of commitment progressively legitimized the idea that management authority depends on employee consent.

IRC has been an important contributor in all three rounds of commitment innovations—welfare work, human relations, and EI. The story I propose to tell about the long-term evolution of work organization leads me to conjecture that unitarist HRM approaches such as those promulgated by IRC will continue to wax and wane in popularity but will tend to become more rather than less popular over the long (that is, very long!) period. These approaches, however, appear to encounter a limit in their ability to acknowledge the divergence of interests that is constitutive of the capitalist employment relation—and the resulting limits of any commitment to commitment.

Acknowledgments

This paper has benefited from the comments of Eileen Appelbaum, Rose Batt, Charles Heckscher, Roy Helfgott, Sue Helper, Sandy Jacoby, Bruce Kaufman, Martin Kenney, Tom Kochan, and Paul Thompson. They are not responsible if I didn't pay more heed.

Notes

1. Adapting Littler's (1982) account of the British case.
2. The subcontractors were sometimes parents who employed family members, which was particularly common in the earlier years of the 4a category. Sometimes the subcontractors were craftsmen, especially in the early years of the 4b category. And sometimes the subcontractors were gang bosses who functioned as small-scale capitalists, which was particularly common in the 4c category.
3. Textile mills had seen a jump in size earlier in the century, but their size then stabilized. By 1900, steel, locomotives, and electrical and agricultural machinery industries had much larger plants, with several employing more than five thousand workers (see Nelson 1975).
4. Unless otherwise noted, the supporting data for this section come from *Historical Statistics* (1975) and *Statistical Abstract* (various years).
5. Here we are discussing what Marx called the "detailed" division of labor—the specialization of tasks within firms, coordinated ex ante by managers—as distinct from the "social" division of labor—the specialization of firms and industries, coordinated ex post by market exchange.
6. Quoted from U.S. House of Representatives, "Investigation by a Select Committee of the House of Representatives Relative to the Causes of the General Depres-

sion in Labor and Business; and as to Chinese Immigration" (Washington, D.C.: GPO, 1879), p. 429, in *The Position of the Worker in American Society 1865–1896* by Irwin Yellowitz (Englewood Cliffs, N.J.: Prentice-Hall, 1969), p. 88.

7. Note, however, that aspirations to economic independence were still significant at mid-century. In Chinoy's 1946–51 study of the GM-Oldsmobile plant in Lansing, Michigan, forty-eight of the sixty-two auto-assembly workers interviewed answered in the affirmative the question "Have you ever thought of getting out of the shop?" Of these forty-eight, thirty-one said their goal was a business of their own, and a further six wanted to become independent farmers (Chinoy 1992, 82). Only six aimed for other wage employment. Even the weekly paper published by the CIO unions in the city frequently carried stories about autoworkers who had ventured into small business (ibid., 4).

8. Whereas many writers assert that Taylor's ideas on functional foremen were antithetical to the doctrine of unity of command and were therefore rarely implemented, Stephen Meyer seems closer to the truth when he writes: "In the new Ford plant [circa 1917], however, the foreman's duties were more circumscribed, and he had assistant foremen, sub-foremen (straw bosses), clerks, inspectors and others to help him. . . . They directed, recorded, or examined the work of others. In fact, each occupation reflected Taylor's notions of 'functional management' and the division of the foreman's job into specific functional tasks" (1981, 54). Taylor's proposal was to divide the traditional tasks of the foremen into these distinct positions. This departed from the well-tested precept of unity of command, but this difficulty was overcome with articulation of the line/staff model by Gulick and Urwick (1937, chaps. I, II).

9. Data from Maddison (1995) indicate that the stock of machinery and equipment per worker increased from $4,115 in 1890 to $6,932 in 1913 and to $39,636 in 1992 (in constant 1990 international dollars).

10. The 1964 study was based on interviews and quantitative data from forty-six establishments (in thirty-six companies) selected as representative of "operating situations where major technological innovation had occurred" (Beaumont and Helfgott 1964, 13) in manufacturing, transportation, and public utilities. The later study (Helfgott 1988) was based on case studies of the impact of computer-based technologies on sixteen companies in a range of relatively high-technology and capital-intensive manufacturing industries.

11. The charismatic basis of authority seems to have been a perennial theme in the management literature, expressed in the continuing interest in leadership as something distinct from (and often superior to) management.

12. Debate continues over the validity of Kondratieff's hypothesis. For the present purposes, I rely only on the rough periodization it offers.

13. It is interesting to note that there is arguably a similar, but inverse, cycle in British industrial relations since the mid-nineteenth-century: Ramsay (1977) argues that worker participation schemes have waxed when employers felt their prerogatives challenged—primarily in more prosperous phases—and waned when managers felt their power was more entrenched—primarily in economic downswings.

14. Feiss's one major alteration of the Taylor system was also motivated by his interest in labor: A standard Taylorist approach to apparel manufacturing would have led him to introduce helpers to move materials around the plant, thus allowing the sewing machine operators to focus on their relatively higher-skilled tasks; but Feiss worried that this restriction on the movements of the operators would create boredom.

15. Osterman's surveys in 1992 and 1997 are described in Osterman (1999). Both

were representative samples of for-profit private-sector establishments with more than fifty employees and asked respondents about practices pertaining to core employees, that is, employees in the largest occupational grouping. Lawler's survey was of *Fortune* 1000 firms and asked corporate HR executives to estimate the proportion of all employees covered by various practices.

16. In Osterman's survey, the respondents were managers, who may not be the most objective or well informed on these questions. However, the results in Table 11.2 are similar to those obtained from workers themselves in the Quality of Employment Survey (Quinn and Staines 1979).

17. MacDuffie and Kochan (1995) found that newly hired auto-assembly-plant production workers received on average 42 hours of training in their first six months in U.S. firms, 225 hours in Japanese transplants, and 364 hours in Japanese plants. Workers with more than one year's experience received 31 hours in the U.S. companies, 52 in the transplants, and 76 in Japan.

18. In the last decades of the century, however, the trend toward internal recruitment slowed and even went into reverse. Observers noted a proliferation of contingent work and a decline in average job tenure. This decline in average tenure was, however, modest in magnitude and restricted to men. Nevertheless, by 1996, only 9 percent of firms offered employment security assurances to more than 80 percent of their employees—down from 26 percent that offered it to more than 80 percent of their employees in 1987 (Lawler et al. 1998). Public debate about employment security grew in intensity: Some observers interpreted the trends as signs of a shift toward a more dynamic economy, while others saw it as an assertion of unrestrained employer power. The positive import of these changes was difficult to see through the human cost of this insecurity, but this shift also seemed to encourage a broadening of identities. The parochial quality of 1950s-style loyalty—the loyalty of the organization man to the closed community of an individual corporation—was in decline, and two images competed to replace it: a hyperindividualistic "free agency" image and a more professional model of "community of purpose" (Heckscher 1995). HRM ideas about employability were often ambiguous enough to encompass the two competing versions.

19. STS and EI proponents started with the same empirical premises—that deskilling was common and that it led to performance benefits far less frequently than its popularity would suggest. Whereas labor process theorists assumed that the frequency of deskilling called for a structural explanation, the proponents of STS and EI assumed that management could be awakened to the superiority of more humane forms of organization (see Helfgott 1992).

20. A Weberian variant of this second view argues that technical rationality is an important force but is itself a sociocultural phenomenon. To this essentially idealist view, this chapter counterposes the first, more materialist view. A related social constructionist variant of the second view grants that work organization is shaped by technology but argues that technology itself is shaped by the broader social structure. It is easy to show some social influence in specific equipment design choices, but it is an altogether more difficult task to show that social factors determine the broad overall trajectory of technological change. For reasons such as those advanced by Hutchby (2001), I find this latter idea quite implausible, so I will leave it aside in the analysis that follows.

21. Available conceptualizations of work organization are strikingly atheoretical. Organization theory does not offer a concept of work organization per se but focuses

on the dimensions of organization structure that have emerged as important in the history of that field. Mintzberg (1979), for example, distinguishes positions (formalization, specialization, training), superstructure (departmentalization), lateral relations (planning and control, liaison devices), and decision making (vertical and horizontal decentralization). Frenkel and associates (1999) adopt a more topological view and distinguish employment relations (recruiting, training, careers, rewards), control (process and output controls, participation), coworker relations (task interdependence, learning interdependence, informal relations, forms of teamwork), work complexity (theoretical knowledge, creativity, social and analytic skills), and customer relations (duration, affectivity, differentiation, standardization). There is a considerable degree of overlap in the substantive areas covered in these different conceptualizations, as with those found elsewhere in the literature. The one striking discrepancy is organization theory's ignorance of compensation systems.

22. Skills also differ in symbolic ways. Most notably, skills are often gendered; for instance, the education and training time required for work designated as women's are often grossly undervalued.

23. Goldin and Katz (1998) review the extensive literature that finds complementarity of skilled labor and capital. They argue that this complementarity is due to two factors. First, it reflects the increase in the ratio of toolmakers (equipment design, manufacture, and maintenance tasks) to tool users—their assumption being that the former's tasks are on average more skilled than the latter's. This raises two problems. First, it is not clear that employment in the two broad families of tasks has evolved in the direction asserted, at least when viewed over the whole economy and clerical and sales occupations are included among tool users. Second, it remains to be shown that skills of the former are in fact generally higher than of the latter. The second reason they give for complementarity is that electrical power replaced many of the least-skilled laborer jobs. The generalization seems plausible, but one wonders why this should be the case. Why technical change has been on average complementary to, rather than a substitute for, skilled labor remains therefore an unresolved puzzle. (For another interesting, but more limited and equally unsatisfying, discussion, see Autor, Levy, and Murnane 2001.) By contrast, it is perhaps easier to see why technical change should tend to broaden interdependencies rather than strengthen autarky. At its core, technical change consists of a progressive extension of rational mastery, and such instrumental rationalization undermines parochial identities, imposing a universal standard of reason where tradition and affect previously dominated people's relations to the material and social world. The social forces discussed in the following section also clearly contribute to the broadening of interdependence: The market undermines particularisms and autarky.

24. In micro-organizational-behavior research, autonomy is often presented as a critical motivating characteristic of jobs—even though the evidence is just as strong that formalization of work procedures reduces stress and increases commitment (see, for example, Rizzo, House, and Lirtzman 1970; Organ and Greene 1981; Jackson and Schuler 1985; Podsakoff, Williams, and Todor 1986). Specialization and the resulting interdependence are assumed to be likely to undermine commitment because they reduce the identity of the worker's task. If interdependence is addressed in this research, it is usually only within the work team, and the focus is once again on autonomy—now, the autonomy of the self-directed work team. Macro–organization theory offers a richer range of concepts for characterizing interdependence and the associated coordination mechanisms—see below.

25. These procedures may originate within the firm, but they can also be purchased, as when firms buy copyrighted forms and procedure manuals. They may also enter the firm as recommended administrative procedures that accompany the purchase of equipment. In more highly institutionalized settings (in the sense of Scott 1995), they may enter the firm in the form of professional norms and regulatory requirements.

26. One example comes from the auto industry's experience of automation (Meyer 1999). Like the nineteenth-century craftsman, the skilled worker in the typical auto engine plant of the 1950s was "far removed from direct production and had considerable autonomy in and control over their work routines." In more highly automated engine plants, by contrast, where continuity of operations was crucial, the skilled maintenance worker became "tightly bound to the assembly line." Further support for the general proposition comes from steel finishing lines in the 1990s. Gant, Ichniowski, and Shaw (1999, 2000) find that in the higher-performing lines, workers' communication networks were considerably denser both within the production worker team and among these workers and managers, staff, and support people. Support also comes from Appelbaum and Berg's (2000, 130) analysis that finds that about a third of their sample of workers in steel, apparel, and medical electronics communicated at least weekly with technical experts outside their workgroup. The ratio was higher in more technologically complex medical electronics than in steel or apparel, and it was higher in settings with self-directed and off-line teams than in settings with more traditional work organization.

27. J.D. Thompson (1967) discusses *types* of interdependence (pooled, sequential, and reciprocal) and the corresponding mechanisms of coordination (standards, plans, and mutual adjustment, respectively), but he pays little attention to the *degree* of interdependence (to the fact that operations may not be coordinated well or coordinated at all) or to the *scope* of interdependence (the scale of operations and the number of people being coordinated).

28. Looking at this evolution through the lens of autonomy, some authors privilege the role of mutual adjustment because this seems to restore autonomy to operating units relative to hierarchical superiors. This, however, is inconsistent with the argument of J.D. Thompson (1967). According to Thompson, the main coordination mechanisms form a Guttman scale: Pooled interdependence relies on standards, where sequentially interdependent operations use plans *and* standards and reciprocally interdependent operations use mutual adjustment *and* plans *and* standards. Self-managed teams, therefore, typically find themselves deeply enmeshed in highly bureaucratic structures (hierarchy, standards, plans) that ensure coordination *across* teams. The kernel of truth to the autonomy thesis is that mutual adjustment requires of individuals and groups, even thus enmeshed, a higher degree of subjective engagement in the coordination task.

29. Within the United States, growing interdependence is evidenced in the growth of interregional labor mobility and the convergence of wage rates across regions. The United States' growing integration into the global economy is evidenced by the growth of exports as a percent of GDP: from 2.5 percent in 1870 to 3.7 percent in 1913 and 8.2 percent in 1992 (Maddison 1995, 38). At a more global level, Lindert and Williamson (2001) mobilize a broad range of data to argue that the degree of integration of the global economy first grew between 1820 and 1914, then regressed between 1914 and 1950, and then grew again between 1950 and 2000. The overall result, they argue, was that commodity price gaps between continents fell some 92

percent and capital markets progressed 60 percent of the way from complete segmentation to global integration.

30. A word on the impact of this globalization on work organization: The argument of this chapter is framed in terms of the United States; one might counter, however, that the progressive features that I identify in the evolution of work organization within the United States may have come at the expense of a degradation of conditions in other countries, in particular less-developed trading partners. Or alternatively, one might argue that past improvements within the United States are being reversed by current globalization trends. I doubt that either argument bears scrutiny. In general, it has been the less-skilled jobs that have gone overseas. This has had terrible effects on the unemployment and wage levels of those less-skilled U.S. workers thrown into competition with workers in low-wage regions. But not all the effects are negative. First, the jobs created overseas are usually more highly skilled and better paid than the alternatives available for workers in those countries. Second, while many U.S. workers have thus lost their jobs and suffered wage cuts, the recent acceleration of globalization appears to have continued to drive in the direction of overall skill upgrading in the United States, and if the adjustment costs are distressingly high for so many workers, it is because our polity has not facilitated this adjustment by socializing its costs.

31. I know of no data that would allow us to test this conjecture. Freeland's (1996) study is probative, but it is difficult to assess the generalizability of GM's early history.

32. To these two features we could plausibly add the critical role of the state (law, regulations) in setting the parameters of competition and of other forms of interaction. If our focus were on the distinctive character of work organization in the United States versus other countries, or on evolution over a shorter time frame, then we would expect to see the state as well as other forces such as politics and ideology—forces closer to the visible surface of social reality—play a more central role in our explanation.

33. Firms have some interest in their reputation as good employers because it attracts higher-quality employees. But reputation is unreliable as a device for holding management to this high road—not only because reputation markets are not well formed, but more fundamentally because profitability (especially over the time horizon relevant to decision makers) can be ensured in many different ways, not all of which require worker commitment.

34. Theoretically, this assertion only applies to general, as distinct from firm-specific, training. But when training aims to prepare workers to use new technologies, it is likely to have a strong general component.

35. I would add two notes concerning this formulation. First, two views have recently come into greater prominence that argue against the idea of cumulative character of technological change: path-dependence theory and the social constructionist view of technology. In the strong version of either of these, technology cannot be said to progress at all. In my opinion, it is only the least plausible components of these views that contradict the broad generalization of cumulative progress. Second, concerning the reproduction of a stable social structure: A more precise formulation would indicate (a) that the social forces tend to reproduce capitalist relations of production on an ever expanding scale and (b) that this reproduction does not exclude some degree of accommodation with subaltern forces when the dominant classes' control is threatened. Keynes was an articulate spokesman for such an accommodation in macroeconomics; IRC represents accommodation in microeconomics.

36. Too slow, as when new technologies could alleviate unsafe or burdensome working conditions but implementation is unprofitable. And too fast, as when technology changes more rapidly than society can absorb the displaced workers. Note that consistent with the previous footnote, this formulation allows social forces to change the rate but not the basic direction of technological change.

37. As Fine (1993) writes: "All the hallmarks of masculinity at the workplace were eradicated by automation, machines, time clocks, as well as new management practices."

38. "Coal mining imposed a degree of vassalage so inconsistent with the American ideal of freedom that resort to arms practically was inevitable. . . . Discipline was maintained by intimidation, and, if need be, by physical assault" (Gitelman 1988, 3). IRC was formed by John D. Rockefeller, Jr., largely in reaction to the massacre at Ludlow in 1914 by government and company-paid militiamen of some 24 men, women, and children striking against despotic conditions in the mining camps run inter alia by Colorado Fuel and Iron Company, of which Rockefeller was the principal shareholder.

39. A 1996 Peter Hart poll found that 83 percent agreed (59 percent strongly) that "average working families have less economic security today because corporations have become too greedy and care more about profits than about being fair and loyal to their employees" (cited in Heckscher 2000).

Section III

Human Resource Management in the
Twenty-First Century

12

HR Today and Tomorrow

Organizational Strategy in Global Companies

Richard A. Beaumont, Carlton D. Becker,
and Sydney R. Robertson

Introduction

To mark its seventy-fifth anniversary, Industrial Relations Counselors, Inc. (IRC) commissioned a study[1] to explore how the human resource (HR) function has changed over time. More importantly, the objective was to illuminate the path ahead. Historically, IRC has been concerned with (and contributed to) ways in which the HR field has shaped and reshaped itself in response to the changing demands of management, business, and the external environment.

Perhaps more than at any other time since IRC helped to give birth to the modern practice of human resource management, businesses are rapidly responding to fundamental changes in the economic, social, and political environment in which business is conducted. Basic organizational structures are being redefined, as are the roles and responsibilities of working people and their relationships at work. It is appropriate, therefore, that we "freeze the frame" to see where the field is at this moment and how it is changing from three viewpoints—those who create HR strategy, those who implement the strategy, and those who are recipients of HR's services.

To that end, in the summer of 2001, the research staff identified and visited ten major multinational companies (see Table 12.1) and interviewed the senior vice presidents of Human Resources, heads of HR at the business-unit level, and senior line executives at both the corporate and business-unit levels.

The companies that participated in the study are large global companies, most headquartered in the United States. In terms of revenues, they are among the 200 largest companies in the world. Because of the way this small but significant sample organizes and operates, it encompasses an interesting ar-

Table 12.1

Study Participants

Alcoa Inc.	International Paper Company
Avon Products, Inc.	Pfizer Inc.
General Motors Corporation	Royal Dutch/Shell Group of Companies
The Goodyear Tire & Rubber Company	Textron Inc.
International Business Machines Corporation	United Parcel Service, Inc.

ray of organizational structures, geographic locations, and product and service mix, which, in turn, requires sophisticated capabilities to respond to the varied HR challenges presented by such a complex set of characteristics. As a result, these companies have highly professional HR leadership known to take leading-edge positions in the field.

The company executives were asked in the interviews to address three main themes: In your company—

- How does HR add value to the business?
- How does HR today differ from HR in the past?
- What will be required of HR in the future, and how should it prepare?

In order to provide some context for our findings, it is helpful to understand the environment in which the HR community, as seen by the interviewees, is operating. Among all companies in the survey sample, change is the order of the day. Underlying this change is the complexity of a global community. Whereas in the past, companies and HR organizations were able to take careful, measured approaches to change, such approaches no longer appear viable. For these companies, evolution as a way of change is unthinkable given the rapid responses required by their businesses as they strive for continued profits in the face of increased competition, talent shortages, increasingly greater government scrutiny and regulations, and volatilities associated with global market conditions.

While some management gurus write of the need for revolutionary change, re-invention, and other dramatic approaches to change, which represent the end of the continuum opposite evolution, we did not find such modes of change as a choice in the study group. If one visualizes this continuum of change as shown in Figure 12.1, the surveyed companies are right of center—in a realm of controlled but rapid change. In light of the many forces to be managed and many uncertainties associated with any course of action, these companies face a difficult challenge: to control the change process and thereby

Figure 12.1 **Continuum of Change**

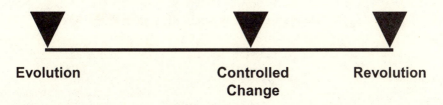

Evolution   **Controlled**   **Revolution**
                                 Change

prevent it from assuming a life of its own, fomenting internal chaos, and, in turn, creating imbalances that require more resources to manage them than are available.

What appears new about the change processes today, as compared to the more or less historical model of measured change, is that companies—including their HR functions—are anticipating future needs and consequently planning and finding ways of controlling their destiny in the face of the challenges and uncertainties. It is in this context then that the role of HR and its leadership is being redefined.

The IRC Study

It is a common generalization that HR no longer functions in a largely administrative capacity, the keeper and controller of a business's HR policies. The findings of our interviews with these constituencies—senior VPs of HR, business-unit HR leaders, and senior line executives—confirm that the HR model today is very different from that traditional model and, in most cases, profoundly so.

Adding Value to the Enterprise

It is significant that the three constituencies interviewed agreed in large part on the sources of HR's value to the business. Table 12.2 illustrates the alignment among their opinions. If the activities in Table 12.2 indicate any critical competencies for HR, they would be change management and leadership, that is, being an active participant in determining both the future course of the business and how HR could further the business objectives.

The senior VPs of HR noted a number of specific ways in which the HR function today adds value, which are listed below along with some illustrative quotes from the interviews:

• *Influences business strategy and plans*
   "My CEO wants me in the room when strategic issues are discussed so

Table 12.2

Alignment of Interviewees' Opinions About HR's Value-Added

Sr. VPs of HR	Line executives	Business-unit HR leaders
• Identify and acquire global talent	• Acquire talent • Assess management capability • Create candidate pools	• Identify HiPo's* on a global basis • Conduct strategic hiring • Lead talent management
• Implement leadership development	• Focus on leadership development	• Develop talent at all levels
• Align HR strategies with the strategic needs across business segments	• Make things work for the business so that business targets can be achieved	• Integrate HR policies and processes with business objectives
• Lead performance improvement efforts throughout the company	• Support the performance management process work	• Make the performance management process
• Provide support to chairman and other members of the management team	• Act as a confidant and advisor to senior management	• Be the organizational conscience
• Lead change efforts	• Lead change efforts are implemented and followed	• Ensure change initiatives

*High-potential candidates

I can help shape the company's plan and comment on the capacity of our human capital to achieve that plan."

- *Leads change*

  "Our company's business model is changing, and there is really only one way to bring about change in an organization—and that's through your people . . . developing and empowering the human capital in the company."

- *Communicates and operationalizes vision and values*

  "We know the people in the company. That is why senior managers come to us for assistance on how to communicate ideas or for opinions on how employees might perceive this. In turn, we work with the vision and values and ensure that they are becoming a part of the company's everyday behaviors . . . assuring a uniform approach, a management style that we all agree on."

- *Creates implementation programs*
  "We know what the needs are, what the issues are, and what programs to deliver."
- *Supports the chairman and management team*
  "Because of our broad exposure to the business and the people, senior management is expecting us to be brutally honest in our communications with them. They really want to know how the employees perceive them. We're also the only ones who can talk to them about their management style."
- *Builds talent assets*
  "I better make sure that [insufficient] talent isn't a roadblock to success. My top priority is to build the bench strength, identify high potentials, and make sure everyone is learning what is needed."
- *Improves organizational effectiveness*
  "We're in a competitive business. If we don't tap into the full creativity of our employees and make this a better place to work, then HR isn't doing its job."
- *Nurtures morale and well-being of the workforce*
  "The trick is to find the right balance between [business and employee] interests so that our workforce is motivated to perform. Paying attention to morale is vital. Without it, we're not going to get the commitment from our people that we need."
- *Interprets emerging social issues*
  "Having a good sense of what is happening allows us to answer important questions impacting our company. For example, what do the demographic studies tell us about our future workforce, or even our current workforce? What is our social responsibility to local communities? How are we going to address the 'graying' of our workforce? . . . [O]n a more global basis, we are confronted with issues around the green movement, religious issues, and country-specific social agendas that may not coincide with our thinking."
- *Delivers fundamental services at/to the highest organizational level*
  "Despite all the talk about being strategic business partners, my manager is still expecting me to deliver fundamental HR services. . . . [For example], I still have to engage in handholding with senior executives so they can get the maximum value from their benefits coverage."

All of the companies studied—even those in old-economy industries where we might expect more conservative tendencies—were faced with the persistent need to change systems, processes, or corporate culture and to develop their leadership capacity. The only distinction was in their approach: to focus change efforts on (1) one area only, (2) some combination of system or process changes, or (3) pursuit of all of the needs cited above.[2]

The list from the senior line executives on HR's value-added was very similar, with a strong emphasis on HR's role as a leader of change and confidant of and advisor to management. However, business-unit line executives were more apt to stress the importance of delivering fundamental HR services (e.g., compensation, staffing) efficiently and effectively. One item that appeared on their list but was absent from that of the senior VPs of HR was "ensuring equity and legal compliance," processes that signal reliance on a more traditional HR role. Unsurprisingly, line executives see these functions as necessary parts of running a business and expect them to be managed so competently that they are "nonissues."

For HR, this means running its own internal operations according to the same principles and strategies utilized by the organization. For example, if continuous improvement, TQM, or some other recognized principle is employed throughout the organization, then the HR function must also adopt that principle and ensure quality and reliability of its services. In this manner, HR establishes its right to be accepted as a full business partner.

Also notable is the degree of alignment between the perspectives of the senior VPs of HR and the business-unit HR leaders. These midlevel HR managers, often the pivot point between HR strategy and implementation, not only understand the corporate vision but also, for the most part, are committed to realizing it. Where they differ from their senior vice presidents is in their greater emphasis on and time commitment to employee relations concerns and activities such as morale, labor relations, and conflict resolution. The business-unit HR leaders were also more likely to attribute HR's value, in part, to its work in interpreting the impact of social issues (e.g., the environmental movement, work/life conflicts, religion) on the business and crafting organizational responses. Whereas some of these issues might be viewed on a strategic scale at the corporate level (for example, how to deal with cultural diversity in a global context), at the business-unit level, HR managers are adding value by figuring out how to manage these issues in a way that maximizes organizational effectiveness.

In response to the question "What else is currently required of the HR function?" we heard a degree of admonition. To paraphrase, avoid being bureaucrats closeted in a functional silo, or do not mistakenly think that U.S. operations have all of the answers (in other words, don't be U.S.-centric in thinking). Line executives, in particular, are looking to HR for more strategic thinking and understanding, to provide the right resources at the right time, and to nurture a high-performance workforce.

How HR Today Differs from the Past

The executives we spoke with talked about four different aspects of the change occurring in HR:

- Rate of change
- Priorities
- Organizational complexity
- Worldview

Rate of Change

Of all the aspects discussed, the most striking is the increase in the rate of change itself. Most companies have had to abandon the evolutionary model by which their organizations adjust slowly and organically to external forces. The outside environment now changes too rapidly for the evolutionary model to accommodate; organizations must now exert some control over their destiny by finding new ways of anticipating, identifying, and staying abreast of environmental changes that could impact the business and then planning well in advance for the changes that might lie ahead.

The faster an organization is forced to change, the more its people and its systems and processes are tested and, in some cases, disrupted. Some companies have recognized this potential for chaos but have decided nevertheless to stay in a state of sustained rapid change—despite the disruption to people and processes. Most companies, however, have opted for a more controlled approach to handling rapid change: Recognizing the need for agility and adaptability, they seek to set a pace for change that challenges their human capital as well as other resources of the organization without losing control of their strategy, structure, and processes. Their challenge is to maintain essential processes, reinvent others, and avoid overstressing the organization or its employees.

Even those taking this more controlled approach, however, are unable to avoid the inevitable gaps in infrastructure that arise during sustained, fast-paced change. They face a continual struggle to patch together or otherwise fix dismembered communications systems and work processes that are critical to the management of global activities, integration of IT and knowledge management, identification of talent, and development of leaders for the future of the business.

Priorities

A comparison of the results of this study with records from IRC's archives shows that over the past sixty years, the focus of HR professionals has been shifting from maintaining the workforce (e.g., addressing compensation, job evaluation, benefits, and labor relations) to advancing the business. This current position is well stated in the top three priorities identified and discussed by the HR and line executives interviewed:

- *Finding and developing needed talent in an environment of short supply*
  "In the past, HR . . . placed newspaper ads, prescreened applicants, and then presented four or five candidates for management's review. . . . [Now] I need my HR rep constantly looking for talent, developing a branding strategy that makes us attractive to recruits, ensuring our diversity, and identifying internal talent that we need to invest in."
- *Leading organizational development and change*
  "HR doesn't have a long history in leading change, so naturally this makes this area different. I'm adding new people on staff in the area of organizational development to meet this challenge."
- *Implementing HR strategies that improve productivity, reduce lead time, and increase return on investment*
  "If HR wants line management to see it as a business partner, then HR had better take on the same practices that make business leaders successful."

One example of this redirection of attention is the HR function's current view of its advocacy role in the organization. In the early decades of the profession, HR was the arbiter of the social contract with the workforce as a whole, helping society define workforce relationships that would benefit both employees and the enterprise. Gradually, HR took on the role of champion of the individual employee, assuring protection of his rights and making sure the corporate welfare system was addressing his needs. Now, as HR seeks to exert its influence directly on the bottom line, there is a tendency among HR people at all levels to minimize and in some cases disavow the advocacy role altogether. At the least, HR is attempting to redefine itself as a facilitator of employee self-service while lowering delivery costs. The common approach is to make resources available to employees, who are then responsible for accessing and applying them, thus bypassing the traditional personal contact and handholding.

HR not only views its role in the organization as more directly related to the business than ever before but is also applying businesslike practices to its internal management. Cost containment is no longer the chief measurement of HR effectiveness. HR programs are now justified by estimates as to contribution to return on investment (ROI) or increases in productivity. HR leaders now challenge their function to re-engineer its own processes in order to improve quality and cycle time.

Organizational Complexity

The typical business organization in this study is relatively flat and highly matrixed. The lines of accountability and responsibility are not always straight or clear. Individuals within these organizations interact with many people in a variety of positions in many different organizational units. Thus, there is fluidity in the behavior of the organization. This fluidity enables greater organizational agility, knowledge transfer, and power sharing, but it also greatly increases the complexity and instability of workplace relationships. Corporate vision is no longer cascaded down a vertical structure but is radiated throughout the company horizontally and obliquely via cross-functional and cross-geographic linkages and teams.

These highly matrixed team environments, although in some ways aiding the alignment of work groups to corporate goals, have nonetheless left a vacuum in the linkage roles formerly filled by midlevel managers who no longer populate the structure as they once did. These midlevel managers had not only disseminated corporate policy and strategy but also verified their implementation. They transmitted lower-level questions, concerns, and observations back up to senior management and resolved conflicts between competing interests.

With the ranks of midlevel managers decimated, the role of facilitating alignment falls increasingly to HR. At the same time, the political sensitivity of HR's role is heightened. Now, HR must not only guide and empower its own matrixed organization, it must also assist line managers in communicating among themselves and with their corporate leaders in order to clarify goals and strategy, resolve conflict, and allocate resources. The successful adoption of this role has also been a significant factor in boosting the image of HR and enabling it to become a part of the management process. It is how HR gets involved, how it gets its "seat at the table."

HR itself has to respond in other ways, as well, to the new organizational complexity and fluidity. Matrix arrangements challenge traditional leadership approaches and make the skill sets of constituent-building and influence more important than ever. Flexibility and agility are new additions to the HR vocabulary, especially in designing service delivery points. Centers of excellence are appearing throughout the global structure, and HR leaders need to learn how to coordinate and integrate activities on a "24/7" basis.

Worldview

The complexity of aligning corporate strategy while empowering local managers increases geometrically with globalization. While most of the multinational corporations studied have a single corporate headquarters, they also have many centers of operation throughout the world. There is no monistic structure—even within a company—for achieving this balance between global direction and local empowerment. Some companies may locate all corporate functions together, while others may locate corporate functions in different regions of the world but coordinate them functionally rather than geographically. Some functions may be centralized but not others; conversely, functions may be decentralized to such a degree that every location has the capacity and autonomy to perform the functions its region requires—not only distribution and marketing, but also HR, R&D, customer service, engineering, etc. In these cases, corporate functions are smaller and tend to be more focused on policy and strategy, while local entities must be able to interpret policy and then design and administer plans that are aligned with the policy and that fit the operating needs at the local level. Where this is the model, it tends to be replicated throughout the major business segments of the company.

What these companies do have in common, however, is that they embrace many cultures, communicate in many languages and through many media, and span many time zones. The complexity of global business manifests itself in every function of HR. Take staffing as one example. These companies no longer view staffing as the sole concern of the local unit. Talent needs throughout the organization must be considered, and processes for deploying people where and when they are required must be established. Staffing strategy requires, therefore, that the skill sets to achieve these tasks be available around the world. Similarly, every system must take into account variations in social, political, and cultural contexts across the globe and must include processes that facilitate smooth handoffs and communications among locations and individuals.

Looking Forward

The research staff asked the executives participating in this study to speculate on how the HR function will operate in the company of the future. Line managers and HR leaders were in considerable agreement on what the function must do to remain viable and valuable going forward. These recommendations address what HR should do in three categories of concern:

- Its relationship with the organization
- The execution of its functional responsibility
- The internal management of the function

HR's Relationship with the Organization

HR leadership has made tremendous strides in moving from its traditional role of administration to becoming a respected business partner. Undoubtedly, HR leaders cannot slow down their progress. Future success will be highly contingent on the ability to provide leadership, strategic input, and bottom-line contributions to the organization. Inherent in this development are issues that concern the following:

- Employee advocacy, the best way for HR to represent and advance the interests of employees
- Organizational conscience, whereby HR asks the questions that might not otherwise get asked, especially from the point of view of impact on the employees
- Trend identification, whereby HR scans the environment to identify the longer-term changes in patterns of employer/employee relationships and their impact on the firm

Execution of HR's Functional Responsibilities

Within the typical portfolio of HR responsibilities, several will assume additional dimensions and greater importance as companies try to groom the kind of workforce capable of managing a global business and responding creatively to continual change:

- Develop a global leadership model that addresses the competencies and attributes of global leaders needed by the organization, and then implement and maintain a process to develop these leaders.
- Create a competitive advantage by developing an effective means of reskilling the workforce on an ongoing basis in response to changes in the competencies critical to business success and the ability of the organization to either develop them internally or obtain them in the marketplace.
- Figure out how to energize the workforce and maintain its commitment in the face of turmoil, turbulence, and change in both the organization and the external world. This includes measuring/monitoring current commitment levels and identifying, actuating, and evaluating levers that can increase/sustain commitment.

Internal Management of the HR Function

The HR function will need to make fundamental structural changes in order to fulfill its mission in the ever-changing business enterprise of today and

Table 12.3

Skill Sets for Future HR Generalists

• Business understanding	• Facilitation	• Internal consulting
• Change management	• Financial understanding	• IT understanding
• Constituent building	• Global experience	• Organization development
• Customer knowledge	• Influence	• Organization effectiveness

Table 12.4

Requirements for Future Senior HR Leaders

• Line experience	• Exceptional change management
• Experience in more than one	capabilities and sensitivities
geographic location	• Ability to represent and balance the
• A minimum of one expatriate assignment	interests of multiple constituencies
• Demonstrated capability for achieving	• Ability to deal with ambiguity
results	• Good interpersonal and group
• Strong political savvy and expertise	leadership skills

tomorrow. The function will have to work in new ways to serve a global client base, ways that will include virtual relationships, teams that form and disband as needed and that span countries and organizational units, shared services, and centers of excellence located throughout its company's worldwide operations. Further investments in technology and infrastructure will be necessary to build and maintain this new organizational concept.

In addition, the HR function will need to concentrate on upgrading the skills of its professionals to cope with new demands. Just as HR must help the company figure out how to keep the workforce as a whole on a path of continual learning and rededication to the organization's mission, so HR itself must pursue these goals for its own staff.

In a response representative of many we heard, one interviewee outlined the skill sets that will be required for HR generalists at the business-unit level (Table 12.3). Respondents also identified what it will take to be a successful senior HR leader in the future (Table 12.4).

Research Staff Observations

For the companies in our study, rapid change continues to impact the existing infrastructure, rendering it ineffective or obsolete. Further, the depletion of the midlevel managerial ranks has removed the linking mechanisms traditionally relied upon to coordinate activities between units and organizational levels and to provide translation between strategic vision and operating realities of the company. HR, given its historical roles of boundary spanner, culture protector, and communicator, is being called upon to fill that organizational void. HR has become, in effect, the "Great Integrator," whereby it performs the following functions:

- Translates strategy into a variety of structural, process, talent, and cultural designs
- Reinforces the company's vision and strategy being broadcast by line management across the organization, and then conducts concerns back to the center
- Moderates the natural tensions that arise between corporate and local levels because of perceived conflicts in objectives—strategic versus tactical, global versus local, etc.

In addition, every company is struggling to understand how globalization will affect its markets, competition, operations, talent supply, people costs, organizational structure, etc. One thing appears certain: Each company's configuration and response will be different. But all must decide, explicitly or implicitly, what the role of their business will be in world society, what kind of leaders they will need in that context, and what the effects of those decisions will be on HR's role and internal structure.

Opponents of globalization complain that the corporation is becoming a world government. There is truth in the observation that the global corporation will exert a significant influence on the economy and society of the geographic regions in which it does business. Business leaders will be forced to consider the impact of their actions on society wherever it operates and on its workforce, both locally and throughout the world. Therefore, companies will require leaders who understand the importance of their role in the broadest sense and who can move comfortably from one culture to another.

Globalization will affect HR not only in how the function organizes to accommodate a global business structure and what competencies are required of its practitioners but also in how it responds to emerging issues. For example, whose job is it to develop culturally competent leaders? The organizational development function? Diversity function? Management development function? Line management? The answer appears to be all these groups. Consequently, greater collaboration and closer partnerships—both within the boundaries of the HR function and with line management—will be required to meet the needs and obligations of businesses in the new global society.

HR's new role is further reflected in the people who are being chosen to head the HR function in these companies. The majority of the senior VPs of HR with whom we talked came to their jobs from other disciplines, other companies, or both. They were chosen deliberately as outsiders in order to recalibrate and create dramatic change within the HR function.

However, while HR's goal may be to change the organization, it cannot accomplish this single-handedly. Not even CEOs can impose change. Organizations have become too complex, a global business is too far-flung in scope and geography, and employees are too cognizant of the fact that the social contract with the workforce recognizes the autonomy of human capital. Instead, HR needs to broker cooperation among many interests and constituencies. It will have to assist in balancing multiple pairs of competing interests—headquarters versus the business units, global versus local, strategic versus operational, the enterprise versus society, shareholders versus employees.

Because HR resides in the interstices of these interests and can communicate in all directions, and because of HR's presumed "soft" skills—facilitating change, provoking re-examination of relationships, influencing line managers —both employees and management are coming to rely more than ever on HR leaders as advisors, confidants, and true business partners.

Conclusions

The complexity of organizations, the dispersion of authority among corporate, business units, and geographical locations, and the agility required to compete globally has virtually killed "me-too-ism" (i.e., the tendency to choose people, strategies, and practices according to what other "best-in-class" companies are doing). HR leaders are finding that while there may be lessons to learn from others' experiences, their own strategies must be tied to the specific demands of their company's business objectives, competitive environment, and marketplace.

The one thing all companies seem to share is the need to build organizations that can change quickly and continually without crippling the ability to operate on a day-to-day basis. Most companies realize that evolutionary change will not advance them quickly enough but have eschewed the other extreme, sometimes referred to as "creative destruction." They prefer to set their change efforts at a pace that can be controlled and maintained over the long haul, given the resources and style of the company.

Concerning its relationship with the organization, HR must be prepared to regularly renegotiate its role vis-à-vis the workforce and management. HR needs to work out if and when it needs to be an employee advocate, the conscience of the institution, provoker of modified managerial behaviors, a sociological soothsayer predicting the effects of external forces on the business, or some combination of all these. Will it be a strategic partner—that is, a codeveloper of business strategy—or a strategic support responsible for translating and implementing strategy, or both?

Companies are clearly looking towards their HR leaders to set and guide the change process in an increasingly complex world. However, being at the center of the organization's political system also puts HR at great risk. Line managers aver that they depend on HR to speak the truth, to tell the emperor when he is wearing no clothes. In many organizations, however, truth does not protect the messenger from retribution.

How to manage risk is just one of many uncertainties remaining for companies and their HR functions to debate and negotiate. Over the coming years, we can expect continued dialogue in the journals and networking forums about the issues encapsulated in the following questions:

- What is HR's role in business change?
- What is required for HR to fulfill this role?
- How can we institutionalize continual change?
- What is the utility of benchmarking in today's world?
- What will HR have to be able to do well to handle the challenges of globalization?
- What changes will be required in how HR is staffed, trained, structured, and managed?
- How can we develop leaders and organizations that are not only open to new ideas but are also capable of assimilating new ideas rapidly?
- How do organizations ensure that their HR leaders will take the risky positions that line management may require but find uncomfortable?

Notes

1. Staff members of Organization Resources Counselors, Inc., conducted this study under a grant from IRC.

2. Half the companies we studied had made deliberate decisions to change their culture. In the other half, the focus was on changing processes with the assumption that cultural changes would follow naturally.

13

Selected HR Issues

William N. Brown, Geoffrey W. Latta,
and Roderick O. Mullett

Introduction

Having seen in Chapter 12 what managers in leading companies perceive to be the future of human resource management, we turn to three specific areas of human resource policy—compensation, international compensation, and Equal Employment Opportunity (EEO)/Diversity. These areas embody powerful tools, processes, and dynamics for creating and sustaining an organization that can respond to the pressures and opportunities of rapid change and globalization.

Part I of this chapter,—"Incentives, Structure, and Strategies: Issues in the Development of Pay Practices for the Twenty-First Century," by William N. Brown of Organization Resources Counselors, Inc. (ORC)—identifies and explores the broader questions about compensation strategy and design posed by the downturn in equity markets, the slowdown in business performance, globalization, short-term economic cycles, and sharper public focus on the relationship between shareholder value and compensation. Part II, Current Trends in International Compensation, by ORC's Geoffrey W. Latta, evaluates how effective the current approaches to expatriate compensation will be at inducing talented individuals to leave their home country for foreign assignments to satisfy the needs of increasingly global business. The third and final section—EEO and Diversity: Capitalizing on Difference, by Roderick O. Mullett (formerly of ORC)—examines the successes and pitfalls of EEO, Affirmative Action, and Diversity efforts and how these programs can be strengthened to enable companies to leverage diversity as an organizational asset.

I. Incentives, Structure, and Strategies: Issues in the Development of Pay Practices for the Twenty-First Century

Compensation for all levels of employees evolved significantly throughout the twentieth century, partly from the initiatives of the governmental sector, but mostly as a result of companies responding to various changes that impacted the way they conducted their business. For example, the growth of equity programs for employees grew because of the favorable tax and accounting treatment that the equity form of compensation received.

For the twenty-first century, compensation will continue to evolve but in a way that is tailored more to the needs and culture of individual companies. There should be less emphasis on doing what other companies are doing and more on "doing the right thing" to meet the company's own business strategies and the needs of its employees. Implicit in this commitment is the consideration and design of programs that add value to the business, recognize the global nature of the corporation, represent investments in people, are flexible, are perceived as equitable, and are cost-effective.

Therefore, there are many specific types of compensation programs for the new millennium, such as team-based, competency-based, individual-based, and other forms of pay delivery. However, there appear to be several macro questions to be considered and resolved before the mechanics of individual compensation programs can be contemplated:

- Should all employees be eligible for and have a portion of their compensation tied to the equity markets?
- Should employees share in the organization's risks by receiving a portion of their compensation in the form of variable pay?
- Because all employees have basic needs for wages and security, should the employees be entitled to participate in the design of such compensation programs?
- In the global economy in which most companies compete, should compensation be viewed from more of a global perspective?
- Because industries and individual businesses can change quickly in response to business and economic cycles, should compensation programs be flexible and agile enough to switch between long-term and short-term performance cycles? Or should there be elements of both in compensation programs?
- For companies, public or private, that have many or few shareholders or investors, how should compensation programs reflect shareholder value?

Equity

During the surge in the U.S. stock market, and particularly the technology-laden NASDAQ, in the late 1990s, there was a rush to expand the eligibility for equity programs, particularly stock option plans. In many instances, organizations pushed the eligibility for equity programs to all employees and strongly encouraged employees to become owners of the company. With the swoon in the U.S. markets in 2000 and 2001, many employees evidenced a desire to have more of their compensation in the form of cash rather than in equity.

Should compensation in the form of equity be embraced again as it was in the nineties, or should it begin to disappear as a form of employee compensation? This question must be considered from several perspectives.

However, as has been seen in the financial debacle with Enron and its 401(k) program, any company programs in which employees are provided the opportunity to invest in company stock and are strongly encouraged by management to do so must have certain safeguards for employees, including at the very least:

- Plan trustees and administrators who understand the business economics of the company *and* their fiduciary responsibilities to the employees *and* who exercise that responsibility
- Financial penalties against such trustees for failure to perform their duties fully
- Educational programs for employees to help them understand the implications of their decision to place a large portion of their retirement assets in the stock of the company for whom they work—including examples of the financial distress that could occur if the company stock price plummets by 75 percent or more
- Limitation on the percentage of employer-matched contributions or employer investment that could be invested in company stock
- Elimination of the restrictions on the sale of company stock beyond some minimal holding period
- Establishment of ground rules that create "blackout" periods for employees—time blocks when the company stock cannot be sold—and that create the same "blackout" periods for all executives and other stock optionees with respect to the exercise of their stock options

Only then, when some or all of the above protections are provided to employees who invest in company stock through various employer-provided company-equity programs, will the employees be able to adequately control their investments in their employer's stock.

Employee ownership in the company is generally a positive situation because having a financial stake in the company engenders more employee involvement and commitment. Therefore, it is desirable that all employees should be *eligible* for equity compensation in some form. The form could be restricted stock, stock options, stock in a Section 423 plan (employee stock purchase plan), or stock within a 401(k) plan. Whatever the form, all employees should be eligible for any plan for which the employer has a choice to make all employees eligible. Whether they receive a grant every year or not is a different issue.

Depending on the type of plan used, there may or will be tax implications and advantages to the company, the employee, or both. There also are accounting implications for the company.

However, at the lower salary levels, below $50,000, the portion of compensation that is in equity should be small and should be additive—not substitutive—compensation. Employees at these lower salary levels have very little discretionary income and are generally more risk-averse. Thus, the portion of their compensation that is in equity should be small and additive to, not a substitute for, cash compensation to minimize the risk of significant fluctuations in their level of total compensation.

Finally, if equity is to become a part of the employee's total rewards package, the advantages and disadvantages, i.e., the risks and benefits, must be explained and communicated in an understandable, complete, and regular manner. That communication needs to be balanced so that the employee is able to understand all of the implications of this type of compensation and of their decisions to invest in company equities.

Variable Pay

During the 1980s and 1990s, variable pay programs became more prolific in all respects—more programs, more employees participating in them, and higher compensation opportunity. Throughout the nineties, however, most organizations were performing so well that the payouts from these variable compensation plans were generally quite good. Now in 2001–2002, with the U.S. economy in a recession and many global economies also experiencing a slowdown, there is no certainty that variable compensation plans will pay as generously as in the past. Because a variable compensation plan is just that —*variable*—the considerations for designing and implementing such plans are many, particularly when they will impact many, or even all, of a company's employees.

Given this, should all employees be eligible for some form of variable compensation, thus sharing the success and suffering the failures of the company? The answer is a qualified yes. All employees would feel very connected to the company because they would share in the company's performance. Some compensation expense would be variable, which would help the business manage its costs and remain competitive. However, the following issues should be considered if an all-employee incentive plan is contemplated:

- What is the culture of the company?
- Are employees knowledgeable about the business?
- Are employees informed about the financial operations of the company?
- Are employees encouraged to be risk-takers?
- Will the employees be motivated by an incentive plan?
- What company measures are appropriate to use for determining the incentive?
- Can these performance elements be measured effectively?
- Should the incentive plan be a substitute for fixed compensation or be additive?
- What are the key design parameters for the plan?
- How will the plan be communicated?

The answers to the above questions have implications for what type of incentive plan would be most effective. Should it be an individual incentive, a group incentive, or a company profit-sharing plan? Should it be self-funding and make payments only when objectives are exceeded, or should it include significant risk of loss of compensation?

These questions are not easy to answer; each company must evaluate the above issues and determine for itself whether an incentive plan is appropriate. For businesses in general, however, the future will include more employees in more variable compensation programs in more organizations.

Employee Involvement in Compensation Design

In a perfect business world and a perfect company, all groups with a stake in the business entity should have a voice in as much of the operations as possible, and particularly for those aspects that affect each employee personally. However, to be involved in the decision making requires full knowledge of the details of the business and its issues in order to evaluate all possible alternatives and to make intelligent decisions.

Because compensation is so personal and involves the basic need for security, all employees have a keen interest in how their compensation plans are designed and function. Thus, the use of employee focus groups to discuss compensation design and performance measurement features could result in employees accepting the program designs more readily than if they had no involvement. However, to be involved and effective, employees must be educated about the financial aspects of the business and the fundamentals of compensation plans and design.

If all of the cultural conditions in the company are positive and the communications are effective, the involvement of employees in compensation design would help to build some ownership of the final plan and thus increase the potential employee satisfaction with compensation processes. The effective and progressive companies will devise a strategy and will implement programs to involve their employees in all facets of the business, including the design of compensation plans.

Compensation Strategy

Just as there are a number of key design considerations for incentive plans, there are critical issues for management to review and discuss in order to establish the appropriate compensation strategy for the corporation and each of its businesses. Effective programs will be those that support the company's strategic business plan, assist in attracting, retaining, and motivating employees, and are cost-effective.

Competing for talent and being cost-effective requires consideration of the appropriate people strategy. Does the company consider its people resources to be a strategic business factor because of knowledge and competencies, because of commitment to the company, or because of cost? The nature of the people strategy assists in framing and defining the debate over the following questions:

- Should the company establish its compensation strategy for the enterprise or on a business unit–by–business unit basis?
- What competitive market is the concern for the company? Is it the relevant industry, the geographical location, or the specific employee disciplines? Or is it a combination of these?
- How should the competitive level reflect business strategy? For example, should an emerging company pay high now to attract the best talent to drive it to success, or must it be successful first before it can afford to be a high payer? Should a company with a low-cost pricing strategy for its products/services pay below the market to keep labor costs down, or should it pay below-market base salary and allow incentives to bring total cash compensation to a competitive level when the firm's annual performance warrants it?
- Should the degree of competitiveness vary by business unit, by employee group?
- Should competitiveness be measured by base salary, by total compensation (including incentive payments), or by total remuneration (which incorporates values for benefits, perquisites, and equity participation)?
- Should noncash factors, e.g., the company's culture, ethics, location, be taken into account?

Global Impact

Major corporations have been multinational, even global, for many years; however, it is only in the last two decades of the twentieth century that the economy has become truly global, and now most companies of any size are expected to think globally in the operation of their business.

What implications does being a global business have for a company's compensation and rewards programs? Globalization raises such questions as

- Should the programs be driven by the parent entity/headquarters, or should they be locally planned, designed, and implemented?
- Should the competitive strategy for the firm's parent location (country) be the same for every other country in which the firm operates?
- What message do employees in the international locations receive if their respective pay strategies are less competitive than the pay strategy for the headquarters location and/or the parent country?
- Should the value of benefits be considered in weighing the total rewards strategy?
- Should equity granting be equal for similar positions?

Whatever decision is reached about the compensation strategy around the world, it must be deliberated and chosen very carefully.

The key HR considerations for a business in the twenty-first century must be the ability to attract, retain, motivate, and reward its key talent and to prepare that talent for future challenges. Therefore, the most important consideration for compensation programs is that the compensation strategy and philosophy should be developed broadly to support the business both locally and globally. No compensation plan or program should be developed outside of the company's overall strategy. However, that does not suggest that all plans in all locations must be identical or even that all locations should be equally competitive. The business and people issues are different in locations around the world.

So the considerations for the twenty-first century should be to plan globally and reward locally, with the exception of senior executive management. For this group, compensation should be linked globally in order to facilitate global executive recruitment, retention, and succession planning and to tie the executives to enterprise-level objectives and performance, which this group can greatly impact.

Economy

Throughout the twentieth century, there have been cycles of accelerating economic growth and recessionary "soft landings" as well as a depression and the boom of the late nineties. In addition, throughout most of the century, the progress of change in compensation programs has been steady, with the exception of the rapid expansion of equity granting in the late nineties.

Should compensation, more appropriately titled "total rewards," be designed to respond to short-term economic cycles, or should it be more thoughtfully planned for the long term? It can and should do both. But how?

At the executive level, the programs already include elements that are affected by both short- and long-term company results, which will reasonably track the economic cycles. Multiple-year, overlapping long-term incentive plans—whether cash, equity-based, or both—typically provide for a measure of reward or risk over three or five years. The granting of stock options with vesting schedules from one to five years and a term of ten years provides for rewards over a few economic cycles. The short-term annual incentive is more appropriately related to shorter-term company results and will thus reflect near-term economic cycles. For the remainder of the employee population, the compensation programs will, to a greater degree, be focused on and impacted by short-term economic cycles because of modest variable pay programs and a smaller amount of equity. Whatever the design of cash and equity programs, such programs require careful planning if they are to meet the different conditions of a changing economy in a changing world.

Shareholder Value

The beginning of the new millennium brings the issue of shareholder value into the sharpest focus in many years. Short-term incentive payments have continued to be significant and longer-term equity grants have continued to rise—in the number of shares being granted and the value of such grants—despite a substantial loss of shareholder value with the 2000–2001 declines in the stock market. Should this situation continue into this century, or should there be a more direct correlation between the gain or loss in shareholder value and the level of compensation for senior executives? That question could drive the philosophy, strategy, and design of all types of executive compensation programs in the near future.

It is clear that companies will not solve this question alone. Employees, shareholders, investors, communities, and the government—all stakeholders—will show an interest and become involved in finding an answer.

Conclusion

Performance of companies in an ever-changing business environment—one that is now more complex because of globalization, more dynamic because of the pace of change, and more performance-driven—will require HR programs that provide the organization with flexibility but have an appropriate amount of structure to ensure that they are fair, equitable, legal, and ethical. All constituencies—executives, other employees, institutional shareholders, other shareholders, communities, and special interest groups—will expect nothing less. Therefore, the nature of compensation will continue to evolve. For most organizations, the movement will be in the direction of broader employee eligibility for those programs that reward them for their work and provide an entrepreneurial connection to the company, along with a greater respect for employees' opinions on programs that impact them personally.

II. Current Trends in International Compensation

Introduction

Any major organization that operates internationally could rely entirely on staff recruited locally and, of course, most do so for the majority of positions. However, most companies also employ expatriates, those who work outside their country of origin, usually because the company has transferred them. These expatriates are used for a variety of reasons. In some cases, they fill skill gaps when local staff is not available; in other cases, they may be sent to train local staff or to install companywide systems in areas like IT and finance. Increasingly, part of the motivation is to ensure that the future top-management cadre of an organization has had some international experience.

Whatever the reason for using expatriates, this group of people—relatively small in number—takes up a quite disproportionate amount of the time of human resource departments around the world. Unlike key local staff, it is not sufficient to pay expatriates well by reference to the local job market or to offer them a challenging job within one country with the prospect of advancement in that country. Expatriates require more than this; they must be viewed by reference to the country they came from, the one they are currently in, the one they will next move to, and the one they will ultimately work in. This is a minimum of two countries, but it could be more.

Expatriates also cost a lot of money. They get cost-of-living and housing allowances; they travel back home at the company's expense; their children have to be educated; they often get additional premiums on top of their basic salary. Indeed, one is often tempted (a temptation shared by many human resource managers) to wonder why there are so many expatriates.

This section will explore some of the key challenges in managing this employee group, focusing primarily on the issue of compensation. It will review current trends and speculate on future developments.

Trends in the Use of Expatriates

As just mentioned, major companies have long used expatriates to address specific needs such as lack of skills in the local market or the need to train local employees. In some cases, the company is seeking to introduce or reinforce company procedures and culture. Expatriates are frequently the advance guard when a company goes into a new market or establishes a new joint venture.

Over the last twenty years, observers have frequently suggested that the number of expatriates would decline as companies became more able to rely on local talent and as the costs of expatriate programs rose. However, in practice, expatriate numbers are growing. One key reason is that international mobility is increasingly tied to the desire to expose future top managers to international assignments. This latter goal is inextricably linked with the stated desire of many companies to become global. Many companies feel that globalization will be enhanced if employees are exposed to international operations to a higher degree than in the past. In order to achieve this, a number of companies are requiring future top managers to have had an international assignment as part of their career development program.

In addition, as companies have expanded into less-developed countries, they have encountered the problem of the scarce availability of certain key technical and managerial skills. The collapse of the Soviet Union opened a number of countries for foreign investment where this situation pertained. The growth of investment in Asia, particularly in China and India, has created similar pressures.

The combination of globalization and new markets has exerted upward pressure on expatriate numbers. It has also broadened the range of countries from which expatriates are drawn, creating a further set of compensation challenges.

Barriers to Employee Mobility

Therefore, despite the cost, companies appear to be using more rather than fewer expatriates. Yet, in the last decade, many companies report that they are finding it increasingly difficult to move people around. There are a number of barriers to mobility. Some are readily understandable, such as language, while others are subtler, such as an unwillingness to abandon certain aspects of a home-country lifestyle. Increasingly, family issues make employees unwilling to become global nomads. What effect will international moves have on a child's education? What happens to aging parents who might need care? What happens to a spouse's career when an employee goes to work for several years in a country where the spouse cannot pursue her (or, with increasing frequency, his) career and may not even be able to find any sort of employment? For all of these reasons, many major companies report that potential expatriates are turning down assignments in increasing numbers.

However, perhaps the single biggest problem is not what happens when the expatriate is on assignment but what happens when he or she returns to the home country. Studies of expatriates show a very high dissatisfaction level on return to the home country; they also show significant numbers of returned expatriates leaving their company within two years of returning home. This problem of so-called repatriation is a major one and one with significant cost implications for companies. If a company sends an employee overseas on a compensation package that costs three to four times the employee's base salary and the employee quits on return, this represents a significant loss on the investment in that employee.

There are many reasons for the dissatisfaction of returning expatriates. These include the following:

- The feeling that overseas experience is not effectively utilized at home
- The perception that the job back home is not as interesting or challenging as the job abroad
- The impact that several years away may have in weakening an employee's network at corporate headquarters
- The perception that peers who stayed at home may have gotten ahead faster than those on overseas assignments

Most companies claim they do a good job in planning the careers of their expatriates and in reintegrating them into the home country. There is much evidence here of a degree of wishful thinking. One simple but often overlooked reason why expatriates are so expensive is that employees make a very rational evaluation of the risks to their careers of an assignment overseas. Those companies that can demonstrate to their employees that an assignment will concretely help their career can generally attract people to accept assignments and can often pay assignees a less generous package than those companies where accepting an assignment is a leap into the unknown.

Patterns of International Mobility

There is a variety of patterns of expatriate use. Organization Resources Counselors, Inc. (ORC) recently conducted a major study of expatriate compensation policies among more than 600 of its clients in North America, Europe, and Japan. For North American companies, the typical assignment pattern (about 65 percent of cases) is still the planned out-and-back assignment where an employee is sent from their home country for a two- to five-year foreign assignment with the intention that they will return to the home country. About 27 percent of assignments are of indefinite duration, which could mean in practice out and back in less than five years, but it could also mean a longer time. The remainder are serial assignments where the employee moves from one assignment country to another. In Europe, this latter pattern is somewhat more common.

When employees are sent to work in another country permanently, most companies will seek to employ them on a local compensation and benefits package. In a sense, such people cease to be expatriates. In some cases, however, local structures may not provide a sufficient incentive to the employee, and there are a number of cases of employees remaining on expatriate packages for years. This can result in having a base salary tied to a country where the expatriate has not worked for many years and will probably not work again. Some companies have a separate international salary structure for those whom they expect to move from country to country throughout their careers. This is true, for example, with some oil companies, where jobs follow the location of exploration and production operations.

The type and pattern of assignments may have a major impact on how assignees are paid. Some companies specifically recognize different assignment types and pay employees differently to reflect them; others are wary that this will create conflict and jealousy and prefer to have a single policy for all assignees.

The trend in recent years that has emerged most clearly is the greater use of short-term assignments of less than a year's duration. Such assignments often involve moving the employee without relocating the family. As such, they are cheaper than a longer assignment. Obviously, not all assignments can be accomplished in less than a year, but companies have found that the possibility of such assignments can offset other problems such as dual-career issues that hamper acceptance of longer-term assignments.

Major Approaches to International Compensation

Home-Country-Based Balance Sheet

A clear majority of companies for a clear majority of assignments pay expatriates on a home build-up, or balance sheet, approach if the assignment is out and back. This is true for 90 percent of North American companies (based on the latest ORC survey). For European companies, it is still the clear majority practice (60 percent), although there is more variety in how it is put into practice. Japanese practice used to be more generous but has now moved toward a balance-sheet approach, with 82 percent of Japanese companies surveyed using this method.

Base salary. A home-country build-up or balance sheet consists first of retaining the expatriate in his or her home-country salary and grading structure. This approach facilitates repatriation at the end of a limited-duration assignment (the vast majority) because the employee has never left the home salary structure, and it provides equity for expatriates of the same nationality at the same assignment location. It provides a way of managing base pay that ensures that the employee is not out of line with peers at home.

Incentives. Retention in home salary structures is only part of this approach. Many companies also pay additional incentives to accept overseas assignments. The traditional form of incentive was the so-called foreign service premium, usually 15 percent of base pay delivered on an ongoing basis. In recent years, many companies have taken a fresh look at these premiums: Some have eliminated them; some have reduced them; and others have replaced an ongoing monthly premium with lump-sum mobility premiums paid at the beginning and end of an assignment. A company in which assignments are well integrated into career planning and clearly aid future career advancement can probably dispense with incentives altogether. On the other hand, for project-type assignments where there is no career advantage, premiums are probably needed. Lump-sum mobility payments have definite advantages. They are more clearly perceived as an incentive to relocate than an ongoing monthly payment, and they are more clearly seen as associated with the act of moving. Their payment can be tax-effective because it can be made in either the home country or the assignment country, depending on the tax impact. Lump sums also help greatly when an employee moves from country A to B to C. Under the traditional approach, the employee gets the same ongoing payment in C as in B. Under a lump-sum mobility-premium approach, the employee receives an additional payment for moving from B to C, which would not have been paid if the employee had stayed in B.

Cost Equalizers. A corollary of the retention of employees in the home-country structure is the payment of a series of cost-related allowances to expatriates. The underlying principle of using cost equalizers as part of the balance sheet approach is to provide broad comparability with home lifestyle and costs. First, most companies pay a cost-of-living allowance if the cost of goods and services is higher in the assignment location than at home (a brave few reduce the package if the cost of living is lower). Second, most companies pay for housing in the assignment location. In North America, most companies calculate their payment for housing taking into account what the employee would have paid at home. Thus, they pay total host-location housing costs (usually rental, not ownership) but deduct a home-housing cost amount that corresponds to an average housing cost (as opposed to the actual costs to the specific employee). In Europe, companies are far less likely to take a home deduction for housing costs. This relates to the fact that European expatriates—for both cultural and legal reasons—are more reticent to rent out their homes and so are more likely to be actually incurring two sets of housing costs. Third, most companies seek to equalize employees' tax payments so that they pay no more or no less than if they had stayed at home. Companies typically also pay education costs for expatriate children as well as other payments such as home leave. Education is a significant issue, as most expatriates want their children educated in the curriculum of the home country so that upon return, the children can progress to the next educational level. In practice, this means expensive private American, French, Japanese, or other international schools. Education fees for a family with several children are such an expensive proposition that companies may occasionally be tempted to avoid sending those with multiple children of school age.

Headquarters-Based Balance Sheet

The second approach that is used by some companies is what is termed a headquarters approach, in which employees on assignment are all put on the headquarters-country salary structure. This assists with equity between expatriates of different nationalities at the cost of making reintegration back home at the end of the assignment more difficult. Companies in industries that rely heavily on project work with closely integrated multinational teams are more likely to see the value of removing home-based differences in compensation levels. If the home country has a high salary structure (e.g., Switzerland or the United States), this approach makes it easy to attract employees to accept assignments. On the other hand, it is costly. The reverse side of the coin is that if the headquarters country has lower salary levels (e.g., the U.K. or Australia), it may be difficult to attract employees from higher paying countries to accept assignments. Typically, this approach includes all the cost equalizers outlined above but related to the headquarters country.

International Pay Scale

In a few cases, companies use a separate pay scale for expatriates that is not explicitly the pay structure of any single country. This approach used to be more common but has fallen into disfavor because it is often difficult to administer and maintain. In practice, the pay scale is often linked implicitly to a particular country. Interest in this method revived with the advent of the euro in Europe. With a common currency for twelve Eurozone countries, it would appear possible that a euro pay structure could be developed. At present, however, salary levels in the twelve countries in gross terms differ considerably, not least because income tax and social security contributions vary widely. Thus, any structure only makes sense in net pay terms, and even in that case, differences are still large. Net pay scales are also much more difficult to maintain, and so it is likely that this approach will remain relatively limited in use.

Host Pay

The major advantages of a host pay approach are clear. It provides equity with host peers and is perceived as administratively easier. For permanent transfers, a host pay approach makes sense. It has disadvantages, however, for typical expatriate assignments. First, it does not provide sufficient inducement for the employee to move when the assignment salary structure is too much below the home structure. For instance, an American going to Bangladesh will not accept being put on a host structure. For an American going to Switzerland, the salary package will be more attractive, but there are still issues with the high cost of living in Switzerland and the need to address housing and education in English-language schools. As a result, even with host pay methods, expatriate package elements typically are added in areas such as education, housing, and home leave. In turn, this reinstates complexity to an approach that initially seems simpler, and it undermines the equity with local nationals. Second, repatriation is more difficult when the assignment salary structure is higher than the home structure. For instance, a Canadian would be willing to go to the United States for the higher salary but may be less willing to accept the lower Canadian structure upon repatriation. Third, differences in the tax structures and social security and pension plans of home and host countries have to be taken into account. A move from the United Kingdom, for instance, with its low public pensions and high private pensions, to Italy, where it is the other way around, cannot simply be addressed through base pay. Managing benefits such as pensions is more complex, so most companies want employees to stay in home benefit plans, which is easily achieved under a balance sheet approach but is more problematic under a host pay approach.

Hybrid Approaches

In Europe, a number of companies use what is termed the "higher of home or host" approach, in which they calculate a home build-up, compare the results of it with a host pay approach, and pay the better of the two. This provides a compromise between home- and host-based systems, but in practice, all moves to countries with higher costs are on a home base.

Overall Evaluation of Compensation Approaches

Many companies find that they use several approaches for different groups of assignees. However, the balance sheet approach remains the most common. Although the system is complex, it has gained wide use for several reasons. First, it is systematic—an approach does not have to be reinvented for each assignment. Its core philosophy of equalization, with no major windfalls and no major losses, seems to be accepted by both expatriates and management. The system minimizes individual bargaining—typical in companies that are sending out their first expatriates—and from an HR perspective, it limits the freedom of line management to cut deals. By maintaining the linkage to home-country pay structures, the system eases reintegration at the end of assignments. The balance sheet is also very flexible and can accommodate many different pay elements. A company can pay incentives or not; it can pay allowances that preserve a full home-country lifestyle or ones that reflect greater adaptation to local conditions, as with ORC's Efficient Purchaser Index (EPI). Housing can be geared to high-priced areas, or through the peer-housing concept, a company can have expatriates living in areas similar to those of the local managers.

A key reason for the popularity of the balance sheet approach is that most alternatives have significant drawbacks. The strength of the balance sheet is that it separates the management of base compensation from issues related to cost differences between home and host locations. It further insists on separating from base salary those payments such as foreign service premiums and hardship allowances that are purely incentives to accept the assignment. For out-and-back assignments, the ease of reintegration into the home salary structure is a major advantage.

Other Issues

There are other issues that companies wrestle with. Some are structural: Should the company have a single compensation policy for all expatriates, or should it have different policies for different types of assignment, different regions, and/or different business units? The single-policy approach is seen as more consistent and fits if a company wants to maintain strong central control. The so-called multitier approach gives flexibility and can address different business needs, but it requires more communication to expatriates on the reasons for variations in policy, and there is a greater need to ensure that line management does not bend the rules (this applies where the policy is based on assignment type).

Many companies in the early 1990s sought to cut the costs of assignment packages, and clearly there were some costs that needed cutting. However, in the last few years, the pendulum has started to swing back to produce a more balanced situation. Companies cannot afford to make the package so unattractive that potential candidates refuse assignments, given employee concerns about possible adverse impacts on their families and their careers. Indeed, in some areas companies are going in the opposite direction and are spending more money. One is the increasing use of cultural adaptability testing and training, language training, and predeparture orientation—often including the entire family. The second is the increasing willingness of companies to pay for pre-assignment trips for the entire family to the location. Both represent an evaluation on the part of companies that this early payment may reduce the risk of sending a family that will be unhappy in the assignment location and may help those who go to integrate more quickly and effectively.

Future Directions

Despite the cost involved, it is clear that the use of expatriates will continue to grow. The key changes that impact how they will be managed relate to several factors. The first is the increasing variety of types of assignment. While the out-and-back assignment of two to five years' duration remains the most common, there has been a growth of short-term assignments of less than a year and even more exotic approaches such as commuter assignments (out on Monday, home on Friday) in some close geographic areas.

In addition, the focus of international assignments has continued to shift to the less-developed parts of the world, where lack of skills locally makes the use of expatriates more pressing. The challenge here is to provide packages attractive enough to convince employees to relocate to locations that have drawbacks from the point of view of daily living conditions. To the extent that assignees are drawn from these less-developed countries, pay approaches need to be carefully reviewed. The balance sheet approach may not be the most appropriate for moves from such countries, but host-based systems also have drawbacks. Creativity is needed to reflect the particular pattern of assignments in such situations.

Both the wider variety in assignment types and the increasing range of home and assignment locations are likely to lead to a wider variety of compensation systems and to the need to maintain sufficient flexibility to respond to differing circumstances.

Managing expatriates is really a balancing act that involves dealing with conflicting pressures. Since expatriates are expensive, there is pressure to reduce costs, but there is also greater difficulty getting potential assignees to accept moves. There is a need for flexibility in policy design, but if this leads to inconsistencies in the treatment of different expatriates, it creates human resource challenges. Companies recognize the need to integrate assignments into career-planning processes, but often the immediate need to have someone accept an assignment outweighs the career considerations. These and other conflicting pressures make the expatriate management field a continuous, but interesting, challenge.

III. EEO and Diversity: Capitalizing on Difference

Introduction

EEO and Diversity[1] are not high management priorities. In ORC's March 2001 survey of the priorities of senior human resource managers, neither EEO nor Diversity made the "hit parade," but recruitment and retention (the highest priority) and people development (the second priority) cannot be optimized without cognizance of EEO and Diversity. Moreover, easily three of the ten items cited by senior HR executives as the ways the HR function adds value to their companies (Chapter 12)—namely, builds talent assets, improves organizational effectiveness, and nurtures morale and well-being of the workforce—will not only require but will also be enhanced by successful EEO/Diversity efforts.

This section of the chapter further argues that complacency with respect to EEO and Diversity is unwise. It explores the reasons in a discussion of the following topics:

- The history of the Civil Rights movement
- The current status of EEO and Diversity in corporate America
- Inherent difficulties with compliance efforts and the synergies between compliance and Diversity efforts
- The evolution of employment-related Affirmative Action (AA)
- The evolution of Diversity initiatives
- The likelihood that deeply felt differences among employees will cause disruptive behavior in the workplace

The low priority being accorded to EEO and Diversity entails risk of liability, damage to reputation, reduced ability to adapt to changing demographics, reduced ability to elicit constructive differences of opinion from workforce members, and a propensity toward "groupthink." It also suggests that HR is failing to fully utilize processes that contribute to an optimized workforce and thereby diminishes its value added to the enterprise.

A Glance at History

Professor Jonathan Leonard has revealed in Chapter 8 of this volume a past of both progress and problem in the EEO/Diversity arena. The present and the near future are more encouraging in some respects, less in others. To consider the momentum and direction of the Civil Rights movement can enhance perspective on where we are and may be going.

Although one can point to isolated successes before the middle of the twentieth century,[2] there was not much momentum until the Supreme Court's 1954 decision in *Brown* v. *Board of Education.* In fact, while *Brown* did not produce immediate tangible results, the 1960s did produce the black protest movement[3] and great momentum—the Civil Rights Act of 1964, the Voting Rights Act of 1965, Executive Order 11246 in 1965,[4] the Open Housing Act of 1968, Nixon's 1970 promulgation of the Philadelphia Plan and extension of its underutilization concept[5] to all federal contractors, the Supreme Court's 1971 decision in *Griggs* v. *Duke Power,*[6] and the Equal Employment Opportunity Act of 1972. This was an era of "a radical shift in national social policy."[7]

Thereafter, Congress enacted antidiscrimination legislation for additional categories of people but did nothing to address the disadvantages brought on subordinated people by prior discrimination. The basic posture of antidiscrimination legislation was present- and future-oriented, but not past-oriented. This worked reasonably well in situations where the exercise of subordinated people's rights did not impinge on anyone else's rights (e.g., access to hotels, voting booths, restaurants, schools, etc.) but not in situations where the selection of one individual precluded the selection of another (e.g., hiring and promotions). Procedural paths were opened, but discriminatory patterns of relationships remained.

The Civil Rights movement put greater emphasis on attacking substantive structures and on reducing inequalities, and it ran into significantly increased societal resistance. It is not as though the movement had not previously sought compensatory justice as well as equality of opportunity or had not met with resistance to this effort;[8] but the emphasis shifted, increasing the tension between antidiscrimination and Affirmative Action. Public opinion surveys indicate increasing support over time for antidiscrimination efforts but relatively constant, perhaps even increasing, resistance to remedies related to proportional representation. In this context, the movement did not make a great deal of progress in the seventies and eighties but did manage to beat back an assault from the Reagan administration.

In the nineties, a well-organized and well-financed anti–Affirmative Action campaign began to make some headway as indicated by the passage of Proposition 209 in California.[9] Moreover, although AA has not been administered the coup de grâce in the courts, the decisional trend is distinctively adverse to AA.

The factors that have influenced the Civil Rights movement's momentum and direction include the following:

- Its focus (focusing exclusively on African-Americans is likely to produce better results for them than investing the same effort in the rights of women, the disabled, etc.)
- Consciousness on the part of both subordinated and dominant people of societal barriers faced by subordinated people
- Perceived tension between antidiscrimination and Affirmative Action efforts
- Religious and ethical mores
- Legislation
- Judicial attitudes
- Presidential leadership or lack thereof
- The degree of assimilation of subordinated people
- Societal perception of the gap between those who have more and those who have less
- The extent to which people feel empathy with people not like themselves
- The way in which discrimination manifests itself (blatant versus subtle/ systemic)

Table 13.1 compares and contrasts the presence of the potentially influential factors in the 1960s with their presence now and in the likely immediate future. The factors that contributed to the success of the movement in the 1960s are present today, but this factor constellation is such that the challenge to the movement is much greater today than it was forty years ago.

Corporate America tends to assess human talent in terms of an individual's current readiness. Civil rights proponents tend to see this as an incomplete assessment. They argue that centuries of enslavement, segregation, and discrimination enabled whites to appropriate socioeconomic resources from African-Americans, with the result that African-Americans[10] are inherently disadvantaged by their group membership.[11] Hence, something must be done to neutralize the inherent disadvantage. As long as it remains legally permissible, Affirmative Action offers at least some basis for reconciling individual

Table 13.1

The Presence of Factors That Influence Progress in Civil Rights: Now vs. Then

Factors	The 1960s	Today/Tomorrow
Focus	Primarily African-Americans; women were covered by Title VII late in the legislative process.	Several other categories of people have become "protected," even white males—the 60s focus has been diluted.
Consciousness of barriers	Barriers were obvious.	Barriers are more subtle but are increasingly recognized, e.g., the "glass ceiling."
Tension between AA and antidiscrimination	The tension existed in the 60s as manifested in the debates over Title VII.	Anti-AA advocates have achieved considerable success in amplifying the perception of tension.
Religious/ethical mores	Consciousness of discrimination grew stronger.	Intentional discrimination is generally perceived to be unethical; limited recognition of systemic discrimination exists.
Legislation	Achievement of the era.	In place to address procedural barriers; disparate impact analysis given a statutory basis in Civil Rights Act of 1991.
Judicial attitudes	Favorable.	Less favorable—especially vis-à-vis AA.
Presidential leadership	Provided by Johnson; also provided by Nixon vis-à-vis Executive Order 11246.	Jury is out with respect to Bush, but no reason to believe he will lead new initiatives.
Assimilation	White ethnics had been assimilated; people of color were not.	People of dark color still unassimilated, but a good number now in middle class; many more women now in midmanagement ranks.
Gap between the have-more and the have-less	Very evident; associated with marches, civil disobedience, and riots.	Actually more pronounced than in 60s, but not perceived as much.
Empathy	Very evident; associated with marches, civil disobedience, and riots.	Diminished relative to the 60s; inverse correlation with anti-AA feelings.
Manifestation of discrimination	Blatant.	Systemic; hard to identify.

and group values, but the voice of those who would preclude any cognizance of an individual's group identity is loud.

Overview of the Present

Women and minorities have come a long way but still have not achieved equal opportunity. The "glass ceiling" is a reality as well as a catchy phrase, but it has not been impervious in some companies. Companies are more open than in the past to difference (Diversity), but expressing an opinion contrary to a prevailing view is still frequently a risky proposition. Some companies have successfully differentiated EEO and Diversity, but many have not; and measures of Diversity performance, other than the representation of women and minorities, are few and far between. Affirmative Action has significantly contributed to greater utilization of women and minorities, but it is under attack. There is a significant gap between companies' EEO/Diversity "talk" and "walk." There is a significant upward trend in employment discrimination charges and lawsuits as well as awards and settlements. Identity formation has become more complex and fluid as indicated by the choices on the U.S. Census form.

A foundation for further progress is in place. Companies have EEO personnel who understand the OFCCP's (Office of Federal Contract Compliance Programs) regulations, and regular analysis of companies' EEO postures takes place under Affirmative Action Plans (AAPs). The Diversity function has been in place in most companies for a decade or more. In companies where the Diversity and EEO functions are combined, the staff tends to have more prestige and clout and to be more involved with line and other staff personnel than staff with only an EEO mandate. The EEO function is less of an occupational cul-de-sac than it once was and is no longer populated only by minorities. Many companies have a form of alternate dispute resolution (ADR)[12] that helps to surface and resolve problems, thus preventing charges or lawsuits. Managers in other functions have heightened understanding as to what constitutes insensitive and/or illegal behavior. Although work demands are increasing at the expense of nonwork interests, programs that seek to help employees achieve an appropriate balance between their work and nonwork lives are in place in most companies and help. Policies are in place and have been blessed by senior managers.

Blatant discrimination (like that acted out by television's Archie Bunker) has been largely stamped out, but we now face second-generation discrimination, which is harder to identify and fight. Senior management has difficulty recognizing that its organization could be racist or sexist; the concept of unintentional discrimination seems counterintuitive. More sophisticated statistical tools for identifying systemic discrimination are needed. EEO has been repair-and-maintenance oriented; more emphasis on prevention is needed, e.g., education and incentives for talent utilization.

Companies understand that American demography is changing and that long-run corporate survival will require broader utilization of nontraditional talent, but short-term fluctuations in the employment market have been such that few companies have felt the need to make it a priority.

Opportunities for Enhancing Compliance and Diversity Efforts

Problems with EEO Compliance Systems

EEO compliance systems have inherent problems that diminish their effectiveness. To begin with, senior managers are subject to asymmetrical incentives. The less spent on compliance—assuming that undetected discrimination does not subsequently surface—the more positive the bottom line. Underenforcement is actually efficient. Unidentified problems that do not surface later are costless, whereas problems that are identified but would not have surfaced subsequent to audit can be costly. Moreover, senior managers suffer little personal exposure when subordinates' violations are detected.

Line managers have a built-in conflict vis-à-vis EEO problem identification in their units, as it can negatively affect their compensation, reputations, and/or bottom lines. Companies recognize this conflict and compensate with staff audits, hot lines, ombuds systems, etc., but these compensations are not costless and underscore the problem of too much reliance on the line.

Supervisors may not "see" discriminatory behavior, may rationalize it, or may take no action in the hope that it will go away. It is unpleasant, after all, to confront a person for inappropriate behavior. Moreover, supervisors tend to vouch for people they hired or manage, and favorable impressions tend to persist. In addition, employees may conceal discriminatory attitudes, and people may have racist/sexist attitudes but be unaware of them, thus making it more difficult to change their behavior. Subtle or unconscious racism is more prevalent today than the more blatant and hence observable Archie Bunker–type is.

Effective compliance requires clear demarcation between acceptable and unacceptable behavior, but the distinctions are hard to grasp for the nonprofessional. The concept of unintentional discrimination (disparate impact) seems counterintuitive. It is clear that people are not supposed to discriminate against minorities and women, but Affirmative Action implies more than just nondiscrimination, and yet AA is supposed to be nonpreferential. Most line personnel have difficulty making sense of this mixed bag of messages.

Auditing by the compliance staff compensates for problems in reliance on line managers and supervisors, but understaffing of the compliance function can reduce its effectiveness. Moreover, the compliance staff may be inhibited from confronting line and senior managers by fear of being identified as "not a team player." On the other hand, aggressive monitoring by staff can create line-staff mistrust, generate line hostility with respect to policy, and/or lead the line to see the process more as a game and less as an adjunct to the goal.

Risk management principles are often not utilized in the design and management of EEO compliance systems. Many EEO compliance systems simply evolved without a great deal of conscious attention to design considerations, and many others were patterned after the programs of other companies without much adaptation. Better results would be obtained if management would determine how much risk of a Title VII and/or OFCCP problem it was willing to assume and then allocated resources to avoid any greater risk.

Problems with Diversity Initiatives

Diversity initiatives are not without problems, but they tend to be from mismanagement (rather than built in) and not to be the same as those of compliance systems. Diversity has positive synergy with compliance but not much negative synergy, i.e., a well-managed Diversity initiative can facilitate compliance, but a poorly managed Diversity initiative is not likely to present compliance problems. The following factors can diminish the effectiveness of a Diversity initiative:

- It is run as an adjunct to AA, focused on representational diversity (i.e., the number of women and minorities in the workforce) to the exclusion of other kinds of diversity.
- Line managers do not buy the business case for increasing diversity.
- It is run like a compliance program—heavy monitoring/exhortation versus letting the business case be the driver—thereby creating line-staff mistrust.
- It is applied as a programmatic overlay rather than being integrated with business management processes.

Improving Current and Future Compliance and Diversity Efforts

Both compliance and Diversity efforts could be made more effective by the following actions:

- Involve counsel, EEO managers, and both line and senior management in a dialog on how much risk of noncompliance the company is willing to assume, the means that will be utilized (including costs) to reduce risk to the acceptable level, and whether there is an appropriate balance between the yield (reduced risk) and the investment. Such a dialog can produce ideas as to better means of compliance, a better match between resources and the objective, and a better understanding of the degree of risk that is being assumed.
- Determine the degree of congruence between the compliance and recognition/rewards systems. Determine if there are incentives other than the avoidance of potential liability and, if not, whether liability avoidance is a sufficient incentive.
- Consider periodic use of outside monitoring/auditing resources. This can be more cost-effective than increasing the internal compliance staff. It can also reduce a number of the line-staff problems associated with compliance.
- Recognizing that standards of acceptable corporate social performance escalate over time and that hindsight evaluations tend to be more rigorous than contemporaneous ones, consider auditing against more demanding standards than exist today.
- Involve line managers in developing improved measures of Diversity performance that relate it to business performance.

Mending Affirmative Action

Affirmative Action Plans need to be mended, not ended. The AAP framework was designed at a time when jobs were defined narrowly (not much emphasis on teamwork), organizations were more hierarchical, one-company careers were the norm, and career paths were less flexible, and AAP design has changed little. As a result, a great deal of time and effort goes into number crunching that does not provide a great deal of insight as to organizational dynamics. EEO managers devote too much time to crunching numbers and defending their organizations to OFCCP and too little to spreading the gospel. OFCCP should revise its requirements to correspond with the realities of today's work world. Whether OFCCP does or (more likely) does not, EEO managers need better tools to really identify organizational dynamics with respect to age, race, sex, etc.

It seems likely that the courts will preclude consideration of race/gender in employment decisions before too many years have past. This will be problematical in that legal review of organizations' performance will continue to take cognizance of race/gender considerations (disparate impact analysis)—since organizations are not insulated from societal race/gender discrimination —but organizations will be limited to remedial action and precluded from preventative action. If the effects of past discrimination did not disadvantage minorities and females, antidiscrimination efforts with respect to current employment-related decisions would suffice, but these groups continue to be disadvantaged. They will continue to perceive discrimination until representation numbers improve significantly, and in the meantime, charges and lawsuits will continue. Unless society determines that representation numbers are not the primary indicator of discrimination, organizations will be required to assume liability when people in protected categories—although treated fairly in terms of what they currently bring to the party—are treated unfairly in terms of what they might have brought to the party had discriminatory societal patterns of relationship been eliminated. Companies need to either mount a more effective defense of AA in the public arena, invent a race/gender-neutral means of undoing the effects of past societal discrimination,[13] or plan/budget for continuing liability.

Diversity: Managing Difference

Three kinds of difference exist in organizations: (1) hidden/suppressed differences,[14] (2) constructive differences of opinion,[15] and (3) troublesome disputes.[16] Diversity strategy should seek to create a difference-friendly environment—to surface type 1 (hidden/suppressed) differences, encourage the expression of type 2 (constructive) differences, and address type 3 (troublesome) differences. Little is done to encourage or nurture constructive differences. Open-door and grievance systems are available for suppressed differences, but the former are generally not utilized sufficiently, and the latter are better at eliciting differences that have escalated into troublesome disputes than more easily resolvable, pre-escalation differences. Making pre-dispute binding arbitration mandatory is the favored means of dealing with troublesome disputes. However helpful it may be in terms of litigation management, it is not employee friendly, it lacks a systemic problem-solving orientation, and it does little to enhance organizational effectiveness.[17]

An effective difference management system should seek to produce data on its systems that identify problems to be solved and from which the organization can learn and establish accountability.[18] Such a system would do the following:

- Describe and assess the existing approach to difference management from a systemic perspective
- Program/encourage difference using structure, training, and processes

- Pay attention to the impact of change
- Balance complexity, simplicity, and comprehensiveness in the design
- Specifically address power and power sharing
- Facilitate employee voice
- Piggyback with other initiatives (EI, TQM, Competency)
- Emphasize learning, reflection, critical thinking
- Provide resources (acquaint all personnel with the principles of critical thinking, group dynamics, problem solving, and the art of balancing *forcing agreement* and *fostering relationships*)
- Anticipate implementation problems (resistance)
- Incorporate collective, as well as individual, outlooks in performance management and compensation (e.g., 60 percent of my rating is based on my personal performance and 40 percent on my unit's performance)
- Provide an employee-friendly way of addressing differences

In sum, there is ample room for improvement in making organizations more difference-friendly, but a solid foundation for the effort exists, and the effort will enhance organizational effectiveness. For as long as it remains legal to do so, the effort will be buttressed by taking cognizance of race and gender, but in view of the threat to Affirmative Action, it is prudent to differentiate between AA and Diversity.

September 11 and the Likelihood of Outbreaks of More Disruptive Difference

The tragedy of September 11 had obvious and perhaps not-so-obvious implications for EEO/Diversity practice. The obvious danger was discrimination against people because of Middle Eastern/Central Asian background and/or appearance in American society at large and, therefore, in the workplace by osmosis. Companies, however, knew how to communicate in order to address this issue, and President Bush's leadership facilitated the effort. This is not to say that there is no issue, but rather that companies recognized it and they have and are utilizing the "technology" to address it. What is not so obvious is that there are deep-seated conflicting beliefs with other discriminatory overtones in American culture with potential to disrupt the workplace.

These beliefs at least border on intolerance of conflicting views, are assuredly not the constructive differences Diversity initiatives seek to encourage, and are sometimes beyond the limits of social cohesion. The beliefs inform what each of us knows as true and meaningful about family, the arts, faith, education, identity, the media, law, and government. Not all have immediate implications for the workplace, but some do. Issues with respect to sexual orientation discrimination and domestic partner benefits are rooted in conflict with respect to the meaning of "family." Gender roles too are related to concepts of family. Conflicts with respect to assimilation versus multiculturalism, as well as those about whether it is proper to take cognizance of an individual's membership in a group in decision making, are rooted in identity concepts. Although some opponents of Affirmative Action may be aversive racists/genderists, many others believe that it is morally wrong to consider at all a person's ethnicity or gender in decision making.

The corporate response to these deep-seated conflicting beliefs has largely been to ignore their existence, and this response has not proved very detrimental to date. It has to be better, however, to employ a strategy of identifying the nature and extent of such beliefs in the workforce on the theory that you cannot manage a problem that you do not know you have. Affinity groups serve this, as well as other, purposes. Employee surveys could be adapted for this purpose. An ombuds system, too, would be helpful. Although corporate activity is unlikely to make much of a dent in societal problems of this kind, these problems have considerable potential for disrupting organizational effectiveness. Moreover, the workplace is the most diversified institution in society and unlikely to remain unaffected.

Companies will be put in the position of forcing true believers to accept decisions that they greatly dislike. At the same time, companies will wish to minimize poor relationships with employees and advocacy groups adversely affected by company decisions. It will be necessary to manage the paradox of forcing decisions on and fostering relationships with disaffected people.

The suggestions below can aid organizations in managing this paradox:

- *Explore other options before forcing.* Fostering generates more and better ideas as well as commitment to the new agreement.
- *Focused forcing is better than wholesale forcing.* Possession of a power advantage does not mean that it is always wise to use it. Cognizance should be taken of the other party's view of what is reasonable, and positions taken should be supported by a persuasive rationale. The rationale may be unlikely to bring about agreement, but it may be able to reduce intense resentment and lubricate post-forcing relations.
- *Do not overestimate your power, and use forms least likely to trigger escalation.* Be thorough in assessing relative power; do not rely on untested assumptions. Too much reliance on attitudinal and interorganizational tactics that seek to undermine the legitimacy of the other side may generate force but also cause the other side to dig in.
- *Make sure the other side understands what you are doing and why.*

With effective communication, differences may remain, but understanding the reasons for the differences is important in terms of avoiding escalation and fostering post-negotiations relations.

- *Progress is built through small steps.* Progress on smaller, simpler issues can facilitate learning to work together, build trust, and inoculate the negotiators against internal attacks because the smaller scope makes the components of progress easier to digest. Recognize, however, that cooperative success has a double-edged quality: It demonstrates capacity to generate joint gain, but it also raises questions about the independence of each party.
- *Constituent education and awareness is critical.* Internal communication breakdowns can cause derailments. Internal education requires listening as well as speaking—i.e., intra-organizational negotiation. The focus cannot be limited to developing cooperative, problem-solving skills; fundamental questions such as "Why change?" must be addressed.
- *Anticipate forcing episodes.* An exclusive focus on teamwork, cooperation, and consensus misses the real world. Distinguish between issues to be fostered and those that are not. If the issues are unrelated, keep them separate; deal with distributive issues by forcing the inevitable win-lose resolution, not by attempting to force win-win issues. If the issues are related, the linkages need to be addressed, and forcing the whole lot may be appropriate.
- *The successful juxtaposition of forcing and fostering drives change in organizational structure and process, giving rise to new organizational forms.* The most challenging task is to create structures and approaches that will allow distributive activities to take place within a fostering regime. Both interpersonal and institutional dimensions must be addressed. Interpersonally, it is important to facilitate both the clarification of core interests and the surfacing of underlying feelings and values. Institutionally, multiple avenues for surfacing and addressing complaints should be made available.

A Final Thought

Although relevant legal problems and threats are clearly significant, they should not cause us to lose sight of the role that EEO and Diversity can play, especially in a time of anticipated talent shortages, in assuring that all the human resources in an organization are fully utilized. And aside from it being the ethical course to take, EEO and Diversity efforts—in their capacity to render organizations more functional, more adaptable, and open to new ideas—should be a management priority.

Notes

1. Diversity, as used herein, refers not only to the group-identity mix of the workforce but also to an organizational effort to capitalize on (versus stifling) differences in perspective, opinion, etc., among employees.

2. E.g., passage of the 19th Amendment in 1920 giving women the right to vote; creation of the Federal Fair Employment Practices Committee with respect to defense industries; passage of the first state FEPC law in New York and New Jersey in 1945; Branch Rickey's hiring of Jackie Robinson and thereby breaking the color barrier in major league baseball in 1947; and the promulgation of desegregation of the armed forces in 1949.

3. E.g., Rosa Parks, Martin Luther King, the Freedom Riders.

4. Requiring Affirmative Action in employment on the part of federal contractors.

5. Comparing a contractor's utilization of minority employees with the availability of those employees in the labor market.

6. Holding that the use of seemingly neutral employment criteria (a high-school degree in this instance) can be a violation of Title VII if its use has an adverse/disparate impact on minorities.

7. Hugh Davis Graham, *The Civil Rights Era* (New York: Oxford University Press, 1990).

8. E.g., the legislative history of the Civil Rights Act of 1964 reflects considerable debate as to whether the proposed statute would entail quotas or preferences.

9. Outlawing Affirmative Action on the part of state entities.

10. And members of other disadvantaged groups.

11. Joe R. Feagin, *Racist America: Roots, Current Realities, & Future Reparations* (New York: Routledge, 2000).

12. E.g., an ombuds system and/or a mediation, peer review, or arbitration process.

13. Easier to say than to do. Medicine is an analogy. It is much further along in remedying disease than in preventing it or promoting general well-being.

14. E.g., the subordinate who is afraid to point out the flaws in the boss's plan, or the use of facially employment-neutral criteria that have a disparate impact.

15. E.g., the dialog between line and HR managers that leads to the conclusion that greater scheduling flexibility for employees could be a productivity plus.

16. E.g., a claim of unfair or illegal treatment.

17. Other more employee-friendly yet litigation-reducing systems include a voluntary postdispute option for the employee to participate in binding arbitration, with arbitration being binding on the employer but not the employee when a statutory issue is involved.

18. Most existing systems stop when the instant problem appears to have been resolved (perhaps, better said, when the symptoms of the problem have been eliminated). The data with respect to the individual problems are not aggregated and examined from a systemic perspective.

14

Challenge and Balance

Richard A. Beaumont

We seek in this chapter to identify major organizational, business, and socio-economic issues that will present significant challenges for the human resource (HR) function in the years ahead. To do so, we have drawn on the lessons learned during the twentieth century and current trends in human resource management (HRM), as detailed in Section II of this volume, as well as the perspectives of HR practitioners about the future direction of HR and HRM policies and practices, discussed in Chapters 12 and 13 of this volume.

Focusing on the Future

Through the ups and downs of the 1970s and 1980s and in the economic expansion of the 1990s, human resource staffs expanded in order to manage new or enhanced HR programs and services of all types for current and retired workers. During this same period, however, American companies faced intensified competition, both foreign and domestic, and the HR function began to shift emphasis from largely serving employee interests to working in support of management's business objectives. In this context, the function began to focus more specifically on the cost and character of its services in relation to business strategy.

In the span of just a few years, HR came under pressure to reduce its operating costs, especially its many transactional expenses. To achieve cost reductions, some companies created centers of excellence to provide corporatewide services that presumably could be more cost-effective than distributed services. Others found that outsourcing was a more effective way to reduce costs, and this continues to be explored today.

Interestingly, outsourcing was soon extended to far more than transactional services, leading some to speculate that the human resource function itself could ultimately be moved to outside service suppliers. And perhaps it can. But can workers be treated as just another input to production? In many, maybe most, cases, organizational performance continues to depend upon well-functioning teams—of managers and/or workers—with their collective knowledge and skills, organized to be highly effective in producing goods and services of value to consumers. To achieve this objective, management will continue to seek a state of balance between its needs and the interests of employees. In this equation, something more is needed than an outsourced function that simply processes a benefit form, creates a slate of job candidates, or develops compensation options. Only an internal HR function is close enough to management to be able to understand strategy and anticipate and translate business needs into organizational and HR strategies and objectives; only an internal HR function is close enough to the workforce to daily facilitate the programs and processes that contribute to organizational effectiveness and continuity. This is especially important when rapidly changing business and environmental forces are present.

Companies and their management continue to confront socioeconomic and political challenges wherever they operate in the world, and many of these involve people both inside and outside the company. It is here that the human resource function may ultimately make its most significant contributions. Let us address ten such challenges that have the potential to be the dominant issues that will demand HR's and management's attention for some time to come. Most represent potential cost and jeopardy to organizations—and perhaps society—if not adequately addressed, and several represent significant opportunities to develop resources and capabilities that can be used to competitive advantage. These challenges, listed below, clearly demonstrate management's need for a thoughtful, skilled, professional human resource staff:

- Challenge One—Reskilling
- Challenge Two—Simultaneous Labor Shortages and Surpluses
- Challenge Three—Income Distribution
- Challenge Four—Employee Quest for Security
- Challenge Five—Social Security and Retirement
- Challenge Six—EEO and Diversity
- Challenge Seven—Corporate Governance
- Challenge Eight—Organization and Structure
- Challenge Nine—Risk
- Challenge Ten—Corporate Codes of Conduct and the Social Behavior of Companies

Challenge One—Reskilling

The current rate of change in market conditions creates the need for companies to rapidly adopt new technologies, business concepts, approaches, and structures that affect the type of work and how it is performed in many—

even all—parts of the company. This new reality is best seen in the techno-logical revolution of the last decade, which introduced information technology into all aspects of work. Reskilling, i.e., imparting the knowledge and behaviors that enable the workforce to function effectively in the changed work environment, will be increasingly critical to business and society—even a condition of survival—now and for the future. Millions have already been invested in new skills development. But as newer technologies are introduced, job requirements change at an accelerated pace and so do ways of working, e.g., work teams that are characterized by collaboration and shifting membership and objectives. The requirement to develop dramatically new skills and knowledge has become a permanent feature of the workplace.

Not all members of the workforce may be trainable for the newer technologies; others may be impeded by seeing their workplace in terms of historical hierarchy and structure and/or the relative stability imposed by fixed equipment and processes. Our failure to reskill quickly or more successfully may leave too many workers behind, thereby creating a social and economic problem of an equal scale and equally difficult nature.

Thus, the beginning of the new millennium poses a compelling need for more deliberate thought and research in five areas important to the development of a workforce that can function in the new world of business:

- Skills
- Work organization systems
- Processes of involvement and socialization at work
- Work support systems to integrate nonparticipants into the workforce
- Work/life-balance support systems

Some of the necessary new skills will be provided by new entrants to the workforce, but as Challenge Two will illustrate later, labor shortages limit what the external marketplace can be counted on to contribute. Much will have to come from training and developing existing employees, who without help could otherwise become a "drag" on their employers and on society. This can only be achieved with more extensive and sophisticated selection and training processes than we have used in the past.

Twenty-first-century training and development strategies must be able to prepare people for new jobs, for new technologies, and even for new modalities of working life. These requirements introduce a new dimension for the HR function—and for the educational establishment. Given the serious performance problems faced by the U.S. public education system, it is difficult at this point to imagine that educational institutions can do the job alone, and the prevalence of low test scores suggests a difficult job made even more difficult. But companies cannot afford to do the required reskilling without help from the educational system. Despite companies' efforts in the past to partner with public education, success has been marginal. However, with cooperative, imaginative efforts dedicated to new strategies for meeting well-defined needs, more may be possible in the future than in the past. Industry will have to invent new ways to work with the educational establishment in curricula development, teaching methods, training, etc. What are called for now are more research and a commitment to dedicate corporate resources to these issues and questions.

But who will pay for this huge and ongoing reskilling effort? It may be necessary—and appropriate—to encourage employees to trade some future increases in pay or leisure time for training and development. Historically, productivity gains made it possible for workers to gain more leisure time and wage and benefit increases and for companies to realize higher profits. American productivity is doing well while increases in unit labor costs remain relatively moderate. According to the U.S. Bureau of Labor Statistics (BLS), productivity will continue to increase, but even if its estimates are too high, we can assume at least a 50 percent increase, and more likely a 70 percent increase, between 1997 and 2020. Certainly some portion of this increase—in the form of trade-offs for some compensation from employees and some profit from employers—can be invested in reskilling the workforce to meet the new demands.

Challenge Two—Simultaneous Labor Shortages and Surpluses

The last few years have given all organizations a preview of a central issue that will characterize the early part of the twenty-first century. Labor shortages have been in sharp focus through the year 2000 as recruitment and retention of people with certain skills and talents were so difficult. In 1999 and 2000, many workers flocked to e-commerce, with its promise of high rewards for what seemed to many (especially younger workers) to be low risk, only to find themselves back on the job market with the turn of the economy and the collapse of the dot-coms.

Short-cycle developments such as these will continue to affect the near-term supply and demand for labor. However, at a more fundamental level, it appears as though for the next several decades, the labor force will grow more slowly, will be older in advanced economies, and in certain segments will have fewer skills, especially in the United States, where immigration from less developed countries will continue to be high. Thus, the issues of retirement, education, and training will come together not only as part of the national debate about the labor force but also as issues to be dealt with at the individual company level. The payroll-trimming practice of encouraging early retirement, common in the past, will come to be seen as contrary to national and business needs.

Given that the economy moves between good times and bad, management is always confronted with the challenge to moderate labor costs but preserve talent. The retention issue is of growing concern to every enterprise that has become more reliant on knowledge workers and their contributions.

In just the short period between 1999 and 2002 in the United States, we have gone from shortages of trained people to the need to cut labor costs. As the economy recovers in 2002–3, the environment of shortages will reappear and with greater intensity. The short economic downturn will not have changed the following longer-term trends reported by the BLS:

- In the decade from 1998 to 2008, employment in engineering will add 290,000 jobs in contrast to 33,000 in the prior decade. Yet engineering school enrollments and graduations are down, with B.S. degrees in engineering actually declining from their 1985 peak of nearly 78,000 to about 64,000 now.
- From 1990 to 1998, the surge period in technological progress, science and engineering graduate school enrollments rose only 2.1 percent. Will that very modest growth rate produce a sufficiently large pool to meet what we can expect to be even greater future demand for scientific and engineering talent?
- In the decade between 1998 and 2008, two fifths of all new jobs in manufacturing will be in computer systems—analysts, engineers, and scientists. Furthermore, BLS estimates that the economy will have to more than double the number of computer engineers in that ten-year period as compared with the prior ten years. The actual numbers of B.S. degrees in one subset, mathematical/computer science, have declined from nearly 59,000 to about 40,000 between 1986 and 1991 and are only at about the 1991 level today.
- A significant portion of the students who earned advanced degrees in engineering and computer science are not U.S. citizens—one third in 1980, growing to one half in 1998—and may not necessarily enter or remain in the U.S. workforce. Even at the teaching level, noncitizens account for about one third of the instructors in critical disciplines.

Global employers, moreover, will be subject to political pressure wherever there is significant unemployment. Thus, they will face demands to hire or support the unemployed as well as feel the pressure to increase rewards in order to recruit or retain employees with critical high-demand skills.

As a consequence, in their attempt to deal rationally with the wide variation in labor costs and the shortage of needed skills, management will further fracture the already weakened pillar of modern human resources: the *doctrine of equality of treatment* in pay, benefits, and developmental opportunities. Occupations in critical areas and in short supply will command higher pay and larger increases than jobs for which demand is less than supply. What will replace equality of treatment is as yet unclear, but companies' adoption of market-based pay systems, which link pay more closely to market conditions and push concepts of internal equity aside, is a giant step toward modifying the doctrine.

Differentiation in treatment in the workplace is likely to extend to promotions, development/training assignments, job security, and other rewards, which will make already visible differences even more evident to employees. Although this may be unavoidable, exquisite communications will not cause employees to easily understand and readily accept rational economic arguments for why such significant differences must exist.

We do not think that there will be a successful single or simple strategy for dealing with such differentiation. But human resource practitioners will be required to aid management in finding effective ways to manage this issue, especially since it will probably be even more difficult to get courts to sanction such differences in the future. We can already sense their unwillingness to allow gender compensation differentials on the basis of market-based pay systems. While this problem may diminish when women achieve "equality" in high-demand/short-supply occupations, this will take time. It is unrealistic to imagine that during the period of dislocation, there will be no push to closely examine whether employer policies/practices have magnified market differentials. Further, unions and others will again raise the debate on comparable worth and focus attention on compensation differentials. In the end, we must learn to deal with differentiation that results from labor surpluses and shortages existing side by side. It is here that the HR staff will be relied upon heavily to use its competencies in such areas as recruitment/employment, reward systems, and employee relations to shape the workforce according to business needs while maintaining a constructive, satisfying work environment for all employees.

Challenge Three—Income Distribution

The matter of what is the appropriate distribution of income for jobs at different levels and between industries reflects a society's values and the country's political and economic conditions, including governmental tax policy. In recent years in the United States, because of the visibility of data during the spring

Securities and Exchange Commission (SEC) filings, executive pay levels have been scrutinized and frequently considered astronomic, especially when including the presumed value of stock options, the use of which has spread under particular accounting principles and current tax laws and the value of which has grown with the bull market of the 1990s. The Enron and ABB Brown Boveri situations have made executive rewards appear excessive and even immoral. Since we may not have seen the last of the Enron-type cases, executive pay will be exposed to further public review and greater regulatory control. At the time of this writing, several bills have been introduced in the U.S. Congress to deal with stock options, and it also seems likely that Federal Accounting Standards Board (FASB) will reconsider the accounting treatment of options.

A comparison of executive pay and wealth-creation systems with the compensation packages for entertainment and sports figures might show that executives at the "star" level are rewarded properly. Nonetheless, when the ratio of pay of the highest job to the lowest job in the organizational hierarchy is the greatest it has ever been—and appears to be growing—many will ask if this ratio is right? Is it fair? Is it necessary? Directors of companies will be called upon to address these issues surrounding executive pay, and the demands imposed on corporate compensation staffs and consultants will become more than a passing concern.

The issue of high pay is news; the underlying philosophical issue of what is the right level of pay for a given job is largely unaddressed. To the compensation professional, the right level is what is required for recruitment and retention, not only of a given executive but also of the stream of talent needed by large, complex business organizations.

It is important to understand that pay and rewards shape behavior and that sophisticated pay and wealth-creation systems are essential for more than reward in large organizations. They attract into a company a flow of viable candidates that ensures an available talent stream. A regularized flow of talent enables an organization to provide developmental opportunities for individuals and observation opportunities regarding performance and ability. It is essential over time for continuity of a business. There may be a successful Gerstner (a CEO of IBM) recruited to a specific company job, but what complex organization could survive by staffing largely through opportunistic recruitment over a long period of time? And besides, would a Gerstner have performed differently if his pay had been lower or higher by 10 percent or 50 percent? Furthermore, sophisticated pay and wealth-creation systems help to retain the talent that has proven its ability to meet goals and produce results.

The purpose of the foregoing is not to justify high levels of pay and the extravagant use of stock options, but it does intend to raise the question of whether executive compensation practice has been far too focused on the "what" and the "how" issues in executive pay and the related legal and tax considerations rather than on the fundamental longer-term issues of maintaining and managing the stream of talent in an organization. These are lifeblood matters to a dynamic business system and if forgotten or undermined can damage a system that has produced extraordinary results.

Will the moderate economic slowdown that began in 2001 significantly temper executive pay-increase levels? Will the war for talent reassert itself? The strong likelihood is that pay and rewards for the higher-level jobs and for those with scarce skills will continue to escalate while pay structures for employees at the middle-management levels and below will advance at relatively more modest rates. While much focus is on executive pay, at the other end of the spectrum, lower-skilled people live the reality of low escalation in pay levels. Will this growing gap lead to realistic demands for higher minimum pay or "living" wage proposals? If the income differentials come to be seen as an unequal distribution of the rewards of the system, it could become a major sociopolitical issue, with consequences for future tax policy, at a minimum. Thus, it is imperative for HR leadership to understand and help to rationalize executive pay not with just an apology for what exists but with a succinct explanation of what is appropriate and why. Although a difficult role, it must be pursued inside corporations, at the board level, and in the public arena.

Challenge Four—Employee Quest for Security

It is axiomatic that the most prized employee benefit is the provision of economic security, but history and current reality demonstrate that even "relative security" is costly and any high degree of security may be impossible—especially in the face of growing competition from emerging economies where the cost of labor is comparatively low. Employees, sensing this, naturally seek to improve their security in a variety of ways. One way, which can be insidious from a management perspective, is to associate with peers, unions, and professional groups to explore common problems and attempt to form a countervailing force to unilateral management actions taken to manage labor costs.

Some will argue that employees' concerns over security have declined in recent years with a tight labor market and greater employee acceptance of corporate shakeouts and restructuring. But it would be folly to rely on it. Employees can be provoked to seek to redress any new threat to their security. We have seen, for example, IBM employees react vigorously in resisting a change from a defined-benefit retirement plan to a defined contribution system, and otherwise "businesslike" unions have done the same in the face of proposals to reduce company-provided employee health care insurance. What may be sound business steps to moderate labor costs in a globally interdependent world, where compensation levels vary dramatically from region to region, are met with actual or implied challenges that could be followed by more adversarial actions. And the challenges are not confined to unionized situations.

Management proclamations that employees' security lies in having marketable skills have shifted employee sentiments from company loyalty to occupational loyalty. This enhances the natural inclination for employees with common personal or occupational interests or characteristics to band together for what they perceive is their mutual advantage. Whether security concerns will now provoke employees to organize directly into unions is not the issue. Employee interest groups can take on the characteristics of a traditional union as they struggle with issues of importance to the members of a group. We need only look at teachers and nurses in the United States to see historical examples of purely professional associations that evolved into powerful unions. The potential will be exacerbated by the growing trend toward "professionalization" of the salaried workforce in general.

In the past, this transition has followed the general pattern described below:

- A distinct group of professionals associates for legitimate "professional" purposes.
- They share and compare job-related data, including pay, benefits, and work conditions.
- They work on developing professional codes regarding entry to the profession and/or work conditions, first for their own interest as "professionals" and perhaps later for presentation to employers.
- If aggrieved, they may try to present issues to one or more employers or to governmental bodies by using the platform of the association.
- If rebuffed, they come to understand that they can gain a protected status by affiliating with or becoming a legally recognized union, as was the case with the nursing and teaching professions.

The more professional the group, the more likely it is that their aim will be to control issues of work and structure, advancement, and the character and quality of supervision. Such issues can pose major operational problems from management's perspective, and in the end, skilled HR professionals will have to take on the role of dealing with the issues.

However, it may be far more productive for HR leaders to spearhead the development of more innovative approaches to preserving a degree of security acceptable to employees at a cost acceptable to the company.

For example, a comprehensive health-care program with first-visit or modest copay coverage might be replaced with a catastrophic plan combined with some form of spendable amount for minor health problems. To suggest something even more heretical, have we—in the light of spiraling private insurance costs—perhaps reached the point where a broad government health-care system is a more feasible and acceptable alternative? In retirement planning, particularly for individuals with skills in short supply, companies might consider an extension of employment beyond normal retirement, on a full-time or part-time basis, combined with lump-sum payments and a concomitant delay in the delivery of retirement benefits.

Might it be time to seriously consider a truly combined public/private structure of health and retirement benefits, one that is far more realistically related to lifetime employment than certain European plans? Joint funding plus a higher degree of cost-effectiveness may be possible. Could we conceive of a public/private unemployment insurance system that combines private severance payments with unemployment insurance in a new way? A systems approach that ties together pension/social security, severance, and health-related benefits—and delivers more "security" for the total expenditure—could also be explored.

Challenge Five—Social Security and Retirement

One special element of the security issue is income protection in retirement. The debate over social security and retirement normally embraces financial issues, birth-rate pressures, longevity trends, and equity with regard to who should pay and how much for sustaining retirees. The restructuring of U.S. industry in the early 1990s has provoked the emergent discussion on the issue. It is now beginning to affect historical employment patterns in other countries as well—the changes in the lifetime employment model in Japan, for example, and the need to reduce the social net in such countries as Germany and France. The flame was further fanned when several large firms in the United States—albeit for what they saw as good business and economic reasons—moved from defined benefit plans to some form of cash-balance retirement plans.

Whatever the sound business or political reasons cited for proposed changes in retirement income support, any prolonged period of slow economic growth will truly exacerbate an issue that smolders just below the surface: the natural conflict that exists over the distribution of wealth between those who are working and those who are retired. This issue may be seen more clearly in mature, large-employer industries—e.g., coal, steel, autos—where there already is an overhang of large numbers of retirees supported by fewer and fewer younger workers. In some companies, for example, there are two or even three retired employees for each active employee, and in at least one industry, the ratio for some companies is as high as 10:1.

It is conceivable that tension between younger workers and retirees could rise to the level of divisiveness. If it does, it is far more than a human resource issue. Nonetheless, it has broad human resource implications in terms of compensation and benefit plans and structures, work opportunity, and—even more importantly—social and working relationships between the young and the old within organizations and within society as a whole.

Today on a national level, the ratio of workers to retirees is 3:1, but by 2030 it will drop to 2:1. Under almost any future economic scenario, it will be difficult to maintain the current level of retiree benefits in the public system. Even private plans will be stressed for several reasons, some of which will also affect the public system. First, morbidity tables are being modified to reflect increasing longevity. This foreshadows longer retirement periods if the retirement age is not increased and, hence, higher costs. Second, baby boomers are inexorably moving toward retirement, with the peak to be reached in 2015, which will bring a commensurate jump in added retirement costs that the system must absorb. Third, pension-fund earnings over the last two years have had negative or only modest increases, making it difficult for employers to meet their future liabilities under their defined benefit plans. This will cause many private employers to shift to some form of defined contribution plan.

How will the nation deal with the increased cost of retirement? One option will be for employers to keep retirement-aged people in the workforce—with or without an increase in the normal retirement age—especially since older people continue to function and remain healthy longer. This may be a feasible way to manage cost assuming that employers will utilize older people where they can perform meaningful work—obviously more feasible with knowledge workers—and that older workers will accept longer working lives. Such an arrangement could help both the public and private systems as long as neither system allows earnings after normal retirement age to increase the cost of retirement benefits (based on earnings and longevity ratios).

Under more favorable economic scenarios, the retirement system might be managed, especially if productivity grows at the projected rates and creative people collaborate on solutions for mitigating costs. It would seem necessary, however, to dedicate resources *today* if viable solutions are to be in place within a decade. Who will put these issues before management and take a leadership position? Isn't this an area where forward-thinking companies need to engage their HR staffs and begin to play a role in shaping what will be a national debate?

Challenge Six—EEO and Diversity

Without getting enmeshed in a discussion of the details of equal employment opportunity (EEO) and Diversity, it is sufficient to observe that this area of human resource management demonstrates better than any other that firms do—and must—respond to sociopolitical and cultural changes. Yet despite the progress, which has been considerable from the perspective of the mid-sixties, there is still a long road ahead regarding equal opportunity. Although legal threats to the viability of Affirmative Action are not insignificant, companies must realize that their claims of equal opportunity will be tested. Given the reality of demographic patterns, which will continue to bring even greater diversity to the general population and the workplace, the public and government will continue to ask whether minorities, women, the disabled, and people of color are fairly represented. Certainly the courts and regulatory agencies will, and in specific situations, so will consumers.

Diversity is too often narrowly thought of as a legal issue and confused with EEO/Affirmative Action, at least in U.S. companies. Diversity efforts strive to make organizations difference-friendly, by which differing values, views, and experience are seen to energize and invigorate an organization. This requires change on the part of all who come together in the workplace. To the extent that work is increasingly team-based and managed through a cooperative matrix rather than an authoritarian hierarchy, a key to organizational effectiveness will be a far greater acceptance of Diversity than exists today. Thus, it is imperative that the human resource practitioner clearly sees this issue in the broader context of organizational dynamics and effectiveness rather than EEO/Affirmative Action.

For a global company, the issue of workforce Diversity is fraught with even greater challenges. Blending and cohering people from different cultures—with fundamentally different perceptions, values, and beliefs—into a global team is a new frontier. And HR, having worked with this issue in the context of the cultural and legal structures of developed nations, may not yet have the skill set to deal with the many other nations that contribute to true world Diversity. HR must prod management to adopt a model that extends opportunity and creates an organizational culture that is receptive to Diversity. HR also has the responsibility to facilitate the transition of minorities and people of other cultures from "outsiders" into active partners inside the economic system.

Challenge Seven—Corporate Governance

If J.P. Morgan should miraculously reappear on earth, it is likely that one of his observations would be that today's corporate boards of directors are more of a cross-section of business and society than boards principally dedicated to advancing the interests of the stockholders. He probably would also question the extent to which directors have become involved, albeit modestly in some companies, in strategic planning and management selection and compensation.

Corporate directors themselves must be confused today about their role because of the complexity of business; public/political perceptions of what a director's responsibility should be; the extent of fiduciary responsibility; the rights of other "stakeholders"—employees, customers, suppliers, the community—vis-à-vis stockholders; and other factors. The collapse of Enron raises concern about whether directors are even sufficiently fulfilling their fundamental obligations to stockholders. Moreover, the boundary between the directors' role vis-à-vis management's is shifting.

The practical issue for a well-managed company is whether the directors' role should evolve willy-nilly or whether some internal function should have a role in raising the level of dialogue about these issues and helping to rationalize a role for the board that best serves the long-term viability of the company. We believe it should be a responsibility of HR, in its integrative role, to help facilitate the exploration of governance questions, such as:

- What is the appropriate role of directors? Is that role changing from simply representing stockholder interests?
- To what extent should a board or its individual members have a "representational" role by reflecting the public's or the customers' views, social or cultural norms, ethical standards? (And is it possible for the board of a global company to be "representative" in global terms?)
- How deeply should a board get involved in strategic issues, which could include social and political issues, while still satisfying its responsibilities to shareholders?
- Is there agreement on how human resource practitioners should serve board members as contrasted with how HR practitioners serve top management (especially in executive compensation and succession planning)?
- What should be the nature of the interaction between board members or committees of the board and members of top management?
- Should HR play any role—e.g., facilitate dialogue among the corporate secretarial function, outside legal counsel, and professional associations—in the exploration of these and related issues?

Challenge Eight—Organization and Structure

Over the last three decades, there has been a noticeable shift from more or less authoritarian organizational structures to ones that could be described as more open, more fluid, more unstructured, more informal, and in some cases more democratic. While no one reason explains the shift, major contributors include changes in society and management orientation and philosophy, the combination of new technologies and more sophisticated methods of work organization and operations, and the rapidly changing competitive environment. Corporate leaders (except possibly in the high-tech world and start-ups) are usually no longer the owners or dominant shareholders in their firms, which has a subtle but perceptible and meaningful influence on the organizational structures those companies tend to adopt.

As we look to the future, we can already discern that the trend toward more flexibility and democracy will continue, but will other features accompany it? Business strategy will demand an organization that is organic in terms of its capacity to change, to adapt, and to integrate capabilities from all parts of the organization and external sources to achieve the results that the firm seeks. The aftermath of September 11, 2001, has shown a clear example of how organizations must achieve rapid operational and cultural change. New forms of cooperation are now demanded among security, HR, legal, financial, and management personnel in order to deal effectively with workplace safety and security and respond to unexpected threats. HR can play an energetic and creative role in such cases—managing team-building processes, adapting reward systems, participating in modifying management processes— to support a dynamic organizational modality.

In their quest for competitive advantage, some companies will focus on amassing superior human competencies such as innovation and risk-taking— in both traditional and new professional areas—and entrepreneurism. Many people with these characteristics, especially younger ones, can be more idiosyncratic and less conforming to organizational norms of behavior. For this to be successful, HR will have to become an organizational broker or impresario who gains acceptance of diverse styles and develops HR systems and processes to support the development of new competencies.

Along with an acceleration of the need to decentralize and the growth of global structures, corporations will struggle with centrifugal forces that arise in all organizations that are functionally, operationally, and/or geographically dispersed. At the same time, there will be a quest at the center to control costs, maintain standards (qualitative and quantitative), and ensure various forms of collaboration by adopting centripetal processes that will cohere and integrate the organization—something increasingly difficult in an era when organizational democracy is growing. Thus, a major organizational and human resource challenge will be how to balance the centripetal forces that serve the needs of the enterprise as a whole—especially in meeting externally imposed standards and challenges—with the decentralization required to meet valid marketing, operating, and employee needs at the local/operating level.

Some believe more matrix organizational processes will help. Although formal matrix organization theory has not been universally successful in practical application, matrices have proven to be extremely useful for responding effectively to some of the new competitive and operational challenges and new business opportunities in the financial services industry, high-tech firms, and professional organizations. Team-based organizations owe much of their fluidity and flexibility to their matrix form, so it may prove to be the model required in a global economy. However, because matrix organizations have proven, up to now, to be notoriously difficult to merge with traditional processes and manage, HR can play a pivotal role in designing and implementing new processes and inculcating the cooperative behaviors needed for the effective functioning and responsiveness of tomorrow's organization.

Challenge Nine—Risk

In visualizing human resource needs of the next decade, it is abundantly clear that HR practitioners of the future, whether from traditional staff jobs or from the line organization, will need to take on far more aggressive roles if the organization is to meet its challenges. As pointed out in Chapter 12 of this volume, they will have to be, at one time or another, philosopher, manager, innovator/developer, and user of new tools. They will have to be not only leaders but also implementers, observers scanning global and local developments, and forceful but effective proponents for change inside the organization. They will need to step up from a staff role in order to join line management as an effective business partner in developing short-term and long-term strategies that steer the organization down the best path for success.

Such roles might require an HR practitioner to persuade a CEO that some portion of short-term gains and earnings per share should be traded off for long-term investments in human resources that will produce longer-term gains. That is a risky stance to take. Furthermore, it is far easier to argue increased costs for recruiting essential talent or retaining key people when the economy is robust and a company is profitable, but what about when business performance declines? The human resource professional will have to know when and how to make such arguments. But however well conceived or skillfully delivered, they are accompanied by risk. The markets punish a company that does not meet its near-term earnings targets, and many line executives will be equally tough on one who takes unpopular positions and aspires to be their organization's philosopher king.

Is the political risk worth it? If the human resource function's model of the future is sitting at the table where business strategy is developed, then the risk is inevitable. But along with acceptance of risk will come first-tier status in management and the concomitant rewards. Getting there will require HR practitioners to thoroughly assess how prepared they are to take on this level of risk.

Challenge Ten—Corporate Codes of Conduct and the Social Behavior of Companies

Beginning in the early 1960s, primarily in Europe, there developed the view that codes of conduct should be used to evaluate, and perhaps even govern, a company's behavior. Some nongovernmental organizations (NGOs) and unions insisted that the development of these codes and monitoring for compliance be done from outside the company. The push for codes of conduct was reminiscent of efforts in the United States over the years by religious leaders who insisted that companies demonstrate social responsibility in their business actions as they relate to employees and the community. The European concept of codes of conduct continued to ripen during the decade and resulted in the International Chamber of Commerce Code on Multinational Behavior, which many major U.S. companies were willing to accept in the late 1960s.

Paralleling this development was—and continues to be—a push for corporate codes of conduct in both the environmental and occupational safety and health areas. Highly visible international child-labor issues and other forms of potentially discriminatory and/or exploitative employment practices have further increased the attention paid to corporate behavior. Many American companies, particularly in apparel and footwear, have dealt with problems of inhumane treatment wherever it has existed in their offshore supplier companies.

Perhaps a signal event in a major corporation's response to public pressure was Royal Dutch Shell's actions regarding the Brent Spar oil platform issue (1991–1999). The company had planned to destroy an oil platform at sea—a practice it deemed safe and cost-effective—but it bowed to public pressure stemming from environmental concerns and towed the platform to shore and demolished it at great cost, perhaps creating a greater environmental problem (many informed people believe) than if it had sunk the platform at sea. Because of the scope and impact of this incident and because Shell had always seen itself as a good corporate citizen, Shell appears to have felt a responsibility to take the most positive course of action. This event undoubtedly added to Shell's decision to report annually on its role in "sustainable development," with its report significantly titled *People, Planet, Profits, An Act of Commitment*.

In this era of social policy, European unions have been very active, and when operating in Europe, U.S. unions and the U.S. Department of Labor (in certain administrations) have been especially supportive of related issues, including the provision of information and consultation. Industry responses to European Union initiatives have been responsible, but the employer camp has been divided over the character of the response whenever new initiatives are proposed. We foresee more efforts by unions and governments in this area in the years ahead, both in Europe and elsewhere in the world.

The Enron and Arthur Andersen debacles in the United States and the special compensation award for a retiring CEO in ABB Brown Boveri all fly in the face of what is acceptable. As a result, they also are likely to provoke changes to regulations and laws that in the end will further constrain and govern the behavior of management in its pursuit of business.

Thus, in the future there will inevitably be mounting pressure to evaluate the behavior of companies as corporate citizens and on many more dimensions than just financial performance. For HR, this means more in-depth scrutiny in such areas as compensation, corporate performance in Diversity, and the utilization and advancement of women and minorities. These are not solely HR issues, so HR will have to interact with many other corporate functions in order to provide the leadership and oversight required for the company to meet its legal/regulatory obligations and society's expectations.

If company behavior is found wanting, outside audits such as compensation reviews will become a new burden. This will complicate interactions with employees and with the outside world. Corporations must focus on thoughtful management planning and behavior. Yet many managers consider the threat of such scrutiny far too remote to even worry about. Can responsible management reasonably believe that it will escape some form of surveillance today, especially given shareholder proposals from pressure groups, trade agreements that contain audit requirements, European laws that require various forms of review, and the fall out from the Enron scandal? HR in its emerging role as organizational conscience may be called upon to convince management otherwise.

Conclusion

These challenges, selected from a larger list, indicate the nature and scope of the issues that the nation, its businesses, and its workforce will face in the years ahead. It represents a ripe agenda for the HR function and will call for broad, strong leadership.

Based on the experience of the past, it is our belief that the capacity to deal with these challenges exists. But for HR to play a role, it will take the willingness of companies to allow it to focus on the longer-term and to work jointly with other institutions to deal with the increasingly complex issues that the future will pose.

15

In Conclusion

Transiting from the Past to the Future

Richard A. Beaumont

If one were to analyze the initiatives that grew out of the massacre at Ludlow, Colorado, in the context of just the surface forces at play at the time, it is possible to conclude that such efforts were designed and executed only to prevent the organization of workers by a union. However, by viewing these initiatives in the broader context of how they subsequently affected other developments, it is possible to conclude from the same set of facts that Ludlow was the first step toward the significant place that human resource management (HRM) now occupies in modern management. It is this latter conclusion that has both shaped my thinking and guided my leadership of the organizations spawned by John D. Rockefeller, Jr., and the work we have done with management during the last forty years of Industrial Relations Counselors, Inc.'s (IRC's), seventy-five-year history.

Without Rockefeller's crusade for a cooperative relationship between employers and employees, one based on mutual respect and the recognition of respective rights and responsibilities, progress in HRM, and in management generally, would have been much less certain. For as this volume demonstrates, our field has had an observably logical development, and the contributions of many of its most influential theorists and managers have their seeds in the ideas and values promoted by Rockefeller. Although the field has evolved far beyond what Rockefeller could have envisioned, he was a prime mover who started us on a journey with outcomes that have contributed much to individual, corporate, and national interests.

Rockefeller also must be credited for his willingness to move so far from what might have been expected—given his background, surroundings, and the laissez-faire autocracy of his peers in industry—as well as for his boldness and persistence in the pursuit of voluntary industrial democracy in a time when it had scant support in the business community. Indeed, for a period when the gulf between all-powerful owners/managers and workers with few rights was broad and deep, Rockefeller's transformation—from "absent landlord" to champion of workers' right to have a voice in determining the conditions under which they worked—was nothing short of revolutionary. His embrace of the concept of the unity of interest between employers and employees and his promotion and implementation of employee representation plans signaled a sea change, a cooperative approach when the only other alternatives seemed to be oppression, adversarialism, or chaos.

In preparing for IRC's seventy-fifth-anniversary symposium, I spent a great deal of time reading material in the Rockefeller archives, including letters to and from Rockefeller, as well as many of the speeches he gave. I was impressed with not only the clarity of his thinking but also the energy he dedicated to the development and articulation of his ideas; for him, it became a mission. And through his efforts, our field and its perspectives have been advanced enormously.

Prime Causes

Turning our attention from Rockefeller's contributions to our field, we, like Rockefeller, seek to understand the prime causes, the larger forces, that will iteratively shape the continuing evolution of the field of HRM as a crucial element in the practice of management. I find three key drivers of persistent change in the field:

- The startling rate of change in markets and technologies
- The constant flux in social thinking about the role and contributions of private organizations and about the roles, needs, and desires of people as members of society
- The changes in the complex matrix of employee views and attitudes (by level and occupation) about their work, their organizations, and their managers

In the years from 1975 to 1990, U.S. industry went through a major period of re-engineering, regrouping, retrenching, and refocusing to meet increasingly aggressive foreign competition in what had been more predictable domestic markets dominated by U.S. companies. The last decade, 1990–2000, brought a tidal wave of investment in and introduction of revolutionary advances in information technology and communications. Both office and production processes changed—from clerks in offices to word processors; from operators on assembly lines and in mills, chemical plants, and refineries to console operators and other classifications heavily reliant on the new technology. These new jobs are now supported by an array of technicians proficient in software development and design and the implementation of new technologies.

There is no gainsaying the fact that markets and technology, while ever changing, did so more quickly in these two periods than in prior ones. More-over, it is likely that rapid change will persist and even accelerate in the future.

Change and the Implicit Disequilibrium

All companies seek to adjust to change and to find a state of operational balance with the marketplace, to find the right balance of resources to pro-duce goods and services that effectively compete with those of other produc-ers who seek to serve the same market. Adjusting its resources to meet the challenges of the market is the relatively complex responsibility of manage-ment. It orchestrates various disciplines, hopefully making the right invest-ments and needed changes in production and distributive processes. Surviving companies manage with more or less success. However, in periods of accel-erated change, the orchestrating process becomes exceedingly complex and competitive.

Indeed, internal structures and organizations require change and adapta-tion as well. Even here, we know enough in order to tweak organizations or to radically change them. However, change may also be required in the mix and/or motivation of employees or in their skills and knowledge. Tradition-ally, employees—managers and workers alike—have had difficulty in ac-cepting organizational and work-process changes. Thus, disequilibrium easily develops in the balance sought by management between the company and its market's demands and between the resources and organization of the com-pany and its employees, a condition illustrated in Figure 15.1. Unfortunately, experience shows that the element in the balance equation represented by employees is the most resistant to the rapid changes that the new technology and market conditions generally require.

Thus, not only do markets drive organizations and their people, but also the equilibrium that management seeks is a never-ending quest that can only be partially successful because of investment lags or resistance to change by institutional and/or human behavior.

The HR Contribution

Trying to aid management to provoke faster change in organizations and to help employees adjust to change, can be seen as the burden or, alternatively, the opportunity of the human resource function. Correspondingly, it has developed—or has had foisted upon it—a panoply of programs, policies, and techniques to achieve employee buy-in, improve organizational struc-tures, and gain acceptance of the need for new processes for the design, manufacture, and distribution of goods and services.

Figure 15.1 **Disequilibrium Model**

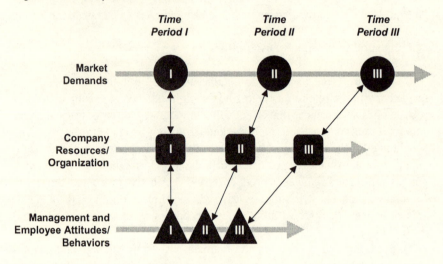

Notes:
a. In Time Period I, equilibrium exists between market, resources/organization, and people.
b. Market demands continuously shift.
c. Company resources/organization move at a pace that lags market changes.
d. Management and employee attitudes/behaviors change slowly.

Despite HR's efforts, long-term skill requirements may demand new personnel with different skill and knowledge bases. However, employees are not fungible, and company philosophy, government regulations, and/or union agreements do not allow a company to freely trade an existing employee for a new one. As HR considers these parameters in its advice and counsel to management, management may perceive HR as standing in the way of the corporation's quickest path to success. The reality is that HR can prepare and aid people and organizations to make needed changes, but the change will be at a pace that will not always be in perfect sync with the pace that management believes necessary to respond to marketplace pressures.

In addition to the rate of market and technological change, the other key drivers of change require other types of contributions from HR. There will always be differing views throughout the society about the respective roles of employees and employers and about the distribution of the fruits of business. Concepts about the role and contributions of employees will change, just as we have seen with knowledge workers, who now, because of the growth of the economy and the expansion of technology, can offer more to organizational productivity than ever before. Thus, another significant role for HR professionals is to help their organizations understand and respond to these changing views and values, be it issues of fair pay, minority rights regarding employment and development, or proposed laws and regulations, to name a few.

This new role, that of the integrating philosopher of the organization, has the potential to extend HR's impact and influence even further beyond what we have seen today. The role is not only a difficult one to play well, but it also carries with it considerable risk—of misjudging the impact of outside forces or the willingness of the organization to make needed changes in policies, behaviors, and the nature and character of management systems.

In Conclusion—Themes and Lessons from History

The material presented by the several authors in this volume reflects certain themes and lessons learned that characterize the arc of HRM's journey from past to present. These can be summarized as follows:

- The traditional method of managing labor in the early years led to significant labor problems that culminated in what is now referred to as the Ludlow Massacre. This event focused Rockefeller's attention on the need to re-examine the then traditional approach toward labor problems.
- During these early years, several approaches were developed to deal with the "Labor Problem." One of the most significant was the highly professional humanistic approach that Rockefeller and IRC pioneered, and this is the story on which the authors of this volume have focused.
- Over the years, labor and management, while having conflicting interests, could not be brought together productively unless ways of balancing or reconciling differences could be achieved. The approach championed by Rockefeller and his advisors was at first heavily influenced by the experience of collective bargaining at that time. Thus, their initial objective was to find a less adversarial model, which is embodied in the employee representation plan.
- Over the twentieth century, the approach espoused by Rockefeller gradually evolved into the HRM approach, which shares many of the same goals but proceeds in a slightly different direction in that it de-emphasizes a collective governing structure and pursues more individual-oriented strategies. Rather than focus on resolving conflicts between interests, it seeks instead to integrate and align interests between a company and its employees. This development owes much to the additions to knowledge about individual and organizational behav-

ior, which stemmed from the behavioral sciences, and to the development of new HRM methods, including pay for performance, employee participation in work-related decisions, and extensive communications between management and employees.

- Over the years, not all employers or employees have behaved rationally, and many firms still find it practical to manage their organizations in ways that largely serve short-term business goals with little concern for the needs and aspirations of workers. Their numbers, however, have declined, and so it is not surprising that union representation has been shrinking. Some of this shrinkage in union membership is also related to a change in the industrial complexion of the nation as it has moved from extractive and manufacturing industries to service industries of one type or another, which now account for a large percentage of employees.

- From the earliest period to the present, the challenge to HR as a management function has been to find the most effective way to balance interests that are not always congruent and may conflict with one another. The objective for doing so is to promote not only the firm's business goals but also the goals of employees. In this manner, it is possible to engender commitment, loyalty, and behaviors that advance productivity, quality, and innovation in the workplace.

It is in the context of the aforementioned key drivers of change, and the accompanying disequilibrium, that IRC has worked and contributed to the evolution of HRM. Seventy-five years ago, IRC studied vacation policy as a new need emerged in the industrial workplace. Since that time we have, as a nation and as responsible businesses, sought to protect workers from the loss of income from unemployment, sickness, and old age. We have learned to mitigate the impact on workers of plant relocations and changes in technology through worker retraining and adjustment programs, and even the impact of personal burdens through family leave policies and employee assistance programs (EAP).

Almost fifty years ago, IRC became deeply concerned about the role of African-Americans in industry—not a prominent issue at that time in either the country or industry. Nevertheless, in advance of the Civil Rights movement, IRC was conscious of this social issue and began to research and alert management to its implications in the workplace.

IRC's 1964 study, *Management, Automation, and People*, sought to understand how the increasing pace of technological development was changing business and what its impact might be on people, society, unions, and governments. The study also identified the need for information technology (IT) specialists and skills in technologies that were then new and/or unrecognized by many in business. The study's conclusions about changes in job content, skill level, workplace relationships, and other areas of impact are in evidence today.

Whenever one concludes that there is no further need of change, social or political processes seem to present yet another new challenge. Someone within a company must be sensitive to the changes in societal views about companies and their behavior and to shifts in the political landscape that may change the way the company interacts with employees, customers, or the public. HR, positioned as it is at the nexus of a business and its people, can play a significant role in helping management understand the forces that do and will shape the environment in which the company operates.

Perhaps the greatest change during IRC's seventy-five-year history has been in the structure of the business organization and the growth in the matrix of skills, talents, knowledge, and experience required to do its work. We may still need experienced miners like those who dug for coal in Ludlow in 1914, but many fewer of them. Today, the requirement includes technologists to operate consoles and other advanced equipment for extracting coal, information specialists to design and apply software to the economic and market analyses essential to a modern coal company competing in a world market, and the availability of the technical capabilities to support these business tools and processes.

This diverse mix of employees has differing perspectives, experience, and values, which affect individual motivation, career aspirations, and responses to rewards. Such differences must first be understood and then productively channeled and managed. It is this ever more complex organization that HR, in concert with the rest of management, must shape and reshape in response to market and technological changes, social pressures, and the constraints of laws and regulations everywhere the company operates.

The period of large-scale corporate downsizing and restructuring has pruned from contemporary HR organizations much of what gave the function a reputation as a bloated bureaucracy. Through outsourcing and/or the development and installation of self-service IT-based information systems, HR is no longer the custodian of large record-keeping systems that require a sizeable payroll dedicated to largely clerical tasks. This development may be the key to the maturation and acceptance of HR. It enables more resources to be dedicated to talent recruitment, development, and succession planning, which given an environment of talent scarcity and globalization, are recognized by top management as keys to business success. Issues such as innovative compensation systems, sophisticated retention systems, and results-oriented development processes have become essential. Paralleling these needs, board members today have a keen interest in succession, which further provokes CEOs to look to HR for more and more support. Staffing, organizational development, compensation/reward/wealth-creation systems, all linked together, have created in HR a powerful capability for support of management in the achievement of business objectives.

Throughout this volume, the authors have focused on streams of events and the evolution of concepts and policies—and in this chapter, I have cast my remarks broadly and in the light of philosophical developments—rather than on the tools and techniques of the field. Too often in the field of HR, there has been a tendency for practitioners to think and behave more like engineers than architects. Architecture is an art form; and despite all it owes to science and systems, despite its quest for professional standardization, HR is most successful when practiced as an art form. Thus, it has the capability to balance many seemingly contradictory forces and find innovative solutions to perplexing business issues.

IRC's role over the years has been to nudge HRM developments along and urge that the test of reasonableness be applied in an ethical, honest, humane manner. This is the way that contributions and innovations can extend the boundaries of art and practice. From this review of IRC's seventy-five years of service, of its role as a central observer and participant in the evolution of human resources into a major contributor to corporate success, it is possible to conclude that Rockefeller would be proud of what we have done. The field has progressed and continues to grow in sophistication and influence, and its practitioners have contributed to the advancement of the art and practice. This, in no small way, has aided our transit from a less enlightened industrial time to this modern, more democratic business system and the new age it has achieved.

References

Chapter 2. The United States in the 1920s: Breaking with European Traditions

Author's note: I used innumerable sources, including almanacs and encyclopedias, for this historical survey, but a few books deserve special mention.

Douglas, Ann. 1995. *Terrible Honesty: Mongrel Manhattan in the 1920s*. Reprint. London: Macmillan Co., Papermac, 1997. Particularly helpful regarding the cultural scene of the period, including the American break with European traditions.

Drucker, Peter. 1970. *Technology, Management, and Society.* Reprint. London: Pan Books, 1972.

Fosdick, Raymond B. 1956. *John D. Rockefeller, Jr.: A Portrait.* New York: Harper & Brothers.

Helfgott, Roy B. 1980. *Labor Economics.* 2d ed. New York: Random House. Economic and labor information for the period.

Time-Life Books. 1969. *This Fabulous Century: Vol. III, 1920/1930.* New York.

Wren, Daniel A. 1972. *The Evolution of Management Thought.* New York: Ronald Press.

Chapter 3. Industrial Relations Counselors, Inc.: Its History and Significance

Adams, Thomas, and Helen Sumner. 1905. *Labor Problems.* New York: Macmillan Co.

Balderston, C. Canby. 1937. *Profit Sharing for Wage Earners.* New York: Industrial Relations Counselors.

———. 1940. *Wage Setting Based on Job Analysis and Evaluation.* New York: Industrial Relations Counselors.

Belknap, Chauncey. 1976. "The Formative Years." In *People, Progress, and Employee Relations, Proceedings of the Fiftieth Anniversary Conference of Industrial Relations Counselors, Inc.,* ed. Richard Beaumont, pp. 9–12. Charlottesville, Va.: University Press of Virginia.

Bendix, Reinhard. 1956. *Work and Authority in Industry.* New York: Wiley.

Bernstein, Irving. 1960. *The Lean Years.* Boston: Houghton Mifflin.

Casebeer, Kenneth. 1987. "Holder of the Pen: An Interview with Leon Keyserling on Drafting the Wagner Act." *University of Miami Law Review* 42 (November): 285–363.

Ching, Cyrus. 1953. *Review and Reflection.* New York: Forbes.

Commons, John. 1913. *Labor and Administration.* New York: Macmillan Co.

————. 1919. *The Functions of the Executive.* Cambridge, MA: Harvard University Press.

————. 1921. *Industrial Government.* New York: Macmillan Co.

————. 1934. *Myself.* Madison, Wis.: University of Wisconsin Press.

Cowdrick, Edward. 1924. *Manpower in Industry.* New York: Henry Holt.

Curtis, Fosdick, and Belknap [Law Firm of]. 1922–1925. "Annual Report of Industrial Relations Activities." Industrial Relations Counselors, Inc., library, New York.

Debs, Eugene. 1948. *The Writings and Speeches of Eugene V. Debs.* New York: Hermitage Press.

Domhoff, G. William. 1990. *The Power Elite and the State: How Policy Is Made in America.* New York: Aldine de Gruyter.

————. 1996. *State Autonomy or Class Dominance: Case Studies on Policy Making in America.* New York: Aldine De Gruyter.

Dulebohn, J., G. Ferris, and J. Stodd. 1995. "The History and Evolution of Human Resource Management." In *Handbook of Human Resource Management,* ed. G. Ferris, S. Rosen, and D. Barnum, pp. 19–41. New York: Blackwell.

Dunn, Robert. 1926. *American Company Unions.* Chicago: Trade Union Educational League.

Fine, Sidney. 1956. *Laissez Faire and the General-Welfare State.* Ann Arbor, Mich.: University of Michigan Press.

Fitch, John. 1924. *The Causes of Industrial Unrest.* New York: Harper.

Fosdick, Raymond. 1921. "Memorandum on a Survey of the Properties of the Consolidated Coal Company" [November 1]. Industrial Relations Counselors, Inc., library, New York.

————. 1951. "Opening Remarks of the Chairman." In *Proceedings of a Conference Commemorating the Twenty-Fifth Anniversary of Industrial Relations Counselors, Inc.,* pp. 1–3. New York: Industrial Relations Counselors.

————. 1956. *John D. Rockefeller, Jr.: A Portrait.* New York: Harper & Bros.

————. 1958. *Chronicle of a Generation.* New York: Harper & Bros.

Fosdick to Rockefeller, 2 June 1921. Industrial Relations Counselors, Inc., library, New York.

Fosdick to Rockefeller, March 1934. John D. Rockefeller, Jr., Papers, Economic Interests, Box 16, Folder 127, Rockefeller Archive Center, New York.

French, Carroll. 1923. *The Shop Committee in the United States.* Baltimore, Md.: Johns Hopkins University Press.

————. 1937. "Recent Developments in Employee Representation." *Personnel* 14 (August): 2–9.

Gibb, George, and Evelyn Knowlton. 1956. *The Resurgent Years: 1911–1927.* New York: Harper & Bros.

Gilman, Nicholas. 1899. *A Dividend to Labor.* New York: Houghton Mifflin.

Gilson, Mary. 1940. *What's Past Is Prologue: Reflections on My Industrial Experience.* New York: Harper & Bros.

Gitelman, Howard M. 1988. *Legacy of the Ludlow Massacre: A Chapter in American Industrial Relations.* Philadelphia: University of Pennsylvania Press.

————. 1991. "The Special Conference Committee: Reality and Illusion in the Industrial Relations of the 1920s." Industrial Relations Counselors, Inc., library, New York.

Gray, Robert. 1943. *Systematic Wage Administration in the Southern California Aircraft Industry.* New York: Industrial Relations Counselors.

Harris, Howell. 1982. *The Right to Manage: Industrial Relations Policies of American Business in the 1940s.* Madison, Wis.: University of Wisconsin Press.

Hicks, Clarence. 1928. "Industrial Relations Trails of Yesterday and Tomorrow." In *Proceedings of the YMCA Human Relations in Industry Conference*, pp. 85–96. (Copy of paper in Industrial Relations Counselors, Inc., library, New York.)
———. 1941. *My Life in Industrial Relations: Fifty Years in the Growth of a Profession*. New York: Harper & Bros.
Hicks to Rockefeller, 1943. John D. Rockefeller, Jr., Papers, Economic Interests, Box 16, Folder 130, Rockefeller Archive Center, New York.
Huthmacher, J. 1968. *Senator Robert F. Wagner and the Rise of Urban Liberalism*. New York: Athenaeum.
Industrial Relations Counselors. [n.d.]. "Industrial Relations Counselors, Inc." (Arthur Young, Counsel). Industrial Relations Counselors, Inc., library, New York.
———. 1940. "Research Program of Industrial Relations Counselors, Inc." Industrial Relations Counselors, Inc., library, New York.
———. 1943. "IRC First Training Course." Industrial Relations Counselors, Inc., library, New York.
———. 1951. *Proceedings of a Conference Commemorating the Twenty-Fifth Anniversary of Industrial Relations Counselors, Inc.*, New York.
———. 1957. "Proposed Research Program, Industrial Relations Counselors, Inc." Industrial Relations Counselors, Inc., library, New York.
———. 1970. "IRC: A Review of Its Contributions, A Preview of Its Future." Industrial Relations Counselors, Inc., library, New York.
———. 1976. "Historical Documents." Industrial Relations Counselors, Inc., library, New York.
———. 1994. *Report on the IRC Survey of Employee Involvement*. New York.
Jacoby, Sanford. 1985. *Employing Bureaucracy: Managers, Unions, and the Transformation of Work in American Industry, 1900–1945*. New York: Columbia University Press.
———. 1997. *Modern Manors: Welfare Capitalism since the New Deal*. Princeton: Princeton University Press.
———. 2000. "A Road Not Taken: Independent Local Unions in the United States since 1935." In *Nonunion Employee Representation: History, Contemporary Practice, and Policy*, ed. Bruce E. Kaufman and Daphne G. Taras, pp. 76–95. Armonk, N.Y.: M.E. Sharpe.
Kaufman, Bruce. 1993. *The Origins and Evolution of the Field of Industrial Relations in the United States*. Ithaca, N.Y.: ILR Press.
———. 2000. "Accomplishments and Shortcomings of Nonunion Employee Representation in the Pre–Wagner Act Years: A Reassessment." In *Nonunion Employee Representation: History, Contemporary Practice, and Policy*, ed. Bruce E. Kaufman and Daphne G. Taras, pp. 21–60. Armonk, N.Y.: M.E. Sharpe.
———. 2001. "The Theory and Practice of Strategic HRM and Participative Management: Antecedents in Early Industrial Relations." *Human Resource Management Review* 11 (4): 505–33.
Kaufman, Bruce E., and Daphne G. Taras, eds. 2000. *Nonunion Employee Representation: History, Contemporary Practice, and Policy*. Armonk, N.Y.: M.E. Sharpe.
King, William Lyon Mackenzie. 1918. *Industry and Humanity*. Toronto: University of Toronto Press.
———. 1919. "Memorandum Respecting Survey of Industrial Relations: The Consolidated Coal Company." Industrial Relations Counselors, Inc., library, New York.
Leiserson, William. 1928. "The Accomplishments and Significance of Employee Representation." *Personnel* 4 (February): 119–35.

————. 1929. "Contributions of Personnel Management to Improved Labor Relations." In *Wertheim Lectures on Industrial Relations*, pp. 125–64. Cambridge, Mass.: Harvard University Press.

Lescohier, Don. 1960. *My Story for the First Seventy-Three Years.* Madison, Wis.: Art Brush Creations.

Lichtenstein, Nelson, and Howell Harris. 1993. *Industrial Democracy: The Ambiguous Promise.* New York: Oxford University Press.

Loth, David. 1958. *Swope of GE: The Story of Gerard Swope and General Electric in American Business History.* New York: Simon & Schuster.

Lubin to Rockefeller, 5 May 1934. John D. Rockefeller, Jr., Papers, Economic Interests, Box 16, Folder 127, Rockefeller Archive Center, New York.

Mandell, Nikki. 2002. *The Corporation as Family: The Gendering of Corporate Welfare, 1890–1930.* Chapel Hill, N.C.: University of North Carolina Press.

McGregor, F.A. 1962. *The Fall & Rise of Mackenzie King: 1911–1919.* Toronto: Macmillan of Canada.

National Labor Relations Board. 1985. *Legislative History of the National Labor Relations Act.* Washington, D.C.: Government Printing Office.

Nelson, Daniel. 2000. "The AFL and Company Unionism, 1915–1937." In *Nonunion Employee Representation: History, Contemporary Practice, and Policy*, ed. Bruce E. Kaufman and Daphne G. Taras, pp. 61–75. Armonk, N.Y.: M.E. Sharpe.

Northrup, Herbert. 1946. *Unionization of Professional Engineers and Chemists.* New York: Industrial Relations Counselors.

Perry, Arthur Latham. 1878. *Elements of Political Economy.* New York: Scribner's.

Rockefeller, John D., Jr. 1923. *The Personal Relation in Industry.* New York: Boni and Liveright.

————. 1933. Radio address, August 26. John D. Rockefeller, Jr., Papers, Personal Speeches, Box 73, Folder 154, Rockefeller Archive Center, New York.

Rubinow, Isaac M. 1934. *The Quest for Security.* New York: Henry Holt.

Scheinberg, Stephen. 1986. *The Development of Corporation Labor Policy, 1900–1940.* New York: Garland.

Schuler, Randall. 1995. *Managing Human Resources.* Minneapolis, Minn.: West.

Selekman, Benjamin, and Mary Van Kleeck. 1924. *Employees' Representation in Coal Mines.* New York: Russell Sage Foundation.

Slichter, Sumner H. 1929. "The Current Labor Policies of American Industries." *Quarterly Journal of Economics* (May): 393–435.

Smith, Robert. 1960. *Mill on the Dan: A History of Dan River Mills, 1882–1950.* Durham, N.C.: Duke University Press.

Spates, Thomas. 1960. *Human Values Where People Work.* New York: Harper.

Talbot, Allan. 1982. "Making It All Work." *The Lamp* (Spring/Summer). Employee magazine of the Exxon Corporation.

Taylor, Frederick. 1895. "A Piece Rate System, Being a Partial Solution to the Labor Problem." *Transactions: American Society of Mechanical Engineers* 16: 856–83.

————. 1911. *Principles of Scientific Management.* New York: Harper & Bros.

Teplow, Leo. 1976. "Industrial Relations Counselors at Fifty Years." In *People, Progress, and Employee Relations, Proceedings of the Fiftieth Anniversary Conference of Industrial Relations Counselors, Inc.*, ed. Richard Beaumont. Charlottesville, Va.: University Press of Virginia.

"Thirty Years of Labor Peace." *Fortune* (November 1946).

Tone, Andrea. 1997. *The Business of Benevolence.* Ithaca, N.Y.: Cornell University Press.

U.S. Congress. 1916. *Industrial Relations: Final Report and Testimony*. Washington, D.C.: Government Printing Office.
U.S. Senate. Committee on Education and Labor. 1939. *Violations of Free Speech and Rights of Labor, Hearings before a Subcommittee of the Committee on Education and Labor*, Part 45. Washington, D.C.: Government Printing Office.
Wall, Bennett, and George Gibb. 1974. *Teagle of Jersey Standard*. New Orleans, La.: Tulane University Press.
Watkins, Gordon, and Paul Dodd. 1940. *Labor Problems*. 3d ed. New York: Cromwell.
Witte, Edwin. 1963. *The Development of the Social Security Act*. Madison, Wis.: University of Wisconsin Press.
Young to Rockefeller, 1926. John D. Rockefeller, Jr., Papers, Economic Interests, Box 16, Folder 127, Rockefeller Archive Center, New York.

Chapter 4. The Quest for Cooperation and Unity of Interest in Industry

Alchian, Armen, and Harold Demsetz. 1972. "Production, Information Costs, and Economic Organization." *American Economic Review* 72 (5): 777–95.
Appelbaum, Eileen, Thomas Bailey, Peter Berg, and Arne Kalleberg. 2000. *Manufacturing Advantage: Why High-Performance Works Systems Pay Off*. Ithaca, N.Y.: Economic Policy Institute and Cornell University Press, ILR Press.
Appelbaum, Eileen, and Rosemary Batt. 1994. *The New American Workplace*. Ithaca, N.Y.: ILR Press.
Argyris, Chris. 1964. *Integrating the Individual and the Organization*. New York: Wiley.
Babbage, Charles. 1833. *On the Economy of Machinery and Manufactures*. London: Charles Knight.
Balderston, Canby. 1935. *Executive Guidance of Industrial Relations*. Philadelphia: University of Pennsylvania Press.
Barnard, Chester. 1938. *The Functions of the Executive*. Cambridge, Mass.: Harvard University Press.
Beer, Michael, and Burt Spector. 1984. "Human Resources Management: The Integration of Industrial Relations and Organizational Development." In *Research in Personnel and Human Resources Management*, vol. 2, ed. K.M. Rowland and G. Ferris, pp. 261–97. Greenwich, Conn.: JAI Press.
Bendix, Reinhard. 1956. *Work and Authority in Industry*. New York: Wiley.
Cappelli, Peter, and David Neumark. 2001. "Do 'High-Performance' Work Practices Improve Establishment-Level Outcomes?" *Industrial and Labor Relations Review* 54 (July): 737–75.
Chandler, Alfred. 1962. *Strategy and Structure: Chapters in the History of the Industrial Enterprise*. Cambridge, Mass.: MIT Press.
Cheung, Steven. 1983. "The Contractual Nature of the Firm." *Journal of Law and Economics* 26 (April): 1–21.
Coase, Ronald. 1937. "The Nature of the Firm." *Economica* 4 (November): 386–405.
Commons, John. 1919. *Industrial Goodwill*. New York: McGraw-Hill.
Delaney, John, and John Godard. 2001. "An Industrial Relations Perspective on the High-Performance Paradigm." *Human Resource Management Review* 11, no. 4: 395–430.
Demsetz, Harold. 1991. "The Theory of the Firm Revisited." In *The Nature of the*

Firm, ed. Oliver Williamson and Sidney Winter, pp. 159–78. New York: Oxford University Press.

Drucker, Peter. 1995. "Mary Parker Follett: Prophet of Management." In *Mary Parker Follett—Prophet of Management*, ed. Pauline Graham, pp. 1–10. Boston: Harvard Business School Press.

Duncan, Jack. 1989. *Great Ideas in Management*. San Francisco: Jossey-Bass.

Fayol, Henri. 1916. *Industrial and General Administration*. Geneva: International Management Institute.

Fine, Sidney. 1956. *Laissez Faire and the General-Welfare State*. Ann Arbor, Mich.: University of Michigan Press.

Follett, Mary Parker. [n.d.]. "Business as an Integrative Unity." Reprinted in *Dynamic Administration: The Collected Papers of Mary Parker Follett*, ed. Henry Metcalf and L. Urwick, pp. 71–94. New York: Harper & Bros., 1940.

Freeman, Richard, and Joel Rogers. 1999. *What Workers Want*. Ithaca, N.Y.: ILR Press.

Furubotn, Erik, and Rudolf Richter. 1997. *Institutions and Economic Theory*. Ann Arbor, Mich.: University of Michigan Press.

Gilman, Nicholas. 1889. *Profit Sharing between Employer and Employee*. New York: Houghton Mifflin.

———. 1899. *A Dividend to Labor: A Study of Employers' Welfare Institutions*. New York: Houghton Mifflin.

Gitelman, Howard M. 1988. *The Legacy of the Ludlow Massacre: A Chapter in American Industrial Relations*. Philadelphia: University of Pennsylvania Press.

Hicks, Clarence. 1941. *My Life in Industrial Relations: Fifty Years in the Growth of a Profession*. New York: Harper.

Hirsch, Barry. 1991. *Labor Unions and the Economic Performance of Firms*. Kalamazoo, Mich.: Upjohn Institute.

Jacoby, Sanford. 1985. *Employing Bureaucracy: Managers, Unions, and the Transformation of Work in American Industry, 1900–1945*. New York: Columbia University Press.

———. 1997. *Modern Manors: Welfare Capitalism Since the New Deal*. Princeton: Princeton University Press.

Kaufman, Bruce. 1997. "Labor Markets and Employment Regulation: The View of the Old Institutionalists." In *Government Regulation of the Employment Relationship*, ed. Bruce Kaufman, pp. 11–55. Ithaca, N.Y.: ILR Press.

———. 2001. "The Theory and Practice of Strategic HRM and Participative Management: Antecedents in Early Industrial Relations." *Human Resource Management Review* 11, no. 4: 505–34.

Kaufman, Bruce, and David Levine. 2000. "An Economic Analysis of Employee Representation." In *Nonunion Employee Representation: History, Contemporary Practice, and Policy*, ed. Bruce E. Kaufman and Daphne G. Taras, pp. 145–79. Armonk, N.Y.: M.E. Sharpe.

King, William Lyon Mackenzie. 1918. *Industry and Humanity*. Toronto: University of Toronto Press.

Kochan, Thomas, and Paul Osterman. 1994. *The Mutual Gains Enterprise*. Boston: Harvard Business School Press.

Laistner, M. 1974. *Greek Economics*. London: Dent & Sons.

Lawler, Edward. 1992. *Ultimate Advantage: Creating the High-Involvement Organization*. San Francisco: Jossey-Bass.

Leiserson, William. 1922. "Constitutional Government in American Industry." *American Economic Review* 12 (Supplement): 56–79.

Likert, Rensis. 1961. *New Patterns of Management.* New York: McGraw-Hill.

Mayo, Elton. 1933. *The Human Problems of an Industrial Civilization.* New York: Macmillan Co.

————. 1945. *The Social Problems of an Industrial Civilization.* Cambridge, Mass.: Harvard Business School Press.

McGregor, Douglas. 1960. *The Human Side of Enterprise.* New York: McGraw-Hill.

McMahan, G., M. Bell, and M. Virick. 1998. "Strategic Human Resource Management, Employee Involvement, Diversity, and International Issues." *Human Resource Management Review* 8, no. 3: 193–214.

Miller, Gary. 1991. *Managerial Dilemmas.* New York: Cambridge University Press.

Nadler, David, and Marc Gerstein. 1992. "Designing High-Performance Work Systems: Organizing People, Work, Technology, and Information." In *Organizational Architecture,* ed. D. Nadler, M. Gerstein, and R. Shaw, pp. 110–32. San Francisco: Jossey-Bass.

Nelson, Daniel. 1975. *Managers and Workers: Origins of the New Factory System in the United States, 1880–1920.* Madison, Wis.: University of Wisconsin Press.

Peters, Thomas, and Robert Waterman. 1982. *In Search of Excellence.* New York: Harper & Row.

Pfeffer, Jeffrey. 1994. *Competitive Advantage through People.* Boston: Harvard Business School Press.

Pomeroy, Sarah. 1994. *Xenophon Oeconomicus: A Social and Historical Commentary.* New York: Clarendon Press.

Rockefeller, John D., Jr. 1923. *The Personal Relation in Industry.* New York: Boni and Liveright.

Simon, Herbert. 1982. *Models of Bounded Rationality,* vol. 2. Cambridge, Mass.: MIT Press.

Smith, Adam. 1776. *An Inquiry into the Nature and Causes of the Wealth of Nations.* New York: Modern Library.

Taylor, Frederick. 1895. "A Piece Rate System, Being a Partial Solution to the Labor Problem." Reprinted in *Early Management Thought,* ed. Daniel Wren, pp. 245–72. Brookfield, Vt.: Dartmouth Publishing, 1997.

————. 1911. *The Principles of Scientific Management.* New York: Harper & Row.

Towne, Henry. 1886. "The Engineer as an Economist." Reprinted in *Early Management Thought,* ed. Daniel Wren, pp. 35–39. Brookfield, Vt.: Dartmouth Publishing, 1997.

Trist, Eric. 1981. *The Evolution of Socio-Technical Systems.* Toronto: Ontario Quality of Working Life Centre.

Voos, Paula. 2001. "An IR Perspective on Collective Bargaining." *Human Resource Management Review* 11, no. 4: 487–504.

Williamson, Oliver. 1985. *The Economic Institutions of Capitalism.* New York: Free Press.

Wren, Daniel, ed. 1997. *Early Management Thought.* Brookfield, Vt.: Dartmouth Publishing.

Chapter 5. A Century of Human Resource Management

Baritz, Loren. 1960. *The Servants of Power.* Middletown, Conn.: Wesleyan University Press.

Barney, Jay. 1991. "Firm Resources and Sustained Competitive Advantage." *Journal of Management* 17 (March): 99–120.

Becker, Brian, and Mark Huselid. 1999. "Strategic HRM in Five Leading Firms." *Human Resource Management* 38 (Winter): 287–301.

Bennett, George K. 1948. "A New Era in Business and Industrial Psychology." *Personnel Psychology* 1 (Winter): 473–77.

Berg, Ivar, Marcia Freedman, and Michael Freeman. 1978. *Managers and Work Reform: A Limited Engagement.* New York: Free Press.

Berkowitz, Edward, and Kim McQuaid. 1978. "Businessman and Bureaucrat: The Evolution of the American Social Welfare System, 1900–1940." *Journal of Economic History* 38 (May): 120–47.

———. 1992. *Creating the Welfare State: The Political Economy of Twentieth-Century Reform.* Lawrence, Kans.: University Press of Kansas.

Berle, Adolf A., and Gardiner C. Means. 1932. *The Modern Corporation and Private Property.* New York: Macmillan Co.

Blair, Margaret, and Lynn A. Stout. 1999. "Team Production in Business Organizations: An Introduction." *Journal of Corporation Law* 24 (Summer): 744–50.

Blake, Robert, and Jane Mouton. 1964. *The Managerial Grid.* Houston, Tex.: Gulf Publishing.

Bluestone, Barry, and Bennett Harrison. 1982. *The Deindustrialization of America.* New York: Basic Books.

Brandes, Stuart. 1976. *American Welfare Capitalism, 1880–1940.* Chicago: University of Chicago Press.

Business Week. 1998. "We Want You to Stay, Really." June 22.

Caimano, Vincent, Pat Canavan, and Linda Hill. 1999. "Trends and Issues Affecting Human Resources and Global Business." In *The New HR: Strategic Positioning of the HR Function,* ed. Karl Price and James W. Walker, pp. 23–38. New York: Human Resource Planning Society.

Cappelli, Peter. 1999. *The New Deal at Work.* Boston: Harvard Business School Press.

Chambers, Elizabeth, Mark Foulon, Helen Jones, Steven Hankin, and Edward Michaels. 1998. "The War for Talent." *McKinsey Quarterly* 3: 44–57.

Chandler, Alfred D. 1956. "Management Decentralization: An Historical Analysis." *Business History Review* 30 (Spring): 111–74.

———. 1962. *Strategy and Structure.* Cambridge, Mass.: MIT Press.

———. 1977. *The Visible Hand: The Managerial Revolution in American Business.* Cambridge, Mass.: Harvard University Press.

Coffee, John C., Jr. 1988. "Shareholders versus Managers: The Strain in the Corporate Web." In *Knights, Raiders and Targets: The Impact of the Hostile Takeover,* ed. John C. Coffee, Jr., Susan Rose-Ackerman, and Louis Lowenstein, pp. 77–134. New York: Oxford University Press.

Conference Board. 1966. *Personnel Administration: Changing Scope and Organization.* New York.

Csoka, Louis. 1995. "Rethinking Human Resources." Conference Board Report no. 1124–95–RR. New York.

Derickson, Alan. 1994. "Health Security for All? Social Unionism and Universal Health Insurance, 1935–58." *Journal of American History* 80 (March): 1333–56.

Dobbin, Frank. 1998. "The Strength of a Weak State: The Rights Revolution and the Rise of Human Resources Management Divisions." *American Journal of Sociology* 104 (September): 441–76.

Domhoff, William. 1996. "How the Rockefeller Network Shaped Social Security." In *State Autonomy or Class Dominance?* ed. William Domhoff. New York: Aldine.

Donaldson, Gordon. 1994. *Corporate Restructuring: Managing the Change Process from Within.* Boston: Harvard Business School Press.

Eilbirt, Henry. 1959. "The Development of Personnel Management in the United States." *Business History Review* 33 (Autumn): 345–64.

Elder, Glen H., Jr. 1974. *Children of the Great Depression: Social Change in Life Experience.* Chicago: University of Chicago Press.

Evans, Chester, and LaVerne N. Laseau. 1950. *My Job Contest.* Washington, D.C.: Personnel Psychology Press.

Fligstein, Neil. 1985. "The Spread of the Multidivisional Form." *American Sociological Review* 50 (June): 377–91.

———. 1990. *The Transformation of Corporate Control.* Cambridge, Mass.: Harvard University Press.

Foss, Nicolai. 1997. *Resources, Firms, and Strategies.* Oxford: Oxford University Press.

Foulkes, Fred K. 1980. *Personnel Policies in Large Nonunion Firms.* Englewood Cliffs, N.J.: Prentice-Hall.

Freedman, Audrey. 1985. *The New Look in Wage Policy and Employee Relations.* New York: Conference Board.

Freeman, Richard, and James Medoff. 1984. *What Do Unions Do?* New York: Basic Books.

Gilson, Mary B. 1940. *What's Past Is Prologue: Reflections on My Industrial Experience.* New York: Harper & Bros.

Gitelman, Howard M. 1984. "Being of Two Minds: American Employers Confront the Labor Problem, 1915–1919." *Labor History* 25 (Spring): 189–216.

———. 1988. *Legacy of the Ludlow Massacre: A Chapter in American Industrial Relations.* Philadelphia: University of Pennsylvania Press.

Gratton, L., V. Hope-Hailey, P. Stiles, and C. Truss. 1999. "Linking Individual Performance to Business Strategy: The People Process Model." In *Strategic Human Resource Management*, ed. Randall Schuler and Susan Jackson. Oxford: Blackwell.

Groves, Martha. 1998. "In Tight Job Market, Software Firm Develops Programs to Keep Employees." *Los Angeles Times*, June 14.

Harris, Howell John. 2000. *Bloodless Victories: The Rise and Fall of the Open Shop in the Philadelphia Metal Trades, 1890–1940.* Cambridge: Cambridge University Press.

Heckscher, Charles. 1988. *The New Unionism: Employee Involvement in the Changing Corporation.* New York: Basic Books.

Herzberg, Frederick. 1968. "One More Time: How Do You Motivate Employees?" *Harvard Business Review* (January/February).

Hicks, Clarence J. 1941. *My Life in Industrial Relations: Fifty Years in the Growth of a Profession.* New York: Harper & Bros.

Jacoby, Sanford M. 1985. *Employing Bureaucracy: Managers, Unions, and the Transformation of American Industry, 1900–1945.* New York: Columbia University Press.

———. 1988. "Employee Attitude Surveys in Historical Perspective." *Industrial Relations* 27 (Winter): 74–93.

———. 1993. "Employers and the Welfare State: The Role of Marion B. Folsom." *Journal of American History* 80 (September): 525–56.

———. 1997. *Modern Manors: Welfare Capitalism since the New Deal.* Princeton: Princeton University Press.

———. 1999. "Are Career Jobs Headed for Extinction?" *California Management Review* (Fall): 123–45.

———. 2000. "A Road Not Taken: Independent Local Unions in the U.S. since 1935." In *Nonunion Employee Representation: History, Contemporary Practice, and Policy*, ed. Bruce E. Kaufman and Daphne G. Taras, pp. 76–95. Armonk, N.Y.: M.E. Sharpe.

Janger, Allen R. 1977. *The Personnel Function: Changing Objectives and Organization*. New York: Conference Board.

Kaufman, Bruce E. 2000. "Personnel/Human Resource Management: Its Roots as Applied Economics." *History of Political Economy* 32 (Annual Supplement): 229–56.

Kevles, Daniel. 1968. "Testing the Army's Intelligence: Psychologists and the Military in World War I." *Journal of American History* 65: 565–81.

Klein, Jennifer. 2000. "The Business of Health Security: Employee Health Benefits, Commercial Insurers, and the Reconstruction of Welfare Capitalism, 1945–1960." *International Labor and Working Class History* 58 (Fall): 293–313.

Kletzer, Lori. 1998. "Job Displacement." *Journal of Economic Perspectives* 12 (Winter): 115–36.

Kochan, Thomas, Harry C. Katz, and Robert McKersie. 1986. *The Transformation of American Industrial Relations*. New York: Basic Books.

Kramer, Robert J. 1998. "Organizing the Corporate Headquarters." *HR Executive Review* 6.

Lafferty, Kevin. 1996. "Economic Short-Termism: The Debate, the Unresolved Issues, and the Implications for Management." *Academy of Management Review* 21 (July): 825–60.

Legge, Karen. 1995. "HRM: Rhetoric, Reality, and Hidden Agendas." In *Human Resource Management: A Critical Text*, ed. John Storey, pp. 33–59. London: Routledge.

Leiserson, William. 1933. "Personnel Problems Raised by the Current Crisis." *Management Review* 22 (April): 114.

Lever, Scott. 1999. "An Analysis of Managerial Motivations Behind Outsourcing Practices." *Human Resource Planning* 20: 27–47.

Ling, Cyril C. 1965. *The Management of Personnel Relations*. Homewood, Ill.: R.D. Irwin.

Litterer, Joseph. 1963. "Systematic Management: Design for Organizational Recoupling in American Manufacturing Firms." *Business History Review* 37 (Winter): 376–89.

Lombardo, Michael, and Robert Eichinger. 1997. "Human Resources' Role in Building Competitive Edge Leaders." In *Tomorrow's HR Management*, ed. Dave Ulrich, Michael Losey, and Gerry Lake. New York: Wiley.

Marginson, Paul, Paul Edwards, John Purcell, and Nancy Hubbard. 1993. "The Control of Industrial Relations in Large Companies: An Initial Analysis of the Second Company-Level Industry Relations Survey." *Warwick Papers in Industrial Relations, No. 45*. Coventry: University of Warwick.

McFarland, Dalton. 1962. *Cooperation and Conflict in Personnel Administration*. New York: American Foundation for Management Research.

McGregor, Douglas. 1960. *The Human Side of Enterprise*. New York: McGraw-Hill.

Milton, Charles R. 1970. *Ethics and Expediency in Personnel Management*. Columbia, S.C.: University of South Carolina Press.

Nelson, Daniel. 1969. *Unemployment Insurance: The American Experience, 1915–1935*. Madison, Wis.: University of Wisconsin Press.

————. 1975. *Managers and Workers: Origins of the New Factory System in the U.S.* Madison, Wis.: University of Wisconsin Press.

Nelson, Daniel, and Stuart Campbell. 1972. "Taylorism versus Welfare Work in American Industry: H.L. Gantt and the Bancrofts." *Business History Review* 46 (Spring): 1–16.

Nestor, Oscar. 1986. *A History of Personnel Administration.* New York: Garland Press.

Ozanne, Robert. 1967. *A Century of Labor-Management Relations at McCormick and International Harvester.* Madison, Wis.: University of Wisconsin Press.

Parker, Mike, and Jane Slaughter. 1988. *Choosing Sides: Unions and the Team Concept.* Boston: South End Press.

Pearse, Robert F. 1964. "Sensitivity Training, Management Development, and Organizational Effectiveness." In *The Personnel Job in a Changing World,* ed. Jerome W. Blood, pp. 273–87. New York: American Management Association.

Pfeffer, Jeffrey. 1997. "Pitfalls on the Road to Measurement: The Dangerous Liaison of Human Resources with the Ideas of Accounting and Finance." *Human Resource Management* 36 (Fall): 357–65.

————. 1998. *The Human Equation: Building Profits by Putting People First.* Boston: Harvard Business School Press.

Purcell, John. 1995. "Corporate Strategy and Its Link with HRM Strategy." In *In Human Resource Management: A Critical Text,* ed. John Storey, pp. 63–86. London: Routledge.

Purcell, John, and Bruce Ahlstrand. 1994. *Human Resource Management in the Multidivisional Company.* Oxford: Oxford University Press.

Reichheld, Frederick F. 1996. *The Loyalty Effect.* Boston: Harvard Business School Press.

Ritzer, George, and Harrison Trice. 1969. *An Occupation in Conflict: A Study of the Personnel Manager.* Ithaca, N.Y.: New York State School of Industrial & Labor Relations.

Rodgers, Daniel. 1998. *Atlantic Crossings: Social Politics in a Progresssive Age.* Cambridge, Mass.: Harvard University Press.

Roethlisberger, F.J., and William J. Dickson. 1939. *Management and the Worker.* Cambridge, Mass.: Harvard University Press.

Rush, Harold M.F. 1969. *Behavioral Science: Concepts and Management Application.* New York: Conference Board.

Sampson, Anthony. 1995. Company Man: *The Rise and Fall of Company Life.* New York: Times Books.

Scheinberg, Stephen J. 1966. "The Development of Corporation Labor Policy, 1900–1940," Ph.D. dissertation, University of Wisconsin.

Strauss, George, et al., eds. 1974. *Organizational Behavior: Research and Issues.* Madison, Wis.: Industrial Relations Research Association.

Sutton, Francis X., Seymour Harris, Carl Kaysen, and James Tobin. 1956. *The American Business Creed.* Cambridge, Mass.: Harvard University Press.

Taylor, Frederick W. 1895. "A Piece Rate System: Being a Partial Step Toward Solution of the Labor Problem." *Transactions of the American Society of Mechanical Engineers* 16: 860–95.

Tedlow, Richard. 1979. *Keeping the Corporate Image: Public Relations and Business.* Greenwich, Conn.: JAI Press.

Teece, David J. 1998. "Capturing Value from Knowledge Assets." *California Management Review* 40: 55–79.

Thompson, C. Bertrand. 1914. "Wages and Wage Systems as Incentives." In *Scientific Management: A Collection of the More Significant Articles Describing the Taylor System of Management*, ed. C.B. Thompson, pp. 684–705. Cambridge, Mass.: Harvard University Press.

Useem, Michael. 1996. *Investor Capitalism.* New York: Basic Books.

Vogel, Steven. 1996. *More Rules: Regulatory Reform in Advanced Industrial Countries.* Ithaca, N.Y.: Cornell University Press.

White, Lawrence J. 2001. "What's Been Happening to Aggregate Concentration in the U.S. (And Should We Care?)." Working Paper no. CLB-01-008, Stern School of Business, New York University.

Whyte, William H. 1956. *The Organization Man.* New York: Simon & Schuster.

Wiebe, Robert H. 1967. *The Search for Order, 1877–1920.* New York: Hill & Wang.

Yeung, Arthur, and Wayne Brockbank. 1999. "Reengineering HR through Information Technology." In *The New HR: Strategic Positioning of the HR Function*, ed. Karl Price and James W. Walker, pp. 161–81. New York: Human Resource Planning Society.

Chapter 6. Employee Benefits and Social Insurance: The Welfare Side of Employee Relations

Beaumont, Richard A. 2001. *Establishing the Roots of Industrial Democracy and Pursuing Its Future.* New York: Industrial Relations Counselors.

Berkowitz, Edward D. 1996. "Review of G. William Domhoff, (October). Available on the Internet at http://www.h-net.msu.edu/reviews/showrev.cgi?path= 7418851737404.

Berkowitz, Edward D., and Monroe Berkowitz. 1985. "Challenges to Workers' Compensation: An Historical Analysis." In *Workers' Compensation Benefits: Adequacy, Equity, and Efficiency*, ed. John D. Worrall and David Appel, pp. 158–79. Ithaca, N.Y.: ILR Press.

Berkowitz, Edward D., and Kim McQuaid. 1992. *Creating the Welfare State: The Political Economy of Twentieth-Century Reform.* Rev. ed. Lawrence, Kans.: University of Kansas Press.

Bernstein, Irving. 1960. *The Lean Years.* Boston: Houghton Mifflin.

Boskin, Michael J. 1986. *Too Many Promises: The Uncertain Future of Social Security.* Homewood, Ill.: Dow Jones–Irwin.

Brandes, Stuart. 1970. *American Welfare Capitalism, 1880–1940.* Chicago, Ill.: University of Chicago Press.

Brody, David. 1993. "The Rise and Decline of Welfare Capitalism." In *Workers in Industrial America: Essays in the Twentieth Century Struggle.* 2d ed. New York: Oxford University Press.

Bureau of the Census. 1975. *Historical Statistics of the United States, Colonial Times to 1970, Part 1.* U.S. Department of Commerce. Washington, D.C.: Government Printing Office.

Bureau of Labor Statistics. 1942. "Union Agreement Provisions." Bulletin 686. U.S. Department of Labor. Washington, D.C.: Government Printing Office.

———. 2001a. "Employer Costs for Employee Compensation—March 2001." Press release U.S. Department of Labor: 01–194. Washington, D.C.

———. 2001b. "Employee Benefits in Private Industry, 1999." Press release U.S. Department of Labor: 01–473. Washington, D.C.

Bureau of National Affairs, Inc. 1950. *Negotiated Pension Plans: Text of 30 Agreements with Editorial Summary*. Washington, D.C.

Clinton, William J. 2001. *Economic Report of the President*. Office of the President. Washington, D.C.: Government Printing Office.

Commons, John R. 1903. "'Welfare Work' in a Great Industrial Plant." *Review of Reviews* 28 (July): 79.

Couper, Walter J., and Roger Vaughan. 1954. *Pension Planning: Experience and Trends*. Monograph No. 16. New York: Industrial Relations Counselors.

Domhoff, G. William. 1996. *State Autonomy or Class Dominance? Case Studies on Policy Making in America*. New York: Aldine de Gruyter.

Dulles, Foster Rhea. 1955. *Labor in America*. New York: Thomas Y. Crowell.

Ely, Richard T. 1903. *Studies in the Evolution of Industrial Society, Volume II*. New York: Macmillan Co.

Epstein, Abraham. 1936. *Insecurity: A Challenge to America*. 3d ed. New York: Random House.

Gilson, Mary Barnett. 1931. *Unemployment Insurance in Great Britain: The National System and Additional Benefit Plans*. New York: Industrial Relations Counselors.

Gottschalk, Marie. 1998. *Labor's Embrace of the Private Welfare State: How Ideas Shaped Health Care Policy in the U.S.* Paper presented at the Ideas, Culture and Political Analysis Workshop. Princeton: Princeton University. Available on the Internet at http://www.ciaonet.org/conf/ssr01/ssr01an.html.

Hansen, Alvin H., Merrill G. Murray, Russell A. Stevenson, and Bryce M. Stewart. 1934. *A Program for Unemployment Insurance and Relief in the United States*. Minneapolis, Minn.: University of Minnesota.

Hicks, Clarence J. 1941. *My Life in Industrial Relations: Fifty Years in the Growth of a Profession*. New York: Harper & Brothers.

Industrial Relations Counselors. 1936. "Industrial Pension Plans." Memo 27. New York.

———. 1945a. "Company-Financed Sickness and Disability Benefit Plans." Memo 78. New York.

———. 1945b. "Stock Ownership for Wage Earners and Executives." Memo 76. New York.

———. 1948. "Extra Pension Payments." Memo 103. New York.

———. 1949. "Pension Planning in the Light of Current Trends—I." Memo 111. New York.

———. 1950. "Pension Planning in the Light of Current Trends—II." Memo 116. New York.

———. 1957. "Major Medical Insurance—An Analysis of Evolving Patterns." Memo 134. New York.

———. 1996. "Social Security: Maintaining a Perspective on Its Problems and Their Possible Solutions." *IRConcepts* (Spring).

Jacoby, Sanford M. 1997. *Modern Manors: Welfare Capitalism since the New Deal*. Princeton: Princeton University Press.

Kaufman, Bruce E. 1997. "Labor Markets and Employment Regulation: The View of the 'Old Institutionalisms.'" In *Government Regulations of the Employment Relationship*, ed. Bruce E. Kaufman. Madison, Wis.: Industrial Relations Research Association.

———. 2001. "HR Management in the Twentieth Century: Milestones and Lessons Learned." *Perspectives on Work* 5, no. 1: 53–56.

Kiehel, Constance A. 1932. *Unemployment Insurance in Belgium: A National Development of the Ghent and Liege Systems*. New York: Industrial Relations Counselors.

Larson, Arthur, and Lex K. Larson. 2001. *Larson's Workers' Compensation Desk Edition*. New York: Lexis Publishing.

Latimer, Murray Webb. 1932a. *Industrial Pension Systems in the United States and Canada*. New York: Industrial Relations Counselors.

————. 1932b. *Trade Union Pension Systems and Other Superannuation and Permanent and Total Disability Benefits in the United States and Canada*. New York: Industrial Relations Counselors.

Latimer, Murray Webb, and Karl Tufel. 1940. "Trends in Industrial Pensions." Monograph No. 5. New York: Industrial Relations Counselors.

Lester, Richard A., and Charles V. Kidd. 1939. "The Case Against Experience Rating in Unemployment Compensation." Monograph No. 2. New York: Industrial Relations Counselors.

Lubove, Roy. 1968. *The Struggle for Social Security, 1900–1935*. Cambridge, Mass.: Harvard College.

Mandell, Nikki. 2002. *The Corporation as Family: The Gendering of Corporate Welfare, 1890–1930*. Chapel Hill, N.C.: University of North Carolina Press.

Mills, Charles M. 1927. *Vacations for Industrial Workers*. New York: Industrial Relations Counselors.

Mitchell, Daniel J.B. 2000. *Pensions, Politics, and the Elderly: Historic Social Movements and Their Lessons for Our Aging Society*. Armonk, N.Y.: M.E. Sharpe.

————. 2001. "Warren's Waterloo: The California Health Plan That Wasn't (And the New York Health Plan That Was and Is)." In *California Policy Options 2001*, ed. Daniel J.B. Mitchell. Los Angeles: UCLA School of Public Policy and Social Research.

Mont, Daniel, John F. Burton, Jr., Virginia Reno, and Cecili Thompson. 2002. *Workers' Compensation: Benefits, Coverage, and Costs, 2000 New Estimates*. Washington, D.C.: National Academy of Social Insurance.

Moore, Michael J., and W. Kip Viscusi. 1990. *Compensation Mechanisms for Job Risks: Wages, Workers' Compensation, and Product Liability*. Princeton: Princeton University Press.

Moss, A. David. 1996. *Socializing Security: Progressive-Era Economists and the Origins of American Social Policy*. Cambridge, Mass.: Harvard University Press.

Munnell, Alicia H., Annika Sunden, and Elizabeth Lidstone. 2002. *How Important Are Private Pensions?* Issue in Brief Number 8. Boston: Center for Retirement Research, Boston College.

National Commission on State Workmen's Compensation Laws. 1972. *The Report of the National Commission on State Workmen's Compensations Laws*. Washington, D.C.

National Industrial Conference Board (NICB). 1921. *Health Service in Industry*. New York.

————. 1923. *Experience with Mutual Benefit Associations in the United States*. New York.

————. 1929a. *Employee Thrift and Investment Plans*. New York.

————. 1929b. *Industrial Relations Programs in Small Plants*. New York.

————. 1931. *The Present Status of Mutual Benefit Associations*. New York.

————. 1934. *Recent Developments in Industrial Group Insurance*. New York.

————. 1935. *Vacations with Pay for Wage Earners*. New York.

————. 1936a. *Savings Plans and Credit Unions in Industry*. New York.

————. 1936b. *What Employers Are Doing for Employees*. New York.

————. 1954. *Fringe Benefit Packages*. New York.

Orloff, Ann. 1993. *The Politics of Pensions*. Madison, Wis.: University of Wisconsin Press.

Poen, Monte M. 1979. *Harry S. Truman versus the Medical Lobby: The Genesis of Medicare*. Columbia, Mo.: University of Missouri Press.

Posner, Richard A. 1972. "A Theory of Negligence." *Journal of Legal Studies* 1, no. 1: 29–96.

Quadagno, Jill. 1984. "Welfare Capitalism and the Social Security Act of 1935." *American Sociological Review* 49 (October): 632–47.

————. 1988. *The Transformation of Old Age Security: Class and Politics in the American Welfare State*. Chicago: The University of Chicago Press.

Reagan, Patricia B., and John A. Turner. 2000. "Did the Decline in Marginal Tax Rates during the 1980s Reduce Pension Coverage?" In *Employee Benefits and Labor Markets in Canada and the United States*, ed. William T. Alpert and Stephen A. Woodbury, pp. 475–95. Kalamazoo, Mich.: Upjohn Institute.

Rowe, Evan Keith. 1955. "Health Insurance and Pension Plans in Union Contracts." Bulletin 1187. Bureau of Labor Statistics, U.S. Department of Labor. Washington, D.C.: Government Printing Office.

Rubinow, Isaac M. 1913. *Social Insurance, with Special Reference to American Conditions*. New York: Henry Holt.

————. 1934. *The Quest for Security*. New York: Henry Holt.

Schlesinger, Arthur M., Jr. 1957. *The Crisis of the Old Order: 1919–1933*. Boston: Houghton Mifflin.

Skocpol, Theda. 1992. *Protecting Soldiers and Mothers: The Political Origins of Social Policy*. Cambridge, Mass.: Belknap Press of Harvard University Press.

Slichter, Summer H. 1929. "The Current Labor Policies of American Industries." *Quarterly Journal of Economics* (May): 393–435.

Social Security Administration. 2000. *Annual Statistical Supplement, 2002, to the Social Security Bulletin*. Washington, D.C.: Government Printing Office.

Somers, Herman Miles, and Anne Ramsay Somers. 1954. *Workmen's Compensation*. New York: Wiley.

Spates, T.G., and G.S. Rabinovitch. 1931. *Unemployment Insurance in Switzerland: The Ghent System Nationalized with Compulsory Features*. New York: Industrial Relations Counselors.

Spieler, Emily A., and John F. Burton, Jr. 1998. "Compensation for Disabled Workers: Workers' Compensation." In *New Approaches to Disability in the Workplace*, ed. Terry Thomason, John F. Burton, Jr., and Douglas Hyatt. Madison, Wis.: Industrial Relations Research Association.

Stein, Bruno. 1979. *Social Security and the Private Pension System*. New York: Industrial Relations Counselors.

Stevens, Beth. 1986. *Complementing the Welfare State: The Development of Private Pensions, Health Insurance, and Other Employee Benefits in the United States*. Labour-Management Relations Series 65. Geneva: International Labour Organization.

Stewart, Bryce M. 1930. *Unemployment Benefits in the United States: The Plans and Their Setting*. New York: Industrial Relations Counselors.

————. 1931. "Summary of Studies on Unemployment Insurance." Pamphlet. New York: Industrial Relations Counselors.

Thomason, Terry, Timothy P. Schmidle, and John F. Burton, Jr. 2001. *Workers' Compensation: Benefits, Costs, and Safety under Alternative Insurance Arrangements.* Kalamazoo, Mich.: W.E. Upjohn Institute for Employment Research.

Tone, Andrea. 1997. *The Business of Benevolence: Industrial Paternalism in Progressive America.* Ithaca, N.Y.: Cornell University Press.

Weinberg, Arthur, and Lila Weinberg. 1961. *The Muckrakers.* New York: Simon & Schuster.

Weinstein, James. 1968. *The Corporate Ideal in the Liberal State, 1900–1918.* Boston: Beacon Press.

Willborn, Steven L., Stewart J. Schwab, and John F. Burton, Jr. 2002. *Employment Law: Cases and Materials.* 3d ed. Newark, N.J.: LexisNexis.

Williams, C. Arthur, Jr., and Peter S. Barth. 1973. *Compendium on Workmen's Compensation.* National Commission on State Workmen's Compensation Laws. Washington, D.C.: Government Printing Office.

Witte, Edwin E. 1962. *The Development of the Social Security Act.* Madison, Wis.: University of Wisconsin Press.

Woodbury, Stephen A., and Wei-Jang Huang. 1991. *The Tax Treatment of Fringe Benefits.* Kalamazoo, Mich.: Upjohn Institute.

Chapter 7. Incentives and Structure: Development of Pay Practices in the Twentieth Century

Alexander, Karen. 2000. "Lost Stock Options Give Rise to Suits over Job Termination." *Los Angeles Times,* November 24.

American Society of Civil Engineers. 1952. *Job Evaluation and Salary Surveys.* New York.

Arnault, E. Jane, Louis Gordon, Douglas H. Joines, and G. Michael Phillips. 2001. "An Experimental Study of Job Evaluation and Comparable Worth." *Industrial and Labor Relations Review* 54 (July): 806–15.

Asch, Beth J., and John T. Warner. 1997. "Incentive Systems: Theory and Evidence." In *The Human Resource Management Handbook,* ed. David Lewin, Daniel J.B. Mitchell, and Mahmood A. Zaidi, pp. 175–215. Greenwich, Conn.: JAI Press.

Ashford, Robert, and Rodney Shakespeare. 1999. *Binary Economics: The New Paradigm.* Lanham, Md.: University Press of America.

Balderston, C. Canby. 1930. *Group Incentives: Some Variations in the Use of Group Bonus and Gang Piece Work.* Philadelphia: University of Pennsylvania Press.

———. 1937. *Profit Sharing for Wage Earners.* New York: Industrial Relations Counselors.

———. 1940. *Wage Setting Based on Job Analysis and Evaluation.* New York: Industrial Relations Counselors. Excerpted in *Management of an Enterprise,* 2d ed., by C. Canby Balderston et al., pp. 371–97. New York: Prentice-Hall, 1949.

Balderston, C. Canby, Robert P. Brecht, Victor S. Karabasz, and Robert J. Riddle. 1949. *Management of an Enterprise.* 2d ed. New York: Prentice-Hall.

Baron, James N., Frank R. Dobbin, P. Devereaux Jennings. 1986. "War and Peace: The Evolution of Modern Personnel Administration in U.S. Industry." *American Journal of Sociology* 28 (September): 350–83.

Baron, James N., P. Devereaux Jennings, and Frank R. Dobbin. 1988. "Mission Control? The Development of Personnel Systems in U.S. Industry." *American Sociological Review* 53 (August): 497–514.

Baumback, Clifford M. 1954. *Arbitration of Job Evaluation Disputes*. Research Series No. 8. Iowa City, Iowa: State University of Iowa, Bureau of Labor and Management.

Becker, William E. 2000. "Teaching Economics in the 21st Century." *Journal of Economic Perspectives* 14 (Winter): 109–19.

Bellamy, Edward. 1887. *Looking Backwards: 2000–1887*. Reprint. New York: Modern Library, 1917.

Benge, Eugene J. 1953. *Compensating Employees Including a Manual of Procedures on Job Evaluation and Merit Rating*. New London, Conn.: National Foremen's Institute.

Benge, Eugene J., Samuel L.H. Burk, and Edward N. Hay. 1941. *Manual of Job Evaluation: Procedures of Job Analysis and Appraisal*. New York: Harper & Bros.

Bewley, Truman F. 1999. *Why Wages Don't Fall During a Recession*. Cambridge, Mass.: Harvard University Press.

Bureau of the Census. 1975. *Historical Statistics of the United States: Colonial Times to 1970*. U.S. Department of Commerce. Washington, D.C.: Government Printing Office.

Bureau of Labor Statistics. 1937. *Strikes in the United States: 1880–1936*. Bulletin 651. U.S. Department of Labor. Washington, D.C.: Government Printing Office.

———. 1942. *Union Agreement Provisions*. Bulletin 686. U.S. Department of Labor. Washington, D.C.: Government Printing Office.

———. 1943. *Effect of Incentive Payments on Hourly Earnings*. Bulletin 742. U.S. Department of Labor. Washington, D.C.: Government Printing Office.

———. 1946. *Union Agreements in the Cotton-Textile Industry*. Bulletin 885. U.S. Department of Labor. Washington, D.C.: Government Printing Office.

———. 1947a. *Guaranteed Wage or Guaranteed Employment Plans*. Bulletin 906. U.S. Department of Labor. Washington, D.C.: Government Printing Office.

———. 1947b. *Economic Analysis of Guaranteed Wages*. Bulletin 907. U.S. Department of Labor. Washington, D.C.: Government Printing Office.

———. 1948a. *Collective Bargaining Provisions: Incentive Wage Provisions; Time Studies and Standards of Production*. Bulletin 908–3. U.S. Department of Labor. Washington, D.C.: Government Printing Office.

———. 1948b. *Collective Bargaining Provisions: General Wage Provisions*. Bulletin 908–8. U.S. Department of Labor. Washington, D.C.: Government Printing Office.

———. 1948c. *Collective Bargaining Provisions: Wage Adjustment Plans*. Bulletin 908–9. U.S. Department of Labor. Washington, D.C.: Government Printing Office.

———. 1999a. *Employee Benefits in Small Private Establishments, 1996*. Bulletin 2507. U.S. Department of Labor. Washington, D.C.: Government Printing Office.

———. 1999b. "Employee Benefits in Medium and Large Private Establishments, 1997." Press release U.S. Department of Labor: 99–02. Washington, D.C.

———. 2000a. "Employer Costs for Employee Compensation—March 2000." Press release U.S. Department of Labor: 00–186. Washington, D.C.

———. 2000b. "Pilot Survey on the Incidence of Stock Options in Private Industry in 1999." Press release U.S. Department of Labor: 00–290. Washington, D.C.

Bureau of National Affairs, Inc. 1961. *Basic Patterns in Union Contracts*. 5th ed. Washington, D.C.

————. 1995. *Basic Patterns in Union Contracts*. 14th ed. Washington, D.C.

Carlson, Norma W. 1982. "Time Rates Tighten Their Grip on Manufacturing Industries." *Monthly Labor Review* 105 (May): 15–22.

Carmichael, H. Lorne, and W. Bentley MacLeod. 2000. "Worker Cooperation and the Ratchet Effect." *Journal of Labor Economics* 18 (January): 1–19.

Chamber of Commerce of the United States. 1999. *The 1999 Employee Benefits Study*. Washington, D.C.

Cox, John Howell. 1971. "Time and Incentive Pay Practices in Urban Areas." *Monthly Labor Review* 94 (December): 53–56.

Dawson, Virginia P. 1999. *Lincoln Electric: A History*. Cleveland, Ohio: Lincoln Electric Co.

Ells, Ralph W. 1945. *Salary and Wage Administration*. New York: McGraw-Hill.

Emmet, Boris. 1917. *Profit Sharing in the United States*. Bulletin 208. Bureau of Labor Statistics, U.S. Department of Labor. Washington, D.C.: Government Printing Office.

Fox, Harland, and Mitchell Meyer. 1962. *Employee Savings Plans in the United States*. New York: Conference Board.

Frutkin, Arnold W. 1955. *The Guaranteed Annual Wage*. Washington, D.C.: Bureau of National Affairs, Inc.

Gilmour, Robert W. 1956. *Industrial Wage and Salary Control*. New York: Wiley.

Gomberg, William. 1947. *A Labor Union Manual on Job Evaluation, The Relationship of Industrial Engineering Techniques to Collective Bargaining*. Chicago: Roosevelt College, Labor Education Division.

Hayes, Krista Read. 2000. "E-Compensation: Recruiting and Rewarding Internet Talent." *WorldatWork Journal* 9: 8–13.

Hicks, Clarence J. 1941. *My Life in Industrial Relations: Fifty Years in the Growth of a Profession*. New York: Harper & Brothers.

Industrial Relations Counselors. 1932. *Job Analysis: A Classified and Annotated Bibliography*. New York.

————. 1944. "A Digest of Selected Articles on Wage Incentive Plans." Memo 72. New York.

————. 1945a. "Profit Sharing to Wage Earners and Executives." Memo 73. New York.

————. 1945b. "Stock Ownership for Wage Earners and Executives." Memo 76. New York.

————. 1948a. "Extra Pension Payments." Memo 103. New York.

————. 1948b. "Guaranteed Employment or Wages as Part of a Security Program." Memo 95. New York.

————. 1953. "The Guaranteed Annual Wage: An Active Issue." Memo 131. New York.

————. 1963. "Restricted Stock Options: The Intent and the Controversy." Memo 143. New York.

Jacoby, Sanford M. 1983. "Industrial Labor Mobility in Historical Perspective." *Industrial Relations* 22 (Spring): 261–82.

————. 1997. *Modern Manors: Welfare Capitalism Since the New Deal*. Princeton: Princeton University Press.

Jacoby, Sanford M., and Daniel J.B. Mitchell. 1988. "Measurement of Compensation: Union and Nonunion." *Industrial Relations* 27 (Spring): 215–31.

Johnson, Forrest Hayden, Robert W. Boyse, Jr., and Dudley Pratt. 1946. *Job Evaluation*. New York: Wiley.

Jones, Derek C., Takao Kato, and Jeffrey Pliskin. 1997. "Profit Sharing and Gainsharing: A Review of Theory, Evidence, and Effects." In *The Human Resource Management Handbook*, ed. David Lewin, Daniel J.B. Mitchell, and Mahmood A. Zaidi, pp. 153–73. Greenwich, Conn.: JAI Press.

Kaufman, Bruce E. 2000. "Accomplishment and Shortcomings of Nonunion Employee Representation in the Pre–Wagner Act Years: A Reassessment." In *Nonunion Employee Representation: History, Contemporary Practice, and Policy*, ed. Bruce E. Kaufman and Daphne G. Taras, pp. 21–60. Armonk, N.Y.: M.E. Sharpe.

Kelso, Louis O., and Mortimer J. Adler. 1958. *The New Capitalists*. New York: Random House.

Kennedy, Van Dusen. 1945. *Union Policy and Incentive Wage Methods*. New York: Columbia University Press.

Kerr, Clark, and Lloyd Fisher. 1950. "Effect of Environment and Administration on Job Evaluation." *Harvard Business Review* 28 (May): 77–96.

King, William Lyon MacKenzie. 1918. *Industry and Humanity*. Abridged version. Toronto: Macmillan Co., 1947.

Knowlton, P.A. 1954. *Profit Sharing Patterns: A Comparative Analysis of the Formulas and Results of the Plans of 300 Companies with 730,000 Employees*. Evanston, Ill.: Profit Sharing Research Foundation.

Kruse, Douglas L., and Joseph R. Blasi. 1997. "Employee Ownership, Employee Attitudes, and Firm Performance: A Review of the Evidence." In *The Human Resource Management Handbook*, ed. David Lewin, Daniel J.B. Mitchell, and Mahmood A. Zaidi, pp. 113–51. Greenwich, Conn.: JAI Press.

———. 2000. "The New Employee-Employer Relationship." In *A Working Nation: Workers, Work, and Government in the New Economy*, ed. David T. Ellwood et al., pp. 42–91. New York: Russell Sage Foundation.

Lanham, Elizabeth. 1955. *Job Evaluation*. New York: McGraw-Hill.

Lebow, David, Louise Sheiner, Larry Slifman, and Martha Starr-McCluer. 1999. "Recent Trends in Compensation Practices." Working paper. Board of Governors of the Federal Reserve System.

Lincoln, James F. 1946. *Lincoln's Incentive System*. New York: McGraw-Hill.

Lott, Merrill R. 1926. *Wage Scales and Job Evaluation: Scientific Determination of Wage Rates on the Basis of Services Rendered*. New York: Ronald Press.

Milkovich, George T., and Jennifer Stevens. 1999. "Back to the Future: A Century of Compensation." Working paper 99–08. Center for Advanced Human Resource Studies, Cornell University.

Mitchell, Daniel J.B. 1985. "Wage Flexibility: Then and Now." *Industrial Relations* 24 (Spring): 266–79.

———. 1992. "Gain-Sharing: An Anti-Inflation Reform." *Challenge* 23 (July-August): 18–25.

———. 1995. "Profit Sharing and Employee Ownership: Policy Implications." *Contemporary Economic Policy* 13 (April): 16–25.

Mitchell, Daniel J.B., David Lewin, and Edward E. Lawler, III. 1990. "Alternative Pay Systems, Firm Performance, and Productivity." In *Paying for Productivity: A Look at the Evidence*, ed. Alan S. Blinder. Washington, D.C.: Brookings Institution.

National Center for Employee Ownership, Inc. 2000. "Seven to 10 Million Employees Now Receive Stock Options." *Employee Ownership Report* 20 (May/June): 1, 10.

National Industrial Conference Board. 1920. *Practical Experience with Profit Sharing in Industrial Establishments*. New York.

———. 1921. *Experience with Trade Union Agreements—Clothing Industries.* New York.

———. 1928a. *The Economic Status of the Wage Earner in New York and Other States.* New York.

———. 1928b. *Employee Stock Purchase Plans in the United States.* New York.

———. 1929a. *Employee Thrift and Investment Plans.* New York.

———. 1929b. *The Five-Day Week in Manufacturing Industries.* New York.

———. 1929c. *Industrial Relations Programs in Small Plants.* New York.

———. 1930a. *Employee Stock Purchase Plans and the Stock Market Crash of 1929.* New York.

———. 1930b. *Lay-Off and Its Prevention.* New York.

———. 1930c. *Systems of Wage Payment.* New York.

———. 1931. *The Present Status of Mutual Benefit Associations.* New York.

———. 1934. *Profit Sharing.* New York.

———. 1936a. *Plans for Stimulating Suggestions from Employees.* New York.

———. 1936b. *Savings Plans and Credit Unions in Industry.* New York.

———. 1936c. *What Employers Are Doing for Employees.* New York.

———. 1940. *Job Evaluation: Formal Plans for Determining Basic Pay Differentials.* New York.

———. 1950. *When Should Wages Be Increased?* New York.

———. 1954. *Fringe Benefit Packages.* New York.

Office of Management and Budget. 2000. *Analytical Perspectives: Budget of the United States Government, Fiscal Year 2001.* Executive Office of the President. Washington, D.C.: Government Printing Office.

Okun, Arthur M. 1973. "Upward Mobility in a High-Pressure Economy." *Brookings Papers on Economic Activity*: 207–52.

Otis, Jay L., and Richard H. Leukart. 1948. *Job Evaluation: A Basis for Sound Wage Administration.* New York: Ronald Press.

Parus, Barbara, and Jeremy Handel. 2000. "Total Salary Increase Budget Survey Results: Companies Battle Talent Drain." *Workspan* 19 (September): 17–25.

Patton, John A., and Reynold S. Smith, Jr. 1949. *Job Evaluation.* Chicago: Irwin.

Peterson, Trond. 1992a. "Individual, Collective, and Systems Rationality in Work Groups: Dilemmas and Market-Type Solutions." *American Journal of Sociology* 98 (November): 469–510.

———. 1992b. "Individual, Collective, and Systems Rationality in Work Groups: Dilemmas and Nonmarket Solutions." *Rationality and Society* 4 (July): 332–55.

Prendergast, Canice, and Robert Topel. 1996. "Favoritism in Organizations." *Journal of Political Economy* 104 (May): 958–78.

Raff, Daniel M.G., and Lawrence H. Summers. 1987. "Did Henry Ford Pay Efficiency Wages?" *Journal of Labor Economics* 5 (October): S57–S86.

Rockefeller, John D., Jr. 1923. *The Personal Relation in Industry.* New York: Boni and Liveright.

Rodrick, Scott S., ed. 1999. *The Stock Options Book.* 3d ed. Oakland, Calif.: National Center for Employee Ownership.

Scott, H. Gordon. 1975. "The Eisenhower Administration: The Doctrine of Shared Responsibility." In *Exhortation & Controls: The Search for a Wage-Price Policy, 1945–1971*, ed. Crauford D. Goodwin. Washington, D.C.: Brookings Institution.

Sheahan, John. 1967. *The Wage-Price Guideposts.* Washington, D.C.: Brookings Institution.

Silverstein, Stuart. 2000. "Job Report Cools Fears of Pending Inflation." *Los Angeles Times*, August 5.

Tarneja, Ram S. 1964. *Profit Sharing and Technological Change*. Madison, Wis.: School of Commerce, University of Wisconsin.

Taylor, Frederic Winslow. 1911. *The Principles of Scientific Management*. Reprint. New York: Dover, 1998.

Urhbrock, Richard Steven. 1935. *A Psychologist Looks at Wage-Incentive Methods*. New York: American Management Association.

War Production Board. 1945. *A Handbook on Wage Incentive Plans*. Washington, D.C.: Government Printing Office.

Weber, Arnold R. 1973. *In Pursuit of Price Stability: The Wage-Price Freeze of 1971*. Washington, D.C.: Brookings Institution.

Weber, Arnold R., and Daniel J.B. Mitchell. 1978. *The Pay Board's Progress: Wage Controls in Phase II*. Washington, D.C.: Brookings Institution.

Weitzman, Martin L. 1984. *The Share Economy: Conquering Stagflation*. Cambridge, Mass.: Harvard University Press.

Wilson, Thomas B. 1999. *Rewards That Drive High Performance: Success Stories from Leading Organizations*. New York: AMACOM.

Chapter 8. Advancing Equal Employment Opportunity, Diversity, and Employee Rights: Good Will, Good Management, and Legal Compulsion

Ashenfelter, Orley, and James Heckman. 1976. "Measuring the Effect of an Antidiscrimination Program." In *Evaluating the Labor Market Effects of Social Programs*, ed. O. Ashenfelter and J. Blum, pp. 46–84. Princeton: Princeton University Press.

Berger, Monroe. 1978. *Equality by Statute: The Revolution in Civil Rights*. New York: Farrar, Straus & Giroux.

Bloch, Farrell. 1994. *Antidiscrimination Law and Minority Employment*. Chicago: University of Chicago Press.

Bound, John, and Richard Freeman. 1992. "What Went Wrong? The Erosion of Relative Earnings and Employment among Young Black Men in the 1980s." *Quarterly Journal of Economics* 107, no. 1: 201–32.

Cain, Glenn. 1986 "Labor Market Discrimination." In *Handbook of Labor Economics*, Vol. 1, ed. O. Ashenfelter and D. Layard, chapter 13. Amsterdam: North-Holland.

Chay, Kenneth. 1998. "The Impact of Federal Civil Rights Policy on Black Economic Progress: Evidence from the Equal Employment Opportunity Act of 1972." *Industrial and Labor Relations Review* 51, no. 4: 608–32.

Collins, William J. 2001. "The Labor Market Impact of State Level Anti-Discrimination Laws 1940–1960." Vanderbilt University.

Dewey, Donald. 1952. "Negro Employment in Southern Industry." *Journal of Political Economy* 60 (August): 279–93.

Donohue, John J., and James Heckman. 1991. "Continuous versus Episodic Change: The Impact of Civil Rights Policy on the Economic Status of Blacks." *Journal of Economic Literature* 29 (December): 1603–43.

Feldman, Herman. 1931. *Racial Factors in American Industry*. New York: Harper & Brothers.

Freeman, Richard. 1973. "Changes in the Labor Market for Black Americans, 1948–1972." *Brookings Papers on Economic Activity* 1: 67–120.

Friedman, Raymond. 1996. "Network Groups: An Emerging Form of Employee Representation." In *Proceedings of the Forty-Eighth Annual Meeting of the Industrial Relations Research Association*, ed. Paula B. Voos, pp. 241–50. Madison, Wis.: Industrial Relations Research Association.

Goldstein, Morris, and Robert Smith. 1976. "The Estimated Impact of the Antidiscrimination Program Aimed at Federal Contractors." *Industrial and Labor Relations Review* 29, no. 3: 524–43.

Graham, Hugh D. 1990. *The Civil Rights Era*. New York: Oxford University Press.

Greenberg, Jack. 1994. *Crusaders in the Courts*. New York: Basic Books.

Heckman, James, and Brook Paynor. 1989. "Determining the Impact of Federal Antidiscrimination Policy on the Economic Status of Blacks: A Study of South Carolina." *The American Economic Review* 79 (March): 138–77.

Heckman, James, and Kenneth Wolpin. 1976. "Does the Contract Compliance Program Work? An Analysis of Chicago Data." *Industrial and Labor Relations Review* 29, no. 3: 544–64.

Helfgott, Roy B. 2000. "The Effectiveness of Diversity Networks in Providing Collective Voice for Employees." In *Nonunion Employee Representation: History, Contemporary Practice, and Policy*, ed. Bruce E. Kaufman and Daphne G. Taras, pp. 348–64. Armonk, N.Y.: M.E. Sharpe.

Hellerstein, Judith K., David Neumark, and Kenneth Troske. 1999. "Wages, Productivity, and Worker Characteristics: Evidence from Plant-Level Production Functions and Wage Equations." *Journal of Labor Economics* 17 (July): 409–46.

Hicks, Clarence. 1941. *My Life in Industrial Relations: Fifty Years in the Growth of a Profession*. New York: Harper & Brothers.

Higgs, Robert. 1989. "Black Progress and the Persistence of Racial Economic Inequalities, 1865–1940." In *The Question of Discrimination: Racial Inequality in the U.S. Labor Market*, ed. Steven Shulman and William Darity, Jr., pp. 9–31. Middletown, Conn.: Wesleyan University Press.

Holzer, Harry, and David Neumark. 1999. "Are Affirmative Action Hires Less Qualified? Evidence from Employer-Employee Data on New Hires." *Journal of Labor Economics* 17, no. 3: 534–69.

———. (forthcoming). "Assessing Affirmative Action." *Journal of Economic Literature*.

Ichniowski, Casey. 1983. "Have Angels Done More? The Steel Industry Consent Decree." *Industrial and Labor Relations Review* 36 (January): 182–98.

Kaufman, Bruce E. and Daphne G. Taras. 1999. "Nonunion Employee Representation: Introduction." *Journal of Labor Research* 20 (Winter): 1–8.

Kesselman, Louis C. 1946. "The Fair Employment Practice Commission Movement in Perspective." *Journal of Negro History* 30, no. 1: 30–46.

King, William Lyon Mackenzie. 1918. *Industry and Humanity*. Toronto: University of Toronto Press.

Leiserson, William M. 1929. "Contributions of Personnel Management to Improved Labor Relations." In *Wertheim Lectures on Industrial Relations, 1928*, pp. 125–64. Cambridge, Mass.: Harvard University Press.

Leonard, Jonathan. 1984a. "Anti-Discrimination or Reverse Discrimination: The Impact of Changing Demographics, Title VII and Affirmative Action on Productivity." *Journal of Human Resources* 19 (Spring): 145–74.

————. 1984b. "Employment and Occupational Advance under Affirmative Action." *Review of Economics and Statistics* 66 (August): 377–85.

————. 1984c. "The Impact of Affirmative Action on Employment." *Journal of Labor Economics* 2 (October): 439–63.

————. 1985a. "Affirmative Action as Earnings Redistribution: The Targeting of Compliance Reviews." *Journal of Labor Economics* 3 (July): 363–84.

————. 1985b. "What Promises Are Worth: The Impact of Affirmative Action Goals." *Journal of Human Resources* 20 (Winter): 3–20.

————. 1986. "Splitting Blacks? Affirmative Action and Earnings Inequality Within and Between Races." *Proceedings of the 39th Annual Meeting of the Industrial Relations Research Association* (Winter): 51–57.

————. 1990. "The Impact of Affirmative Action Regulation and Equal Employment Law on Black Employment." *Journal of Economic Perspectives* 47, no. 3: 47–64.

Maloney, Thomas. 1995. "Degrees of Inequality: The Advance of Black Workers in the Northern Meat Packing and Steel Industries before World War II." *Social Science History* 19 (Spring): 31–61.

Maloney, Thomas, and Warren Whatley. 1995. "Making the Effort: The Contours of Racial Discrimination in Detroit's Labor Markets, 1920–1940." *Journal of Economic History* 55 (September): 465–93.

Margo, Robert. 1990. *Race and Schooling in the South, 1880–1950: An Economic History*. Chicago: University of Chicago Press.

Marshall, Ray. 1965. *The Negro and Organized Labor.* New York: Wiley.

Mayo, Elton. 1929. "The Maladjustment of the Industrial Worker." In *Wertheim Lectures on Industrial Relations, 1928*, pp. 165–96. Cambridge, Mass.: Harvard University Press.

Myrdal, Gunnar. 1944. *An American Dilemma: The Negro Problem and Modern Democracy.* New York: Harper and Row.

Neumark, David, and Wendy Stock. 2001. "The Effect of Race and Sex Discrimination Legislation: A Historical View." Working paper. Michigan State University.

Norgren, Paul, and Samuel Hill. 1964. *Toward Fair Employment.* New York: Columbia University Press.

Norgren, Paul, Albert Webster, Roger Borgeson, and Maud Patten. 1959. *Employing the Negro in American Industry: A Study of Management Practices*. Monograph No. 17. New York: Industrial Relations Counselors.

Northrup, Herbert R. 1944. *Organized Labor and the Negro.* New York: Harper & Brothers.

————. 1970. *Negro Employment in Basic Industry.* Philadelphia: University of Pennsylvania.

Ozanne, Robert W. 1967. *A Century of Labor-Management Relations at McCormick and International Harvester.* Madison, Wis.: University of Wisconsin Press.

Rockefeller, John D., Jr. 1923. *The Personal Relation in Industry.* New York: Boni and Liveright.

Rodgers, William M., and William E. Spriggs. 1996. "The Effect of Federal Contractor Status on Racial Differences in Establishment-Level Employment Shares: 1979–1992." *American Economic Review* 86, no. 2: 290–93.

Ruchames, Louis. 1953. *Race, Jobs, and Politics: The Story of the FEPC.* New York: Columbia University Press.

Smith, James. 1984. "Race and Human Capital." *American Economic Review* 74 (September): 685–98.

Smith, James, and Finis Welch. 1984. "Affirmative Action and Labor Markets." *Journal of Labor Economics* 2, no. 2: 269–301.

Sniderman, Paul, and Thomas Piazza. 1993. *The Scar of Race*. Cambridge, Mass.: Harvard University Press, The Belknap Press.

Treplow, Leo. 1976. "Industrial Relations Counselors at Fifty Years." In *People, Progress and Employee Relations, Proceedings of the Fiftieth Anniversary Conference of Industrial Relations Counselors, Inc.*, ed. Richard Beaumont, pp. 3–8. Charlottesville, Va.: University Press of Virginia.

Whatley, Warren. 1990. "Getting a Foot in the Door: Learning, State Dependencies and the Racial Integration of Firms." *Journal of Economic History* 50 (March): 43–66.

Wright, Gavin. 1986. *Old South, New South*. New York: Basic Books.

Chapter 9. Voice in the North American Workplace: From Employee Representation to Employee Involvement

Abella, Irving M. 1973. *Nationalism, Communism, and Canadian Labour: The CIO, the Communist Party, and the Canadian Congress of Labour 1935–1956*. Toronto: University of Toronto Press.

Appelbaum, Eileen, Thomas Bailey, Peter Berg, and Arne Kalleberg. 2000. *Manufacturing Advantage: Why High Performance Work Systems Pay Off*. Ithaca, N.Y.: Economic Policy Institute and Cornell University Press, ILR Press.

Balderston, C. Canby. 1937. *Profit Sharing for Wage Earners*. New York: Industrial Relations Counselors.

———. 1940. *Wage Setting Based on Job Analysis and Evaluation*. New York: Industrial Relations Counselors.

Basset, William Rupert. 1919. *When the Workmen Help You Manage*. New York: Century Co.

Batt, Rosemary, and Eileen Appelbaum. 1995. "Worker Participation in Diverse Settings: Does the Form Affect the Outcome, and If So, Who Benefits?" *British Journal of Industrial Relations* 33, no. 3: 353–77.

Becker, Brian, and Mark A. Huselid. 1998. "High Performance Work Systems and Firm Performance: A Synthesis of Research and Managerial Implications." In *Research in Personnel and Human Resources Management*, vol. 16, ed. K.M. Rowland and G. Ferris, 53–101. Greenwich, Conn.: JAI Press.

Belknap, Chauncey. 1976. "The Formative Years [of IRC]." In *People, Progress and Employee Relations, Proceedings of the Fiftieth Anniversary Conference of Industrial Relations Counselors, Inc.*, ed. Richard Beaumont. Charlottesville, Va.: University Press of Virginia.

Bercuson, David Jay. 1990. *Confrontation at Winnipeg: Labour, Industrial Relations and the General Strike*. Montreal: McGill-Queen's University Press.

Blasi, Joseph, and Douglas Kruse. 2000. "High Performance Work Practices at Century's End: Incidence, Diffusion, Industry Group Differences and the Economic Environment." Working paper. Rutgers University School of Management and Labor Relations.

Brandes, Stuart. 1976. *American Welfare Capitalism, 1880–1940*. Chicago: University of Chicago Press.

Brody, David. 1960. *Steelworkers in America: The Nonunion Era*. New York: Russell & Russell.

Bureau of Labor Statistics. 1937. "Characteristics of Company Unions: 1935." Bulletin No. 634. U.S. Department of Labor. Washington, D.C.: Government Printing Office.

Ching, Cyrus S. 1953. *Review and Reflection: A Half-Century of Labor Relations.* New York: B. C. Forbes and Sons.

————. 1973. "The Reminiscences of Cyrus Ching." Manuscript, Oral History Research Office, Columbia University.

Cohen, Lizabeth. 1990. *Making a New Deal: Industrial Workers in Chicago, 1919–1939.* Cambridge: Cambridge University Press.

Commons, John R. 1921. *Industrial Government.* New York: Macmillan Co.

Cotton, John L. 1993. *Employee Involvement.* Newbury Park, Calif.: Sage.

Cotton, J.L., D.A. Vollrath, K.L. Froggatt, M.L. Lengnick-Hall, and K.R. Jennings. 1988. "Employee Participation: Diverse Forms and Different Outcomes." *Academy of Management Journal* 13: 147–53.

Craven, Paul. 1980. *"An Impartial Umpire": Industrial Relations and the Canadian State 1900–1911.* Toronto: University of Toronto Press.

Delaney, John, David Lewin, and Casey Ichniowski. 1989. "Human Resource Policies and Practices in American Firms." BLMR Report No. 137, U.S. Department of Labor. Washington, D.C.

Douglas, Paul M. 1921. "Shop Committees: Substitute for, or Supplement to, Trades-Unions?" *Journal of Political Economy* 29, no. 2: 89–107.

Estreicher, Samuel. 2000. "Nonunion Employee Representation: A Legal/Policy Perspective." In *Nonunion Employee Representation: History, Contemporary Practice, and Policy,* ed. Bruce E. Kaufman and Daphne G. Taras. Armonk, N.Y.: M.E. Sharpe.

Ewing, David W. 1989. *Justice on the Job: Resolving Grievances in the Nonunion Workplace.* Boston: Harvard Business School Press.

Ewing, John S. 1951. "History of Imperial Oil." Prepared for Business History Foundation, Inc., Harvard Business School. Unpublished. Imperial Oil Archives, Toronto.

Fosdick, Raymond B. 1952. *The Story of the Rockefeller Foundation.* New York: Harper & Brothers.

Foulkes, Fred K. 1980. *Personnel Policies in Large Nonunion Companies.* Englewood Cliffs, N.J.: Prentice-Hall.

Freeman, Richard, and Joel Rogers. 1999. *What Workers Want.* Ithaca, N.Y.: Cornell University Press, ILR Press, and New York: Russell Sage Foundation.

Ghent, William J. 1903. *Our Benevolent Feudalism.* New York: Macmillan Co.

Gibb, George Sweet, and Evelyn H. Knowlton. 1956. *History of Standard Oil Company (New Jersey): The Resurgent Years 1911–1927.* New York: Harper & Brothers.

Gitelman, H.M. 1988. *Legacy of the Ludlow Massacre: A Chapter in American Industrial Relations.* Philadelphia: University of Pennsylvania Press.

Grant, H.M. 1998. "Solving the Labour Problem at Imperial Oil: Welfare Capitalism in the Canadian Petroleum Industry, 1919–1929." *Labour/Le Travail* 41 (Spring): 69–95.

Hammer, Tova Helland. 2000. "Nonunion Representation Forms: An Organizational Behavior Perspective." In *Nonunion Employee Representation: History, Contemporary Practice, and Policy,* ed. Bruce E. Kaufman and Daphne G. Taras. Armonk, N.Y.: M.E. Sharpe.

Hanson, Randall, Rebecca I. Porterfield, and Kathleen Ames. 1995. "Employee Empowerment at Risk: Effect of Recent NLRB Rulings." *Academy of Management Executive* 9, no. 2: 45–54.

Harris, Howell John. 2000. *Bloodless Victories: The Rise and Fall of the Open Shop in the Philadelphia Metal Trades, 1890–1940*. Cambridge and New York: Cambridge University Press.

Hein, Kenneth. 1996. "Clinton Vetoes TEAM Act." *Incentive* 170 (September): 16.

Hicks, Clarence J. 1941. *My Life in Industrial Relations: Fifty Years in the Growth of a Profession*. New York: Harper & Bros.

Industrial Relations Counselors. 1936. *Industrial Pension Systems in the United States and Canada: Certain Phases of Pension Activities for the Years 1931–1934*. New York.

———. 1945. "National Collective Bargaining Policy." Monograph 9. New York.

———. 1954. "Steadier Jobs: A Handbook for Management on Stabilizing Employment." New York.

———. 1962. "Group Wage Incentives: Experience with the Scanlon Plan." Memo 141. New York.

———. 1994. *Report on the IRC Survey of Employee Involvement*. New York.

Jacoby, Sanford. 1997. *Modern Manors: Welfare Capitalism Since the New Deal*. Princeton: Princeton University Press.

———. 2000. "A Road Not Taken: Independent Local Unions in the United States since 1935." In *Nonunion Employee Representation: History, Contemporary Practice, and Policy*, ed. Bruce E. Kaufman and Daphne G. Taras. Armonk, N.Y.: M.E. Sharpe.

Jacoby, Sanford, and Anil Verma. 1992. "Enterprise Unions in the Modern Era." *Industrial Relations* 31, no. 1: 137–58.

Kaufman, Bruce E. 1996. "Why the Wagner Act?: Reestablishing Contact with its Original Purpose." In *Advances in Industrial and Labor Relations*, vol. 7, ed. David Lewin, Bruce Kaufman, and Donna Sockell, pp. 15–68. Greenwich, Conn.: JAI Press.

———. 1999. "Does the NLRA Constrain Employee Involvement and Participation Programs in Nonunion Companies?: A Reassessment." *Yale Law and Policy Review* 17 (no. 2): 729–811.

———. 2000. "Accomplishments and Shortcomings of Nonunion Employee Representation in the Pre–Wagner Act Years: A Reassessment." In *Nonunion Employee Representation: History, Contemporary Practice, and Policy*, ed. Bruce E. Kaufman and Daphne G. Taras. Armonk, N.Y.: M.E. Sharpe.

Kaufman, Bruce E., and David I. Levine. 2000. "An Economic Analysis of Employee Representation." In *Nonunion Employee Representation: History, Contemporary Practice, and Policy*, ed. Bruce E. Kaufman and Daphne G. Taras. Armonk, N.Y.: M.E. Sharpe.

Kaufman, Bruce E., David Lewin, and John A. Fossum. 2000. "Nonunion Employee Involvement and Participation Programs: The Role of Employee Representation and the Impact of the NLRA." In *Nonunion Employee Representation: History, Contemporary Practice, and Policy*, ed. Bruce E. Kaufman and Daphne G. Taras. Armonk, N.Y.: M.E. Sharpe.

Kaufman, Bruce E., and Daphne G. Taras, eds. 2000. *Nonunion Employee Representation: History, Contemporary Practice, and Policy*. Armonk, N.Y.: M.E. Sharpe.

King, William Lyon Mackenzie. 1893–1950. *The Mackenzie King Diaries*. With Index. Toronto: University of Toronto Press, 1973–1980.

———. 1918. *Industry and Humanity*. Toronto: Thomas Allen; Boston and New York: Houghton Mifflin.

Kraut, Allen I., and Abraham K. Korman, eds. 1999. *Evolving Practices in Human*

Resource Management: Responses to a Changing World of Work. San Francisco: Jossey-Bass.

La Dame, M. 1930. *The Filene Store.* New York: Russell Sage Foundation.

Latimer, Murray Webb. 1932. *Industrial Pension Systems in the United States and Canada.* New York: Industrial Relations Counselors.

Latimer, Murray Webb, and Karl Tufel. 1940. "Trends in Industrial Pensions." Monograph no. 5. New York: Industrial Relations Counselors.

Lauck, W. Jett. 1926. *Political and Industrial Democracy: 1776–1926.* New York: Funk and Wagnalls.

Lawler, Edward E., III. 1999. "Employee Involvement Makes a Difference." *Journal for Quality and Participation* 22, no. 5: 18–38.

Leitch, John. 1919. *Man-to-Man: The Story of Industrial Democracy.* New York: Forbes.

LeRoy, Michael. 1997. "Dealing with Employee Involvement in Nonunion Workplaces: Empirical Research Implications for the TEAM Act and Electromation." *Notre Dame Law Review*: 31–82.

———. 1999. "Employee Participation in the New Millennium: Redefining a Labor Organization Under Section 8(a)(2) of the NLRA." *Southern California Law Review* 72 (no. 6): 1651–723.

———. 2000. "Do Employee Participation Groups Violate Section 8(a)(2) of the National Labor Relations Act? An Empirical Analysis." In *Nonunion Employee Representation: History, Contemporary Practice, and Policy,* ed. Bruce E. Kaufman and Daphne G. Taras. Armonk, N.Y.: M.E. Sharpe.

Lipset, Seymour Martin, and Noah M. Meltz. 2000. "Estimates of Nonunion Employee Representation in the United States and Canada: How Different Are the Two Countries?" In *Nonunion Employee Representation: History, Contemporary Practice, and Policy,* ed. Bruce E. Kaufman and Daphne G. Taras. Armonk, N.Y.: M.E. Sharpe.

Litchfield, Paul W. 1946. *The Industrial Republic: Reflections of an Industrial Lieutenant.* Cleveland, Ohio: Corday & Gross.

MacIsaac, Merle. 1993. "Born-Again Basket Case." *Canadian Business* (May): 38–44.

Mahoney, Thomas A., and Mary R. Watson. 1993. "Evolving Modes of Work Force Governance: An Evaluation." In *Employee Representation: Alternatives and Future Directions,* ed. Bruce E. Kaufman and Morris M. Kleiner. Madison, Wis.: Industrial Relations Research Association Series.

Marshall, F. Ray. 1961. "Independent Unions in the Gulf Coast Petroleum Refining Industry—The Esso Experience." *Labor Law Journal* (September): 823–40.

McCabe, Douglas M. 1988. *Corporate Nonunion Complaint Procedures and Systems.* New York: Praeger.

McCabe, Douglas M., and David Lewin. 1992. "Employee Voice: A Human Resource Management Perspective." *California Management Review* 34 (Spring): 112–24.

McGregor, Frank A. 1962. *The Fall and Rise of Mackenzie King: 1911–1919.* Toronto: Macmillan of Canada.

Mills, Charles M. 1927. *Vacations for Industrial Workers.* N.Y.: Industrial Relations Counselors.

National Industrial Conference Board. 1922. "Experience with Works Councils in the United States." Research Report No. 50. New York.

Nelson, Daniel. 1982. "The Company Union Movement, 1900–1937: A Re-examination." *Business History Review* 56: 335–57.

―――. 2000. "The AFL and the Challenge of Company Unionism, 1915–1937." In *Nonunion Employee Representation: History, Contemporary Practice, and Policy*, ed. Bruce E. Kaufman and Daphne G. Taras. Armonk, N.Y.: M.E. Sharpe.

Norgren, Paul H., Albert N. Webster, Roger B. Borgeson, and Maud B. Patten. 1959. *Employing the Negro in American Industry: A Study of Management Practices*. New York: Industrial Relations Counselors.

Osterman, Paul. 1994. "How Common Is Workplace Transformation and Who Adopts It?" *Industrial and Labor Relations Review* 47, no. 2: 173–89.

Ozanne, Robert. 1967. *A Century of Labor-Management Relations at McCormick and International Harvester*. Madison, Wis.: University of Wisconsin Press.

Pivec, Mary, and Howard Z. Robbins. 1996. "Employee Involvement Remains Controversial." *HR Magazine* (November): 145–50.

Rockefeller, John D. [Sr.] 1909. *Random Reminiscences of Men and Events*. Toronto: McClelland & Goodchild.

Rockefeller, John D., Jr. 1916. *The Colorado Industrial Plan*. Standard Oil (New Jersey).

Roethlisberger, F. J., and W. J. Dickson. 1939. *Management and the Worker*. Reprint. London: Oxford University Press, 1964.

Schacht, John N. 1975. "Toward Industrial Unionism: Bell Telephone Workers and Company Unions, 1919–1937." *Labor History* 16 (Winter): 5–36.

Scheinberg, Stephen J. 1978. "Rockefeller and King: The Capitalist and the Reformer." In *Mackenzie King: Widening the Debate*, ed. J. English and J. O. Stubbs. Toronto: Macmillan of Canada.

―――. 1986. *The Development of Corporation Labor Policy, 1900–1940*. New York: Garland.

Seager, Henry R. 1923. "Company Unions vs. Trade Unions." *American Economic Review* 13, no. 1: 1–13.

Selekman, Ben M., and Mary Van Kleeck. 1924. *Employees' Representation in Coal Mines: A Study of the Industrial Relations Representation Plan of the Colorado Fuel and Iron Company*. New York: Russell Sage Foundation.

Smith, Robert Sidney. 1960. *Mill on the Dan: A History of Dan River Mills, 1882–1950*. Durham, N.C.: Duke University Press.

Stewart, Bryce M., and Walter J. Couper. 1945. *Profit Sharing and Stock Ownership for Wage Earners and Executives*. Monograph No. 10. New York: Industrial Relations Counselors.

Taras, Daphne Gottlieb. 1997. "Why Nonunion Representation Is Legal in Canada." *Relations industrielles/Industrial Relations* 52, no. 4: 761–80.

―――. 2000a. "Contemporary Experience with the Rockefeller Plan: Imperial Oil's Joint Industrial Council." In *Nonunion Employee Representation: History, Contemporary Practice, and Policy*, ed. Bruce E. Kaufman and Daphne G. Taras. Armonk, N.Y.: M.E. Sharpe.

―――. 2000b. "Portrait of Nonunion Employee Representation in Canada: History, Law, and Contemporary Plans." In *Nonunion Employee Representation: History, Contemporary Practice, and Policy*, ed. Bruce E. Kaufman and Daphne G. Taras. Armonk, N.Y.: M.E. Sharpe.

Taras, Daphne Gottlieb, and Jason Copping. 1998. "The Transition from Formal Nonunion Representation to Unionization: A Contemporary Case." *Industrial and Labor Relations Review* 52, no. 1: 22–44.

Taras, Daphne Gottlieb, and Bruce E. Kaufman. 1999. "What Do Non-Unions Do?

What Should We Do About Them?" United States Task Force on Reconstructing America's Labor Market Institutions, part of the secretary of labor's project "The Workforce/Workplace of the Future." U.S. Department of Labor. (Also published on the Internet as MIT Task Force Working Paper # WP14 at http://mitsloan.mit.edu/iwer/taskforce.html.)

Taylor, Frederick Winslow. 1916. "The Principles of Scientific Management." *Bulletin of the Taylor Society* (December). Reprinted in *Classics of Organization Theory*, 4th. ed., ed. J.M. Shafritz and J. Steven Ott. Fort Worth, Tex.: Harcourt Brace, 1995.

Teplow, Leo. 1976. "Industrial Relations Counselors at Fifty Years." In *People, Progress and Employee Relations, Proceedings of the Fiftieth Anniversary Conference of Industrial Relations Counselors, Inc.,* ed. Richard Beaumont. Charlottesville, Va.: University Press of Virginia.

Verma, Anil. 2000. "Employee Involvement and Representation in Nonunion Firms: What Canadian Employers Do and Why?" In *Nonunion Employee Representation: History, Contemporary Practice, and Policy,* ed. Bruce E. Kaufman and Daphne G. Taras. Armonk, N.Y.: M.E. Sharpe.

Chapter 10. Industrial Relations in the Global Economy

Alcock, Antony. 1971. *The History of the International Labour Organization.* London: Macmillan Co.

Aligisakis, Maximos. 1997. "Labour Disputes in Western Europe: Typology and Tendencies." *International Labour Review* 136: 73–94.

Aparicio-Valdez, Luis. 1995. "Hemispheric Integration and Labour Laws." *International Journal of Comparative Labour Law and Industrial Relations* 11 (Summer): 99–111.

Bellace, Janice R., and Geoffrey Latta. 1983. "Making the Corporation Transparent: Prelude to Multinational Bargaining." *Columbia Journal of World Business* 18 (Summer). Special issue on International Labor, ed. David Lewin: 64–72.

Bercuson, David Jay. 1973. Introduction to reprint of *Industry and Humanity,* by William Lyon MacKenzie King, 1918. Toronto: University of Toronto Press.

Bhagwati, Jagdish. 1994. "Fair Trade, Reciprocity and Harmonization: The New Challenge to the Theory and Policy of Free Trade." In *Analytical and Negotiating Issues in the Global Trading System,* ed. Alan Deardorf and Robert Stern. Ann Arbor, Mich.: University of Michigan Press.

Bhagwati, J.N., and R.E. Hudec. 1996. *Fair Trade and Harmonization: Prerequisites for Free Trade?* Cambridge, Mass.: MIT Press.

Blainpain, Roger, ed. 2000. *Bulletin of Comparative Labour Relations* 37. Special Issue on Multinational Enterprises and the Social Challenges of the XXIst Century: The ILO Declaration on Fundamental Principles at Work, Public and Private Corporate Codes of Conduct.

Charnovitz, Steve. 1987. "The Influence of International Labour Standards on the World Trading Regime." *International Labour Review* 126: 565–84.

———. 1992. "Environmental and Labour Standards and Trade." *The World Economy* 15: 335–56.

Compa, Lance A., and Tashia Ainchcliffe Darricarrère. 1996. "Private Labor Rights Enforcement Through Corporate Codes of Conduct." In *Human Rights, Labor*

Rights, and International Trade, ed. Lance A. Compa and Stephen F. Diamond, pp. 181–98. Philadelphia: University of Pennsylvania Press.

Compa, Lance A., and Stephen F. Diamond, eds. 1996. *Human Rights, Labor Rights, and International Trade*. Philadelphia: University of Pennsylvania Press.

Dahlby, Bev. 1993. "Payroll Taxes." In *Business Taxation in Canada*, ed. A. Maslov. Toronto: University of Toronto Press.

De Wet, Erika. 1995. "Labour Standards in the Globalized Economy: The Inclusion of a Social Clause in the General Agreement on Tariffs and Trade/World Trade Organization." *Human Rights Quarterly* 17: 443–62.

Diamond, Stephen F. 1996. "Labor Rights in the Global Economy: A Case Study of the North American Free Trade Agreement." In *Human Rights, Labor Rights, and International Trade*, ed. Lance A. Compa and Stephen F. Diamond, pp. 199–226. Philadelphia: University of Pennsylvania Press.

Due, Jasper, Jorgen Steen Madsen, and Carston Stroby-Jensen. 1991. "The Social Dimension: Convergence or Divergence of IR in the Single European Market." *Industrial Relations Journal* (Summer): 85–102.

Ehrenberg, Ronald E. 1994. *Labor Markets and Integrating National Economies.* Washington, D.C.: Brookings Institution.

Erickson, Christopher L., and Daniel J. B. Mitchell. 1996. "Labour Standards in International Trade Agreements." *Labour Law Journal* 47 (December): 763–73.

Fields, Gary. 1995. *Trade and Labour Standards: A Review of the Issues*. Paris: Organization for Economic Cooperation and Development.

Freeman, Richard B. 1994. "A Hard-Headed Look at Labour Standards." In *Creating Economic Opportunities: The Role of Labour Standards in Economic Restructuring*, ed. Warner Sengenberger and Duncan Campbell, pp. 79–92. Geneva: International Labour Organization.

Gadbaw, Michael R., and Michael T. Medwig. 1996. "Multinational Enterprises and International Labor Standards." In *Human Rights, Labor Rights, and International Trade*, ed. Lance A. Compa and Stephen F. Diamond, pp. 141–62. Philadelphia: University of Pennsylvania Press.

"Globalization: Context and Practicalities." 2001. *IRConcepts* (Winter): 1–10.

Gomez, Rafael, and Morley Gunderson. 2002. "The Integration of Labour Markets in North America." In *North American Integration: Economic, Cultural and Political Dimensions*, ed. G. Hoberg. Toronto: University of Toronto Press.

Gunderson, Morley. 1998. "Harmonization of Labour Policies Under Trade Liberalization." *Relations Industrielles/Industrial Relations* 53, no. 1: 24–52.

———. 1999. "Labour Standards, Income Distribution and Trade." *Integration and Trade* 3 (January): 82–104.

Gunderson, Morley, and Douglas Hyatt. 1996. "Do Injured Workers Pay for Reasonable Accommodation?" *Industrial and Labor Relations Review* 50: 92–104.

Gunderson, Morley, and W. Craig Riddell. 1995. "Jobs, Labour Standards and Promoting Competitive Advantage: Canada's Policy Challenge." *Labour* (special issue): S125–48.

Gunderson, Morley, and Anil Verma. 1992. "Canadian Labour Policies and Global Competition." *Canadian Business Law Journal* 20: 63–89.

———. 1994. "Free Trade and Its Implications for Industrial Relations and Human Resource Management." In *Regional Integration and Industrial Relations in North America*, ed. Maria Cook and Harry Katz, pp. 167–79. Ithaca, N.Y.: ILR Press.

————. 1999. "Canadian Labour in the Global Economy." *Journal of Canadian Studies* 19: 160–71.

Gunter, Hans. 1992. "The Tripartite Declaration of Principles concerning Multinational Enterprises and Social Policy." In *International Encyclopedia for Labour Law and Industrial Relations*, ed. R. Blanpain. London: Kluwer.

Hansson, Gote. 1983. *Social Clauses and International Trade*. New York: St. Martin's Press.

Helfgott, Roy B, 1983. "American Unions and Multinational Enterprises: A Case of Misplaced Emphasis." *Columbia Journal of World Business* 18 (Summer). Special issue on International Labor, ed. David Lewin: 81–86.

Herzenberg, Stephen A., and Jorge Perez-Lopez, eds. 1990. *Labor Standards and Development in the Global Economy*. Washington, D.C.: U.S. Department of Labor.

Hicks, Clarence. 1941. *My Life in Industrial Relations: Fifty Years in the Growth of a Profession*. New York: Harper & Brothers.

International Labour Office. 1997. *The ILO, Standard Setting and Globalization: Report of the Director General*. Geneva.

International Labour Organization. 1999. *Decent Work*. Geneva.

Johnston, George A. 1970. *The International Labour Organization: Its Work for Social and Economic Progress*. London: Europa Publications.

Kaufman, Bruce E., and Daphne Gottlieb Taras. 1999. "Nonunion Employee Representation: Introduction." *Journal of Labor Research* 20 (Winter): 1–8.

————, eds. 2000. *Nonunion Employee Representation: History, Contemporary Practice, and Policy*. Armonk, N.Y.: M.E. Sharpe.

Kenner, Jeff. 1995. "EC Labour Law: The Softly, Softly Approach." *International Journal of Comparative Labour Law and Industrial Relations* 11 (Winter): 307–26.

King, William Lyon Mackenzie. 1918. *Industry and Humanity*. Reprint. Toronto: University of Toronto Press, 1973.

Kochan, Thomas A., and Willis Nordlund. 1989. *Reconciling Labor Standards and Economic Goals: An Historical Perspective:* Washington, D.C.: U.S. Department of Labor.

Krugman, P. 1994. "Competitiveness: Does It Matter?" *Journal of Economic Literature* 32: 109–15.

————. 1997. "What Should Trade Negotiators Negotiate About?" *Journal of Economic Literature* 35, no. 1: 113–20.

Kuhn, Peter. 1992. "Mandatory Notice." *Journal of Labor Economics* 10: 117–37.

Langille, Brian A. 1996. "General Reflections on the Relationship of Trade and Labor (Or: Fair Trade Is Free Trade's Destiny)." In *Fair Trade and Harmonization: Vol. 2, Legal Analysis*, ed. Jagdish Bhagwati and Robert Hudec, pp. 231–66. Cambridge, Mass.: MIT Press.

Lazear, Edward. 1990. "Job Security Provisions and Employment." *Quarterly Journal of Economics* 105 (August): 699–726.

Leary, Virginia A. 1996. "Workers' Rights and International Trade: The Social Clause." In *Fair Trade and Harmonization: Vol. 2, Legal Analysis,* ed. Jagdish Bhagwati and Robert Hudec, pp. 177–230. Cambridge, Mass.: MIT Press.

Lee, Eddy. 1996. "Globalization and Employment: Is Anxiety Justified?" *International Labour Review* 135, no. 5: 485–97.

————. 1997. "Globalization and Labour Standards: A Review of Issues." *International Labour Review* 136, no. 2: 173–89.

Lipsig-Mummé, Carla. 2001. "Trade Unions and Labour Relations Systems in Comparative Perspective." In *Union-Management Relations in Canada*, ed. Morley Gunderson, Allen Ponak, and Daphne Gottlieb Taras, pp. 521–38. Toronto: Pearson.

Maskus, Keith. 1997. "Should Core Labor Standards Be Imposed through International Trade Policy?" World Bank Working Paper 1817. Washington, D.C.

Murray, Gregor. 2001. "Unions: Membership, Structures, Actions, and Challenges." In *Union-Management Relations in Canada*, ed. Morley Gunderson, Allen Ponak, and Daphne Gottlieb Taras, pp. 79–116. Toronto: Pearson.

Neumark, David, and Wendy A. Stock. 1999. "Age Discrimination Laws and Labor Market Efficiency." *Journal of Political Economy* 107: 1081–125.

Northrup, Herbert R., and Richard Rowan. 1979. *Multinational Collective Bargaining Attempts*. Philadelphia: Wharton School, Industrial Research Unit.

Organization for Economic Cooperation and Development. 1996. *Trade, Employment and Labour Standards: A Study of Core Workers' Rights and International Trade*. Paris.

Portes, Alejandro. 1990. "When More Can Be Less: Labor Standards, Development and the Informal Economy." In *Labor Standards and Development in the Global Economy*, ed. Stephen A. Herzenberg and Jorge Perez-Lopez. Washington, D.C.: U.S. Department of Labor.

Rhodes, Martin. 1992. "The Future of the 'Social Dimension': Labour Market Regulation in Post-1992 Europe." *Journal of Common Market Studies* 30 (March): 23–51.

Rodrik, Dani. 1997. *Has Globalization Gone Too Far?* Washington, D.C.: Institute for International Economics.

Rowan, Richard, and Duncan C. Campbell. 1983. "The Attempt to Regulate Industrial Relations through International Codes of Corporate Conduct." *Columbia Journal of World Business* 18 (Summer). Special issue on international labor, ed. David Lewin: 64–72.

Ruhm, Christopher J. 1998. "The Economic Consequences of Parental Leave Mandates: Lessons from Europe." *Quarterly Journal of Economics* 113: 285–318.

———. 2000. "Parental Leave and Child Health." *Journal of Health Economics* 19: 931–60.

Sabel, Charles, Dara O'Rourke, and Archon Fung. 2000. "Ratcheting Labor Standards." Paper prepared for World Bank.

Schoepfle, Gregory K., and Kenneth A. Swinnerton, eds. 1994. *International Labor Standards and Global Economic Integration: Proceedings of a Symposium*. Washington, D.C.: U.S. Department of Labor.

Sengenberger, Warner, and Duncan C. Campbell, eds. 1994. *Creating Economic Opportunities: The Role of Labour Standards in Economic Restructuring*. Geneva: International Labor Organization.

Servais, J.-M. 1989. "The Social Clause in Trade Agreements: Wishful Thinking or an Instrument of Social Progress?" *International Labour Review* 128: 423–33.

Stewart, Bryce M. 1927. "Labor Standards and Competition Between the United States and Canada." *The American Labor Legislation Review* 17: 176–80.

Swinnerton, Kenneth A., and Gregory K. Schoepfle. 1994. "Labor Standards in the Context of a Global Economy." *Monthly Labor Review* 117 (September): 52–58.

Teplow, Leo. 1976. "Industrial Relations Counselors at Fifty Years." In *People, Progress and Employee Relations, Proceedings of the Fiftieth Anniversary Conference of*

Industrial Relations Counselors, Inc., ed. Richard A. Beaumont, pp. 3–8. Charlottesville, Va.: University Press of Virginia.

Trejo, Stephen. 1991. "Compensating Differentials and Overtime Pay Regulation." *American Economic Review* 81 (September): 719–40.

Valticos, Nicolas. 1969. "Fifty Years of Standards-Setting Activities by the International Labour Organization." *International Labour Review* 100: 201–37.

van Liemt, Gijsbert. 1989. "Minimum Labour Standards and International Trade: Would a Social Clause Work?" *International Labour Review* 128: 433–48.

Verma, Anil. 1997. "Labour, Labour Markets and Economic Integration of Nations." In *Regionalization and Labour Market Interdependence in East and Southeast Asia*, ed. Duncan Campbell, Aurelio Parisotto, Anil Verma, and Asma Lateef, pp. 260–78. New York: St. Martin's Press.

———. 2001. "Corporate Codes of Conduct and the North-South Divide: What Can Governments Do?" In *Promoting Harmonious Labour Relations in India*, ed. A.S. Oberai, A. Sivananthiran, and C.S. Venkata Ratnam, pp. 168–88. New Delhi: South Asia Multidisciplinary Advisory Team, International Labour Organization, and Indian Industrial Relations Association.

Wever, Kirsten S., and Lowell Turner. 1995. *The Comparative Political Economy of Industrial Relations*. Madison, Wis.: Industrial Relations Research Association.

Windmuller, John P. 1987. *Collective Bargaining in Industrialised Market Economies: A Reappraisal*. Geneva: International Labour Office.

———. 1992. "European Regional Organizations." In *European Labor Unions*, ed. J. Campbell, pp. 527–44. London: Greenwood Press.

Chapter 11. Toward Collaborative Interdependence: A Century of Change in the Organization of Work

Abrahamson, Eric. 1997. "The Emergence and Prevalence of Employee Management Rhetorics: The Effects of Long Waves, Labor Unions, and Turnover, 1875 to 1992." *Academy of Management Journal* 40 (June): 491–533.

Abramowitz, Moses, and Paul A. David. 1996. "Technological Change and the Rise of Intangible Investments: The U.S. Economy's Growth Part in the Twentieth Century." In *Employment and Growth in the Knowledge-Based Economy*, pp. 35–60. Paris: Organization for Economic Cooperation and Development.

Addams, Jane. 1902. *Democracy and Social Ethics*. Reprint. Cambridge, Mass.: Harvard University Press, 1964.

Adler, Paul S. 1986. "New Technologies, New Skills." *California Management Review* (Fall): 9–28.

———. 1988. "Managing Flexible Automation." *California Management Review* (Spring): 34–56.

———. 1993. "The Learning Bureaucracy: New United Motors Manufacturing, Inc." In *Research in Organizational Behavior*, vol. 15, ed. Barry M. Staw and Larry L. Cummings, pp. 111–94. Greenwich, Conn.: JAI Press.

———. 2001. "Market, Hierarchy, and Trust: The Knowledge Economy and the Future of Capitalism." *Organization Science* (March–April): 214–34.

Appelbaum, Eileen, and Peter Berg. 2000. "High-Performance Work Systems: Giving Workers a Stake." In *The New Relationship: Human Capital and the American Corporation*, ed. Margaret M. Blair and Thomas A. Kochan, pp. 102–37. Washington, D.C.: Brookings Institution.

Autor, D.H., F. Levy, and R.J. Murnane. 2001. "The Skill Content of Recent Technological Change: An Empirical Exploration." Working paper 8337. National Bureau of Economic Research.

Barker, James R. 1999. *The Discipline of Teamwork*. Thousand Oaks, Calif.: Sage.

Barley, Stephen R. 1996. "Technicians in the Workplace: Ethnographic Evidence for Bringing Work into Organization Studies." *Administrative Science Quarterly* 41 (September): 404ff.

Barley, Stephen R., and Gideon Kunda. 1992. "Design and Devotion: Surges of Rational and Normative Ideologies of Control in Managerial Discourse." *Administrative Science Quarterly* 37: 363–99.

Barley, S. R., and J. E. Orr, eds. 1997. *Between Craft and Science: Technical Work in U.S. Settings*. Ithaca, N.Y.: ILR Press.

Baron, James N., Frank R. Dobbin, and P. Devereaux Jennings. 1986. "War and Peace: The Evolution of Modern Personnel Administration in U.S. Industry." *American Journal of Sociology* 92 (September): 350–83.

Beaumont, Richard A., and Roy B. Helfgott. 1964. *Management, Automation, and People*. Monograph No. 24. New York: Industrial Relations Counselors.

Bhaskar, Roy. 1978. *A Realist Theory of Science*. 2d ed. Leeds, U.K.: Leeds Books.

Bielby, W.T., and J.N. Baron. 1986. "Men and Women and Work: Sex Segregation and Statistical Discrimination." *American Journal of Sociology* 91: 759–99.

Blackburn, Phil, Rod Coombs, and Kenneth Green. 1985. *Technology, Economic Growth, and the Labour Process*. New York: St. Martin's Press.

Blauner, Bob. 1964. *Alienation and Freedom: The Factory Worker and His Industry*. Chicago: University of Chicago Press.

Braverman, Harry. 1974. *Labor and Monopoly Capital*. New York: Monthly Review Press.

Bronfenbrenner, K. 2000. "Uneasy Terrain: The Impact of Capital Mobility on Workers, Wages, and Union Organizing." Submitted to the U.S. Trade Deficit Review Commission, U.S. Congress.

Bureau of the Census. 1975. *Historical Statistics of the United States*. U.S. Department of Commerce. Washington, D.C.: Government Printing Office.

———. 1992. *Census of Manufacturing 1987*. U.S. Department of Commerce. Washington, D.C.: Government Printing Office.

Burgelman, R. 1983. "A Process Model of Internal Corporate Venturing in the Diversified Major Firm." *Administrative Science Quarterly* 28: 223–44.

Cappelli, P., L. Bassi, H. Katz, D. Knoke, P. Osterman, and M. Useem. 1997. *Change at Work*. New York: Oxford University Press.

Champy, James. 1995. *Reengineering Management*. New York: HarperBusiness.

Chandler, Alfred D. 1962. *Strategy and Structure*. Cambridge, Mass.: MIT Press.

———. 1977. *The Visible Hand*. Cambridge, Mass.: Harvard University Press.

Chinoy, Ely. 1992. *Automobile Workers and the American Dream*. 2d ed. Urbana, Ill.: University of Illinois Press.

Daft, Richard L. 1989. *Organization Theory and Design*. 3d ed. St. Paul, Minn.: West.

Daft, R.L., and A.Y. Lewin. 1993. "Where are the Theories for the 'New' Organizational Forms?" *Organization Science* 4 (November): i–vi.

Daft, R.L., and N. Macintosh. 1978. "A New Approach to Design and Use of Management Information." *California Management Review* 21: 82–92.

Dewey, John. 1930. *Individualism Old and New*. New York: Minton, Balch & Co.

Edwards, Richard. 1979. *Contested Terrain*. New York: Basic Books.

Edwards, Richard, Michael Reich, and Thomas E. Weisskopf, eds. 1986. *The Capitalist System: A Radical Analysis of American Society.* Engelwood Cliffs, N.J.: Prentice-Hall.

Fine, Lisa. 1993. "'Our Big Factory Family': Masculinity and Paternalism at the Reo Motor Car Company of Lansing, Michigan." *Labor History* 34: 274–91.

Freeland, R.F. 1996. "The Myth of the M-Form? Governance, Consent, and Organizational Change." *American Journal of Sociology* 102, no. 2: 483–526.

Freeman, Richard, and Joel Rogers. 1999. *What Workers Want.* Ithaca, N.Y.: Cornell University Press.

Frenkel, S.J., M. Korczynski, K.A. Shire, and M. Tam. 1999. *On the Front Line: Organization of Work in the Information Economy.* Ithaca, N.Y.: ILR/Cornell University Press.

Freyssenet, M. 1974. *Le Processus de Dequalification-Surqualification de la Force de Travail.* Paris: Centre de Sociologie Urbane.

Gallie, Duncan. 1978. *In Search of the New Working Class.* Cambridge: Cambridge University Press.

Gant, Jon, Casey Ichniowski, and Kathryn Shaw. 1999. "Getting the Job Done: Inside the Production Functions of High-Involvement and Traditional Organizations." Unpublished.

———. 2000. "Social Capital and Organizational Change in High-Involvement and Traditional Work Organizations." Paper presented at the 2000 Organization Science Winter Conference. Available on the Internet at http://faculty.fuqua.duke.edu/oswc/.

Gitelman, Howard M. 1988. *Legacy of the Ludlow Massacre: A Chapter in American Industrial Relations.* Philadelphia: University of Pennsylvania Press.

Gittell, J.H. (forthcoming). "Supervising Complex Interdependent Work." *Organization Science.*

Goldberg, David J. 1992. "Richard A. Feiss, Mary Barnett Gilson, and Scientific Management at Joseph & Feiss, 1909–1925." In *A Mental Revolution: Scientific Management since Taylor*, ed. Daniel Nelson, pp. 40–57. Columbus, Ohio: Ohio State University.

Goldin, C., and L.F. Katz. 1995. "The Decline of Non-Competing Groups: Changes in the Premium to Education." Working paper 5202. National Bureau of Economic Research.

———. 1996. "The Origins of Technology-Skill Complementarity." Working paper 5657. National Bureau of Economic Research.

———. 1998. "The Origins of Technology-Skill Complementarity." *Quarterly Journal of Economics* 113 (August): 693–732.

———. 1999. "The Returns to Skill in the United States Across the Twentieth Century." Working paper 7126. National Bureau of Economic Research.

Gordon, David M. 1996. *Fat and Mean.* New York: Free Press.

Guest, D.E. 1989. "Human Resource Management: Its Implications for Industrial Relations and Trade Unions." In *New Perspectives on Human Resource Management*, ed. John Storey, pp. 41–55. London: Routledge.

Guillén, Mauro F. 1994. *Models of Management: Work, Authority, and Organization in a Comparative Perspective.* Chicago: University of Chicago Press.

Gulick, Luther, and L. Urwick, eds. 1937. *Papers on the Science of Administration.* New York: Institute of Public Administration.

Hammer, Michael. 1996. *Beyond Reengineering.* New York: HarperBusiness.

Hammer, Michael, and James Champy. 1993. *Reengineering the Corporation.* New York: HarperBusiness.

Hamper, Ben. 1992. *Rivethead.* New York: Warner Books.

Heckscher, Charles C. 1995. *White Collar Blues: Management Loyalties in an Age of Corporate Restructuring.* New York: Basic Books.

———. 2000. "HR Strategy and Nonstandard work: Dualism versus True Mobility." In *Nonstandard Work: The Nature and Challenges of Changing Employment Relations,* ed. F. Carre, M. Ferber, L. Golden, and S.A. Herzenberg, pp. 267–90. Madison, Wis.: Industrial Relations Research Association.

Helfgott, Roy B. 1965. "Easing the Impact of Technological Change on Employees: A Conspectus of United States Experience." *International Labour Review* 91, no. 6: 3–20.

———. 1966. "EDP and the Office Work Force." *Industrial and Labor Relations Review* 19, no. 4: 503–16.

———. 1988. *Computerized Manufacturing and Human Resources.* Lexington, Mass.: Lexington Books.

———. 1992. "Labor Process Theory vs. Reform in the Workplace." *Critical Review* 6, no. 1: 11–27.

Hicks, Clarence. 1941. *My Life in Industrial Relations: Fifty Years in the Growth of a Profession.* New York: Harper.

Hobsbawn, E.J. 1964. *Labouring Men.* New York: Basic Books.

Hutchby, I. 2001. "Technologies, Texts and Affordances." *Sociology* 35, no. 2: 441–56.

Hyman, R. 1987. "Strategy or Structure? Capital, Labour and Control." *Work, Employment and Society* 1, no. 1: 25–55.

Jackson, Susan E., and Randall S. Schuler. 1985. "A Meta-Analysis and Conceptual Critique of Research on Role Ambiguity and Role Conflict in Work Settings." *Organizational Behavior and Human Decision Processes* 36: 17–78.

Kaufman, Bruce E. 1993. *The Origins and Evolution of the Field of Industrial Relations.* Ithaca, N.Y.: ILR Press.

———. 2001. "The Employee Participation/Representation Gap: An Assessment and Proposed Solution." *University of Pennsylvania Journal of Labor and Employment Law* 3, no. 3: 491–550.

Kenney, M., and R. Florida. 1988. "Beyond Mass Production: The Social Organization of Production and Innovation in Japan." *Politics and Society* 16, no. 1: 121–58.

Kern, H., and M. Schumann. 1972. *Industriearbeit und Arbeiterbewusstsein.* Frankfurt: Europaische Verlagsanstalt.

Knights, David, and Hugh Willmott, eds. 1986. *Managing the Labour Process.* Aldershot, Hants, U.K.: Gower.

Lawler, Edward E., III. 1979. "The New Plant Revolution." *Organizational Dynamics* (Winter): 2–12.

Lawler, Edward E., III, Susan A. Mohrman, and Gerald E. Ledford, Jr. 1995. *Creating High Performance Organizations.* San Francisco: Jossey-Bass.

———. 1998. *Strategies for High Performance Organizations.* San Francisco: Jossey-Bass.

Lewchuk, Wayne A. 1993. "Men and Monotony: Fraternalism as a Managerial Strategy at the Ford Motor Company." *Journal of Economic History* 53 (December): 824–56.

Lindert, P.H., and J.G. Williamson. 2001. "Does Globalization Make the World More Unequal?" Working paper 8228. National Bureau of Economic Research.

Littler, C. 1982. "Deskilling and the Changing Structure of Control." In *The Degradation of Work*, ed. S. Wood. London: Hutchinson.

MacDuffie, John Paul, and Thomas A. Kochan. 1995. "Do U.S. Firms Invest Less in Human Resources? Training in the World Auto Industry." *Industrial Relations* 34, no. 2: 147–68.

Maddison, Angus. 1995. *Monitoring the World Economy, 1820–1992*. Paris: Organization for Economic Cooperation and Development.

Mallet, Serge. 1963. *La Nouvelle Classe Ouvrière*. Paris: Seuil.

March, James G., and Herbert A. Simon. 1958. *Organizations*. New York: Wiley.

Melman, S. 1951. "The Rise of Administrative Overhead in the Manufacturing Industries of the United States, 1899–1947." *Oxford Economic Papers* 3: 62–112.

Meyer, Stephen, III. 1981. *The Five Dollar Day*. Albany, N.Y.: State University of New York Press.

———. 1999. "'An Economic Frankenstein': Workers and Automation in the Ford Brook Park Plant in the 1950s." Unpublished. Available on the Internet at http://uwp.edu/~meyer/frank.htm.

Mintzberg, Henry. 1979. *The Structuring of Organizations*. Englewood Cliffs, N.J.: Prentice-Hall.

Montgomery, David. 1979. *Workers' Control in America*. New York: Cambridge University Press.

Nelson, Daniel. 1975. *Managers and Workers: Origins of the New Factory System in the United States, 1880–1920*. Madison, Wis.: University of Wisconsin Press.

Nichols, Theo, and Huw Beynon. 1977. *Living with Capitalism: Class Relations and the Modern Factory*. London: Routledge-Kegan Paul.

Nyland, C. 1998. "Taylorism and the Mutual Gains Strategy." *Industrial Relations* 37 (no. 4): 519–42.

Organ, Dennis W., and Charles N. Greene. 1981. "The Effects of Formalization on Professional Involvement: A Compensatory Process Approach." *Administrative Science Quarterly* 26: 237–52.

Osterman, Paul. 1994. "How Common Is Workplace Transformation and How Can We Explain Who Adopts It?" *Industrial and Labor Relations Review* (January): 175–88.

———. 1999. *Securing Prosperity*. Princeton: Princeton University Press.

Pasmore, W., C. Francis, and J. Haldeman. 1982. "Socio-Technical Systems: A North American Reflection on Empirical Studies on the Seventies." *Human Relations* 35 (no. 12): 1179–204.

Peterson, Joyce Shaw. 1987. *American Automobile Workers, 1900–1933*. Albany, N.Y.: State University of New York Press.

Pine, B. Joseph, II. 1993. *Mass Customization: The New Frontier in Business Competition*. Boston: Harvard Business School Press.

Podsakoff, Philip M., Larry J. Williams, and William T. Todor. 1986. "Effects of Organizational Formalization on Alienation of Professionals and Non-Professionals." *Academy of Management Journal* 29, no. 4: 820–31.

Pryor, Frederic L. (forthcoming). "Will Most of Us Be Working for Giant Enterprises by 2028?" *Journal of Economic Behavior and Organization*. Available on the Internet at http://papers.ssrn.com/sol3/papers.cfm?cfid=808862&cftoken=93887417&abstract_id=25596.

Quinn, Robert P., and Graham L. Staines. 1979. *The 1977 Quality of Employment Survey: Descriptive Statistics, with Comparison Data from the 1969–70 and the 1972–73 Surveys.* Ann Arbor, Mich.: University of Michigan, Institute for Social Research, Survey Research Center.

Ramsay, H. 1977. "Cycles of Control: Worker Participation in Sociological and Historical Perspective." *Sociology* 11: 481–505.

Rizzo, John R., Robert J. House, and Sidney I. Lirtzman. 1970. "Role Conflict and Ambiguity in Complex Organizations." *Administrative Science Quarterly* 15: 150–63.

Roethlisberger, F.H., and William J. Dickson. 1939. *Management and the Worker.* Cambridge, Mass.: Harvard University Press.

Rogers, Daniel T. 1974. *The Work Ethic in Industrial America 1850–1920.* Chicago: University of Chicago Press.

Schultze, Charles L. 2000. "Has Job Security Eroded for American Workers?" In *The New Relationship: Human Capital in the American Corporation*, ed. Margaret M. Blair and Thomas A. Kochan, pp. 28–65. Washington, D.C.: Brookings Institution.

Scott, W. Richard. 1995. *Institutions and Organizations.* Thousand Oaks, Calif.: Sage.

Scranton, Philip. 1997. *Endless Novelty.* Princeton: Princeton University Press.

Tannenbaum, A., and R.L. Kahn. 1957. "Organizational Control Structure." *Human Relations* 10: 127–40.

Thompson, E.P. 1967. "Time, Work Discipline, and Industrial Capitalism." *Past and Present* 38: 56–97.

Thompson, James D. 1967. *Organizations in Action.* New York: McGraw-Hill.

Touraine, A. 1954. *L'Evolution du travail aux usines Renault.* Paris: Editions du CRNS.

Tushman, Michael L., and Charles A. O'Reilly, III. 1997. *Winning through Innovation.* Boston: Harvard Business School Press.

Van Norst, J., and M. Van Norst. 1903. *The Woman Who Toils.* New York: Page.

Walker, Charles R., and Robert H. Guest. 1952. *Man on the Assembly Line.* Cambridge, Mass.: Harvard University Press.

Woodward, Joan. 1965. *Industrial Organization: Theory and Practice.* London: Oxford University Press.

Zuboff, Shoshana. 1988. *In the Age of the Smart Machine.* New York: Basic Books.

List of Contributors

Paul S. Adler is a professor in the Department of Management and Organization, School of Business Administration, at the University of Southern California.

Richard A. Beaumont is the chairman of Organization Resources Counselors, Inc., and director of research for Industrial Relations Counselors, Inc.

Carlton D. Becker is a senior consultant with Organization Resources Counselors, Inc.

William N. Brown is vice president and director of Compensation Consulting for Organization Resources Counselors, Inc.

John F. Burton, Jr., is a professor in the Department of Labor Studies and Employment Relations, School of Management and Labor Relations, at Rutgers University.

Morley Gunderson is the CIBC Professor of Youth Employment in the Department of Economics and the Centre for Industrial Relations at the University of Toronto.

Roy B. Helfgott is president of Industrial Relations Counselors, Inc.

Sanford M. Jacoby is a professor of management, history, and policy studies in the Anderson Graduate School of Management at the University of California at Los Angeles.

Bruce E. Kaufman is a professor of economics and senior associate of the W.T. Beebe Institute of Personnel and Employment Relations at Georgia State University.

Geoffrey W. Latta is executive vice president and director of International Compensation for Organization Resources Counselors, Inc.

Jonathan S. Leonard is a professor in the Haas School of Business at the University of California at Berkeley.

Daniel J.B. Mitchell is the Ho-su Wu Professor in the Anderson Graduate School of Management and the Department of Policy Studies, School of Public Policy and Social Research, at the University of California at Los Angeles.

Roderick O. Mullett is vice president emeritus and the former director of the EEO/Diversity practice for Organization Resources Counselors, Inc.

Sydney R. Robertson is executive vice president of Organization Resources Counselors, Inc.

Daphne G. Taras is the associate dean of research in the Faculty of Management and a professor of Industrial Relations at the University of Calgary.

Anil Verma is a professor at the Centre for Industrial Relations and the Rotman School of Management at the University of Toronto.

Index